International Rare Book Prices

SCIENCE & MEDICINE

1991

International Rare Book Prices

SCIENCE & MEDICINE

Series Editor: Michael Cole

1991

The Clique

International Rare Book Prices – Science & Medicine

ISBN 1 870773 24 1

North America

Spoon River Press, P.O. Box 3676
Peoria, Illinois 61614, U.S.A.

Typesetting by Maxiprint, York, England
Printed and bound by Biddles Ltd., Guildford, England

Contents

Introduction and Notes

Science & Medicine is the fourth title in the annual series *International Rare Book Prices*. The other titles in the series are *The Arts & Architecture, Early Printed Books, Modern First Editions, Voyages, Travel & Exploration, Literature*.

The series, generally referred to as *IRBP*, provides annual records of the pricing levels of out-of-print, rare or antiquarian books within a number of specialty subject areas and gives likely sources and suppliers for such books in Britain and the United States of America. It is intended to be used by both the experienced bookman and the newcomer to book-collecting.

Sources of information:

The books recorded each year in the various subject volumes of *IRBP* have been selected from catalogues of books for sale issued during the previous year by numerous bookselling firms in Britain and the United States. These firms, listed at the end of this volume, range in nature from the highly specialized, handling books solely with closely defined subject areas, through to large concerns with expertise across a broad spectrum of interests.

Extent of coverage:

IRBP concentrates exclusively on books published in the English language and, throughout the series as a whole, encompasses books published between the 16th century and the 1970s.

The 30,000 or so separate titles recorded in the annual volumes of *IRBP* vary greatly from year to year although naturally there is a degree of overlap, particularly of the more frequently found titles. Consecutive annual volumes do not, therefore, merely update pricings from earlier years; they give substantially different listings of books on each occasion. The value of the *IRBP* volumes lies in providing records of an ever-increasing range of individual titles which have appeared for sale on the antiquarian or rare book market.

Emphasis is placed throughout on books falling within the lower to middle range of the pricing scale (£10 - £250; $20 - $500) rather than restricting selection to the unusually fine or expensive. In so doing, *IRBP* provides a realistic overview of the norm, rather than the exception, within the booktrade.

Authorship and cross-references:

Authors are listed alphabetically by surname.

Whenever possible, the works of each author are grouped together under a single form of name irrespective of the various combinations of initials, forenames and surnames by which the author is known.

Works published anonymously, or where the name of the author is not recorded on the title-page, are suitably cross-referenced by providing the main entry under the name of the author (when mentioned by the bookseller) with a corresponding entry under the first appropriate word of the title. In cases of unknown, or unmentioned, authorship, entry is made solely under the title.

Full-titles:

Editorial policy is to eschew, whenever possible, short-title records in favour of full-, or at least more complete and explanatory, titles. Short-title listings do little to convey the flavour, or even the content, of many books - particularly those published prior to the nineteenth century.

Descriptions:

Books are listed alphabetically, using the first word of the title ignoring, for alphabetical purposes, the definite and indefinite articles *the*, *a* and *an*. Within this alphabetical grouping of titles, variant editions are not necessarily arranged in chronological order, i.e., a 2nd, 3rd or 4th edition might well be listed prior to an earlier edition.

Subject to restrictions of space and to the provisos set out below, the substance of each catalogue entry giving details of the particular copy offered for sale has been recorded in full.

The listings have been made so as to conform to a uniform order of presentation, viz: Title; place of publication; publisher or printer; date; edition; size; collation; elements of content worthy of note; description of contents including faults, if any; description and condition of binding; bookseller; price; approximate price conversion from dollars to sterling or vice versa.

Abbreviations of description customary within the booktrade have generally been used. A list of these abbreviations will be found on page *x*.

Collations:

Collations, when provided by the bookseller, are repeated in toto although it should be borne in mind that booksellers employ differing practices in this respect; some by providing complete collations and others by indicating merely the number of pages in the main body of the work concerned. The same edition of the same title catalogued by two booksellers could therefore have two apparently different collations and care should be taken not to regard any collation recorded in *IRBP* as being a definitive or absolute record of total content.

Currency conversion:

IRBP lists books offered for sale priced in either pounds sterling (£) or United States dollars ($). For the benefit of readers unaccustomed to one or other of these currencies, an approximate conversion figure in the alternative currency has been provided in parentheses after each entry, as, for example, "**£100 [≃ $191]**", or, "**$60 [≃ £31]**". The conversion is based upon an exchange rate of £1 sterling ≃ US $1.91 (US $1 ≃ £0.525 sterling), the approximate rate applicable at the date of going to press.

It must be stressed that the conversion figures in parentheses are provided merely as an indication of the approximate pricing level in the currency with which the reader may be most familiar and that fluctuations in exchange rates will make these approximations inaccurate to a greater or lesser degree.

Acknowledgements:

We are indebted to those booksellers who have provided their catalogues during 1990 for the purposes of *IRBP*. A list of the contributing booksellers forms an appendix at the rear of this volume.

This appendix forms a handy reference of contacts in Britain and the United States with proven experience of handling books within the individual specialist fields encompassed by the series. The booksellers listed therein are able, between them, to offer advice on any aspect of the rare and antiquarian booktrade.

Many of the listed books will still, at the time of publication, be available for purchase. Readers with a possible interest in acquiring any of the items may well find it worth their while communicating with the booksellers concerned to obtain further and complete details.

Caveat:

Whilst the greatest care has been taken in transcribing entries from catalogues, it should be understood that it is inevitable that an occasional error will have passed unnoticed. Obvious mistakes, usually typographical in nature, observed in catalogues have been corrected. We have not questioned the accuracy in bibliographical matters of the cataloguers concerned.

The Clique

Abbreviations

advt(s)	advertisement(s)	intl	initial
addtn(s)	addition(s)	iss	issue
a.e.g.	all edges gilt	jnt(s)	joint(s)
ALS	autograph letter signed	lge	large
altrtns	alterations	lea	leather
Amer	American	lib	library
bibliog(s)	bibliography(ies)	ltd	limited
b/w	black & white	litho(s)	lithograph(s)
bndg	binding	marg(s)	margin(s)
bd(s)	board(s)	ms(s)	manuscript(s)
b'plate	bookplate	mrbld	marbled
ctlg(s)	catalogue(s)	mod	modern
chromolitho(s)	chromo-lithograph(s)	mor	morocco
ca	circa	mtd	mounted
cold	coloured	n.d.	no date
coll	collected	n.p.	no place
contemp	contemporary	num	numerous
crnr(s)	corner(s)	obl	oblong
crrctd	corrected	occas	occasional(ly)
cvr(s)	cover(s)	orig	original
dec	decorated	p (pp)	page(s)
detchd	detached	perf	perforated
diag(s)	diagram(s)	pict	pictorial
dw(s)	dust wrapper(s)	port(s)	portrait(s)
edn(s)	edition(s)	pres	presentation
elab	elaborate	ptd	printed
engv(s)	engraving(s)	qtr	quarter
engvd	engraved	rebnd	rebind/rebound
enlgd	enlarged	rec	recent
esp	especially	repr(d)	repair(ed)
ex lib	ex library	rvsd	revised
f (ff)	leaf(ves)	roy	royal
f.e.p.	free end paper	sep	separate
facs	facsimile	sev	several
fig(s)	figure(s)	sgnd	signed
fldg	folding	sgntr	signature
ft	foot	sl	slight/slightly
frontis	frontispiece	sm	small
hand-cold	hand-coloured	t.e.g.	top edge gilt
hd	head	TLS	typed letter signed
ill(s)	illustration(s)	unif	uniform
illust	illustrated	v	very
imp	impression	vell	vellum
imprvd	improved	vol(s)	volume(s)
inc	including	w'engvd	wood-engraved
inscrbd	inscribed	w'cut(s)	woodcut(s)
inscrptn	inscription	wrap(s)	wrapper(s)

Science & Medicine 1990 Catalogue Prices

Abbott, C.G.
- The Home-Life of the Osprey. London: 1911. 4to. 40 mtd photo plates. half mor, spine faded. *(Grayling)* £35 [≃ $67]

Abbott, Maude
- Atlas of Congenital Cardiac Disease. New York: 1936. 1st edn. Folio. 62 pp. Ills. Orig bndg. *(Fye)* $250 [≃ £130]
- Atlas of Congenital Cardiac Disease. New York: 1954. 1st edn, reprinted. Folio. 62 pp. Ills. Orig bndg. *(Fye)* $125 [≃ £65]

Abbott, Maude (ed.)
- Appreciations and Reminiscences: Sir William Osler, Bart. Montreal: 1926. 1st printing. One of 1500. 633 pp. Ports. Orig bndg. *(Fye)* $200 [≃ £104]

Abel, Thomas
- Subtensial Plain Trigonometry, wrought with a Sliding-Rule, with Gunter's Lines: and also Arithmetically, in a Very Concise Manner ... Phila: 1761. 12mo. [2],86 pp (6 pp misnumbered). 7 fldg plates. Sm lib stamp. Foxed, sm repr to 1 plate. Mod three qtr calf. *(Reese)* $900 [≃ £468]

Abercrombie, J.
- The Gardener's Pocket Journal. London: 1807. 10th edn. 12mo. 324 pp. Half calf. *(Wheldon & Wesley)* £30 [≃ $57]
- The Gardener's Pocket Journal, and Daily Assistant. London: 1821. 16th edn. 12mo. 324 pp. Frontis. Half calf gilt. *(Wheldon & Wesley)* £20 [≃ $38]

Abercrombie, John
- Pathological and Practical Researches on Diseases of the Brain and Spinal Cord. Phila: 1831. 1st Amer edn. 464 pp. Orig bndg. *(Fye)* $250 [≃ £130]

Abercromby, R.
- Seas and Skies in many Latitudes. or Wanderings in Search of Weather. London: 1888. xvi,447 pp. 9 photos, 3 maps (sl foxing on versos), 33 engvs. Orig pict cloth, rear inner hinge sl loose. *(Whitehart)* £18 [≃ $34]

Abernethy, J.P.
- The Modern Service of Commercial and Railway Telegraphy. 1884. 3rd edn. 333 pp. Orig bndg. *(New Wireless)* $40 [≃ £20]

Abernethy, John
- Introductory Lectures, exhibiting some of Mr. Hunter's Opinions respecting Life and Diseases, delivered before the Royal College of Surgeons ... London: 1815. 97-136 pp. Later half cloth & mrbld bds. *(Whitehart)* £40 [≃ $76]
- Surgical Observations on Injuries of the Head; and on Miscellaneous Subjects. Phila: for Thomas Dobson, 1811. 162 pp. Frontis. Orig bds, uncut, spine chipped, hinges cracked. *(Karmiole)* $150 [≃ £78]
- Surgical Observations on the Constitutional Origin and Treatment of Local Diseases; and on Aneurisms ... Phila: 1811. 1st Amer edn. 325 pp. Leather. *(Fye)* $250 [≃ £130]
- Surgical Observations. On the Constitutional Origin and Treatment of Local Diseases; and on Aneurisms ... Phila: for Thomas Dobson ..., 1811. 1st Amer edn. 8vo. ix, [2],352 pp. Sl browning & spotting. Contemp tree calf, sm split in hinge. *(Hemlock)* $225 [≃ £117]
- Surgical Observations on the Constitutional Origin and Treatment of Local Diseases; and on Aneurisms ... Volume I [all published]. London: 1828. 10th edn. xii,346 pp. Orig bds, paper label, spine ends sl defective, label half missing, edges uncut. *(Whitehart)* £40 [≃ $76]

Abney, W. de W.
- Colour Vision being the Tyndall Lectures

delivered in 1894 at the Royal Institution.
London: 1895. ix,231 pp. Cold frontis, text
diags. Inscrptn on half-title. Orig bndg.
(Whitehart) **£25 [≈ $47]**

Abraham, J.J.
- Lettsom, His Life, Times, Friends and
Descendants. London: Heinemann, 1933. 1st
edn. Lge 8vo. xx,498 pp. Fldg table, num ills.
Orig cloth, upper cvr sl splashed.
(Bow Windows) **£65 [≈ $124]**
- Lettsom. His Life, Times, Friends and
Descendants. London: 1933. xx,498 pp.
Plates, ills. Half-title sl loose. Cloth, sl faded.
(Whitehart) **£25 [≈ $47]**

Abramson, Albert
- Electronic Motion Pictures: A History of the
Television Camera. 1955. 1st edn. 212 pp. 93
ills. Lib marks. Orig bndg.
(New Wireless) **$45 [≈ £24]**

An Account of the Tenia ...
- See Simmons, S.F.

Accum, Friedrich Christian (Frederick)
- An Explanatory Dictionary of the Apparatus
and Instruments employed in Various
Operations of Philosophical and
Experimental Chemistry. London: Thomas
Boys, 1824. 8vo. vii, 295 pp. 70 plates (sl
foxed). Cloth, rebacked.
(Gemmary) **$475 [≈ £247]**
- A Practical Essay on the Analysis of Minerals.
London: for the author, 1804. 1st edn. Sm
8vo. xvi,183 pp. 1 text fig. Some foxing.
Rebound in cloth. *(Gemmary)* **$225 [≈ £117]**
- A Treatise on the Art of making Wine from
Native Fruits ... London: Longman ..., 1820.
1st edn. 12mo. Half-title. 24 advt pp at end.
Hand cold vignette on title. Old half mor,
rubbed, edges worn. *(Ximenes)* **$375 [≈ £195]**

Acheta Domestica (pseud.)
- Episodes of Insect Life ... see Budgen, M.L.

Acland, Henry W.
- The Harveian Oration. London: 1865. 8vo.
85 pp. Orig bndg.   *(Goodrich)* **$45 [≈ £24]**

Acton, Eliza
- Modern Cookery, in all its Branches ...
Eighth Edition. To which are added,
Directions for Carving. London: Longman,
1848. Fcap 8vo. xlviii,608,4,32 pp. 8 plates,
text ills. Some foxing, mainly to the plates.
Orig cloth gilt, faded, backstrip relaid.
(Spelman) **£65 [≈ $124]**

Adam, C.
- Ophthalmoscopic Diagnosis based on Typical
Pictures of the Fundus of the Eye ...
Translated by M.L. Foster. New York: 1913.
4to. 229 pp. 86 cold plates. Orig bndg.
(Goodrich) **$75 [≈ £39]**

Adams, Edward Dean
- Niagara Power. 1928. 1st edn. 2 vols. 949 pp.
277 ills. Orig bndg.
(New Wireless) **$110 [≈ £57]**

Adams, F.D.
- The Birth and Development of the Geological
Sciences. London: 1936. 506 pp. Frontis, 14
plates, 79 figs. Orig cloth. Author's pres copy.
V. & J. Eyles copy with marg pencil notes.
(Baldwin) **£175 [≈ $335]**
- The Birth and Development of the Geological
Sciences. New York: Dover (1936) 1954. 506
pp. Frontis, 14 plates, 79 figs. Orig wrappers,
used copy, inner hinges sellotaped.
(Baldwin) **£28 [≈ $53]**

Adams, G.
- Astronomical and Geographical Essays.
London: the author, 1790. 8vo. xix,599,15
advt pp. 21 fldg plates. New half leather.
(Gemmary) **$600 [≈ £312]**
- An Essay on Electricity. London: R.
Hindmarch for the author, 1787. 8vo. lxxxvi,
473 pp. 10 fldg plates. Leather, rebacked.
(Gemmary) **$750 [≈ £390]**

Adams, H.G.
- Beautiful Shells their Nature, Structure, and
Uses familiarly explained ... London: 1887.
8vo. [iv],156 pp. 8 cold plates, 90 text figs.
Front fly leaf removed. Orig illust cloth.
(Bow Windows) **£28 [≈ $53]**
- Humming Birds, Described and Illustrated ...
London: Groombridge, 1856. Sm 8vo. 71,1
advt pp. 8 hand cold plates, 6 w'engvs. Orig
green cloth, faded, spine rather worn with a
fragment missing. *(Beech)* **£48 [≈ $92]**
- Humming Birds Described and Illustrated.
London: n.d. 8vo. 8 hand cold plates. Orig
dec cloth, a.e.g., recased.
(Henly) **£95 [≈ $182]**

Adams, Harriet
- Wild Flowers of the British Isles ... Revised
by James E. Bagnall. London: Heinemann,
1910. 2 vols. 4to. 137 cold plates. Sl marg
foxing. Orig cloth. *(Beech)* **£45 [≈ $86]**

Adams, Joseph
- Observations on Morbid Poisons, Chronic

and Acute ... Second Edition ... London:
1807. 4to. 406 pp. 4 cold mezzotint engvs.
Orig cloth backed bds, untrimmed, label
defective, 2 inches missing from hd of
backstrip.   *(Fye)* **$325 [≈ £169]**

Adams, Lionel E.
- The Collector's Manual of British Land and
Freshwater Shells. London: 1884. 8vo. 125
pp. 1 plain & 8 hand cold plates. Cloth.
          (Wheldon & Wesley) **£25 [≈ $47]**
- The Collector's Manual of British Land and
Fresh-Water Shells ... London: George Bell &
Sons, 1884. 1st edn. 125 pp. 8 hand cold
plates, 1 plain plate. V occas sl spotting. Orig
pict green cloth gilt.   *(Gough)* **£35 [≈ $67]**
- The Collector's Manual of British Land and
Freshwater Shells ... Leeds: 1896. 2nd edn.
[6], ii,214, [12 advt] pp. Cr 8vo. 11 plates (9
cold). Orig cloth gilt. *(Fenning)* **£28.50 [≈ $55]**

Adams, R., et al.
- Diseases of Muscle. A Study in Pathology.
London: 1962. 2nd edn. xvi,735 pp. Frontis,
438 ills. Orig cloth, sl worn & marked.
          (Whitehart) **£25 [≈ $47]**

Adams, William
- Lectures on the Pathology and Treatment of
Lateral and Other Forms of Curvature of the
Spine. London: 1865. 334 pp. 5 litho plates,
61 w'cuts. Orig bndg, recased.
          (Fye) **$450 [≈ £234]**

Addison, Thomas
- A Collection of the Published Writings.
London: 1868. 1st edn. 242 pp. Lacks front
endpaper. Orig bndg.   *(Fye)* **$250 [≈ £130]**

Adelmann, Howard B.
- Marcello Malpighi and the Evolution of
Embryology. New York: Cornell UP, 1966. 5
vols. Folio. 5 frontis, 11 cold fldg plates in vol
2. Orig cloth. Slipcase.
          (Karmiole) **$225 [≈ £117]**

Adrian, E.D.
- The Basis of Sensation. New York: 1928. 1st
Amer edn. 122 pp. Orig bndg.
          (Fye) **$60 [≈ £31]**

Agassiz, A.
- The Coral Reefs of the Tropical Pacific.
Cambridge, MA: 1903. 2 vols. 4to. xxxiii,410
pp. Sections, text figs. With an atlas of 238
plates. Sm blind stamp on titles & plates. Half
mor, rubbed.
          (Wheldon & Wesley) **£180 [≈ $345]**

Agassiz, E.C.
- Louis Agassiz. His Life and Correspondence.
Boston: 1897. 11th edn. Cr 8vo. xviii,794 pp.
10 plates, 2 vignettes. Cloth gilt.
          (Henly) **£35 [≈ $67]**

Agassiz, J.L.R.
- Contributions to the Natural History of the
United States of America. Boston: 1857-62. 4
vols, all published. Roy 8vo. 77 plates (2
cold). Orig cloth, 1 vol rebacked.
          (Wheldon & Wesley) **£200 [≈ $383]**

Agassiz, Louis
- Bibliographia Zoologiae et Geologiae. A
General Catalogue of Books, Tracts and
Memoirs on Zoology and Geology. Edited by
H.E. Strickland. London: Ray Society,
1848-54. 4 vols. 8vo. A few lib stamps. Orig
cloth, 2 vols rebacked.
          (Wheldon & Wesley) **£120 [≈ $230]**
- Methods of Study in Natural History.
London: 1896. Cr 8vo. viii,319 pp. Text ills.
Cloth gilt.   *(Henly)* **£18 [≈ $34]**

Aiken, H.H.
- Synthesis of Electronic Computing and
Control Circuits. Cambridge: Harvard UP,
1951. 4to. 278 pp. Num text figs. Cloth. Dw.
          (Gemmary) **$50 [≈ £26]**

Aikin, Arthur
- A Manual of Mineralogy. London: 1814. 1st
edn. Cr 8vo. lx,164 pp. Contemp half calf.
          (Fenning) **£45 [≈ $86]**

Airy, Sir George Biddell
- Account of Observations of the Transit of
Venus, 1874, December 8 ... London:
HMSO, 1881. 1st edn. 4to. viii,256, [2],
257-512,21 pp. 17 litho plates. Some foxing &
dust soiling. Orig cloth.
          (Gaskell) **£120 [≈ $230]**
- Account of the Northumberland Equatoreal
and Dome, attached to the Cambridge
Observatory. Cambridge: UP, 1844. 1st edn.
4to. [ii],39 pp. 17 plates. Last plate foxed,
traces of foxing on the other plates. Lib stamp
on title. Orig cloth. *(Gaskell)* **£350 [≈ $671]**
- On the Undulatory Theory of Optics.
London: Macmillan, 1877. Cr 8vo. viii,159
pp. 2 plates. Cloth. *(Gemmary)* **$45 [≈ £23]**
- Six Lectures on Astronomy ... London:
[1851]. 2nd edn. xx,247 pp. 7 fldg plates
(foxed). Orig cloth, leather reback.
          (Whitehart) **£35 [≈ $67]**
- Six Lectures on Astronomy ... London: [ca
1860]. 4th edn. ix,222 pp. 7 fldg plates. Occas

sl foxing. Orig cloth, rubbed.
(Whitehart) **£20 [≈ $38]**

Aitken, R.B.
- Great Game Animals. New York: 1968. 192 pp. Cold & b/w ills. Dw.
(Trophy Room) **$125 [≈ £65]**
- Great Game Animals of the World. London: 1969. Lge 4to. Num cold & other ills. Dw.
(Grayling) **£60 [≈ $115]**

Aitken, W.
- The Science and Practice of Medicine. London: 1866. 4th edn, rvsd. 2 vols. 54 + 33 figs. Orig cloth, dust stained, spines faded, vol 2 backstrip relaid, new endpapers.
(Whitehart) **£35 [≈ $67]**

Akeley, Carl E.
- Taxidermy and Sculpture. The Work of Carl E. Akely in Field Museum of Natural History. Chicago: [ca 1927]. 4to. [4] pp. 48 photo plates. In portfolio. Ptd slipcase (cracked, reprd).
(Karmiole) **$125 [≈ £65]**

Albee, Fred
- Bone-Graft Surgery. Phila: 1915. 1st edn. 417 pp. Orig bndg.
(Fye) **$250 [≈ £130]**
- Orthopedic and Reconstructive Surgery. Phila: 1919. 1st edn. 1138 pp. Orig bndg.
(Fye) **$200 [≈ £104]**

Albin, E.
- A Natural History of English Insects ... London: 1720. 1st edn. 4to. 100 hand cold plates. Calf, rebacked.
(Wheldon & Wesley) **£1,650 [≈ $3,167]**

Albucasis
- On Surgery and Instruments. London: Wellcome, 1973. Thick 4to. 850 pp. Orig cloth. Dw.
(Moon) **£28 [≈ $53]**

Alcock, Thomas
- Lectures on Practical and Medical Surgery ... London: 1830. 1st edn. 302 pp. 12 engvd plates. Half leather.
(Fye) **$200 [≈ £104]**

Alderson, Ralph
- A Chemical Analysis and Medical Treatise on the Shap Spaw, In Westmorland ... Kendal: R. Lough, 1828. 1st edn. 88 pp. 4 pp subscribers. Orig bds, worn, hinges broken but 1 cord holding.
(Hollett) **£250 [≈ $479]**

Ali, Salim A.
- The Birds of Travancore & Cochin. London: Oxford, [ca 1953]. 1st edn. 8vo. xviii,436 pp.

Ills (inc cold). Dw. *(McBlain)* **$100 [≈ £52]**

Ali, Salim A. & Ripley, S.D.
- Handbook of the Birds of India and Pakistan together with those of Nepal, Sikkim, Bhutan and ceylon. London: 1968-74. 1st edn. 10 vols. Roy 8vo. Cloth.
(Wheldon & Wesley) **£200 [≈ $383]**

Alken, Henry T.
- The Beauties & Defects in the Figure of the Horse Comparatively Delineated in a Series of Engravings. Boston: 1830. 1st Amer edn. 4to. 18 plates, with facing text. Some foxing. Orig cloth, pict label (rubbed), rebacked, ink sgntrs on cvrs & endsheets. Anon.
(Reese) **$950 [≈ £494]**

All About the Telephone ...
- All About the Telephone and Phonograph ... London: Ward, Lock, [1878]. Sm 8vo. [iv], 9-99, [24 ctlg] pp. Text ills. Advt pastedowns & endpapers. Orig pict paper bds, recased, most of spine preserved, rubbed.
(de Beaumont) **£100 [≈ $191]**

Allan, Mea
- The Tradescants, their Plants, Gardens, and Museums, 1570-1662. London: Joseph, (1964). 1st edn. 8vo. 345 pp. Fldg table, 27 plates. Orig cloth. Dw.
(Bookpress) **$135 [≈ £70]**

Allbutt, T. Clifford
- The Historical Relations of Medicine and Surgery to the End of the 16th Century. London: 1905. 1st edn. 125 pp. Orig bndg.
(Fye) **$100 [≈ £52]**
- Science and Medieval Thought. London: 1901. 1st edn. 116 pp. Orig bndg.
(Fye) **$75 [≈ £39]**
- Science and Medieval Thought. The Harveian Oration ... London: Clay, 1901. 8vo. 116 pp. Orig bndg, front jnt starting.
(Goodrich) **$45 [≈ £24]**

Allen, Charles
- The Operator for the Teeth. With a New Introduction by R.A. Cohen. London: 1969. One of 250. Sm 4to. [vi],x,[ii],22 pp. 3 plates, facs of orig title. Orig bndg.
(Bow Windows) **£75 [≈ $143]**

Allen, E.A.
- The Prehistoric World or Vanished Races. Cincinnati: Central Publishing House, 1885. 8vo. 820 pp. Num plates & text figs. Leather.
(Gemmary) **$50 [≈ £26]**

Allen, Grant
- Falling in Love. With Other Essays on more Exact Branches of Science. London: Smith, Elder, 1889. 1st edn. 8vo. [viii],356 pp,2 advt ff. Orig cloth.   *(Bickersteth)* £38 [≈ $72]

Allen, J. Fenwick
- Some Founders of the Chemical Industry. Manchester: Sherratt & Hughes, 1907. 2nd edn. 29,289,6 pp. Orig blue cloth, somewhat worn, inner jnt cracked.   *(Bell)* £45 [≈ $86]

Allen, John
- Synopsis Medicinae: or, A Summary View of the Whole Practice of Physick ... London: W. Innys ..., 1749. 3rd edn. 2 vols. 8vo. [viii], 400; [iv],356, [43],[1] pp. Contemp calf, hinges & spines cracked.
      (Bookpress) $285 [≈ £148]

Allis, Oscar
- Scoliosis: a New Study of an Old Problem. Phila: privately ptd, 1938. 1st edn. 168 pp. 102 ills. Orig wraps.   *(Fye)* $100 [≈ £52]

Allman, George James
- A Monograph of the Fresh-Water Polyzoa. London: Ray Society, 1856. Folio. viii,119 pp. 11 plates (10 cold). Lib stamps. Half calf.   *(Baldwin)* £45 [≈ $86]
- A Monograph of the Gymnoblastic or Tubularian Hydroids ... London: Ray Society, 1871. Folio. xxii,450 pp. 1 plain & 22 hand cold plates. Occas sl spotting. Contemp blue half mor, gilt dec spines, t.e.g.
      (Gough) £195 [≈ $374]

Allsop, F.C.
- Induction Coil and Coil Making. 1899. 3rd edn. 172 pp. 125 ills. Orig bndg.
      (New Wireless) $75 [≈ £39]
- Practical Electrical Light Fitting. 1895. 2nd edn. 275 pp. 221 ills. Orig bndg.
      (New Wireless) $45 [≈ £23]
- Telephones; Their Construction and Fitting. London: Spon, 1892. 2nd edn, rvsd & enlgd. Cr 8vo. xvi,256,28 pp. Fldg plates, num ills. A few faint marks. Orig bndg.
      (Ash) £25 [≈ $47]
- Telephones: Their Construction and Fitting. 1899. 5th edn. 184 pp. 15 fldg plates, 156 ills. Orig bndg.   *(New Wireless)* $65 [≈ £34]

Althaus, Julius
- On Sclerosis of the Spinal Cord ... London: Longmans, 1885. 8vo. 394 pp. 9 engvs. Orig bndg.   *(Goodrich)* $175 [≈ £91]

Amuchastegui, Axel
- Studies of Birds and Mammals of South America. With Descriptive Text by Helmut Sick. London: The Tryon Gallery, 1967. 1st edn. Sm folio. 63 pp. Frontis, 24 cold plates. Sl damage to endpaper. Orig mor backed mrbld bds, vellum tips.
      (Claude Cox) £32 [≈ $61]

Anderson, J.W.
- The Prospector's Handbook. London: Crosby Lockwood, 1887. 2nd edn. Sm 8vo. xii,198 pp. 69 text figs. Orig cloth.
      (Gemmary) $30 [≈ £15]
- The Prospector's Handbook. London: Crosby Lockwood, 1904. 10th edn. Sm 8vo. xii,176 pp. 70 text figs. Orig cloth.
      (Gemmary) $35 [≈ £18]

Anderson, James
- The New Practical Gardener and Modern Horticulturist. London: William Mackenzie, [ca 1870]. 1st edn (?). 988 pp. 27 chromolitho & 12 plain plates, num text ills. Contemp half calf, gilt spine.   *(Gough)* £150 [≈ $287]

Anderson, McC.
- On the Parasitic Affections of the Skin. London: 1868. 2nd edn. xi,250 pp. Frontis, 1 plate, 33 ills. Occas foxing. Cloth, rather worn, marked, dust stained.
      (Whitehart) £25 [≈ $47]

Anderson, Richard
- Lightning Conductors Their History, Nature and Mode of Application. London: Spon, 1880. 1st edn. 8vo. Num ills. Orig cloth, recased. Pres copy.   *(Young's)* £60 [≈ $115]

Andral, Gabriel
- A Treatise on Pathological Anatomy. Translated from the French by Richard Townsend and William West. Dublin: Hodges & Smith, 1829. 1st edn in English. 2 vols. 8vo. xiii,698; xxii,808 pp. 2 lib stamps. Mod qtr mor.   *(Bickersteth)* £120 [≈ $230]

Andrews, James (illustrator)
- Choice Garden Flowers: their Cultivation and General Treatment ... London: Houlston & Wright, (1860). 1st edn. 12mo. (202) pp. 12 hand cold plates inc frontis. Orig green cloth, sl soiled.   *(Chapel Hill)* $75 [≈ £39]

Andrews, W.
- The Diuturnal Theory of the Earth. Or, Nature's System of Constructing a Stratified Physical World. London: 1900. xxiv,551 pp.

Port, 2 maps. Orig cloth, dust stained.
(Whitehart) £18 [≈ $34]

Andrews, William
- The Doctor in History, Literature, Folk-Lore, etc. London: 1896. 1st edn. 287 pp. Orig bndg.   *(Fye)* $175 [≈ £91]

Andry, Nicolas
- An Account of the Breeding of Worms in Human Bodies ... London: H. Rhodes, 1701. 1st edn. 8vo. xl,[iv],120 pp, 121-176 ff, 177-266, [xxvi] pp. 5 plates. Later sheep.
(Bookpress) $600 [≈ £312]
- Orthopaedia: or the Art of Correcting and Preventing Deformities in Children ... Translated from the French. London: 1743. 1st English edn. 2 vols. 8vo. viii,230,[8]; vi, 310 pp. 16 (of 21) plates. Lacks frontis. Title browned & mtd. Mod half calf gilt.
(Hemlock) $475 [≈ £247]
- Orthopaedia. Phila: 1961. Facs of London 1743 edn. 2 vols. Orig leatherette. Slipcase.
(Fye) $225 [≈ £117]

Angot, A.
- The Aurora Borealis. London: International Scientific Series, 1896. xii,264 pp. 18 plates, 2 text ills. Orig cloth, sl dust stained, ft of spine sl worn.   *(Whitehart)* £18 [≈ $34]

Annandale, Thomas
- The Malformation, Diseases, and Injuries of the Fingers and Toes and their Surgical Treatment. Edinburgh: 1865. 1st edn. 292 pp. 12 engvd plates. Orig bndg.
(Fye) $750 [≈ £390]
- Observations and Cases in Surgery. Edinburgh: 1865. 1st edn. 80 pp. Orig wraps.
(Fye) $125 [≈ £65]

Ansted, David T.
- The Applications of Geology to the Arts and Manufactures ... Lectures ... delivered before the Society of Arts ... London: Hardwicke, 1865. 1st coll edn. Sm 8vo. iv, [3], 300,[4 advt] pp. 18 ills. Orig cloth gilt, discold.
(Fenning) £45 [≈ $86]
- Elementary Course of Geology, Mineralogy, and Physical Geography. London: 1869. Enlgd reissue. xvi,606 pp. 250 text figs. Lib stamp on title verso. Orig cloth, spine ends sl worn.   *(Whitehart)* £25 [≈ $47]
- Geological Gossip: or, Stray Chapters on Earth and Ocean. London: 1860. 1st edn. Sm 8vo. viii,325,[3] pp. 8 figs. Few sm marks. Orig cloth.   *(Bow Windows)* £40 [≈ $76]
- Geology, Introductory, Descriptive, &

Practical. London: 1844. 1st edn. 2 vols. 8vo. Num text diags. Lacks half-titles. Sl marg stain 2 ff. Contemp half calf, rubbed, mor labels chipped. *(Bow Windows)* £95 [≈ $182]

Ansted, David T., et al.
- Geology, Mineralogy and Crystallography. London: Houlston & Stoneman, 1855. Cr 8vo. xvi, 587 pp. 396 text figs. Half leather, worn.   *(Gemmary)* $100 [≈ £52]

Appleyard, Rollo
- The History of the Institution of Electrical Engineers (1871-1931). London: 1939. 342 pp. Cold frontis, 37 plates. Orig bndg.
(Whitehart) £18 [≈ $34]

Arago, D. Francois J.
- Biographies of Distinguished Scientific Men. London: 1857. viii,607 pp. A few figs. Cloth, sl dusty & worn, rebacked, sl weak.
(Whitehart) £40 [≈ $76]
- Popular Astronomy. Translated ... and edited by Admiral W.H. Smyth ... and Robert Grant ... London: Longman ..., 1855-58. 1st edn of this translation. 2 vols. 8vo. 25 plates, 358 ills. Contemp calf, sides strengthened with cloth.   *(Fenning)* £65 [≈ $124]

Aran, Francois Amilcar
- Practical Manual of the Heart and Great Vessels. Translated from the French by William A. Haris. Phila: Barrington & Haswell, 1843. 12mo. 296,[4 ctlg] pp. Lib stamp on title. Orig cloth.
(Hemlock) $120 [≈ £62]

Arber, Agnes
- The Gramineae. A Study of Cereal, Bamboo & Grass. London: 1934. xvii,480 pp. Cold frontis, 212 figs. Orig cloth.
(Baldwin) £45 [≈ $86]
- Herbals. Their Origin and Evolution. A Chapter in the History of Botany 1470-1670. London: 1912. xviii,253 pp. 21 plates, 113 figs. Orig cloth.   *(Baldwin)* £85 [≈ $163]
- Herbals: their Origin and Evolution ... New Edition, rewritten and enlarged. Cambridge: UP, 1938. 8vo. 26 plates, 131 text figs.
(Georges) £75 [≈ $143]
- The Mind and the Eye. A Study of the Biologist's Standpoint. Cambridge: 1954. 1st edn. xi,146 pp. Orig bndg.
(Whitehart) £12 [≈ $23]
- Monocotyledons, a Morphological Study. Cambridge: 1925. Roy 8vo. xv,258 pp. Frontis, 160 text figs. Orig cloth, spotted.
(Wheldon & Wesley) £25 [≈ $47]

- The Natural Philosophy of Plant Form. London: 1950. xiv,247 pp. 47 figs. Orig cloth. *(Baldwin)* **£25 [≈ $47]**
- Water Plants. A Study of Aquatic Angiosperms. London: 1920. xvi,436 pp. 171 figs. Orig cloth. *(Baldwin)* **£35 [≈ $67]**

Archer, G. & Godman, E.M.
- The Birds of British Somaliland and the Gulf of Aden. London: 1937-61. 4 vols. Imperial 8vo. 4 maps, 34 cold & 24 plain plates. Occas v sl foxing. Orig buckram. Dws (those to vols 1 & 2 sl water stained). *(Wheldon & Wesley)* **£585 [≈ $1,123]**

Archer, Gleason L.
- History of Radio to 1926. 1938. 1st edn. 421 pp. 20 photos. Orig bndg, fine. *(New Wireless)* **$95 [≈ £50]**

Archer, Mildred
- Natural History Drawings in the India Office Library. London: 1964. 2nd imp. ix,116 pp. Cold frontis, 25 plates. Orig bndg. *(Whitehart)* **£18 [≈ $34]**

Ardenne, Manfred von
- Television Reception. 1936. 1st edn in English. 121 pp. 50 photos, 46 ills. Orig bndg, sm tear hd of spine. *(New Wireless)* **$50 [≈ £26]**

Aristotle (pseud.)
- The Works of Aristotle. In Four Parts. London: 1798. 407 pp. Leather. *(Fye)* **$100 [≈ £52]**

Arjunba, Sakharam
- Principles and Practice of Medicine designed for the Students of the Vernacular Class, Grant Medical College, Bombay. Indu Prakash Press: 1869. 8vo. Panelled sheep, gilt inner dentelles. Author's pres inscrptn to the dedicatee. *(Goodrich)* **$250 [≈ £130]**

Arkell, W.J.
- The Geology of Oxford. London: 1947. viii, 267 pp. 6 plates, 49 figs. Orig cloth. Dw. *(Baldwin)* **£38 [≈ $72]**
- The Geology of Oxford. Oxford: 1947. 8vo. viii, 267 pp. 2 maps, 6 plates. Cloth. *(Wheldon & Wesley)* **£45 [≈ $86]**
- The Jurassic System in Great Britain. London: 1933. xii,681 pp. 41 plates. Orig cloth. *(Baldwin)* **£55 [≈ $105]**
- The Jurassic Geology of the World. London: 1956. xv,806 pp. 46 plates. Orig cloth. Dw. *(Baldwin)* **£55 [≈ $105]**

- The Jurassic System in Great Britain. London: (1933). 1970. Reprint. xii,681 pp. 41 plates. Orig cloth. *(Baldwin)* **£45 [≈ $86]**

Armatage, G.
- Memoranda for Emergencies; or, the Veterinarian's Pocket Remembrancer: being Concise Directions for the Treatment of Urgent or Rare Cases ... London: 1870. xi,168 pp. New cloth. *(Whitehart)* **£25 [≈ $47]**

Armstrong, Edward A.
- The Folklore of Birds. London: Collins New Naturalist, 1958. 1st edn. 8vo. xvi,272 pp. 1 cold & 32 plain plates. Orig cloth. *(Henly)* **£60 [≈ $115]**
- The Folklore of Birds ... London: Collins New Naturalist, 1958. 1st edn. 272 pp. Cold frontis, ills. Orig cloth gilt. Price-clipped Dw. *(Hollett)* **£80 [≈ $153]**
- The Wren. London: Collins New Naturalist, 1955. 1st edn. 8vo. viii,312 pp. 8 plates. Orig cloth. *(Henly)* **£36 [≈ $69]**
- The Wren. London: Collins New Naturalist, 1955. 1st edn. 312 pp. Plates, ills. Orig cloth gilt. Dw (v sm chips spine ends). *(Hollett)* **£75 [≈ $143]**

Armstrong, H.G.
- Principles and Practice of Aviation Medicine. London: 1939. xii,496 pp. Frontis, 86 text figs. Orig bndg. *(Whitehart)* **£25 [≈ $47]**

Armstrong, Harry (ed.)
- Aero-Space Medicine. Baltimore: 1961. 1st edn. 633 pp. Orig bndg, owner's name in magic marker on foredge. *(Fye)* **$100 [≈ £52]**

Arnold, F.H.
- Flora of Sussex ... New Edition, with Numerous Additions. London: 1907. 8vo. xxi, 154 pp. Cold frontis, map. Some foxing & dust marks. Orig cloth, cvrs dull. *(Bow Windows)* **£30 [≈ $57]**

Arnott, Neil
- Elements of Physics, or Natural Philosophy, General and Medical ... London: Longman ..., 1828. 3rd edn. xlviii,647 pp. Ills. Orig cloth backed bds, uncut. *(Young's)* **£58 [≈ $111]**
- Elements of Physics, or Natural Philosophy, General and Medical ... Fifth Edition. London: 1833. 2 vols. Vol 2 described as Part 1 (all published). 8vo. Num text figs. Orig half calf. *(Bickersteth)* **£35 [≈ $67]**

Arrhenius, S.
- Text-Book of Electrochemistry. New York: Longmans, Green, 1902. 8vo. xi,344 pp. 58 text figs. Ex-lib. Cloth.
(Gemmary) **$40 [≈ £20]**

The Art of Tanning and Currying Leather ...
- See Vallancey, Charles.

Arthur, R.
- A Popular Treatise on the Diseases of the Teeth: including a Description of their Structure and Modes of Treatment; together with the Usual Mode of Inserting Artificial Teeth. Phila: 1846. 187 pp. 28 text ills. Sl discold. New cloth, orig front cvr laid on.
(Whitehart) **£60 [≈ $115]**

Artis, E.T.
- Antediluvian Fossil Phytology Illustrated by a Collection of the Fossil Remains of Plants, peculiar to the Coal Formations of Great Britain. London: 1838. 2nd edn. 4to. xiii, 24 pp. 24 plates. Some marg browning & staining. New buckram.
(Baldwin) **£85 [≈ $163]**
- Antediluvian Phytology Illustrated by a Collection of the Fossil Remains of Plants peculiar to the Coal Formations of Great Britain. London: 1838. 4to. xiv,24 pp. 25 plates. Few minor stains. Cloth, rebacked.
(Wheldon & Wesley) **£120 [≈ $230]**

Aschoff, Ludwig
- Lectures on Pathology delivered in the United States. New York: Hoeber, 1959. 8vo. 365 pp. Orig bndg, some spotting to cvrs.
(Goodrich) **$45 [≈ £23]**

Ashhurst, John
- Injuries of the Spine. With an Analysis of nearly Four Hundred Cases. Phila: 1867. 1st edn. 127 pp. Orig bndg, fine.
(Fye) **$200 [≈ £104]**

Ashley, Charles & Hayward, Charles
- Wireless Telegraphy and Wireless Telephony. 1912. 1st edn. 141 pp. 7 photos, 90 ills. Orig bndg, sl faded.
(New Wireless) **$90 [≈ £46]**
- Wireless Telegraphy and Wireless Telephony. 1916. 2nd edn. 141 pp. 7 photos, 90 ills. Orig bndg.
(New Wireless) **$90 [≈ £46]**

Ashton, John
- Curious Creatures in Zoology. London: Nimmo, 1890. 1st edn. xi,348 pp. 130 plates

& ills. Orig pict green cloth, t.e.g., fine.
(Gough) **£60 [≈ $115]**

Ashton, T.J.
- On the Diseases, Injuries, and Malformations of the Rectum and Anus, with Remarks on Habitual Constipation. Phila: 1860. 1st Amer edn. 292 pp. W'cut ills. Orig bndg, fine.
(Fye) **$150 [≈ £78]**

Astley, Hubert D.
- My Birds in Freedom and Captivity. London: Dent, 1900. 1st edn. xvi,254 pp. Plates, ills. Orig pict 2-tone cloth gilt, t.e.g.
(Gough) **£35 [≈ $67]**

Astley, Philip
- Astley's System of Equestrian Education, exhibiting the Beauties and Defects of the Horse ... Dublin: Thomas Burnside, 1802. 8th edn. xvi,197 pp. Frontis port, 9 plates. Extra map dated 1808 bound in. Orig bds, rebacked.
(Bookline) **£180 [≈ $345]**

Astruc, Jean
- A General and Compleat Treatise on all the Diseases incident to Children ... London: John Nourse, 1746. 1st English edn. 8vo. [x], 229,[1] pp. Edges on 2 ff reinforced. Contemp calf, rebacked.
(Bookpress) **$750 [≈ £390]**

Atchley, Shirley C.
- Wild Flowers of Attica. London: 1938. 4to. xix, 59 pp. 22 cold plates. Cloth.
(Henly) **£68 [≈ $130]**
- Wild Flowers of Attica. London: 1938. 4to. 22 cold plates. Prelims foxed. Buckram, sl discold.
(Grayling) **£30 [≈ $57]**

Atkins, William
- A Discourse Shewing the Nature of the Gout ... London: for Tho. Fabian ... & the author, 1694. xvi,128 pp. Port frontis. Browned, few sm tears & flaws not affecting text. Old sheep, worn. Wing A.4125. *(Clark)* **£750 [≈ $1,439]**

Atkinson, Herbert
- The Old English Game Fowl: Its History, Description, Management, Breeding and Feeding. London: Fanciers' Gazette, (1891). 1st edn. One of 100. 4to. 66 pp. Ills. Occas foxed (a few ff inc title heavily). Orig cloth gilt.   *(Respess)* **$200 [≈ £104]**

Atkinson, John C.
- British Birds' Eggs and Nests, Popularly Described. New Edition. London: Routledge, 1870. Lge 12mo. viii,182 pp, advt leaf. 12

cold plates by W.S. Coleman, lge fldg chart in pocket. Orig cloth gilt, a.e.g., spine faded, inner hinges cracked.
(Fenning) **£24.50 [≃ $47]**

- British Birds' Eggs and Nests, Popularly Described. Illustrated by W.S. Coleman. London: Routledge, [1880s]. 8vo. viii,182 pp, advt leaf. 12 chromolitho plates, lge fldg chart in pocket. Orig cloth pict blocked in gold & black.   *(Claude Cox)* **£20 [≃ $38]**

Atkinson, Philip

- The Elements of Electric Lighting. 1889. 3rd edn. 260 pp. 102 ills. Orig bndg.
(New Wireless) **$65 [≃ £34]**

Atkinson, W.N. & J.B.

- Explosions in Coal Mines. London: 1886. 1st edn. 8vo. [iv],144 pp. 13 cold plans. Orig illust wraps, rather marked, spine sl defective at ends, sgntr on cvr.
(Bow Windows) **£55 [≃ $105]**

Atlee, Washington

- General and Differential Diagnosis of Ovarian Tumours, with Special Reference to the Operation of Ovariotomy ... Phila: 1873. 1st edn. 482 pp. Orig bndg.
(Fye) **$350 [≃ £182]**

Attman, Artur

- L.M. Ericsson Telephone Co. 100 Years. 1977. 1st edn. 3 vols. 1181 pp. Num ills. Orig bndgs. Dws.   *(New Wireless)* **$95 [≃ £50]**

Audubon, John James

- The Original Water-Colour Paintings for The Birds of America. Reproduced in Colour ... New York: American Heritage; Crown, 1966. 2 vols in one. 4to. 431 cold plates, 21 figs. Orig buckram. Dw. *(Claude Cox)* **£40 [≃ $76]**

Augusta, J. & Burian, Z.

- Prehistoric Animals; Prehistoric Man; The Age of Monsters; Prehistoric Sea Monsters; Prehistoric Reptiles & Birds. London: 1960-65. 4 vols. Roy 4to & 1 vol 8vo. Together 5 vols. Num cold plates. Orig cloth. Dws. 4to vols in slipcases.
(Baldwin) **£100 [≃ $191]**

Austin, J.A.

- Ambulance Sermons. Being a Series of Popular Essays on Medical and Allied Subjects. London: 1887. xvi,384 pp. Occas foxing. Orig cloth, sl marked & worn.
(Whitehart) **£25 [≃ $47]**

The Autocar Handbook ...

- The Autocar Handbook. A Guide to the Motor Car. Fifth Edition. Entirely revised. London: Iliffe, [1913]. 8vo. 297,[7],xvi pp. Fldg sectional drawing, num text ills. Orig ptd & pict cloth, extremities sl worn.
(Claude Cox) **£25 [≃ $47]**

Aveling, James Hobson

- English Midwives, their History and Prospects. Reprint of the 1872 Edition with an Introduction ... London: 1967. 8vo. [xxxi], [vii], 186 pp. Port. Orig cloth.
(Bickersteth) **£25 [≃ $47]**

Axe, J. Wortley (ed.)

- The Horse, Its Treatment in Health and Disease ... London: Gresham Publ Co, 1906. 9 vols. Cold plates, photos, text ills. Orig dec dark green cloth.   *(Bookline)* **£70 [≃ $134]**

Ayre, Joseph

- Pathological Researches into the Nature and Treatment of Dropsy of the Brain, Chest, Abdomen, Ovarium, and Skin ... Second Edition illustrated with Cases. London: Longman ..., 1829. 8vo. xii,287 pp. Sl foxing. Half roan.   *(Goodrich)* **$195 [≃ £101]**

B., J.

- The Epitome of the Art of Husbandry ... see Blagrave, Joseph.

Babbage, Charles

- The Ninth Bridgewater Treatise. A Fragment ... Second Edition. London: Murray, 1838. 2nd edn, enlgd. 8vo. viii, xxii, 23-270, [4], [4 advt dated Feb 1838] pp. W'cut ills. Marg lib stamps. Orig cloth, paper label, upper jnt cracked.   *(Gaskell)* **£350 [≃ $6,719]**

Babington, Charles Cardale

- Flora of Cambridgeshire. London: 1860. lvi, 327 pp. Fldg map. Orig cloth, dull.
(Whitehart) **£18 [≃ $34]**

Babington, Churchill

- Catalogue of the Birds of Suffolk. London: Van Voorst, 1884-86. 1st edn. 8vo. [viii],281 pp. Map, 7 photo plates. Orig cloth gilt spine (sl worn at ends).   *(Gough)* **£50 [≃ $95]**

Babson, G.K.

- A Descriptive Catalogue of the Grace K. Babson Collection of the Works of Sir Isaac Newton. New York: Herbert Reichner, 1950. 8vo. xv,228 pp. Num plates. Cloth.
(Gemmary) **$150 [≃ £78]**

Bacon, Sir Francis, Lord Verulam

- Baconiana. Or certain Genuine Remains ... London: J.D. for Richard Chiswell, 1679. 1st edn. Issue with imprimatur on B4v. 8vo. Engvd & ptd titles, [viii],104,270 pp. Divisional title B1. Contemp calf, upper jnt split but holding. Wing B.269..
(Gaskell) **£350 [≈ $671]**
- The Two Bookes of Sr Francis Bacon, of the Proficience and Advancement of Learning, Divine and Humane. Oxford: L.L. for Thomas Huggins, 1633. 4to. [ii], 1-166, 169-335, [i] pp. Last few ff creased. Mod half calf. STC 1166.   *(Clark)* **£285 [≈ $547]**

Bacon, Roger

- The Cure of Old Age ... Translated out of Latin; with Annotations ... Account of his Life ... By Richard Browne ... also A Physical Account of the Tree of Life ... London: 1683. 1st edn in English. [xl], 156, [vi], 108,[8] pp. 19th c mor gilt, a.e.g., sl rubbed. Wing B.372
(Clark) **£480 [≈ $921]**

Badger, John

- A Collection of Remarkable Cures of the King's Evil, Perfected by the Royal Touch. Collected from the Writings of many Eminent Physicians and Surgeons ... London: Cooper, 1748. 8vo. Half-title,64 pp. Some foxing & early underlining. Antique style bds.
(Goodrich) **$135 [≈ £70]**

Badham, Charles David

- Prose Halieutics or Ancient and Modern Fish Tattle. London: Parker, 1854. 1st edn. 8vo. Orig cloth.   *(Ximenes)* **$100 [≈ £52]**
- A Treatise on the Esculent Funguses of England. London: 1847. 1st edn. Roy 8vo. x, 138 pp. Cold frontis, 17 cold & 3 plain plates. Sound ex-lib, stamp on title. Some soiling. Orig cloth, reprd.
(Wheldon & Wesley) **£100 [≈ $191]**
- A Treatise on the Esculent Funguses of England. London: 1863. 2nd edn. 8vo. xvi,152 pp. 12 hand cold plates. Orig cloth, sl worn.   *(Wheldon & Wesley)* **£80 [≈ $153]**

Badt, Francis B.

- Dynamo Tenders' Handbook. 1892. 2nd edn. 226 pp. 140 ills. Orig bndg, some wear to crnrs. Sgnd by the author.
(New Wireless) **$65 [≈ £34]**
- Electric Transmission Hand-Book. 1891. 1st edn. 97 pp. 22 ills. Orig bndg.
(New Wireless) **$55 [≈ £29]**

Bagnall, J.E.

- The Flora of Warwickshire ... London: 1891. One of 500 sgnd. 8vo. xxxiv,579 pp. Map in pocket. Cloth, trifle used.
(Wheldon & Wesley) **£50 [≈ $95]**

Bailes, G.M. (ed.)

- Modern Mining Practice. A Practical Work of Reference on Mining Engineering. Sheffield: J.H. Bennett & Co, [ca 1915]. 5 vols. 4to. Num photos & figs. Cloth.
(Gemmary) **$100 [≈ £52]**

Bailey, P.

- Intracranial Tumours. Springfield: 1948. 2nd edn. xxiv,478 pp. Frontis, 16 plates, text ills. Orig cloth, recased, new endpapers.
(Whitehart) **£40 [≈ $76]**

Bailey, Pearce

- Accident and Injury, their Relations to Diseases of the Nervous System. New York: 1899. 1st edn. 430 pp. Orig bndg, fine.
(Fye) **$150 [≈ £78]**

Baillie, Matthew

- A Series of Engravings, accompanied with Explanations, which are intended to illustrate the Morbid Anatomy of ... the Human Body. London: 1985. Facs reprint of the 1799 edn. One of 520. 235 pp. 73 plates. leather gilt. Slipcase.   *(Whitehart)* **£200 [≈ $383]**

Baily, W.H.

- Figures of Characteristic British Fossils. Vol. 1 Palaeozoic [all published]. London: [1867-] 1875. 8vo. lxxx,126 pp. 42 plates. Orig cloth.
(Wheldon & Wesley) **£30 [≈ $57]**

Bain, Alexander

- Mental and Moral Science: a Compendium of Psychology and Ethics. London: Longmans, Green, 1868. Contemp half calf, rubbed, front jnt cracked. *(Waterfield's)* **£60 [≈ $115]**

Baines, Sir Jervoise A.

- Ethnography (Castes and Tribes) ... Strassburg: 1912. 1st edn. Roy 8vo. [4],211, [2] pp. Contemp cloth. *(Fenning)* **£45 [≈ $86]**

Baker, A.L.

- Elliptic Functions. An Elementary Text-Book for Students of Mathematics. New York: 1890. v,118 pp. 3 figs. Orig bndg.
(Whitehart) **£25 [≈ $47]**

Baker, E.C.S.

- Fauna of British India. Birds. London:

1922-30. 2nd edn. 8 vols. 8vo. 35 cold & 4 plain plates. Cloth.
(Wheldon & Wesley) **£180 [≈ $345]**
- The Game Birds of India, Burma and Ceylon. London: 1921-30. 3 vols. Roy 8vo. 2 maps, 60 cold & 18 plain plates. Paper of vol 1 plates sl browned. Vols 1 & 2 orig half mor, vol 3 orig cloth, as issued, vols 1 & 2 spines sl faded.   *(Wheldon & Wesley)* **£300 [≈ $575]**
- Indian Pigeons and Doves. London: 1913. Roy 8vo. xv,260 pp. 27 cold plates. Orig half mor.   *(Wheldon & Wesley)* **£175 [≈ $335]**

Baker, H.
- Of Microscopes and the Discoveries made thereby. Vol. I. The Microscope Made Easy. London: Dodsley, 1785. 2nd edn. 8vo. xxiii, 324 pp. 14 plates. New leather.
(Gemmary) **$325 [≈ £169]**
- The Well-Spring of Sciences ... London: 1650. Sm 8vo. [4],312,[21] pp. Lacks last leaf of index. Sm crnr torn from 1 leaf affecting text. Later half leather, sl worn, front hinge cracked.   *(Whitehart)* **£135 [≈ $259]**

Baker, J.G.
- Handbook of the Amaryllideae. London: 1888. 8vo. xii,216 pp. Cloth, good ex-lib.
(Wheldon & Wesley) **£35 [≈ $67]**
- Handbook of the Amaryllideae. London: (1888) 1972. 8vo. xii,216 pp. Wraps.
(Wheldon & Wesley) **£15 [≈ $28]**
- North Yorkshire, Studies of its Botany, Geology, Climate and Physical Geography. London: 1863. 8vo. xii,353 pp. 4 cold maps. Orig cloth, sl worn.
(Wheldon & Wesley) **£70 [≈ $134]**

Baker, T. Thorn
- The Spectroscope. London: Bailliere, Tindall & Cox, 1923. 2nd edn. 8vo. x,208 pp. 98 text figs. Cloth.   *(Gemmary)* **$35 [≈ £18]**
- Wireless Pictures and Television. 1926. 1st edn. 188 pp. 99 ills. Orig bndg.
(New Wireless) **$160 [≈ £83]**

Bakewell, R.
- An Introduction to Geology ... London: 1815. 2nd edn. 8vo. xxviii,492 pp. Geological map, 4 sections, 2 plates, 4 hand cold & 3 fldg [sic]. Contemp calf, rebacked.
(Henly) **£235 [≈ $451]**
- An Introduction to Geology. Edited by B. Silliman ... New Haven: 1829. 1st Amer edn. 8vo. xx,400,128 pp. Cold map, 6 plates. New bds.   *(Wheldon & Wesley)* **£75 [≈ $143]**

Baldwin, J.H.
- The Large and Small Game of Bengal and the North Western Provinces of India. London: 1876. 8vo. Frontis, text ills. Sl browning. New half mor.   *(Grayling)* **£87 [≈ $167]**

Balfour, F.M.
- A Treatise on Comparative Embryology. London: 1885. 2nd edn. 2 vols. 429 figs. Lib stamps, few sm reprs. Lib bndgs.
(Whitehart) **£60 [≈ $115]**

Ball, James Moores
- The Sack-'Em-Up Men. An Account of the Rise and Fall of the Modern Resurrectionists. London: 1928. xxxi,216 pp. Frontis, 60 plates, 18 text figs. Dw.
(Whitehart) **£40 [≈ $76]**

Ball, Sir R.
- The Story of the Sun. London: 1893. 1st edn. xii,376 pp. 11 plates, 82 text figs. Orig cloth, t.e.g.   *(Whitehart)* **£15 [≈ $28]**

Ball, W.W.R.
- A Short Account of the History of Mathematics. London: Macmillan, 1919. Stereotype edn. 8vo. xxiv,522 pp. Leather, some edge wear.   *(Gemmary)* **$75 [≈ £39]**

Ballance, Sir Charles Alfred
- Essays on the Surgery of the Temporal Bone. London: 1919. 1st edn. 2 vols. 4to. 612 pp. Ills. Orig bndg, front inner hinge vol 1 cracked.   *(Fye)* **$750 [≈ £390]**
- Some Points in the Surgery of the Brain and its Membranes. London: 1907. 1st edn. 451 pp. Orig bndg, fine.   *(Fye)* **$500 [≈ £260]**

Ballance, Sir Charles Alfred & Green, Charles D.
- Essays on the Surgery of the Temporal Bone. London: Macmillan, 1919. 1st edn. 2 vols. 4to. Frontis port, 125 plates (many cold, 2 addtnl outline plates on tissue), 120 text figs. Orig cloth. Sgnd pres inscrptn by Ballance.
(Rootenberg) **$2,500 [≈ £1,302]**

Ballenger, Edgar (ed.)
- History of Urology. Baltimore: 1933. 1st edn. 2 vols. 385; 361 pp. Orig bndg.
(Fye) **$350 [≈ £182]**

Balston, Thomas
- William Balston, Paper-Maker 1759-1849. London: Methuen, 1954. 8vo. xii,171 pp. 14 plates, 18 text ills. Orig cloth. Dw.
(de Beaumont) **£68 [≈ $130]**

Bampfield, Robert William
- A Practical Treatise on Tropical Dysentery, more particularly as it occurs in the East Indies ... London: Burgess & Hill, 1819. 1st edn. 8vo. 3 ff,x,352,11 pp. Fldg table. 19th c calf, backstrip relaid.
(Offenbacher) **$450 [≈£234]**

Bancroft, E.
- An Essay on the Natural History of Guiana, in South America ... London: 1769. 8vo. iv, 402, [2] pp. Frontis. Lib blind stamp on title. Contemp calf, rebacked. Anon.
(Wheldon & Wesley) **£300 [≈$575]**

Banfield, A.W.F.
- The Mammals of Canada. London: 1974. Folio. Maps, cold plates, text ills. Dw (sl torn).
(Grayling) **£35 [≈$67]**

Bankoff, George
- The Story of Plastic Surgery. London: 1952. 1st edn. 224 pp. Orig bndg.
(Fye) **$100 [≈£52]**

Banks, John
- On the Power of Machines, etc., including Doctor Barker's Mill, Westgarth's Engine, Cooper's Mill ... Kendal: W. Pennington, sold by W.J. & J. Richardson, 1803. 1st edn. viii, 127 pp. 3 fldg plates. Orig bds, uncut, edges worn, backstrip sl defective.
(Hollett) **£450 [≈$863]**
- A Treatise on Mills. London: W. Richardson, 1795. 1st edn. 8vo. xxiv,172,[4] pp. 10 pp subscribers. 3 fldg plates. Later half calf.
(Bookpress) **$585 [≈£304]**

Banks, W.L.
- Flora Exotica; or Companion to the Green-House ... London: [1893]. Only edn. 12mo. 40 hand cold aquatint plates. Contemp mor, gilt spine, a.e.g. *(Burmester)* **£200 [≈$383]**

Bannerman, David A.
- Birds of the Maltese Archipelago. Malta: 1976. 22 cold plates, text ills. Dw.
(Grayling) **£50 [≈$95]**
- The Birds of Tropical West Africa ... London: 1930-51. Only edn. 8 vols. Imperial 8vo. 7 maps, 83 cold & 3 plain plates, 710 text figs. Some foxing. Sl worm end of vol 5. Orig buckram, t.e.g., vol 5 sl rubbed. 7 dws (worn).
(Sotheran's) **£698 [≈$1,340]**
- The Birds of Tropical West Africa ... London: 1930-51. 8 vols. Imperial 8vo. 7 maps, 83 cold & 3 plain plates, 695 text figs. Vol 1 endpapers trifle water stained, occas

foxing (mainly of endpapers). Orig cloth, trifle used, early vols sl faded & marked.
(Wheldon & Wesley) **£550 [≈$1,055]**
- The Birds of West and Equatorial Africa. London: 1953. 2 vols. 8vo. 30 cold & 24 other plates, 433 text figs. Orig cloth. Dws.
(Henly) **£80 [≈$153]**
- Handbook of the Birds of Cyprus & Migrants of the Middle East. London: 1971. Num cold plates. *(Grayling)* **£35 [≈$67]**
- Handbook of the Birds of the British Isles. Volume 12 [only]. London: 1963. Imperial 8vo. 31 cold plates. Dw (sl frayed).
(Grayling) **£25 [≈$47]**

Bannerman, D.A. & W.M.
- Birds of Cyprus. London: 1958. Imperial 8vo. lxix, 384 pp. Map, 16 cold & 15 other plates, 2 line drawings. Orig cloth.
(Wheldon & Wesley) **£100 [≈$191]**
- Birds of the Atlantic Islands. London: 1963-68. 4 vols. Roy 8vo. 11 maps, 47 cold & 54 plain plates, num text figs. Orig cloth.
(Wheldon & Wesley) **£420 [≈$806]**
- Birds of the Atlantic Islands. London: 1963-68. 4 vols. Roy 8vo. 11 maps, 47 cold & 54 plain plates, num text figs. V sl foxing & staining. Cloth. Dws (worn).
(Wheldon & Wesley) **£350 [≈$671]**

Bannerman, D.A. & Vella-Gaffiero, J.A.
- Birds of the Maltese Archipelago. Valetta: 1976. 570 pp. Map, 22 cold plates, over 200 ills. *(Wheldon & Wesley)* **£25 [≈$47]**

Barbette, Paul
- The Practice of the most successful Physitian Paul Barbette, Doctour of Physick. With the Notes and Observations of Frederick Deckers ... London: 1675. [xvi],272 pp. Frontis. Last page in facs on old paper. Cambridge style calf antique. *(Whitehart)* **£380 [≈$729]**

Barbut, J.
- The Genera Vermium exemplified by various Specimens of the Animals contained in the Orders of the Intestina et Mollusca Linnaei [Part 1, only]. London: 1783. 4to. [ii],xx, ii, 101 pp. Engvd title, 11 hand cold plates (sl offset). Qtr calf, rebacked.
(Wheldon & Wesley) **£160 [≈$307]**

Barclay, D., Bolus, H.M., & Steer, E.J.
- A Book of South African Flowers. Cape Town: 1925. Cr 4to. xvii,174 pp. 30 cold plates, 50 other ills. Orig buckram.
(Wheldon & Wesley) **£45 [≈$86]**

Barclay, John
- A Series of Engravings, representing the Bones of the Human Skeleton; with the Skeletons of some of the Lower Animals. By Edward Mitchell, engraver, Edinburgh ... Edinburgh: 1820. Folio. 2 parts in one vol. 32 + 3 plates. Orig ptd bds, rebacked, sl worn.
(Spelman) **£180 [≃ $345]**

Bard, Samuel
- A Guide for Young Shepards or Facts and Observations on the Character and Value of Merino Sheep: with Rules and Precepts for their Management, and the Treatment of their Diseases ... New York: Collins, 1811. 12mo. vi, 112 pp. Orig qtr sheep, mrbld bds.
(Goodrich) **$495 [≃ £257]**

Bardeen, Charles
- Anatomy in America. Madison: 1905. 1st edn. 205 pp. Orig wraps, uncut.
(Fye) **$100 [≃ £52]**

Barker, Fordyce
- On Sea-Sickness. New York: Appleton, 1870. 8vo. 36 pp. Limp bds, a.e.g., stained.
(Goodrich) **$85 [≃ £44]**

Barker, Lewellys
- The Nervous System and its Constituent Neurons ... New York: Appleton, 1901. Later imp. 8vo. xxxii,1122 pp. 676 ills. Orig half calf, sl worn. *(Goodrich)* **$225 [≃ £117]**
- The Nervous System and its Constituent Neurones. New York: 1899. 1st edn. 1132 pp. Orig bndg. *(Fye)* **$250 [≃ £130]**
- The Young Man and Medicine. New York: 1928. 8vo. 202 pp. Orig bndg. Author's pres copy. *(Goodrich)* **$65 [≃ £33]**

Barker, T.V.
- Graphical and Tabular Methods in Crystallography. London: Thomas Murby & Co, 1922. 8vo. xvi,152 pp. 99 text figs. Cloth.
(Gemmary) **$60 [≃ £31]**

Barlow, A.E.
- Corundum, Its Occurrence, Distribution, Exploitation, and Uses. Ottawa: Department of Mines, 1915. 8vo. vii,377 pp. Cold frontis, 28 plates. Fine ex-lib. orig wraps.
(Gemmary) **$65 [≃ £34]**

Barlow, P., et al.
- A Treatise on the Strength of Materials. London: 1867. xii,396 pp. 19 plates (sl foxed), num text figs. Orig cloth, new endpapers.
(Whitehart) **£50 [≃ $95]**

Barlow, W.
- New Theories of Matter and of Force. London: Sampson Low, 1885. 8vo. xii,395 pp. 35 text figs. Ex-lib. Cloth, unopened.
(Gemmary) **$50 [≃ £26]**

Barnard, George P.
- The Selenium Cell; Its Properties and Applications. 1930. 1st edn. 331 pp. 258 ills. Orig bndg. *(New Wireless)* **$50 [≃ £26]**

Barnes, H.T.
- Ice Formation with special reference to Anchor-Ice and Frazil. New York: 1906. x,260 pp. 40 text ills. Orig cloth, sl faded & sl worn. *(Whitehart)* **£18 [≃ $34]**

Baron, John
- The Life of Edward Jenner, M.D. With Illustrations of his Doctrines, and Selections from his Correspondence. London: Colburn, 1827. 1st issue of the 1st vol. 8vo. xxiv, 624 pp. Port. Few sm lib stamps. Orig bds, uncut, rebacked. *(Bickersteth)* **£90 [≃ $172]**

Barrett, C.G.
- The Lepidoptera of the British Islands ... London: 1892-1907. Large Paper. 11 vols. Roy 8vo. 504 hand cold plates. Sl foxing. Half morocco, t.e.g.
(Wheldon & Wesley) **£1,150 [≃ $2,207]**

Barrett-Hamilton, G.E.H.
- A History of British Mammals. Continued by M.A.C. Hinton. London: 1910-21. Parts 1-21, all published. Bound in 3 vols. Roy 8vo. 2 ports, 14 cold & 57 plain plates. Cloth, trifle marked. *(Wheldon & Wesley)* **£100 [≃ $191]**

Barrow, Isaac
- The Usefullness of Mathematical Learning Explained and Demonstrated ... London: 1734. 1st edn. xxxii,440,[23] pp. Frontis port, fldg plate. Contemp calf, rebacked, crnrs worn. *(Whitehart)* **£150 [≃ $287]**

Barsky, Arthur
- Plastic Surgery. Phila: 1938. 1st edn. 355 pp. 432 ills. Ink notes on endpapers, front endpaper torn. Orig bndg, cvrs spotted.
(Fye) **$100 [≃ £52]**

Bartholow, Roberts
- Medical Electricity. 1881. 1st edn. 256 pp. 96 ills. Orig bndg. *(New Wireless)* **$120 [≃ £63]**

Barth, M. & Roger, Henry
- A Practical Treatise on Auscultation.

Translated with Notes, by Francis Smith. Phila: 1845. 1st Amer edn. 160 pp. Orig bndg.   *(Fye)* **$200 [≈£104]**

Bartlett, Elisha
- The History, Diagnosis, and Treatment of Typhoid and Typhus Fever; with an Essay on the Diagnosis of Bilious Remittent and of Yellow fever. Phila: 1842. 1st edn. 393 pp. Half leather, hinges weak, hd of backstrip defective.   *(Fye)* **$300 [≈£156]**

Barton, B.H. & Castle, T.
- The British Flora Medica: a History of the Medicinal Plants of Great Britain. A New Edition by J.R. Jackson. London: 1877. 8vo. xxii, 447 pp. 48 cold plates (soiled). New cloth.   *(Wheldon & Wesley)* **£65 [≈$124]**

Barton, Clara
- The Red Cross in Peace and War. Washington: 1899. 1st edn. 703 pp. Num photo ills. Orig bndg.   *(Fye)* **$100 [≈£52]**

Barton, F.T.
- Pheasants in Covert and Aviary. London: 1912. 4to. 288 pp. 4 cold plates, 56 ills. Orig cloth, trifle worn, trifle loose.
          (Wheldon & Wesley) **£35 [≈$67]**

Barton, J.
- A Lecture on the Geography of Plants. London: 1827. Post 8vo. [4],94 pp. 4 fldg maps. Orig bds, uncut, rebacked.
          (Wheldon & Wesley) **£30 [≈$57]**

Barwick, P.
- The Life of the Reverend Dr. John Barwick, D.D. ... London: 1724. London: 1724. [28], 552, [38] pp. 2 frontis ports. Some pp dusty, last index page remargd with v sl loss of text. New three qtr leather.
                    (Whitehart) **£50 [≈$95]**

Bary, A. de
- Comparative Anatomy of the Vegetative Organs of the Phanerogams and Ferns. Oxford: 1884. xvi,659 pp. 241 text figs. Binder's cloth.   *(Whitehart)* **£35 [≈$67]**

Bashforth, F.
- An Attempt to test the Theories of Capillary Action by comparing the Theoretical and Measured Forms of Drops of Fluids ... Cambridge: 1883. Lge 4to. 80,59 pp. Frontis. Outer edge of cvrs water stained.
                    (Whitehart) **£25 [≈$47]**

Baskin, Leonard
- Ars Anatomica. New York: 1972. One of 2500. Folio. 13 sep plates with commentary laid into cloth backed folder. Slipcase. Sgnd by Baskin.   *(Fye)* **$300 [≈£156]**

Bastholm, E.
- The History of Muscle Physiology. Copenhagen: Acta Hist Scient Nat Med Vol 7, 1950. 8vo. Ills. Orig bndg, uncut & unopened.   *(Goodrich)* **$75 [≈£39]**
- The History of Muscle Physiology. Copenhagen: 1950. 1st edn. 257 pp. Orig wraps.   *(Fye)* **$60 [≈£31]**

Bastian, H.C.
- The Brain as an Organ of Mind. Fourth Edition. London: International Scientific Series, 1890. 8vo. xvi,708 pp. Ca 180 text ills. Orig cloth, jnts sl rubbed.
                (Bow Windows) **£25 [≈$47]**

Bateman, Thomas
- Delineations of Cutaneous Diseases exhibiting the Characteristic Appearances ... comprised in the Classification of the late Dr. Willans ... London: 1849. New edn. Folio. viii pp. 72 hand cold plates, with accompanying text. Contemp half mor, fine.
                (Hemlock) **$600 [≈£312]**
- A Practical Synopsis of Cutaneous Diseases, according to the Arrangement of Dr. Willan. Phila: 1818. 1st Amer edn. 348 pp. Cold frontis. Leather.   *(Fye)* **$300 [≈£156]**

Bateson, Beatrice
- William Bateson, F.R.S., Naturalist: His Essays & Addresses together with a Short Account of his Life. Cambridge: 1928. 1st edn. 469 pp. Orig bndg.   *(Fye)* **$75 [≈£39]**

Bateson, William
- Materials for the Study of Variation treated with especial regard to Discontinuity in the Origin of Species. London: 1894. 8vo. xvi, 598 pp. 209 text figs. Sl foxing & signs of use. Orig cloth, sl used, inner jnts reprd..
          (Wheldon & Wesley) **£120 [≈$230]**
- Mendel's Principles of Heredity. Cambridge: 1906. 1st edn. xiv,396 pp. 3 ports, 6 cold plates, 33 text figs. 2 sm marg ink stains. Rebound in cloth, leather label.
                    (Whitehart) **£65 [≈$124]**
- Mendel's Principles of Heredity. Cambridge: 1913. 3rd imp, with addtns. xiv, 413 pp. 3 ports, 6 cold plates, 38 text figs. Orig cloth, spine v sl worn.   *(Whitehart)* **£38 [≈$72]**
- Problems of Genetics. New Haven: 1913.

8vo. ix,258 pp. 4 plates (2 cold), text figs. Reviews &c pasted to endpapers. Cloth, trifle used, front inner jnt taped.
(Wheldon & Wesley) **£50 [≈ $95]**

- Scientific Papers of William Bateson, edited by R.C. Punnett. Cambridge: 1928. 2 vols. 4to. 36 plates (16 cold). Vol 1 f.e.p. sl marked. Orig cloth, hd of spines v sl worn.
(Wheldon & Wesley) **£100 [≈ $191]**

Battershall, Jesse P.
- Food Adulteration and its Detection. New York: Spon, 1887. 1st edn. 8vo. 328 pp. Cold frontis, plates. Orig cloth, hd of spine sl rubbed.   *(Chapel Hill)* **$65 [≈ £33]**

Baudelocque, Jean Louis
- An Abridgment of Mr. Heath's Translation of Baudelocque's Midwifery. With Notes, by William P. Dewees, M.D. Phila: Thomas Dobson ..., 1811. 1st Amer edn. 8vo. xvi,588 pp. 7 plates. Title browned & backed. Sl browning & foxing. Mod half calf.
(Hemlock) **$150 [≈ £78]**

Bauer, Max
- Precious Stones. Translated from the German with additions by L.J. Spencer. London: Griffin, 1904. Cr 4to. xv,627 pp. 8 cold & 12 b/w plates, 94 text ills. Foxed. Rebound in leather.   *(Gemmary)* **$275 [≈ £143]**
- Precious Stones. Translated from the German with additions by L.J. Spencer. London: Griffin, 1904. Cr 4to. xv,627 pp. 8 cold & 12 b/w plates, 94 text ills. Half mor, t.e.g., spine v sl rubbed.   *(Gemmary)* **$450 [≈ £234]**

Bauerman, H.
- Text-Book of Systematic Mineralogy. New York: Appleton, 1881. Cr 8vo. vii,367 pp. 373 text figs. Rebound in cloth.
(Gemmary) **$45 [≈ £23]**
- Text-Book of Systematic Mineralogy. New York: Appleton, 1903. Cr 8vo. vii,367 pp. 373 text figs. V.g. ex-lib. Cloth.
(Gemmary) **$40 [≈ £20]**
- Textbook of Systematic Mineralogy. London: 1881. vii,367 pp. 373 ills. Ink stamp & sgntr on title. Half leather, edges rubbed, sm label at ft of spine.   *(Whitehart)* **£15 [≈ $28]**

Baumgartner, Leona
- John Howard, Hospital and Prison Reformer: A Bibliography. Baltimore: 1939. 8vo. 77 pp. Orig bndg. Author's pres inscrptn.
(Goodrich) **$65 [≈ £33]**

Baumgartner, Leona & Fulton, John F.
- A Bibliography of the Poem Syphilis sive Morbus Gallicus by Girolamo Fracastoro of Verona. Yale: UP, 1935. Med 8vo. 10 plates. Orig bndg.   *(Georges)* **£50 [≈ $95]**

Bausch, E.
- Manipulation of the Microscope. Rochester, New York: Bausch & Lomb Optical Co, 1891. 2nd edn. Cr 8vo. 127 pp. 31 ills. Cloth.   *(Gemmary)* **$30 [≈ £15]**

Bax, Edmund I.
- Popular Electric Lighting, being Practical Hints to Present and Intending Users of Electric Energy ... Second Edition. London: Biggs & Co, 1892. 2nd edn, enlgd. Cr 8vo. viii, 159,xi advt pp. 45 ills. Orig pict cloth.
(Fenning) **£18.50 [≈ $36]**

Baxter, E.V. & Rintoul, L.J.
- The Birds of Scotland ... London: 1953. 2 vols. Roy 8vo. 2 cold & 24 photo plates. Cloth, inner jnts vol 1 strained & reprd. Dws.   *(Wheldon & Wesley)* **£120 [≈ $230]**

Bayliss, William M.
- Principles of General Physiology. London: 1915. 1st edn. 850 pp. Orig bndg.
(Fye) **$150 [≈ £78]**
- Principles of General Physiology. London: 1918. 2nd edn, rvsd. xxiv,858 pp. 260 text figs. Orig cloth.   *(Whitehart)* **£30 [≈ $57]**
- The Vaso-Motor System. London: 1923. 1st edn. 163 pp. Orig bndg. *(Fye)* **$100 [≈ £52]**

Bayma, Joseph
- The Elements of Molecular Mechanics. London: Macmillan, 1866. 1st edn. [2 advt], xviii, 266,[2 advt] pp. 3 plates. Orig cloth.   *(Fenning)* **£65 [≈ $124]**

Bayne, David, alias Kinneir
- A New Essay on the Nerves and the Doctrine of the Animal Spirits ... London: Innys & Manby, 1738. 1st edn. 4to. vi,167,19 advt pp. A few stains. Sm hole affecting 1 letter. Contemp calf, rebacked.
(Rootenberg) **$400 [≈ £208]**

Bayne, P.
- The Life and Letters of Hugh Miller. London: 1871. 1st edn. 2 vols. 8vo. Frontis ports, 1 cold plate, facs letter, title vignettes. Some dust & other marks. 2 gatherings sl loose. Orig cloth, some crnrs bumped.
(Bow Windows) **£120 [≈ $230]**

Bazin, Gilles Auguste
- The Natural History of Bees ... Translated from the French. London: Knapton, Vaillant, 1744. 1st edn in English. 8vo. [xvi],542, [xvi] pp. 12 fldg plates. Orig calf, rebacked. Anon.
(Bickersteth) £280 [≈ $537]

Beale, L.S.
- How to Work with the Microscope. London: Harrison, 1868. 4th edn. 8vo. xix,383 pp. 69 plates, text figs. Cloth, v loose, spine torn..
(Gemmary) $50 [≈ £26]
- How to Work with the Microscope. London: Harrison, 1880. 5th edn. 8vo. xvi,518 pp. 99 plates, text figs. Cloth.
(Gemmary) $100 [≈ £52]
- The Microscope and its Application to Practical Medicine. London: 1867. 3rd edn. xxiv, 320 pp. 58 plates. Sm tear in half-title. Cloth worn, spine defective, new endpapers.
(Whitehart) £35 [≈ $67]
- The Microscope in Medicine. Phila: Lindsay & Blakiston, 1878. 4th edn. 8vo. xxviii,539 pp. 86 plates. Rebound in cloth, sl loose.
(Gemmary) $100 [≈ £52]

Beale, Lionel J.
- A Treatise on Deformities exhibiting a Concise View of the Nature and Treatment of the Principle Distortions and Contractions of the Limbs, Joints, and Spine. London: 1830. 1st edn. 248 pp. 4 litho plates, sev w'cut ills. Orig bndg. Inscrbd by the author.
(Fye) $1,000 [≈ £520]

Beale, Sir William Phipson
- An Amateur's Introduction to Crystallography. New York: Longmans, Green, 1915. 8vo. vii,220 pp. 136 text figs. Good ex-lib. Cloth. *(Gemmary)* $35 [≈ £18]

Beamish, Richard
- Memoirs of the Life of Sir Marc Isambard Brunel. London: Longman, Green ..., 1862. 8vo. Orig green cloth, crnrs sl bumped, sm tear hd of spine. *(Georges)* £50 [≈ $95]
- Memoirs of the Life of Sir Marc Isambard Brunel. Second Edition Revised and Corrected. London: Longman, Green ..., 1862. 8vo. xviii, [1], 357, [2 advt] pp. Port, 8 plates, 8 ills. Orig cloth gilt, inner jnts reprd.
(Fenning) £85 [≈ $163]

Bean, Percy & McCleary, William
- The Chemistry and Practice of Finishing. Manchester: Hutton, Hartley, 1926. 3rd edn. 2 vols. Sm 4to. 96 cloth samples, num plates. Orig cloth. *(Bookpress)* $175 [≈ £91]

Beard, George
- Stimulants and Narcotics; Medically, Philosophically, and Morally Considered. New York: 1871. 1st edn. 155 pp. Orig bndg.
(Fye) $100 [≈ £52]

Beasley, Henry
- The Book of Prescriptions, containing 3000 Prescriptions, collected from the Practice of the most Eminent Physicians and Surgeons ... Second Edition. London: Churchill, 1859. 12mo. [2 advt], xvi,548 pp. Occas sl dusty. Rec bds. *(Fenning)* £32.50 [≈ $63]

Beaumont, R.
- Woollen and Worsted. The Theory and Technology of the Manufacture of Woollen, Worsted and Union Yarns and Fabrics. London: 1916. 2 vols. xxxvi,640 pp. 42 plates, 469 text ills. Occas sl stains. Sm lib stamp on verso of some plates. Orig bndg.
(Whitehart) £40 [≈ $76]
- Woollen and Worsted ... London: 1919. 3rd rvsd edn. xxxix,716 pp. 42 plates, ca 500 text ills, 18 tables. Orig half rexine, t.e.g., edges worn, rear cvr stained.
(Whitehart) £35 [≈ $67]

Beaumont, William
- Experiments and Observations on the Gastric Juice, and the Physiology of Digestion. Plattsburgh: F.P. Allen, 1833. 1st edn. 8vo. 280 pp. 3 w'engvs. Usual light browning. Orig bds, rebacked in cloth. Half mor slipcase. *(Rootenberg)* $2,500 [≈ £1,302]
- Experiments and Observations on the Gastric Juice, and the Physiology of Digestion. Plattsburgh: 1833. 1st edn. Sm repr to crnr of title. Orig bds, rebacked, new endpapers.
(Fye) $1,750 [≈ £911]
- Experiments and Observations on the Gastric Juice ... Reprinted from the Plattsburgh Edition, with Notes by Andrew Combe, M.D. Edinburgh: 1838. 1st British edn. Lge 12mo. xix,319 pp. Text figs. 2 lib stamps. Lacks half-title. Title rehinged. Rec qtr mor.
(Bickersteth) £220 [≈ $422]
- Experiments and Observations on the Gastric Juice, and the Physiology of Digestion. Reprinted from the Plattsburgh Edition, with Notes by Andrew Combe, MD. Edinburgh: 1838. 1st British edn. 8vo. Half-title ,xx,319, advt pp. Orig cloth, some wear to headband.
(Goodrich) $775 [≈ £403]

Beauties ...
- The Beauties & Defects in the Figure of the Horse ... see Alken, Henry. T.

Beaven, E.W.
- Tales of the Divining Rod. London: Stockwell, 1899. Only edn. 8vo. 322 pp. Orig cloth.   *(Young's)* **£40 [≈ $76]**

Beck, C.
- The Microscope. A Simple Handbook. London: 1921-4. 1st edn. 2 vols. 144; 231 pp. 301 figs. Orig cloth, faint stain front cvr vol 2.   *(Whitehart)* **£35 [≈ $67]**

Beck, Carl
- The Crippled Hand and Arm. Phila: 1925. 1st edn. 243 pp. 302 ills. Orig bndg.
                    (Fye) **$200 [≈ £104]**

Beck, L.C.
- Mineralogy of New York. Albany: Nat Hist of New York Part 3, 1842. 4to. xxiv,536 pp. 8 plates, 533 ills. Sl foxing throughout. Orig dec cloth, lacks backstrip.
                    (Gemmary) **$100 [≈ £52]**

Beck, R.
- A Treatise on the Construction, Proper Use, and Capabilities of Smith, Beck and Beck's Achromatic Microscopes. London: Van Voorst, 1865. Roy 8vo. viii,144 pp. 28 plates. Cloth.   *(Gemmary)* **$375 [≈ £195]**

Beck, T.R.
- Elements of Medical Jurisprudence. Vol 2 [only]. Albany: 1823. 471 pp. Occas foxing. Leather, rebacked.   *(Whitehart)* **£45 [≈ $86]**

Becker, Friedrich
- The Breed of the Racehorse: its Developments and Transformations. London: British Bloodstock Agency, (1936). 4to. 267,[1] pp. Frontis, 2 fldg tables. Orig cloth gilt.   *(Fenning)* **£55 [≈ $105]**

Beckett, Joseph
- Elements & Practice of Mensuration and Land Surveying ... With an Appendix ... London: Lackington, Allen, 1804. 1st edn. 8vo. xv,342 pp, advt leaf. 4 fldg plates, text figs. Orig bds, uncut, rebacked.
                    (Bickersteth) **£85 [≈ $163]**

Beclard, P.A.
- Elements of General Anatomy: translated from the last Edition of the French ... Notes and Corrections by Robert Knox. Edinburgh: 1830. 8vo. xxvii,399 pp. Title damp stained. Orig bds, uncut, worn. Translator's pres copy.   *(Goodrich)* **$195 [≈ £101]**

Beddard, Frank E.
- Animal Coloration ... London: Swan Sonnenschein, 1892. 1st edn. 8vo. viii,288 pp. 4 hand cold lithos, num text ills. Publisher's pres stamp on title. Orig pict cloth gilt, backstrip relaid.   *(Gough)* **£65 [≈ $124]**
- A Book of Whales. London: Murray, 1900. 1st edn. xv,320 pp. 22 plates, 40 text ills. Orig red pict cloth, faded.   *(Gough)* **£50 [≈ $95]**

Bedini, S.A.
- Early American Scientific Instruments and their Makers. Washington: US Natl Museum Bulletin 231, 1964. 8vo. xii,184 pp. 85 ills. Wraps.   *(Gemmary)* **$75 [≈ £39]**

Beebe, William
- Pheasants. Their Lives and Homes. Garden City, New York: Doubleday, Doran, 1936. 1st edn. 2 vols. 4to. xxviii,258; xv,310 pp. 64 plates, mostly cold. Orig green cloth gilt, hd of spines v sl frayed. *(Karmiole)* **$150 [≈ £78]**
- Pheasants, their Lives and Homes. London: 1937. Sheets of the Amer 1936 edn with a new London title-page. 2 vols in one. Sm 4to. xxviii, 309 pp. 32 cold & 32 plain plates. Buckram, sl faded.
                    (Wheldon & Wesley) **£100 [≈ $191]**

Beebe, William, et al.
- Tropical Wild Life in British Guiana; Zoological Contributions from the Tropical Research Station of the New York Zoological Society. Volume 1 [all published]. New York: 1917. 8vo. xx,504 pp. 144 photo plates. Orig pict green cloth gilt.   *(Gough)* **£45 [≈ $86]**

Beetham, Bentley
- The Home-Life of the Spoonbill; The Stork and Some Herons. London: Witherby, 1910. 1st edn. Sm 4to. viii,47 pp. 32 mtd photo plates. Occas sl foxing as usual. Orig green cloth gilt.   *(Gough)* **£40 [≈ $76]**

Beeton, Mrs Isabella
- The Book of Household Management ... London: S.O. Beeton, 1861. 1st edn. 8vo. One vol in 2. xxxix, 1112 pp. Hand cold frontis & title (green & grey), 12 chromolitho plates, num w'engvs in text. Occas spotting & soiling. Contemp cloth.
                    (Frew Mackenzie) **£795 [≈ $1,526]**
- The Book of Household Management ... London: S.O. Beeton, 1861. 1st edn. One vol in 2. Cold frontis, pict title, 12 cold plates. Contemp half roan & mrbld bds, gilt spines, a trifle rubbed.   *(Ximenes)* **$1,600 [≈ £833]**
- The Book of Household Management ...

London: S.O. Beeton, 1861. 1st edn. 8vo.
One vol in 2. xxxix, 1112 pp. Hand cold title
(green & pink), 12 chromolitho plates, num
w'engvs in text. Occas sl soiling. Orig mor
backed cloth gilt, backstrip sl defective &
relaid.   *(Frew Mackenzie)* **£495 [≈ $950]**
- The Book of Household Management ... One
Hundred and Eighty-Seventh Thousand.
London: Ward, Lock & Tyler, [1869]. 8vo.
[2],xl,[1], 1139 pp. 12 cold litho plates,
w'engvd vignettes. Trimmed (no loss). Some
marks & use. Early half roan, rather worn.
                    (Beech) **£85 [≈ $163]**
- The Book of Household Management ... New
Edition. London: Ward, Lock, n.d. 3rd edn
(?). 8vo. xli,1139 pp. Half-title. 12 cold plates.
Frontis laid down & rehinged. 1 leaf
strengthened at edge. Orig purple cloth,
recased, rebacked in mor.
                    (Gough) **£100 [≈ $191]**

Behrens, Charles (ed.)
- Atomic Medicine. New York: 1949. 416 pp.
Orig bndg.   *(Fye)* **$150 [≈ £78]**

Beigelman, M.N. & P.M.
- 400 Books from a Private Library. Los
Angeles: 1967. Lge 8vo. 291 pp. Orig bndg.
                 (Goodrich) **$150 [≈ £78]**

Belcher, C.F.
- The Birds of Nyasaland ... London: 1930.
8vo. Prelims v sl spotted. Orig bndg, spotted.
                (Central Africana) **£75 [≈ $143]**
- The Birds of the District of Geelong,
Australia. Geelong: 1914. xxix,384 pp. 50
photos. Orig bndg. Sgnd by the author.
                 (Whitehart) **£40 [≈ $76]**

Belcher, T.W.
- Memoir of Sir Patrick Dun (Knt.) M.D.,;
M.P.; Physician-General to the Army ...
Second Edition, revised and enlarged.
Dublin: 1866. 8vo. 80 pp. Ptd slip. Port. Orig
cloth gilt.   *(Fenning)* **£75 [≈ $143]**

Bell, Alexander Graham
- The Mechanism of Speech. 1916. 8th edn.
133 pp. Orig bndg.
                 (New Wireless) **$110 [≈ £57]**
- The Telephone. A Lecture entitled
Researches in Electric Telephony. London &
New York: Spon, 1878. 1st sep edn. 8vo. 32
pp, 16 blank ff. 30 text ills. Rec cloth, orig
front wrapper bound in.
                 (Rootenberg) **$750 [≈ £390]**

Bell, Benjamin
- A System of Surgery. Phila: 1791. 1st Amer
edn. 570,xxx pp. Leather, inner hinges taped,
front outer hinge cracked, half backstrip
missing.   *(Fye)* **$200 [≈ £104]**
- A System of Surgery. Worcester, Mass.:
1791. 1st Amer edn. 4 vols. 100 w'cut ills.
Foxed. Leather, scuffed & worn, hinges
cracked.   *(Fye)* **$300 [≈ £156]**

Bell, Sir Charles
- The Anatomy and Philosophy of Expression
as Connected with the Fine Arts. London:
1847. 4th edn. 275 pp. Num engvs. Leather.
                 (Fye) **$400 [≈ £208]**
- The Hand Its Mechanism and Vital
Endowments as Evincing Design. London:
Pickering, 1834. 3rd edn. 8vo. xvi,348 pp.
Num w'engvs in text. Orig half calf, front jnt
split.   *(Goodrich)* **$250 [≈ £130]**
- The Nervous System of the Human Body;
embracing the Papers delivered to the Royal
Society on the Subject of the Nerves.
Washington: 1833. 1st Amer edn. 8vo. 233
pp. 12 engvd plates. Some foxing. Unabused
ex-lib. Contemp half calf.
                 (Goodrich) **$595 [≈ £309]**
- A System of Operative Surgery, founded on
the Basis of Anatomy. Hartford: 1812. 1st
Amer edn. 2 vols. 323; 272 pp. 19 plates. Rec
leatherette, new endpapers.
                 (Fye) **$400 [≈ £208]**

Bell, E.T.
- The Development of Mathematics. New
York: 1945. 2nd edn. xiii,637 pp. Traces of
lib stamp erasure on title & spine.
                 (Whitehart) **$25 [≈ $47]**

Bell, F.D. & Young, Frederick
- Reasons for Promoting and Cultivating New
Zealand Flax. London: Smith Elder ..., 1842.
1st edn. 8vo. 34,[4 advt] pp. Stitched as
issued.   *(Young's)* **£40 [≈ $76]**

Bell, J. & Redwood, T.
- Historical Sketch of the Progress of Pharmacy
in Great Britain. London: 1880. [iv], 415 pp.
Orig cloth, sl dust stained.
                 (Whitehart) **£35 [≈ $67]**
- Historical Sketch of the Progress of Pharmacy
in Great Britain. London: 1880. [iv], 415 pp.
Sgntr on title. Sm nick front endpaper. Cloth,
sl dusty.   *(Whitehart)* **£40 [≈ $76]**

Bell, John
- Discourses on the Nature and Cure of
Wounds. Walpole: 1807. 1st Amer edn.

192,180 pp. 2 plates. Rec half leather.
(Fye) **$300 [≈ £156]**

Bell, John & Charles
- Anatomy of the Human Body. From the
Fourth London Edition ... New York: Collins
& Perkins, 1809-10. 4 vols in 2. 8vo. xxviii,
284; xxiv, 309; x,308; v,243 pp. 33 plates.
Foxed. Contemp leather, scuffed, vol 1 jnts
weak, lacks 1 label.   *(Schoyer)* **$150 [≈ £78]**

Bell, L.
- The Telescope. New York: 1922. 1st edn, 6th
imp. ix,287 pp. Frontis, 190 figs.
(Whitehart) **£35 [≈ $67]**

Bell, Thomas
- A History of British Quadrupeds including
the Cetaceae. London: 1874. 2nd edn. xviii,
474, 2 pp. 160 w'engvs. Cloth, spine faded.
(Henly) **£30 [≈ $57]**
- A History of British Reptiles. London: 1849.
2nd edn. 8vo. xxiv,159 pp. 50 ills. Cloth,
spine faded.   *(Henly)* **£30 [≈ $57]**
- A History of the British Stalk-Eyed
Crustacea. London: 1853. 1st edn. 8vo. lxv,
386 pp. 174 w'cut engvs. Some contemp
annotations. Sm lib stamp on title. Calf,
backstrip relaid.   *(Henly)* **£45 [≈ $86]**

Bell, W.G.
- The Great Plague in London in 1665.
London: (1924) 1951. xiii,361 pp. Frontis, 40
ills. Occas foxing on page edges. Spine faded.
(Whitehart) **£25 [≈ $47]**

Belt, Elmer
- Leonardo the Anatomist. Lawrence: 1955.
8vo. 76 pp. Ills. Dw. *(Goodrich)* **$30 [≈ £15]**

Benjamin, Park
- The Age of Electricity. 1887. 1st edn. 381 pp.
143 ills. Orig bndg, hd of spine chipped.
(New Wireless) **$55 [≈ £29]**

Bennett, A.W.
- The Flora of the Alps. London: 1897. 2 vols.
8vo. 120 cold plates. Lib stamps on titles. Sl
foxing, mostly of text. Cloth.
(Wheldon & Wesley) **£60 [≈ $115]**

Bennett, J.W.
- A Selection of Rare and Curious Fishes found
upon the Coast of Ceylon. London: 1851. 3rd
edn. 4to. 30 hand cold plates. Sm hole in
lower blank marg of 1st 11 plates reprd.
Margs at beginning trifle frayed & brittle.
Mod calf backed bds.

(Wheldon & Wesley) **£1,100 [≈ $2,111]**

Bennett, N.
- The Science and Practice of Dental Surgery.
London: 1931. 2nd edn. 2 vols. 1230 figs.
Orig bndg.   *(Whitehart)* **£35 [≈ $67]**

Bennion, E.
- Antique Medical Instruments. London:
Sotheby's, 1979. xiii,355 pp. Num ills. Dw.
(Whitehart) **£35 [≈ $67]**

Benson, C.W. & White, C.H.N.
- Check List of the Birds of Northern
Rhodesia. Lusaka: 1957. 8vo. Maps, ills. Orig
bndg.   *(Central Africana)* **£55 [≈ $105]**

Bentham, George
- Flora Hongkongensis: a Description of the
Flowering Plants and Ferns of the Island of
Hongkong. London: 1861. 8vo. 20,li,482 pp.
Map. New cloth.
(Wheldon & Wesley) **£140 [≈ $268]**

Bentham, George & Hooker, Sir J.D.
- Handbook of the British Flora ... Fifth
Edition. London: L. Reeve, 1887. 8vo. lxxx,
584 pp. Contemp prize calf gilt, sm wormhole
in upper jnt.   *(Gough)* **£30 [≈ $57]**
- Handbook of the British Flora, together with
Illustrations of the British Flora and Further
Illustrations of British Plants. London:
1946-49. 3 vols. Cr 8vo. Cloth.
(Henly) **£30 [≈ $57]**

Bentham, George & Mueller, F.
- Flora Australiensis: a Description of the
Plants of the Australian Territory. London:
1863-78. 7 vols. 8vo. Vol 3 lacks pp 1-32.
Sound ex-lib. Cloth, jnts of 2 vols torn.
(Wheldon & Wesley) **£200 [≈ $383]**

Berdoe, Edward
- Dying Scientifically; A Key to St. Bernard's.
By Aesculapius Scalpel [pseud.]. London:
Swan Sonnenschein ..., 1888. 2nd edn. 8vo.
120 pp. Orig yellowback bds, some wear to
cvrs but spine mostly intact.
(de Beaumont) **£38 [≈ $72]**
- The Origin and Growth of the Healing Art:
a Popular History of Medicine. London:
1893. 8vo. 509 pp. Orig bndg.
(Goodrich) **£35 [≈ £18]**
- The Origin and Growth of the Healing Art.
A Popular History of Medicine ... London:
1893. xii,509 pp. Frontis, 4 plates. Top edge
of cloth v worn.   *(Whitehart)* **£25 [≈ $47]**

Bergman, E. von, et al.
- A System of Practical Surgery. New York: 1904. 1st English transl. 5 vols. Orig bndg, fine.   *(Fye)* **$250 [≈ £130]**

Bergman, Torbern Olof
- A Dissertation on Elective Attractions ... Translated from the Latin by the Translator of Spallanzani's Dissertations [Thomas Beddoes]. London: Murray, 1785. 1st edn in English. 8vo. xiv,[2],382,[2] pp. 4 fldg plates, 3 fldg tables. Few marg water stains Half calf.
               (Rootenberg) **$500 [≈ £260]**

Berkeley, George
- The Medicinal Virtues of Tar Water fully explained ... Dublin Printed. London: reprinted for the proprietors of the Tar Water Warehouse, & sold by M. Cooper, 1744. 8vo. Sm tear on 2 ff (no loss). Sewn as issued, uncut.   *(Waterfield's)* **£235 [≈ $451]**

Berkeley, M.J.
- Handbook of British Mosses. London: 1863. 1st edn. 8vo. xxxvi,324 pp. 1 plain & 23 hand cold plates. Orig cloth, rebacked.
               (Wheldon & Wesley) **£40 [≈ $76]**
- Introduction to Cryptogamic Botany. London: 1857. 8vo. ix,604 pp. 127 text figs. Cloth, trifle used & faded.
               (Wheldon & Wesley) **£30 [≈ $57]**
- Outlines of British Fungology. London: 1860. 8vo. xvii,442 pp. 1 plain & 23 hand cold plates. Ex-lib. Orig cloth, spine worn.
               (Wheldon & Wesley) **£60 [≈ $115]**
- Outlines of British Fungology. London: 1860. 8vo. xvii,442 pp. 1 plain & 23 hand cold plates. Half mor.
               (Wheldon & Wesley) **£80 [≈ $153]**

Berkenhout, J.
- Clavis Anglica Linguae Botanicae; or, a Botanical Lexicon; in which the Terms of Botany, particularly those ... of Linnaeus ... are explained. London: 1764. Sm 8vo. xii, [215] pp. Lib b'plate. Contemp sheep.
               (Wheldon & Wesley) **£35 [≈ $67]**

Berly, J.A.
- The Voltaic Accumulator. 1889. 1st edn. 202 pp. 62 ills. Orig bndg.
               (New Wireless) **$55 [≈ £29]**

Berry, R.J.
- Inheritance and Natural History. London: Collins New Naturalist, 1977. 1st edn. 8vo. 350 pp. 4 cold & 8 plain plates. Orig cloth. dw.   *(Henly)* **£35 [≈ $67]**

- The Natural History of Orkney. London: Collins New Naturalist, 1985. 1st edn. The true 1st issue. 8vo. 304 pp. Ills. Inscrptn on flyleaf. Orig cloth gilt. Dw.
               (Hollett) **£100 [≈ $191]**

Berry, R.J. & Johnston, J.L.
- The Natural History of Shetland. London: Collins New Naturalist, 1980. 1st edn. The true 1st issue. 8vo. 380 pp. Ills. Orig cloth gilt. Dw.   *(Hollett)* **£120 [≈ $230]**

Bertin, R.J.
- Treatise on the Diseases of the Heart. Phila: 1833. 1st English translation. 449 pp. Rec qtr leather & mrbld bds.   *(Fye)* **$250 [≈ £130]**

Berzelius, J.J.
- An Attempt to Establish a Pure Scientific System of Mineralogy by the Application of the Electro-Chemical Theory and Chemical proportions. L: Baldwin, 1814. Cr 8vo. 144 pp. Qtr leather, bds loose, rubbed.
               (Gemmary) **$375 [≈ £196]**
- The Use of the Blowpipe in Chemical Analysis and in the Examination of Minerals. London: 1822. 8vo. xxxix,344 pp. Lge fldg table, 3 plates. Half calf, rebacked.
               (Henly) **£140 [≈ $268]**

Bessemer, Sir Henry
- Sir Henry Bessemer, F.R.S.: an Autobiography. London: 1905. Thick 4to. Num plates. Sm lib stamps throughout. Buckram, rubbed.   *(Bell)* **£80 [≈ $153]**

Best, Charles H.
- Selected Papers. Toronto: 1963. 1st edn. 723 pp. Orig bndg.   *(Fye)* **$100 [≈ £52]**

Beth, E.W.
- The Foundations of Mathematics. A Study in the Philosophy of Science. Amsterdam: 1959. xxvi, 741 pp. Cloth sl dusty.
               (Whitehart) **£35 [≈ $67]**

Bettany, G.T.
- Eminent Doctors: their Lives and their Work. London: 1885. 2nd edn. 2 vols. 311; 318 pp. Orig bndg, uncut.   *(Fye)* **$150 [≈ £78]**
- Eminent Doctors: Their Lives and their Work. London: [1885]. 2nd edn. 2 vols. Few marg cold pencil notes. Orig bndg.
               (Whitehart) **£38 [≈ $72]**

Bettmann, Otto
- A Pictorial History of Medicine. Springfield: 1956. 4to. 318 pp. Num plates & ills. Orig

bndg.   *(Goodrich)* **$45 [≈ £23]**

Bevan, E.
- The Honey Bee, its Natural History, Physiology and Management. London: 1838. 8vo. xxiv, 447 pp. Frontis, vignette, text figs. Blind stamp on title. Cloth, rebacked.
(Wheldon & Wesley) **£50 [≈ $95]**

Bewick, Thomas
- History of British Birds. London: 1797-1804. 1st edn. 2 vols. xxx,335; xx,400 pp. 218 figs, 227 vignettes & tailpieces. Contemp calf, jnts sl weak. Roscoe 14d & 17d, both variant B; the indelicate vignette p 289 is in the inked state, before the bar. *(Henly)* **£285 [≈ $547]**
- A History of British Birds. Newcastle upon Tyne: 1809. 3rd edn. 2 vols in one. 8vo. Num engvs. Trifle used. Contemp calf, v used.
(Wheldon & Wesley) **£100 [≈ $191]**
- A History of British Birds. Newcastle: 1847. 10th edn vol 1, 8th edn vol 2. 2 vols. 8vo. 318 w'cut figs, 310 vignettes & tail-pieces, 14 text figs. Orig brown cloth.
(Spelman) **£160 [≈ $307]**
- A History of British Birds. Newcastle: 1847. 2 vols. 8vo. xxxix, xxxvi, 374; xxiii, 406, xi pp. Num w'engvs. Cloth gilt, partly unopened. *(Henly)* **£150 [≈ $286]**
- A General History of Quadrupeds ... Third Edition. Newcastle upon Tyne, 1792. 8vo. x, 483 pp. Occas sl spotting & browning. W'engvs. Rebound in green half mor gilt.
(Frew Mackenzie) **£125 [≈ $239]**
- A General History of Quadrupeds ... Fourth Edition. Newcastle upon Tyne: 1800. 8vo. [i advt], x, 525 pp. W'engvd ills. Contemp half calf, gilt spine, sm repr hd of spine.
(Gough) **£225 [≈ $431]**
- A General History of Quadrupeds ... Seventh Edition. Newcastle upon Tyne: for T. Bewick, 1820. iv,528,x pp. Contemp red half mor. Roscoe 7(a) or (b) - this copy having a page size 25 x 17 cm which is half way between Roscoe's Extra Imperial & Royal octavo. *(Bickersteth)* **£165 [≈ $316]**
- A General History of the Quadrupeds. London: 1970. Reprint of 5th edn. 8vo. 225 figs, 111 vignettes & tailpieces. Cloth. Dw.
(Henly) **£28 [≈ $53]**
- A Supplement to the History of British Birds. Newcastle: 1821. 2 parts in one vol. 8vo. Num w'cuts. Some foxing, trifle soiled. Orig bds, uncut. *(Wheldon & Wesley)* **£45 [≈ $86]**

Beyschlag, F., et al.
- The Deposits of the Useful Minerals and Rocks: Their Origin, Form, and Content.

London: Macmillan, 1914. 2 vols, all published. 8vo. 467 ills. Orig cloth, hinges cracking. *(Gemmary)* **$125 [≈ £65]**

Bibliotheca Walleriana ...
- See Sallander, Hans.

Bichat, Marie-Francois-Xavier
- Physiological Researches on Life and Death ... Translated by F. Gold, Notes by F. Magendie. Boston: Richardson & Lord, 1827. 1st Amer edn. 8vo. 334 pp. Frontis port. Browned. Orig calf, somewhat stained.
(Rootenberg) **$250 [≈ £130]**
- A Treatise on the Membranes in general, and on Different Membranes in Particular ... New Edition, Enlarged ... Boston: Summings & Hilliard ..., 1813. 1st Amer edn. 8vo. 251, [1] pp. Errata on verso of last leaf. Three qtr calf gilt. *(Hemlock)* **$350 [≈ £182]**

Bickerton, Thomas H.
- A Medical History of Liverpool from the Earliest Days to the Year 1920 ... London: Murray, 1936. 1st edn. Sm thick 4to. xx,313 pp. 8 maps & plans, 24 plates, 50 ports. Orig cloth gilt. Interesting pencil notes.
(Hollett) **£75 [≈ $143]**

Bidwell, S.
- Curiosities of Light and Sight. London: 1899. xii,226 pp. 50 text ills. Perf lib stamp on title & preface, other lib stamps. Spine reprd, inner hinge v sl cracked.
(Whitehart) **£35 [≈ $67]**

Bigsby, J.J.
- The Flora and Fauna of the Devonian and Carboniferous Periods. The Genera and Species arranged in Tabular Form ... London: 1878. 4to. x,[i],447 pp. Fldg table. Ex-lib. Cloth.
(Wheldon & Wesley) **£80 [≈ $153]**

Billings, E.R.
- Tobacco: Its History, Varieties, Culture, Manufacture and Commerce ... Hartford: Amer Publ Co, 1875. 1st edn. Lge 8vo. 486 pp. Frontis, ills. Orig cloth.
(Karmiole) **$150 [≈ £78]**

Billmeir, J.A.
- A Supplement to a Catalogue of Scientific Instruments. London: Frank Partridge, 1957. Roy 8vo. 99 pp. 21 plates. Cloth.
(Gemmary) **$50 [≈ £26]**

Billroth, Theodor
- Clinical Surgery. Extracts from the Reports of Surgical Practice between the Years 1860-1876. London: New Sydenham Soc, 1881. xx,518 pp. 9 plates, 29 figs. Orig cloth.
(Whitehart) £40 [≈ $76]
- Clinical Surgery. Extracts from the Reports of Surgical Practice between the Years 1860-1876. London: 1881. 1st English translation. 518 pp. Litho plates, w'cuts. Orig bndg, fine.
(Fye) $275 [≈ £143]
- General Surgical Pathology and Therapeutics, in Fifty-one Lectures ... Translated from the Fourth German Edition ... by Charles E. Hackley. New York: Appleton, 1883. 8vo. xvi,835 pp. Orig cloth, rubbed.
(Goodrich) $65 [≈ £33]
- Lectures on Surgical Pathology and Therapeutics. London: 1877-78. 1st English translation. 2 vols. 438; 543 pp. 200 w'cut ills. Orig bndgs, sm hole spine vol 2.
(Fye) $150 [≈ £78]
- The Medical Sciences in the German Universities ... New York: Macmillan, 1924. 8vo. xiv,292 pp. Orig bndg.
(Goodrich) $65 [≈ £34]

Binz, C.
- Lectures on Pharmacology for Practitioners and Students. London: New Sydenham Society, 1895-97. 1st edn in English. 2 vols. 8vo. Text figs. Lib stamp on vol 2 title. Orig brown cloth gilt.
(Gough) £35 [≈ $67]
- Lectures on Pharmacology for Practitioners and Students. London: New Sydenham Society, 1895-97. 2 vols. Orig cloth.
(Whitehart) £25 [≈ $47]

Birch, Thomas
- The Life of the Honourable Robert Boyle. London: A. Millar, 1744. 1st edn. 8vo. [ii], [iv], 458,[14], [2] pp. Frontis. Contemp calf, hinges starting, sl worn. Contains a port not called for by Fulton. *(Bookpress)* $185 [≈ £96]

Birkett, John
- The Diseases of the Breast, and their Treatment. London: 1850. 1st edn. 264 pp. 11 partly hand cold plates. Orig bndg, fine.
(Fye) $400 [≈ £208]

Bischof, G.
- Elements of Chemical and Physical Geology. Translated by Benjamin H. Paul and J. Drummond. London: Cavendish Society, 1854-55-59. 3 vols. 8vo. Num tables. Good ex-lib. Orig dec cloth, worn.
(Gemmary) $500 [≈ £260]

Blackall, John
- Observations on the Nature and Cure of Dropsies, and particularly on the Presence of the Coagulable Part of the Blood in Dropsical Urine ... Appendix ... Angina Pectoris ... London: 1818. 3rd edn. 416 pp. Qtr leather.
(Fye) $200 [≈ £104]

Blackburn, I.W.
- Intracranial Tumors among the Insane ... Washington: GPO, 1903. 8vo. 6,94,index pp. 30 photo plates, 65 ills. Orig cloth, worn, old label removed. *(Goodrich)* $145 [≈ £76]

Blackfan, K.D. & Diamond, L.K.
- Atlas of the Blood in Children. New York: 1944. 8vo. 320 pp. 70 cold plates. Orig bndg.
(Goodrich) $60 [≈ £31]

Blackham, G.E.
- On Angular Aperture of Objectives for the Microscope. Read before the Microscopical Congress, at Indianapolis, August 15th, 1878. New York: 1880. 1st edn. 8vo. 21 pp. 18 fldg plates. Orig bndg.
(Bow Windows) £50 [≈ $95]

Blackwall, John
- A History of the Spiders of Great Britain and Ireland. London: Ray Society, 1861-64. 2 vols in one. Folio. 29 hand cold plates (minor foxing, upper blank marg of 1 plate water stained, margs of 2 plates reprd). Buckram.
(Wheldon & Wesley) £300 [≈ $575]
- A History of the Spiders of Great Britain and Ireland. London: Ray Society, 1861. 1st edn. Folio. vi,384 pp. 29 hand cold plates. Contemp green half mor, gilt dec spine, t.e.g.
(Gough) £350 [≈ $671]

Blackwell, J. Kenyon
- Explosions in Coal Mines, their Causes, and the Means available for their Prevention and Control ... London: Taylor & Francis, 1853. 1st edn. 8vo. Title dusty. Disbound.
(Young's) £26 [≈ $49]

Blagrave, Joseph
- Blagrave's Astrological Practice of Physick ... London: for Obadiah Blagrave, 1689. 2nd edn. 8vo. [xvi],139,[5 advt] pp. Upper marg trimmed close. Mod half calf antique. Wing B.3114. *(Bickersteth)* £300 [≈ $575]
- The Epitome of the Art of Husbandry. Comprising all necessary directions for the improvement of it ... By J.B. Gent. London: for Ben. Billingsley, 1669. 1st edn. Engvd title, ptd title,306,6 advt pp. V sl browning.

Contemp sheep, rebacked. Wing B.3115.
(*C.R. Johnson*) **£1,500** [≈ **$2,879**]

Blaine, Delabere
- Canine Pathology or a Full Description of the Diseases of Dogs ... London: Boosey, 1817. 1st edn. 8vo. 3 ff,50,184 pp. W'cut title vignette, 3 text vignettes by Austin. Old three qtr calf, gilt spine.
(*Offenbacher*) **$450** [≈ **£234**]

Blair, Revd David
- The Universal Preceptor; or, General Grammar of Arts, Sciences, and Useful Knowledge, for the Use of Schools. London: Phillips, 1831. 25th edn. Sm 8vo. Frontis, num engvs. Contemp mor (sl worn).
(*Stewart*) **£25** [≈ **$47**]

Blake, E.
- Constipation and some Associated Disorders. London: 1900. 2nd edn. xv,286 pp. 29 text figs. Orig cloth, dust stained & sl worn, hinge cracked, sm tear in spine.
(*Whitehart*) **£18** [≈ **$34**]

Blakston, W., Swaysland, W., & Wiener, A.F.
- The Illustrated Book of Canaries and Cage-Birds, British and Foreign. London: Cassell, [ca 1890]. 4to. viii,448 pp. 56 cold plates. Orig dec cloth, recased.
(*Wheldon & Wesley*) **£150** [≈ **$287**]

Blancard or Blankaart, Steven
- The Physical Dictionary. Wherein the Terms of Anatomy, the Names and Causes of Diseases, Chyrurgical Instruments ... are accurately described ... London: 1708. 5th edn, enlgd. 8vo. [iv],318,[2 advt] pp. Plate. Sl foxed at ends. Rec qtr calf.
(*Burmester*) **£85** [≈ **$163**]
- The Physical Dictionary. Wherein the Terms of Anatomy, the Names and Causes of Diseases, Chirurgical Instruments ... are accurately described ... London: 1726. 7th edn. [iv],370 pp. Marg damp stain to prelims. Some pp sl discold. Orig leather, v worn.
(*Whitehart*) **£120** [≈ **$230**]

Bland, M.
- Algebraical Problems, producing Simple and Quadratic Equations, with their Solutions, designed as an Introduction to the Higher Branches of Analytics ... Appendix ... Cambridge: 1832. 6th edn. viii,438 pp. A few v sl stains. Orig bds, rebacked in leather.
(*Whitehart*) **£35** [≈ **$67**]

Blandford, G. Fielding
- Insanity and Its Treatment: Lectures on the Treatment, Medical and Legal of Insane Patients. Edinburgh: 1871. 1st edn. 8vo. viii, 435 pp. Orig cloth, spine faded.
(*Bickersteth*) **£40** [≈ **$76**]

Blankaart, Steven
- See Blancard or Blankaart, Steven.

Blatter, E.
- Beautiful Flowers of Kashmir. London: 1928-29. Vol 2 a later issue. 2 vols. 8vo. 1 plain & 63 cold plates. Cloth, not uniform, vol 2 faded.
(*Wheldon & Wesley*) **£65** [≈ **$124**]

Blogg, M.W.
- Bibliography of the Writings of Sir William Osler ... Revised and Enlarged with an Index. Baltimore: 1921. 8vo. 96 pp. Orig bndg.
(*Goodrich*) **$85** [≈ **£44**]

Blunt, David E.
- Elephant. London: 1933. 8vo. Ills. Prelims sl foxed. Orig cloth, sl marked.
(*Grayling*) **£300** [≈ **$575**]

Blunt, W.
- The Art of Botanical Illustration. London: Collins New Naturalist, 1950. 1st edn. 8vo. xxxi, 304 pp. 46 cold & 32 plain plates. Orig cloth.
(*Henly*) **£60** [≈ **$115**]
- Flora Magnifica ... see Jones, Paul.

Blyth, A.W.
- A Dictionary of Hygiene and Public Health ... London: 1876. xii,672 pp. Fldg cold map. Orig bndg, sl worn. (*Whitehart*) **£25** [≈ **$47**]

Bockenheimer, P. & Frohse, F.
- Atlas of Typical Operations in Surgery. Edited by J.H. Evans. New York & London: 1906. 252 pp. 60 ills. Half mor, rather worn.
(*Whitehart*) **£35** [≈ **$67**]

Bolton, H.
- The Geology of Rossendale. Bacup: [1890]. Cr 8vo. 167 pp, subscribers. Text ills. Cloth.
(*Henly*) **£28** [≈ **$53**]

Bolton, John
- Geological Fragments collected principally from Rambles among the Rocks of Furness and Cartmel. Ulverston: 1869. 1st edn. 264 pp. 5 plates (sl spotted). Orig cloth gilt.
(*Hollett*) **£85** [≈ **$163**]

Bolus, H.M.L.
- Notes on Mesembrianthemum and some Allied Genera with . Descriptions of a Hundred New Species. Part 1. Cape Town: 1928. 8vo. 156 pp. 21 cold & num other ills. Cloth.   *(Wheldon & Wesley)* **£80 [≈ $153]**

Bonavia, E.
- The Cultivated Oranges and Lemons etc. of India and Ceylon, with Researches into their Origin and the Derivation of their Names and other Useful Information. London: 1888-90. 1st edn. 2 vols. 8vo & oblong 4to. 260 (1-259, 116a) plates. Good ex-lib. Cloth.
    (Wheldon & Wesley) **£80 [≈ $153]**

Bonhote, J. Lewis
- Birds of Britain. London: A. & C. Black, 1907. 1st edn. 8vo. x,405 pp. 100 cold plates. Orig pict brown cloth gilt.
    (Gough) **£40 [≈ $76]**

Boni, N., Russ, M. & Laurence, D.H.
- A Bibliographical Checklist and Index to the Published Writings of Albert Einstein. New Jersey: 1960. [2],84 pp. 4 ports, 2 text ills.
    (Whitehart) **£21 [≈ $40]**

Bonner, James
- A New Plan for Speedily increasing the Number of Bee-Hives in Scotland. Edinburgh: 1795. 8vo. xx,260 pp. Crude plain cloth.
    (Wheldon & Wesley) **£80 [≈ $153]**
- A New Plan for Speedily Increasing the Number of Bee-Hives in Scotland; and which may be extracted, with equal Success, to England, Ireland, America ... Edinburgh: J. Moir, 1795. Half-title, 258,[1] pp. Advt, errata leaf. Qtr calf, rebacked.
    (C.R. Johnson) **£225 [≈ $431]**

Bonney, Thomas G.
- Flowers from the Upper Alps, with Glimpses of Their Homes. London: W.M. Thompson, 1869. 1st edn. Folio. viii,[24] pp. 12 mtd chromolitho plates. Orig yellow cloth gilt, a.e.g., repr to spine. *(Fenning)* **£135 [≈ $259]**

Bonnycastle, John
- A Treatise on Plane and Spherical Trigonometry ... London: for J. Johnson, 1806. 1st edn. 8vo. 419 pp. Engvd vignette title. Orig bds, paper label, front hinge cracked, crnrs rubbed.
    (Chapel Hill) **£150 [≈ $78]**

The Book of the Household ...
- The Book of the Household; or, Family Dictionary of Everything connected with Housekeeping and Domestic Medicine ... London: London Printing & Publ Co, [ca 1857]. 1st edn. 2 vols in one. Roy 8vo. 576; 576 pp. 20 tinted plates, sev text ills. Contemp half calf, backstrip relaid.
    (Gough) **£90 [≈ $172]**

Boole, George
- An Investigation of the Laws of Thought, on which are founded the Mathematical Theories of Logic and Probabilities. London: Macmillan, 1854. 1st edn. 8vo. v,[1], iv, [4], 424 pp. Errata. Leaf of notes. Lib stamp in title marg. Half mor over cloth.
    (Rootenberg) **$3,200 [≈ £1,666]**

Booth, A.D. & K.H.V.
- Automatic Digital Calculators. London: 1953. 1st edn. Frontis, 2 plates, text figs.
    (Whitehart) **£35 [≈ $67]**

Borden, William C.
- The Use of the Roentgen Ray by the Medical Department of the United States Army in the War with Spain. Washington: GPO, 1900. 4to. 98 pp. Plates. Endleaves dusty. Ex-lib. Orig cloth, worn. *(Goodrich)* **$125 [≈ £65]**
- The Use of the Roentgen Ray by the Medical Department of the United States Army in the War with Spain. Washington: GPO, 1900. Lge 4to. 98 pp. 38 plates. Orig bds, worn, some staining. *(Goodrich)* **$150 [≈ £78]**

Born, Ignaz von
- New Process of Amalgamation of Gold and Silver Ores, and Other Metallic Mixtures ... Translated into English by R.E. Raspe. London: Cadell, 1791. 1st edn in English. 4to. xxxiv,256 pp. 22 plates. A few marg stains. Contemp bds, rebacked.
    (Rootenberg) **$750 [≈ £390]**

Born, Max
- Natural Philosophy of Cause and Chance. Oxford: 1949. 1st edn. vii,215 pp. Dw.
    (Whitehart) **£35 [≈ $67]**
- Problems of Atomic Dynamics. Cambridge: MIT, 1926. 1st edn. 8vo. xiv,200 pp. Cloth.
    (Gemmary) **$125 [≈ £65]**

Borrer, William
- The Birds of Sussex. London: 1891. 1st edn. 8vo. xviii,385,[5 advt] pp. Cold map, 6 cold litho plates by Keulemans. Sm tear on fly. Orig cloth, marked, sl rubbed, inner hinges

strained. *(Bow Windows)* **£95 [≈ $182]**
- The Birds of Sussex. London: R.H. Porter, 1891. 1st edn. xviii,390,8 advt pp. Fldg map, 6 hand cold plates by Keulemans. Orig blue cloth gilt, sl bumped. Pres copy.
(Gough) **£80 [≈ $153]**

Borthwick, George
- A Treatise upon the Extraction of the Crystalline Lens. Edinburgh: for Charles Elliot, 1775. 1st edn. 4to. viii,30 pp. Thick paper. Half mor, mrbld bds, mor label.
(Rootenberg) **$500 [≈ £260]**

Boscovich, Roger Joseph
- A Theory of Natural Philosophy ... Latin-English Edition from the Text of the First Venetian Edition ... Chicago: Open Court Publ Co, 1922. 1st English edn. Large Paper. Folio. xviii,[2],463,[6] pp. Orig green cloth.
(Rootenberg) **$500 [≈ £260]**

The Botanist's Calendar ...
- The Botanist's Calendar, and Pocket Flora: arranged according to the Linnaean System ... London: Bensley for B. & J. White, 1797. 1st edn. 2 vols. Sm 8vo. vi, [ii],264; [iv], 265-396, [92] pp. Half-titles. Sm reprs to titles. 19th c half cloth, hd of spines v sl frayed.
(Burmester) **£90 [≈ $172]**

Bottone, S.R.
- A Guide to Electric Lighting. 1892. 1st edn. 189 pp. 77 ills. Orig soft cvr bndg.
(New Wireless) **$55 [≈ £28]**
- Wireless Telegraphy and Hertzian Waves. 1900. 1st edn. 116 pp. 34 ills. Orig bndg.
(New Wireless) **$165 [≈ £86]**
- Wireless Telegraphy and Hertzian Waves. 1901. 2nd edn. 123 pp. 35 ills. Ex-lib. rebound in half leather.
(New Wireless) **$95 [≈ £49]**

Bottone, S.R. & Beale, Alfred
- Electro-Motors - How Made and How Used. 1891. 1st edn. 168 pp. 78 ills. Lacks front f.e.p. Orig bndg. *(New Wireless)* **$65 [≈ £34]**

Boutcher, William
- A Treatise on Forest-Trees ... Edinburgh: ptd by R. Fleming, & sold by the author, J. Murray, London ..., 1775. 1st edn. Lge 4to. Half-title. Subscribers. Orig tree calf, gilt dec spine sl worn, front hinge cracked but firm.
(Vanbrugh) **£175 [≈ $335]**
- A Treatise on Forest-Trees ... Dublin: Wilson & Exshaw, 1776. 1st Dublin edn. 8vo. xvi, [iv],311 pp. Plate. Occas marg staining.

Contemp calf, v worn, lacks label.
(Finch) **£45 [≈ $86]**
- A Treatise on Forest-Trees ... Dublin: for William Wilson ..., 1784. 3rd edn. 8vo. xxviii, [4],307 pp. Old calf, rebacked.
(Young's) **£90 [≈ $172]**

Bowden, B.V. (ed.)
- Faster than Thought. 1955. 1st edn. 2nd printing. 416 pp. 18 photos, 50 ills. Orig bndg. *(New Wireless)* **$45 [≈ £23]**

Bowden, J.
- The Naturalist in Norway. Notes on the Wild Animals, Birds, Fishes and Plants of that Country ... London: 1869. Tinted litho plates. Orig cloth, unevenly faded, stitching sl loose. *(Grayling)* **£40 [≈ $76]**

Bowditch, W.R.
- The Analysis, Technical Valuation, Purification and Use of Coal Gas. London: 1867. 1st edn. 8vo. iv,300 pp. Fldg table, num text figs. Orig cloth, recased, backstrip relaid, crnr tips worn.
(Bow Windows) **£35 [≈ $67]**

Bowerbank, J.S.
- A Monograph of the British Spongidae. London: Ray Society, 1864-882. 1st edn. 4 vols. 146 plates. Occas sl foxing. Orig blue cloth gilt, t.e.g., crnrs sl bumped.
(Gough) **£145 [≈ $278]**

Bowles, E.A.
- A Handbook of Crocus and Colchicum for Gardeners. Revised Edition. London: 1952. 8vo. 222 pp. 12 cold & 20 plain plates. Orig bndg. *(Henly)* **£18 [≈ $34]**

Bowman, A.K.
- The Life and Teaching of Sir William Macewen. A Chapter in the History of Surgery. London: 1942. 4to. x,425 pp. Port. Ink name on title. Marg pencil notes. Orig bndg. *(Whitehart)* **£30 [≈ $57]**

Bowman, William
- Lectures on the Parts concerned in the Operations on the Eye, and on the Structure of the Retina, delivered at the Royal Ophthalmic Hospital, Moorfields, June 1847 ... London: Longman ..., 1849. 1st edn. 8vo. xii, 143 pp. text figs. Sev lib stamps. Orig cloth. *(Bickersteth)* **£250 [≈ $479]**

Bowyer, William & Nichols, John (eds.)
- The Origin of Printing. In Two Essays ...

Second Edition: With Improvements. London: for W. Bowyer & J. Nichols, 1776. 8vo. viii, 176 pp. Mod lib cloth, spine ends sl rubbed. Anon.   *(Finch)* **£300 [≃ $575]**

Boyd, A.W.
- A Country Parish. Great Budworth in the County of Chester. London: Collins New Naturalist Series, 1951. 1st edn. 8vo. xvi, 278 pp. 32 cold plates. Orig cloth gilt. Dw.
        (Hollett) **£75 [≃ $143]**
- A Country Parish. London: Collins New Naturalist, 1951. 1st edn. 8vo. xvi,278,2 pp. 32 cold & 32 plain plates. Orig cloth.
        (Henly) **£48 [≃ $92]**

Boyle, F.
- The Culture of Greenhouse Orchids, Old System and New ... London: 1902. 1st edn. 8vo. 3 cold plates, 50 ills. Orig cloth, stained & dull, spine ends fingered.
        (Bow Windows) **£30 [≃ $57]**

Boyle, Sir Robert
- New Experiments and Observations touching Cold ... London: 1683. [xlii],325,20,29 pp. 2 plates in facs. Contemp leather, rubbed, hinges cracked, casing sl torn, torn patch on front inner cvr. *(Whitehart)* **£400 [≃ $767]**

Bradley, O.C.
- History of the Edinburgh Veterinary College. Edinburgh: 1923. xi,101 pp. 17 plates. Vellum v dust stained & spotted.
        (Whitehart) **£35 [≃ $67]**

Bradley, Richard
- A Complete Body of Husbandry ... London: Woodman & Lyon, 1727. 1st edn. 8vo. [iv],xi, 372, [4] pp. 4 plates. Contemp calf, respined. Fitzwilliam b'plate.
        (Bookpress) **$385 [≃ £200]**
- A Philosophical Account of the Works of Nature .... London: 1721. 4to. [xix],194,[1] pp. 28 hand cold engvd plates. Inscrptn & blind stamp on title. Some offsetting (12 plates seriously affected), minor foxing. Sm marg worm at end. Contemp calf, rebacked, trifle worn.
        (Wheldon & Wesley) **£220 [≃ $422]**
- A Philosophical Account of the Works of Nature. London: W. Mears, 1721. 1st edn. 4to. [20],194 pp,advt leaf. 8 pp subscribers. Red & black title. 28 full page ills (many hand cold, 1 fldg) by James Cole. Sl browning prelims. Contemp calf, rebacked.
        (Rootenberg) **$800 [≃ £416]**
- The Plague at Marseilles consider'd; with

remarks upon the Plague in General ... London: for W. Mears, 1721. 1st edn. 8vo. [16], 60, [6 advt] pp. Title stained, minor spotting. Calf backed mrbld bds, mor label.
        (Rootenberg) **$900 [≃ £468]**

Brady, G.S.
- A Monograph of the Free and Semi-Parasitic Copepoda of the British Islands. London: Ray Society, 1878-80. 3 vols. 8vo. 96 plates (some cold). Ex-lib. Cloth, sl worn, vol 2 rebacked.
        (Wheldon & Wesley) **£50 [≃ $95]**

Bragg, W.H.
- Studies in Radioactivity. London: Macmillan's Science Monographs, 1912. x,196 pp. Diags, tables. Orig cloth, stained, spine faded.   *(Whitehart)* **£35 [≃ $67]**

Bragg, W.H. & W.L.
- X Rays and Crystal Structure. London: G. Bell & Sons, 1915. 1st edn. 8vo. viii,229 pp. 4 plates, 75 text figs. Rebound in cloth.
        (Gemmary) **$90 [≃ £46]**
- X Rays and Crystal Structure. London: G. Bell & Sons, 1916. 2nd edn. 8vo. viii,229 pp. 4 plates, 75 text figs. Cloth.
        (Gemmary) **$80 [≃ £41]**

Bragg, W.L.
- Atomic Structure of Minerals. Ithaca, New York: Cornell UP, 1937. 8vo. xiii,292 pp. Port, 144 text figs. Cloth.
        (Gemmary) **$65 [≃ £33]**
- The Crystalline State: Vol I - A General Survey. London: G. Bell & Sons, 1939. 8vo. xiv, 352 pp. 32 plates, 187 text figs. Cloth.
        (Gemmary) **$35 [≃ £18]**
- The Crystalline State: Vol III - The Determination of Crystal Structures. London: G. Bell & Sons, 1953. 8vo. ix,345 pp. 8 plates, 325 text figs. Cloth. Dw.
        (Gemmary) **$65 [≃ £33]**
- An Introduction to Crystal Analysis. New York: Van Nostrand, 1929. 8vo. vii,168 pp. 105 text figs. Ex-lib. Cloth.
        (Gemmary) **$50 [≃ £26]**

Braid, James
- Neurypnology; or, the Rationale of Nervous Sleep, considered in relation with Animal Magnetism. London: Churchill, 1843. 1st edn. 8vo. xxii,265,[3] pp. Errata. 2 advt pp. Orig cloth, backstrip relaid. Author's pres inscrptn.   *(Rootenberg)* **$2,000 [≃ £1,041]**

Braithwaite, R.
- The British Moss Flora. London: 1887-1905.

3 vols. Roy 8vo. 128 plates. Cloth.
(Wheldon & Wesley) £135 [≃ $259]
- The Sphagnaceae or Peat-Mosses of Europe
and North America. London: 1880. Imperial
8vo. 91 pp. 29 plain plates. Cloth, spine sl
faded. *(Henly)* £42 [≃ $80]

Bramwell, Byrom
- Anaemia and some of the Diseases of the
Blood-Forming Organs and Ductless Glands.
Edinburgh: 1899. [vii],450 pp. Cloth, stained
& dusty, spine ends & crnrs worn.
(Whitehart) £40 [≃ $76]
- Diseases of the Spinal Cord. Edinburgh:
1884. 2nd edn. 359 pp. Chromolitho ills.
Orig bndg. *(Fye)* $100 [≃ £52]

Bramwell, J. Milne
- Hypnotism. Its History, Practice and Theory.
New York: 1956. Reissue of the 1903 edn,
with new introduction. 8vo. xvi,480 pp. Orig
cloth. Dw. *(Bickersteth)* £24 [≃ $46]

Bransby, John
- The Use of Globes, containing an
Introduction to Astronomy & Geography ...
Ipswich: 1791. 8vo. x,216 pp. 2 fldg plates.
Mod buckram gilt. *(Lamb)* £30 [≃ $57]

Brasher, Rex
- Birds and Trees of North America ... New
York: Rowman & Littlefield, 1961-62. 1st edn
thus. 4 vols. Oblong folio. 875 cold plates.
Orig mor backed bds gilt, top edges of vol 4
spotted. *(Hollett)* £350 [≃ $671]
- Birds and Trees of North America. New
York: 1962. The 2nd reprint, omitting plates
37-54, 127-144, 673-690. Oblong folio. 794
cold plates. Cloth backed bds.
(Wheldon & Wesley) £120 [≃ $230]

Bree, Charles Robert
- A History of the Birds of Europe, not
Observed in the British isles. London:
Groombridge, 1859-63. 1st edn. 4 vols. Roy
8vo. xv,206, & 1*,203*; iv,203, & 117*; iv,
247; iv,250 pp, errata leaf. 180 & 58 cold
plates. Some foxing. Contemp half mor,
t.e.g., sl worn & rubbed.
(Sotheran's) £625 [≃ $1,199]

Brehaut, Thomas Collings
- Cordon Training of Fruit Trees ... London:
Longman, Green, 1860. 1st edn. 119 pp.
Frontis, plates. Front jnt sl worn, crnrs
bumped. *(Wreden)* $79.50 [≃ £41]

Brera, Valerian Lewis
- A Treatise on Verminous Diseases, preceded
by the Natural History of Intestinal Worms ...
Translated from the Italian, with Notes by
Messrs J. Bartoli and Calvet. Boston: 1817.
8vo. 367 pp. 5 fldg plates. Foxed & damp
stained. Calf. *(Goodrich)* $125 [≃ £65]

Brett, R.D.
- History of British Aviation 1908-1914.
London: 1934. 2 vols. 216; 207 pp. 64 plates,
7 diags. Orig bndg. *(Whitehart)* £40 [≃ $76]

Brewington, M.V.
- The Peabody Museum Collection of
Navigating Instruments with Notes on their
Makers. Salem, Mass.: Peabody Museum,
1963. Roy 8vo. xii,155 pp. 57 plates. Cloth.
(Gemmary) $250 [≃ £130]

Brewster, Sir David
- Letters on Natural Magic, addressed to Sir
Walter Scott. London: 1832. xi,351 pp. Lib
label. Endpapers sl foxed. Orig cloth, sl
marked & dusty, sl weak.
(Whitehart) £25 [≃ $47]
- The Life of Sir Isaac Newton. London:
Murray, 1831. 1st edn. 12mo. xvi,366 pp.
Port (name clipped from marg). Orig ptd
linen, a bit rubbed & dark.
(Burmester) £60 [≃ $115]
- The Life of Sir Isaac Newton. London:
Murray, 1831. 1st edn. 18mo. xv,366 pp.
Port. Frontis & title foxed. Contemp half calf,
gilt spine, green label.
(Frew Mackenzie) £85 [≃ $163]
- The Life of Sir Isaac Newton. London:
Murray, Family Library vol 24, 1831. 1st
edn. 8vo in 16s. xvi,366 pp. Port, title
vignette, text ills. Frontis sl foxed & offset
onto title. Orig drab glazed ptd cloth, dated
1831 on upper bd, backstrip relaid.
(Gaskell) £100 [≃ $191]
- Memoirs of the Life, Writings, and
Discoveries of Sir Isaac Newton. Edinburgh:
1855. 1st edn. 2 vols. 478; 564 pp. Half
leather, part of 1 hinge cracked.
(Fye) $150 [≃ £78]
- Memoirs of the Life, Writings, and
Discoveries of Sir Isaac Newton. Edinburgh:
Constable, 1855. 1st edn. 2 vols. 8vo. xxii,
[ii], 478, [2 blank]; xii,564, [4 advt] pp. 2
frontis (foxed). Orig brown cloth, jnts reprd.
(Gaskell) £250 [≃ $479]
- More Worlds than One. The Creed of the
Philosopher and the Hope of the Christian.
London: Murray, 1854. Cr 8vo. vii,259 pp.
Dec cloth. *(Gemmary)* $100 [≃ £52]

- A Treatise on Optics. A New [2nd] Edition. London: Lardner's Cabinet Cyclopaedia, 1833. Sm 8vo. Orig cloth, paper label.
(*Fenning*) **£32.50 [≈ $63]**
- A Treatise on the Kaleidoscope. Edinburgh: Constable ..., 1819. 1st edn. 8vo. 7 plates. Half-title. Advt leaf at end. Orig bds, uncut, edges rubbed, paper cvring lacking from backstrip. (*Georges*) **£300 [≈ $575]**
- A Treatise on the Microscope. Edinburgh: Adam & Charles Black, 1837. Cr 8vo. 193 pp. 14 plates, 48 text figs. Rebound in buckram.
(*Gemmary*) **$250 [≈ £130]**

Brian, M.V.
- Ants. London: Collins New Naturalist, 1977. 1st edn. 8vo. Ills. Dw.
(*Wheldon & Wesley*) **£25 [≈ $47]**
- Ants. London: Collins New Naturalist, 1977. 1st edn. 8vo. 225 pp. 2 cold & 16 plain plates. Orig cloth. Dw. (*Henly*) **£30 [≈ $57]**

Bridge, B.
- A Treatise on the Elements of Algebra. London: 1821. 5th edn. [vi],227 pp. Paper cvrd bds, worn, new spine & endpapers.
(*Whitehart*) **£35 [≈ $67]**

Bridgeman, Thomas
- The Florist's Guide. New York: W. Mitchell, 1835. 1st edn. 12mo. 120 pp. Occas foxing. The 2 intl blank ff defective. Orig cloth backed ptd bds, lower crnrs worn.
(*Bookpress*) **$250 [≈ £130]**
- The Florist's Guide. New York: Mitchell & Turner, 1836. 2nd edn. 12mo. 128 pp. Water stained. Orig cloth backed ptd bds, some wear. (*Bookpress*) **$150 [≈ £78]**

Bridgman, Percy
- Collected Experimental Papers. Cambridge: 1964. 1st edn. 7 vols. 4721 pp. Orig bndg.
(*Fye*) **$100 [≈ £52]**

Briffault, Robert
- The Mothers: a Study of the Origins of Sentiments and Institutions. New York: 1927. 1st edn. 3 vols. 781; 789; 841 pp. Orig bndg. (*Fye*) **$250 [≈ £130]**

Briggs, G.A.
- Audio Biographies. 1961. 1st edn. 343 pp. 90 photos. Dw. (*New Wireless*) **$40 [≈ £20]**

Briggs, L. Vernon
- Occupation as a Substitute for Restraint in the Treatment of the Mentally Ill. A History of the Passage of Two Bills through the

Massachusetts Legislature. Boston: 1923. 8vo. 205 pp. Plates. Orig bndg. Author's pres copy. (*Goodrich*) **$65 [≈ £33]**

Brigham, Amariah
- Remarks on the Influence of Mental Cultivation and Mental Excitement upon Health. London & Manchester: 1839. 8vo. iv,48 pp. Dble columns. Inner marg of title torn & reprd without loss. Mod bds.
(*Bickersteth*) **£45 [≈ $86]**

Bright, Richard
- Clinical Memoirs on Abdominal Tumours and Intumescence. London: 1860. 1st edn. 326 pp. Orig bndg, outer hinges torn.
(*Fye*) **$250 [≈ £130]**

Bright, Richard, et al.
- Fatal Epilepsy, from Suppuration between the Dura Matter and Arachnoid ... [In] Guy's Hospital Reports, No. 1. Edited by George Barlow & James Babington. London: January, 1836. 8vo. [2],xii,188,[4] pp. 5 plates (4 hand cold). Orig ptd wraps, soiled, edges fray
(*Rootenberg*) **$600 [≈ £312]**

Brillat-Savarin, Jean Anthelme
- The Physiology of Taste. London: Davies, 1925. One of 750. Imperial 8vo. xx,326 pp. Ills. Orig vellum backed mrbld bds. Dw.
(*Ash*) **£150 [≈ $287]**

Brisbin, James S.
- Trees and Tree-Planting. New York: Harper, 1888. 1st edn. 8vo. xxxii, 258, [4 advt] pp. Port. Orig cloth. (*Fenning*) **£24.50 [≈ $47]**

Bristow, H.W.
- The Geology of the Isle of Wight. Second Edition by C. Reid and A. Strahan. London: Geol. Survey, 1889. 8vo. xv,349 pp. 5 fldg maps & sections. Ex-lib. Binder's cloth.
(*Wheldon & Wesley*) **£50 [≈ $95]**

Bristowe, J.S.
- A Treatise on the Theory and Practice of Medicine. London: 1876. xxxiii,1166 pp. 10 diags. Occas sl foxing, few marg pencil notes. Orig cloth, dusty & worn, new endpapers.
(*Whitehart*) **£35 [≈ $67]**
- A Treatise on the Theory and Practice of Medicine. London: 1887. 6th edn. xliv,1269 pp. 113 text figs. New cloth.
(*Whitehart*) **£25 [≈ $47]**

Bristowe, W.S.
- The Comity of Spiders. London: Ray Society,

1939-41. 1st edn. 2 vols. 8vo. 22 plates, 96 text figs. Minor marg stains vol 1. Cloth, trifle faded. *(Wheldon & Wesley)* **£75** [≈ $143]
- The World of Spiders. London: Collins New Naturalist, 1958. 1st edn. 8vo. xiii,304 pp. 4 cold & 32 plain plates. Orig cloth. *(Henly)* **£22** [≈ $42]

The British Jewel ...
- The British Jewel, or Complete Housewife's best Companion ... London: J. Miller, 1782. New edn. 8vo. 112 pp. Frontis defective, some soiling. Contemp wraps, wear ft of spine. *(Chapel Hill)* **$175** [≈ £91]

British Pharmacopoeia
- British Pharmacopoeia 1867. London: 1867. xxiv, 434 pp. Pencil notes on final blank. Spine reprd. *(Whitehart)* **£40** [≈ $76]
- British Pharmacopoeia 1885. London: (1885) 1887. xxx,536 pp. Lib stamps, ink notes. Cloth, dull & worn, lib label, inner hinge weak. *(Whitehart)* **£35** [≈ $67]
- British Pharmacopoeia 1898. London: 1898. 1st issue (not later reprint). xxxii,534 pp. Cloth, dusty & sl worn, sm dents edges. *(Whitehart)* **£28** [≈ $53]

Britten, Emma Hardinge
- The Electric Physician. 1875. 1st edn. 59 pp. Orig bndg. *(New Wireless)* **$65** [≈ £34]

Britten, J.
- European Ferns. London: [1881]. 4to. xliv, 196 pp. 30 cold plates. Orig dec cloth gilt, trifle used. *(Wheldon & Wesley)* **£30** [≈ $57]
- European Ferns. London: [1881]. 1st edn. 4to. xliv,196 pp. 30 cold plates. Half leather, sm split upper jnt, crnrs bumped. *(Henly)* **£35** [≈ $67]

Britton, N.L. & Rose, N.J.
- The Cactaceae, Descriptions and Illustrations of Plants of the Cactus Family. Washington: 1919-23, facs reprint 1964. 4 vols in 2. 4to. 1068 pp. 137 uncold plates, 1120 ills. *(Wheldon & Wesley)* **£52** [≈ $99]

Broad, C.D.
- The Mind and its Place in Nature. London: Kegan Paul, 1925. Times Book Club label on pastedown. Orig cloth, sl rubbed, spine dull. *(Sanders)* **£30** [≈ $57]

Broadbent, Sir William
- Heart Disease: with Special Reference to Prognosis and Treatment. New York: 1893.

1st Amer edn. 331 pp. Orig bndg. *(Fye)* **$100** [≈ £52]
- Selections from the Writings Medical and Neurological of Sir William Broadbent. London: 1908. 1st edn. 444 pp. Orig bndg. *(Fye)* **$100** [≈ £52]

Brockbank, William
- Ancient Therapeutic Art. The Fitzpatrick Lectures ... London: 1955. 1st reprinting. 8vo. 162 pp. Ills. Dw. *(Goodrich)* **$45** [≈ £23]

Brocklehurst, H.C.
- Game Animals of the Sudan ... London: 1931. 8vo. xix,170 pp. Map, 12 cold & 14 plain plates. Occas sl foxing. Orig cloth. *(Wheldon & Wesley)* **£90** [≈ $172]

Brodetsky, S.
- The Mechanical Principles of the Aeroplane. London: 1921. vii,272 pp. 119 figs. Orig cloth, faded, sl marked, sm nick on spine. *(Whitehart)* **£35** [≈ $67]

Brodie, B.C.
- Lectures on Diseases of the Urinary Organs. London: 1832. 1st edn. 8vo. viii,306 pp. 8 pp ctlg at front. Title & prelims sl spotted. Orig bds, uncut, respined. *(Bickersteth)* **£160** [≈ $307]

Brooke, Jocelyn
- The Wild Orchids of Britain. London: 1950. One of 1140. Folio. 139 pp. Frontis (a duplicate of plate 23) & 40 cold plates. Cloth, trifle faded. *(Wheldon & Wesley)* **£110** [≈ $211]

Brookes, R.
- An Introduction to Physic and Surgery ... London: 1754. viii,536 pp. Top marg of title & some ff discold. Contemp leather, rebacked. *(Whitehart)* **£185** [≈ $355]
- A New and Accurate System of Natural History; containing the History of Quadrupeds, Birds, Fishes and Serpents, Insects, Waters, Earths, Stones, Fossils, Minerals and Vegetables. London: 1763. 6 vols. 12mo. 144 plates. Contemp calf, jnts weak. *(Wheldon & Wesley)* **£200** [≈ $383]

Brouzet, Pierre
- An Essay on the Medicinal Education of Children; and the Treatment of their Diseases. London: for Thomas Field, 1755. 1st edn in English. 8vo. xxi,[5], 364,3 advt pp. Sl browned. Contemp calf, rebacked. *(Rootenberg)* **$1,500** [≈ £781]

Browinowski, Gracius J.
- The Birds of Australia ... Melbourne: Charles Stuart, 1890. 1st edn. 6 vols. Lge 4to. 301 chromolitho plates. Lib stamps on titles only. Contemp half mor, gilt dec spines.
(Gough) **£3,350 [≈ $6,431]**

Brown, Alfred
- Old Masterpieces in Surgery. Being a Collection of Thoughts and Observations engendered by a Perusal of Some of the Works of Our Forbears in Surgery. Omaha: privately ptd, 1928. 4to. 262 pp. Plates. Orig bndg.
(Goodrich) **$125 [≈ £65]**
- Old Masterpieces in Surgery. Omaha: 1928. 1st edn. 263 pp. Num ills. Orig bndg.
(Fye) **$200 [≈ £104]**

Brown, H.T.
- Five Hundred and Seven Mechanical Movements ... New York: 1884. 14th edn. 122 pp. Sm lib stamp. Orig cloth, dull, sl worn.
(Whitehart) **£25 [≈ $47]**

Brown, J.C.
- A History of Chemistry from the Earliest Times till the Present Day. London: 1913. xxix, 543 pp. 106 ills. Orig cloth, dull & sl worn, inner hinges cracked but bndg firm.
(Whitehart) **£25 [≈ $47]**

Brown, James
- The Forester being Plain and Practical Directions for the Planting, Rearing and General Management of Forest Trees. Edinburgh & London: Blackwood, 1847. 1st edn. 8vo. viii, 215 pp. Orig cloth, uncut, sl marked.
(Claude Cox) **£28 [≈ $53]**
- The Forester, a Practical Treatise on the Planting, Rearing and General Management of Forest Trees ... Second Edition. Edinburgh: 1851. 8vo. xiv,526,16 advt pp. Dble-page plate. Some marks & pencillings. Orig green cloth, spine faded.
(Bow Windows) **£65 [≈ $124]**
- The Forester, a Practical Treatise on Planting, Rearing and General Management of Forest Trees. London: 1861. 3rd edn. Roy 8vo. x, 700, 16 pp. Diag, charts, 149 text figs. Half calf, backstrip relaid.
(Henly) **£54 [≈ $103]**
- The Forester, or, a Practical Treatise on the Planting, Rearing, and General Management of Forest-Trees. Fifth Edition, enlarged and improved. Edinburgh: 1882. Roy 8vo. xiv,898, [1] pp. Fldg plate, 4 fldg tables, 185 ills. Lacks a blank flyleaf. Orig cloth.
(Fenning) **£48.50 [≈ $94]**

Brown, L.
- British Birds of Prey. London: Collins New Naturalist, 1976. 2nd edn. 8vo. xiv,400 pp. 16 plates. Orig cloth. Dw.
(Henly) **£24 [≈ $46]**

Brown, P.
- American Martyrs to Science through the Roentgen Rays. Springfield: 1936. xv,276 pp. 55 figs. Cloth, sl dusty.
(Whitehart) **£40 [≈ $76]**

Brown, Thomas
- The Elements of Conchology ... according to the Linnean System ... London: for Lackington, Allen ..., 1816. 1st edn. [4 advt], [ix], 168 pp. 9 hand cold plates. Some contemp MS marg notes. Occas foxing. Orig bds, uncut, rebacked. *(Gough)* **£250 [≈ $479]**
- Illustrations of the Fossil Conchology of Great Britain and Ireland with Descriptions and Localities of all the Species. London: 1849. 4to. ix,274 pp. 115 plain plates (17 bis). Plate 3* called for but does not appear to have been issued. Orig cloth, rebacked.
(Baldwin) **£100 [≈ $191]**
- The Zoologist's Text-Book. Glasgow: 1833. 2 vols. Post 8vo. xii,13-578, 15,[1] pp. 107 plates (1-106, 42*). Orig cloth.
(Wheldon & Wesley) **£48 [≈ $92]**

Brown, W.R.
- The Horse of the Desert ... Arabian Horse. New York: Derrydale Press, 1929. One of 750. Lge 4to. 218 pp. Ills. Dw.
(Trophy Room) **$800 [≈ £416]**

Browne, D.J.
- The American Muck Book ... all the Principal Fertilisers & Manures in Common Use ... New York: C.M. Saxton, 1851. 1st edn. 429, [2 advt] pp. 22 text figs. Occas sl foxing, tip torn from endpaper. Orig cloth gilt.
(Petrilla) **$60 [≈ £31]**

Browne, M.
- Artistic & Scientific Taxidermy and Modelling. London: 1896. xii,463 pp. 22 plates, 11 figs. Orig cloth. ALS by the author inserted.
(Baldwin) **£55 [≈ $105]**

Browne, Sir Thomas
- Certain Miscellany Tracts ... London: for Charles Mearne, & sold by Henry Bonwick, 1684. 1st edn, 2nd issue. 8vo. [viii], 215, [i blank], [vi] pp. Port frontis. Sl browned. Mod qtr calf. Wing B.5152.
(Frew Mackenzie) **£175 [≈ $335]**

- Certain Miscellany Tracts. London: Charles Mearne, 1684. 1st edn. 8vo. viii,215,[6] pp. Frontis (chipped). Later bds. Wing B.5152.
(Bookpress) **$350 [≈ £182]**
- Letter to a Friend. London: Etchells, Haslewood Reprints, 1924. One of 425. Sm folio. Orig bndg. *(Goodrich)* **$60 [≈ £31]**
- Pseudodoxia Epidemica ... London: T.H. for Edward Dod, 1646. 1st edn. Folio. [xviii],386 pp. Lacks imprimatur leaf. Few sm reprs, minor damp stain at ends, title sl browned. Rec half calf. Wing B.5159.
(Clark) **£280 [≈ $537]**
- Pseudodoxia Epidemica; or, Enquiries into very many received Tenets, and commonly presumed Truths. The Second Edition, Corrected and much enlarged by the Author. London: 1650. Sm folio. [8],329,[5] pp. Sl browning. Later calf, a.e.g., gilt dentelles. Wing B.5160. *(Goodrich)* **$795 [≈ £414]**
- Pseudodoxia Epidemica ... Whereunto is added Religio Medici. London: Nath. Ekins, 1659. Folio. [xii], 326,[10], [iv],64 pp. Calf.
(Bookpress) **$450 [≈ £234]**
- Works. Edited by Simon Wilkins. London: Pickering, 1836. 4 vols. 8vo. Plates. Calf, jnts split, 1 vol lacks front bd.
(Goodrich) **$150 [≈ £78]**
- The Works ... Edited by Geoffrey Keynes. London: Faber & Gwyer, 1964. 4 vols. 8vo. Orig cloth. Dws.
(Frew Mackenzie) **£225 [≈ $431]**

Brownrigg, William
- The Art of Making Common Salt, as now Practised ... London: Davis, Millar, Dodsley, 1748. 1st edn. 8vo. xxiv,295 pp, errata leaf. 6 fldg plates. Orig calf, rebacked.
(Bickersteth) **£320 [≈ $614]**

Bruel, Walter
- Praxis Medicinae, or, The Physicians Practice. London: William Sheares, 1632. 1st edn. Sm 4to. [iv],407,[4] pp. Later endpapers. Royal College of Physicians' stamp & b'plate. Contemp calf. *(Bookpress)* **$1,250 [≈ £651]**

Brunings, W.
- Direct Laryngoscopy, Bronchoscopy, and Oesophagoscopy. London: 1912. xiv,370 pp. 114 text ills. Orig bndg, lib label on cvr.
(Whitehart) **£25 [≈ $47]**

Brunschwig, Hieronymus
- The Book of Chirurgia ... Strassburg, 1497. With a Study on Hieronymus Brunschwig and his Work by Henry Sigerist. Milano: 1923. Folio. Unabused ex-lib. Half linen.

(Goodrich) **$75 [≈ £39]**

Brunton, T. Lauder
- Collected Papers on Circulation and Respiration. First Series. London: 1907. 1st edn. 696 pp. Orig bndg. *(Fye)* **$200 [≈ £104]**
- Lectures on the Actions of Medicines. New York: 1897. 1st Amer edn. 673 pp. Orig bndg. *(Fye)* **$125 [≈ £65]**
- Modern Developments of Harvey's Work. London: 1894. 1st edn. 35 pp. Orig bndg.
(Fye) **$60 [≈ £31]**
- Pharmacology and Therapeutics; or, Medicine Past and Present. London: 1880. 1st edn. 212 pp. Orig bndg.
(Fye) **$125 [≈ £65]**
- Therapeutics of the Circulation. London: 1914. 2nd edn. 536 pp. Orig bndg.
(Fye) **$75 [≈ £39]**

Bryan, G.H.
- Stability in Aviation. An Introduction to Dynamical Stability as applied to the Motions of Aeroplanes. London: 1911. x,192 pp. 9 ills, 38 text figs. Orig cloth, edges water stained. *(Whitehart)* **£18 [≈ $34]**

Bryan, Margaret
- Lectures on Natural Philosophy ... with an Appendix ... London: George Kearsley, 1806. 1st edn. 388 pp. Frontis port, 36 engvd plates. Contemp three qtr calf, sl worn, jnts starting.
(Wreden) **$325 [≈ £169]**

Bryce, James
- Practical Observations on the Inoculation of Cowpox ... The Second Edition. With an Appendix ... Edinburgh & London: 1809. 8vo. xix,[i], 214,132 pp. 3 cold plates on 2 ff. 3 lib stamps. Contemp half calf, rebacked.
(Bickersteth) **£185 [≈ $355]**

Bryk, Felix
- Circumcision in Man and Woman. Its History, Psychology and Ethnology. New York: 1934. 1st English translation. 342 pp. Num ills. Orig bndg. *(Fye)* **$100 [≈ £52]**

Buchan, A.
- A Handy Book of Meteorology. Edinburgh & London: 1867. [vi],204 pp. 5 plates, 53 text diags. Inscrptn on half-title. Cloth sl worn, spine faded. *(Whitehart)* **£25 [≈ $47]**

Buchan, William
- Domestic Medicine; or, the Family Physician. Edinburgh: Balfour, Auld, & Smellie, 1769. 1st edn. 8vo. xv,[i],624 pp.

Browned. Later bds.
(Bookpress) **$400** [≈ **£208**]
- Domestic Medicine ... London: for W. Strahan ..., 1772. 2nd edn, enlgd. 8vo. 2 ctlg pp. 2 ff sl soiled. New cloth.
(Stewart) **£125** [≈ **$239**]
- Domestic Medicine ... Second Edition, with considerable additions. London: 1772. 8vo. xxxvi, 758 pp. Contemp half calf, worn.
(Goodrich) **$250** [≈ **£130**]
- Domestic Medicine ... A New Stereotype Edition. London: J. Smith, [ca 1860]. Sm 8vo. "581" pp (prelims erratically paginated). 12 plates. Illust title. Orig blue cloth gilt spine.
(Beech) **£18** [≈ **$34**]
- A Letter to the Patentee, concerning the Medical Properties of the Fleecy Hosiery ... Second American Edition, with Additional Notes and Observations. Providence: Carter & Wilkenson ..., 1795. 8vo. 34,[1] pp. Sl browned. Mod qtr calf.
(Hemlock) **$175** [≈ **£91**]

Buck, A.H.
- The Growth of Medicine from the Earliest Times to about 1800. New Haven: 1917. xviii, 582 pp. 28 figs. Few marg pencil marks. Cloth, worn & sl marked, inner hinge sl worn.
(Whitehart) **£25** [≈ **$47**]

Buckland, William
- Geology and Mineralogy considered with reference to Natural Theology. London: William Pickering, 1836. 2 vols. 8vo. xv,468; vii,131 pp. Hand cold fldg plate, 87 engvd plates. 1 crnr water stained vol 2. Cloth, vol 1 unopened.
(Gemmary) **$200** [≈ **£104**]
- Geology and Mineralogy considered with reference to Natural Theology. London: 1837. 2nd edn. 2 vols. 8vo. xvi,619; 4,ix,129 pp. Hand cold fldg section, 87 plain plates. Orig cloth.
(Henly) **£85** [≈ **$163**]
- Geology and Mineralogy considered with reference to Natural Theology. Phila: Lea & Blanchard, 1837. 1st Amer edn. 2 vols. 8vo. xv,468; vii,131 pp. Hand cold fldg plate, 87 engvd plates. Sl foxed. New cloth.
(Gemmary) **$250** [≈ **£130**]
- Geology and Mineralogy considered with reference to Natural Theology. London: 1858. 3rd edn. 2 vols. 8vo. Frontis, 90 plates. Sm lib stamps on title versos. Some plates sl foxed. Tree calf, backstrips relaid.
(Henly) **£75** [≈ **$143**]
- Life and Correspondence ... By his Daughter, Mrs. Gordon. New York: Appleton, 1894. 8vo. xvi,288 pp. 6 plates, 15 text figs. Cloth.
(Gemmary) **$50** [≈ **£26**]

- Reliquiae Diluvianae; or, Observations on the Organic Remains contained in Caves, Fissures, and Diluvial Gravel ... London: Murray, 1823. 1st edn. 4to. vii,303 pp. Fldg table, 27 litho plates (3 cold, 1 fldg)). Rec half calf antique.
(Bickersteth) **£285** [≈ **$547**]
- Reliquiae Diluvianae; or Observations on the Organic Remains contained in Caves, Fissures and Diluvial Gravel. London: 1824. 2nd edn. 4to. viii,303 pp. 27 plates & maps (3 hand cold). Some offsetting from plates. Half mor, rebacked.
(Henly) **£180** [≈ **$345**]

Buckler, W.
- The Larvae of the British Butterflies and Moths. Edited by H.T. Stainton and G.T. Porritt. London: Ray Society, 1866-1901. 9 vols. 8vo. 164 cold plates (the 1st 105 hand cold). New cloth, vol 1 jnts reprd.
(Wheldon & Wesley) **£500** [≈ **$959**]

Bucknill, John
- The Psychology of Shakespeare. London: 1859. 1st edn. 264 pp. Orig bndg, backstrip defective.
(Fye) **$150** [≈ **£78**]

Bucknill, John A.
- The Birds of Surrey. London: R.H. Porter, 1900. 1st edn. 8vo. lvi,374 pp. Fldg map, 6 gravure & 13 b/w plates. Frontis a trifle foxed. Orig pict brown cloth gilt.
(Gough) **£45** [≈ **$86**]
- The Birds of Surrey. London: R.H. Porter, 1900. 1st edn. lvi,374 pp. Fldg map, 6 gravures, 13 b/w ills. Orig pict cloth gilt.
(Gough) **£45** [≈ **$86**]

Buckton, George Bowdler
- Monograph of the British Cicadae or Tettigidae. London: Macmillan, 1890. 1st edn. 2 vols. 82 plates, mostly cold. Occas sl foxing. Contemp maroon half mor, gilt dec spines, t.e.g.
(Gough) **£145** [≈ **$278**]

Budgen, Miss M.L.
- Episodes of Insect Life by Acheta Domestica M.E.S. London: 1849-51. 3 vols. 8vo. 3 frontis, engvd decs. Good ex-lib. Half mor gilt, trifle rubbed.
(Wheldon & Wesley) **£110** [≈ **$211**]

Buffon, Georges-Louis Leclerc, Comte de
- The History of Singing Birds containing an Exact Description of their Habits and Customs ... Edinburgh: for Silvester Doig, 1791. 1st edn. 12mo. 192 pp. Engvd half-title & title, plates. Orig calf, hinges cracking.
(Chapel Hill) **$150** [≈ **£78**]

- Natural History ... Occasional Notes and Observations by the Translator (William Smellie). Edinburgh: Creech, 1780. 1st edn thus. 8 vols. 8vo. 299 engvs. Contemp three qtr leather & mrbld bds, hd of spines & some bds sl rubbed.   *(Schoyer)* **$1,000 [≈ £520]**
- Natural History, General and Particular. London: 1785. 2nd edn. 9 vols. Num engvs. Contemp calf, hinges weak, lacks labels.
  (Grayling) **£150 [≈ $287]**
- Natural History. London: 1792. 2 vols. 8vo. Frontis, 2 engvd titles with vignettes, 107 plates. Sm water stains on 4 plates. Calf backed bds, jnts starting to crack.
  (Henly) **£45 [≈ $86]**
- Natural History, General and Particular. London: Cadell & Davies, 1812. 20 vols. Demy 8vo. Over 650 engvd plates. A few sl marks. Contemp half gilt, a few chips.
  (Ash) **£750 [≈ $1,439]**
- A Natural History, General and Particular ... Translated from the French by W. Smellie. A New Edition ... added ... Birds, Fishes, Reptiles, and Insects ... London: T. Kelly, [ca 1817]. 2 vols. 4to. Port (duplicated), 52 cold plates. Contemp calf, sl worn.
  (Wheldon & Wesley) **£120 [≈ $230]**

Bull, Henry Graves
- Notes on the Birds of Herefordshire. London: 1888. Photo frontis. Orig pict cloth, sl rubbed & marked.   *(Grayling)* **£65 [≈ $124]**
- Notes on the Birds of Herefordshire. Contributed by Members of the Woolhope Club ... London & Hereford: 1888. 1st edn. 8vo. xxxii, 274,[2] pp. Port. Orig pict cloth.
  (Bow Windows) **£55 [≈ $105]**

Bullard, W.H.G.
- Naval Electrician's Text Book. 1917. 4th edn. 2 vols. 1386 pp. 842 ills. Orig bndg.
  (New Wireless) **$75 [≈ £39]**

Buller, Sir Walter L.
- A History of the Birds of New Zealand. Edited and Revised by E.G. Turbott. New Zealand: 1967. Folio. 48 mtd cold plates. Dw (sl marked).   *(Grayling)* **£75 [≈ $143]**
- A History of the Birds of New Zealand. Edited and Revised by E.G. Turbott. New Zealand: 1967. Folio. 48 mtd cold plates. Dw. Slipcase.   *(Grayling)* **£90 [≈ $172]**

Bulloch, William
- The History of Bacteriology. London: 1938. xii, 422 pp. 16 plates, 36 figs. Ink name on title. Orig bndg.   *(Whitehart)* **£35 [≈ $67]**
- The History of Bacteriology. OUP: (1938)

1960. 8vo. Plates, text ills.
  (Georges) **£35 [≈ $67]**

Bullock, W.
- A Companion to Mr. Bullock's Museum, containing a Brief Description of upwards of Ten Thousand Natural and Foreign Curiosities ... London: 1811. 10th edn. Sm 8vo. vi,150, [6,1 advt] pp. Frontis. Orig bds, rebacked.   *(Wheldon & Wesley)* **£45 [≈ $86]**

Bunyard, E.A.
- Old Garden Roses. London: 1936. 1st edn. 4to. xvi,163 pp. 1 cold & 32 plain plates. Orig cloth, sl faded, backstrip relaid.
  (Henly) **£24 [≈ $46]**

Burbidge, Frederick William
- Cool Orchids and How to Grow Them, with a Descriptive List of all the Best Species in Cultivation. London: Hardwicke, 1874. 1st edn. Sm 8vo. [vi],160 pp. Frontis, 4 hand cold plates, 17 plates & ills. Orig green cloth gilt.
  (Gough) **£45 [≈ $86]**
- Domestic Floriculture, Window Gardening and Floral Decorations ... London: Blackwood, 1874. 8vo. [2 advt],xviii,396 pp. 200 ills. Orig dec green cloth gilt, v sl rubbed.   *(Beech)* **£38 [≈ $72]**
- The Narcissus: its History and Culture ... London: 1875. Roy 8vo. xvi,95 pp. 48 hand cold plates. Orig dec cloth, trifle used.
  (Wheldon & Wesley) **£450 [≈ $863]**
- The Narcissus: its History and Culture. London: 1875. Roy 8vo. xvi,95 pp. 48 hand cold plates. New half mor.
  (Wheldon & Wesley) **£500 [≈ $959]**

Burchard, H.H.
- A Text-Book of Dental Pathology and Therapeutics, including Pharmacology. Being a Treatise on ... Dental Medicine ... Philadelphia & New York: 1898. 587 pp. 2 cold plates, 388 text engvs. Page edges soiled. Orig leather, spine ends chipped.
  (Whitehart) **£25 [≈ $47]**

Burkill, Isaac H.
- A Dictionary of the Economic Products of the Malay Peninsula ... London: 1935. 1st edn. 2 vols. Roy 8vo. Orig buckram gilt, sl marked.   *(Fenning)* **£85 [≈ $163]**

Burmeister, Hermann
- A Manual of Entomology. Translated by W.E. Shuckard. London: 1836. 8vo. xii,654 pp. 33 plates (8 cold). Half calf, sl used.
  (Wheldon & Wesley) **£50·[≈ $95]**

- A Manual of Entomology, translated from the German by W.E. Shuckard. With Additions ... London: Edward Churton, 1836. 1st edn in English. 8vo. xii,654 pp. Hand cold frontis, 32 plates. Sl spotting. Contemp binder's cloth.   *(Claude Cox)* **£35 [≈ $67]**
- The Organisation of Trilobites ... Edited from the German by Professor Bell and Professor E. Forbes. London: Ray Society, 1846. 1st English edn. 4to. xii,136 pp. 6 plates. Some marks. Old cloth backed bds, rebacked.   *(Bow Windows)* **£80 [≈ $153]**

Burn, A.
- Geodosia Improved; or, a New and Correct Method of Surveying ... In Two Parts ... London: T. Evans, 1775. 1st edn. 8vo. x,355 pp. 5 fldg plates. Some browning. Contemp calf, edges sl rubbed. *(Gough)* **£65 [≈ $124]**

Burns, Allen
- Observations on Some of the Most Frequent and Important Diseases of the Heart ... Edinburgh: James Muirhead for Thomas Bryce, 1809. 1st edn. 8vo. iv,[ii],322 pp. Steeven's Hospital lib stamps on title. Contemp half calf.
        (Rootenberg) **$1,800 [≈ £937]**

Burr, Malcolm
- A Synopsis of the Orthoptera of Western Europe. London: Oliver Janson, 1910. 1st edn. 8vo. 160 pp. Orig wraps.
        (Gough) **£20 [≈ $38]**

Burrell, H.
- The Platypus, its Discovery, Zoological Position, Form and Characteristics. Sydney: 1927. 8vo. viii,227 pp. 35 plates (1 cold). Cloth.   *(Wheldon & Wesley)* **£60 [≈ $115]**

Burton, Robert
- The Anatomy of Melancholy ... The Eighth Edition, corrected and augmented. London: Peter Parker, 1676. Folio. Sl foxing. Later calf.   · *(Goodrich)* **$495 [≈ £257]**
- The Anatomy of Melancholy ... To which is prefixed an Account of the Author. London: for Vernor, Hood ..., 1806. 11th edn, crrctd. 2 vols. 8vo. xxiv,461; 601,[12] pp. New half calf.   *(Young's)* **£78 [≈ $149]**
- The Anatomy of Melancholy. Now for the First Time with the Latin completely given in Translation and embodied in an All-English Text ... New York: 1927. 8vo. xix,1036 pp. Orig cloth. Dw.   *(Bickersteth)* **£25 [≈ $47]**

Butcher, R.W.
- A New Illustrated British Flora. London: 1961. 2 vols. 8vo. 1825 ills. Cloth, trifle used.   *(Wheldon & Wesley)* **£30 [≈ $57]**

Butler, Arthur G.
- Birds of Great Britain and Ireland; Order Passeres. London: Brumby & Clarke, [ca 1908]. 1st edn. 2 vols. 4to. 210; 216 pp. 115 chromolitho plates. Orig cloth backed bds, faded.   *(Gough)* **£295 [≈ $566]**
- Foreign Birds for Cage and Aviary. London: [ca 1900]. 2 vol. 4to. Plates, text ills. Sl rubbed.   *(Grayling)* **£35 [≈ $67]**
- Foreign Finches in Captivity. London: 1899. 2nd edn. 4to. 60 cold plates by F.W. Frohawk. Qtr leather, rebacked.
        (Henly) **£165 [≈ $316]**
- Foreign Finches in Captivity. London: 1899. 2nd edn. Roy 8vo. 60 cold plates by Frohawk. Orig half buckram, trifle used.
        (Wheldon & Wesley) **£160 [≈ $307]**
- Foreign Finches in Captivity. London: 1899. 2nd edn. Roy 8vo. 60 cold plates by Frohawk. Half buckram, rather crudely rebacked.
        (Wheldon & Wesley) **£120 [≈ $230]**

Butler, Arthur G. & Frohawk, F.W.
- Birds' Eggs of the British Isles. London: Upcott Gill, 1904. 1st edn. Sm 4to. ix,105 pp. 24 cold plates. Occas sl spotting. Orig green cloth gilt, t.e.g, fine. *(Gough)* **£60 [≈ $115]**

Butler, C.G.
- The World of the Honeybee. London: Collins New Naturalist, 1954. 1st edn. 8vo. xiv,226 pp. 2 cold & 40 plain plates. Orig cloth.
        (Henly) **£22 [≈ $42]**

Butter, William
- An Improved Method of Opening the Temporal Artery. Also, a New Proposal for extracting the Cataract. London: for J. Robson, 1783. 1st edn. 8vo. viii,213,[1] pp,advt leaf. Fldg plate. Half calf, mrbld bds. Anon.   *(Rootenberg)* **$500 [≈ £260]**

Buxton, J.
- The Redstart. London: Collins New Naturalist, 1950. 1st edn. 8vo. xii,180 pp. 1 cold & 16 other plates. Orig cloth.
        (Henly) **£28 [≈ $53]**
- The Redstart. London: Collins New Naturalist, 1950. Cold frontis, ills. Orig cloth.   *(Grayling)* **£25 [≈ $47]**

Buxton, P.A.
- The Natural History of Tsetse Flies. An

Account of the Biology of the Genus Glossina (Diptera). London: 1955. Cr 4to. xviii,816 pp. 47 plates, text figs. Blind stamps at beginning. Cloth, spine spotted.
(Wheldon & Wesley) **£40 [≃ $76]**

Byfield, Timothy
- Some Plain Directions for the Use of our Sal Oleosum Volatile. [London: ca 1710?]. Sm 8vo. 8 pp. Stitched, as issued.
(Burmester) **£250 [≃ $479]**

Byng, M. & Bell, F.G.
- A Popular Guide to Commercial and Domestic Telephony. General Electric Co.: 1898. 1st edn. 152 pp. 2 fldg plates, 165 ills. Orig bndg. *(New Wireless)* **$65 [≃ £34]**

Byrne, Muriel St Clare (ed.)
- The Elizabethan Zoo. A Book of Beasts both Fabulous and Authentic ... London: Etchells & Macdonald, 1926. One of 525. xiv,171 pp. Fldg map, ills. Orig cloth backed bds, partly unopened, crnrs bumped, cvrs sl darkened.
(Wreden) **$75 [≃ £39]**

Byrne, O.
- Handbook for the Artisan, Mechanic, and Engineer. Phila: Henry Carey Baird, 1898. 8vo. 463,[32 advt] pp. 185 ills. Cloth.
(Gemmary) **$45 [≃ £23]**

Bywater, John
- An Essay on the History, Practice, and Theory, of Electricity. London: for the author ..., 1810. Sole edn. 8vo. [2],iii,[2], 127 pp. 2 fldg plates. Orig bds, uncut, rebacked.
(Fenning) **£110 [≃ $211]**

Cabot, R.C.
- A Guide to the Clinical Examination of the Blood for Diagnostic Purposes. London: 1897. xix, 405 pp. 3 cold plates, 28 figs. Occas foxing. Orig bndg, inner hinges sl cracked. *(Whitehart)* **£25 [≃ $47]**

Cabot, Richard
- Facts on the Heart. Phila: 1926. 1st edn. 981 pp. Orig bndg. *(Fye)* **$50 [≃ £26]**

Cadbury, D.A., Hawkes, J.G. & Readett, R.C.
- A Computer Mapped Flora of Warwickshire. London: 1971. 4to. ix,768 pp. Cold map, 979 other maps with 10 transparent overlays. Cloth. *(Wheldon & Wesley)* **£30 [≃ $57]**

Cady, W.G.
- Piezoelectricity. New York: McGraw Hill, 1946. 1st edn. 8vo. xxiii,806 pp. 168 text figs. Cloth. *(Gemmary)* **$50 [≃ £26]**

Cahen, E. & Wooton, W.O.
- The Mineralogy of the Rarer Metals. A Handbook for Prospectors. London: Griffin, 1912. 12mo. xxviii,211 pp. Cloth.
(Gemmary) **$35 [≃ £18]**
- The Mineralogy of the Rarer Metals. A Handbook for Prospectors. London: Griffin, 1920. 2nd edn. 12mo. xxxii,246 pp. Cloth.
(Gemmary) **$37.50 [≃ £19]**

Caird, James
- English Agriculture in 1850-51. London: Longman, 1852. 1st edn. 8vo. xxvi,550,32 ctlg pp. Frontis map. Orig cloth, hd of spine v sl frayed. *(Burmester)* **£85 [≃ $163]**

Caldwell, H.R. & J.C.
- South China Birds, a Complete Popular and Scientific Account ... Shanghai: 1931. 8vo. [xiii], 447 pp. 6 cold plates, over 75 ills on 32 plates. Cloth, inner jnts cracking.
(Wheldon & Wesley) **£140 [≃ $268]**

Caldwell, J.W.
- Full and Comprehensive Instructions How to Mesmerize, Ancient and Modern Miracles by Mesmerism, also Is Spiritualism true? ... Second Edition. Boston: the author, 1882. 8vo. 128 pp. Port. Orig ptd wraps, 2 lower crnrs torn away. *(Bickersteth)* **£65 [≃ $124]**

Calkins, A.
- Opium and the Opium-Appetite: with Notices of Alcoholic Beverages, Cannabis Indica, Tobacco and Coca, and Tea and Coffee, in their Hygienic Aspects and Pathologic Relations. Phila: 1871. 1st edn. 390 pp. Lib stamp. Edges worn, spine defective. *(Whitehart)* **£40 [≃ $76]**

Calot, F.
- Indispensable Orthopaedics. London: 1914. 1st English transl. 1175 pp. 1252 ills. Orig bndg. *(Fye)* **$200 [≃ £104]**

Calvert, A.F.
- Mineral Resources of Minas Geraes (Brazil). London: 1915. 1st edn. 8vo. xvi,100 pp. 9 maps, 118 ills. 1 plate sl torn in marg. Occas spots. Orig cloth.
(Bow Windows) **£105 [≃ $201]**

Calvert, J.
- The Gold Rocks of Great Britain and Ireland, with a Treatise on the Geology of Gold. London: 1853. 8vo. xx,324,2,x pp. Rec calf.
(Henly) £150 [≈ $287]

Cameron, E.N.
- Pegmatite Investigations, 1942-45. New England. Washington: 1954. 4to. 352 pp. 48 pocket maps, 139 text figs. Wrappers.
(Gemmary) $75 [≈ £39]

Cameron, G.R.
- Pathology of the Cell. Edinburgh: 1952. xv, 840 pp. 64 plates, 41 figs. Bottom crnr sl knocked. Dw.   *(Whitehart)* £48 [≈ $92]
- Pathology of the Cell. London: 1952. 1st edn. xv,840 pp. 64 plates, 41 text figs. Orig bndg.
(Whitehart) £35 [≈ $67]

Cameron, P.
- A Monograph of the British Phytophagous Hymenoptera ... Vol 2 [only]. London: Ray Society, 1885. vi,233 pp. 27 plates (some cold). Lib stamp on 1st page of text. Orig cloth, faded, rebacked.
(Whitehart) £28 [≈ $53]
- A Monograph of the British Phytophagous Hymenoptera. London: Ray Society, 1882-93. 4 vols. 8vo. 84 plates (55 cold). Orig cloth, vol 2 spine worn.
(Wheldon & Wesley) £150 [≈ $287]

Camm, F.J.
- Newnes Television and Shortwave Handbook. 1934. 1st edn. 256 pp. 61 photos, 169 ills. Orig bndg.
(New Wireless) $25 [≈ £13]

Campbell, Frank
- Memoranda on Noses. London: T. Richards, 1874. Sole edn. 8vo. vi,34 pp. 1 plate. Disbound. Anon.   *(Bickersteth)* £38 [≈ $72]

Campbell, George Ashley
- The Collected Papers. American Telephone & Telegraph Co.: 1937. 1st edn. 548 pp. Orig bndg.   *(New Wireless)* $45 [≈ £24]

Campbell, J.M.
- Notes on the Natural History of the Bell Rock. Edinburgh: David Douglas, 1904. 1st edn. 8vo. Orig cloth (stained).
(Young's) £24 [≈ $46]

Campbell, L. & Garnett, W.
- The Life of James Clerk Maxwell with a Selection from his Correspondence and

Occasional Writings ... London: 1882. 1st edn. xvi,662 pp. 4 cold plates, 3 ports. New endpapers. Cloth, sl worn.
(Whitehart) £75 [≈ $143]
- The Life of James Clerk Maxwell. London: Macmillan, 1884. 8vo. 421 pp. Prize calf gilt, sl worn.   *(Gemmary)* $150 [≈ £78]

Campbell, W.W.
- Stellar Motions with Special reference to Motions determined by Means of the Spectrograph. London: Henry Frowde, 1913. 8vo. xi,328 pp. Ex-lib. Cloth.
(Gemmary) $50 [≈ £26]

Candolle, A.P. de & Sprengel, K.
- Elements of the Philosophy of Plants; containing the Principles of Scientific Botany, translated from the German. Edinburgh: 1821. 8vo. xxxii,486 pp. 8 plates. Sl foxing. Half calf, sl rubbed.
(Wheldon & Wesley) £60 [≈ $115]

Cantor, G.
- Contributions to the Founding of the Theory of Transfinite Numbers. Translated by P.E.B. Jourdain. Chicago: Open Court Classics of Science and Philosophy, 1915. vii,211,14 pp. Lib stamps on front endpaper. Spine ends nicked. *(Whitehart)* £25 [≈ $47]

Capper, James
- Meteorological and Miscellaneous Tracts, applicable to Navigation, Gardening, and Farming ... Cardiff: J.D. Bird ..., 1809. 1st edn. 8vo. xx,211,[1] pp. Half-title. 6 fldg tables. Rec bds, uncut. Inscrbd "From the Author".   *(Burmester)* £120 [≈ $230]

Carey, George A.
- 500 Useful and Amusing Experiments in the Arts and Manufactures; With Observations on the Properties of the Substances employed, and their Application to useful Purposes. London: J. Johnston, 1822. 1st edn. 8vo. xxiv, 306 pp. 4 plates. Occas foxing. Contemp half calf, rebacked.   *(Gough)* £125 [≈ $239]

Carlisle, Sir Anthony
- An Essay on the Disorders of Old Age ... Phila: Edward Earle ..., 1819. 1st Amer edn. 8vo. 74 pp. Orig blue bds, cloth spine, paper label (defective).   *(Hemlock)* $150 [≈ £78]

Carneal, Georgette
Conqueror of Space; The Life of Lee DeForest. 1930. 1st edn. 296 pp. Wraps. Dw.
(New Wireless) $55 [≈ £29]

Carnegie, Andrew
- James Watt. Edinburgh & London: Oliphant Anderson & Ferrier, [1905]. 12mo. 164,4 advt pp. Orig cloth stamped in gilt & yellow, sl fading of spine & edges. Sgnd by the author.
(Schoyer) **$150 [≈ £78]**

Carpenter, W.B.
- The Microscope and its Revelations. London: John Churchill & Sons, 1875. 5th edn. 8vo. xxxii,848 pp. 25 plates, 449 text figs. Ex-lib. Qtr leather, worn. *(Gemmary)* **$100 [≈ £52]**
- The Microscope & Its Revelations. London: Churchill, 1881. 6th edn. 8vo. xxxii,882 2 advt pp. 26 plates, 502 ills. Some spotting endpapers. Orig cloth, a few stains rear bd, inner hinges sl cracked. *(Savona)* **£40 [≈ $76]**
- The Microscope and its Revelations. London: J. & A. Churchill, 1881. 6th edn. 8vo. xxxii,882 pp. 26 plates, 502 text figs. Ex-lib. Cloth. *(Gemmary)* **$125 [≈ £65]**
- The Microscope and Its Revelations. Seventh Edition. London: Churchill, 1891. xviii, 1099,xvi advt pp. 20 plates (some cold), 756 text ills. Orig green cloth, gilt spine.
(Gough) **£45 [≈ $86]**
- The Microscope and its Revelations. London: J. & A. Churchill, 1891. 7th edn. 8vo. xviii,1099,28 ctlg pp. 21 plates, 800 text figs. Cloth, sl loose. *(Gemmary)* **$125 [≈ £65]**

Carpenter, William B.
- Introduction to the Study of Foraminifera. London: Ray Society, 1862. 1st edn. Folio. xxii, 319 pp. 22 lithos. Occas sl spotting. Contemp black half mor, gilt dec spine, t.e.g.
(Gough) **£125 [≈ $239]**
- Principles of Mental Physiology, with their Application to the Training and Disciplining of the Mind, and the Study of its Morbid Conditions. Fifth Edition. London: 1879. 8vo. lxiii,737 pp. Orig cloth.
(Bickersteth) **£35 [≈ $67]**

Carpue, Joseph Constantine
- An Introduction to Electricity and Galvanism, shewing their Effects in the Cure of Diseases. London: Phillips, 1803. 1st edn. 8vo. viii,112 pp. 3 fldg plates. 1st & last ff stained. Contemp calf backed mrbld bds, rubbed. Prospectus for a related work dated Feb 10 1803 inserted.
(Rootenberg) **$950 [≈ £494]**

Carrel, Alexis & Dahelly, G.
- The Treatment of Infected Wounds. New York: 1917. 1st English translation. 238 pp. Orig bndg. *(Fye)* **$150 [≈ £78]**

Carrington, Charles (ed.)
- Untrodden Fields of Anthropology ... By a French Army-Surgeon. Paris: 1898. 2nd ltd edn, one of 1000. 2 vols. Lge 8vo. Orig cloth, gilt lettering faded. *(Hollett)* **£75 [≈ $143]**

Carter, Francis
- An Account of the Various Systems of Medicine ... London: for the author ... particularly from the Works of John Brown, M.D. ... 1788. 1st edn. 2 vols in one. 8vo. vi,200; 239 pp, errata leaf. Orig half calf, jnts cracked, spine ends worn.
(Bickersteth) **£185 [≈ $355]**

Casper, Johann
- A Handbook of the Practice of Forensic Medicine, based upon Personal Experience. London: 1861-65. 1st English translation. 4 vols. Orig bndg. *(Fye)* **$300 [≈ £156]**

Casper, M.
- Kepler. London: Abelard-Schuman, 1959. 8vo. 401 pp. Cloth. Dw.
(Gemmary) **$45 [≈ £23]**

Cassar, Paul
- Medical History of Malta. London: Wellcome, 1964. 8vo. xi,586 pp. Ills. Orig bndg. *(Goodrich)* **$65 [≈ £33]**

Cassell's Cyclopaedia ...
- Cassell's Cyclopaedia of Mechanics. Containing Receipts, Processes, and Memoranda for Workshop Use ... Special Edition ... London: Cassell, n.d. 8 vols. Lge 8vo. 32 cold & 8 other plates, num ills. Orig gilt & black blocked cloth, sev cvrs sl mottled.
(Bow Windows) **£80 [≈ $153]**

Castellani, Aldo & Chalmers, Albert J.
- Manual of Tropical Medicine. Third Edition. London: 1919. Thick 8vo. x,2436 pp. 16 cold plates, num text figs. Orig cloth, sl worn.
(Bickersteth) **£40 [≈ $76]**

Castiglioni, Arturo
- A History of Medicine. New York: 1941. 1st edn. 1013 pp. Ex-lib. Orig bndg.
(Fye) **$150 [≈ £78]**

Castle, Thomas
- An Introduction to Medical Botany. London: E. Cox, 1829. 1st edn. 12mo. 172,8 advt pp. 3 hand cold plates. Orig bds, uncut, rebacked.
(Gough) **£75 [≈ $143]**

Cathcart, Charles W. & Caird, F.M.
- Johnston's Students Atlas of Bones and Ligaments. Edinburgh & London: W. & A.K. Johnston, 1885. 1st edn. Folio. 63 ff. 30 chromolitho plates. Orig cloth. Cathcart's copy. *(Chapel Hill)* **$225** [≈ £117]

Catlow, Joseph Peel
- On the Principles of Aesthetic Medicine ... London: John Churchill; Birmingham: Hudson, 1867. 1st edn. 8vo. 325 pp. Orig maroon cloth, hd of spine chipped, tears in lower jnt. Pres inscrptn. *(Burmester)* **£48** [≈ $92]

Catlow, M.E.
- Popular British Entomology. London: 1852. 2nd edn. 8vo. x,280 pp. 16 hand cold plates. Sm blind stamp on title & plates. Cloth, sl worn, hd of spine defective. *(Wheldon & Wesley)* **£20** [≈ $38]
- Popular British Entomology. London: 1852. 2nd edn. 8vo. x,280 pp. 16 hand cold plates. Inscrptn on half-title. Cloth, rebacked. *(Wheldon & Wesley)* **£30** [≈ $57]
- Popular Geography of Plants ... Edited by Charles Daubeny. London: Lovell Reeve, 1855. 1st edn. Sm sq 8vo. xl,370 pp. 29 chromolitho plates. Orig pict cloth gilt, jnts rubbed. *(Gough)* **£65** [≈ $124]

Caux, J.W. de
- The Herring and the Herring Fishery ... London: Hamilton, Adams, 1881. 8vo. viii,159 pp. Orig cloth. *(Lamb)* **£25** [≈ $47]

Cave, F.O. & MacDonald, J.D.
- Birds of the Sudan ... London: 1955. 8vo. xxvii,444 pp. 12 cold plates, 2 maps, 12 pp of photos. Orig cloth. Dw. *(Wheldon & Wesley)* **£200** [≈ $383]

Cavendish, Henry
- The Electrical Researches ... Written between 1771 and 1781, edited from the Original Manuscripts ... by J. Clerk Maxwell. Cambridge: UP, 1879. 1st edn. 8vo. lxvi,454, [2], 48 advt pp. Lib blind stamp on title. Orig cloth, rubbed, spine ends chipped. *(Rootenberg)* **$450** [≈ £234]

Cayley, A.
- An Elementary Treatise on Elliptic Functions. London: 1895. 2nd edn. xiii,386 pp. A few figs. Orig bndg. *(Whitehart)* **£40** [≈ $76]

Chaloner & Fleming
- The Mahogany Tree. Liverpool: Rockliff & Sons, (1850). 1st edn. 8vo. x,5-117 pp. Fldg map, fldg table, 7 litho plates. Occas foxing. Orig cloth, spine extremities chipped. *(Bookpress)* **$235** [≈ £122]

Chambers, Abraham Henry
- Observations on the Formation, State and Condition of Turnpike Roads and Other Highways with Suggestions for their Permanent Improvement on Scientific Principles ... London: for the author, 1820. 28 pp. Sewn, uncut, as issued. *(C.R. Johnson)* **£85** [≈ $163]

Chambers, Robert
- Ancient Sea-Margins, as Memorials of Changes in the Relative Level of Sea and Land. Edinburgh: Chambers; London: Orr, 1848. 1st edn. 8vo. 337 pp. Mtd litho frontis, fldg map, text ills. Orig cloth, some dust soiling. *(Chapel Hill)* **$250** [≈ £130]
- Vestiges of the Natural History of Creation. Tenth Edition, with Extensive Additions and Emendations ... London: John Churchill, 1853. 1st 8vo edn. 8vo. xii,325, [3], lxvii,[1], 32 ctlg pp. Ills. Orig cloth, partly unopened. Anon. *(Claude Cox)* **£75** [≈ $143]

Chaney, H.J.
- Our Weights and Measures. London: Eyre & Spottiswoode, 1897. 8vo. viii,163 pp. 35 text figs. Qtr leather, backstrip defective. *(Gemmary)* **$75** [≈ £39]

Chapin, J.P.
- The Birds of the Belgian Congo. New York: Bull Amer Mus Nat Hist Vols 65 & 75, 1932-54. 4 vols. Roy 8vo. Map, 73 plates (some cold), 328 text figs. Mod cloth. *(Wheldon & Wesley)* **£500** [≈ $959]

Chapman, N.
- Lectures on the more Important Diseases of the Thoracic and Abdominal Viscera. Phila: 1844. 1st edn. 383 pp. Title & prelims water stained. Leather, rec label. *(Fye)* **$75** [≈ £39]

Chapman, T.A.
- The Genus Acronytca and its Allies ... London: R.H. Porter, 1893. 1st book edn. iv, 116 pp. 6 cold & 3 other plates. Some foxing. Orig cloth, gilt spine. *(Gough)* **£40** [≈ $76]

Chapple, H.J.
- Television for the Amateur Constructor. 1934. 2nd edn. 266,44 advt pp. 58 photos,

124 ills. Orig bndg.
(New Wireless) **$85 [≈ £44]**

Chaptal, M.I.A.
- Elements of Chemistry. Translated from the French. Phila: 1796. 3 vols in one. 8vo. 673 pp. Title mtd. Lib stamp. Old calf, rebacked.
(Goodrich) **$195 [≈ £101]**

Charcot, J.M.
- Clinical Lectures on the Diseases of the Nervous System delivered at the Infirmary of La Salpetriere. Second Series. Translated by G. Sigerson. London: New Sydenham Soc, 1881. xvi, 399 pp. 17 plates. Orig cloth, 3 v sm worm holes in rear hinge.
(Whitehart) **£90 [≈ $172]**
- Clinical Lectures on Diseases of the Nervous System delivered at the Infirmary of La Salpetriere. Vol. III. Translated by T. Savill. London: New Sydenham Soc, 1889. xviii, 438 pp. 86 ills. Orig cloth, bottom crnr sl marked. *(Whitehart)* **£90 [≈ $172]**
- Clinical Lectures on Senile and Chronic Diseases. London: New Sydenham Soc, 1881. xvi, 307 pp. 6 plates. Orig cloth.
(Whitehart) **£90 [≈ $172]**
- Lectures on Bright's Disease of the Kidneys. Delivered at the School of Medicine of Paris ... Translated by ... Henry B. Millard. New York: Wood, 1878. 8vo. x,100 pp. 2 cold plates. Orig red cloth gilt.
(Goodrich) **$125 [≈ £65]**
- Lectures on Diseases of the Nervous System. Second Series. London: 1881. 1st edn. 399 pp. 10 partly cold engvd plates. Orig bndg.
(Fye) **$200 [≈ £104]**
- Lectures on Localisation of Cerebral and Spinal Diseases. London: 1883. 1st English translation. 341 pp. Orig bndg.
(Fye) **$250 [≈ £130]**
- Lectures on the Localisation of Cerebral and Spinal Diseases delivered at the Faculty of Medicine of Paris. Translated by W.B. Hadden. London: New Sydenham Soc, 1883. xxxii, 341 pp. 89 figs. Orig cloth.
(Whitehart) **£90 [≈ $172]**

Charlesworth, J.K.
- The Quaternary Era. London: 1957. 2 vols. 1700 pp. 325 figs. Orig cloth. Dws.
(Baldwin) **£60 [≈ $115]**

Charleton, A.G.
- Tin. London: Spon, 1884. 8vo. xi,83 pp. 15 plates, text figs. Cloth.
(Gemmary) **$75 [≈ £40]**

Charlton, Jasper
- The Ladies Astronomy and Chronology, in Four Parts ... and the Machine called the Assimilo, explained. London: Thomas Gardner, for the author ..., 1735. 1st edn. 8vo. Errata leaf. 9 fldg plates. Contemp calf gilt. *(Ximenes)* **$300 [≈ £156]**

Charnley, John
- The Closed Treatment of Common Fractures. Edinburgh: 1950. 1st edn. 190 pp. 133 ills. Dw. *(Fye)* **$100 [≈ £52]**

Chaumont, F.S.B.F.
- Lectures on State Medicine delivered before the Society of Apothecaries. London: 1875. vi,196 pp. 20 fldg charts. Sm lib stamp on a few pp. Half roan, v rubbed & worn.
(Whitehart) **£38 [≈ $72]**

Chemistry, Theoretical, Practical and Analytical..
- See Mackenzie, W. (publisher).

Cheselden, William
- The Anatomy of the Human Body. London: Knapton, 1726. 3rd edn. 8vo. [xvi],376 pp. 34 plates. Contemp calf, jnts reprd.
(Bookpress) **$325 [≈ £169]**
- The Anatomy of the Human Body. London: 1750. 7th edn. [vi],334,[16] pp. Frontis, 40 plates. 1 plate reprd. Orig leather, sl worn & marked, backstrip relaid.
(Whitehart) **£120 [≈ $230]**

Cheshire, F.R.
- Bees and Bee-Keeping: Scientific and Practical. London: 1886-88. 2 vols. Cr 8vo. 1 plate, 197 text ills. Cloth gilt, sl faded & soiled. *(Henly)* **£45 [≈ $86]**

Cheyne, George
- The English Malady: or, A Treatise of Nervous Disorders of all Kinds; as Spleen, Vapours, Lowness of Spirits, Hypochondriacal and Hysterical Distempers ... Fourth Edition. London: Strahan, 1734. 8vo. xxxi,370,advt pp. Some foxing. Contemp calf, jnts cracked.
(Goodrich) **$195 [≈ £101]**
- An Essay on Health and Long Life. London: 1724. 1st edn. 8vo. Contemp calf, jnts cracked. *(Goodrich)* **$295 [≈ £154]**
- An Essay on Health and Long Life. London: 1725. 4th edn. 232 pp. Title wrinkled & stained, with old repr. Rec qtr leather.
(Fye) **$150 [≈ £78]**
- An Essay on Health and Long Life. London:

1725. 5th edn. xx,[xxiv],232 pp. Bottom marg
of title reprd. New leather backed bds.
(Whitehart) **£150 [≈ $287]**
- An Essay on Regimen. Together with Five
Discourses, Medical, Moral, and
Philosophical ... London: 1740. 1st edn. 344
pp. Rec qtr leather.   *(Fye)* **$300 [≈ £156]**

Cheyne, W.W.
- Manual of the Antiseptic Treatment of
Wounds for Students and Practitioners.
London: 1885. xiii,151 pp. 51 figs. Leather
gilt.   *(Whitehart)* **£40 [≈ $76]**

Chickering, Mrs Francis E.
- Cloud Crystals; a Snow-Flake Album.
Collected and Edited by a Lady. New York:
Appleton, 1865 sic. 4to. 158 pp. Addtnl litho
title & 28 plates. Some offsetting from plates.
2 blanks sl water stained. Orig mor gilt, a.e.g.
Anon.   *(Beech)* **£110 [≈ $211]**

Child, Charles G., et al.
- The Hepatic Circulation and Portal
Hypertension. Philadelphia & London: 1954.
1st edn. 8vo. xiii,444 pp. Text figs. Orig
cloth.   *(Bickersteth)* **£18 [≈ $34]**

Chilton, C. (ed.)
- The Subantarctic Islands of New Zealand,
Reports on the Geophysics, Geology, Zoology
and Botany of the Islands lying to the South
of New Zealand. Wellington, NZ: 1909. 2
vols. 4to. 25 plates (3 cold). Sound ex-lib.
Orig cloth.
(Wheldon & Wesley) **£100 [≈ $191]**

Chisholm, Alec H.
- Birds and Green Places. A Book of Australian
Nature Gossip. London: Dent, 1929. 1st edn.
xiv,224 pp. Cold frontis, 78 photo plates.
Orig green cloth. Pres copy.
(Gough) **£45 [≈ $86]**

Chisholm, Colin
- An Essay on the Malignant Pestilential Fever
introduced into the West Indian Islands from
Boullam, on the Coast of Guinea ... Phila:
Thomas Dobson, 1799. 8vo. xvi,308 pp.
Some browning & spotting. Contemp calf,
crnrs worn, front hinge split.
(Hemlock) **$275 [≈ £143]**

Chittenden, J.F. (ed.)
- Dictionary of Gardening ... see Royal
Horticultural Society.

Chopra, R.N.
- Indigenous Drugs of India. Their Medical
and Economic Aspects. Calcutta: 1933. xxii,
655 pp.   *(Whitehart)* **£35 [≈ $67]**

Choulant, Ludwig
- History and Bibliography of Anatomic
Illustration ... New York: Schuman's, 1945.
Med 8vo. Num plates & text ills. Orig bndg,
sl soiled.   *(Georges)* **£85 [≈ $163]**

Christison, Robert
- Dispensatory, or Commentary on the
Pharmacopoeias of Great Britain. London:
1848. 2nd edn. xlii,1003 pp. Traces of label
removal from endpaper. Sgntr on title. Orig
cloth, sl dusty, edges sl worn.
(Whitehart) **£40 [≈ $76]**
- A Treatise on Poisons, in relation to Medical
Jurisprudence, Physiology and the Practice of
Physic. Edinburgh: 1836. 3rd edn. 876 pp.
Rec qtr leather. Author's inscrptn.
(Fye) **$250 [≈ £130]**

Chubb, John
- On the Construction of Locks and Keys.
Excerpt Minutes of Proceedings of the
Institute of Civil Engineers, Vol IX. London:
[1850]. 8vo. 36 pp. Engvd title, 8 text ills.
Orig cloth, endpapers sl dusty.
(Rankin) **£25 [≈ $47]**

Church, A.H.
- Types of Floral Mechanisms ... Part 1, Types
1-12 [all published]. Oxford: 1908. 4to.
viii,211 pp. 38 cold plates. Cloth.
(Wheldon & Wesley) **£50 [≈ $95]**

Churchill, Fleetwood (ed.)
- Essays on the Puerperal Fever and Other
Diseases peculiar to Women. Selected from
the Writings of British Authors previous to
the Close of the Eighteenth Century. London:
Sydenham Society, 1849. 8vo. 552 pp. Orig
bndg.   *(Goodrich)* **$95 [≈ £49]**
- Essays on the Puerperal Fever and Other
Diseases peculiar to Women ... Phila: Lea &
Blanchard, 1850. 1st Amer edn. 8vo. 444 pp.
1st few pp v sl spotted. Orig cloth.
(Hemlock) **$50 [≈ £26]**

Churchill, Frederick
- Face and Foot Deformities. Phila: 1885. 1st
Amer edn. 195 pp. Litho plates (3 cold),
w'cuts. Orig bndg, spine ends chipped & torn,
spine faded.   *(Fye)* **$450 [≈ £234]**

Churchman, John
- An Explanation of the Magnetic Atlas, or Variation Chart ... Phila: James & Johnson, 1790. 1st edn. 8vo. 2 lge fldg tables. Some foxing. Lacks chart as usual. Sewn as issued, uncut. *(Ximenes)* **$850 [≈ £442]**

Claiborne, John
- An Inaugural Essay on Scurvy ... Phila: Stephen C. Ustick, 1798. 1st edn. 8vo. [viii], 35 pp. Disbound. *(Bookpress)* **$185 [≈ £96]**

Clancey, P.A.
- The Birds of Natal and Zululand. London: 1964. Roy 8vo. xxxiv,511 pp. Fldg map, 30 cold plates, 17 photos, 40 text figs. Cloth. *(Wheldon & Wesley)* **£50 [≈ $95]**
- The Birds of Natal and Zululand. London: 1964. Imperial 8vo. Map, 41 cold plates, text figs. Dw. *(Grayling)* **£70 [≈ $134]**

Claridge, John
- The Shepherd of Banbury's Rules to judge of the Changes of the Weather ... Second Edition, Corrected [by John Campbell]. London: for T. Waller, 1748. 8vo. x,54 pp. Sl used. Mod bds. *(Hannas)* **£20 [≈ $38]**

Clark, Alonzo
- Lectures on Diseases of the Heart. New York: 1884. 1st edn. 251 pp. Orig bndg. *(Fye)* **$50 [≈ £26]**

Clark, J.W. & Hughes, T.M.
- Life and Letters of the Reverend Adam Sedgwick. London: 1890. 2 vols. xiii,539; vii,640 pp. 2 frontis. Orig cloth, fine. *(Baldwin)* **£85 [≈ $163]**
- Life and Letters of the Reverend Adam Sedgwick. London: (1890) 1970. Reprint. 2 vols. xiii,539; vii,640 pp. 2 frontis. Orig cloth. *(Baldwin)* **£50 [≈ $95]**
- The Life and Letters of the Reverend Adam Sedgwick. London: (1890) 1970. Reprint. 2 vols. xiii,539; vii,640 pp. Maps, plates. Cloth. *(Henly)* **£28 [≈ $53]**

Clark, R.H.
- The Development of the English Steam Wagon. Norwich: Goose & Son, 1963. 4to. xvii, 207, appendices pp. Dw. *(Peter Taylor)* **£22 [≈ $42]**

Clark-Kennedy, A.E.
- Stephen Hales, D.D., F.R.S. An Eighteenth Century Biography. Cambridge: 1929. 1st edn. 256 pp. Orig bndg. *(Fye)* **$65 [≈ £33]**

Clarke, Charles Baron
- Illustrations of Cyperaceae. London: 1909. All published. Roy 8vo. 144 plates. Cloth. *(Wheldon & Wesley)* **£45 [≈ $86]**
- Illustrations of the Cyperaceae. London: Williams & Norgate, 1909. 1st edn. Imperial 8vo. 144 b/w plates. Orig green cloth, spine gilt, fine. *(Gough)* **£60 [≈ $115]**

Clarke, Edwin & Dewhurst, Kenneth
- An Illustrated History of Brain Function. Oxford: 1972. Lge 4to. 154 pp. 157 figs. Dw. *(Goodrich)* **$115 [≈ £60]**
- An Illustrated History of Brain Function. Berkeley: (1972) 1974. [xii],154 pp. Frontis, 157 figs. Water stains top margs most pp, some pp edges sl torn. *(Whitehart)* **£35 [≈ $67]**

Clarke, Edwin & O'Malley, C.D.
- The Human Brain and Spinal Cord: a Historical Study illustrated by Writings from Antiquity to the Twentieth Century. Berkeley: 1968. 1st edn. 926 pp. Orig bndg. *(Fye)* **$200 [≈ £104]**

Clarke, L.L.
- Objects for the Microscope. London: Groombridge, 1870. 3rd edn. Cr 8vo. xv,248 pp. 8 cold plates (some loose). Dec cloth. *(Gemmary)* **$45 [≈ £23]**
- Objects for the Microscope ... London: Groombridge, 1871. 4th edn. 8vo. viii,230,6 advt pp. 8 cold plates, text figs. Orig dec bds, sl worn, new endpapers. *(Savona)* **£25 [≈ $47]**
- Objects for the Microscope ... London: Groombridge, 1887. 7th edn. 8vo. viii,230,2 advt pp. 8 cold plates, 4 text figs. Orig dec bds, darkened, crnrs worn, backstrip relaid, new endpapers. *(Savona)* **£25 [≈ $47]**

Clarke, William Eagle
- Studies in Bird Migration. London: Gurney & Jackson, 1912. 1st edn. 2 vols. 25 plates. Orig green cloth, gilt spines, t.e.g. *(Gough)* **£60 [≈ $115]**
- Studies in Bird Migration. London: 1912. 2 vols. Maps, photo plates, ills. Orig bndg, t.e.g., sl rubbed. *(Grayling)* **£85 [≈ $163]**

Clarke, William Eagle & Roebuck, Wm. Denison
- A Handbook of the Vertebrate Fauna of Yorkshire ... London: Lovell Reeve, 1881. 1st edn. 8vo. xlviii,149 pp. Some spotting. Orig cloth gilt, spine faded. *(Hollett)* **£30 [≈ $57]**

Claude, G.
- Liquid Air Oxygen Nitrogen. Translated by H.E.P. Cottrell. London: 1913. xxv,418 pp. 151 text ills.   *(Whitehart)* **£18 [≃ $34]**

Clay, R.S. & Court, T.H.
- The History of the Microscope. London: Charles Griffin, 1932. 4to. xiv,266 pp. 163 ills. Few ff loose. Cloth.
        (Gemmary) **$150 [≃ £78]**
- The History of the Microscope. London: Holland Press, 1975. Reprint of 1932 edn. 8vo. xiv,266 pp. 164 ills. Cloth. Dw.
        (Gemmary) **$50 [≃ £26]**

Clayton, E.G.
- A Compendium of Food-Microscopy. London: Bailliere, Tindall & Cox, 1909. 1st edn. 8vo. 431 pp. Frontis, 282 figs. Orig cloth, v sl nick hd of spine.
        (Savona) **£30 [≃ $57]**

Cleaveland, P.
- An Elementary Treatise on Mineralogy and Geology. Boston: 1816. 8vo. xii,668 pp. Fldg cold map, 5 plates. 1 plate reprd at fold. New half calf. *(Wheldon & Wesley)* **£360 [≃ $691]**
- Elementary Treatise on Mineralogy & Geology. Boston: Cummings & Hilliard, 1822. 2nd edn. 2 vols in one. 8vo. xii,818 pp. Frontis cold map, 5 engvd plates. Moderately foxed. Contemp leather.
        (Gemmary) **$450 [≃ £234]**

Clerk, D.
- The Gas and Oil Engine. London: (1899) 1902. Rvsd edn. xii,588 pp. 228 ills. Occas sm marg lib stamps. Cloth sl worn, sl loose.
        (Whitehart) **£25 [≃ $47]**

Clerke, A.M.
- Problems in Astrophysics. London: 1903. xvi,567 pp. 31 plates, 50 text figs. Orig cloth.
        (Whitehart) **£25 [≃ $47]**

Cloud Crystals ...
- See Chickering, Mrs Francis E.

Clow, A. & N.L.
- The Chemical Revolution. A Contribution to Social Technology. London: 1952. xvi,680 pp. Ills. Front inner hinge cracked but bndg firm.   *(Whitehart)* **£25 [≃ $47]**

Cobb, J.H.
- A Manual containing Information respecting the Growth of the Mulberry Tree, with Suitable Directions for the Culture of Silk.

Boston: Carter, Hendee, 1833. New edn. 12mo. 98 pp. 3 plates (2 hand cold). Old damp stain through text. Orig cloth backed ptd bds.   *(Respess)* **$60 [≃ £31]**

Cobbett, William
- The Woodlands: or, a Treatise on the Preparing of Ground for Planting; on the Cultivating; on the Pruning ... London: for William Cobbett ..., 1825. 1st edn. 8vo. [344] pp. Advt leaf at end. Occas spots. 2 sm reprs. Lacks front fly leaf. Contemp cloth.
        (Bow Windows) **£125 [≃ $239]**

Coburn, Alvin
- The Factor of Infection in the Rheumatic State. Baltimore: 1931. 1st edn. 288 pp. Orig bndg.   *(Fye)* **$75 [≃ £39]**

Cockburn, W.
- The Symptoms, Nature, Cause and Cure of a Gonorrhoea. London: Strahan, 1728. 4th edn. 8vo. [xxxvi],332 pp. Contemp calf, spine sl worn.   *(Bookpress)* **$350 [≃ £182]**

Cocker, Edward
- Cocker's Arithmetic ... published by John Hawkins ... Forty Third Edition ... amended by George Fisher. London: Edw. Midwinter, [ca 1725]. 12mo. vi,183,[1 advt] pp. Frontis port. Contemp sheep.
        (Spelman) **£140 [≃ $268]**
- Cocker's Decimal Arithmetic ... London: 1695. [16],436 pp. Foxed. Sm marg repr. New leather. *(Whitehart)* **£120 [≃ $230]**

Cocking, W.T.
- Television Receiving Equipment. 1944. 1st edn. 298 pp. 14 photos, 100 ills. Orig bndg.
        (New Wireless) **$30 [≃ £15]**

Cocks, W.P.
- Pathological Anatomy of the Brain, Spinal Cord, and their Membranes ... London: S. Highley, 1831. 1st edn. Sm 8vo. xvi,175 pp. 13 hand cold litho plates. Orig bds, cloth spine, uncut, rebacked, rubbed.
        (Bickersteth) **£880 [≃ $1,689]**

Coffey, Walter, et al.
- Angina Pectoris: The Anatomy, Physiology and Surgical Treatment. New Orleans, 1927. 1st edn. 393 pp. Ills. Orig bndg.
        (Fye) **$200 [≃ £104]**

Coffin, Albert Isaiah
- A Treatise on Midwifery, and the Diseases of Women and Children ... First Thousand.

Manchester: British Medico-Botanic Press ...,
1849. 1st edn. 8vo. [x],vi,9-184 pp. Litho
port, 4 litho plates. Text sl discold. Contemp
half roan, sl worn. *(Gaskell)* £95 [≈ $182]

Cohnheim, Julius
- Lectures on General Pathology ... Translated
from the Second German Edition by
Alexander B. McKee. With Memoir by the
Translator. London: New Sydenham Society,
1889-90. 3 vols. 8vo. Orig cloth, worn, jnts
cracked, internally unmarked ex-lib.
(Goodrich) $175 [≈ £91]

Cohnheim, P.
- Diseases of the Digestive Canal ... Translated
from the 2nd German Edition by D. Fulton.
Phila: [1909]. xxi,373 pp. 45 text figs. Orig
cloth, marked, new endpapers.
(Whitehart) £25 [≈ $47]

Colburn, Zerah & Holley, Alexander L.
- The Permanent Way and Coal-Burning
Locomotive Boilers of European Railways;
with a Comparison of ... European and
American Lines ... New York: 1858. Folio.
xxiii,168 pp. 2 maps, 49 plates. Lib stamps.
Orig cloth, faded, crude reprs to spine ends,
front hinge broken. *(Reese)* $275 [≈ £143]

Colden, Cadwallader D.
- The Life of Robert Fulton ... Comprising
Some Account of ... Steam-Boats ... Canals ...
New York: 1817. vi,371 pp. Fldg table, port.
Foxed. Mod cloth, orig front & rear ptd paper
preserved. *(Reese)* $225 [≈ £117]

The Cole Library ...
- The Cole Library of Early Medicine and
Zoology. Catalogue of Books and Pamphlets.
Reading: 1969. 2 vols. 4to. Orig bndgs.
(Goodrich) $115 [≈ £59]
- The Cole Library of Early Medicine and
Zoology. Catalogue of Books and Pamphlets
[1472 to the present day]. Reading: 1969-75.
2 vols. Part 1 cloth, part 2 wrappers.
(Whitehart) £40 [≈ $76]

Cole, F.J.
- A History of Comparative Anatomy from
Aristotle to the Eighteenth Century. London:
Macmillan, 1944. 8vo. Num ills. Orig bndg.
(Georges) £35 [≈ $67]
- A History of Comparative Anatomy from
Aristotle to the Eighteenth Century. London:
1949. 1st reprinting. 8vo. 524 pp. Dw.
(Goodrich) $65 [≈ £33]
- A History of Comparative Anatomy from

Aristotle to the Eighteenth Century. London:
(1944) 1949. viii,524 pp. 200 figs. Orig bndg.
(Whitehart) £45 [≈ $86]

Cole, R.V.
- British Trees Drawn and Described. London:
1907. 2 vols. Lge 4to. 430 plates, text ills.
Prelims foxed. Orig bndgs, sl rubbed.
(Grayling) £35 [≈ $67]

Coleman, W.S.
- British Butterflies ... Eighteenth Edition.
London: Routledge, 1886. vii,179 pp. 13 cold
& 2 other plates. Orig elab pict blue cloth gilt.
(Gough) £35 [≈ $67]

Colgan, Nathaniel
- Flora of the County Dublin ... Dublin: 1904.
[With] A Supplement to Colgan's Flora of the
County Dublin. Dublin: 1961. 1st edns. 2
vols. 8vo. 2 maps. Orig cloth, t.e.g., & orig
ptd wraps. *(Fenning)* £65 [≈ $124]

Collectanea for a Flora of Moray ...
- See Gordon, G.

College of Physicians
- Medical Transactions published by the
College of Physicians in London. Volume the
First. London: 1785. xv,474 pp. Title sl
marked. Later bds. *(Whitehart)* £60 [≈ $115]

Colles, Abraham
- Selections from the Works ... Edited with
Annotations by Robert McDonnell. London:
1891. 1st edn. 431 pp. Orig bndg.
(Fye) $150 [≈ £78]
- Selections from the Works ... Edited with
Annotations by R. McDonnell. London: New
Sydenham Soc, 1891. xvi,431 pp. Port. Orig
cloth, sl worn, lib marks on spine &
elsewhere. *(Whitehart)* £35 [≈ $67]

Collins, A. Frederick
- The Book of Wireless. 1915. 1st edn. 222 pp.
219 ills. Orig illust bndg.
(New Wireless) $45 [≈ £23]
- Experimental Television. 1932. 1st edn. 313
pp. 185 ills. Orig bndg.
(New Wireless) $165 [≈ £85]
- Manual of Wireless Telegraphy and
Telephony. 1906. 1st edn. 1st printing (of
1000 copies). 232 pp. 90 ills. Orig bndg.
(New Wireless) $115 [≈ £59]
- Wireless Telegraphy - Its History, Theory
and Practice. 1905. 1st edn. 2 pp torn. 299
pp. 122 photos, 200 ills. Orig bndg.
(New Wireless) $175 [≈ £91]

Collins, E.T. & Law, F.W.
- The History & Traditions of the Moorfield's
  Eye Hospital ... London: 1929-75. 2 vols.
  xii,226; xvi,299 pp. 1 frontis, 27 + 1 plates,
  69 ills. Orig cloth.   *(Whitehart)* £35 [≈ $67]

Collins, H.F.
- The Metallurgy of Lead & Silver. London:
  Charles Griffin, 1899. 2 vols. 8vo. xvi,368;
  xvi,352 pp. 231 text figs. Cloth.
                      (Gemmary) $225 [≈ £117]

Collins, J.H.
- A First Book of Mineralogy. London:
  William Collins, 1876. Sm 8vo. 160 pp. 159
  text figs. Cloth, worn.
                      (Gemmary) $25 [≈ £13]
- Observations on the West of England Mining
  Region ... Plymouth: 1912. 1st edn. 8vo. xxiv,
  683,[1] pp. 18 plates. Endpapers marked.
  Orig cloth.   *(Bow Windows)* £80 [≈ $153]

Collins, Samuel
- Paradise Retriev'd: plainly and fully
  demonstrating the most beautiful, durable,
  and beneficial Method of managing and
  improving Fruit-Trees ... London: John
  Collins, Seedsman, 1717. 8vo. [2],v,[5],6-106
  pp. 2 fldg plates. 1 tear reprd. Contemp calf,
  rebacked.   *(Spelman)* £180 [≈ $345]

Colyer, F.
- Old Instruments used for Extracting Teeth.
  London: 1952. [xvi],7-244 pp. 283 figs.
  Cloth, sl marked.   *(Whitehart)* £40 [≈ $76]
- Variations and Diseases of the Teeth of
  Animals. London: 1936. viii,750 pp. 1007
  text figs. Ink stamp removed from title. Half
  cloth. Inscrbd by the author.
                      (Whitehart) £50 [≈ $95]

Colyer, James Frank
- John Hunter and Odontology. London:
  Claudius Ash, 1913. 1st edn. 4to. 214 pp.
  Port frontis, text ills. Traces of sl foxing on
  frontis & tissue. Orig cloth, a.e.g.
                      (Chapel Hill) $150 [≈ £78]

Combe, Andrew
- The Physiology of Digestion considered with
  relation to the Principles of Dietics ...
  Edinburgh: MacLachlan & Stewart ..., 1836.
  2nd edn, rvsd & enlgd. 8vo. xxviii,350, [8] pp.
  Half-title. Orig cloth backed bds, label
  chipped.   *(Young's)* £180 [≈ $345]
- The Physiology of Digestion considered with
  relation to the Principles of Dietetics. Boston:
  1836. 1st Amer edn. 328 pp. Orig bndg.

                      (Fye) $100 [≈ £52]
- The Principles of Physiology applied to the
  Preservation of Health, and the Improvement
  of Physical and Mental Education. Fifth
  Edition, revised and enlarged. Edinburgh:
  1836. 8vo. vi,438,6 advt pp. Orig cloth,
  spotted, jnt ends sl worn.
                      (Bickersteth) £38 [≈ $72]

Combe, George
- The Life and Correspondence of Andrew
  Combe. Edinburgh: 1850. 1st edn. 8vo.
  xii,563 pp. Port. Contemp blue half mor,
  t.e.g.   *(Bickersteth)* £48 [≈ $92]
- The Life and Correspondence of Andrew
  Combe. Edinburgh: 1850. 1st edn. 8vo. xii,
  563, [1] pp. Port. Half calf, gilt spine, mor
  labels, t.e.g.   *(Bow Windows)* £135 [≈ $259]

A Comparative View ...
- A Comparative View of the State and
  Faculties of Man ... see Gregory, John.

Complete ...
- The Complete English Farmer ... see Henry,
  David.
- The Complete Family-Piece: and, Country
  Gentleman, and Farmer's Best Guide ...
  Physick and Surgery; Cookery ... Hunting ...
  Fishing ... Gardens ... Improving of Land ...
  London: J. Roberts, 1736. 1st edn. 12mo.
  Contemp calf, hinges splitting.
                      (Jarndyce) £380 [≈ $729]
- The Complete Farmer: or, a General
  Dictionary of Husbandry, in all its Branches
  ... By a Society of Gentlemen. Fourth
  Edition, considerable improved ... London:
  Longman, [1793]. Folio. Engvd frontis, 34
  plates. Final leaf creased. Contemp mor,
  backstrip relaid.   *(Spelman)* £200 [≈ $383]
- The Complete Grazier: or, Gentleman and
  Farmer's Directory ... London: for J. Almon,
  1767. 1st edn. 12mo. [iii]-xii,252,[ii] pp. Intl
  advt leaf bound in at end. 1 w'cut in text.
  Contemp calf, mor label, extremities worn,
  jnts cracked but firm. *(Finch)* £130 [≈ $249]

Comrie, J.D.
- History of Scottish Medicine. London: 1932.
  2nd edn. 2 vols. 852 pp. Cold frontis, num
  ills. Orig bndg.   *(Whitehart)* £50 [≈ $95]

Comstock, J.A.
- Butterflies of California. 1927. 4to. 334 pp.
  63 cold plates. Margs sl discold, sm blind
  stamp on half-title. Cloth.
                      (Wheldon & Wesley) £200 [≈ $383]

Comstock, J.L.
- An Introduction to Mineralogy. New York: Pratt, Woodford, 1851. 16th edn. Cr 8vo. 369 pp. W'cut ills. Foxed. Leather, worn.
(Gemmary) **$100 [≈ £52]**

Condry, W.M.
- The Natural History of Wales. London: Collins New Naturalist, 1981. 1st edn. 8vo. 287 pp. 24 plates. Orig cloth. Dw.
(Henly) **£24 [≈ $46]**
- The Snowdonia National Park. London: Collins New Naturalist, 1966. 1st edn. 8vo. xvii,238 pp. 4 cold & 24 plain plates. Orig cloth. Dw.
(Henly) **£18 [≈ $34]**

Conrady, A.E.
- Applied Optics and Optical Design Part One. London: OUP, 1929. Roy 8vo. ix,518 pp. 102 text figs. Cloth.
(Gemmary) **$65 [≈ £33]**

Conversations ...
- Conversations on Botany ... see Fitton, E. & S.M.
- Conversations on Geology; comprising a Familiar Explanation of the Huttonian and Wernerian Systems; the Mosaic Geology ... late Discoveries ... London: for Samuel Maunder, 1828. 8vo. xxii,[ii],371 pp. 12 plates (4 hand cold). Orig cloth backed bds, sl worn.
(Burmester) **£125 [≈ $239]**

Cook, E.T. (ed.)
- The Century Book of Gardening. A Comprehensive Work for Every Lover of the Garden. London: Country Life, 1908. 4to. ix, 610, xiii pp. Cold frontis, num ills. Orig illust cloth, sl worn, front hinge reprd.
(Bernett) **$50 [≈ £26]**

Cook, Sir Edward
- The Life of Florence Nightingale. New York: 1913. 1st edn. 2 vols. 507; 510 pp. Lib b'plates. Orig bndg.
(Fye) **$100 [≈ £52]**
- The Life of Florence Nightingale. London: 1913. 2 vols. 8vo. 6 ports, 1 facs. Occas spots. Hd of a few ff sl bumped. Orig cloth, t.e.g.
(Bow Windows) **£48 [≈ $92]**

Cook, Moses
- The Manner of Raising, Ordering, and Improving Forest-Trees ... Second Edition, very much Corrected. London: for Daniel Browne ..., 1717. 8vo. [iii]-xix, [i],276 pp. Frontis, 4 fldg plates (1 sl defective). Sl damp stain throughout. Contemp calf, sl worn.
(Finch) **£55 [≈ $105]**
- The Manner of Raising, Ordering, and

Improving Forest-Trees ... Second Edition, very much Corrected. London: 1717. 8vo. xix,[i], 276 pp, inc frontis. 4 fldg diags. Contemp Cambridge style calf, rebacked, crnrs worn.
(Bow Windows) **£205 [≈ $393]**

Cooke, C.W.R.
- A Book about Cider and Perry. London: 1898. 1st edn. Sm 8vo. viii,120,[8 advt] pp. Frontis. Orig cloth.
(Bow Windows) **£48 [≈ $92]**

Cooke, John
- A Treatise of Pathology and Therapeutics. Lexington: 1828. 1st edn. 2 vols (all published). 566; 520 pp. Leather.
(Fye) **$100 [≈ £52]**

Cooke, M.C.
- British Edible Fungi. How to Distinguish and Cook Them ... London: 1891. 1st edn. 8vo. 237 pp. 12 cold plates. Orig cloth, a little marked & rubbed.
(Bow Windows) **£40 [≈ $76]**
- Edible and Poisonous Mushrooms; What to Eat and What to Avoid. London: SPCK, 1894. 1st edn. 126,8 ctlg pp. 18 chromolithos. Orig pict green cloth, spine lettering faded.
(Gough) **£30 [≈ $57]**
- Freaks and Marvels of Plant Life; or, Curiosities of Vegetation. London: 1882. viii, 463 pp. 97 text ills. Orig pict cloth, dull, spine marked.
(Whitehart) **£15 [≈ $28]**
- Illustrations of British Fungi ... London: 1881-91. 8 vols. 8vo. 1198 cold plates. Plates renumbered in MS. Mor, 2 vols rebacked, trifle rubbed, few jnts just cracking.
(Wheldon & Wesley) **£3,000 [≈ $5,759]**
- Introduction to the Study of Fungi. Their Organography, Classification and Distribution. London: 1895. x,360 pp. 148 text figs. Orig cloth, inner hinges cracked but firm.
(Whitehart) **£18 [≈ $34]**
- Our Reptiles ... Lizards, Snakes, Newts, Toads, Frogs and Tortoises Indigenous to Great britain. London: Hardwicke, 1865. 1st edn. 12mo. vii,199 pp. 11 hand cold plates, num text ills. Orig green cloth, gilt spine, fine.
(Gough) **£40 [≈ $76]**
- Rust, Smut, Mildew & Mould. An Introduction to the Study of Microscopic Fungi. London: Hardwicke, 1870. 2nd edn. 8vo. 242 pp. 26 cold plates. Orig dec cloth.
(Savona) **£30 [≈ $57]**
- Rust, Smut, Mildew and Mould; An Introduction to the Study of Microscopic Fungi. Fifth Edition, Revised and Enlarged. London: W.H. Allen, 1886. 12mo. 262 pp. 16

cold plates. V occas sl spotting. Orig brown cloth, spine gilt, fine.　*(Gough)* **£25 [≈ $47]**

Cooke, T. & Sons
- The Adjustment & Testing of Telescope Objectives. London: 1921. 123 pp. 3 plates. Cloth, rather worn.　*(Whitehart)* **£35 [≈ $67]**

Cooke, William
- A Commentary of Medical and Moral Life; or Mind and the Emotions, considered in relation to Health, Disease, and Religion. London: Longman, 1852. 1st edn. 8vo. xvi,304,[2] pp. Orig cloth, largely unopened. Inscrbd "from the Author".
(Burmester) **£80 [≈ $153]**

Coolidge, J.L.
- A History of the Conic Sections and Quadric Surfaces. Oxford: 1945. xi,214 pp. 42 figs. Sm lib stamp on title verso. Traces of label removal from endpapers.　*(Whitehart)* **£35 [≈ $67]**
- A Treatise on the Circle and the Sphere. Oxford: 1916. 603 pp. Sev text figs.
(Whitehart) **£25 [≈ $47]**

Coombs, Carey
- Rheumatic Heart Disease. New York: 1924. 1st Amer edn. 376 pp. Orig bndg.
(Fye) **$100 [≈ £52]**

Cooper, Astley
- The Anatomy and Surgical Treatment of Abdominal Hernia. Phila: 1844. 1st Amer edn. 427 pp. 26 engvd plates. Name clipped from crnr of title. Leather.
(Fye) **$350 [≈ £182]**
- A Treatise on Dislocations and Fractures of the Joints. A New Edition, much enlarged. Edited by Bransby B. Cooper. Phila: 1851. 496 pp. Leather.　*(Fye)* **$200 [≈ £104]**

Cooper, Bransby B.
- Surgical Essays: The Result of Clinical Observations made at Guy's Hospital. London: 1843. 8vo. 4 cold litho plates. Orig bds.　*(Goodrich)* **$300 [≈ £156]**

Cooper, D.
- Flora Metropolitana or Botanical Rambles within Thirty Miles of London. London: 1836. Post 8vo. xvi,139 pp. Cloth, trifle used.
(Wheldon & Wesley) **£35 [≈ $67]**

Cooper, H.J.
- Scientific Instruments. New York: Hutchinson, 1946. 8vo. 293 pp. Num text figs. Ex-lib. Cloth.　*(Gemmary)* **$45 [≈ £23]**

Cooper, Samuel
- A Dictionary of Practical Surgery ... with Notes and Additions by John Syng Dorsey. Phila: 1816. 2nd Amer edn. 2 vols. 531; 522 pp. Leather, fine.　*(Fye)* **$325 [≈ £169]**
- Dictionary of Practical Surgery ... London: 1825. 5th edn. viii,1264 pp. Lacks half-title. A little underlining, names on title. Contemp leather, rebacked.　*(Whitehart)* **£40 [≈ $76]**
- A Dictionary of Practical Surgery ... With Numerous Notes ... by David Meredith Reese. New York: 1830. 2 vols. 489; 510 pp. Leather.　*(Fye)* **$150 [≈ £78]**

Cooper, William
- Practical Remarks on Near Sight, Aged Sight, and Impaired Vision; with Observations upon the Use of Glasses and on Artificial Light. London: 1847. 1st edn. 216 pp. Orig bndg, fine.　*(Fye)* **$100 [≈ £52]**

Corbet, P.S., Longfield, C. & Moore, N.W.
- Dragonflies. London: Collins New Naturalist, 1961. 1st edn. 8vo. xii,260 pp. 24 cold & 8 plain plates. Orig cloth. Dw.
(Henly) **£60 [≈ $115]**

Corbin, Henry
- Avicenna and the Visionary Recital. Translated from the French by Willard R. Trask. New York: 1960. 8vo. 452 pp. Orig bndg.　*(Goodrich)* **$65 [≈ £33]**

Cornaro, Lewis (Luigi)
- Discourses on a Sober and Temperate Life. London: Benjamin White, 1768. 8vo. 281 pp. Contemp calf, elab gilt spine, split upper hinge.　*(Hemlock)* **$125 [≈ £65]**

Cornaro, Lewis (Luigi), et al.
- The Temperate Man, or the Way of Preserving Life and Health. London: John Starkey, 1678. 12mo. [xxxvi],168 pp. Contemp sheep. Anon.
(Bookpress) **$450 [≈ £234]**

Correvon, H. & Robert, P.
- The Alpine Flora. Translated by E.W. Clayforth. Geneva: [1912]. 8vo. 436 pp. 1 plain & 100 cold plates. Cloth.
(Wheldon & Wesley) **£25 [≈ $47]**

Corrington, J.D.
- Adventures with the Microscope. Rochester, New York: 1934. 8vo. ix,445 pp. Cold frontis, 352 text ills. Cloth.
(Henly) **£25 [≈ $47]**

Corvisart, J.N.
- An Essay on the Organic Diseases and Lesions of the Heart and Great Vessels. Boston: 1812. 1st English translation. 344 pp. Foxed, some tears in title. Rec leather.
  (Fye) **$350 [≈ £182]**
- A Treatise on the Diseases and Organic Lesions of the Heart and Great Vessels. London: 1813. 1st British edn. 404 pp. Half leather. *(Fye)* **$400 [≈ £208]**

Cory, R.
- Lectures on the Theory and Practice of Vaccination. London: 1898. [ix],122 pp. 14 plates. Cloth, marked, dusty, sl worn.
  (Whitehart) **£25 [≈ $47]**

Cotes, R.
- Hydrostatical and Pneumatical Lectures ... Published from the Author's Original Manuscript, with Notes by Robert Smith. London: 1775. 3rd edn. 8vo. [xvi],288,[8] pp. Fldg plates. Occas sl foxing. Half mor gilt, uncut. *(Whitehart)* **£150 [≈ $287]**

Cotton, William Charles
- My Bee Book. London: Rivington, 1842. 8vo. 368 pp. 72 w'cut text ills. Orig cloth gilt, mottled & faded. *(Hollett)* **£95 [≈ $182]**

Couch, Jonathan
- A History of the Fishes of the British Islands. London: George Bell & Son, 1877. 4 vols. 252 chromolitho plates. V occas sl foxing. Contemp blue half mor, gilt dec spines v sl faded, t.e.g. *(Gough)* **£750 [≈ $1,439]**

Coursey, Philip R.
- Telephony Without Wires. 1919. 1st edn. 414 pp. 249 ills. Orig bndg.
  (New Wireless) **$50 [≈ £26]**

Court, T.H. & Von Rohr, M.
- On the Development of Spectacles in London from the End of the Seventeenth Century and A History of the Development of the Telescope from about 1675 to 1830. London: Optical Soc Trans XXX, 1928-29. 8vo. xiv,272 pp. Buckram.
  (Gemmary) **$60 [≈ £31]**

Coward, T.A.
- The Birds of the British Isles and their Eggs. London: Warne, 1923. 4th imp. 3 vols. 12mo. 591 cold plates, num photo plates. Orig pict brown cloth gilt. *(Gough)* **£25 [≈ $47]**

Coward, T.A. & Oldham, Charles
- The Birds of Cheshire. Manchester: 1900. 278 pp. Map, 6 plates. Cloth, uncut.
  (Wheldon & Wesley) **£45 [≈ $86]**
- The Birds of Cheshire. Manchester: Sherratt & Hughes, 1900. 1st edn. 278 pp. Fldg map, 6 plates. V occas sl spotting. Orig green cloth, t.e.g. *(Hollett)* **£55 [≈ $105]**
- The Vertebrate Fauna of Cheshire and Liverpool Bay. London: Witherby, 1910. 2 vols. 8vo. Fldg map, 55 ills. Orig cloth gilt, spine browned. *(Hollett)* **£75 [≈ $143]**

Coward, T.A. (ed.)
- The Vertebrate Fauna of Cheshire and Liverpool Bay. London: Witherby, 1910. 1st edn. 2 vols. Fldg map, 54 photo plates. Orig cloth, t.e.g., v sl marked. *(Gough)* **£55 [≈ $105]**

Cowell, John
- The Curious and Profitable Gardener ... London: Weaver Bickerton, 1730. 1st edn. 8vo. iv, [iv],126, [ii],67, [1] pp. Frontis, fldg plate. Contemp sheep, worn.
  (Bookpress) **$650 [≈ £338]**

Cox, E., & Son, publishers
- Medical Botany. London: for E. Cox & Son, 1821. 2 vols. Roy 8vo. 138 hand cold plates. Some discoloration to inner marg of 9 plates, a few faint marks, some sl browning. Contemp half calf, sl rubbed.
  (Ash) **£1,000 [≈ $1,919]**

Cox, E.H.M.
- Plant Hunting in China. London: 1945. 1st edn. 8vo. 230 pp. 1 cold & 24 plain plates. Orig cloth, spine faded, cvrs damp stained.
  (Henly) **£20 [≈ $38]**

Cox, Herbert E.
- A Handbook of the Coleoptera (or Beetles) of Great Britain and Ireland. London: E.W. Janson, 1874. 1st edn. 2 vols. 8vo. viii,527; 366 pp. Half calf, vol 1 rebacked.
  (Gough) **£45 [≈ $86]**

Cox, I. (ed.)
- The Scallop. Studies of a Shell and its Influences on Humankind. London: 1957. 4to. 135 pp. Num cold ills. Orig cloth gilt.
  (Wheldon & Wesley) **£15 [≈ $28]**

Coxe, John Redman
- The Philadelphia Medical Dictionary ... Second Edition. Phila: 1817. 8vo. viii,433, [2] pp. Sl browning. Contemp calf, worn.
  (Hemlock) **$75 [≈ £39]**

Crabb, G.

- Universal Technological Dictionary or Familiar Explanation of the Terms used in all Arts and Sciences ... London: 1823. 2 vols. 60 plates, text ills. Cloth backed bds, paper labels. *(Whitehart)* **£180** [≈ **$345**]

Crabtre, A.D.

- The Funny Side of Physic ... Medical Humbugs, Quacks, and Charlatans in all Ages and all Countries. Hartford: 1880. 1st edn. 816 pp. W'cut ills. Orig bndg. *(Fye)* **$175** [≈ **£91**]

Cramer, Johann Andreas

- Elements of the Art of Assaying Metals ... Translated from the Latin ... With an Appendix ... London: Woodward, Davis, 1741. 1st edn in English. 8vo. [xii],208, 201-470, [8] pp. 6 fldg plates. Sl water stain. 19th c half calf, rubbed. *(Burmester)* **£250** [≈ **$479**]

Crampton, Josiah

- The Lunar World: its Scenery, Motions, etc ... Dublin: George Herbert; London: Hamilton, Nisbet ..., 1853. 1st edn. Sq 12mo. viii,100 pp. 7 plates. Contemp mor, sl scuffed. *(Burmester)* **£40** [≈ **$76**]

Crane, W.R.

- Index of Mining Engineering Literature. New York: John Wiley, 1909. 1st edn. 8vo. xii, 812 pp. Cloth. *(Gemmary)* **$50** [≈ **£26**]

Crawley, Chetwode

- From Telegraphy to Television. 1931. 1st edn. 212 pp. 24 photos. Orig bndg, cvrs stained. *(New Wireless)* **$55** [≈ **£28**]

Creighton, Charles

- A History of Epidemics in Britain ... Cambridge: UP, 1891-94. 1st edn. 2 vols. Orig cloth. *(Wreden)* **$150** [≈ **£78**]
- The Natural History of Cow-Pox and Vaccinal Syphilis. London: Cassell, 1887. 1st edn. 8vo. 160,8 advt pp. Orig red cloth. *(Rootenberg)* **$250** [≈ **£130**]

Crellin, J.K.

- Medical Ceramics. A Catalogue of the English and Dutch Collections in the Museum of the Wellcome Institute of the History of Medicine. London: 1969. vii,304 pp. Cold frontis, num plates. Orig bndg. *(Whitehart)* **£38** [≈ **$72**]

Creuze, Augustin Francis Bullock

- Treatise on the Theory and Practice of Naval Architecture ... Edinburgh: Adam & Charles Black, 1848. 1st edn. 4to. 90 pp. 15 plates. Orig cloth, sl worn & rubbed. *(Chapel Hill)* **$150** [≈ **£78**]

Crichton, Alexander

- Practical Observations on the Treatment and Cure of Several Varieties of Pulmonary Consumption ... London: Lloyd & Son, 1823. 1st edn. 8vo. 261 pp. Crnr lacking from flyleaf. Orig bds, spine worn. *(Chapel Hill)* **$150** [≈ **£78**]

Crile, George

- Anemia and Resuscitation: An Experimental and Clinical Research. New York: 1914. 1st edn. 305 pp. Rec qtr leather. *(Fye)* **$200** [≈ **£104**]
- Blood-Pressure in Surgery, and Experimental and Clinical Research. Phila: 1903. 1st edn. 422 pp. Ex-lib. Orig bndg. *(Fye)* **$150** [≈ **£78**]
- George Crile. An Autobiography. Philadelphia & London: 1947. 1st edn. 2 vols. 8 dble-sided plates. Dws. *(Whitehart)* **£25** [≈ **$47**]

Cripps, E.C.

- Plough Court: the Story of a Notable Pharmacy 1715-1927. London: Allen & Hanburys, 1927. 1st edn. 8vo. xviii,227 pp. 43 plates. Orig cloth. *(Bow Windows)* **£20** [≈ **$38**]

Crocker, Francis B.

- Electric Lighting. Volume I. The Generating Plant. 1896. 1st edn. 450 pp. 152 ills. Orig bndg. *(New Wireless)* **$55** [≈ **£29**]

Crocker, Francis B. & Wheeler, Schuyler S.

- Practical Management of Dynamos and Motors. 1896. 5th edn. 206 pp. 99 ills. Orig bndg. *(New Wireless)* **$40** [≈ **£21**]

Croker, Temple Henry

- Experimental Magnetism, or the Truth of Mr. Mason's Discoveries ... Proved and Ascertained. London: for J. Coote, 1761. Only edn. 8vo. Half-title, title, iii-x,72 pp. Frontis, fldg plate. Rec wraps. *(Gaskell)* **£325** [≈ **$623**]

Croll, James

- Autobiographical Sketch of James Croll with Memoir of his Life and Work by J.C. Irons. London: 1896. 553 pp. Port. Orig cloth,

partly unopened. *(Whitehart)* £35 [≈ $67]
- Climate and Time in their Geological Relations: a Theory of Secular Changes of the Earth's Climate. New York: 1887. xvii,577 pp. 8 plates. New endpapers. Cloth, sl worn. *(Whitehart)* £38 [≈ $72]
- Climate and Time in their Geological relations: a Theory of Secular Changes of the Earth's Climate. London: 1897. 4th edn. xvii, 577 pp. 8 plates. *(Whitehart)* £35 [≈ $67]

Crompton, R.E.
- Reminiscences. 1928. 1st edn. 238 pp. Orig bndg. *(New Wireless)* $45 [≈ £23]

Crook, Ronald E.
- A Bibliography of Joseph Priestley 1733-1804. London: Library Association, 1966. Roy 8vo. Dw. *(Georges)* £50 [≈ $95]

Crookes, W.
- Diamonds. London: Harper & Bros, 1909. Sm 8vo. xvi,146 pp. 24 mtd photo ills. Orig cloth. *(Gemmary)* $80 [≈ £41]
- Select Methods in Chemical Analysis (Chiefly Inorganic). London: Longman, Green, 1886. 2nd edn. 8vo. xxii,725 pp. 39 text figs. Ex-lib. Cloth. *(Gemmary)* $125 [≈ £65]

Crosby, James M.
- Diseases of the Lungs and Air-Vessels; comprising Asthma, Chronic Bronchitis, Influenza, Pulmonary Consumption, &c. &c. ... Scarborough: for the author ..., 1881. 8vo. 82 pp. Orig ptd wraps. *(Bickersteth)* £26 [≈ $49]

Cross, J.E.
- The Berries and Heaths of Rannoch. By a Snowdrop. London: 1881. Roy 8vo. 24 pp. 13 hand cold plates. Sl foxing. Cloth, trifle marked. Anon.. *(Wheldon & Wesley)* £40 [≈ $76]

Cross, M.I. & Cole, M.J.
- Modern Microscopy. London: Tindall & Cox, 1895. 2nd edn. 8vo. 182 pp. 40 text figs. Cloth. *(Gemmary)* $50 [≈ £26]
- Modern Microscopy. London: Tindall & Cox, 1903. 3rd edn. 8vo. xvi,292 pp. 76 text figs. Cloth. *(Gemmary)* $50 [≈ £26]
- Modern Microscopy. London: Tindall & Cox, 1912. 4th edn. 8vo. xvii,325 pp. 6 plates, 87 text figs. Cloth, spotted. *(Gemmary)* $50 [≈ £26]
- Modern Microscopy. London: Tindall & Cox, 1922. 5th edn. 8vo. x,315 pp. 12 plates, 114 text figs. Ex-lib. Cloth.

(Gemmary) $50 [≈ £26]

Crosse, John Green
- Cases in Midwifery ... arranged by Edward Copeman ... London: Churchill; Norwich: Stevenson & Matchett, 1851. Sole edn. 8vo. xi, 228 pp, advt leaf. Orig cloth, uncut & largely unopened. *(Bickersteth)* £85 [≈ $163]

Crowther, A.H.
- A Quantum Theory of the Scattering of X-Rays by Light Elements. Lancaster, PA: The Physical Review, 2nd Series, Vol 21, No. 5, Amer Physical Soc, May, 1923. 8vo. 483-584 pp. Text figs. Wraps.
(Gemmary) $125 [≈ £65]

Crowther, J.
- The Microscope and Its Lessons. London: George Cauldwell, 1891. 8vo. 286 pp. Num text figs. Dec cloth, a.e.g.
(Gemmary) $65 [≈ £33]

Crowther, J.G.
- British Scientists of the Nineteenth Century. London: 1935. xii,332 pp. Frontis, 12 ports. *(Whitehart)* £18 [≈ $34]

Cudworth, W.
- Life and Correspondence of Abraham Sharp, the Yorkshire Mathematician and Astronomer, and Assistant of Flamsteed. London: 1889. xvi, 342 pp. Port, 5 plates, 2 pedigrees, num text ills. Orig half parchment, dust stained, sm splits in jnts.
(Whitehart) £65 [≈ $124]

Cullen, William
- First Lines of the Practice of Physic ... New York: Samuel Campbell, 1793. 2 vols. 8vo. 438,[2]; vi, (9)-410,21 pp. Contemp calf.
(Bookpress) $225 [≈ £117]
- Lectures on the Materia Medica ... Phila: Robert Bell, 1775. 1st Amer edn. "Second American Printing" not stated on title. 4to. viii, 512 pp. Foxed. Later calf.
(Bookpress) $500 [≈ £260]
- A Treatise on the Materia Medica. Dublin: Luke White, 1789. 2 vols. 8vo. xxiii,351; viii, 511 pp. Contemp calf, dull, hinges cracked but holding. Amer inscrptn dated 1800.
(Hemlock) $700 [≈ £364]

Culley, George
- Observations on Live Stock ... Fourth Edition, with an Appendix. London: Wilkie & Robinson, 1807. 8vo. viii,274,[vi] pp. 2 plates. Sl wear & tear. Period half sheep.
(Rankin) £45 [≈ $86]

Culley, R.S.
- A Handbook of Practical Telegraphy. London: 1878. 7th edn. xi,468 pp. 18 plates (some fldg), 147 text figs. Orig cloth, spine faded, sl marked, inner hinges cracked but bndg firm.   *(Whitehart)* **£25 [≈ $47]**
- A Handbook of Practical Telegraphy. Eighth Edition. London: 1885. 8vo. viii,442 pp. 152 figs. Some foxing of blank end ff. Contemp prize calf gilt.   *(Bow Windows)* **£42 [≈ $80]**

Culpeper, Nicholas
- The Complete Herbal ... added ... The English Physician Enlarged. London: 1850. 4to. vi,398,[2] pp. Port frontis, 20 hand cold plates of 180 figs. Somewhat foxed, a little soiled. Title reprd. Contemp roan, rubbed, front jnt broken.
          (Wheldon & Wesley) **£75 [≈ $143]**
- Culpeper's Complete Herbal ... [vignette title] The British Herbal and Family Physician. Halifax: Milner & Sowerby, 1862. 16mo. xiv,431 pp. Cold vignette title, 25 hand cold plates (1 fldg). Sl foxed & used. Orig cloth, recased, worn & reprd, new endpapers. *(Wheldon & Wesley)* **£45 [≈ $86]**
- The Complete Herbal. A New Edition ... annexed The English Physician ... Key to Physic. Kynoch Press: privately ptd, 1953. Lge 8vo. x,603 pp. Frontis, 16 cold plates. Orig red half mor, cloth bds a little dusty.
          (Spelman) **£40 [≈ $76]**
- The English Physician Enlarged, with 369 Medicines made of English Herbs. London: 1788. 12mo. xii,371 pp. Antique style calf.
          (Henly) **£90 [≈ $172]**
- Culpeper's English Physician and Complete Herbal ... Illustrated with Notes ... by E. Sibly ... London: for the author ..., [1793]. 4to. xvi,396,256 pp. Port, 29 hand cold (v occas sl spotting) & 13 sepia (damp marked) plates. Contemp calf, rebacked.
          (Gough) **£325 [≈ $623]**
- Pharmacopoeia Londinensis: or the London Dispensatory ... London: peter Cole, 1655. [With] A Key to Galen's Method of Physick. London: Peter Cole, 1654. 6th edn. 8vo. [xxiv],294 (paginated 1-106,106, 191-377), [32] pp. Port frontis. Sl used. Contemp sheep, rebacked. Wing C.7528
          (Sotheran's) **£1,250 [≈ $2,399]**

Culpeper, Nicholas & Parkins, Dr.
- The English Physician, enlarged with 369 Medicines made of English Herbs ... Family Physician ... Crosby's Improved Edition. London: Crosby, 1814. Bound in 6's. xxiv,389, [7] pp. 8 hand cold plates. Contemp

tree calf gilt.   *(Gough)* **£145 [≈ $278]**

Cunningham, B.
- A Treatise on the Principles and Practice of Dock Engineering. London: 1922. 3rd edn. xviii,600 pp. 49 fldg plates, 613 text figs. Orig pict cloth, sl marked, hd of spine sl torn.
          (Whitehart) **£25 [≈ $47]**
- A Treatise on the Principles and Practice of Harbour Engineering. London: 1928. 3rd edn. xvi,432 pp. 35 plates, 294 text ills. Orig bndg.   *(Whitehart)* **£25 [≈ $47]**

Curiosities of Entomology ...
- See Wood, T.W.

Curle, R.
- The Ray Society a Bibliographical History. London: Ray Society & Quaritch, 1954. 1st edn. 8vo. vi,99 pp. 2 plates. Orig cloth.
          (Bow Windows) **£30 [≈ $57]**

Curling, T.B.
- Observations on the Diseases of the Rectum. London: 1851. 1st edn. 123 pp. Orig bndg, spine chipped.   *(Fye)* **$150 [≈ £78]**
- A Practical Treatise on the Diseases of the Testes and of the Spermatic Cord and Scrotum. Phila: 1843. 1st Amer edn. 568 pp. W'cut ills. Leather.   *(Fye)* **$150 [≈ £78]**

Currie, James
- Medical Reports, on the Effects of Water ... as a Remedy in Fever and Febrile Diseases ... Volume 2, Consisting of the Author's Experience of this Remedy, subsequent to the Second Edition of Volume I, in 1798. London: 1805. 2nd edn. 284,55 pp. Leather, 1 bd detached.   *(Fye)* **$100 [≈ £52]**
- Medical Reports, on the Effects of Water ... Phila: 1808. 1st Amer edn. 2 vols in one. 430 pp. Ex-lib. Leather.   *(Fye)* **$150 [≈ £78]**

Currie, William
- A Sketch of the Rise and Progress of the Yellow Fever, and of the Proceedings of the Board of Health, in Philadelphia, in the year 1799 ... Phila: Budd & Bartram, 1800. 1st edn. 8vo. 112 pp. Rec half calf.
          (Hemlock) **$300 [≈ £156]**
- Synopsis or General View of the Principal Theories or Doctrines of Diseases ... Phila: 1815. 1st edn. 8vo. viii,172 pp. Contemp calf, rubbed, front bd loose.
          (Hemlock) **$300 [≈ £156]**

Curtis, C.H.
- Orchids, their Description and Cultivation.

London: 1950. Cr 4to. 288 pp. 30 cold & 48 plain plates. Cloth.
(Wheldon & Wesley) **£25 [≈ $47]**

Curtis, John
- British Entomology: Diptera. London: 1862. 8vo. 103 hand cold plates. Title sl foxed. Cloth. *(Wheldon & Wesley)* **£350 [≈ $671]**
- British Entomology: Hymenoptera. London: 1862. 8vo. 125 hand cold plates. Cloth.
(Wheldon & Wesley) **£400 [≈ $767]**
- A Guide to an Arrangement of British Insects. London: 1829 [-31]. 8vo. vi,256 columns,[i] pp. Half mor, trifle rubbed.
(Wheldon & Wesley) **£75 [≈ $143]**
- Farm Insects ... London: Blackie & Son, [1857]. 1st edn. Imperial 8vo. xiv,528 pp. 16 hand cold plates. Prelims spotted. Orig pict brown cloth gilt, repr to 1 jnt.
(Gough) **£100 [≈ $191]**

Curtis, John
- Harvey's Views on the Use of the Circulation of the Blood. New York: 1915. 8vo. 195 pp. Frontis (loose). Unabused ex-lib. Orig bndg.
(Goodrich) **$50 [≈ £26]**

Curtis, Thomas Stanley
- High Frequency Apparatus. 1920. 2nd edn. 269 pp. 150 ills. Orig bndg.
(New Wireless) **$65 [≈ £34]**

Curtis, William
- Practical Observations on the British Grasses ... Fifth Edition, with Additions by John Lawrence and Sir Joseph Banks. London: H.D. Symonds, 1812. 8 hand cold plates (1 fldg). Contemp half calf, backstrip relaid.
(Gough) **£48 [≈ $92]**

Cushing, Harvey
- Consecratio Medici and Other Papers. Boston: 1928. 1st edn, 1st printing. 276 pp. Orig bndg. *(Fye)* **$150 [≈ £78]**
- From a Surgeon's Journal. Boston: 1936. 1st edn, 1st printing. 534 pp. Orig bndg. Sgnd by the author. *(Fye)* **$400 [≈ £208]**
- The Life of Sir William Osler. Oxford: 1925. 1st edn, 1st printing. 2 vols. 685; 728 pp. Orig bndg. *(Fye)* **$300 [≈ £156]**
- The Life of Sir William Osler. Oxford: 1925. 1st edn, 2nd imp. 2 vols. 8vo. 2 frontis, ills. Orig cloth, spine ends v sl fingered, sm mark on 1 cvr. *(Bow Windows)* **£80 [≈ $153]**
- The Life of Sir William Osler. Oxford: 1925. 1st edn, 2nd imp. 2 vols. Orig cloth.
(Goodrich) **$135 [≈ £70]**

- The Life of Sir William Osler. Oxford: 1925. 1st edn, 3rd printing. 2 vols. 685; 728 pp. Orig cloth. *(Fye)* **$125 [≈ £65]**
- The Life of Sir William Osler. Oxford: 1926. 1st edn, 3rd imp. 2 vols. Orig cloth.
(Goodrich) **$125 [≈ £65]**
- The Life of Sir William Osler. Oxford: 1926. 1st edn, 4th printing. 2 vols. 685; 728 pp. With the Corrigenda & Addenda published in 1936. Orig bndg, fine. *(Fye)* **$250 [≈ £130]**
- The Medical Career. Hanover: 1930. 1st edn in book form. 53 pp. Orig bndg.
(Fye) **$100 [≈ £52]**
- The Meningiomas arising from the Olfactory Groove and their Removal by Aid of Electro-Surgery. Offprint from The Lancet: 1927. 11 pp. *(Fye)* **$150 [≈ £78]**
- The Meningiomas arising from the Olfactory Groove and their Removal by Aid of Electrosurgery. Glasgow: 1927. 1st edn. 53 pp. Orig wraps, fine. *(Fye)* **$200 [≈ £104]**
- Papers relating to the Pituitary Body, Hypothalamus and Parasympathetic Nervous System. Springfield: 1932. 1st edn. 234 pp. Dw. *(Fye)* **$450 [≈ £234]**
- The Pituitary Body and its Disorders. Phila: 1912. 1st edn, 1st printing. 341 pp. Orig bndg. *(Fye)* **$500 [≈ £260]**
- Selected Papers on Neurosurgery edited by Donald Matson. New Haven: 1969. 1st edn. 669 pp. Orig bndg. *(Fye)* **$150 [≈ £78]**
- Tumors of the Nervus Acusticus. Phila: 1917. 1st edn. 269 pp. New front endpapers and pastedown. Orig bndg.
(Fye) **$500 [≈ £260]**

Cuthill, James
- The Culture of the Strawberry ... Third Edition. London: Groombridge, [ca 1860]. Sm 8vo. 24 pp. Orig dec cloth gilt.
(Gough) **£28 [≈ $53]**

Cuvier, Georges L.C.F.D. de, Baron
- The Animal Kingdom, arranged after its Organization. New Edition with considerable additions by W.B. Carpenter and J.O. Westwood. London: 1863. Roy 8vo. xxii,706 pp. Vignette, 4 plain & 40 cold plates. Orig cloth, recased, trifle worn.
(Wheldon & Wesley) **£70 [≈ $134]**
- Discourse on the Revolutions of the Surface of the Globe, and the Changes thereby produced in the Animal Kingdom. Phila: Carey & Lea, 1831. 12mo. iv,252 pp. Foxed, some pencilling. Orig cloth & bds, spine label defective. *(Schoyer)* **$115 [≈ £59]**
- Essay on the Theory of the Earth. Translated

from the French ... by Robert Kerr. With
Mineralogical Notes ... by Professor Jameson.
Edinburgh: Blackwood ..., 1813. 1st edn
thus. 8vo. xiii,265,[1] pp. Half-title. 2 plates.
Contemp half calf. *(Fenning)* **£185 [≈$355]**
- Essay on the Theory of the Earth. New York:
Kirk & Mercein, 1818. 8vo. xxiii,431 pp.
Many pp water stained, foxed. Cloth.
(Gemmary) **$200 [≈£104]**

Da Costa, Emanuel Mendes
- Elements of Conchology; or, an Introduction
to the Knowledge of Shells. London:
Benjamin White, 1776. 1st edn. vi, 318, [i
errata,i advt] pp. 7 hand cold plates.
Occas v sl spotting. 19th c green half calf.
(Gough) **£225 [≈$431]**
- A Natural History of Fossils. Volume 1 Part
1. London: 1757. All published. 4to. viii, 294
pp. Plate. Old blind stamp on title, occas sl
foxing. New half calf, antique style.
(Wheldon & Wesley) **£200 [≈$383]**

Da Costa, J.M.
- Harvey and his Discovery. Phila: 1879. 1st
edn. 57 pp. Orig bndg.   *(Fye)* **$50 [≈£26]**

Daglish, E.F.
- The Birds of the British Islands. London:
1948. 4to. xviii,222 pp. 48 plates (25 hand
cold). Buckram, t.e.g. *(Henly)* **£85 [≈$163]**

Dallas, Robert Charles
- Elements of Self-Knowledge: intended to lead
Youth into an Early Acquaintance with the
Nature of Man, by an Anatomical Display of
the Human Frame ... London: for Murray &
Highley, 1802. 1st edn. 8vo. xxxiv,464 pp.
Hand cold frontis. Sl spots. Contemp calf, sl
worn.   *(Burmester)* **£100 [≈$191]**

Dallimire, W.
- Holly, Yew & Box with Notes on Other
Evergreens ... London: 1908. 1st edn. 8vo.
xiv, 284 pp. 175 ills. Some spotting. Orig
illust cloth, t.e.g. *(Bow Windows)* **£45 [≈$86]**

Dalyell, J.G.
- Rare and Remarkable Animals of Scotland,
represented from Living Subjects. London:
1847-48. 2 vols. 4to. 110 cold plates
(numbered 1-53, 44A, 1-56). Stamps on
reverse of plates. Mod lib cloth.
(Wheldon & Wesley) **£250 [≈$479]**

Damon, Robert
- Geology of Weymouth, Portland and Coast of
Dorsetshire. London: 1884. 2nd edn. xii,250

pp. Map, 60 figs. Orig cloth.
(Baldwin) **£38 [≈$72]**
- Handbook to the Geology of Weymouth and
the Island of Portland. With Notes on the
Natural History ... London: (1860). 1st edn.
Sm 8vo. xii,199,[1] pp. Hand cold fldg map,
fldg table, fldg view, figs. Some ink notes.
Orig cloth, spine ends v sl fingered.
(Bow Windows) **£50 [≈$95]**
- Handbook to the Geology of Weymouth and
the Island of Portland. London: 1860. 1st
edn. 12mo. xii,199 pp. Map (reprd at hinge),
58 figs. Lacks half of fly leaf. Orig cloth.
(Baldwin) **£40 [≈$76]**

**Dampier-Whetham,   William   Cecil
Dampier**
- A History of Science and its Relations with
Philosophy & Religion. Cambridge: UP,
1929. Med 8vo. Orig bndg, sl soiled.
(Georges) **£35 [≈$67]**

Dana, Edward S. & James D.
- A Text-Book of Mineralogy. With an
Extended Treatise on Crystallography and
Physical Mineralogy ... on the Plan and with
the Co-operation of Professor James D. Dana.
New York: 1877. 1st edn. 8vo. [x],485,16
advt pp. Cold frontis, num figs. Orig cloth,
backstrip relaid. *(Bow Windows)* **£40 [≈$76]**
- A Textbook of Mineralogy. New York: John
Wiley, 1877. 1st edn. 8vo. viii,485 pp. Cold
plate, num w'cuts. V.g. ex-lib. Cloth.
(Gemmary) **$45 [≈£23]**
- A Textbook of Mineralogy. New York: John
Wiley, 1884. 10th edn. 8vo. ix,521 pp. Cold
plate, num w'cuts. V.g. ex-lib. Cloth.
(Gemmary) **$45 [≈£23]**
- A Textbook of Mineralogy. New Edition.
New York: John Wiley, 1909. 8vo. vii,593
pp. Cold plate, num w'cuts. V.g. ex-lib.
Cloth.   *(Gemmary)* **$45 [≈£23]**

Dana, James D.
- Corals and Coral Islands. New York: 1872.
398 pp. Plates, text ills. Orig pict cloth,
reprd, new endpapers.
(Whitehart) **£25 [≈$47]**
- Corals and Coral Islands. London: 1875. xx,
348 pp. Cold frontis, fldg maps, text ills. Orig
cloth, sl dust stained & marked.
(Whitehart) **£25 [≈$47]**
- Corals and Coral Islands. Third Edition.
New York: (1890). 8vo. [iv],440 pp. 16 plates
(3 cold), num figs. Sm lib stamps of the Royal
Society of Edinburgh. Orig cloth, t.e.g.
Author's pres inscrptn to the R.S.E. & with
ALS.   *(Bow Windows)* **£205 [≈$393]**

- Descriptive Mineralogy. London: 1883. 5th edn. 8vo. Num text figs. Orig cloth, backstrip relaid. *(Henly)* **£65 [≈ $124]**
- Manual of Mineralogy. Including Observations on Mines, Rocks, reduction of Ores, and the Application of the Science to the Arts ... New Edition, Revised and Enlarged. London: 1872. 8vo. 456 pp. 260 text ills. Some browning & finger marks. Orig cloth, backstrip relaid.
  (Bow Windows) **£60 [≈ $115]**
- Rudimentary Treatise on Mineralogy. London: John Weale, 1859. 4th edn. Sm 8vo. 191 pp. Cold plate, 63 text figs. V.g. ex-lib. Rebound in cloth. *(Gemmary)* **$100 [≈ £52]**
- A System of Mineralogy. New York: Putnam, 1854. 4th edn. 2 vols in one. 8vo. 320; 533 pp. Num w'cuts. Orig cloth, sl worn, loose.
  (Gemmary) **$325 [≈ £169]**
- A System of Mineralogy. New York: John Wiley, 1869. 5th edn. 8vo. xlviii,827 pp. Num w'cuts. Cloth, spine torn.
  (Gemmary) **$175 [≈ £91]**
- A System of Mineralogy. New York: John Wiley, 1880. 5th edn. "9th sub-edition with two appendixes and corrections". 8vo. xlviii, 827, iv,19,x,64 pp. Num w'cuts. Orig cloth, spine torn. *(Gemmary)* **$250 [≈ £130]**
- A System of Mineralogy. New York: John Wiley, 1884. 5th edn. "9th sub-edition with three appendixes and corrections". 8vo. xlviii, 827, iv,19,x,64,134 pp. Num w'cuts. Crudely rebound. *(Gemmary)* **$250 [≈ £130]**
- The System of Mineralogy of James Dwight Dana. New York: John Wiley, 1900. 6th edn. Roy 8vo. lxiii,1134,ix,75 pp. Num figs. Rebound in cloth. *(Gemmary)* **$275 [≈ £143]**
- The System of Mineralogy of James Dwight Dana. New York: John Wiley, 1909. 6th edn. Roy 8vo. lxiii,1134,ix,75 pp. Num figs. V.g. ex-lib. Rebound in buckram, sl worn.
  (Gemmary) **$300 [≈ £156]**

Dana, James Freeman
- An Epitome of Chymical Philosophy ... Concord, NH: ptd by Isaac Hill, 1825. 1st edn. 8vo. 231,[1] pp. Some MS doodles on blanks. Sl browning, some stains. Orig bds, uncut, rebacked. *(Rootenberg)* **$450 [≈ £234]**

Dance, S.P.
- Rare Shells. London: 1969. Roy 8vo. 128 pp. 24 cold plates. Cloth.
  (Wheldon & Wesley) **£25 [≈ $47]**

Dandy, Walter
- Intracranial Arterial Aneurysms. Ithaca: 1944. 1st edn, 2nd printing. 147 pp. Fldg

charts. Orig bndg.   *(Fye)* **$175 [≈ £91]**

Darling, F. Fraser
- West Highland Survey. An Essay in Human Ecology. OUP: 1955. 8vo. Frontis. Dw.
  (Grayling) **£60 [≈ $115]**
- Wild Country. A Highland Naturalist's Notes and Pictures. London: 1938. Num photo ills. Orig bndg. *(Grayling)* **£35 [≈ $67]**

Darling, F.F.
- Natural History in the Highlands and Islands. London: Collins New Naturalist, 1947. 1st edn. 8vo. xv,303 pp. 32 cold & 32 plain plates. Orig cloth. *(Henly)* **£18 [≈ $34]**

Darnell, A.W.
- Hardy and Half Hardy Plants ... suitable for Outdoor Culture in the British Isles. London: privately ptd, 1930. 2 vols. 4to. 504 ills (12 cold). Orig cloth gilt. *(Henly)* **£65 [≈ $124]**

Darwin, Charles
- The Descent of Man and Selection in Relation to Sex. London: 1887. 2nd edn, rvsd. 8vo. xvi,639 pp. Orig cloth.
  (Henly) **£28 [≈ $53]**
- The Descent of Man, and Selection in Relation to Sex. Second Edition, revised and augmented. Twenty-Ninth Thousand. London: 1890. 8vo. xvi,693 pp. Figs. Orig cloth. Freeman 971.
  (Bow Windows) **£40 [≈ $76]**
- The Different Forms of Flowers on Plants of the Same Species. London: Murray, 1877. 1st edn. 8vo. viii,352,[32 advt dated March 1877] pp. Text ills. Orig green cloth, b'plate. Freeman 1277. *(Rootenberg)* **$500 [≈ £260]**
- The Expression of the Emotions in Man and Animals. London: 1872. 1st edn, 1st issue. 8vo. vi,374,4 advt pp. 7 heliotype plates, 21 text ills. Orig cloth, sl worn.
  (Henly) **£240 [≈ $460]**
- The Expression of the Emotions in Man and Animals. London: 1872. 1st edn. vi,374 pp. 7 plates, 21 figs. Lacks half-title. Port stuck to endpaper. Orig cloth, sl worn, sl loose at beginning of book. *(Whitehart)* **£95 [≈ $182]**
- Expression of the Emotions in Man and Animals. London: 1872. 1st edn, 2nd issue. vi, 374 pp. 7 plates, 21 figs. Tears in 2 plates reprd. Some foxing. Orig cloth. Freeman 1142. *(Baldwin)* **£150 [≈ $287]**
- The Expression of the Emotions in Man and Animals ... New York: Appleton, 1873. 1st Amer edn. v,374,[14 advt] pp. 7 plates (3 fldg), ills. Some marg damp stains. Orig dec cloth, sl tear in spine, jnts somewhat worn,

hinges starting. Freeman 1143.
(Wreden) **$250 [≈ £130]**
- The Expression of the Emotions in Man and Animals. Tenth Thousand. London: 1873. 8vo. vi,374 pp, advts dated 1872 & 1883. 7 plates, ills. Occas spotting. Orig cloth, sl tear in jnt. Freeman 1144.
(Bow Windows) **£75 [≈ $143]**
- The Formation of Vegetable Mould, through the Action of Worms ... Fifth Thousand, corrected. London: Murray, 1881. 8vo. viii, 326, [2] pp. Orig cloth. Freeman 1361.
(Burmester) **£55 [≈ $105]**
- The Foundations of the Origin of Species, a Sketch written in 1842 ... Edited by his son Francis Darwin. Cambridge: UP, 1909. 1st edn. 8vo. 53 pp. Port, facs. Orig vellum backed bds, some soiling.
(Chapel Hill) **$75 [≈ £39]**
- Geological Observations on the Volcanic Islands and Parts of South America visited during the Voyage of H.M.S. 'Beagle'. London: 1876. 2nd edn. xiii,647 pp. 2 maps, cold sections, 4 plates. Orig cloth. Freeman 276.
(Baldwin) **£130 [≈ $249]**
- Insectivorous Plants. Second Thousand. London: Murray, 1875. 1st edn, 2nd thousand. 8vo. x,462 pp. 6-line errata slip. Ills. Orig cloth gilt. Freeman 1218.
(Claude Cox) **£75 [≈ $143]**
- Journal of Researches. London: 1860. 10th thousand. xv,519 pp. Ills. Calf, gilt spine. Freeman 20.
(Baldwin) **£75 [≈ $143]**
- The Life and Letters ... including an Autobiographical Chapter. Edited by his Son, Francis Darwin. Seventh Thousand Revised. London: 1883. 3 vols. 8vo. Orig cloth, spines faded & frayed at hd.
(Bickersteth) **£40 [≈ $76]**
- On the Origin of Species by Means of Natural Selection ... London: Murray, 1859. 1st edn. 8vo in 12s. ix, [1],502, [32 advt dated June 1859] pp. Fldg plate. Orig cloth, spine reprd. Half mor box. Freeman 373, advts variant 3, bndg variant a.
(Rootenberg) **$18,000 [≈ £9,375]**
- The Variation of Animals and Plants under Domestication. Second Edition, Revised. Fifth Thousand. London: Murray, 1882. 2 vols. 8vo. Orig cloth, mostly unopened, v sl string mark vol 1. Freeman 883.
(Bow Windows) **£65 [≈ $124]**

Darwin, R.W.
- Principia Botanica: or, a Concise and Easy Introduction to the Sexual Botany of Linnaeus. Newark: 1787. 1st edn. 8vo. vii, 280, [1] pp. Contemp calf, lower jnt

beginning to crack but sound.
(Wheldon & Wesley) **£180 [≈ $345]**

Daubeny, C.
- Lectures on Roman Husbandry delivered before the University of Oxford. Oxford: 1857. 8vo. xvi,328 pp. 12 plates (1 cold). Blind stamp on title. Cloth, reprd.
(Wheldon & Wesley) **£50 [≈ $95]**

Davenport, John
- Aphrodisiacs and Anti-aphrodisiacs. Three Essays ... London: privately ptd, 1869. 1st edn. xii,154 pp. Frontis, plates. Orig half mor, t.e.g., extremities sl chafed.
(Wreden) **$100 [≈ £52]**

Davenport, Walter Rice
- Thomas Davenport. 1929. 1st edn. 165 pp. 18 photo ills. Orig bndg.
(New Wireless) **$45 [≈ £24]**

Davidson, A.
- Hygiene & Diseases of Warm Climates. Edinburgh: 1893. xvii,1016 pp. 97 figs. Sev sm lib stamps. Orig cloth, dusty, marked, worn.
(Whitehart) **£22 [≈ $42]**

Davie, O.
- Methods in the Art of Taxidermy. London: 1900. xiv,359 pp. 90 plates. Orig cloth, hinges loose, spine worn.
(Baldwin) **£40 [≈ $76]**

Davies, C.
- Elements of Geometry and Trigonometry, from the Works of A.M. Legendre. New York: 1864. viii,259, 134,62 pp. Title edges sl discold. Front endpaper edges ragged. Contemp sheep, leather label (sl defective).
(Whitehart) **£30 [≈ $57]**
- Elements of Surveying. New York: Wiley & Long, 1836. 8vo. viii,158, 62,91 pp. 6 fldg plates, text figs. Sl foxed. Leather, rubbed.
(Gemmary) **$100 [≈ £52]**
- Elements of Surveying and Navigation. New York: A.S. Barnes, 1853. Rvsd edn. 8vo. viii, 222, 100 pp. 6 fldg plates. Leather, spine worn, sl loose.
(Gemmary) **$90 [≈ £46]**

Davies, John
- The Innkeeper and Butler's Guide, or a Directory in the making and managing of British Wines ... Third Edition. Leeds: 1807. 8vo. [4],200 pp. Orig bds, uncut, engvd dec paper cvrs laid down & refolded, edges dusty, cvrs soiled.
(Spelman) **£120 [≈ $230]**

Davis, Daniel, Jr.
- A Manual of Magnetism. 1854. 6th edn. 322

pp. 184 ills. Orig illust bndg, some wear to spine, chipped at hd.
(New Wireless) **$85 [≈ £45]**

Davis, G.E.
- Practical Microscopy. London: David Bogue, 1882. 2nd edn. 8vo. viii,335 pp. 257 text figs. Ex-lib. Cloth, backstrip torn.
(Gemmary) **$75 [≈ £39]**

Davis, James W. & Lees, F. Arnold
- West Yorkshire: An Account of its Geology, Physical Geography, Climatology, and Botany. London: L. Reeve, 1878. xl,414,16 pp. 2 lge fldg cold maps in pocket, 5 fldg cold sections, 16 plain plates. Mod half calf gilt.
(Hollett) **£120 [≈ $230]**

Davis, John S.
- Plastic Surgery: its Principles and Practice. Phila: 1919. 1st edn. 720 pp. 864 ills. Orig bndg, fine.
(Fye) **$650 [≈ £338]**

Davis, R.H.
- Breathing in Irrespirable Atmospheres, and, in some cases, also Under Water ... London: [1948]. xi,386 pp. Num ills. Dw (rather worn).
(Whitehart) **£35 [≈ $67]**

Davis, T.L.
- The Chemistry of Powder and Explosives. New York: John Wiley & Sons, 1943. 8vo. xiv,490 pp. 106 text figs. Cloth.
(Gemmary) **$60 [≈ £31]**

Davison, C.
- A Study of Recent Earthquakes. London: Contemporary Science Series, 1905. xii,355 pp. 80 text ills. Orig cloth.
(Whitehart) **£15 [≈ $28]**

Davy, Sir Humphry
- Conversations on Chemistry. North Haven: Sidney's Press, 1813. Cr 8vo. xi,358,17 pp. 10 plates. Leather, worn.
(Gemmary) **$50 [≈ £26]**
- Elements of Agricultural Chemistry, in a Course of Lectures for the Board of Agriculture. London: Bulmer for Longman ..., 1813. 1st edn. Folio. viii,323,lxiii pp. 10 plates (1 fldg). 1st blank loose. Orig bds, uncut. William A. Cole b'plate.
(Rootenberg) **$550 [≈ £286]**
- Elements of Agricultural Chemistry, in a Course of Lectures ... London: for Longman ..., 1814. 2nd edn. 8vo. vii,479,[9] pp. 10 fldg plates. Rec half calf. *(Young's)* **£60 [≈ $115]**

- Elements of Agricultural Chemistry, in a Course of Lectures ... London: for Longman ... & Constable & Co., Edinburgh, 1821. 3rd edn. 8vo. x,415 pp. Half-title. 10 fldg plates. Contemp half russia.
(Burmester) **£80 [≈ $153]**
- Elements of Agricultural Chemistry, in a Course of Lectures ... A New Edition, with ... Notes ... by John Shier. Glasgow: 1845. 1st edn thus. 8vo. x,293 pp. Rec half calf.
(Young's) **£55 [≈ $105]**

Davy, J.
- Memoirs of the Life of Sir Humphry Davy, Bart. by his Brother ... London: 1836. 2 vols. xii,507; vii,420 pp. Frontis port, 1 page of figs. Occas sl foxing. Half leather, mrbld bds.
(Whitehart) **£125 [≈ $239]**

Dawkins, W. Boyd
- Early Man in Britain and his Place in the Tertiary Period. London: 1880. 1st edn. Thick 8vo. xxiv,537 pp. 168 text ills. Occas sl foxing. Brown half niger mor, t.e.g.
(Bow Windows) **£48 [≈ $92]**

Dawson, J.W.
- The Geological History of Plants. London: 1888. Cr 8vo. x,290 pp. Frontis, text figs. Cloth, stained.
(Wheldon & Wesley) **£20 [≈ $38]**

Dawson, John Frederic
- Geodaphaga Britannica. A Monograph of the Carnivorous Ground-Beetles indigenous to the British Isles. London: Van Voorst, 1854. 8vo. xx, 224 pp. 3 hand cold plates. Orig cloth gilt, faded & rubbed, hinges reprd.
(Hollett) **£75 [≈ $143]**

Dawson, William Leon
- The Birds of California. A Complete Scientific and Popular Account ... Booklovers' Edition. San Diego, 1923. One of 1000. 4 vols. 4to. Num cold & other plates & ills. Orig green embossed fabricoid.
(Karmiole) **$350 [≈ £182]**

Day, F.
- The Fishes of Great Britain and Ireland ... London: 1880-84. 2 vols. Roy 8vo. 180 plates (1-179, 172A). Some foxing. New cloth.
(Wheldon & Wesley) **£300 [≈ $575]**
- The Fishes of India ... London: 1876-88. 2 vols. 4to. xx,816 pp. 198 plates (1-195, 51a-c). Half mor, trifle rubbed.
(Wheldon & Wesley) **£750 [≈ $1,439]**
- The Fishes of Malabar. London: 1865. 4to.

xxxii,293 pp. 20 plates. New half mor.
(Wheldon & Wesley) **£330** [≈ **$633**]

Day, J.
- An Introduction to Algebra, being the First
Part of a Course of Mathematics, adapted to
the Method of Instruction in the American
Colleges. New Haven & New York: 1838.
32nd edn. viii,332 pp. 2 fldg plates. Occas
foxing. Title marg defective. Contemp
leather, rubbed & worn.
(Whitehart) **£40** [≈ **$76**]

Day, L. Meeker
- The Improved Family Physician ... also a
Complete Digest on Midwifery. New York:
1833. 1st edn. 12mo. viii,(9)-120,24 pp.
Contemp roan backed bds.
(Hemlock) **$175** [≈ **£91**]

Deakin, R.
- The Ferns of Britain and their Allies.
London: 1848. 8vo. 138 pp. 28 plates. Bds.
(Wheldon & Wesley) **£18** [≈ **$34**]

D'Albe, E.E. Fournier
- The Life of Sir William Crookes. 1923. 1st
edn. 413 pp. 5 photos. Orig bndg.
(New Wireless) **$45** [≈ **£23**]
- The Moon-Element: An Introduction to the
Wonders of Selenium. 1924. 1st edn. 166 pp.
32 ills. Orig bndg.
(New Wireless) **$85** [≈ **£44**]

Dealtry, W.
- The Principles of Fluxions: designed for the
Use of Students in the Universities.
Cambridge: 1816. 2nd edn. v,466 pp. Diags.
Orig bds, paper spine, new label, sl worn.
(Whitehart) **£50** [≈ **$95**]

De Broglie, M.
- Matter and Light. New York: Dover, 1947.
8vo. 300 pp. Cloth. *(Gemmary)* **$30** [≈ **£15**]
- X-Rays. London: Methuen, 1925. 8vo. xii,
204 pp. 7 plates, 39 text figs. Cloth.
(Gemmary) **$50** [≈ **£26**]

Debye, P.
- The Dipole Moment and Chemical
Structure. London: Blackie, 1931. 8vo. x,134
pp. Num text figs. Cloth.
(Gemmary) **$50** [≈ **£26**]

De Crespigny, E.C.
- A New London Flora ... London: 1877. Cr
8vo. xxiv,179,20 advt pp. Some underlining.
Orig cloth. *(Henly)* **£15** [≈ **$28**]

Dedekind, R.
- Essays on the Theory of Numbers.
Translated by W.W. Beman. Chicago: 1901.
1st English edn. 115 pp.
(Whitehart) **£50** [≈ **$95**]

De Forest, Lee
- Father of Radio. 1950. 1st edn. 502 pp. Dw.
(New Wireless) **$65** [≈ **£33**]
- Father of Radio. 1950. 1st edn. 502 pp. Dw.
Sgnd by the author.
(New Wireless) **$125** [≈ **£65**]
- Television - Today and Tomorrow. 1942. 1st
edn. 361 pp. 76 ills. Dw.
(New Wireless) **$55** [≈ **£29**]

de la Beche, Sir Henry T.
- The Geological Observer. London: 1853. 2nd
edn. 8vo. xxviii,740 pp. 306 text figs. Cloth.
(Henly) **£80** [≈ **$153**]
- The Geological Observer. Second Edition,
revised. London: 1853. Thick 8vo. xxviii,740
pp. 308 text figs. Some marks, some crnr tips
folded. Endpapers defaced, inner hinges torn.
Orig cloth, faded, tiny tears hd of jnts.
(Bow Windows) **£105** [≈ **$201**]

Delacour, J.
- Birds of Malaysia. New York: 1947. 8vo.
xii,382 pp. 84 ills. Cloth.
(Wheldon & Wesley) **£35** [≈ **$67**]
- The Pheasants of the World. London: 1951.
1st imp. Cr 4to. 347 pp. 16 cold & 16 plain
plates, 21 maps & diags. Minor damage to a
few margs. Cloth.
(Wheldon & Wesley) **£150** [≈ **$287**]
- The Pheasants of the World. London: (1951)
1965. Cr 4to. 347 pp. 16 cold & 16 plain
plates, 21 maps & diags. Orig cloth.
(Wheldon & Wesley) **£140** [≈ **$268**]

Delacour, J. & Mayr, E.
- Birds of the Philippines. New York: 1946.
8vo. xv,309 pp. 69 text figs. Cloth.
(Wheldon & Wesley) **£35** [≈ **$67**]

Delacour, J. & Scott, Peter
- The Waterfowl of the World. London:
1954-64. 1st edn. 4 vols. Cr 4to. 66 cold
plates, num maps & text figs. Cloth. Ink
sketch by Peter Scott on vol 1 endpaper.
(Wheldon & Wesley) **£200** [≈ **$383**]

De Launay, L.
- The World's Gold. New York: Putnam,
1908. 8vo. xxxii,242 pp. Cloth.
(Gemmary) **$50** [≈ **£26**]

Deleuze, J.P.F.
- Practical Instruction in Animal Magnetism. Translated by Thomas C. Hartshorn. Revised Edition. With an Appendix ... New York: Fowler & Wells, 1890. Sm 8vo. 524,[12],8 advt pp. Orig dec gilt cloth, extremities a bit rubbed. *(Karmiole)* **$40 [≈£20]**

De Moivre, Abraham
- Annuities upon Lives ... The Second Edition, corrected. London Printed. 1st Irish edn. 8vo. 6,viii,122 pp. Contemp calf, new label, sl marked. *(Fenning)* **£350 [≈$671]**
- The Doctrine of Chances: or, a Method of Calculating the Probability of Events in Play. London: W. Pearson, for the author, 1718. 1st edn. 4to. [6],[xiv],175 pp. Num blanks bound in at end. Contemp calf, backstrip relaid. *(Rootenberg)* **$1,500 [≈£781]**

De Morgan, Augustus
- The Differential and Integral Calculus ... London: Baldwin & Cradock, 1842. 1st edn. 8vo. xx,785,64 pp. Contemp calf gilt, mor label, by Maclehose of Glasgow. *(Frew Mackenzie)* **£195 [≈$374]**

De Morgan, S.E.
- Memoir of Augustus de Morgan by his Wife ... with Selections from his Letters. London: 1882. x,422 pp. Port frontis. Occas sl foxing. Spine faded, inner hinges sl cracked but firm. *(Whitehart)* **£45 [≈$86]**

Dempsey, G. Drysdale
- The Practical Railway Engineer ... Fourth Edition, Revised and greatly extended. London: John Weale, 1855. 4to. [viii],428,44 pp. Port, 71 dble-page plates, 72 w'cut ills. Occas sl spotting. Orig yellow cloth, backstrip relaid. *(Gough)* **£125 [≈$239]**

Dendy, Walter Cooper
- On the Phenomena of Dreams, and other Transient Illusions. London: Whittaker, Treacher, 1832. 1st edn. Sm 8vo. Early gatherings loose. Orig blue cloth, paper label (darkened & chipped). *(Sanders)* **£30 [≈$57]**
- On the Phenomena of Dreams, and other Transient Illusions. London: Whittaker, Treacher, 1832. 1st edn. Sm 8vo. Orig purple cloth backed drab bds, paper label, spine faded, sm white spot. *(Ximenes)* **$150 [≈£78]**

Denman, James L.
- The Vine and Its Fruit. London: Longman ..., 1864. 1st edn. Cr 8vo. xii,346,[2],32 pp.

Orig dec cloth gilt, largely unopened, rebacked in mor gilt, some sl wear. *(Ash)* **£200 [≈$383]**

Denman, Thomas
- Aphorisms on the Application and Use of the Forceps and Vectis ... From the 7th London Edition. Boston: Wells & Lilly, 1822. 3rd Amer edn. 95 pp. Orig bds, cvrs & some sections loose. *(Hemlock)* **$225 [≈£117]**

Denny, G.A.
- Diamond Drilling for Gold and Other Minerals. London: Crosby, Lockwood, 1900. 8vo. x,158 pp. 37 ills. Cloth. *(Gemmary)* **$125 [≈£65]**

Denton, S.F.
- Moths and Butterflies of the United States, East of the Rocky Mountains. Boston: 1900. 2 vols. Imperial 8vo. 50 (of 56) cold plates, over 400 photo ills. A few lib blind stamps. Half mor. *(Wheldon & Wesley)* **£350 [≈$671]**

Derham, W.
- Astro-Theology; or a Demonstration of the Being and Attributes of God from a Survey of the Heavens ... Third Edition Improv'd. London: Innys, 1719. 8vo. [xvi],lvi,[viii], 246, [x] pp. 3 fldg plates. Contemp calf. *(Lloyd-Roberts)* **£90 [≈$172]**

De St. Marthe, Scevole
- Paedotrophia, or the Art of Nursing and Rearing Children. London: the author, 1797. 1st edn in English. 8vo. [cxcii],224 pp. Later calf. Translated by H.W. Tytler. *(Bookpress)* **$425 [≈£221]**

Desmond, R.
- Dictionary of British and Irish Botanists and Horticulturists, including Plant Collectors and Botanical Artists. London: 1977. Roy 8vo. xxvi,747 pp. Cloth. *(Wheldon & Wesley)* **£67 [≈$128]**

De Takats, Geza
- Vascular Surgery. Phila: 1959. 1st edn. 726 pp. Orig bndg. *(Fye)* **$75 [≈£39]**

D'Urban, W.S.M. & Mathew, Murray
- The Birds of Devon. London: R.H. Porter, 1892. 1st edn. lxxxvii,459,7 subscribers pp. 3 fldg maps, 5 cold plates, 4 mtd photos. Inner hinges strengthened. Orig pict blue cloth gilt. *(Gough)* **£65 [≈$124]**
- The Birds of Devon. London: 1895. 2nd edn, with supplement. 8vo. lxxxviii,459,31 pp. 3

maps, 5 plates (1 cold) of views, 4 hand cold plates of birds. Orig dec cloth, trifle worn.
(Wheldon & Wesley) **£75 [≈ $143]**

Deutsch, Felix & Kauf, Emil
- Heart and Athletics. Clinical Researches upon the Influence of Athletics upon the Heart. St. Louis: 1927. 1st English translation. 187 pp. Orig bndg.
(Fye) **$100 [≈ £52]**

Dewar, G.A.B.
- Wild Life in Hampshire Highlands. L: 1899. 8vo. x,304 pp. 2 cold & 5 plain plates, head & tail pieces by Arthur Rackham. Cloth gilt.
(Henly) **£35 [≈ $67]**

Dewar, M.J.S.
- The Electronic Theory of Organic Chemistry. Oxford: 1949. x,324 pp. Text diags. Dw (sl marked).
(Whitehart) **£18 [≈ $34]**

Dewees, William
- A Treatise on the Physical and Medical Treatment of Children. Phila: 1825. 1st edn. 496 pp. Occas foxing, water stain affecting index. New endpapers. Rec qtr leather.
(Fye) **$400 [≈ £208]**

Dewhurst, H.W.
- The Natural History of the Order Cetacea ... London: the author, 1834. 8vo. xx,331 pp. Engvd dedic, 23 plates, text figs. Plate margs browned, occas sl browning & foxing. Half calf, rebacked.
(Wheldon & Wesley) **£360 [≈ $691]**

Dewhurst, Kenneth
- John Locke. A Medical Biography with an Edition of the Medical Notes in his Journals. London: 1963. 8vo. 331 pp. Ills. Dw.
(Goodrich) **$45 [≈ £23]**

Dibner, Bern
- Heralds of Science, as represented by Two Hundred Epochal Books and Pamphlets selected from the Burndy Library. Norwalk: Burndy Library, 1955. 4to. Ills. Rebound in buckram. *(Georges)* **£25 [≈ $47]**

Dickie, George
- A Flora of Ulster and Botanist's Guide to the North of Ireland. Belfast: C. Aitchison, 1864. 1st edn. Lge 12mo. xix,176 pp. Orig cloth.
(Fenning) **£45 [≈ $86]**

Dickinson, H.W. & Jenkins, R.
- James Watt and the Steam Engine. The Memorial Volume prepared for the Committee of the Watt Centenary Commemoration at Birmingham 1919. Oxford: 1927. 1st edn. Lge 4to. xvi,415 pp. Frontis port, 2 maps, 104 plates, 39 text ills. Orig cloth gilt, marked.
(Whitehart) **£125 [≈ $239]**

Dickinson, Joseph
- The Flora of Liverpool. London: Van Voorst, 1851. 1st edn. 8vo. 166 pp. Occas sl browning. Mod half mor gilt.
(Hollett) **£75 [≈ $143]**

Dickson, W.E. Carnegie
- The Bone-Marrow, a Cytological Study ... London: 1908. 1st edn. 4to. 160 pp. 12 chromolitho plates, 51 photomicrographs. Orig bndg. *(Fye)* **$100 [≈ £52]**

A Dictionary of Natural History ...
- A Dictionary of Natural History; or, Complete Summary of Zoology ... Illustrated with Accurate Engravings ... London: for Scatcherd & Letterman ..., 1815. 16mo. Ca 400 pp. 47 plates, each with 3 figs. Contemp green half calf, mrbld paper sides.
(Claude Cox) **£45 [≈ $86]**

Dieserud, J.
- The Scope and Content of the Science of Anthropology. Chicago: 1908. 200,[16] pp. Orig cloth, sl stained.
(Whitehart) **£18 [≈ $34]**

Dieulefait, L.
- Diamonds and Precious Stones. London: Blackie & Son, 1874. 8vo. xii,292 pp. 126 w'engvs. Orig dec cloth.
(Gemmary) **$80 [≈ £41]**

Digby, Sir Kenelm   ·
- Two Treatises: in the One of which, The Nature of Bodies; In the other The Nature of Mans Soul, is Looked Into. London: Williams, 1658. 4to. Text diags. Panelled calf. Wing D.1450.
(Rostenberg & Stern) **$675 [≈ £351]**

Dillenius, John James
- Historia Muscorum: a general History of Land and Water & Mosses and Corals ... London: J. Millan, 1768. 4to. [ii],13,10 pp. 85 plates. Some marg pencil notes. Contemp tree calf, rebacked. *(Bookpress)* **$425 [≈ £221]**

Dillwyn, L.
- Hortus Collinsonianus. An Account of the Plants cultivated by the late Peter Collinson, Esq., F.R.S. Swansea: Not Published, 1843. 8vo. vii,64 pp. Half calf. Anon.
(Wheldon & Wesley) **£75 [≈ $143]**

Dilworth, Thomas
- The Schoolmasters Assistant: being a Compendium of Arithmetic, both Practical and Theoretical. Second Edition. London: Henry Kent, 1744. 8vo. xv,[9],168 pp. Frontis, fldg tables, num tables in text. Contemp calf, jnts cracked, spine ends worn, crnrs bumped. *(Spelman)* **£50 [≈ $95]**
- The Schoolmasters Assistant: being a Compendium of Arithmetic, both Practical and Theoretical ... Twentieth Edition. London: Causton, 1780. Frontis. Few ink scrawls. Lacks free endpaper. Contemp sheep, rubbed, wear to spine ends.
(Jarndyce) **£40 [≈ $76]**

Dinsdale, Alfred
- Television (Seeing by Wire or Wireless). 1926. 1st edn. 62 pp. 6 photos, 6 ills. Orig soft cvr, dw. *(New Wireless)* **$345 [≈ £179]**
- Television. 1928. 2nd edn, enlgd. 180 pp. 33 photos, 38 ills. Orig bndg.
(New Wireless) **$125 [≈ £65]**
- Television. London: Television Press Ltd, 1928. 2nd edn, enlgd. 8vo. xx,180,2 advt pp. Photo frontis, 32 photo plates, num text figs. Edge of flyleaf clipped. Orig cloth.
(Rootenberg) **$200 [≈ £104]**

Dirac, P.A.M.
- The Principles of Quantum Mechanics. Oxford: Clarendon Press, 1947. 3rd edn. 8vo. xii, 312 pp. Cloth. Dw.
(Gemmary) **$60 [≈ £31]**
- The Principles of Quantum Mechanics. Oxford: Clarendon Press, 1958. 4th edn. 8vo. xii, 312 pp. Cloth. Dw.
(Gemmary) **$60 [≈ £31]**

Dircks, H.
- Contribution toward a History of Electro-Metallurgy Establishing the Origin of the Art. London: 1863. xvi,102 pp. Frontis port, 1 plate. Orig pebble dash cloth.
(Whitehart) **£40 [≈ $76]**
- The Life, Times and Scientific Labours of the Second Marquis of Worcester. To which is added a Reprint of his Century of Inventions, 1663, with a Commentary thereon. London: 1865. xxiv,624 pp. Frontis, fldg plan, num engvs. Frontis sl water

stained. New cloth. *(Whitehart)* **£35 [≈ $67]**

A Discourse on the Emigration of British Birds ...
- See Edwards, George.

Disney, A.N., et al.
- Origin and Development of the Microscope. London: Royal Microscopical Soc, 1928. 8vo. xi,303 pp. 30 plates, 35 text figs. Cloth, faded. *(Gemmary)* **$250 [≈ £130]**
- Origin and Development of the Microscope. London: RMS, 1928. 1st edn. 8vo. 303 pp. 30 plates, 36 text figs. Cloth bds, sl faded.
(Savona) **£40 [≈ $76]**

Dixon, Charles
- Among the Birds in Northern Shires. London: Blackie, 1900. 1st edn. 8vo. 303 pp. Cold frontis & 40 text ills by Whymper. Few marg reprs, few spots to half-title. Near contemp half mor gilt, a.e.g.
(Hollett) **£45 [≈ $86]**
- The Game Birds and Wild Fowl of the British Islands. Sheffield: 1900. 2nd edn. 4to. xxviii,476 pp. 41 chromolitho plates. Orig pict cloth, trifle marked & faded.
(Gough) **£365 [≈ $700]**
- Lost and Vanishing Birds ... London: John Macqueen, 1898. 1st edn. 295 pp. 10 plates. Orig blue cloth gilt. *(Gough)* **£25 [≈ $47]**

Dixon, Frederic
- The Geology and Fossils of the Tertiary and Cretaceous Formations of Sussex. London: Privately published, 1850. Lge 4to. xvi,422, [2] pp. 41 plates (3 hand cold). Damp stain to lower marg of all plates. Sm lib blind stamp on title. Mod polished half calf gilt.
(Hollett) **£250 [≈ $479]**
- The Geology of Sussex. Second Edition by T.R. Jones. London: 1878. 4to. xxiv,469 pp. Map, 64 plates (2 cold). Some foxing. Sl water mark on some plates. Orig cloth, spine ends & hinges worn. *(Baldwin)* **£140 [≈ $268]**

Dobbin, L.
- Occasional Fragments of Chemical History. Edinburgh: privately ptd, 1942. vii,85 pp. A few diags. Limp bds. Author's pres copy.
(Whitehart) **£35 [≈ $67]**

Dobell, H.
- On Winter Cough, Catarrh, Bronchitis, Emphysema, Asthma: A Course of Lectures ... London: 1872. 2nd edn. xviii,238 pp. 2 plates, 3 w'cuts. Orig cloth, sl worn. Inscrbd by the author. *(Whitehart)* **£38 [≈ $72]**

Dobson, Matthew
- A Medical Commentary on Fixed Air ... Chester: ptd by J. Monk, 1779. 1st edn. 198 pp. Half-title, dedic leaf. Occas spotting or browning. Old mrbld bds, edges darkened & worn, some time rebacked in calf, few sm worm holes, jnts cracking.
(Hollett) **£140 [≈ $268]**

Doby, Tibor
- Discoverers of Blood Circulation from Aristotle to the Times of Da Vinci and Harvey. New York: 1963. 1st edn. 285 pp. Orig bndg. Dw.   *(Fye)* **$50 [≈ £26]**

Dock, George & Bass, Charles C.
- Hookworm Disease. Etiology, Pathology, Diagnosis, Prophylaxis and Treatment ... St. Louis: 1910. 8vo. 250 pp. Cold frontis, ills. Orig cloth, sl worn.   *(Goodrich)* **$65 [≈ £33]**

Dodson, J.
- The Mathematical Repository containing Analytical Solutions of near Five Hundred Questions ... London: 1775. 2nd edn. xi,336 pp. V sl tear in 1st few pp reprd. Contemp leather, v worn with large piece missing from front cvr, front hinge weak.
(Whitehart) **£120 [≈ $230]**

Doe, Janet
- A Bibliography of the Works of Ambroise Pare. Chicago: 1937. 8vo. 266 pp. Errata leaf. Plates. Orig bndg, sl worn.
(Goodrich) **$125 [≈ £65]**

Dolbear, A.E.
- The Telephone. 1877. 1st edn. 128 pp. 17 ills. Orig pict bndg, some wear on spine.
(New Wireless) **$195 [≈ £101]**
- The Telephone. 1877. 1st edn. 128 pp. 17 ills. Orig pict bndg, fine.
(New Wireless) **$215 [≈ £113]**

Donders, F.C.
- On the Anomalies of Accommodation and Refraction of the Eye. With a Preliminary Essay ... Translated by W.D. Moore. London: New Sydenham Soc, 1864. 1st edn. xvii,635 pp. Fldg chart, 175 figs. Orig cloth.
(Whitehart) **£80 [≈ $153]**
- On the Anomalies of Accomodation and refraction of the Eye. London: 1864. 1st English edn. 635 pp. Orig bndg.
(Fye) **$150 [≈ £78]**
- On the Anomalies of Accommodation and Refraction of the Eye. With a Preliminary Essay ... Translated by W.D. Moore.

London: 1952. Reprint of 1864 1st edn. xvii,635 pp. 175 figs. Orig bndg.
(Whitehart) **£35 [≈ $67]**

Donovan, E.
- The Natural History of British Fishes. London: 1802-08. 5 vols in 2. 120 cold plates. 1 plate foxed. Calf, rebacked.
(Wheldon & Wesley) **£2,000 [≈ $3,839]**

Dorsey, John Syng
- Elements of Surgery: for the Use of Students; with Plates. Phila: 1818. 2nd edn. 2 vols. 422; 474 pp. 25 plates. Water stain affecting vol 2. Leather, bds detached, bndgs dry, lacks vol 2 label.   *(Fye)* **$250 [≈ £130]**

Dossie, Robert
- The Elaboratory Laid Open, or the Secrets of Modern Chemistry and Pharmacy revealed ... London: Nourse, 1758. 1st edn. 8vo. xi,[3], 375, [9] pp. Old lib stamp. Contemp calf gilt, rebacked, crnrs rubbed. Anon.
(Rootenberg) **$750 [≈ £390]**

Dotter, Charles & Steinberg, Israel
- Angiocardiography. New York: 1952. 1st edn. 304 pp. Ills. Orig bndg.
(Fye) **$125 [≈ £65]**

Douglas, Sir Howard
- An Essay on the Principles and Construction of Military Bridges, and the Passage of Rivers in Military Operations. London: 1832. 2nd edn, enlgd. 8vo. vi,417,28 pp. Frontis, 12 fldg plates. Orig cloth, rebacked, uncut & unopened.   *(Young's)* **£148 [≈ $284]**

Dove, H.W.
- The Distribution of Heat over the Surface of the Globe, illustrated by Isothermal ... and other Curves of Temperature. London: 1853. 1st edn. 4to. [iv],27,[1] pp. 9 plates. Orig cloth, hd of spine & crnr tips sl worn.
(Bow Windows) **£85 [≈ $163]**

Dover, A.T.
- Electric Traction: a Treatise on the Application of Electric Power to Tramways and Railways. London: 1919. 2nd imp. xix,670 pp. 5 fldg plates, 518 ills. Half-title reprd. Orig cloth, rebacked.
(Whitehart) **£35 [≈ $67]**

Dowding, G.V.
- Book of Practical Television. 1935. 1st edn. 320 pp. 62 photos, 232 ills. Orig bndg.
(New Wireless) **$45 [≈ £23]**

Dowsett, H.M.
- Wireless Telegraphy and Telephony: First Principles, Present Practice and Testing. 1920. 1st edn. 331 pp. 305 ills. Orig bndg. *(New Wireless)* **$45** [≈ £23]
- Wireless Telephony and Broadcasting. London: 1924. 1st edn. 2 vols. 442 pp. Num ills. *(New Wireless)* **$125** [≈ £65]

Drachman, Julian M.
- Studies in the Literature of Natural Science. New York: Macmillan, 1930. 8vo. 6 plates. Orig bndg. *(Georges)* **£35** [≈ $67]

Draper, John William
- A Treatise on the Forces which produce the Organization of Plants ... New York: Harper, 1844. 1st edn. 4to. xi,[1],108,216 pp. Hand cold frontis, 3 plates (1 dble-page). Orig cloth, backstrip detached. Half mor box. *(Rootenberg)* **$400** [≈ £208]

Dresser, H.E.
- A Manual of Palaearctic Birds. London: 1902-03. 2 vols. 8vo. 922 pp. 2 plates (1 cold). New cloth. *(Wheldon & Wesley)* **£45** [≈ $86]

Driesch, Hans A.E.
- The Science and Philosophy of the Organism. The Gifford Lectures ... London: A. & C. Black, 1908. 1st edn. 2 vols. 8vo. Orig cloth. *(Fenning)* **£75** [≈ $143]

Drinker, H.S.
- Tunneling, Explosive Compounds & Rock Drills. New York: John Wiley & Sons, 1878. Roy 4to. 1031,xliii pp. 19 fldg plates, 1086 text figs. Cloth, rebacked. *(Gemmary)* **$150** [≈ £79]

Druce, G.C.
- The Flora of Northamptonshire. Arbroath: 1930. 8vo. cxlii,304 pp. Binder's cloth. *(Wheldon & Wesley)* **£35** [≈ $67]
- The Flora of Oxfordshire. London: 1886. 1st edn. Cr 8vo. lii,452 pp. Cold map in pocket. Rebound in cloth. *(Henly)* **£48** [≈ $92]
- The Flora of Oxfordshire. Oxford: 1927. 2nd edn, rewritten. Cr 8vo. cxxxii,538 pp. Cloth, trifle used. *(Wheldon & Wesley)* **£80** [≈ $153]

Drude, P.
- The Theory of Optics. New York: Longmans, Green, 1902. 8vo. xxi,546 pp. 110 text figs. Ex-lib. Cloth. *(Gemmary)* **$45** [≈ £23]

Drummond, W.H.
- The Large Game & Natural History of South & South-East Africa. Rhodesia: 1972. Reprint of the 1st edn. One of 1000. 8vo. Cold frontis & title, tinted plates, text ills. Dw (frayed). *(Grayling)* **£55** [≈ $105]

Dubois, E.
- The Climates of the Geological Past and their Relation to the Evolution of the Sun. London: 1895. viii,167 pp. Orig bndg. *(Whitehart)* **£18** [≈ $34]
- The Climates of the Geological Past and their relation to the Evolution of the Sun. London: 1895. viii,167 pp. Sm 8vo. Lib stamp on title & preface. Orig cloth, edges sl worn. *(Whitehart)* **£18** [≈ $34]

Duchene, M.
- The Mechanics of the Aeroplane. A Study of the Principles of Flight. Translated J.H. Ledeboer and T. O'B. Hubbard. London: 1912. 1st English edn. x,231 pp. 91 text figs. Orig cloth. *(Whitehart)* **£35** [≈ $67]

Du Moncel, Th., Count
- Electric Lighting. 1882. 1st edn. 318 pp. 76 ills. Orig bndg. *(New Wireless)* **$115** [≈ £59]
- Electric Lighting. 1883. 2nd edn. 318 pp. 76 ills. Orig bndg. *(New Wireless)* **$110** [≈ £58]
- Elements of Construction for Electro-Magnets. 1883. 1st edn. 86 pp. Orig bndg, sl worn. *(New Wireless)* **$85** [≈ £45]
- The Telephone, The Microphone, and The Phonograph. 1879. 1st English edn. 277 pp. 74 ills. Orig bndg, moderate wear on spines & cvr. *(New Wireless)* **$110** [≈ £57]
- The Telephone, The Microphone, and the Phonograph. New York: 1879. 277 pp. 70 w'engvs. Remains of lib label on endpaper. Orig cloth, spine ends chipped, cloth dusty, hinges weak. *(Whitehart)* **£60** [≈ $115]

Dunbar Brander, A.A.
- Wild Animals in Central India. London: Arnold, 1927. 2nd edn. xv,296,16 advt pp. Frontis, ills. Orig cloth. *(Bates & Hindmarch)* **£75** [≈ $143]

Duncan, A.
- Memorials of the Faculty of Physicians and Surgeons of Glasgow 1588-1850 ... Glasgow: 1896. 4to. xiii,[i],307 pp. Frontis, 3 ills. Cloth, dull & marked. *(Whitehart)* **£35** [≈ $67]

Duncan, Andrew
- Observations on the Distinguishing

Symptoms of Three Different Species of Pulmonary Consumption ... with some Remarks on the Remedies ... Edinburgh: 1816. 2nd edn. 195 pp. Rec qtr leather.
(Fye) **$100 [≈ £52]**

Duncan, J.M.
- Papers on the Female Perineum. London: 1879. viii,156 pp. Cloth, sl worn. Author's inscrptn.   *(Whitehart)* **£40 [≈ $76]**

Duncan, James
- Beetles. Edinburgh: Jardine's Naturalist's Library, 1835. Sm 8vo. viii,17-269 pp, complete. Port, cold vignette, 30 cold plates. Frontis & title trifle foxed & soiled. Diced calf, trifle rubbed, jnts weak.
(Wheldon & Wesley) **£45 [≈ $86]**
- British Butterflies ... London: W.H. Allen, Jardine's Naturalist's Library, [ca 1870]. New edn. 12mo. 246 pp. Port, hand cold vignette, 34 hand cold plates. Orig blue cloth gilt, fine.
(Gough) **£50 [≈ $95]**
- British Moths ... London: W.H. Allen, Jardine's Naturalist's Library, [ca 1890]. New edn. 12mo. 268 pp. Port, 30 hand cold plates. Orig blue cloth gilt, fine.
(Gough) **£45 [≈ $86]**
- Exotic Moths. London: Bohn, Jardine's Naturalist's Library, n.d. Sm 8vo. Port, cold vignette, 29 cold & 3 plain plates. Orig red cloth.   *(Wheldon & Wesley)* **£40 [≈ $76]**
- Introduction to Entomology. London: Bohn, Jardine's Naturalist's Library, 1860. Cr 8vo. Port, cold vignette, 32 hand cold plates. Cloth, trifle worn.
(Wheldon & Wesley) **£40 [≈ $76]**
- The Natural History of Bees. Edinburgh: Jardine's Naturalist's Library, 1840. Cr 8vo. x,301 pp.Pp 1-16 were not published. Port, cold vignette, 19 cold & 11 plain plates. Orig cloth, sl spotted.
(Wheldon & Wesley) **£50 [≈ $95]**

Dunell, H.
- British Wire-Drawing and Wire-Working Machinery. London: 1925. Lge 4to. xv,188 pp. 181 text ills. Orig bndg.
(Whitehart) **£25 [≈ $47]**

Dunglison, Robley
- History of Medicine from the Earliest Ages to the Commencement of the Nineteenth Century. Phila: 1872. 1st edn. 287 pp. Orig bndg.   *(Fye)* **$150 [≈ £78]**
- Medical Lexicon. A Dictionary of Medical Science. Phila: 1848. 7th edn. 912 pp. Orig leather, fine.   *(Fye)* **$75 [≈ £39]**

- Medical Lexicon. A Dictionary of Medical Science. Phila: 1865. 1047 pp. Leather.
(Fye) **$100 [≈ £52]**

Dunlap, Orrin E.
- Marconi: The Man and His Wireless. 1937. 1st edn. 360 pp. 15 photo ills. Orig bndg, hd of spine worn.   *(New Wireless)* **$40 [≈ £21]**
- Radio's 100 Men of Science. 1944. 4th edn. 294 pp. 98 photos. Dw.
(New Wireless) **$45 [≈ £23]**

Dunn, Matthias
- A Treatise on the Winning and Working of Collieries ... Newcastle upon Tyne: 1848. 8vo. [4 advt],372 pp. 28 plates (1 fldg). Orig cloth, most of orig backstrip relaid, later endpapers.   *(Spelman)* **£75 [≈ $143]**

Duns, J.
- Biblical Natural Science: being the Explanation of all the References in Holy Scripture to Geology, Botany, Zoology, and Physical Geography. London: [1863]. 2 vols. Roy 8vo. 9 maps & charts, 45 plates. Sm repr to 1 plate (no loss), vol 2 title sl foxed. Half calf.   *(Wheldon & Wesley)* **£70 [≈ $134]**

Duparcque, F.
- A Treatise on the Functional and Organic Diseases of the Uterus. From the French. Translated with Notes by Joseph Warrington, MD. Phila: 1837. 8vo. 455 pp. Foxed. New antique style cloth. *(Goodrich)* **$125 [≈ £65]**

Dupouy, Edmond
- Medicine in the Middle Ages. Translated by T.C. Minor. Reprinted from Cincinnati Lancet: 1889. 8vo. 99 pp. Bds.
(Goodrich) **$75 [≈ £39]**

Dupuytren, Guillaume
- On Lesions of the Vascular System, Diseases of the Rectum, and Other Surgical Complaints. London: 1854. 1st English translation. 378 pp. Orig bndg.
(Fye) **$150 [≈ £78]**

Durand, W.F.
- Aerodynamic Theory. A General Review of Progress. Berlin: 1934-36. 6 vols. 18 plates, num figs. Dws.   *(Whitehart)* **£75 [≈ $143]**

Durkheim, Emile
- Suicide. A Study in Sociology. Translated by John A. Spalding and George Simpson. London: 1952. 8vo. 404 pp. Orig cloth. Dw.
(Bickersteth) **£20 [≈ $38]**

Durling, Richard J.
- A Catalogue of Sixteenth Century Printed Books in the National Library of Medicine. Bethesda, Maryland, Natl Lib of Medicine, 1967. 4to. Orig bndg.
(Georges) £125 [≈ $239]
- A Catalogue of Sixteenth Century Printed Books in the National Library of Medicine. Bethesda: 1967. 1st edn. 698 pp. Orig bndg.
(Fye) $125 [≈ £65]

DuToit, A.L.
- Geology of South Africa. Edinburgh: Oliver & Boyd, 1939. 2nd edn. 8vo. xii,515 pp. 41 plates, geological map, 68 text figs. Ex-lib. Cloth.
(Gemmary) $65 [≈ £34]

Dutton, C.E.
- Earthquakes in the Light of the New Seismology. London: 1905. xxiii,314 pp. 10 plates, 63 text figs. Front endpaper sl marked. Orig cloth, sl dusty, lib label on spine, front hinge sl weak.
(Whitehart) £15 [≈ $28]

Earhart, John F.
- The Color Printer. A Treatise on the Use of Colors in Typographic Printing. Cincinnati: Earhart & Richardson, 1892. Only edn. 4to. 137 pp. 90 plates ptd in colour (sev with embossing &c.). Orig dec cloth, new endpapers.
(Spelman) £350 [≈ $671]

Earle, A.M.
- Sun-Dials and Roses of Yesterday. New York: Macmillan, 1902. 8vo. xxiii,461 pp. Num plates & text figs. Dec cloth.
(Gemmary) $75 [≈ £39]

Eastman, W.R. & Hunt, A.C.
- The Parrots of Australia. London: 1966. Roy 8vo. xiv,194 pp. Num cold & plain ills. Cloth.
(Wheldon & Wesley) £25 [≈ $47]

Eastwood, B.
- A Complete Manual for the Cultivation of the Cranberry, With a Description of the Best Varieties. New York: C.M. Saxton, Barker, 1860. Sm 8vo. [2],120 pp. 10 litho plates. Orig green cloth.
(Karmiole) $65 [≈ £33]

Eaton, H.S.
- Catalogue of the Library of the Institution of Civil Engineers. Second Edition. Corrected to December 31, 1865. 2nd edn, enlgd. 8vo. viii,378 pp. Contemp binder's cloth.
(Gaskell) £60 [≈ $115]

Eaton, Richard
- A Book of Rates, Inwards and Outwards ... The Method of making Entries Inwards and Outwards ... New and useful Tables ... Second Edition. Dublin: Boulter Greirson, 1767. 8vo. [iv],xxiv,279 pp. Contemp calf, red mor label.
(Finch) £320 [≈ $614]

Eberhart, Noble M.
- A Working Manual of High Frequeny Currents. 1916. 4th edn. 320 pp. 69 ills. Orig bndg.
(New Wireless) $65 [≈ £34]
- A Working Manual of High Frequency Currents. 1923. 8th edn. 320 pp. 68 ills. Orig bndg.
(New Wireless) $55 [≈ £28]

Eccles, W.H.
- Wireless Telegraphy and Telephony. 1918. 2nd edn. 514 pp. 434 ills. Orig bndg.
(New Wireless) $65 [≈ £33]

Eckhardt, George H.
- Electronic television. 1936. 1st edn. 162 pp. 83 ills. Orig bndg.
(New Wireless) $55 [≈ £29]

Eckstein, G.F.
- A Practical Treatise on Chimneys; with a Few Remarks on Stoves, the Consumption of Smoke, and Coal, Ventilation, &c. London: John Weale, 1852. 1st edn. 8vo. xii,153,9 pp. Orig brown cloth gilt.
(Gough) £45 [≈ $86]

Eddington, A.S.
- New Pathways in Science. London: Cambridge UP, 1935. 1st edn. 8vo. 333 pp. Cloth.
(Gemmary) $45 [≈ £23]
- Stars and Atoms. Oxford: 1927. 1st edn. 127 pp. Frontis, 10 ills. Name in ink on title, lib stamp on verso. Orig bndg.
(Whitehart) £15 [≈ $28]

Eddy, Mary Baker
- Science and Health by Mary Baker Glover. Boston: Christian Scientist Publishing Co, 1875. 1st edn. Thick 8vo. Errata sheet bound in at rear. Sm paper loss at front. Orig cloth gilt, rubbed & darkened, spine ends worn. Slipcase.
(Horowitz) $2,500 [≈ £1,302]

Edelman, Philip E.
- Experimental Wireless Stations. 1920. 3rd edn. 392 pp. 167 ills. Orig bndg.
(New Wireless) $30 [≈ £15]

Edinburgh New Dispensatory ...
- See Rotheram, J.

Edlin, H.L.
- Woods and Man. London: Collins New Naturalist, 1956. 1st edn. 8vo. xv,272 pp. 24 cold & 24 plain plates. Orig cloth.
(Henly) £22 [≈ $42]

Edwards, E.
- The American Steam Engineer. Theoretical and Practical. With Examples ... Design and Construction of Steam Engines ... Phila: 1888. xlix,50-419 pp. 77 ills inc plates. Orig bndg. *(Whitehart)* £38 [≈ $72]

Edwards, Ethel
- Psychedelics and Inner Space. Cincinnati: The Psyche Press, [1969]. 8vo. viii,253 pp. Bds, cloth spine. *(Bickersteth)* £25 [≈ $47]

Edwards, F.W., et al.
- British Blood-Sucking Flies. London: BM, 1939. Roy 8vo. viii,156 pp. 45 plates (44 cold), 64 ills. Orig cloth.
(Fenning) £45 [≈ $86]

Edwards, George
- A Discourse on the Emigration of British Birds ... By a Naturalist. The Second Edition. London: for Stanley Crowder; & B.C. Collins, Salisbury, [1781]. 2nd edn. 8vo. [ii], ix, [i],45 pp, advt leaf. Half-title sl browned & frayed. Old wraps. Anon.
(Burmester) £65 [≈ $124]

Edwards, James
- The Hemiptera-Hemoptera (Cicadina and Psyllina) of the British Islands ... London: L. Reeve, 1896. 1st edn. Large Paper. Roy 8vo. xii,271 pp. 28 hand cold & 2 plain plates. Occas spotting. Contemp green half mor, elab gilt spine, t.e.g. *(Gough)* £250 [≈ $479]

Edwards, K.C.
- The Peak District. London: Collins New Naturalist, 1962. 1st edn. 8vo. xvi,240 pp. 4 cold & 24 plain plates. Orig cloth. Dw.
(Henly) £25 [≈ $47]

Eiffel, G.
- The Resistance of the Air and Aviation. Experiments conducted at the Champ-de-Mars Laboratory. Translated by J.C. Hunsaker. London: 1913. 2nd edn. Lge 4to. xvi,242 pp. 27 fldg plates, 136 diags. Lib stamps on title verso & last page. Dw (rather worn). *(Whitehart)* £120 [≈ $230]

Eimer, G.H.T.
- Organic Evolution as the result of the

Inheritance of Acquired Characters according to the Laws of Organic Growth ... London: 1890. 1st edn in English. 8vo. xxviii,435,[1 blank] pp. Orig cloth.
(Bow Windows) £40 [≈ $76]

Einstein, Albert
- Relativity. The Special and the General Theory. New York: Henry Holt, 1920. 1st Amer edn. Orig blue cloth gilt. Dw (1 crnr wrinkled, minor ageing).
(MacDonnell) $375 [≈ £195]

Eissler, M.
- The Cyanide Process for the Extraction of Gold. London: Crosby Lockwood, 1902. 3rd edn. 8vo. xviii,184 pp. 150 text figs. Cloth.
(Gemmary) $85 [≈ £45]
- The Metallurgy of Gold. London: Crosby Lockwood, 1889. 2nd edn. 8vo. xiv,340 pp. 132 text figs. Cloth, sl stained.
(Gemmary) $125 [≈ £65]
- The Metallurgy of Gold. London: Crosby Lockwood, 1900. 5th edn. 8vo. xxvi,638 pp. Num fldg plates & text ills. Cloth, spine worn, outer hinge torn.
(Gemmary) $150 [≈ £79]

The Elaboratory Laid Open ...
- See Dossie, Robert.

Elam, Charles
- Winds of Doctrine: being an Examination of Modern Theories of Automatism and Evolution. London: Smith, Elder, 1876. 1st edn. 8vo. viii, 163 pp, 2 advt ff. Orig cloth, uncut, largely unopened.
(Bickersteth) £120 [≈ $230]

The Elephant ...
- The Elephant. Principally Viewed in relation to Man. London: 1844. 2nd edn, rvsd. 8vo. text ills. Top crnr of some pp v sl damp marked. Orig cloth, sl rubbed.
(Grayling) £50 [≈ $95]

Ellacombe, H.N.
- The Plant-Lore and Garden-Craft of Shakespeare. London: 1884. 2nd edn. Cr 8vo. 438 pp. Cloth, trifle used.
(Wheldon & Wesley) £40 [≈ $76]

Ellerman, J.R.
- The Families and Genera of Living Rodents ... London: 1940-41. 1st edn. 2 vols. Cr 4to. 239 text figs. Cloth. *(Henly)* £125 [≈ $239]

Ellerman, J.R. & Morrison-Scott, T.C.S.
- Checklist of Palaearctic and Indian Mammals 1758 to 1946. London: BM, 1951. Cr 4to. 810 pp. Map. Buckram, spine faded.
(Wheldon & Wesley) £40 [≈ $76]
- Checklist of Palaearctic and Indian Mammals. London: BM, 1966. 2nd edn. Roy 8vo. 810 pp. Cloth.
(Wheldon & Wesley) £60 [≈ $115]

Elliot, John
- An Account of the Nature and Medicinal Virtues of the Principal Mineral Waters of Great Britain and Ireland ... Second Edition, Corrected and Enlarged. London: for J. Johnson, 1789. 8vo. Fldg plate. Contemp calf, gilt spine. *(Waterfield's)* £200 [≈ $383]

Elliott, D.G.
- The Birds of Daniel Giraud Elliott, a Selection of Pheasants and Peacocks painted by Joseph Wolf and taken from the Original Monograph published in New York in 1872 ... London: Ariel Press, 1979. One of 1000. Imperial folio. 12 cold plates. Orig green cloth. Dw *(Henly)* £95 [≈ $182]

Ellis, E.A.
- The Broads. London: Collins New Naturalist, 1965. 1st edn. 8vo. Ills. Dw.
(Wheldon & Wesley) £45 [≈ $86]
- The Broads. London: Collins New Naturalist, 1965. 1st edn. 8vo. xii,401 pp. 1 cold & 28 other plates. Orig cloth. Dw.
(Henly) £48 [≈ $92]
- The Broads. London: Collins New Naturalist Series, 1965. 1st edn. 8vo. xii,401 pp. 28 plates. Orig cloth gilt. Price-clipped dw.
(Hollett) £75 [≈ $143]

Ellis, William
- New Experiments in Husbandry, for the Month of April ... London: for the author, sold by Fox, Meadows, Astley, Bickerton, 1736. 1st edn. 8vo. [viii],124,[4] pp. Plate (backed). Contemp underlining & notes. Rec bds. *(Burmester)* £85 [≈ $163]

Eltringham, H.
- African Mimetic Butterflies. Oxford: 1910. 4to. 136 pp. Map, 10 cold plates. Lib stamp title verso. Binder's cloth.
(Wheldon & Wesley) £80 [≈ $153]

Emanuel, H.
- Diamonds and Precious Stones. London: Hotten, 1867. 2nd edn. 8vo. xvii,266 pp. 5 plates, 27 text figs. Orig gilt dec cloth.

(Gemmary) $80 [≈ £41]
- Diamonds and Precious Stones: their History, Value, and Distinguishing Characteristics. With Simple Tests for their Identification. Second Edition. London: 1867. 8vo. [ii],xxii,266,6 advt pp. Cold litho title, 4 tinted plates, table. Sl marks. Orig cloth, recased. *(Bow Windows)* £60 [≈ $115]

Emerson, William
- The Mathematical Principles of Geography ... [with] Dialling, or the Art of Drawing Dials. London: 1770. 2 parts in one vol. 8vo. [ii], viii,ii,172; iv,164 pp. 4 + 18 fldg plates. Orig tree calf, spine ends chipped.
(Vanbrugh) £175 [≈ $335]
- The Principles of Mechanics ... New Edition, Corrected. London: 1836. 8vo. xxiv, [x], 320 pp. 83 plates, num text figs. Some spots & dust marks. Rec calf.
(Bow Windows) £90 [≈ $172]

Emmerson, Joan S.
- Catalogue of the Pybus Collection of Medical Books. Manchester: UP, (1981). 1st edn. 4to. xiv,271 pp. Ills. Orig cloth.
(Bookpress) $85 [≈ £44]

Emmet, T.A.
- The Principles and Practice of Gynaecology. Second Edition. Phila: 1880. 8vo. xix,875,82 advt pp. 163 ills. Orig sheep, rubbed.
(Goodrich) $65 [≈ £33]

Emmons, Ebenezer
- Manual of Mineralogy and Geology: designed for the Use of Schools; and for Persons attending Lectures on these Subjects. Albany: Websters & Skinners, 1826. 1st edn. 12mo. xxiii, [1],229,[1] pp, inc addenda & errata. Browned. Contemp qtr calf. Author's inscrptn. *(Rootenberg)* $300 [≈ £156]

Enfield, Charles D.
- Radiography. 1925. 1st edn. 299 pp. 194 ills. Orig bndg. *(New Wireless)* $25 [≈ £13]

Enfield, William
- Institutes of Natural Philosophy, Theoretical and Experimental. Second Edition, with Corrections and Considerable Additions ... London: J. Johnson, 1799. 4to. xvi,428 pp. 13 plates. Minor spotting. Orig bds, untrimmed, rebacked, crnrs sl worn.
(Clark) £160 [≈ $307]

Engineering Research Associates
- High-Speed Computing Devices. 1950. 1st

edn. 451 pp. Orig bndg.
(New Wireless) **$60 [≈ £31]**

English Forests ...
- English Forests and Forest Trees, Historical, Legendary, and Descriptive. London: Ingram, Cooke, 1853. 8vo. 406 pp. Engvd title, frontis, num ills. Contemp calf gilt, jnts sl rubbed.   *(Spelman)* **£65 [≈ $124]**

The Entomologist's Annual ...
- The Entomologist's Annual. London: Van Voorst, 1855-74. 1st edns (vol 1 2nd edn). 20 vols. 12mo. 10 hand cold & 10 plain plates. 2 frontises spotted. Contemp half calf (1-8), orig ptd bds (9-20), 3 backstrips relaid.
   (Gough) **£125 [≈ $239]**
- The Entomologist's Annual. London: Van Voorst, 1855-74. 1st edns. 20 vols (all published). 12mo. 9 hand cold plates, some highlighted in gold, & 11 plain plates. Contemp blue half calf, gilt spines.
   (Gough) **£195 [≈ $374]**

Epps, J.
- The Life of John Walker. London: 1832. 2nd edn. viii,342 pp. Sm lib stamp on title. Cloth backed bds, sl dusty. *(Whitehart)* **£30 [≈ $57]**

Ercker, Lazarus
- Lazarus Ercker's Treatise on Ores and Assaying. Translated from the German Edition of 1580 by Sisco & Smith. Chicago: UP, 1951. Cr 4to. xxxiii, 360 pp. Num ills. Cloth.   *(Gemmary)* **$100 [≈ £52]**

Erichsen, J.E.
- The Science and Art of Surgery ... London: 1864. 4th edn. xxiv,1280 pp. 517 w'engvs. Half leather, rebacked in cloth.
   (Whitehart) **£35 [≈ $67]**

Erichsen, John
- Observations on Aneurism selected from the Works of the Principal Writers on that Disease ... London: 1844. 1st edn. 524 pp. Orig bndg.   *(Fye)* **$200 [≈ £104]**
- Observations on Aneurysms selected from the Works of the Principal Writers on that Disease ... London: Sydenham Society, 1844. 8vo. xii,524 pp. Orig cloth, worn.
   (Goodrich) **$125 [≈ £65]**

Esdaile, J.
- Mesmerism in India and its Practical Application in Surgery and Medicine. London: [1902]. 165 pp. Name and date on title. Orig cloth, worn, marked & stained.

(Whitehart) **£40 [≈ $76]**

Espagnet, Jean d'
- Enchyridion Physicae Restitutae, or, the Summary of Physicks recovered. London: 1651. 1st edn in English. 12mo. [xx],167,[1] pp. Lacks A1 (blank except for sgntr) & A12 as usual. Dust soiling & damp stains, a few headlines just shaved. Contemp mor gilt, rebacked. Wing E.3276A.
   (Gaskell) **£800 [≈ $1,535]**

Esquirol, Jean Etienne
- Mental Maladies. A Treatise on Insanity. Translated from the French, with Additions, by E.K. Hunt, M.D. Phila: 1845. 1st English translation. 496 pp. Inscrptn & stamp on pastedown. Occas foxing. Front bd detached, rear hinge cracked, bd held by cords.
   (Fye) **$1,000 [≈ £520]**

An Essay on the Natural History of Guiana ...
- See Bancroft, E.

Etheridge, R.
- Fossils of the British Islands, Stratigraphically and Zoologically arranged. Vol. 1, Palaeozoic ... Oxford: 1888. All published. 4to. viii,468 pp. Orig cloth.
   (Wheldon & Wesley) **£90 [≈ $172]**

Euclid
- Euclid's Elements ... from the Latin ... of Commandine ... Preface ... by John Keill ... Revised ... by Samuel Cunn. The Eleventh Edition ... London: Strahan ..., 1772. 8vo. [16], 399,[1 advt] pp. 14 fldg plates (1 with 5 onlays). Rec bds.   *(Fenning)* **£85 [≈ $163]**

Euler, L.
- Letters of Euler on Different Subjects in Physics and Philosophy ... addressed to a German Princess. London: for Murray & Highley, 1802. 2nd edn. 2 vols. 8vo. xii,507, xi; lxvii,451,vi pp. 20 plates. Orig bds, spines sl defective.   *(Gemmary)* **$500 [≈ £260]**

Evans, J.
- A History of Jewellery 1100-1870. Boston: Boston Book & Art, 1970. New edn. 8vo. 224 pp. 12 cold plates, 192 photo ills, 35 text figs. Endpapers glued down. Cloth.
   (Gemmary) **$75 [≈ £39]**

Evans, U.R.
- Metals and Metallic Compounds. London: 1923. 4 vols. Text figs. Orig bndg.
   (Whitehart) **£38 [≈ $72]**

Eve, A.S. & Creasey, C.H.

- Life and Work of John Tyndall. With a Chapter on Tyndall as a Mountaineer. London: 1945. xxxii,404 pp. Frontis port & 12 plates. Traces of label removal from endpaper. Faint lib number on spine.
  (Whitehart) £35 [≈ $67]
- Life and Work of John Tyndall. London: 1945. xxxii,404 pp. Frontis, text ills. Lib stamp. Lib bndg. *(Whitehart)* £25 [≈ $47]

Evelyn, John

- Acetaria, a Discourse of Sallets. London: 1706. 2nd edn. 8vo. [xl],190,[49] pp. Fldg table. Pp 33 to end foxed. Mod half calf gilt.
  (Wheldon & Wesley) £200 [≈ $383]
- Fumifugium: or, the Inconvenience of the Aer, and Smoake of London Dissipated. Together with some Remedies humbly proposed by J.E. ... London: for B. White, 1772. 4to. Advt leaf at end. New bds.
  (Georges) £150 [≈ $287]
- Kalendarium Hortense: or, the Gard'ners Almanac, directing what he is to do monthly throughout the year ... London: 1673. 5th edn. Sm 8vo. 127,[8] pp. Lacks half-title. Blind stamp on title. New calf.
  (Wheldon & Wesley) £90 [≈ $172]
- Kalendarium Hortense: or, the Gard'ners Almanac. London: 1706. 10th edn. 8vo. [vi], x,[xiv], 170,[14] pp. Frontis, plates. Mod half calf. *(Wheldon & Wesley)* £80 [≈ $153]
- Sylva, or a Discourse of Forest Trees. London: 1670. 2nd edn, enlgd. Folio. [xlviii], 247,[iv], 67,33,[2] pp. Imprimatur leaf (mtd, old notes on reverse), errata leaf, insert *Z. 5 engvs. Mod calf.
  (Wheldon & Wesley) £200 [≈ $383]
- Sylva: or A Discourse of Forest Trees and the Propagation of Timber in His Majesty's Dominions. London: 1776. 1st Hunter edn. 4to. liv,649,ix pp. Fldg table, 40 plates. Contemp diced calf, backstrip relaid.
  (Henly) £245 [≈ $470]

Ewald, C.A.

- Lectures on Diseases of the Digestive Organs. London: New Sydenham Society, 1891-92. 2 vols. [vii],680 pp. Ills. Occas sl foxing. Inscrptn on half-title. Orig cloth.
  (Whitehart) £25 [≈ $47]

Ewart, J.

- The Poisonous Snakes of India, for the Use of Officials and Others residing in the Indian Empire. London: 1878. Sm 4to. viii,64 pp. 21 plates (19 cold). Cloth (stained), rather loose,
  (Wheldon & Wesley) £160 [≈ $307]

Ewing, Alexander

- Practical Astronomy ... Edinburgh: 1797. Sole edn. 8vo. xi,268,143 pp. Fldg plate. Orig tree calf, spine sl rubbed.
  (Bickersteth) £55 [≈ $105]

Exley, Thomas

- Physical Optics; or, the Phenomena of Optics explained according to Mechanical Science; and on the Known Principles of Gravitation. London: for Longman ..., 1834. 1st edn. 8vo. xix,[v], 206,[2] pp. Errata slip. 2 plates. Orig drab bds, cloth spine, label (chipped).
  (Burmester) £45 [≈ $86]

Eyre, J.

- The Stomach and its Difficulties. London: 1852. 2nd edn. xvi,154 pp. Sm lib stamp on title. Orig cloth, worn & dusty.
  (Whitehart) £35 [≈ $67]

Eyton, T.C.

- A Synopsis on the Anatidae or Duck Tribe. Wellington: 1869. Post 8vo. [vi],141 pp. Orig cloth backed wraps, trifle used, backstrip sl defective. H.F. Witherby's b'plate.
  (Wheldon & Wesley) £125 [≈ $239]

Fabricius, Hieronymus

- The Embryological Treatises ... Facsimile Edition, with an Introduction, a Translation and a Commentary by Howard B. Adelmann. New York: Cornell UP, 1942. Sm 4to. xxiii,883 pp. Facs plates. Orig qtr cloth.
  (Gough) £50 [≈ $95]

Fagge, Charles Hilton

- The Principles and Practice of Medicine. Edited and completed by P.H. Pye-Smith. London: 1888. 2nd edn. 2 vols. New cloth.
  (Whitehart) £35 [≈ $67]

Fahie, J.J.

- Galileo. His Life and Work. London: 1903. xvi, 451 pp. Frontis port, 17 plates, few text diags. Orig cloth gilt, rather worn marked & dust stained. *(Whitehart)* £38 [≈ $72]
- A History of Wireless Telegraphy 1838-1899. 1902. 3rd edn. 348 pp. 85 ills. Orig bndg.
  (New Wireless) £165 [≈ £85]

Fairbairn, Sir William

- Useful Information for Engineers ... Second Series. London: 1860. 1st edn. 8vo. xvi, [1],329 pp, advt leaf. 4 fldg plates, 72 ills. Orig cloth, spine faded.
  (Fenning) £28.50*[≈ $55]

Fairbairn, W.
- Some Game Birds of West Africa. Edinburgh: 1952. 1st edn. 92 pp. 9 cold plates. Dw.
  (Trophy Room) **$100 [≈ £52]**

Falconer, William
- An Account of the Efficacy of the Aqua Mephitica Alkalina ... London: Cadell, 1792. 4th edn. 8vo. iv,208 pp. Half calf, upper bd loose.   *(Hemlock)* **$275 [≈ £143]**
- A Dissertation on the Influence of the Passions upon Disorders of the Body ... London: for C. Dilly, 1791. 2nd edn. Sm 8vo. iv, 148 pp. Port. Sl damp stain. Rec bds.
  (Burmester) **£175 [≈ $335]**
- Observations respecting the Pulse ... London: Cadell & Davies, 1796. 1st edn. Sm 8vo. [ii],158 pp. Lacks half-title. Tables. 2 sm marg tears. Rec bds.
  (Burmester) **£250 [≈ $479]**

Fang, J.
- Mathematicians from Antiquity to Today. Volume I [all published]. Studies in the Nature of Modern Mathematics 12, [1972]. 341 pp.   *(Whitehart)* **£25 [≈ $47]**

Faraday, Michael
- A Course of Six Lectures on the Chemical History of a Candle ... added, a Lecture on Platinum ... London: Griffin, Bohn, 1861. 1st edn. Cr 8vo. viii,208,8 advt pp. 38 ills. Orig red cloth, sl dull.   *(Fenning)* **£85 [≈ $163]**
- Experimental Researches in Electricity. Reprinted from the Philosophical Transactions, with Other Electrical Papers. Facsimile Edition. London: Taylor, 1839-44-55. 1st edn in book form. 3 vols. 8vo. 17 plates. Vols 1 & 3 lacks 1st blank. Orig cloth.   *(Rootenberg)* **$950 [≈ £494]**
- The Selected Correspondence ... Edited by L.P. Williams. Cambridge: 1971. 2 vols. 4to. xii,538; viii, 539-1079 pp. Port, diags. Orig bndg.   *(Whitehart)* **£40 [≈ $76]**

Farber, E.
- The Evolution of Chemistry. A History of its Ideas, Methods, and Materials. New York: 1952. ix,349 pp. 30 figs. Orig bndg.
  (Whitehart) **£25 [≈ $47]**

Farley, John
- The London Art of Cookery. London: for John Fielding ..., 1783. 1st edn. Demy 8vo. [xx], [460] pp. Port frontis, 12 plates. Rec mor gilt.   *(Ash)* **£400 [≈ $767]**

The Farmer's Guide ...
- The Farmer's Guide to Hiring and Stocking Farms ... see Young, Arthur.

Farnsworth, S.
- Illumination and its Development in the Present Day. London: [1922]. 8vo. [4],267 pp. 21 plates (4 cold). Orig cloth gilt.
  (Fenning) **£45 [≈ $86]**

Farrer, R.
- Among the Hills. London: 1927. 2nd imp. 8vo. 326,2 pp. Map, 14 cold & 8 plain plates. Orig cloth.   *(Henly)* **£48 [≈ $92]**
- The English Rock Garden. London: 1930. 5th imp. 2 vols. Roy 8vo. 102 plates. Orig cloth, new endpapers. *(Henly)* **£55 [≈ $105]**
- The Rainbow Bridge. London: 1926. 3rd imp. 8vo. xi,383,16 pp. Map, 16 plates. Orig cloth.   *(Henly)* **£52 [≈ $99]**

Farrington, O.C.
- Catalogue of the Meteorites of North America to January 1, 1909. Washington: Nat Acad of Science Vol 13, 1915. 4to. 513 pp. 36 map plates. Orig cloth. *(Gemmary)* **$175 [≈ £91]**
- Catalogue of the Meteorites of North America to January 1, 1909. Washington: Nat Acad of Science Vol 13, 1915. 4to. 513 pp. 36 map plates. Cloth, lacks backstrip.
  (Gemmary) **$125 [≈ £65]**
- Gems and Gem Minerals. Chicago: A.W. Mumford, 1903. 8vo. xii,229 pp. 16 cold plates, 61 text figs. Cloth.
  (Gemmary) **$125 [≈ £65]**
- Gems and Gem Minerals. Chicago: A.W. Mumford, 1903. 8vo. xii,229 pp. 16 cold plates, 61 text figs. Good ex-lib. Rebound in cloth.   *(Gemmary)* **$50 [≈ £26]**

Fauntleroy, A.M.
- Report on the Medico-Military Aspects of the European War: from Observations taken behind the Allied Armies in France. Washington: 1915. vii,146 pp. 218 ills & plates. Orig cloth, spine faded & sl frayed at ft.   *(Whitehart)* **£35 [≈ $67]**

Fawcett, W. & Rendle, A.B.
- Flora of Jamaica containing Descriptions of the Flowering Plants known from the Island. London: BM, 1910-36. 5 vols (1, 3, 4, 5, 7, all published). 8vo. 37 plates, 483 text figs. Good ex-lib. Orig cloth.
  (Wheldon & Wesley) **£150 [≈ $287]**

Federal Communications Commission
- Petition of RCA and NBC for Approval of

Color Standards for the RCA Color TV. 1953. 1st edn. 695 pp. Num ills. Orig wraps. *(New Wireless)* **$95 [≈ £49]**

Feinagle, Gregor von
- The New Art of Memory ... Third Edition, Corrected and Enlarged. London: R. Edwards for the proprietor ..., 1813. 12mo. xix, [ii], 467,[i] pp. Port, 5 fldg plates, text figs. Orig bds, cloth spine, paper label, uncut, label rubbed & chipped.
(Bickersteth) **£300 [≈ $575]**

Felix, Edgar H.
- Television - Its Methods and Uses. 1931. 1st edn. 272 pp. 73 ills. Orig bndg.
(New Wireless) **$90 [≈ £46]**

Felton, S.
- On the Portraits of English Authors on Gardening, with Biographical Notices. Second Edition, with considerable Additions. London: 1830. 8vo. [xl],221,[1 blank] pp. Some browning & spots. Later half mor, t.e.g.
(Bow Windows) **£165 [≈ $316]**

Fenn, Lady
- A Short History of Insects ... A Pocket Companion for those who visit the Leverian Museum. Norwich: [1797]. Sm 8vo. xxiv,107 pp. 8 cold plates. Outer crnr of 1st few margs stained. Contemp half calf. Anon.
(Wheldon & Wesley) **£100 [≈ $191]**

Fenning, Daniel
- The British Youth's Instructor: or, A New and Easy Guide to Practical Arithmetic ... The Eighth Edition ... London: for S. Crowder, 1775. 12mo. Contemp sheep, sm splits in hinges. *(Jarndyce)* **£90 [≈ $172]**
- The Ready Reckoner; or, Trader's most useful Assistant ... Ninth Edition. With Additions ... Corrected by Joseph Moon. London: for S. Crowder; & B.C. Collins, salisbury, 1788. 12mo. Staining. Early coarse brown cloth. *(Jarndyce)* **£35 [≈ $67]**
- The Young Man's Book of Knowledge: being a proper Supplement to the Young Man's Companion in Six Parts. The Fourth Edition, revised ... London: S. Crowder & B.C. Collins, 1786. 12mo. xiv,381, errata pp. Diag, fldg tables. Contemp calf, rebacked.
(Lamb) **£35 [≈ $67]**

Fenwick, E. Hurry
- The Electric Illumination of the Bladder and Urethra as a Means of Diagnosis of Obscure Vesico-Urethral Diseases. London: 1888. 1st edn. 176 pp. Orig bndg. *(Fye)* **$300 [≈ £156]**

Ferguson, James, 1710-1776
- The Art of Drawing in Perspective made easy to those who have no previous Knowledge of the Mathematics. London: Strahan & Cadell, 1775. 1st edn. 12mo. xii,123,[1 advt] pp. 9 fldg plates. Contemp calf, rebacked.
(Gaskell) **£385 [≈ $739]**
- Astronomy Explained upon Sir Isaac Newton's Principles ... London: Rivington ..., 1790. 8th edn. 8vo. viii,503,xvi pp. 17 fldg plates. Crnr of pp damp stained. Leather, crnrs worn. *(Gemmary)* **$175 [≈ £91]**
- An Easy Introduction to Mechanics, Geometry, Plane Trigonometry ... Optics, Astronomy. To which is prefixed, an Essay [by John Ryland] ... London: Dilly, 1768. Only edn. 12mo. [ii],lii, 161,[1] pp. 12 plates. 2 tears reprd. Contemp sheep, rebacked, crnrs reprd, stained. *(Burmester)* **£350 [≈ $671]**
- Lectures on Select Subjects in Mechanics, Hydrostatics, Pneumatics, and Optics ... London: for A. Millar, 1760. 1st edn. 8vo. [viii], 418,[vi] pp. 23 plates. Occas sl browning. Contemp calf, new label, inner jnts strengthened, spine ends sl chipped.
(Rankin) **£150 [≈ $287]**
- Lectures on Select Subjects in Mechanics, Hydrostatics, Hydraulics ... Edinburgh: Stirling & Slade, 1823. 3rd edn. 2 vols. 8vo. xxiv, 335; iv,400 pp. Plates (foxed). Half leather, jnts worn. *(Gemmary)* **$125 [≈ £65]**
- Lectures on Select Subjects in Mechanics, Hydrostatics, Pneumatics, Optics and Astronomy. A New and Improved Edition, adapted ... London: for Thomas Tegg, 1843. 8vo. [viii], xvii-xlvii, [i], 463,[8 advt] pp. Frontis & 10 plates. Sl foxing & water staining. Orig cloth. *(Burmester)* **£50 [≈ $95]**
- Tables and Tracts, relative to Several Arts and Sciences. London: Millar & Cadell, 1767. 1st edn. 8vo. xvi,328 pp. 3 plates. Contemp polished sprinkled calf, citron mor label, fine.
(Gaskell) **£550 [≈ $1,055]**

Ferguson, John
- Bibliotheca Chemica. A Bibliography of Books on Alchemy, Chemistry and Pharmaceutics. London: Verschoyle, (1906) 1954. 2 vols. Med 8vo. Orig buckram, v sl marked. *(Georges)* **£100 [≈ $191]**

Fergusson, Sir William
- A System of Practical Surgery. London: 1852. 3rd edn, with addtns. Lge 12mo. [4], (vii)-xiii, 846 pp, complete. 393 ills. Contemp half calf, worn but sound.
(Fenning) **£35 [≈ $67]**

Ferrel, W.
- A Popular Treatise on the Winds; comprising the General Motions of the Atmosphere, Monsoons, Cyclones, Tornadoes, Waterspouts, Hail-Storms ... London: 1893. 1st edn. vii,505 pp. Frontis, 36 figs, 7 tables. Sm lib stamp on title. Orig cloth, sl used.
  (Whitehart) **£35 [≈ $67]**

Ferrier, David
- The Functions of the Brain. New York: 1876. 1st Amer edn. 323 pp. Rec qtr leather.
  (Fye) **$500 [≈ £260]**

Festschriften
- Festschrift in Honor of Abraham Jacobi to Commemorate the Seventieth Anniversary of his Birth, May Sixth 1900. New York: 1900. 8vo. 496 pp. Frontis. Later cloth.
  (Goodrich) **$95 [≈ £49]**
- Problems of Continuum Mechanics. Contributions in honor of the Seventieth Birthday of Academician N.I. Muskhelishvili. Edited by I.E. Block and J.R.M. Radok. Phila: 1961. xx,601 pp. Figs.
  (Whitehart) **£35 [≈ $67]**
- Contributions to Medical and Biological Research dedicated to Sir William Osler. In Honour of his Seventieth Birthday ... New York: 1919. One of 1600. 2 vols. Orig bndgs.
  (Goodrich) **$95 [≈ £49]**
- The Ranshoff Memorial Volume. A Collection of Papers representing Original Contributions to the Art and Science of Medicine by Colleagues and Students of Joseph Ranshoff. Cincinnati: 1921. Roy 8vo. 574 pp. Ex-lib. Orig bndg.
  (Goodrich) **$65 [≈ £33]**
- Victor Robinson Memorial Volume. Essays on History of Medicine. In Honor of Victor Robinson on his Sixtieth Birthday, August 16, 1946. Edited by S.R. Kagan. New York: 1948. One of 350. xxi,447 pp. Port, plates. Cloth, sl worn.   *(Whitehart)* **£30 [≈ $57]**
- Contributions to Medical Science dedicated to Aldred Scott Warthin. Ann Arbor: 1927. 8vo. 720 pp. Frontis. Orig bndg, inner hinges weak.   *(Goodrich)* **$35 [≈ £18]**

Feuchtersleben, E. von
- The Principles of Medical Psychology being the Outline of a Course of Lectures ... Translated by H.E. Lloyd. London: Sydenham Society, 1847. xx,[12],392 pp. Orig cloth, t.e.g., backstrip relaid, crnrs worn.   *(Whitehart)* **£40 [≈ $76]**

Feuchtwanger, L.
- A Treatise on Gems, in reference to their Practical and Scientific Value ... New York: 1838. 8vo. 178 pp. Lib blind stamp on title, b'plate. 1st few ff sl foxed. Cloth, spine worn. Author's pres inscrptn.
  (Wheldon & Wesley) **£350 [≈ $671]**

Field, H.
- Memoirs, Historical and Illustrative, of the Botanick Garden at Chelsea, belonging to the Society of Apothecaries of London. London: 1820. 1st edn. 8vo. v,111 pp. Cloth. Anon.
  (Wheldon & Wesley) **£80 [≈ $153]**

Fifield, Lionel
- Infections of the Hand. London: 1926. 1st edn. 192 pp. Ex-lib. Orig bndg.
  (Fye) **$100 [≈ £52]**

Figuier, Louis
- The Insect World ... New Edition, Revised and Corrected by P. Martin Duncan. London: Cassell, Petter & Galpin, [ca 1870]. 538 pp. 579 plates & ills. Orig pict blue cloth gilt.   *(Gough)* **£25 [≈ $47]**

Finn, Frank
- Eggs and Nests of British Birds. London: Hutchinson, 1910. 1st edn. 12mo. xvi,231 pp. 32 cold & b/w plates. Orig elab pict blue cloth gilt, fine.   *(Gough)* **£25 [≈ $47]**

First Elements of Astronomy ...
- First Elements of Astronomy and Natural Philosophy ... For the Use of Private Families, and Public Schools. London: for G. Sael, 1798. 4th edn, crrctd. Cr 8vo. Plate. Contemp mor backed mrbld bds.
  (Stewart) **£45 [≈ $86]**

Fishberg, A.M.
- Heart Failure. London: 1940. 2nd edn. 829 pp. 25 diags. Orig bndg.
  (Whitehart) **£25 [≈ $47]**

Fisher, James
- The Fulmar. London: Collins New Naturalist, 1952. 1st edn. 8vo. Ills. Orig cloth, trifle used, faded.
  (Wheldon & Wesley) **£50 [≈ $95]**
- The Fulmar. London: Collins New Naturalist, 1952. 1st edn. 8vo. xv,496 pp. 4 cold & 48 plain plates. Orig cloth.
  (Henly) **£60 [≈ $115]**

Fisher, James & Lockley, R.M.
- Sea-Birds. Boston: 1954. 1st Amer edn. 8vo.

xvi,320 pp. 77 photos (9 cold). Trifle foxed at ends. Cloth. *(Wheldon & Wesley)* £35 [≈ $67]
- Sea-Birds. London: Collins New Naturalist, 1954. 1st edn. 8vo. xvi,320 pp. 8 cold & 40 plain plates. Orig cloth. *(Henly)* £42 [≈ $80]

Fisher, James (ed.)
- New Naturalist. A Journal of British Natural History. London: 1948. 4to. 216 pp. 12 cold plates, 175 ills. Orig cloth. Dw.
(Henly) £25 [≈ $47]

Fisher, James, et al. (eds.)
- The Birds of the London Area since 1900 ... London: Collins New Naturalist, 1957. 1st edn. 305 pp. Maps, ills. Few faint spots front endpapers. Orig cloth. dw (sl used).
(Hollett) £70 [≈ $134]

Fisher, Lydia
- Memoir of W.H. Harvey, M.D., F.R.S., etc., late Professor of Botany, trinity College, Dublin ... London: Bell & Daldy, 1869. 1st edn. 8vo. xvi,372 pp. Port. Rec bds. Anon.
(Fenning) £55 [≈ $105]

Fisher, W.A.
- Ophthalmoscopy, retinoscopy and Refraction. Chicago: (1922). 8vo. 5 ff, 218, [6] pp. 248 ills inc 48 cold plates & 4-page foldout. Some marg fraying last foldout. Orig cloth. *(Hemlock)* $125 [≈ £65]

Fishman, Alfred & Richards, Dickinson (eds.)
- Circulation of the Blood: Men and Ideas. New York: 1964. 1st edn. 859 pp. Ills. Orig bndg. *(Fye)* $90 [≈ £46]

Fiske, John
- Excursions of an Evolutionist. London: Macmillan, 1884. 1st English edn. 8vo. 379,[5 advt] pp. Orig cloth, v sl rubbed.
(Burmester) £30 [≈ $57]

Fitch, Samuel Sheldon
- Six Lectures on the Functions of the Lungs ... also a Treatise on Medicated Inhalations. New York: 1856. 24th edn. 8vo. xviii,19-384 pp. Port, 30 w'cut plates. 3 advt ff. Orig cloth. *(Hemlock)* $125 [≈ £65]

Fitter, R.S.R.
- London's Natural History. London: Collins New Naturalist, 1945. 1st edn. 8vo. xii,282 pp. 40 cold & 32 plain plates. Orig cloth, faded. *(Henly)* £12 [≈ $23]

Fitton, E. & S.M.
- Conversations on Botany. London: 1828. 6th edn. Post 8vo. xx,278 pp. 21 hand cold plates. Mod cloth. Anon.
(Wheldon & Wesley) £40 [≈ $76]

Fitzgerald, George Francis
- The Scientific Writings ... Edited by J. Larmor. London: 1902. lxiv,576 pp. Port. Traces of label removal from endpaper. Inner jnt sl weak. *(Whitehart)* £95 [≈ $182]

FitzRoy, R.
- The Weather Book: a Manual of Practical Meteorology. London: 1863. 2nd edn (?). xi, 464 pp. 16 plates. Sm tear at edge of 1 plate. Cloth rather worn. *(Whitehart)* £40 [≈ $76]
- The Weather Book: a Manual of Practical Meteorology. London: 1863. 2nd edn. xi,480 pp. 16 fldg plates, some text figs. Sm tear at crnr of 1 plate. Inscrptn on title. Cloth marked & worn, spine edges frayed.
(Whitehart) £35 [≈ $67]
- The Weather Book: a Manual of Practical Meteorology. London: 1863. x,464 pp. 16 plates. Cloth, trifle used.
(Wheldon & Wesley) £50 [≈ $95]

Flaxman, John
- Anatomical Studies of the Bones and Muscles, for the Use of Artists, Engraved by Henry Landseer; with Two Additional Plates, and Explanatory Notes by William Robertson. London: Nattali, 1833. 1st edn. Folio. Port, 21 plates. Orig red cloth, extremities rubbed.
(Rootenberg) $600 [≈ £312]

Fleming, Alexander & Florey, Howard
- The Nobel Lecture on Penicillin. Les Prix Nobel en 1945. Stockholm: 1947. 8vo. Orig bndg. *(Goodrich)* $125 [≈ £65]

Fleming, Alexander (ed.)
- Penicillin. Its Practical Application. London: 1946. 1st edn. 380 pp. Orig bndg.
(Fye) $125 [≈ £65]

Fleming, John
- History of British Animals. Edinburgh: 1828. 1st edn. 8vo. xxiii,565, corrigenda pp. Cloth & bds, label worn. *(Schoyer)* $60 [≈ £31]

Fleming, John Ambrose
- Electrons, Electric Waves and Wireless Telephony. London: The Wireless Press, 1922. 8vo. viii,326 pp. 112 text figs. Cloth.
(Gemmary) $50 [≈ £26]

- An Elementary Manual of Radiotelegraphy and Radiotelephony. 1908. 1st edn. 340 pp. Ills. Rebound. *(New Wireless)* **$125 [≈ £65]**
- An Elementary Manual of Radiotelegraphy [and] Radiotelephony for Students and Operators. London: Longmans, Green, 1908. 8vo. xiv,340 pp. Num text figs. Cloth. *(Gemmary)* **$150 [≈ £78]**
- An Elementary Manual of Radiotelegraphy and Radiotelephony. 1918. 3rd edn. 360 pp. 30 photos, 131 ills. Orig bndg. *(New Wireless)* **$40 [≈ £20]**
- Fifty Years of Electricity. The Memories of an Electrical Engineer. London: The Wireless Press, 1921. 8vo. xi,371 pp. Num plates & text figs. Cloth. *(Gemmary)* **$90 [≈ £46]**
- Magnets and Electric Currents. London: Spon, 1898. 8vo. xv,408 pp. 136 text figs. Cloth. *(Gemmary)* **$50 [≈ £26]**
- The Principles of Electric Wave Telegraphy. 1906. 1st edn. 671 pp. Num ills. Orig bndg. *(New Wireless)* **$185 [≈ £96]**
- The Principles of Electric Wave Telegraphy and Telephony. 1916. 3rd edn. 911 pp. 490 ills. Orig bndg. *(New Wireless)* **$140 [≈ £72]**
- The Propagation of Electric Currents in Telephone and Telegraph Conductors. London: 1912. 2nd edn, rvsd. xiv,316 pp. Text figs. Orig bndg. *(Whitehart)* **£18 [≈ $34]**
- Short Lectures to Electrical Artisans. 1892. 4th edn. 210 pp. 74 ills. Orig bndg, faded & stained. *(New Wireless)* **$60 [≈ £31]**
- The Thermionic Valve and its Developments in Radiotelegraphy and Telephony. 1919. 1st edn. 279 pp. 144 ills. Orig bndg. *(New Wireless)* **$85 [≈ £44]**
- Waves & Ripples in Water, Air & Ether. London: SPCK, 1902. Cr 8vo. xii,299 pp. 85 text figs. Ex-lib. Half-title loose. Cloth. *(Gemmary)* **$25 [≈ £13]**
- Waves & Ripples in Water, Air & Ether. 1923. 1st edn. 4th printing. 299 pp. 84 ills. Orig bndg. *(New Wireless)* **$55 [≈ £28]**
- The Wireless Telegraphist's Pocket Book of Notes, Formulae, and Calculations. 1915. 1st edn. 347 pp. 38 ills. Orig bndg, a.e.g. *(New Wireless)* **$40 [≈ £20]**

Fletcher, A.
- The Universal Measurer. In Two Parts ... Whitehaven: ptd by W. Masheder, 1752/53. 1st edn. 2 parts in one vol. 8vo. xiv,[2 advt], 282; vi, 284 pp. Num text engvs. 2 sm reprs. Half-title creased. Old calf, sl worn. *(Young's)* **£300 [≈ $575]**

Fletcher, H.R.
- The Story of the Royal Horticultural Society, 1804-1968. Roy 8vo. xii,564 pp. Cold frontis, 3 cold & 24 plain plates. Cloth. *(Wheldon & Wesley)* **£35 [≈ $67]**

Fletcher, T.
- Practical Dental Metallurgy. Warrington: 1890. viii,72,15,42 illust advt pp. 42 ills. Crnrs sl worn. *(Whitehart)* **£35 [≈ $67]**

Fleure, H.J.
- The Natural History of Man in Britain. London: Collins New Naturalist, 1951. 1st edn. 8vo. xviii,349 pp. 32 cold & 32 plain plates. Orig cloth. *(Henly)* **£12 [≈ $23]**

Flint, Austin
- Clinical Medicine: A Systematic Treatise of the Diagnosis and Treatment of Diseases. Phila: 1879. 1st edn. 795 pp. Orig bndg, inner hinges cracked, backstrip defective. *(Fye)* **$100 [≈ £52]**
- A Manual of Auscultation and Percussion ... Phila: 1885. 5th edn. 280 pp. Orig bndg. *(Fye)* **$50 [≈ £26]**
- Medicine of the Future. New York: 1886. 1st edn. 37 pp. Port frontis. Orig bndg. *(Fye)* **$75 [≈ £39]**
- Physical Exploration and Diagnosis of Diseases affecting the Respiratory Organs. Phila: 1856. 1st edn. 636 pp. Orig bndg, few holes in spine. *(Fye)* **$125 [≈ £65]**
- A Practical Treatise on the Diagnosis, Pathology, and Treatment of the Heart. Phila: 1859. 1st edn. 473 pp. Orig bndg. *(Fye)* **$400 [≈ £208]**
- A Practical Treatise on the Diagnosis, Pathology and Treatment of Diseases of the Heart. Phila: 1859. 1st edn. 473 pp. Plate water stained. Orig bndg. *(Fye)* **$300 [≈ £156]**
- A Practical Treatise on the Physical Exploration of the Chest, and the Diagnosis of Diseases affecting the Respiratory Organs. Phila: 1866. 2nd edn. 595 pp. Perf stamp on title. Rec cloth. *(Fye)* **$100 [≈ £52]**
- A Treatise on the Principles and Practice of Medicine. Phila: 1867. 2nd edn. 967 pp. Leather, dry & rubbed. *(Fye)* **$75 [≈ £39]**
- A Treatise on the Principles and Practice of Medicine ... Third Edition. Phila: Henry C. Lea, 1868. 8vo. 1002,32 ctlg pp. Leather, shaken & scuffed. *(Schoyer)* **$65 [≈ £33]**
- A Treatise on the Principles and Practice of Medicine. Phila: 1873. 4th edn. 1070 pp. Leather. *(Fye)* **$50 [≈ £26]**

Flora Domestica ...
- See Kent, E.

The Flower Garden ...
- The Flower Garden; Containing Directions for the Cultivation of all known Garden Flowers ... London: Wm. S. orr, 1838. 1st edn. Sm 8vo. iv,515 pp. Hand cold vignette title, 10 hand cold plates, num other plates & text ills. Orig dec cloth gilt.
(Gough) **£150 [≈ $287]**
- See also M'Intosh, Charles.

Flower, W.H.
- An Introduction to the Osteology of the Mammalia ... London: 1876. xi,339 pp. 126 text figs. Orig cloth, dull, sl dust stained.
(Whitehart) **£18 [≈ $34]**

Fluckiger, F. & Hanbury, D.
- Pharmacographia. A History of the Principal Drugs of Vegetable Origin met with in Great Britain and British India. London: 1879. 2nd edn. 803 pp. Qtr leather. *(Fye)* **$150 [≈ £78]**

Flugge, C.
- Micro-Organisms with Special reference to the Etiology of the Infective Diseases. London: 1890. 1st English translation. 826 pp. Orig bndg.   *(Fye)* **$125 [≈ £65]**

Forbes, Edward
- A History of British Starfishes, and Other Animals of the Class Echinodermata. London: 1841. 8vo. xx,270 pp. Num w'cuts. Orig cloth. *(Wheldon & Wesley)* **£40 [≈ $76]**
- A Monograph of the British Naked-Eyed Medusae: with Figures of all the Species. London: 1848. Folio. 104 pp. 13 cold plates. Lib stamps. Half calf. *(Baldwin)* **£48 [≈ $92]**

Forbes, F.B. & Hemsley, W.B.
- An Enumeration of all the Plants known from China Proper, Formosa, Hainan, Corea, the Luchu Archipelago and the Island of Hongkong ... London: Linnean Society of London Journal, Botany vols 23,26,36, 1886-1905. 3 vols. 8vo. Map, 23 plates. Buckram, sound ex-lib
(Wheldon & Wesley) **£250 [≈ $479]**

Forbes, H.O.
- A Handbook to the Primates. London: 1896. 2 vols. Num cold plates. Contemp half calf.
(Grayling) **£35 [≈ $67]**

Forbes, R.J.
- Studies in Early Petroleum History ... [With]

More Studies in Early Petroleum History, 1860-1880. Leiden: Brill, 1958-59. 2 vols. 4to. Ills. Orig cloth gilt, spines faded.
(Karmiole) **$85 [≈ £44]**

Forbush, E.
- Birds of Massachusetts and other New-England States. Boston: 1929-27-29. Vol 1 2nd imp. 3 vols. Roy 8vo. 93 cold plates, 97 figs, 35 maps & text figs. Orig green cloth.
(Wheldon & Wesley) **£160 [≈ $307]**

Forbush, E.H. & May, J.B.
- Natural History of the Birds of Eastern and Central North America. Boston: (1939) 1955. 4to. xxvii,554 pp. 1 plain & 96 cold plates. Cloth.   *(Wheldon & Wesley)* **£35 [≈ $67]**

Ford, E.B.
- Butterflies. London: Collins New Naturalist, 1945. 1st edn. 8vo. xiv,368 pp. 48 cold & 24 plain plates, 32 maps. Ends sl foxed. Orig cloth, spine sl faded.   *(Henly)* **£14 [≈ $26]**
- Butterflies. London: Collins New Naturalist, 1946. 2nd edn. 8vo. xiv,368 pp. 48 cold & 24 plain plates, 32 maps. Orig cloth.
(Henly) **£12 [≈ $23]**
- Moths. London: Collins New Naturalist, 1955. 1st edn. 8vo. xix,266,2 pp. 32 cold & 24 plain plates. Orig cloth. *(Henly)* **£28 [≈ $53]**

Fordyce, G.
- Elements of the Practice of Physic, in Two Parts ... London: 1771. 3rd edn. viii,380 pp. Sm lib stamp on title & 1 marg. Contemp leather, rebacked. *(Whitehart)* **£180 [≈ $345]**

Foreign Essays ...
- Foreign Essays on Agriculture and the Arts. Consisting Chiefly of the Most Curious Discoveries ... Communicated ... for the Improvement of British Husbandry ... London: for R. Davis ..., 1766. 1st edn. 8vo. viii, 392 pp. Sl marg worm. Orig calf.
(Bickersteth) **£120 [≈ $230]**

Forrest, H.E.
- The Vertebrate Fauna of North Wales. London: 1907. 8vo. lxxii,537 pp. 28 plates. Rebound in cloth.   *(Henly)* **£65 [≈ $124]**

Forshaw, J.M.
- Parrots of the World. Melbourne: 1973. 1st edn. Imperial 4to. 584 pp. 158 cold plates by W. Cooper. Orig cloth, upper outer crnrs trifle creased. Dw.
(Wheldon & Wesley) **£350 [≈ $671]**
- Parrots of the World. New York: 1973.

Imperial 4to. 584 pp. 158 cold plates by W.T. Cooper. Dw (reprd).
(Wheldon & Wesley) **£325 [≈ $623]**

Forster, J. Cooper
- The Surgical Diseases of Children. London: Parker, 1860. 8vo. 343 pp. 10 cold plates, text engvs. Orig cloth, sl shaken.
(Goodrich) **$395 [≈ £205]**

Forster, T.
- The Pocket Encyclopaedia of Natural Phenomena. London: 1827. Sm 8vo. xlviii,440 pp. Orig cloth, trifle used, new endpapers. *(Wheldon & Wesley)* **£35 [≈ $67]**

Forster, Thomas
- Observations on the Brumal Retreat of the Swallow ... Third Edition Corrected. London: Thomas Underwood, 1813. 8vo. Paper cvrd bds. *(Young's)* **£60 [≈ $115]**

Forster, W.
- A Treatise on a Section of the Strata from Newcastle upon Tyne to Cross Fell. London: 1883. 3rd edn. lvi,208 pp. 14 plates. New buckram. *(Baldwin)* **£40 [≈ $76]**

Forsyth, A.R.
- Theory of Differential Equations. Cambridge: 1890-1906. 6 vols. Occas sl foxing on endpapers. Sm ink sgntr on half-titles. Orig bndgs. *(Whitehart)* **£180 [≈ $345]**

Forsyth, William, the elder, 1734-1804
- A Treatise on the Culture and Management of Fruit Trees. London: 1803. 2nd edn. 8vo. xxvii, 523 pp. 13 plates. Calf, rebacked.
(Wheldon & Wesley) **£55 [≈ $105]**
- A Treatise on the Culture and Management of Fruit Trees ... London: Longman ..., 1803. 3rd edn. 8vo. iii-xxx,523 pp. 13 fldg engvd plates. Lacks half-title. Minor foxing. Contemp crimson straight grained half mor, gilt spine, bd edges worn.
(Gaskell) **£185 [≈ $355]**
- A Treatise on the Culture and Management of Fruit Trees ... London: 1818. 6th edn. 8vo. xxviii,481 pp. Port, 13 plates (sl offsetting). Sl foxing, 2 margs at end defective. Mod buckram. *(Wheldon & Wesley)* **£35 [≈ $67]**

Foster, C.L. & Cox, S.H.
- A Text-Book of Ore and Stone Mining. London: Charles Griffin, 1894. 7th edn. 8vo. xxx,799 pp. Frontis, 715 ills. Cloth, sl loose.
(Gemmary) **$75 [≈ £39]**

Foster, G.C. & Porter, A.W.
- Elementary Treatise on Electricity and Magnetism. New York: Longmans, Green, 1903. 2nd edn. 8vo. xix,568 pp. 374 text figs. Ex-lib. Cloth. *(Gemmary)* **$50 [≈ £26]**

Foster, Sir Michael
- Lectures on the History of Physiology during the Sixteenth, Seventeenth and Eighteenth Centuries. Cambridge: 1901. 1st edn. 310 pp. Ills. Orig bndg, backstrip torn, front inner hinge cracked. *(Fye)* **$60 [≈ £31]**
- Lectures on the History of Physiology during the Sixteenth, Seventeenth and Eighteenth Centuries. Cambridge: UP, Natural Science Manuals, 1901. 8vo. Frontis. Some neat marginalia in cold pencil. Orig bndg.
(Georges) **£40 [≈ $76]**
- Lectures on the History of Physiology during the Sixteenth, Seventeenth and Eighteenth Centuries. Cambridge: (1901) 1924. [ix],306 pp. Frontis. Ink sgntr on title. Dw.
(Whitehart) **£38 [≈ $72]**
- A Text Book of Physiology. New York: Macmillan, 1893. Mixed 5th & 6th edns. 4 vols. 8vo. Orig matching green cloth, quite worn, some bndgs shaken.
(Goodrich) **$295 [≈ £153]**

Fothergill, J. Milner
- Digitalis: Its Mode of Action and its Use. An Enquiry ... Phila: 1871. 1st edn. 89 pp. Orig bndg. *(Fye)* **$125 [≈ £65]**
- The Heart and its Diseases, with their Treatment including the Gouty Heart. Phila: 1879. 2nd edn. 476 pp. Orig bndg.
(Fye) **$50 [≈ £26]**

Fourier, J.
- The Analytical Theory of Heat. Translated by A. Freeman. Cambridge: 1878. 1st English edn. xxiii,466 pp. Advts dated April 1878. A few text figs. Orig cloth.
(Whitehart) **£95 [≈ $182]**
- The Analytical Theory of Heat. Cambridge: UP, 1878. 8vo. xxiii,466,[51 ctlg] pp. 20 text figs. Orig cloth, tear in jnt.
(Gemmary) **$300 [≈ £156]**

Fowler, John Coke
- Collieries and Colliers. A Handbook of the Law and Leading Cases relating thereto. London: Longman ..., 1861. 1st edn. 8vo. xiv, 352 pp. Orig cloth. *(Gough)* **£25 [≈ $47]**

Fowler, R.H.
- Statistical Mechanics. Cambridge: UP, (1936) 1955. 2nd edn. 4to. 864 pp. 101 text

figs. Cloth. *(Gemmary)* **\$70 [≈ £36]**

Fowler, R.S.
- The Operating Room and the Patient. Second Edition, Revised and Enlarged. Phila: 1910. 8vo. 284 pp. Ills. Orig bndg.
(Goodrich) **\$125 [≈ £65]**

Fowler, W.W. & Donisthorpe, H.St.J.
- The Coleoptera of the British Islands. London: 1887-91. 5 vols. 180 hand cold & 2 plain plates. [With] Supplement. London: 1913. 20 hand cold & 3 plain plates. Together 6 vols. Large Paper. Roy 8vo. Orig cloth.
(Wheldon & Wesley) **£1,000 [≈ \$1,919]**

Fox, Wilson
- The Diseases of the Stomach. London: 1872. 236 pp. Orig bndg. *(Fye)* **\$100 [≈ £52]**

Fracastorius, Hieronymus
- Contagion, Contagious Diseases and their Treatment. Translation by Wilmer Cave Wright. New York: 1930. 8vo. 356 pp. Dw.
(Goodrich) **\$45 [≈ £23]**

Francatelli, Charles Elme
- The Royal English and Foreign Confectioner. London: Chapman & Hall, 1862. 1st edn. Post 8vo. [xxviii],422,18 pp. Chromolitho plates, w'engvs. Advts. Orig dec cloth gilt, reprd, a few sl marks & flaws.
(Ash) **£250 [≈ \$479]**

Francis, G.W.
- An Analysis of the British Ferns and their Allies. Fifth Edition, revised and enlarged by Arthur Henfrey. London: Simpkin, Marshall, 1855. 8vo. viii,92 pp. Engvd title, 10 engvd plates. Orig cloth gilt. *(Gough)* **£25 [≈ \$47]**
- Electrical Experiments; Illustrating the Theory, Practice and Applications of the Science of Free or Frictional Electricity; Containing the Methods of Making and Managing Electrical Apparatus ... London: 1854. [2],91 pp. Text ills. Orig cloth.
(Whitehart) **£40 [≈ \$76]**

Francis, J.G.
- Beach Rambles in Search of Sea-side Pebbles and Crystals. L: Routledge ..., 1861. 2nd edn. Cr 8vo. iv,186 pp. 8 cold plates. Cloth, sl loose. *(Gemmary)* **\$100 [≈ £52]**

Francis, William
- The Gentleman's, Farmer's & Husbandman's most useful Assistant, in measuring and expeditiously computing the amount of any

quantity of Land ... Maidenhead: T. Clayton, 1806. 1st edn. 12mo. vi,45,[3],48 pp. Diags & tables (1 fldg). Contemp half calf, sl worn.
(Burmester) **£125 [≈ \$239]**

Frankel, J. & Hutter, R.
- A Practical Treatise on the Manufacture of Starch, Glucose, Starch-Sugar, and Dextrine. Phila: 1881. 344 pp. 58 text figs. New cloth.
(Whitehart) **£18 [≈ \$34]**

Frazer, J.E.
- The Anatomy of the Human Skeleton. London: 1920. 2nd edn. 4to. viii,284 pp. 219 ills. New cloth. *(Whitehart)* **£25 [≈ \$47]**

Frazer, R.A., et al.
- Elementary Matrices and some Applications to Dynamics and Differential Equations. Cambridge: 1938. xvi,416 pp.
(Whitehart) **£35 [≈ \$67]**

Freeman, R.B.
- The Works of Charles Darwin. An Annotated Bibliographical Handlist. Folkestone: 1977. 2nd edn. 235 pp. Frontis. Orig cloth.
(Whitehart) **£16 [≈ \$30]**
- The Works of Charles Darwin. An Annotated Bibliographical Handlist. London: Dawson, (1977). 2nd edn, rvsd & enlgd. 8vo. 236 pp. Orig cloth. *(Oak Knoll)* **\$50 [≈ £26]**

Freeman-Mitford, A.B.
- The Bamboo Garden. London: 1896. 8vo. xii, 224 pp. 9 plates. Sl foxing. Orig buckram gilt, sl soiled, crnrs trifle bumped.
(Wheldon & Wesley) **£40 [≈ \$76]**

Freind, John
- Nine Commentaries upon Fevers: and Two Epistles concerning the Small-Pox ... London: T. Cox, 1730. 1st edn in English. Sm 8vo. [xii], 137 pp. Name removed from title. Later mor. *(Bookpress)* **\$300 [≈ £156]**

French, J.W.
- Modern Power Generators. Steam, Electric and Internal-Combustion and their Applications to Present-Day Requirements. London: 1908. 2 vols. 4to. xix,201; xiv,203 pp. 11 composite sectional models, 500 text ills. Orig bndgs. *(Whitehart)* **£95 [≈ \$182]**

Fresenius, C.R.
- Instruction in Chemical Analysis (Quantitative). Edited by J. Lloyd Bullock. London: 1846. 1st edn in English. 8vo. Ills. Orig bndg. *(Bow Windows)* **£45 [≈ \$86]**

Freud, Sigmund
- Civilisation and its Discontents. London: 1930. 1st English edn. 144 pp. Orig cloth.
(Whitehart) **£25 [≈ $47]**
- Psychopathology of Everyday Life. Authorized English Edition, with Introduction by A. Brill. New York: [1938]. 8vo. vii,342 pp. Orig cloth.
(Bickersteth) **£38 [≈ $72]**

Frobenius, Leo
- The Childhood of Man. A Popular Account of the Lives, Customs and Thoughts of the Primitive Races. London: Seeley & Co, 1909. 8vo. 415 ills. Orig cloth.
(Young's) **£40 [≈ $76]**

Frohawk, F.W.
- British Birds. London: Ward Lock, 1958. 1st edn. 8vo. 256 pp. 31 cold plates, num ills. Orig cloth.   *(Gough)* **£18 [≈ $34]**
- The Complete Book of British Butterflies. London: 1934. 8vo. 384 pp. 32 cold plates, 160 text figs. Cloth, trifle used.
(Wheldon & Wesley) **£30 [≈ $57]**
- Natural History of British Butterflies ... London: [1924]. 2 vols. Folio. 60 cold & 5 plain plates. Orig cloth, stained.
(Wheldon & Wesley) **£160 [≈ $307]**
- Varieties of British Butterflies. London: 1938 [1946]. 2nd issue. Roy 8vo. 200 pp. 48 cold plates. Orig cloth. Dw.
(Wheldon & Wesley) **£65 [≈ $124]**
- Varieties of British Butterflies. London: 1946. Roy 8vo. 200 pp. 48 cold plates. Cloth.
(Henly) **£40 [≈ $76]**

Frost, W. Adams
- The Fundus Oculi with an Ophthalmoscopic Atlas illustrating its Physiological & Pathological Conditions. Edinburgh: 1896. 1st edn. 4to. 228 pp. Orig bndg.
(Fye) **$250 [≈ £130]**

Frost, W.E. & Brown, M.E.
- The Trout. London: Collins New Naturalist, 1972. 2nd edn. 8vo. 286 pp. 1 cold & 16 other plates, 25 text figs. Orig cloth. Dw. Inscrptn.
(Henly) **£25 [≈ $47]**

Fuller, Henry
- On Rheumatism, Rheumatic Gout, and Sciatica. New York: 1854. 1st Amer edn. 322 pp. Orig bndg.   *(Fye)* **£125 [≈ $65]**

Fuller, Samuel
- Practical Astronomy ... Collected from the Best Authors ... For the Use of Young Students. Dublin: by and for Samuel Fuller, 1732. 1st edn. 8vo. x,237,[1 advt] pp. 10 fldg plates. 1 plate reprd. Contemp calf, spine ends reprd, label chipped.
(Gaskell) **£400 [≈ $767]**

Fuller, Thomas
- Exanthematologia: or, An Attempt to Give a Rational Account of Fevers, especially Measles and Small Pox ... Appendix concerning Inoculation. London: 1730 [-29]. 1st edn. 2 parts & appendix in 1 vol with continuous pagination. 4to. xxvi,[17]-439 pp, advt leaf. Orig calf, rebacked.
(Bickersteth) **£440 [≈ $844]**

Fullmer, Jane Z.
- Sir Humphry Davy's Published Works. Harvard: UP, 1969. Dw. *(Clark)* **£28 [≈ $53]**

Fulop-Miller, Rene
- Triumph Over Pain. Translated by E. & C. Paul. London: (1938). 1st edn in English. 8vo. [vi],438 pp. Frontis, ills. Orig cloth, sunned.   *(Bow Windows)* **£60 [≈ $115]**
- Triumph Over Pain [the history of anaesthesia]. Translated by Eden and Cedar Paul. London: Hamish Hamilton, 1938. 8vo. Num ills.   *(Georges)* **£40 [≈ $76]**

Fulton, John F.
- A Bibliography of the Honourable Robert Boyle, Fellow of the Royal Society. OUP: 1932. 4to. 171 pp. Frontis loose. Ex-lib. Lib buckram.   *(Goodrich)* **$95 [≈ £49]**
- A Bibliography of the Honourable Robert Boyle ... Oxford: Clarendon Press, 1961. 2nd edn. 4to. xxvi,218 pp. 26 text figs. Cloth. Dw.
(Gemmary) **$175 [≈ £91]**
- A Bibliography of the Honourable Robert Boyle, Fellow of the Royal Society. Second Edition. OUP: 1961. Roy 8vo. Frontis, ills. Dw (sl faded).   *(Georges)* **£85 [≈ $163]**
- Frontal Lobotomy and Affective Behaviour. A Neurophysiological Analysis. New York: Norton, 1951. 8vo. Dw.
(Goodrich) **$75 [≈ £39]**
- Functional Localization in the Frontal Lobes and Cerebellum with particular reference to the Operation of Frontal Lobotomy. Being the William Withering Memorial Lectures ... OUP: 1949. 8vo. Orig bndg.
(Goodrich) **$85 [≈ £44]**
- The Great Medical Bibliographers. A Study in Humanism. Phila: 1951. 8vo. 107 pp. Ills. Dw.   *(Goodrich)* **$75 [≈ £39]**
- Harvey Cushing: a Biography. Springfield: 1946. 1st edn. 754 pp. Dw. Sgnd by the

author.   *(Fye)* **$200** [≈ £104]
- Harvey Cushing: a Biography. Springfield: 1946. 1st edn. 754 pp. Orig bndg.
                            (Fye) **$40** [≈ £20]
- Humanism in an Age of Science. Being a Ludwig Mond Lecture. New York: Schuman, 1950. 8vo. 26 pp. Orig ptd wraps.
                        (Goodrich) **$25** [≈ £13]
- Humanism in an Age of Science. Being a Ludwig Mond Lecture. New York: Schuman, 1950. 8vo. Orig ptd wraps. Author's pres copy.   *(Goodrich)* **$75** [≈ £39]
- Michael Servetus. Humanist and Martyr. With a Bibliography of his Works and Census of Known Copies by Madeline E. Stanton. New York: Reichner, 1954. One of 750. 8vo. 98 pp. Frontis, 2 figs. Orig bndg.
                        (Goodrich) **$75** [≈ £39]
- Muscular Contraction and the Reflex Control of Movement. Baltimore: 1926. 1st edn. 644 pp. Orig bndg.   *(Fye)* **$150** [≈ £78]
- Physiology. New York: 1931. 1st edn. 141 pp. Orig bndg.   *(Fye)* **$45** [≈ £23]
- Selected Readings in the History of Physiology. Springfield: 1966. 2nd edn. 492 pp. Ex-lib. Orig bndg.   *(Fye)* **$100** [≈ £52]
- Vesalius Four Centuries Later. Medicine in the Eighteenth Century. (Logan Clendenning Lectures). Lawrence: 1950. 8vo. 52 pp. Dw.
                        (Goodrich) **$35** [≈ £18]

Fulton, Robert
- A Treatise on the Importance of Canal Navigation ... London: 1796. 1st edn. 4to. [2], vii-xvi, 144 pp, advt leaf. 17 plates. Lacks half-title & dedic ff. Contemp calf.
                        (Fenning) **£200** [≈ $383]

Furneaux, W.
- Life in Ponds and Streams. London: Longmans, Green, 1896. 1st edn. xix,406 pp. 8 chromolitho plates, 311 plates & text ills. Orig pict green cloth gilt.
                        (Gough) **£30** [≈ $57]

Furnival, W.J.
- Researches on Leadless Glazes. London: Furnival, 1898. 135 pp. Orig cloth, some wear.   *(Reference Works)* **£38** [≈ $72]

Fussell, G.E.
- The Old English Farming Books from Fitzherbert to Tull 1523-1730. [With his] More Old English Farming Books from Tull to the Board of Agriculture 1731-1793. London: 1947-50. 2 vols. Plates. Dws.
                        (Lamb) **£40** [≈ $76]

Fyfe, Andrew
- A System of Anatomy and Physiology, with the Comparative Anatomy of Animals. Compiled from the Latest and Best Authors ... Edinburgh: 1791. 3 vols. 506; 471; 467 pp. 20 plates. Leather, bds detached or missing, backstrips intact.   *(Fye)* **$100** [≈ £52]
- A System of the Anatomy of the Human Body; Illustrated by Upwards of Two Hundred Tables ... Second Edition, with Alterations and Improvements. Edinburgh: J. Pillans, 1806. 4to. 213 engvd plates (some hand cold). Lacks 1 text leaf. Qtr mor, uncut.
                        (Goodrich) **$1,500** [≈ £781]

Gadow, Hans
- Jorullo: The History of the Volcano of Jorullo and the Reclamation of the Devastated District by Animals and Plants. Cambridge: UP, 1930. 1st edn. 8vo. xviii,100 pp. Fldg map, 3 plates. Dw (sl chipped).
                        (Gough) **£20** [≈ $38]

Gairdner, Andrew
- An Historical Account of the Old Peoples Hospital, commonly called the Trinity Hospital, in Edinburgh ... Edinburgh: ptd in the year, 1734. 2nd (?) edn. 8vo. viii,56 pp. Disbound.   *(Bickersteth)* **£130** [≈ $249]

Galen of Pergamon
- Galen on Anatomical Procedures ... Translation of the Surviving Books with Introduction and Notes by Charles Singer. Oxford: 1956. 8vo. 289 pp. Dw.
                        (Goodrich) **$75** [≈ £39]
- Galen on Anatomical Procedures. The Later Books. A Translation by W.L.H. Duckwork ... Cambridge: 1962. 8vo. 278 pp. Lacks front fly. B'plate removed. Orig bndg.
                        (Goodrich) **$60** [≈ £31]
- Galen's Method of Physick: or, his Great Master-Peece ... translator, Peter English. Edinburgh: 1656. Only edn. 12mo. [4],344 pp. Some quires loose. Contemp calf, front hinge & spine split. Wing G.161.
                        (Hemlock) **$750** [≈ £390]

Galloe, O.
- Natural History of the Danish Lichens. Original Investigations based on New Principles. Copenhagen: 1927-72. 10 vols. 4to. 1397 plates (some cold). Orig wraps.
                    (Wheldon & Wesley) **£120** [≈ $230]

Galton, Sir Francis
- Finger Prints. London: Macmillan, 1892. 1st edn. 8vo. xvi,216 pp. 16 plates, 34 tables, text

ills. Orig cloth, extremities somewhat rubbed.
(Rootenberg) **$500 [≈ £260]**
- Finger Prints. London: Macmillan, 1892. 1st
edn. 8vo. 216 pp. Plates. Orig maroon cloth,
unopened.   *(Chapel Hill)* **$475 [≈ £247]**
- Hereditary Genius: an Inquiry into Its Laws
and Consequences. London: Macmillan,
1869. 1st edn. 8vo. vi,[2],390 pp. 2 fldg
plates. Contemp half calf.
(Rootenberg) **$400 [≈ £208]**

Gamow, G.
- Constitution   of   Atomic   Nuclei   &
Radioactivity. Oxford: Clarendon Press,
1931. 8vo. 114 pp. 40 text figs. Cloth.
(Gemmary) **$50 [≈ £26]**

Gardiner, J.S.
- Coral Reefs and Atolls. London: 1931. 8vo.
xiii, 181 pp. Map, 15 plates, text figs. Cloth.
(Wheldon & Wesley) **£40 [≈ $76]**

Gardiner, W.
- The Flora of Forfarshire. London &
Edinburgh: 1848. 12mo. xxiv,308,4 pp. 2
plates. Stamp on title & reverse of frontis.
New cloth. *(Wheldon & Wesley)* **£55 [≈ $105]**

Gardner, J.
- Household Medicine ... London: 1861.
viii,520 pp. Sev ills. Sl foxing. Later cloth, sl
marked.   *(Whitehart)* **£35 [≈ $67]**

Gardner, Phyllis
- The Irish Wolfhound, a Short Historical
Sketch. Dundalk: Dundalgan, 1931. 8vo. 253
pp. Over 100 ills. Orig cloth bds.
(Emerald Isle) **£45 [≈ $86]**

Garner, R.L.
- Gorillas & Chimpanzees. London: 1896. 8vo.
Ills. Orig cloth, sl marked.
(Grayling) **£50 [≈ $95]**

Garnett, Thomas
- A Lecture on the Preservation of Health.
London: Cadell & Davies, 1800. 2nd edn.
12mo. [iv], vi,115 pp. Port, title vignette.
Lacks half-title. 19th c cloth.
(Burmester) **£70 [≈ $134]**

Garratt, Alfred
- Electro-Physiology   and   Electro-
Therapeutics; showing the Best Methods for
the Medical Use of Electricity. Boston: 1861.
2nd edn. 716 pp. 97 ills. Orig bndg.
(Fye) **$150 [≈ £78]**

Garretson, James E.
- A System of Oral Surgery. Phila: 1881. 3rd
edn. 916 pp. 9 plates, over 500 w'cuts.
Leather.   *(Fye)* **$275 [≈ £143]**

Garrison, Fielding
- History of Neurology ... see McHenry,
Lawrence.
- An Introduction to the History of Medicine.
Phila: 1914. 1st edn, 2nd printing. 763 pp.
Orig bndg.   *(Fye)* **$100 [≈ £52]**
- An Introduction to the History of Medicine.
Third Edition. Phila: 1924. 8vo. Orig cloth.
(Goodrich) **$75 [≈ £39]**
- An Introduction to the History of Medicine.
Phila: 1924. 3rd edn. 942 pp. Orig bndg.
(Fye) **$50 [≈ £26]**
- An Introduction to the History of Medicine.
Phila: 1963. 4th edn. 996 pp. Orig bndg.
(Fye) **$60 [≈ £31]**
- Notes on the History of Military Medicine.
Washington: 1922. 1st edn. 206 pp. Orig
wraps, chipped & taped. *(Fye)* **$125 [≈ £65]**
- The Principles of Anatomic Illustration
before Vesalius ... New York: 1926. 1st edn.
58 pp. Ex-lib.   *(Fye)* **$80 [≈ £41]**

Garrod, A.E.
- An Introduction to the Use of the
Laryngoscope. London: 1886. [vii],54 pp. 17
figs.   *(Whitehart)* **£35 [≈ $67]**

Gataker, T.
- Essays on Medical Subjects, originally
printed separately; to which is now prefixed
an Introduction relating to the Use of
Hemlock   and   Corrosive   Sublimate   ...
London: 1764. lii,284 pp. Contemp leather,
hinges sl weak.   *(Whitehart)* **£180 [≈ $345]**

Gatke, H.
- Heligoland as a Bird Observatory. The Birds
of Heligoland. London: 1895. Ills. Orig cloth,
t.e.g.   *(Grayling)* **£60 [≈ $115]**

Gatty, Mrs A.
- British Sea-Weeds, drawn from Professor
Harvey's "Phycologia Britannica". London:
1872. 2 vols. Roy 8vo. 80 cold plates (some sl
spotted). Orig cloth.
(Wheldon & Wesley) **£120 [≈ $230]**

Gee, G.E.
- The Goldsmith's Handbook. London: Crosby
Lockwood, 1881. Cr 8vo. xxii,259 pp. Cloth,
sl loose.   *(Gemmary)* **$75 [≈ £39]**
- The Practical Gold-Worker. London: Crosby

Lockwood, 1877. 8vo. xix,229 pp. Cloth.
(Gemmary) **$75 [≈ £39]**
- Recovering Precious Metals from Liquid Waste Residues. New York: Spon & Chamberlain, 1920. 8vo. viii,380 pp. 29 text figs. Cloth. *(Gemmary)* **$75 [≈ £40]**
- Silversmith's Handbook. London: Crosby Lockwood, 1921. 5th edn. Cr 8vo. xxx,222 pp. 40 text figs. Cloth.
(Gemmary) **$60 [≈ £31]**

Geikie, Archibald
- Earth Sculpture. London: 1909. 2nd edn. 8vo. xvi,320 pp. 10 plates, text figs. Orig cloth. *(Henly)* **£12 [≈ $23]**
- The Founders of Geology. Second Edition. London: Macmillan, 1905. 8vo. Sl foxing. Cvrs a little soiled, edges browned.
(Georges) **£50 [≈ $95]**
- The Founders of Geology. London: Macmillan, 1905. 2nd edn. 8vo. xi,486 pp. Some foxing. Cloth. *(Gemmary)* **$125 [≈ £65]**
- Fragments of Earth Lore, Sketches and Addresses, Geological and Geographical. London: 1893. Roy 8vo. v,428 pp. 6 fldg cold maps. Orig cloth. *(Henly)* **£18 [≈ $34]**
- Geological Sketches at Home and Abroad. London: 1882. x,382 pp. 29 text ills. Orig cloth, spine sl marked.
(Whitehart) **£18 [≈ $34]**
- Landscape in History and Other Essays. London: 1905. viii,352 pp. Orig cloth, sl dust stained. *(Whitehart)* **£18 [≈ $34]**
- Life of Sir Roderick Murchison. London: 1875. 2 vols. 2 pp carelessly opened. Orig cloth. *(Baldwin)* **£150 [≈ $287]**
- Prehistoric Europe. A Geological Sketch. Phila: Lippincott, 1881. 8vo. xviii,592 pp. 5 cold plates. Good ex-lib. Cloth, loose.
(Gemmary) **$40 [≈ £20]**
- The Scenery of Scotland Viewed in Connection with its Physical Geology. London: Macmillan, 1887. 2nd edn. xx,481 pp. 2 maps, 85 text figs. Cloth, unopened.
(Gemmary) **$50 [≈ £26]**
- The Scenery of Scotland Viewed in Connection with its Physical Geology. London: 1901. 3rd edn. xx,540 pp. 4 fldg maps, 110 figs. Orig cloth, dull, sl marked, front inner hinge cracked but firm.
(Whitehart) **£18 [≈ $34]**
- The Story of a Boulder or Gleanings from the Note-Book of a Field Geologist. London: 1858. xvi,263 pp. 34 text figs. Orig cloth, dull & dust stained, spine reprd.
(Whitehart) **£18 [≈ $34]**
- Text-Book of Geology. London: 1882. 1st

edn. 8vo. Frontis, text figs. Orig cloth, backstrip relaid. *(Henly)* **£28 [≈ $53]**
- Text-Book of Geology. London: Macmillan, 1882. 1st edn. 8vo. xi,971 pp. Orig green cloth, gilt spine, inner hinges cracked.
(Frew Mackenzie) **£40 [≈ $76]**
- Text-Book of Geology. Fourth Edition, revised and enlarged. London: 1903. 2 vols. 8vo. xxii,702,[2]; x,705-1472 pp. Fldg frontis, 508 figs. Endpapers spotted. Orig green cloth. *(Bow Windows)* **£48 [≈ $92]**

Geikie, James
- Fragments of Earth Lore: Sketches and Addresses, Geological and Geographical. Edinburgh: John Bartholomew, 1893. 1st edn. 8vo. [vii],428 pp. 6 cold fldg maps, sev text ills. Orig blue cloth, gilt spine.
(Gough) **£30 [≈ $57]**
- The Great Ice Age and its relation to the Antiquity of Man. London: 1874. 8vo. xxiii, 575 pp. 17 maps etc. Orig cloth.
(Wheldon & Wesley) **£40 [≈ $76]**
- Mountains, Their Origin, Growth and Decay. Edinburgh: 1913. 1st edn. 8vo. xix,311 pp. 82 plates, 57 text figs. Cloth.
(Bickersteth) **£20 [≈ $38]**
- Prehistoric Europe: a Geological Sketch. London: 1881. 1st edn. 8vo. xvi,592,[6 advt] pp. 5 cold plates, sev text figs. Sl marks. Inner hinges torn. Orig cloth, dull, spine ends & crnr tips worn. *(Bow Windows)* **£30 [≈ $57]**

Geminus, Thomas
- Compendiosa totius Anatomiae Delineatio. (Facsimile of the First English Edition of 1553). Introduction by Charles D. O'Malley. London: 1959. Folio. Sl foxing. Orig parchment bds, sl soiled.
(Goodrich) **$195 [≈ £101]**

Genet, Edmond Charles
- Memorial on the Upward Forces of Fluids, and their Applicability to Several Arts, Sciences, and Public Improvements ... Albany: Packard & Van Benthuysen, 1825. 1st edn. 8vo. 112 pp. 6 plates, fldg table. Minor browning. Red mor by Hembra.
(Rootenberg) **$1,750 [≈ £911]**

A Geological Primer ...
- A Geological Primer in Verse: with a Poetical Geognosy ... London: Longman, 1820. 1st edn. 8vo. xii, 68,[12 ctlg] pp. Orig bds, later cloth spine. Possibly by John Scafe.
(Burmester) **£85 [≈ $163]**

George, J.N.
- English Guns and Rifles ... An Account of the Development, Design & Usage of English Sporting Rifles & Shotguns from the 15th Century to the 19th Century. London: 1947. 1st edn. 8vo. Num ills. Dw.
  (Grayling) £70 [≈ $134]
- English Guns and Rifles. Being an Account of the Development, Design and Usage of English Sporting Rifles and Shotguns ... Plantersville, SC: Small-Arms Technical Publ Co, 1947. 344 pp. Ills. Orig cloth.
  (Moon) £45 [≈ $86]

Georgii, A. (ed.)
- Kinetic Jottings: Miscellaneous Extracts from Medical Literature, Ancient and Modern ... London: 1880. vii,267 pp. Occas sl foxing. Orig cloth, sl marked & worn.
  (Whitehart) £25 [≈ $47]

Gerhard, W.W.
- Lectures on the Diagnosis, Pathology, and Treatment of the Diseases of the Chest. Phila: 1842. 1st edn. 157 pp. Fldg cold plate. Half leather. *(Fye)* $250 [≈ £130]

Gesner, Abraham
- A Practical Treatise on Coal, Petroleum, and Other Distilled Oils. New York: Bailliere Bros, 1861. 1st edn. 8vo. 134,24 advt pp. Frontis. Orig cloth, rear cvr sl spotted.
  (Chapel Hill) $450 [≈ £234]

Gharpurey, K.G.
- The Snakes of India. Second Edition. Bombay: 1937. 8vo. [iv],[xii],167 pp. Plates, ills. Orig cloth. Dw (worn).
  (Bow Windows) £30 [≈ $57]

Gibbs, J.W. & Wilson, E.B.
- Vector Analysis. A Text-Book for the Use of Students of Mathematics and Physics. New Haven: (1901) 1922. xix,436 pp. Diags. Endpapers sl marked. Cloth, sl worn.
  (Whitehart) £38 [≈ $72]

Gibson, Charles R.
- Wireless Telegraphy and telephony without Wires. 1914. 1st edn. 156 pp. 9 photos, 19 ills. Orig bndg. Sgnd by the author.
  (New Wireless) $75 [≈ £50]
- Wireless Telegraphy and Telephony without Wires. 1914. 1st edn. 156 pp. 9 photos, 19 ills. Orig bndg. *(New Wireless)* $40 [≈ £20]

Gibson, Thomas
- The Anatomy of Human Bodies Epitomized.

Wherein all the Parts of Man's Body, with their Actions and Uses, are succinctly described ... Sixth Edition. London: 1703. 8vo. [xvi],vii,632 pp. 20 plates. V sl hole in title. Sl marg waterstain to a few ff. Orig calf.
  (Bickersteth) £225 [≈ $431]

Gibson, William
- A New Treatise on the Diseases of Horses ... London: A. Millar, 1751. 1st edn. Large Paper. 4to. [12],464,[12] pp. Frontis, 31 plates. Contemp MS receipts on intl blanks. Contemp calf, rebacked.
  (Rootenberg) $650 [≈ £338]

Gibson, William
- Young Endeavour. Contributions to Science by Medical Students of the Past Four Centuries. Foreword by Sir Henry Dale. Springfield: 1958. 8vo. Orig bndg.
  (Goodrich) $45 [≈ £23]

Gifford, Isabella
- The Marine Botanist ... British Sea-Weeds ... London: Darton & Co, [1848]. 1st edn. Sm 8vo. xxvii, 15-141 pp. 11 litho plates (3 & the title vignette hand cold). Orig cloth gilt, v sl faded & soiled. Some relevant insertions.
  (Beech) £45 [≈ $86]
- The Marine Botanist and Introduction to the Study of British Sea-Weeds. Brighton: 1853. 3rd edn, enlgd. Post 8vo. xl,357,[1] pp. 6 cold & 6 plain plates. Cloth.
  (Wheldon & Wesley) £30 [≈ $57]
- The Marine Botanist ... British Sea-Weeds ... Third Edition, greatly improved and enlarged ... Brighton: R. Folthorp, 1853. Lge 12mo. xl,357 pp, errata leaf, 8 advt pp. 12 plates (7 cold). Orig cloth. *(Fenning)* £38.50 [≈ $74]

Gihon, A.L.
- Practical Suggestions in Naval Hygiene. Washington, 1871. [8],151 pp. Sm lib stamp on title & endpaper. Orig linen bds, mrbld edges. *(Whitehart)* £20 [≈ $38]

Gilbert, W.
- The De Mundo of William Gilbert. A Facsimile with Commentary by S. Kelly. Amsterdam: 1965. 2 vols. Orig bndg.
  (Whitehart) £50 [≈ $95]
- On the Magnet. New York: Basic Books, 1958. 4to. xii,xiv, 247,67 pp. Text figs. Cloth. *(Gemmary)* $50 [≈ £26]

Gillespie, N.A.
- Endotracheal Anaesthesia. Wisconsin: 1941. xii, 187 pp. Cold frontis, 44 figs. Sm lib

stamp title verso. Orig bndg.
(Whitehart) £25 [≈ $47]

Gilmour, J. & Walters, M.
- Wild Flowers. London: Collins New naturalist, 1954. 1st edn. 8vo. xiv,242 pp. 32 cold & 24 plain plates. Orig cloth.
(Henly) £15 [≈ $28]

Gladstone, J.H.
- Michael Faraday. 1872. 1st edn. 223 pp. Orig bndg.   *(New Wireless)* $65 [≈ £33]

Glaister, J. & Brash, J.C.
- Medico-Legal Aspects of the Ruxton Case. Edinburgh: 1937. 1st edn. xvi,284 pp. 172 ills. Orig bndg.   *(Whitehart)* £40 [≈ $76]

Glanvil, Joseph
- Sadducismus Triumphatus: or, a Full and Plain Evidence concerning Witches and Apparitions ... The Fourth Edition, with Additions ... London: 1726. 8vo. [12],35, [10], 161,[4], [12], 223-498, [4 advt] pp. Frontis, 2 plates. Rec qtr calf.
(Fenning) £225 [≈ $431]

Glass, Samuel
- An Essay on Magnesia Alba ... Oxford: for R. Davies, 1764. Only edn. 8vo. 6,38 pp. Stitched as issued, uncut.
(Young's) £120 [≈ $230]

Glasse, Hannah
- The Art of Cookery made Plain and Easy ... A New Edition, with Modern Improvements. Alexandria (VA): Cotton & Stewart, 1805. 1st Amer edn. 12mo. Some water stains, sl foxing. Lacks a flyleaf. Contemp half calf, gilt spine, rubbed.   *(Ximenes)* $1,500 [≈ £781]
- The Complete Confectioner ... London: for J. Cooke, [ca 1765]. 8vo. iv,304,xvi pp. Some spotting, lacks endpapers. Contemp sheep, spine worn but sound.
(Burmester) £200 [≈ $383]

Glassington, C.W.
- Dental Materia Medica, Pharmacology and Therapeutics. London: 1896. ix,266 pp. Front jnt cracked but firm, cloth sl dull.
(Whitehart) £35 [≈ $67]

Glazebrook, R.T.
- Heat. Cambridge: UP, 1896. Stereotyped edn. Cr 8vo. x,230 pp. 88 text figs. Sl foxed. Ex-lib. Cloth.   *(Gemmary)* $37.50 [≈ £19]
- Light. Cambridge: UP, 1895. 2nd edn. Cr 8vo. x,213 pp. 134 text figs. Ex-lib. Cloth.

(Gemmary) $37.50 [≈ £19]

Glenister, A.G.
- The Birds of the Malay Peninsula, Singapore and Penang. London: (1951) 1955. 8vo. 296 pp. 8 cold plates, 74 ills. Cloth, inner jnts loose.   *(Wheldon & Wesley)* £30 [≈ $57]
- The Birds of the Malay Peninsula, Singapore & Penang. London: (1951) 1959. 8vo. 282 pp. Cold plates. Orig cloth. Dw.
(Terramedia) $50 [≈ £26]

Glover, Mary Baker
- Science and Health ... see Eddy, Mary Baker.

Goddard, Robert H.
- A Method of reaching Extreme Altitudes. Washington: Smithsonian, 1919. 1st edn. 8vo. [4],69,[1] pp. 10 plates from photos. Orig wraps, uncut. *(Rootenberg)* $2,200 [≈ £1,145]

Godlee, Sir R.J.
- Lord Lister. Oxford: 1924. 8vo. 15 plates (1 cold), sev text ills. Sev ff carelessly opened. Orig bndg.   *(Bow Windows)* £40 [≈ $76]

Godman, John D.
- Addresses delivered on Various Public Occasions ... A Brief Explanation of the Injurious Effects of Tight Lacing ... Phila: 1829. 8vo. 194 pp. Orig bds, uncut, rebacked.
(Goodrich) $125 [≈ £65]

Godwin, H.
- The History of the British Flora; A Factual Basis for Phytogeography. Cambridge: UP, 1956. 4to. viii,384 pp. 26 plates, 118 text ills. Orig cloth.   *(Gough)* £28 [≈ $53]

Goebel, K. von & Bower, H.M.
- Wilhelm Hofmeister. The Work and Life of a 19th Century Botanist. With Biographical Supplement ... London: Ray Society, 1926. xi, 202 pp. Frontis, 2 facs letters, 3 text figs.
(Whitehart) £18 [≈ $34]

Golding, Benjamin
- Historical Account of the Origin and Progress of St Thomas's Hospital, Southwark. London: Longman ..., [1819]. 1st edn. 12mo. xxiii, 245 pp, errata leaf. Lib stamp on title. Orig bds, uncut, spine ends sl worn, upper jnt cracked.   *(Bickersteth)* £65 [≈ $124]

Goldsmith, Alfred N.
- Radio Facsimile. 1938. 1st edn. 353 pp. Orig wraps.   *(New Wireless)* $25 [≈ £13]
- Radio Telephony. 1918. 1st edn. 247 pp. 110

photos, 116 ills. Orig bndg.
(New Wireless) **$25 [≈ £13]**

Goldsmith, Oliver
- Natural History with Notes. Edited by Henry Innes. A Complete Vade-mecum of Modern Discovery, with a Life of Goldsmith by Moir Bussey. London: [ca 1850]. 472,7 pp. Num w'cut ills. Sl browning. Qtr leather, rebacked, shelf wear.   *(Boswell)* **$50 [≈ £26]**

Goodchild, W.
- Precious Stones. London: Constable, 1908. 8vo. x,309 pp. Ills. Cloth.
(Gemmary) **$50 [≈ £26]**

Gooders, J. (ed.)
- Birds of the World. London: [1969-71]. 10 vols (inc vol 10 'Gallery of Birds'). 4to. 3040 pp. Num ills. Titles supplied in xerox. Orig loose leaf binders, vol 9 binder sl worn.
(Wheldon & Wesley) **£100 [≈ $191]**

Goodeve, T.M.
- Text-Book on the Steam Engine. Fifth Edition. London: Crosby Lockwood, 1883. 8vo. viii,296, [32,16 ctlg] pp. Frontis, text ills. Orig cloth, a little rubbed.
(Claude Cox) **£25 [≈ $47]**

Goodfield, G.J.
- The Growth of Scientific Physiology: The Physiological Method and the Mechanist-Vitalist Controversy ... London: 1960. 1st edn. 174 pp. Dw.   *(Fye)* **$30 [≈ £15]**

Goodison, N.
- English Barometers 1680-1860. A History of Domestic Barometers and their Makers and Retailers. London: Cassell, 1977. 2nd edn. 4to. 388 pp. 194 text ills. Cloth. Dw.
(Gemmary) **$65 [≈ £33]**

Goodman, Herman
- Story of Electricity. 1928. 1st edn. 62 pp. 12 ills. Orig bndg.   *(New Wireless)* **$35 [≈ £18]**

Goodspeed, T.H.
- Plant Hunters in the Andes. London: n.d. 8vo. xvi,429 pp. 65 plates. Orig cloth.
(Henly) **£30 [≈ $57]**

Gordon, C.F.C.
- Clockmaking Past and Present ... London: 1925. viii,232 pp. 35 plates, 29 text figs. 1 plate loose. Orig cloth.
(Whitehart) **£35 [≈ $67]**

Gordon, Charles
- Experiences of an Army Surgeon in India. London: 1872. 1st edn. 168 pp. Ex-lib.
(Fye) **$150 [≈ £78]**

Gordon, G.
- Collectanea for a Flora of Moray. Elgin: 1839. viii,40 pp. Orig bds, cloth spine. Anon.
(Wheldon & Wesley) **£35 [≈ $67]**

Gordon, George
- An Introduction to Geography, Astronomy, and Dialling ... London: Senex, Strahan ... & the author, 1726. 1st edn. 8vo. [xii],iv, 188, 40 pp. 11 engvs on 10 fldg plates. 19th c half calf, rubbed, rebacked.
(Burmester) **£120 [≈ $230]**

Gordon, J.E.H.
- A Physical Treatise on Electricity and Magnetism. London: Sampson Low, 1891. 3rd edn. 2 vols. 8vo. xx,343; xx,332 pp. 73 cold & b/w plates, 312 text figs. Orig dec cloth.   *(Gemmary)* **$125 [≈ £65]**

Gordon, Maurice
- Aesculapius Comes to the Colonies. The Story of the Early Days of Medicine in the Thirteen Original Colonies. Ventnor, NJ: Ventnor Publishers, 1949. 8vo. Plates. Dw (sl frayed).   *(Georges)* **£35 [≈ $67]**

Gore, G.
- The Art of Electro-Metallurgy including All Known Processes of Electro-Deposition. London: 1877. xx,391 pp. Frontis, 56 text ills. Orig cloth, dull. *(Whitehart)* **£25 [≈ $47]**

Gore, George
- The Art of Scientific Discovery of the General Conditions and Methods of Research in Physics and Chemistry. London: Longman, 1876. 1st edn. 8vo. xx,648 pp. Ctlg at end. Orig tan cloth, sl rubbed.
(Burmester) **£55 [≈ $105]**

Gosse, Philip Henry
- Actinologia Britannica, a History of the British Sea-Anemones and Corals. London: 1860. 8vo. xl,362 pp. 12 plates (11 cold). Orig dec cloth, sm split rear jnt.
(Wheldon & Wesley) **£70 [≈ $134]**
- The Aquarium ... Second Edition, Revised and Enlarged. London: Van Voorst, 1856. 8vo. xvi, 304, 6 advt pp. 6 mtd cold lithos, 7 w'engvs. A few sl marks. Orig green cloth, a.e.g., recased.   *(Beech)* **£48 [≈ $92]**
- The Birds of Jamaica. London: 1847. Cr 8vo.

x,447 pp. Half mor, trifle rubbed.
(Wheldon & Wesley) **£75** [≈ **$143**]
- Evenings at the Microscope. New York: P.F.
Collier, 1895. 8vo. xvi,434 pp. Text figs.
Cloth, faded.   *(Gemmary)* **$30** [≈ **£15**]
- A Naturalist's Rambles on the Devonshire
Coast. London: 1853. 1st edn. xvi,451 pp. 28
plates (some cold). 1 advt leaf. Ink inscrptn on
endpaper. Orig cloth, rather faded, sl worn.
(Whitehart) **£50** [≈ **$95**]
- The Ocean. London: [1854]. xii,360 pp. 52
ills. Page edges sl foxed. Orig cloth, sl worn,
new front endpaper. *(Whitehart)* **£40** [≈ **$76**]
- The Romance of Natural History, with
Illustrations by Wolf. London: James Nisbet,
n.d. 2 vols. 368; 393 pp. Some spotting.
Green buckram, wear & darkening to spines.
(Boswell) **$68** [≈ **£35**]
- Tenby: A Seaside Holiday. London: Van
Voorst, 1856. 1st edn. 8vo. xix,400,[12 advt]
pp. 24 cold lithos. Orig green cloth, spine sl
discold, sl rubbed.
(Frew Mackenzie) **£140** [≈ **$268**]
- Tenby: A Seaside Holiday. London: 1856.
12mo. xviii,400 pp. 20 cold & 4 plain plates.
Orig cloth.   *(Henly)* **£98** [≈ **$188**]
- A Text-Book of Zoology, for Schools.
London: SPCK, 1851. 1st edn. 12mo. [ii],450
pp. W'engvd ills. New front endpaper. Orig
cloth, spine ends sl worn.
(Claude Cox) **£30** [≈ **$57**]
- A Year at the Shore. London: 1865. 1st edn.
8vo. xii,330,[2 advt] pp. 36 cold ills (1 sl
marked). Orig cloth.
(Bow Windows) **£80** [≈ **$153**]

Gould, G.M. & Pyle, W.L.
- Anomalies and Curiosities of Medicine being
an Encyclopedic Collection of Rare and
Extraordinary Cases ... New York: 1956.
Reprint of 1896 edn. 12 plates, 295 ills. Dw.
(Goodrich) **$75** [≈ **£39**]

Gould, John
- Birds of New Guinea. Text by A. Rutgers.
London: 1970. Roy 8vo. 160 cold plates.
Cloth.   *(Wheldon & Wesley)* **£25** [≈ **$47**]
- Birds of South America ... Text by A.
Rutgers. London: (1972). Lge 8vo. 321 pp,
inc 160 cold plates. Orig cloth. Dw.
(Bow Windows) **£30** [≈ **$57**]
- An Introduction to the Birds of Great Britain.
London: for the author, 1873. 1st edn.
iv,135,14 subscribers, 4 prospectus pp. Orig
red cloth gilt, fine.   *(Gough)* **£60** [≈ **$115**]
- Mr. Gould's Tropical Birds, comprising 24
Plates selected from John Gould's Folios ...

Edited by E. Mannering. London: 1955. One
of 1000. Folio. 24 cold plates. Cloth backed
bds, slipcase.
(Wheldon & Wesley) **£50** [≈ **$95**]

Gould, William
- An Account of English Ants ... London: for
A. Millar, 1747. 1st edn. Sm 8vo. Final advt
leaf. New sprinkled calf, label.
(Georges) **£400** [≈ **$767**]

Gowers, W.R.
- The Diagnosis and Diseases of the Spinal
Cord. London: 1881. 2nd edn. 86 pp. Ills.
Orig bndg, fine.   *(Fye)* **$200** [≈ **£104**]
- The Diagnosis of Diseases of the Spinal Cord.
With Additions and Illustrations ... Second
Edition. London: 1881. 8vo. viii,86 pp. Ills.
Hole in a front blank. Orig bndg.
(Goodrich) **$175** [≈ **£91**]
- Diagnosis of Diseases of the Brain and Spinal
Cord. New York: 1885. 1st Amer edn. 293
pp. Orig bndg.   *(Fye)* **$150** [≈ **£78**]
- Epilepsy and Other Chronic Convulsive
Diseases: their Causes, Symptoms, and
Treatment. London: 1901. 2nd edn. 320 pp.
Orig bndg.   *(Fye)* **$125** [≈ **£65**]
- Lectures on the Diagnosis of Diseases of the
Brain. Phila: 1885. 1st Amer edn. 246 pp.
Orig bndg.   *(Fye)* **$225** [≈ **£117**]
- Subjective Sensations of Sight and Sound,
Abiotrophy, and Other Lectures. Phila:
Blakiston, 1904. 8vo. 250 pp. Ills. Orig bndg,
internally good ex-lib.
(Goodrich) **$125** [≈ **£65**]

Gowland, W.
- The Metallurgy of Non-Ferrous Metals.
London: Griffin, 1943. 8vo. xxxii,633 pp. 5
plates, 217 text figs. Cloth.
(Gemmary) **$50** [≈ **£26**]

Graham, Harvey
- Eternal Eve. London: 1950. xx,699 pp.
Frontis, 20 plates, 20 text figs. Orig cloth.
(Whitehart) **£25** [≈ **$47**]
- Eternal Eve. The History of Gynaecology and
Obstetrics. Garden City: 1951. 1st Amer edn.
8vo. 699 pp. Ills. Dw. *(Goodrich)* **$65** [≈ **£33**]
- The Story of Surgery. With a Foreword by
Oliver St. John Gogarty. New York: 1939. 1st
edn. 8vo. 425 pp. Orig bndg.
(Goodrich) **$25** [≈ **£13**]
- Surgeons All. London: [1939]. xv,17-426 pp.
Frontis, 23 plates. Orig bndg.
(Whitehart) **£18** [≈ **$34**]

Graham, Henry Davenport
- The Birds of Iona and Mull, 1852-1870 . . Edinburgh: David Douglas, 1890. 1st edn. xv, 279, 15 advt pp. 78 plates & ills. Occas sl spotting. Orig green cloth, sl faded.
(Gough) £55 [≈$105]

Graham, James
- The General State of Medical Chirurgical Practice, Exhibited, shewing them to be Inadequate, Ineffectual, Absurd and Ridiculous ... Sixth Edition. London: 1779. 12mo. 248 pp. Rec leatherette.
(Hemlock) $300 [≈£156]

Graham, T. (ed.)
- Chemical Reports and Memoirs, on Atomic Volume, Isomorphism, Endosmosis ... London: Cavendish Society, 1848. vii,370,15 pp. 2 fldg plates. Sm lib stamp on title. Orig cloth, t.e.g., stained, edges worn, rebacked.
(Whitehart) £35 [≈$67]

Graham, Thomas J.
- A Treatise on Indigestion. With Observations on some Painful Complaints ... Tic Doloureux, Nervous Disorders ... Phila: 1831. 1st Amer edn. 8vo. Orig bndg, uncut.
(Goodrich) $45 [≈£23]
- A Treatise on Indigestion: with Observations on some Painful Complaints originating in Indigestion, especially Mental Aberration. London: Simpkin, 1833. 3rd edn, rvsd. 8vo. Cloth backed bds.
(Young's) £28 [≈$53]

Graham, William
- The Art of Making Wines from Fruits, Flowers, and Herbs, all the Native growth of Great Britain ... New Edition. Revised, Corrected, and greatly Enlarged. London: for R. Baldwin, 1783. 8vo. [iv],68 pp. New bds.
(Georges) £250 [≈$479]

Graham-Smith, G.S.
- Flies in Relation to Disease. Non-Bloodsucking Flies. Cambridge: 1914. 2nd edn. 8vo. xvi,389 pp. 27 plates, 20 charts, 32 text figs. Lib stamp on title. Orig cloth, sl rubbed & discold. *(Bickersteth)* £28 [≈$53]

Grainger, R.D.
- Elements of General Anatomy, containing an Outline of the Organization of the Human Body. London: 1829. 1st edn. xxvi,526 pp. New linen backed bds.
(Whitehart) £40 [≈$76]
- Elements of General Anatomy, containing an Outline of the Organization of the Human Body. London: 1829. 1st edn. xxvi,526 pp. Occas foxing. Ink sgntr on blank. Half cloth, sl rubbed & worn. *(Whitehart)* £25 [≈$47]

Grant, J.C. Boileau
- A Method of Anatomy, Descriptive and Deductive. London: 1938. 1st edn. 8vo. xx,650 pp. Orig cloth.
(Bickersteth) £25 [≈$47]

Grant, R.
- Catalogue of 6415 Stars for the Epoch 1870 ... Glasgow: 1883. lxvi,793 pp. Orig cloth.
(Whitehart) £35 [≈$67]
- History of Physical Astronomy, from the Earliest Ages to the Middle of the Nineteenth Century ... London: [1852]. xx,638 pp. Title sl foxed. New amateur qtr leather, paper label. *(Whitehart)* £30 [≈$57]

Graves, R.J.
- Clinical Lectures on the Practice of Medicine. Dublin: 1864. 2nd edn. xxvii,873 pp. Orig cloth, backstrip relaid.
(Whitehart) £45 [≈$86]

Gravesande, W.J.
- Mathematical Elements of Natural Philosophy confirmed by Experiments, or an Introduction to Sir Isaac Newton's Philosophy [Vol 1] ... London: 1720. 1st English edn. xxii, 259, [2] pp. 33 fldg plates (2 loose). 2 sm marg reprs. Contemp leather, new endpapers, spine sl worn. Vol 2 was published later (1721).
(Whitehart) £180 [≈$345]

Gray, A.
- Absolute Measurements in Electricity & Magnetism. London: Macmillan, 1889. 2nd edn. Sm 8vo. xix,384 pp. 66 text figs. Ex-lib. Cloth. *(Gemmary)* $50 [≈£26]
- The Botanical Text-Book. New York: 1842. 1st edn. 8vo. 413 pp. 78 text figs. Sound ex-lib. Sl foxed. Cloth.
(Wheldon & Wesley) £38 [≈$72]

Gray, Henry
- Anatomy Descriptive and Surgical. London: John W. Parker, 1858. 1st edn. 8vo (258 x 154 mm). 750,4 advt pp. Half-title. 363 text ills. Orig cloth, backstrip relaid.
(Rootenberg) $2,500 [≈£1,302]
- Anatomy, Descriptive and Surgical. Phila: 1862. 2nd Amer edn. 816 pp. Ills. Leather, 1-inch tear in hinge. *(Fye)* $300 [≈£156]
- Anatomy Descriptive and Surgical. Edited by T. Holmes. London: 1864. 3rd edn. xxxii,

788 pp. 394 ills. Orig cloth, worn, sl marked, rebacked. *(Whitehart)* **£60 [≈ $115]**
- Anatomy Descriptive and Surgical. London: 1866. 4th edn. xxiv,788 pp. 394 text ills. Orig cloth, worn, part of backstrip relaid, edges & crnrs worn. *(Whitehart)* **£40 [≈ $76]**
- Anatomy Descriptive and Surgical. London: 1890. 12th edn. xxxvi,1051 pp. 605 text ills. Orig cloth, v sl worn. *(Whitehart)* **£15 [≈ $28]**
- On the Structure and Use of the Spleen. London: 1854. 8vo. 380 pp. Text ills. Lib stamp on title. Orig cloth.
 (Goodrich) **$495 [≈ £257]**

Gray, John
- A Treatise on Gunnery. London: for William Innys, 1731. 2nd edn. 8vo. [iv],xliii,94 pp. 1 fldg plate, 2 engvd text figs, num w'cut text figs. Orig calf. *(Bickersteth)* **£350 [≈ $671]**

Gray, Robert & Anderson, Thomas
- The Birds of Ayrshire and Wigtown. Glasgow: Thomas Murray & Son, 1849. 1st edn. 62 pp. Cold litho frontis. Contemp qtr roan, uncut, spine sl worn at ft.
 (Gough) **£60 [≈ $115]**

Gray, S.F.
- The Operative Chemist; being a Practical Display of the Arts and Manufactures which depend upon Chemical Principles. London: 1828. xiv,882 pp. 100 plates & figs. Marg reprs at start. Sl foxing. Orig bds, rubbed & worn, new cloth spine.
 (Whitehart) **£120 [≈ $230]**
- A Supplement to the Pharmacopoeia: being a Treatise on Pharmacology in General ... together with a Collection of the most useful Medical Formulae ... London: 1828. 4th edn. lvi, 528,[1] pp. Edges last few pp sl water stained. New three qtr roan, uncut.
 (Whitehart) **£45 [≈ $86]**

Gray, Samuel O.
- British Sea-Weeds ... London: L. Reeve, [1867]. 1st edn. xxiii,312,16 advt pp. 16 cold plates. Orig pict green cloth gilt.
 (Gough) **£38 [≈ $72]**

Green, A.R.
- Sundials. New York: Macmillan, 1926. 8vo. 203 pp. Num ills. Cloth.
 (Gemmary) **$60 [≈ £31]**

Green, E.R.R.
- The Industrial Archaeology of County Down. Belfast: 1963. 4to. Ills. Dw.
 (Emerald Isle) **£45 [≈ $86]**

Green, Henry
- A Treatise on the Diseases of the Air Passages ... New York: 1846. 1st edn. 276 pp. 7 hand cold plates. Orig bndg, fine. Ex-lib U.S. Patent Office. *(Fye)* **$400 [≈ £208]**

The Green-House Companion ...
- See Loudon, J.C.

Greene, W.T. (ed.)
- Birds I Have Kept in Years Gone By. London: 1885. 8vo. viii,198 pp. 16 hand cold plates. Orig cloth.
 (Wheldon & Wesley) **£36 [≈ $69]**
- Favourite Foreign Birds for Cages and Aviaries. London: 1891. 8vo. vii,124 pp. 38 text figs. Cloth, spine soiled.
 (Wheldon & Wesley) **£20 [≈ $38]**
- Notes on Cage Birds: by Various Hands. First and Second Series. London: 1882-89. 2 vols. Cr 8vo. Orig cloth, vol 1 rather used with lower jnt torn.
 (Wheldon & Wesley) **£36 [≈ $69]**

Greenewalt, Crawford H.
- Humming Birds. New York: 1960. 1st printing. 4to. xxi,250 pp. 70 cold plates, num ills. Buckram.
 (Wheldon & Wesley) **£160 [≈ $307]**
- Hummingbirds. Garden City, New York: Doubleday & Page for the Amer Museum of Nat Hist, (1960). 4to. xvi,250,xxi pp. 69 mtd cold plates inc frontis, text ills. Orig cloth gilt. Dw. *(Karmiole)* **$200 [≈ £104]**

Greenish, H.G. & Collin, E.
- An Anatomical Atlas of Vegetable Powders. London: Churchill, 1904. 1st edn. 4to. 287 pp. 128 plates. Orig cloth, sl wear to edges, rehinged, new endpapers.
 (Savona) **£35 [≈ $67]**

Greenstreet, W.J. (ed.)
- Isaac Newton 1642-1727. A Memorial Volume edited for the Mathematical Association. London: 1927. viii,181 pp. Frontis port, 8 plates. Endpapers v sl foxed. Spine faded. *(Whitehart)* **£30 [≈ $57]**

Greenwood, George
- The Tree-Lifter; or, a New Method of Transplanting Forest Trees. London: Longman ..., 1844. 1st edn. 8vo. 112,32 ctlg pp. Fldg frontis (sl foxed). Orig dec green cloth, uncut & unopened, spine sunned & cloth splitting, crnrs knocked.
 (Finch) **£48 [≈ $92]**

Greenwood, Major
- Epidemics and Crowd-Diseases. An Introduction to the Study of Epidemiology. London: Williams & Norgate, 1935. 1st edn. 8vo. 409 pp. Orig cloth gilt, spine sl faded.
(Hollett) **£40 [≈ $76]**

Greenwood, W.H.
- A Manual of Metallurgy. London: 1885. 2 vols. 344; 371 pp. 139 ills. Name on titles. Three qtr roan, v sl rubbed.
(Whitehart) **£45 [≈ $86]**

Greg, R.P. & Lettsom, W.G.
- Manual of the Mineralogy of Great Britain and Ireland. London: Van Voorst, 1858. 8vo. xvi, 483 pp. Num text ills. Cloth, worn.
(Gemmary) **$175 [≈ £91]**
- Manual of the Mineralogy of Great Britain and Ireland (London, 1858). Kent: Lapidary Publications, 1977. 8vo. xvi,483,lxvii pp. Num text ills. Cloth. Dw.
(Gemmary) **$60 [≈ £31]**

Gregory, D.F.
- Examples of the Processes of the Differential and Integral Calculus. Cambridge: 1841. 1st edn. viii,524 pp. 62 figs on fldg plates. Some marks, ink notes on 1st few pp. Orig cloth, sl marked & warped. *(Whitehart)* **£40 [≈ $76]**
- Examples of the Processes of the Differential and Integral Calculus. Edited by W. Walton. Cambridge: 1846. 2nd edn. x,529 pp. 62 figs on fldg plates. Later cloth.
(Whitehart) **£40 [≈ $76]**
- Examples of the Processes of the Differential and Integral Calculus ... Edited by William Walton. Cambridge: 1846. 2nd edn. 8vo. x,529 pp. 4 fldg diags. Contemp half calf, sl rubbed. *(Young's)* **£24 [≈ $46]**

Gregory, George
- The Economy of Nature explained and illustrated on the Principles of Modern Philosophy ... London: J. Johnson, 1796. 1st edn. 3 vols. xxiii,543; xv,592; xvi,569,[6] pp. Plates. New cloth. *(Wreden)* **$275 [≈ £143]**
- Treatise on the Theory and Practice of Physic. With Notes and Additions, adapted to the Practice of the United States by Nathaniel Potter and S. Calhoun. Phila: 1836. 1st Amer edn. 2 vols. 8vo. 2 plates (1 cold). Some foxing. Sheep, sl worn.
(Goodrich) **$95 [≈ £49]**

Gregory, J.C.
- A Short History of Atomism from Democritus to Bohr. London: 1931. 258 pp.

A few text figs.   *(Whitehart)* **£30 [≈ $57]**

Gregory, John
- A Comparative View of the State and Faculties of Man with those of the Animal World. London: Dodsley, 1765. 1st edn. Sm 8vo. Contemp calf gilt, spine worn. Anon.
(Hannas) **£75 [≈ $143]**
- A Comparative View of the State and Faculties of Man with those of the Animal World. A New Edition. London: Dodsley, 1785. 8vo. [4],xx,286,[9] pp. Half-title. Lacks a blank flyleaf. Contemp calf gilt.
(Hannas) **£45 [≈ $86]**

Gregory, Olinthus
- Elements of Plane & Spherical Trigonometry. With their Applications to Heights and Distances, Projections of the Sphere, Dialling Astronomy ... London: 1816. 1st edn. x,[1],244, [245-52 ctlg] pp. Orig bds, uncut.
(Whitehart) **£25 [≈ $47]**
- Mathematics for Practical Men: being a Commonplace Book of Pure and Mixed Mathematics chiefly designed for the Use of Civil Engineers, Architects and Surveyors. London: 1848. 3rd edn, rvsd by Henry Law. xix, 392,118 pp. Lge fldg table, 13 plates. Three qtr leather, sl worn.
(Whitehart) **£40 [≈ $76]**
- Memoirs of the Life, Writings, and Character of the late John Mason Good, MD ... London: 1828. 8vo. [4],472 pp. Frontis. Polished calf. Author's pres copy to David Hosack. *(Goodrich)* **$150 [≈ £78]**

Gregory, William
- Letter to a Candid Inquirer on Animal Magnetism. London: Taylor, Walton, Maberley; Edinburgh: MacLachlan & Stewart, 1851. 1st edn. 8vo. xxii, [2],528 pp. Orig blue cloth, uncut, dust soiled, sl rubbed.
(Claude Cox) **£40 [≈ $76]**

Greig, John
- The Flower-Grower's Instructor; or, the Temple of Flora: comprising the Rudiments of Botany, and Instructions for ... Cultivation ... London: Dean & Munday, [ca 1840]. Sm 8vo. 68 pp. 6 plates (inc 4 hand cold). Orig limp cloth, rear cvr mottled. MS insert.
(Spelman) **£60 [≈ $115]**

Greville, R.K.
- Scottish Cryptogamic Flora ... Edinburgh: 1823-28. 1st edn. 6 vols. 8vo. 360 hand cold plates. Contemp MS indexes. Lacks half-titles. Contemp diced calf gilt.
(Henly) **£990 [≈ $1,900]**

Grew, Nehemiah
- The Anatomy of Plants ... London: 1682. Folio. [xxii],24,[x], 304,[20] pp. Usual mispagination at pp 213-220. 83 plates (plate 15 is numbered 6). Sl used, last 3 plates mtd. Mod calf, antique style.
(Wheldon & Wesley) **£550 [≈ $1,055]**
- The Anatomy of Vegetables Begun ... London: for Spencer Highman, 1672. 1st edn. 8vo. 16 ff, 198 pp, 11 ff. 2 (of 3) plates. Contemp calf, front hinge starting. Wing G.1946. *(Hemlock)* **$875 [≈ £455]**
- Musaeum Regalis Societatis ... whereunto is subjoyned the Comparative Anatomy of Stomachs and Guts. London: W. Rawlins, for the author, 1681. 1st edn. 2 parts in one vol. Folio. [12],386,[4], [2],43 pp. 31 plates. Port frontis. Orig calf, rebacked. Wing G.1952
(Rootenberg) **$950 [≈ £494]**

Grey of Falloden, Viscount
- The Charm of Birds. London: 1927. 1st edn, 1st imp. 8vo. xii,243 pp. W'cut decs. Orig cloth, spine faded. *(Henly)* **£25 [≈ $47]**

Grey, C.H.
- Hardy Bulbs. Vol.1. Iridaceae. London: 1937. Roy 8vo. xxvi,403 pp. 15 cold plates, 32 ills. Ownership labels inside front cvr. Orig cloth, front cvr marked.
(Wheldon & Wesley) **£80 [≈ $153]**
- Hardy Bulbs. Vol.2. Amaryllidaceae ... London: 1938. Roy 8vo. viii,368 pp. 10 cold plates, 37 ills. V sl foxing. Cloth, sl marked.
(Wheldon & Wesley) **£80 [≈ $153]**

Grey, Thomas de
- The Compleat Horseman and Expert Farrier. In Two Books. London: Thomas Harper ..., 1639. 1st edn. Folio. Frontis, facing leaf of explanation. Sl soil at beginning, few minor stains. Contemp calf, some rubbing, spine sl worn. STC 12206.
(Ximenes) **$1,200 [≈ £625]**

Griesinger, W.
- Mental Pathology and Therapeutics. Translated by C.L. Robertson and J. Rutherford. London: New Sydenham Soc, 1867. xiv, 530 pp. Page edges marked. Orig cloth. *(Whitehart)* **£40 [≈ $76]**

Grieve, M.
- A Modern Herbal ... Edited by Mrs C.F. leyel. London: 1931. 2 vols. 8vo. 96 plates. Orig cloth, crnrs sl bumped.
(Wheldon & Wesley) **£70 [≈ $134]**

Grieve, S.
- The Great Auk, or Garefowl (Alca impennis, Linn.) Its History, Archaeology, and Remains. London: 1885. 4to. xi,141,58 pp. Cold map, 4 plates (2 cold), 6 ills. Trifle foxed. Lib b'plate. Orig cloth, trifle used.
(Wheldon & Wesley) **£185 [≈ $355]**

Griffin, J.J.
- A System of Crystallography with Its Application to Mineralogy. Glasgow: Richard Griffin, 1841. 8vo. xxvii,346,143 pp. Num diags. Cloth, worn. *(Gemmary)* **$375 [≈ £195]**

Griffith, J.E.
- The Flora of Anglesey and Carnarvonshire. Bangor: [1895]. 8vo. xx,288 pp. Map. Cloth.
(Wheldon & Wesley) **£40 [≈ $76]**

Griffith, John W.
- An Elementary Text-Book of the Microscope. London: Van Voorst, 1864. Lge 12mo. 16 inserted advt pp at end dated January 1863. Frontis & 11 other hand cold plates. Orig cloth, gilt spine (sl chipped at hd).
(Sanders) **£22 [≈ $42]**
- An Elementary Text-Book of the Microscope ... London: Van Voorst, 1864. 1st edn. Sm 8vo. [10],192,16 advt pp. 12 cold plates. Front flyleaf removed. Orig cloth.
(Fenning) **£28.50 [≈ $55]**

Griffith, John W. & Henfrey, A.
- The Micrographic Dictionary: a Guide to the Examination and Investigation of the Structure and Nature of Microscopic Objects. London: 1856. xl,696 pp. 41 plates, 816 w'cuts. Occas foxing. Titled in ink on bottom page edges. Mrbld endpapers with linen at hinges *(Whitehart)* **£35 [≈ $67]**
- The Micrographic Dictionary. London: Van Voorst, 1860. 2 vols in one (text & plates). 8vo. xl,752 pp. 45 plates (many cold). Half leather & bds, worn.
(Gemmary) **$175 [≈ £91]**
- The Micrographic Dictionary: a Guide to the Examination and Investigation of the Structure and Nature of Microscopic Objects. London: 1875. 3rd edn. 2 vols. xli,845 pp. 48 plates, 812 text fig. Half roan, rubbed & worn. *(Whitehart)* **£40 [≈ $76]**

Griffith, R. Eglesfeld
- Medical Botany: or Descriptions of the most Important Plants used in Medicine ... Phila: 1847. 1st edn. 704 pp. Over 300 w'cut ills. Orig bndg, front bd detached, part of lower spine missing. *(Fye)* **$175 [≈ £91]**

Griffits, Thomas Edgar
- Colour Printing. A Practical Demonstration of Colour Printing, by Letter-Press, Photo-Offset Lithography and Drawn Lithography ... London: Faber, 1948. 2 vols. Lge 8vo. 10 lge fldg colour charts in cloth folder. Cut-out guide. Slipcase, rubbed.
(Spelman) **£45 [≈ $86]**

Grigg, E.R.N.
- The Trail of the Invisible Light. From X-Strahlen to Radio(bio)logy. Springfield: 1965. xlii,974 pp. Num text ills. Orig bndg.
(Whitehart) **£60 [≈ $115]**

Grimshaw, A.
- The Horse. A Bibliography of British Books 1851-1976. London: 1982. One of 1000 sgnd. xxxiv, 474 pp. Ills. Cloth. Dw.
(Henly) **£33 [≈ $63]**

Grindon, Leo H.
- The Manchester Flora: a Descriptive List of the Plants growing within Eighteen Miles of Manchester. London: 1859. Cr 8vo. ix,575 pp. Orig cloth, trifle worn.
(Wheldon & Wesley) **£30 [≈ $57]**
- The Shakespere Flora ... With Comments and Botanical Particulars. Manchester: Palmer & Howe, 1883. 2nd edn. xi,318 pp. 5 plates. Orig dec blue cloth, gilt spine, t.e.g., back bd v sl marked. *(Gough)* **£40 [≈ $76]**

Grodzinski, P.
- Diamond Technology. London: N.A.G. Press, 1953. 2nd edn. 8vo. xxiv,784 pp. 486 ills, 93 tables. Cloth. *(Gemmary)* **$75 [≈ £40]**

Grollman, Arthur
- The Cardiac Output of Man in Health and Disease. Springfield: 1932. 1st edn. 325 pp. Orig bndg. *(Fye)* **$150 [≈ £78]**

Gross, Robert E.
- The Surgery of Infancy and Childhood. Its Principles and Techniques. Phila: 1953. 1000 pp. Ills. Orig bndg. *(Goodrich)* **$65 [≈ £33]**

Gross, Samuel D.
- Elements of Pathological Anatomy. Phila: 1857. 3rd edn. 770 pp. 342 w'cut ills. Leather. *(Fye)* **$250 [≈ £130]**
- A Practical Treatise on Foreign Bodies in the Air-Passages. Phila: 1854. 1st edn. 468 pp. Orig bndg. *(Fye)* **$400 [≈ £208]**
- A Practical Treatise on the Diseases and Injuries of the Urinary Bladder, the Prostate Gland, and the Urethra. Phila: 1851. 1st edn.

726 pp. Orig bndg. *(Fye)* **$400 [≈ £208]**
- A System of Surgery. Phila: 1872. 5th edn. 2 vols. Lge 8vo. 1400 engvs. Sheep, some scuffing. *(Goodrich)* **$125 [≈ £65]**
- A System of Surgery: Pathological, Diagnostic, Therapeutic, and Operative. Phila: 1882. 6th edn. 2 vols. 1194; 1174 pp. Over 1600 w'cuts. Leather.
(Fye) **$300 [≈ £156]**

Gross, Samuel W.
- A Practical Treatise on Tumors of the Mammary Gland ... New York: 1880. 1st edn. 8vo. 246 pp. Ills. Orig linen.
(Hemlock) **$350 [≈ £182]**

Grossman, M.L. & Hamlet, J.
- Birds of Prey of the World. New York: 1964. 1st edn. 4to. 496 pp. Num ills. Cloth. Dw (worn). *(Wheldon & Wesley)* **£50 [≈ $95]**
- Birds of Prey of the World. New York: (1964) 1965. 4to. 496 pp. Num ills. Cloth.
(Wheldon & Wesley) **£35 [≈ $67]**

Grosvenor, Benjamin
- Health, an Essay on its Nature, Value, Uncertainty, Preservation, and Best Improvement. The Second Edition. London: for H. Piers, R. Hett, 1748. 12mo. [viii],xi,242 pp, advt leaf. Orig calf, rebacked.
(Bickersteth) **£85 [≈ $163]**

Grubb, N.H.
- Cherries. London: 1949. 4to. 12 cold & 16 plain plates. Orig cloth. Dw.
(Henly) **£20 [≈ $38]**

Gubelin, E.
- The Color Treasury of Gemstones. New York: Thomas Y. Crowell, 1975. 4to. 138 pp. 80 cold plates. Cloth. Dw.
(Gemmary) **$60 [≈ £78]**
- International World of Gemstones. Zurich: ABC Edition, 1974. 1st edn. 4to. 234 pp. Num cold ills. Pict bds.
(Gemmary) **$150 [≈ £78]**

Guenther, Albert
- Catalogue of the Fishes in the British Museum. London: BM, 1859-70. 8 vols. 8vo. Sound ex-lib. Orig cloth.
(Wheldon & Wesley) **£240 [≈ $460]**
- Catalogue of Fishes in the British Museum. London: BM, 1859-70. 8 vols. 8vo. 4268 pp. Blind stamps on titles. Mod cloth.
(Wheldon & Wesley) **£275 [≈ $527]**
- An Introduction to the Study of Fishes. Edinburgh: 1880. 8vo. xvi,720 pp. 321 ills.

Sound ex-lib. Cloth, reprd.
(Wheldon & Wesley) **£40** [≈ $76]
- The Reptiles of British India. London: Ray Society, 1864. One of 750. Folio. xxvii,452 pp. 26 lithos. Occas mostly sl foxing. Contemp red half mor, gilt dec spine, t.e.g.
(Gough) **£495** [≈ $950]

Guerra, Francisco
- American Medical Bibliography 1639-1783. New York: 1962. Thick 8vo. 885 pp. Orig bndg. *(Goodrich)* **£115** [≈ £59]
- American Medical Bibliography 1639-1783. New York: 1962. Thick 8vo. 885 pp. 187 ills. Few pp creased. Orig bndg.
(Whitehart) **£48** [≈ $92]

Guillemin, A.
- The Application of Physical Forces. London: Macmillan, 1877. Roy 8vo. xxxvii,741 pp. 4 cold plates, 467 text figs. Cloth, spine sl torn.
(Gemmary) **$125** [≈ £65]
- The Application of Physical Forces. Translated from the French ... and edited ... by J. Norman Lockyer. London: 1877. 1st edn. Lge 8vo. [xl],741,[1] pp. 4 cold & 21 engvd plates, num figs. Occas marg marks. Contemp calf, sl rubbed, spine ends chipped.
(Bow Windows) **£60** [≈ $115]
- The Heavens. An Illustrated Handbook of Popular Astronomy. Edited by J.N. Lockyer. London: 1867. 2nd edn. xxiii,524 pp. 39 plates, 191 text figs. Sm lib stamp on 1st page. Half mor, rubbed, edges worn.
(Whitehart) **£28** [≈ $53]

Gummere, John
- An Elementary Treatise on Astronomy. In Two Parts ... Second Edition, Enlarged and Improved. Phila: Kimber & Sharpless, 1837. 8vo. 372,104 pp. 7 fldg plates. Many pp sl spotted, a few browned. Orig tree calf.
(Bickersteth) **£35** [≈ $67]
- A Treatise on Surveying. Phila: Thomas, Cowperthwait & Co, 1846. 14th edn. 8vo. 266, 152 pp. 11 plates, 152 tables. Leather, sl worn. *(Gemmary)* **$100** [≈ £52]

The Gun at Home and Abroad ...
- The Gun at Home and Abroad. London: The London & Counties Press Assoc, 1912-15. One of 500. 4 vols. 4to. Port frontis, num cold & other plates. Orig brown mor gilt, t.e.g., some rubbing *(Sotheran's)* **£1,500** [≈ $2,879]

Gunn, John
- Memorials of ... Being Some Account of the Cromer Forest Bed and its Fossil Mammalia

... With a Memoir of the Author. Norwich: W.A. Nudd, 1891. 1st edn. Tall 8vo. xii,120 pp. Port, 12 plates, ills. Some marks. Orig cloth, cvr edges sl string-cut.
(Bow Windows) **£55** [≈ $105]

Gunter, E.
- The Works. London: Francis Eglesfield, 1662. 4th edn. Cr 8vo. x,152,40, 111,166, 64, 150 pp. Rebound in leather.
(Gemmary) **$1,250** [≈ £651]

Gunter, R.T.
- Dr. Plot and the Correspondence of the Philosophical Society of Oxford. Oxford: Early Science in Oxford XII, (1939) 1968. Reprint. xvii,434 pp. Orig cloth.
(Baldwin) **£35** [≈ $67]
- Early Science in Oxford. Vol III. I. The Biological Sciences. II. The Biological Collections. Oxford: (1925), Dawson reprint 1968. xii,564 pp. 47 plates, 74 figs. Orig buckram. *(Baldwin)* **£40** [≈ $76]
- Early Science in Oxford. Vol IV. The Philosophical Society.Oxford: (1925), Dawson reprint 1968. viii,259 pp. 4 plates. Orig buckram. *(Baldwin)* **£20** [≈ $38]
- The Life & Work of Robert Hooke (Pt. IV). Tract on Capillary Attraction, 1661; Diary, 1688 to 1693. Oxford: Early Science in Oxford X, 1935. xliv,294 pp. Orig cloth, spine sl dull. *(Baldwin)* **£45** [≈ $86]
- Life and Letters of Edward Lhwyd. Oxford: Early Science in Oxford XIV, 1945. xv,576 pp. 14 plates, num ills. Orig cloth.
(Baldwin) **£65** [≈ $124]
- Oxford Colleges and their Men of Science. Oxford: Early Science in Oxford XI, 1937. xvi, 429 pp. 68 ports. Orig cloth, spine sl faded. *(Baldwin)* **£55** [≈ $105]

Gurley, W. & L.E.
- A Manual of the Principal Instruments used in American Engineering and Surveying. New York: Gurley, 1921. 48th edn. Sm 8vo. 333 pp. 3 plates, 120 text figs. Flexi-cloth.
(Gemmary) **$45** [≈ £23]

Gurney, J.H.
- Early Annals of Ornithology. London: 1921. 8vo. [viii],240 pp. 36 ills. Cloth, trifle used.
(Wheldon & Wesley) **£30** [≈ $57]
- Rambles of a Naturalist in Egypt and Other Countries ... Ornithological Notes. London: Jarrold, [1877]. 1st edn. 8vo. viii,307 pp. Occas sl spotting. Orig pict cloth gilt. Author's pres copy. *(Gough)* **£35** [≈ $67]

Guthrie, Douglas
- A History of Medicine. London: 1945. 1st edn. 8vo. xvi,448 pp. 72 plates. Orig cloth.
        (Bickersteth) **£45 [≈ $86]**

Guy's Hospital Reports ...
- See Bright, Richard, et al.

Guy, William
- Principles of Forensic Medicine. First American Edition with Notes and Additions by Charles A. Lee. New York: 1845. 711 pp. Leather.   *(Fye)* **$300 [≈ £156]**

Guye, S. & Michel, H.
- Time & Space. New York: Praeger, 1971. Sq 4to. 289 pp. 20 cold & 259 b/w photos, num text figs. Cloth. Dw.
        (Gemmary) **$125 [≈ £65]**

Gwei-Djen, L. & Needham, Joseph
- Celestial Lancets. A History and Rationale of Acupuncture and Moxa. Cambridge: UP, 1980. 4to. xxi,427 pp. 82 ills, 24 tables. Dw.
        (Peter Taylor) **£49 [≈ $94]**

H., J., F.R.S.
- Astronomical Dialogues ... see Harris, John.

Hachisuka, M.
- The Birds of the Philippine Islands, with Notes on the Mammal Fauna. London: 1931-35. 2 vols. Cr 4to. 2 maps, 2 charts, 57 cold & 44 plain plates, 54 text figs. Half mor, orig wraps bound in.
        (Wheldon & Wesley) **£600 [≈ $1,151]**

Haeckel, Ernst
- The Last Link: Our Present Knowledge of the Descent of Man. With Notes and Biographical Sketches by Hans Gadow. London: Adam & Charles Black, 1898. 1st edn in English. Sm 8vo. viii,156,[4] pp. Occas spotting. Orig cloth.
        (Bow Windows) **£48 [≈ $92]**

Haggard, H.W.
- The Doctor in History. New Haven: 1934. xiii, 408 pp. text ills. *(Whitehart)* **£35 [≈ $67]**

Hahnemann, Samuel
- Samuel Hahnemann. His Life and Work. Based on Recently Discovered State Papers, Documents, Letters, &c. ... London: [1922]. 2 vols. 4to. Num figs. Some ink notes. Orig bndg.   *(Whitehart)* **£50 [≈ $95]**

Haines, C. Reginald
- Notes on the Birds of Rutland. London: R.H. Porter, 1907. 1st edn. xlvii,175 pp. Fldg map, cold frontis, 7 plates. Orig green cloth gilt, crnr sl frayed.   *(Gough)* **£38 [≈ $72]**

Haldane, J.B.S.
- New Paths in Genetics. London: 1941. 1st edn. 206 pp. Orig bndg.
        (Whitehart) **£15 [≈ $28]**

Haldane, John Scott
- Respiration. New Haven: 1922. 1st edn. 427 pp. Orig bndg.   *(Fye)* **$175 [≈ £91]**

Hale, A. Creighton
- The Art of Massage ... London: The Scientific Press, [1893]. 1st edn. 8vo. xvi, 144 pp. Num ills. Prelims spotted. Orig cloth, somewhat soiled, lower edge of upper cvr sl marked by damp. *(Claude Cox)* **£25 [≈ $47]**

Hale, Edwin Moses
- A Systematic Treatise on Abortion. Chicago: C.S. Halsey, 1866. 1st edn. 8vo. xvi, 347 pp, advt leaf. 3 plates (2 cold), text ills. Prelims foxed, some underlining. Orig cloth.
        (Rootenberg) **$550 [≈ £286]**

Hale, W.G.
- Waders. London: Collins New Naturalist, 1980. 1st edn. 8vo. 320 pp. 24 plates. Orig cloth. Dw.   *(Henly)* **£16 [≈ $30]**

Hale-White, W.
- Great Doctors of the Nineteenth Century. London: [1935]. vii,325 pp. 1 page sl dusty, few marg pencil lines. Orig bndg.
        (Whitehart) **£35 [≈ $67]**

Hales, Stephen
- Statical Essays: containing Haemastaticks; or, an Account of some Hydraulic and Hydrostatical Experiments made on the Blood and Blood-Vessels of Animals. London: 1740. 2nd edn. 356,index pp. Leather, front bd detached, rear hinge strengthened.
        (Fye) **$500 [≈ £260]**
- Statical Essays: containing Haemastatics; or, an Account of some Hydraulic and Hydrostatical Experiments made on the Blood and Blood-Vessels of Animals. London: 1769. 3rd edn. 356 pp. Leather, front bd detached, spine & rear hinge cracked.
        (Fye) **$375 [≈ £195]**
- Vegetable Staticks ... Being an Essay towards a Natural History of Vegetation. London: 1727. 1st edn. [vii],vii, [ii],376 pp. 19 plates.

Contemp calf, rebacked.
(Wheldon & Wesley) £600 [≈ $1,151]

Half-Hours Underground ...
- Half-Hours Underground. London: James Nisbet, 1905. Cr 8vo. xii,369 pp. Num text figs. Dec cloth. *(Gemmary)* $50 [≈ £26]

Hall, Sir A.D.
- The Genus Tulipa. London: RHS, 1940. 1st edn. Lge 8vo. viii,171 pp. 40 cold plates, 23 other ills. Orig cloth, sl faded.
(Bow Windows) £50 [≈ $95]

Hall, Marshall
- A Critical and Experimental Essay on the Circulation of the Blood ... [Bound with] Researches principally relative to the ... Effects of Loss of Blood (Second American Edition). Phila: Carey & Hart, 1836. 8vo. 168; 257 pp. 10 plates. Foxed. Sheep, rebacked. *(Goodrich)* $295 [≈ £153]
- A Descriptive, Diagnostic and Practical Essay on Disorders of the Digestive Organs and General Health ... Keene, NH: 1823. 1st Amer edn. 192 pp. Orig bds, paper label, uncut, some v sl water staining of bds.
(Whitehart) £80 [≈ $153]
- A Descriptive, Diagnostic, and Practical Essay on Disorders of the Digestive Organs and General Health ... Second Edition. Keene, NH: 1823. 8vo. 142 pp. Some marg damp staining of prelims. Orig bds, uncut, spine worn. *(Goodrich)* £110 [≈ $57]
- Principles of the Theory and Practice of Medicine. First American Edition. Revised and Much Enlarged by Jacob Bigelow and Oliver Wendell Holmes. Boston: Little & Brown, 1839. 8vo. iv,724 pp. Text engvs. Usual foxing. Calf, worn, externally unmarked ex-lib. *(Goodrich)* $250 [≈ £130]

Hall, Percy
- Ultra-Violet Rays in the Treatment and Cure of Disease ... London: Heinemann, 1924. 1st edn. 8vo. xvi,110 pp. 20 ills. Lib stamp on title. Orig cloth. *(Claude Cox)* £18 [≈ $34]

Hall, Samuel
- Samuel Hall's Improvements in Steam Engines ... Nottingham: Samuel Bennett, [ca 1838]. 1st edn. 8vo. 16 pp. Fldg plate (partly hand cold). Disbound.
(Burmester) £90 [≈ $172]

Hall, T.Y.
- Treatises on Various British and Foreign Coal and Iron Mines and Mining. Newcastle upon Tyne: 1853-54. 8vo. 297 pp. Maps & plates inc lge fldg hand cold map. New cloth.
(Wheldon & Wesley) £50 [≈ $95]

Halliwell, James Orchard (ed.)
- A Collection of Letters illustrative of the Progress of Science in England from the Reign of Queen Elizabeth to that of Charles the Second. London: 1841. xvii,124 pp. Orig cloth, sl dust stained. *(Whitehart)* £40 [≈ $76]

Halsted, C.A.
- The Little Botanist. London: 1835. 2 vols. Sm 8vo. 2 cold frontis, 26 plates. Qtr leather, worn, 1 jnt broken.
(Wheldon & Wesley) £30 [≈ $57]

Halsted, William
- Surgical Papers. Baltimore: 1924. 1st edn. 2 vols. 586; 603 pp. Ills. Orig bndg.
(Fye) $375 [≈ £195]
- Surgical Papers. Baltimore: Hopkins, 1952. 2nd printing. 2 vols. Roy 8vo. Orig bndg.
(Goodrich) $175 [≈ £91]

Hamilton, Alexander
- Outlines of the Theory and Practice of Midwifery. From the Last British Edition. The Third American Edition. Northampton: 1797. 8vo. 288 pp. Browned & foxed. Orig calf, worn. *(Goodrich)* $135 [≈ £70]

Hamilton, formerly Buchanan, F.
- An Account of the Fishes found in the River Ganges and its Branches. Edinburgh: 1822. 2 vols. Cr 4to & oblong 4to. vii,405 pp. 39 plates in atlas. Plates foxed, old stamp on title. Calf.
(Wheldon & Wesley) £320 [≈ $614]

Hamilton, J.
- Observations on the Utility and Administration of Purgative Medicines in several Diseases. Edinburgh: 1806. 2nd edn. xx, 349 pp. Contemp tree calf, worn, hd of spine sl defective. *(Whitehart)* £40 [≈ $76]
- Observations on the Utility and Administration of Purgative Medicines in Several Diseases. Edinburgh: 1815. 5th edn, rvsd. xxxii,213 pp. Some ink notes. Mod half leather gilt. *(Whitehart)* £60 [≈ $115]

Hamilton, W.R.
- Lectures on Quaternions: containing a Systematic Statement of a New Mathematical Method ... Dublin: 1853. 1st edn. 64,lxxix, 737 pp. Orig cloth, spine faded, edges worn.
(Whitehart) £150 [≈ $287]

Hamlin, A.C.
- The History of Mount Mica of Maine, U.S.A. and its Wonderful Deposits of Matchless Tourmalines. Bangor, ME: Augustus Choate Hamlin, 1895. 8vo. 72 pp. 43 chromolitho plates, 4 photo ills, 8 plates of line drawings. Cloth, spotted.
(Gemmary) **$425 [≈ £221]**

Hammond, N.
- The Elements of Algebra in a New and Easy method ... London: 1752. 2nd edn. xxiv,328 pp. New leather. *(Whitehart)* **£80 [≈ $153]**

Hammond, Robert
- The Electric Light in Our Homes. London: Warne, [1884]. 1st edn. 8vo. xii,205,[6 ctlg] pp. 3 photo ills, 64 w'engvs in text. Occas spotting & thumbing. Orig pict cloth gilt, sl marked. *(de Beaumont)* **£88 [≈ $168]**
- The Electric Light in Our Homes. 1884. 1st edn. 205 pp. 64 ills. Orig bndg. Sgnd "With the Author's Compliments".
(New Wireless) **$120 [≈ £62]**

Hammond, William
- Lectures on Venereal Diseases. Phila: 1864. 1st edn. 287 pp. Orig bndg.
(Fye) **$200 [≈ £104]**
- Sexual Impotence in the Male and Female. Detroit: 1887. 1st edn. 305 pp. Orig bndg.
(Fye) **$250 [≈ £130]**
- A Treatise on Insanity in its Medical Relations. New York: 1883. 1st edn. 767 pp. Orig bndg. *(Fye)* **$300 [≈ £156]**
- A Treatise on the Diseases of the Nervous System. New York: 1871. 1st edn. 754 pp. Orig bndg, fine. *(Fye)* **$500 [≈ £260]**

Hammond, William A.
- Spiritualism and Allied Causes and Conditions of Nervous Derangement. London: Lewis, 1876. 8vo. xii,366 pp. 9 text engvs. Orig cloth, some wear.
(Goodrich) **$125 [≈ £65]**

Hancock, H.
- Foundations of the Theory of Algebraic Numbers. New York: 1931-32. 2 vols. Sm lib stamps throughout. Vol 2 cloth sl frayed.
(Whitehart) **£35 [≈ $67]**
- Lectures on the Theory of Elliptic Functions. Volume I. Analysis [all published]. New York: 1910. 1st edn. xxiii, 498 pp. 76 figs. Spine faded. Sgnd by the author.
(Whitehart) **£35 [≈ $67]**

Hancock, J. & Elliott, H.F.I.
- The Herons of the World. London: 1978. 4to. 300 pp. 64 cold plates, maps, ills. Cloth.
(Wheldon & Wesley) **£50 [≈ $95]**

Hancock, John
- A Catalogue of the Birds of Northumberland and Durham. London: 1874. Litho plates (3 sl stained). Lacks f.e.p. Orig cloth, sl rubbed & marked. *(Grayling)* **£40 [≈ $76]**

Hancock, Thomas
- Essay on Instinct, and its Physical and Moral Relations. London: William Phillips, 1824. 1st edn. 8vo. 551 pp. Contemp half mor gilt.
(Chapel Hill) **$135 [≈ £70]**
- Personal Narrative of the Origin and Progress of the Caoutchouc or India-Rubber Manufacture in England ... London: 1857. 1st edn. viii,283 pp. Litho port frontis, fldg view, 18 litho plates, text ills. Sl foxing. Contemp polished calf, sl scuffed. Sgnd author's pres to his son.
(Gaskell) **£1,200 [≈ $2,303]**
- Personal Narrative of the Origin and Progress of ... India-Rubber Manufacture in England. London: Longman ..., 1857. 1st edn. Demy 8vo. [viii],284,24 pp. Litho plates. Occas sl foxing. Orig cloth, spine sl sunned.
(Ash) **£250 [≈ $479]**

Handerson, H.E.
- Gilbertus Anglicus. Cleveland: 1918. One of 500. 8vo. 77 pp. Orig wraps.
(Goodrich) **$65 [≈ £33]**

Handfield-Jones, R.M.
- Surgery of the Hand. Edinburgh: 1940. 1st edn. 140 pp. Photo ills. Orig bndg.
(Fye) **$150 [≈ £78]**

Handley, John
- Catalogue of Plants growing in the Sedbergh District ... Leeds: 1898. Sl foxed. Orig ptd wraps. *(Grayling)* **£30 [≈ $57]**

Haraszthy, A.
- Grape Culture, Wines, and Wine-Making with Notes upon Agriculture and Horticulture. New York: Harper, 1862. 1st edn. Tall 8vo. 420 pp. Ills. Orig cloth, some wear at spine tips, crnrs bumped, sm gouge in spine. *(Respess)* **$850 [≈ £442]**

Hardy, Sir A.C.
- The Open Sea. The World of Plankton. London: Collins New Naturalist, 1956. 1st edn. 8vo. xv,335 pp. 24 cold & 24 plain

plates. Ends sl foxed. Orig cloth.
(Henly) **£18 [≃ $34]**
- The Open Sea: Part II. Fish and Fisheries. London: Collins New Naturalist, 1959. 1st edn. 8vo. xiv,322 pp. 16 cold & 32 plain plates. Orig cloth. *(Henly)* **£25 [≃ $47]**

Hardy, Eric
- The Birds of the Liverpool Area ... Arbroath: 1941. 1st edn. 279 pp. 29 plates. Dw (sl chipped). *(Gough)* **£25 [≃ $47]**

Harison, Charles & John
- The Photographer's Handbook. London: John Lane; Bodley Head, [1908]. Sm 8vo. [xii], 152, [4 ctlg] pp. 20 photo ills, num text ills. Orig gilt dec cloth.
(de Beaumont) **£35 [≃ $67]**

Harkins, Henry
- The Treatment of Burns. London: 1942. 1st edn. 457 pp. 120 ills. Orig bndg.
(Fye) **$150 [≃ £78]**

Harmsworth's Wireless Encyclopaedia ...
- See Lodge, Oliver, et al.

Harper, John
- The Sea-Side and Aquarium: or, Anecdote and Gossip on Marine Zoology. Second Edition. Edinburgh: Nimmo, 1859. 8vo. xii,188 pp. Frontis, text vignettes. Orig pict gilt green cloth, upper cvr sl faded.
(Claude Cox) **£18 [≃ $34]**

Harris, C.A.
- The Principles and Practice of Dental Surgery. Phila: 1863. xxiii,869 pp. 320 ills. Sl damp stain in a few bottom margs. Leather, rebacked, rather worn.
(Whitehart) **£40 [≃ $76]**

Harris, E.C.
- New Zealand Berries - New Zealand Flowers - New Zealand Ferns. Nelson, NZ: [1894]. 3 vols in one. 4to. 3 litho titles, 36 plates. Occas sl foxing. Binder's cloth.
(Wheldon & Wesley) **£75 [≃ $143]**

Harris, J.R.
- An Angler's Entomology. London: Collins New Naturalist, 1952. 1st edn. 8vo. xv,268,4 pp. 32 cold & 16 plain plates. Orig cloth.
(Henly) **£22 [≃ $42]**

Harris, John, ?1666-1719
- Astronomical Dialogues between a Gentleman and a Lady ... The Second

Edition. By J.H. F.R.S. London: for John Horsfeild, 1725. 8vo. [2], vi, 184 pp. 6 plates. Calf antique. *(Fenning)* **£125 [≃ $239]**
- The Description and Use of the Celestial and Terrestrial Globes; and of Collins's Pocket Quadrant. London: 1703. 1st edn. 8vo. [vi], 62, [4 advt] pp. Frontis. Contemp sheep, rubbed, crnrs worn, upper jnt split at hd.
(Gaskell) **£600 [≃ $1,151]**
- The Description and Use of the Celestial and Terrestrial Globes ... The Sixth Edition. London: for D. Midwinter, 1725. Sm 8vo. [vi], 62, 4 advt pp. Frontis. Orig calf, front hinge cracked, sl damage to spine ends.
(Vanbrugh) **£75 [≃ $143]**
- The Description and Use of the Globes, and the Orrery. To which is prefixed ... a Brief Account of the Solar System. London: 1734. 3rd edn. viii,190 pp. Frontis, 5 fldg plates. Water stain on top & outer marg of most pp. Contemp leather, rebacked.
(Whitehart) **£140 [≃ $268]**

Harris, M.
- An Exposition of British Insects ... Bees, Flies and Libellulae. London: 1786. 2nd edn, 2nd issue. 4to. viii, 9-166, [4] pp. Engvd title, cold chart, plain plate, 50 hand cold plates. Minor browning. Contemp calf, rebacked, trifle worn. *(Wheldon & Wesley)* **£600 [≃ $1,151]**

Harris, T.Y.
- Wild Flowers of Australia. Sydney, 1938. 1st edn. 8vo. xix,198 pp. 55 cold plates. Orig cloth, spine sl faded. *(Henly)* **£22 [≃ $42]**

Harris, Thaddeus William
- A Treatise on Some of the Insects Injurious to Vegetation. Third Edition. Boston: Crosby & Nichols, 1862. 8vo. xi,640 pp. 8 hand cold plates. Lib stamps on endpaper. Orig pict cloth gilt, faded. *(Gough)* **£40 [≃ $76]**

Harris, William Snow
- Rudimentary Electricity, being a Concise Exposition of the General Principles of Electrical Science ... London: John Weale, 1848. 1st edn. 12mo. 160 pp. Frontis, text ills. Some damp staining rear endpapers. Orig cloth, spotted. Author's pres copy.
(Chapel Hill) **$150 [≃ £78]**

Harrison, R.
- Lectures on the Surgical Disorders of the Urinary Organs. London: 1887. 3rd edn. xi,583 pp. 117 figs & plates in text. Orig cloth, sl water stained.
(Whitehart) **£25 [≃ $47]**

Hart, Ernest
- Hypnotism, Mesmerism and the New Witchcraft. London: Smith, Elder, 1893. 1st edn. 8vo. 20 ills. Orig cloth, extremities rubbed. *(Clark)* £35 [≈ $67]

Hart, I.B.
- The Mechanical Investigations of Leonardo da Vinci. London: 1925. vi,240 pp. 7 plates, 136 text figs. Occas sl foxing. Cloth sl dusty. *(Whitehart)* £38 [≈ $72]

Hartelius, T.J.
- Home Gymnastics for the Preservation and Restoration of Health, for Children and Young and Old People ... Translated ... London: Isbister, [1881]. 1st edn in English. 8vo. [x], 94 pp. 46 text figs. Orig ptd wraps. Translator's inscrptn. *(Bickersteth)* £40 [≈ $76]

Harthan, A.J.
- The Birds of Worcestershire. Worcester: Littlebury, [ca 1947]. 1st edn. Sm 4to. 79 pp. Map, num plates. Dw (chipped). *(Gough)* £25 [≈ $47]

Harting, J.E.
- British Animals Extinct within Historic Times with some Account of British Wild Cattle. London: 1880. x,258 pp. 36 ills. Orig gilt dec cloth. *(Baldwin)* £30 [≈ $57]
- Rambles in Search of Shells, Land and Fresh-Water. London: 1875. 8vo. viii,110,2 pp. 10 hand cold plates. Cloth gilt. *(Henly)* £32 [≈ $61]

Harting, J.E. & Robert, L.P.
- Glimpses of Bird Life Pourtrayed with Pen and Pencil. London: Swann Sonnenschein, 1880. Folio. 20 chromolitho plates, 43 w'cuts & intls. Sl offsetting, 2 ff sl defective. Orig cloth gilt, edges worn & darkened. *(Hollett)* £75 [≈ $143]

Hartwig, G.
- The Subterranean World. London: Longmans, Green, 1871. 8vo. xix,522 pp. 3 maps, num w'engvs. Prize calf, rebacked. *(Gemmary)* $150 [≈ £79]

Harvey, James
- Praesagium Medicum, or the Prognostick Signs of Acute Diseases ... London: 1706. xxix, 216 pp. New qtr leather, garish endpapers. *(Whitehart)* £160 [≈ $307]
- Praesagium Medicum, or the Prognostick Signs of Acute Diseases; Established by

Ancient Observations, and Explain'd by the Best Modern Discoveries. London: Strahan, 1706. 1st edn. 8vo. xxix,216 pp. Panelled calf. *(Goodrich)* $395 [≈ £205]

Harvey, L.A. & St Leger-Gordon, D.
- Dartmoor. London: Collins New Naturalist, 1953. 1st edn. 8vo. xiv,273 pp. 16 cold & 24 plain plates. Orig cloth. *(Henly)* £18 [≈ $34]

Harvey, W.H.
- A Manual of the British Marine Algae. London: 1849. 2nd edn. lii,252 pp. Port (foxed), 27 plates. Num ink notes. New cloth. *(Wheldon & Wesley)* £80 [≈ $153]
- A Manual of the British Marine Algae. London: 1849. 2nd edn. 8vo. lii,252 pp. Port, 27 plates (partly ptd in colours). New cloth. *(Wheldon & Wesley)* £50 [≈ $95]
- Nereis Boreali-Americana, or Contributions to a History of the Marine Algae of North America. Part 1, Melanospermeae. Washington: Smithsonian, 1852. 4to. 149 pp. 12 cold plates. Wraps. *(Wheldon & Wesley)* £60 [≈ $115]

Harvey, William
- An Anatomical Dissertation upon the Movement of the Heart and Blood in Animals, being a Statement of the Discovery of the Circulation of the Blood. Canterbury: privately ptd, 1894. x,73,91 pp. Port. Imitation qtr vellum, endpapers discold. *(Whitehart)* £45 [≈ $86]
- The Anatomical Exercises of Dr. William Harvey ... added the Discourse of James de Back ... London: Lowndes, 1673. 2nd edn in English. Sm 8vo. [xxiv],107, [xx],172 pp. Title mtd & reprd. Contemp calf, reprd. *(Bookpress)* $1,200 [≈ £625]
- The Anatomical Exercises of Dr. William Harvey. London: Nonesuch Press, 1928. One of 1450. 8vo. xiv,202 pp. Fldg plate. Niger mor. *(Goodrich)* £195 [≈ £101]
- The Anatomical Exercises of Dr. William Harvey ... Newly Edited by Geoffrey Keynes. London: 1928. One of 1450. Mor gilt. *(Fye)* £325 [≈ £169]
- William Hervey's De Motu Locali Animalium. Edited and Translated by G. Whitteridge. Cambridge: 1959. One of 1000. 4to. 162 pp. Dw (torn). *(Goodrich)* £45 [≈ £23]
- De Motu Locali Animalium, 1627. Edited by G. Whitteridge. Cambridge: 1959. Ltd edn. 4to. 163 pp. Dw. *(Fye)* $100 [≈ £52]
- Movement of the Heart and Blood in Animals. Translated by K.J. Franklin.

Springfield: 1957. Ltd edn. 209 pp. Orig bndg. Dw.   *(Fye)* **$60 [≈ £31]**
- The Works ... Translated from the Latin with the Life of the Author by Robert Willis, MD. London: Sydenham Society, 1847. 8vo. xcvi, 624 pp. Orig cloth. *(Goodrich)* **$195 [≈ £101]**
- The Works ... Translated from the Latin by Robert Willis, M.D. London: Sydenham Society, 1847. xcvi,624 pp. Lib number on title. Sl underlining on 2 pp, ink notes in index. Orig cloth, new endpapers, spine sl worn at hd, lib number on spine.
                    (Whitehart) **£50 [≈ $95]**
- The Works ... Translated from the Latin with a Life of the Author by Robert Willis. London: 1847. 1st edn. 624 pp. Orig bndg.
                    (Fye) **$250 [≈ £130]**
- See also Mitchell, S. Weir.

Hasse, C.E.
- An Anatomical Description of the Organs of Circulation and Respiration. London: 1846. 1st English translation. 400 pp. Orig bndg.
                    (Fye) **$125 [≈ £65]**
- An Anatomical Description of the Diseases of the Organs of Circulation and respiration. London: Sydenham Society, 1846. xiv,400 pp. Orig cloth, sl worn & dust stained.
                    (Whitehart) **£40 [≈ $76]**

Hastings, John
- The Practice of Surgery: embracing Minor Surgery and the Application of Dressings. Phila: 1850. 1st edn. 479 pp. W'cut ills. Occas foxing. Orig bndg, fine. *(Fye)* **$300 [≈ £156]**

Haswell, G.C.
- On the Silurian Formation in the Pentland Hills. Edinburgh: 1865. 1st edn. 8vo. 47,[1 blank] pp. Errata slip. Frontis, 1 table, 2 sections, 4 plates. Orig limp cloth, ends sl torn & frayed. Author's inscrptn.
                    (Bow Windows) **£48 [≈ $92]**

Hathaway, Kenneth A.
- Television. 1936. 1st edn. 169 pp. 64 ills. Orig bndg, rear cvr stained.
                    (New Wireless) **$40 [≈ £21]**

Hatton, R.G.
- The Craftsman's Plant-Book: or Figures of Plants selected from the Herbals of the Sixteenth Century. London: 1909. Imperial 8vo. ix,539 pp. Cold frontis, over 1000 ills. Sm lib stamps on title. Qtr mor, sl rubbed.
                    (Henly) **£40 [≈ $76]**

Haverschmidt, F.
- Birds of Surinam. London: 1968. Roy 8vo. xxix, 445 pp. Map, 40 cold & 30 plain plates, num text figs. Cloth. Dw (somewhat used).
                    (Wheldon & Wesley) **£200 [≈ $383]**

Hawkins, C.C. & Wallis, F.
- The Dynamo. 1896. 2nd edn. 526 pp. 190 ills. Orig bndg.   *(New Wireless)* **$65 [≈ £33]**

Hawney, William
- The Complete Measurer ... The Sixteenth Edition revised and corrected ... Appendix ... London: 1789. 12mo. x,[iii], 346 pp, advt leaf. Orig sheep.   *(Bickersteth)* **£38 [≈ $72]**

Hayes, Richard
- Interest at One View calculated to a Farthing ... The Seventh Edition, with Additions. London: for W. Meadows, 1747. 16mo. Contemp calf, rebacked, crnrs reprd.
                    (Waterfield's) **£75 [≈ $143]**

Hayes, S.
- A Practical Treatise on Planting and the Management of Woods and Coppices. Dublin: 1794. 1st edn. 8vo. ix,iii, 189,2 pp. Advt leaf. Engvd title & vignette, 5 plates, 10 text engvs. Contemp half mor, upper bd reprd.   *(Henly)* **£190 [≈ $363]**

Hayward, George
- Surgical Reports and Miscellaneous Papers on Medical Subjects. Boston: 1855. 1st edn. 452 pp. Orig bndg.   *(Fye)* **$225 [≈ £117]**

Haywood, James
- Letters to Farmers. London: Simpkin, Marshall; Worksop: Robert White, 1852. 1st edn. 8vo. Final advt leaf. Minor foxing. Orig cloth, spine faded & sl worn at ends.
                    (Clark) **£30 [≈ $57]**

Head, Henry
- Studies in Neurology. Oxford: 1920. 2 vols. 4to. Lib stamp on titles. Orig cloth, recased.
                    (Goodrich) **$225 [≈ £117]**
- Studies in Neurology. Oxford: 1920. 2 vols. 4to. Lib perf stamp on titles. New cloth.
                    (Goodrich) **$175 [≈ £91]**

Headrick, J.
- General View of the Agriculture of the County of Angus or Forfarshire. Edinburgh: 1813. 8vo. xxxi,589,120 pp. Cold map, plate, 3 fldg tables. Half calf antique style.
                    (Wheldon & Wesley) **£60 [≈ $115]**

Healde, Thomas

- The New Pharmacopoeia of the Royal College of Physicians of London. Translated into English, with Notes ... Third Edition, corrected. London: J.W. Galabin, for T. Longman, 1788. 8vo. xvi,368 pp. Approbation leaf. Contemp calf, green edges.
(*Finch*) **£120 [≃ $230]**

Hearn, Charles W.

- The Practical Printer: A Complete Manual of Photographic Printing ... Phila: Edward L. Wilson, 1878. 2nd edn. 220 pp. Orig mtd albumen photo, num text ills. Orig blue cloth gilt.   (*Karmiole*) **$100 [≃ £52]**

Heath, Christopher

- A Course of Operative Surgery with Plates Drawn from Nature by M. Lebeille and Coloured by Hand under his Direction. London: Churchill, 1877. Sm folio. 130 pp. 20 plates (lacks plate 16). Orig cloth, worn.
(*Goodrich*) **$95 [≃ £49]**

Heath, F.G.

- The Fern Paradise: a Plea for the Culture of Ferns. London: 1878. 5th edn. 8vo. 12 plates, num ills. Cloth, trifle used.
(*Wheldon & Wesley*) **£20 [≃ $38]**
- The Fern Portfolio. London: 1885. Folio. 15 plates of 45 cold figs, with descriptive text. Orig cloth, rebacked.
(*Wheldon & Wesley*) **£30 [≃ $57]**

Heath, R.S.

- A Treatise on Geometrical Optics. Cambridge: UP, 1887. 8vo. xvii,356 pp. Num text figs. Ex-lib. Cloth.
(*Gemmary*) **$65 [≃ £33]**

Heath, T.

- The Twentieth Century Atlas of Popular Astronomy ... Edinburgh & London: 1908. 2nd edn. 4to. [ix],134 pp. Cold frontis, 22 cold plates. Lacks free endpaper. Orig cloth, sl dust stained.   (*Whitehart*) **£25 [≃ $47]**
- Twentieth Century Atlas of Popular Astronomy. New York: Stokes, [ca 1910]. 4to. 126 pp. 22 cold plates. Cloth.
(*Gemmary*) **$200 [≃ £104]**

Heavisides, Michael (ed.)

- The True Invention of the Lucifer Match, ny John Walker, of Stockton-on-Tees, in 1827 ... Stockton: Heavisides, 1909. 1st edn. 12mo. 32 pp. Text ills. Orig ptd wraps.
(*Chapel Hill*) **$35 [≃ £18]**

Hebert, Luke

- The Engineer's and Mechanic's Encyclopaedia. Comprehending Practical Illustrations of the Machinery and Processes employed in Every Description of Manufacture of the British Empire ... London: Kelly, 1848. 2 vols. 2 frontis, ca 2000 text engvs. Rec cloth.
(*Gough*) **£65 [≃ $124]**

Hebra, F.

- On Diseases of the Skin, including the Exanthemata. Translated by C.H. Fagge. London: New Sydenham Soc, 1866-80. 5 vols. Occas sl foxing. Orig cloth, sl worn.
(*Whitehart*) **£90 [≃ $172]**

Hecker, J.F.C.

- The Epidemics of the Middle Ages ... Translated by B.G. Babington. London: Sydenham Society, 1844. 8vo. xxviii,418 pp. A few sm lib stamps. rebound in cloth.
(*Bickersteth*) **£38 [≃ $72]**
- The Epidemics of the Middle Ages. London: Sydenham Society, 1844. 8vo. xx,418 pp. Lib stamps on endpapers. Orig cloth, minor nicks to spine ends. (*Frew Mackenzie*) **£54 [≃ $103]**
- The Epidemics of the Middle Ages. London: Sydenham Society, 1846. 8vo. xxviii,380 pp. Orig blue cloth gilt.   (*Gough*) **£40 [≃ $76]**

Heer, O.

- The Primaeval World of Switzerland. Translated by W.S. Dallas. London: 1876. 2 vols. xv,393; vii,324 pp. 5 plates, 372 text figs. Sl foxing. Orig pict cloth, spines marked & faded.   (*Whitehart*) **£50 [≃ $95]**

Heider, M. & Wedl, C.

- Atlas to the Pathology of the Teeth. Leipzig: 1869. Lge 4to. xii,44 pp. 16 plates. 2 v sm ink stamps on title. Paper cvrd bds, rebacked, inner hinge sl cracked but firm.
(*Whitehart*) **£55 [≃ $105]**

Heilmann, G.

- The Origin of Birds. London: 1926. [v],208 pp. 2 cold plates, 140 text figs. Orig bndg.
(*Whitehart*) **£25 [≃ $47]**

Heiniger, E.A. & J.

- The Great Book of Jewels. Lausanne: Edita S.A., 1974. Imperial 4to. 316 pp. Num photo ills, inc cold. Cloth. (*Gemmary*) **$50 [≃ £26]**

Heisenberg, W.

- Cosmic Radiation. New York: Dover, 1946. 8vo. 192 pp. Text figs. Cloth.

(Gemmary) **$35 [≈£18]**

Helferich, H.
- Fractures and Dislocations. Translated by J. Hutchinson. London: New Sydenham Society, 1897. 3rd edn. 162 pp. 68 plates, 126 text figs. Orig cloth, spine sl faded.
(Whitehart) **£40 [≈$76]**
- On Fracture and Dislocations. Translated by J. Hutchinson. London: 1899. 162 pp. 68 plates, 126 text figs. Orig cloth.
(Whitehart) **£35 [≈$67]**

Helsham, Richard
- A Course of Lectures in Natural Philosophy ... Published by Bryan Robinson. The Sixth Edition. Dublin: Sleater & M'Kenzie, 1793. 8vo. 11 plates, some fldg. Contemp mottled sheep, sl wear to spine ends & hinges.
(Jarndyce) **£58 [≈$111]**
- A Course of Lectures in Natural Philosophy ... Published by Bryan Robinson ... The Sixth Edition. Dublin: Sleater & M'Kenzie, 1793. 1st Irish edn. 11 fldg plates. Contemp half russia. *(Waterfield's)* **£115 [≈$220]**
- A Course of Lectures in Natural Philosophy. London: 1855. 3rd edn. x,404 pp. 11 fldg plates. Contemp calf, rebacked.
(Whitehart) **£80 [≈$153]**

Henckel, J.F.
- Pyritologia: or, a History of the Pyrites, the Principal Body in the Mineral Kingdom. London: 1757. 8vo. xviii,382 pp. Frontis. Blind stamp on title. New cloth.
(Wheldon & Wesley) **£150 [≈$287]**

Henderson, J.S.
- M.R.C.O.G. Examination Case Records and Commentaries. London: [1950]. [v],368 pp. Num ills. Lib stamp on endpaper. Spine faded & top 2-inches torn, cloth sl marked.
(Whitehart) **£40 [≈$76]**

Henderson, William Augustus
- The Housekeeper's Instructor; or, Universal Family Cook ... London: W. & J. Stratford, [1790]. 1st edn. 8vo. 456,[xxiv] pp. Frontis, 10 plates (2 fldg). Occas trivial spotting. Rebound (1957) in crushed mor.
(Finch) **£240 [≈$460]**
- The Housekeeper's Instructor. London: W. & J. Stratford, [1790?]. 1st edn in book form, bound from the magazine parts. Fcap 4to. 456, [xxiv] pp. 12 engvd plates. Some discoloration & sl flaws. Later panelled calf.
(Ash) **£350 [≈$671]**

Henoch, Edward
- Lectures on Children's Diseases. Translated from the Fourth Edition (1889) by John Thompson. London: 1889. 2 vols. 493; 455 pp. Orig bndg.   *(Fye)* **$150 [≈£78]**

Henrey, Blanche
- British Botanical and Horticultural Literature before 1800. London: 1975. 3 vols. Roy 8vo. 1128 pp. 32 cold & num other ills. Cloth.   *(Wheldon & Wesley)* **£150 [≈$287]**

Henry, David
- The Complete English Farmer. London: for F. Newbery, 1771. 1st edn. Demy 8vo. [xxviii], 432, 2 pp. 2 plates. Sl foxing. Mod half calf gilt. Anon.   *(Ash)* **£200 [≈$383]**

Henry, William
- The Elements of Experimental Chemistry. The Fourth American, from the Seventh London Edition, Greatly Enlarged ... Phila: James Webster, 1817. xxx, [2], 656, xcvi pp. Fldg table, 10 plates. Contemp calf, extremities rubbed. *(Karmiole)* **$100 [≈£52]**
- An Epitome of Chemistry, in Three Parts. Phila: James Humphreys, 1802. 1st Amer edn. 12mo. Contemp tree sheep, gilt spine.
(Ximenes) **$225 [≈£117]**

Henslow, J.S.
- A Dictionary of Botanical Terms. London: [1858]. New edn. 12mo. xv,319 pp. Ends sl browned. Orig cloth gilt. *(Henly)* **£24 [≈$46]**

Henslow, J.S. & Skepper, E.
- Flora of Suffolk ... London: (1860). 1st edn. Sm 8vo. [xii],140 pp. Some browning & spots. Orig green cloth. *(Bow Windows)* **£48 [≈$92]**
- Flora of Suffolk. London: [1860]. Sm 8vo. x, 140 pp. Title sl foxed, endpapers discold. Orig cloth. *(Wheldon & Wesley)* **£25 [≈$47]**

Hepburn, L.
- Flowers of the Coast. London: Collins New Naturalist, 1952. 1st edn. 8vo. xiv,236,6 advt pp. 16 cold & 40 other plates. Orig cloth. Dw.
(Henly) **£48 [≈$92]**
- Flowers of the Coast. London: Collins New Naturalist, 1952. 1st edn. 8vo. xiv,236,6 advt pp. 16 cold & 40 plain plates. Orig cloth. Dw.
(Henly) **£48 [≈$92]**
- Flowers of the Coast. London: Collins New Naturalist, 1952. 1st edn. 8vo. xiv,236,6 advt pp. 16 cold & 40 plain plates. Orig cloth.
(Henly) **£36 [≈$69]**

Herbert, William
- Amaryllidaceae: preceded by an Attempt to arrange the Monocotyledonous Orders ... London: James Ridgway & Sons, 1837. 2nd edn. vi, 428 pp. 48 plates (the deluxe issue with all but 5 of the plates hand cold). V clean. Contemp half russia, a.e.g., backstrip relaid.   *(Claude Cox)* £650 [≃ $1,247]

Hereman, S.
- Blight on Flowers; or Figures and Descriptions of Insects infesting the Flower Garden. London: 1840. 8vo. xi,242 pp. 17 plates (16 hand cold). Plates more or less foxed; sm stain on frontis. New cloth.
        (Wheldon & Wesley) £48 [≃ $92]

Herrick, James
- A Short History of Cardiology. Springfield: 1942. 1st edn. 258 pp. Dw.
        (Fye) $125 [≃ £65]
- A Short History of Cardiology. Springfield: 1942. 1st edn. 258 pp. Ex-lib. Orig bndg.
        (Fye) $75 [≃ £39]

Herrlinger, Robert
- History of Medical Illustration from Antiquity to 1600. New York: 1970. 1st English translation. 4to. 178 pp. Ills. Orig bndg. Slipcase.   *(Fye)* $125 [≃ £65]

Herschel, John Frederick William
- Familiar Lectures on Scientific Subjects. London: 1867. 1st edn. 8vo. xii,507 pp. Orig cloth, inner hinges strained.
        (Bow Windows) £60 [≃ $115]
- Meteorology. From the Encyclopaedia Britannica. Edinburgh: 1861. viii,288 pp. 3 fldg plates, text figs. Orig cloth.
        (Whitehart) £25 [≃ $47]
- Outlines of Astronomy. London: Longman ..., 1849. 1st edn. 8vo. xiv,[i errata, verso blank], 661, [32 advt] pp. 6 engvd plates (foxed). Orig ochre cloth, spine faded, sm repr to hd of spine.   *(Gaskell)* £165 [≃ $316]
- Outlines of Astronomy. Ninth Edition. London: 1867. 8vo. xxiv,741, [1],[2 advt] pp. 9 plates. Occas spotting. Orig cloth, hd of spine sl fingered, spine rubbed, extreme crnr tips a trifle faded.
        (Bow Windows) £55 [≃ $105]
- A Preliminary Discourse on the Study of Natural Philosophy. London: for Longman & John Taylor, 1831. 1st edn. 8vo. viii,372 pp. 12 advts at front dated March 1831. Addtnl letterpress title at end. Addtnl engvd title (dated 1830). Orig cloth, paper label.
        (Gaskell) £125 [≃ $239]

- A Treatise on Astronomy. London: Cabinet Cyclopaedia, 1833. 1st edn. Sm 8vo. 16 advt, viii, 422, [2] pp. Addtnl engvd title, 3 plates, num text ills. Orig cloth, reprd.
        (Fenning) £65 [≃ $124]

Hertz, Heinrich
- Electric Waves. 1893. 1st edn in English. 278 pp. 40 ills. Orig bndg, spine sl worn.
        (New Wireless) $400 [≃ £208]
- Electric Waves. London: Macmillan, 1893. 8vo. xvii,279 pp. 40 text figs. Ex-lib. Cloth, unopened.   *(Gemmary)* $325 [≃ £169]
- Miscellaneous Papers. 1896. 1st edn. 340 pp. 34 ills. Port frontis in facs. Orig bndg, sl bumped.   *(New Wireless)* $180 [≃ £94]

Hertzler, A.E.
- Clinical Surgery by Case Histories. London: 1921. 2 vols. xvi,546; xii,547-1106 pp. 483 ills. Cloth, sl worn & dust stained, spines faded, hd of vol 2 spine reprd.
        (Whitehart) £40 [≃ $76]

Hewitson, William C.
- British Oology. Newcastle upon Tyne: [1831-38]. 2 vols. 155 hand cold plates. Orig cloth, rebacked with calf. [With] Supplement. Newcastle: [1842]. As issued without a title-page. 14 hand cold plates. Together 3 vols. Half mor, hd of spine worn..
        (Wheldon & Wesley) £280 [≃ $537]
- Coloured Illustrations of the Eggs of British Birds. With Descriptions of their Nests and Nidification. London: 1856. 3rd edn. 2 vols. Num hand cold plates. Contemp half mor, sl scuffed.   *(Grayling)* £150 [≃ $287]

Hewson, William
- The Works of William Hewson, F.R.S., edited with an Introduction and Notes by George Gulliver. London: 1846. 1st edn. 360 pp. Orig bndg.   *(Fye)* $250 [≃ £130]

Hey, M.H.
- Catalogue of Meteorites. London: BM, 1966. 3rd edn. 8vo. lxviii,637 pp. Cloth. Dw.
        (Gemmary) $50 [≃ £26]

Hey, William
- Practical Observations in Surgery, illustrated with Cases and Plates. Phila: 1805. 1st Amer edn. 332 pp. Orig bndg. *(Fye)* $300 [≃ £156]

Heynes, S.
- A Treatise of Trigonometry, Plane and Spherical, Theoretical and Practical ... Treatise of Stereographic and Orthographic

Projection of the Sphere ... London: 1701. [2], 135, [52], [92], 8 pp. Sep titles for 1st 3 sections. 16 plates. Sl marks. Old calf, sl worn. *(Whitehart)* **£150 [≈ $287]**

Hibberd, Shirley
- The Amateur's Flower Garden. London: 1875. 8vo. v,284 pp. 6 cold plates (foxed), num text figs. Orig dec cloth gilt.
  (Wheldon & Wesley) **£30 [≈ $57]**
- The Amateur's Flower Garden ... New Edition, Revised ... London: Collinridge, 1897. 8vo. 347 pp. Fldg cold frontis, num w'cut plates & ills. Orig pict cloth gilt.
  (Gough) **£25 [≈ $47]**
- The Amateur's Flower Garden ... New Edition. London: Collingridge, 1897. 8vo. 347 pp. Fldg chromolitho frontis, num plates. V occas sl spotting. Orig pict cloth gilt.
  (Gough) **£25 [≈ $47]**
- The Book of the Aquarium and Water Cabinet. London: Groombridge, n.d. 8vo. [150] pp. 2 plates, text ills. Orig cloth gilt, a.e.g. *(Sotheran's)* **£125 [≈ $239]**
- The Fern Garden. How to Make, Keep and Enjoy It ... Second Edition. London: Groombridge, 1869. 8vo. vi,148,6 illust advt pp. 8 cold lithos, text engvs. Orig elab gilt cloth, a.e.g., inner jnts cracked.
  (Beech) **£30 [≈ $57]**
- The Fern Garden. London: 1877. 7th edn. Post 8vo. vi,148 pp. 8 cold plates, 40 w'cuts. Orig cloth. *(Wheldon & Wesley)* **£20 [≈ $38]**
- The Ivy, a Monograph ... London: 1872. 1st edn. 8vo. [viii],115 pp. Cold frontis, cold ornamental title, 2 cold plates. Minor foxing. Deleted inscrptns on reverse of frontis. Orig dec cloth gilt, a.e.g., trifle worn.
  (Wheldon & Wesley) **£135 [≈ $259]**

Hickson, S.J.
- An Introduction to the Study of Recent Corals. Manchester: 1924. xiv,157 pp. 110 ills. Sm lib stamp on title & inside cvr. Orig bndg, top edge sl worn. *(Whitehart)* **£18 [≈ $34]**

Hill, Claude W.
- Electric Crane Construction. London: 1911. xx,313 pp. Num fldg diags. Some dust staining & foxing. Orig bndg.
  (Whitehart) **£25 [≈ $47]**

Hill, J.B. & MacAllister, D.A.
- The Geology of Falmouth and Truro and of the Mining District of Cambrone and Redruth. London: Geol Survey Memoirs, 1906. 8vo. x,335 pp. 24 plates, 65 text figs. Some foxing. Cloth gilt, rebacked.

(Henly) **£95 [≈ $182]**

Hill, "Sir" John
- Essays in Natural History and Philosophy. Containing a Series of Discoveries, by the Assistance of Microscopes. London: J. Whiston & B. White, 1752. 415 pp. Contemp calf, red label. *(C.R. Johnson)* **£260 [≈ $499]**
- The Family Herbal ... Bungay: 1812. 8vo. viii, 376 pp. 54 hand cold plates. Sl used. Mod half calf antique style.
  (Wheldon & Wesley) **£120 [≈ $230]**
- A General Natural History or New and Accurate Description of the Animals, Vegetables and Minerals of the Different Parts of the World. London: 1748-52. 3 vols. Folio. Fldg table, 56 plates. Few sl blemishes. Rec half calf, antique style.
  (Wheldon & Wesley) **£450 [≈ $863]**
- A General Natural History. Volume I. A History of Fossils. London: 1748. Folio. [xii], 1-228, 333-592, 457-654,[6] pp, complete. Fldg table, 12 hand cold plates. Some foxing & browning. Marg MS notes. Old half calf, worn, jnts cracked.
  (Wheldon & Wesley) **£300 [≈ $575]**
- A Method of Producing Double Flowers from Single by a Regular Course of Culture. London: 1758. 2nd edn. 8vo. 40 pp. 8 plates. Mod bds. Anon.
  (Wheldon & Wesley) **£75 [≈ $143]**

Hill, Robin
- Australian Birds ... New York: Funk & Wagnalls, 1967. Folio. Num cold plates. Dw.
  (Terramedia) **$75 [≈ £39]**

Hillary, William
- Observations on the Changes of the Air, and Concomitant Epidemical Diseases in the Island of Barbadoes, to which is added A Treatise on the ... Yellow Fever ... with Notes by Benjamin Rush. Phila: 1811. 1st Amer edn. 8vo. xii-260, [4] pp. Foxing. Sheep, rebacked. *(Goodrich)* **$175 [≈ £91]**
- Observations on the Changes of the Air, and the Concomitant Epidemical Diseases in the Island of Barbados ... With Notes, by Benjamin Rush ... Phila: B. & T. Kite ..., 1811. 1st Amer edn. 8vo. xiii,[blank], 15-260, [4] pp. Contemp calf, rubbed, jnt cracked.
  (Hemlock) **$325 [≈ £169]**

Hilton-Simpson, M.W.
- Arab Medicine and Surgery. A Study of the Healing Art in Algeria. London: 1922. 8vo. viii, 96 pp. Ills. Orig bndg, ex-lib.
  (Goodrich) **$65 [≈ £33]**

Himes, Norman E.
- Medical History of Contraception. Baltimore: The Williams & Wilkins Co, 1936. 8vo. Ills. Orig bndg, trifle soiled. *(Georges)* £50 [≈ $95]

Hincks, T.
- A History of the British Hydroid Zoophytes. London: 1868. 2 vols. 8vo. 68 plates. Clean ex-lib, b'plates only. Cloth.
  (Wheldon & Wesley) £60 [≈ $115]

Hind, John
- The Elements of Algebra: Designed for the Use of Students in the University. Cambridge: J. Smith ..., 1830. 2nd edn. 8vo. ix,530 pp. Contemp diced calf.
  (Young's) £40 [≈ $76]

Hind, W.M. & Babington, C.
- The Flora of Suffolk ... London: 1889. 8vo. xxxiv,508 pp. Cold map. Orig cloth.
  (Wheldon & Wesley) £40 [≈ $76]

Hinton, John W.
- Organ Construction. Third Edition. Revised and Enlarged. London: Weekes & Co, 1910. 4to. [8], 190, [4 advt] pp. Fldg plan, 37 plates & ills. Orig cloth. *(Fenning)* £35 [≈ $67]

Hippocrates
- The Genuine Works. Translated from the Greek with a Preliminary Discourse and Annotations by Francis Adams. London: Sydenham Society, 1849. 2 vols. 8vo. 8 plates. Orig cloth, worn. *(Goodrich)* $175 [≈ £91]
- The Genuine Works. Translated by F. Adams. London: Sydenham Society, 1849. 2 vols. 872 pp. 6 plates. Orig cloth, rubbed.
  (Peter Taylor) £52 [≈ $99]
- Hippocrates Upon Air, Water, and Situation; upon Epidemical Diseases; and upon Prognosticks ... London: J. Watts, 1734. 1st edn. 8vo. [viii], xxiv, [xviii], 389, [1] pp. Frontis. Contemp calf, hinges cracked.
  (Bookpress) $375 [≈ £195]

Hirsch, August
- A Handbook of Geographical and Historical Pathology. London: 1883-86. 1st English translation. 3 vols. Orig bndg, fine.
  (Fye) $300 [≈ £156]
- Handbook of Geographical and Historical Pathology. Translated by C. Creighton. London: New Sydenham Soc, 1883-86. 3 vols. Orig cloth. *(Whitehart)* £120 [≈ $230]

Hirschfelder, Arthur
- Diseases of the Heart and Aorta. Phila: 1913.

2nd edn. 738 pp. Ills. Orig bndg.
  (Fye) $100 [≈ £52]

Hirst, Barton (ed.)
- A System of Obstetrics by American Authors. Phila: 1888. 1st edn. 2 vols. 808; 854 pp. Over 500 ills. Orig bndg, fine.
  (Fye) $150 [≈ £78]

Hirst, L.F.
- The Conquest of Plague. A Study of the Evolution of Epedemiology. Oxford: 1953. xvi, 478 pp. A few diags. Cloth, a little marked. *(Whitehart)* £25 [≈ $47]

Hiscox, G.D.
- Gas, Gasoline and Oil Vapour Engines. A New Book Descriptive of their Theory and Power ... London: 1897. [vi],279 pp. 206 text ills. Title sl loose. Piece torn from back endpaper. Spine ends worn.
  (Whitehart) £35 [≈ $67]

Hiscox, G.D. (ed.)
- The Twentieth Century Book of Recipes, Formulas and Processes ... London: 1907. 787 pp. Cloth sl worn.
  (Whitehart) £35 [≈ $67]

An Historical Account ...
- An Historical Account of the Origin, Progress, and Present State of the Bethlehem Hospital, founded by Henry the Eighth, for the Cure of Lunatics ... London: ptd in the year, 1783. 16 pp. Engvd frontis. Disbound.
  (C.R. Johnson) £1,250 [≈ $2,399]

History and Description of Fossil Fuel ...
- See Holland, John.

Hitchcock, E.
- Report on the Geology, Mineralogy, Botany, & Zoology of Massachusetts. Amherst: J.S. & C. Adams, 1833. 8vo. xii,692 pp. Num w'cuts. rebound in cloth. Without the atlas of plates. *(Gemmary)* $80 [≈ £41]
- Supplement to the Ichnology of New England. Boston: 1865. 4to. 96 pp. 20 plates (plates 13-19 are mtd photos). Lib b'plate, lib blind stamp on title. Cloth, reprd.
  (Wheldon & Wesley) £70 [≈ $134]

Hitt, Thomas
- A Treatise of Fruit Trees ... London: for the author, & sold by T. Osborne, 1755. 1st edn. 8vo. [xvi],392 pp. 7 fldg engvd plates (1 or 2 tears). Contemp sprinkled calf, upper jnt cracked but sound. *(Gaskell)* £300 [≈ $575]

- A Treatise of Fruit Trees. London: 1768. 3rd edn. 8vo. viii,394,[6] pp. 7 fldg plates. Tear in 1 plate reprd. Contemp calf, jnts weakening. *(Henly)* £95 [≈ $182]
- A Treatise of Fruit-Trees. London: for Robinson & Roberts, 1768. 3rd edn. viii, 394, [iv] pp. 7 fldg plates. Contemp calf gilt, spine darkened, sm defect in bottom panel. *(Hollett)* £150 [≈ $287]

Hobbs, W.H.
- Earth Features and Their Meaning. An Introduction to Geology for the Student and the General Reader. New York: 1912. xxxix,506 pp. 24 plates, 493 figs. Sm blind stamp on title. Orig cloth, spine sl dull, sm nick hd of spine, lib number on spine. *(Whitehart)* £18 [≈ $34]

Hochberg, Lew
- Thoracic Surgery before the 20th Century. New York: 1960. 1st edn. 858 pp. Orig bndg. *(Fye)* $125 [≈ £65]

Hocking, A.
- Oppenheimer and Son. Johannesburg: McGraw Hill, 1973. 8vo. 526 pp. Num photo ills. Leather. *(Gemmary)* $125 [≈ £65]

Hodgson, Joseph
- Engravings, intended to illustrate some of the Diseases of the Arteries, accompanied with Explanations ... London: for Thomas Underwood, 1815. 1st edn. Sm folio. 27 pp. 8 plates. Orig calf, some rubbing & spotting. *(Chapel Hill)* $600 [≈ £312]

Hoe, Robert
- A Short History of the Printing Press ... New York: Robert Hoe, 1902. 1st edn. 4to. Num ills. Orig wraps (edges chipped). *(Oak Knoll)* $95 [≈ £49]

Hoff, E.C. & Fulton, J.F.
- A Bibliography of Aviation Medicine. Springfield: 1942. xv,237 pp. Cloth, sl marked. *(Whitehart)* £35 [≈ $67]

Hoff, J.H. van't
- Lectures on Theoretical and Physical Chemistry. Translated by R.A. Lehfeldt. London: 1899-1900. 254; 156; 143 pp. 103 figs. Prize leather gilt. *(Whitehart)* £95 [≈ $182]

Hoffer, Raimund
- A Practical Treatise on Caoutchouc and Gutta Percha ... Phila: Henry Carey Baird,

1883. 1st edn in English. 8vo. 278 pp. 9 text ills. Orig cloth. *(Gough)* £25 [≈ $47]

Hofmann, E.
- The Young Beetle-Collector's Handbook. London: Swan Sonnenschein, 1897. 1st edn. 8vo. viii,178 pp. 20 cold plates. Foredge sl spotted. Orig pict cloth gilt. *(Gough)* £45 [≈ $86]
- The Young Beetle-Collector's Handbook. Second Edition. London: Swan Sonnenschein, 1902. 8vo. 178 pp. 20 cold plates. Orig pict cloth gilt. *(Gough)* £20 [≈ $38]

Hofmeister, Wilhelm
- On the Germination, Development, and Fructification of the Higher Cryptogamia, and on the Fructification of the Coniferae. London: Ray Society, 1862. 1st edn in English. 8vo. xvii,506 pp. 65 plates. Orig cloth, backstrip relaid, cvrs & spine faded. *(Rootenberg)* $500 [≈ £260]

Hogg, J.
- The Microscope: Its History, Construction and Application. London: Ingram & Co, 1854. 1st edn. xvi,440 pp. Upwards of 500 engvs. Cloth, backstrip v loose & worn. *(Gemmary)* $75 [≈ £39]
- The Microscope: Its History, Construction and Applications ... London: 1854. 1st edn. xvi, 440 pp. Frontis, engvd title, 14 plates, 169 text figs. Orig pict cloth, sm repr to spine. *(Whitehart)* £48 [≈ $92]
- The Microscope: its History, Construction, and Application. London: 1858. 3rd edn. 8vo. xiv, 607 pp. Frontis, num text figs. Signs of use. Cloth, rebacked. *(Wheldon & Wesley)* £30 [≈ $57]
- The Microscope. London: Routledge, 1869. 7th edn. 8vo. 762 pp. 8 cold plates, 362 text figs. Some spotting to half-title & frontis. New cloth. *(Savona)* £35 [≈ $67]
- The Microscope: Its History, Construction and Application. London: Routledge, 1869. 7th edn. 8vo. xii,762 pp. 9 plates, over 500 text figs. Cloth, v loose, worn, spine torn. *(Gemmary)* $50 [≈ £26]
- The Microscope: Its History, Construction and Application. London: Routledge, 1871. 8th edn. 8vo. xii,762 pp. 9 plates, over 500 text figs. Dec cloth, inner hinge cracked. *(Gemmary)* $80 [≈ £41]
- The Microscope, its History, Construction and Application. London: 1883. 10th edn. Cr 8vo. xx,764 pp. 9 plates (8 cold), 354 text figs. Orig cloth. *(Wheldon & Wesley)* £30 [≈ $57]

- The Microscope: Its History, Construction and Application. London: Routledge, 1886. 11th edn. 8vo. xx,764 pp. 9 plates, 356 text figs. Dec cloth, worn, v loose.
(Gemmary) **$50 [≈ £26]**
- The Microscope. London: 1887. 12th edn. 8vo. 764 pp. 8 cold plates, over 500 engvs. Cloth, trifle used.
(Wheldon & Wesley) **£25 [≈ $47]**
- The Microscope: Its History, Construction and Application. London: Routledge, 1887. 12th edn. 8vo. xx,764 pp. 9 plates, 356 text figs. Ex-lib. Dec cloth.
(Gemmary) **$75 [≈ £39]**
- The Microscope. London: Routledge, 1898. 15th edn. 704 pp. Frontis, 20 plates, 445 text figs. New cloth, orig backstrip preserved.
(Savona) **£28 [≈ $53]**
- The Microscope: Its History, Construction and Application. London: Routledge, 1898. 15th edn. 8vo. xxiv,704 pp. Ills. Dec cloth.
(Gemmary) **$80 [≈ £41]**

Holden, A.E.
- Plant Life in the Scottish Highlands. London: 1952. 1st edn. 8vo. xv,319 pp. 64 plates. Orig cloth. Dw. *(Henly)* **£25 [≈ $47]**
- Plant Life in the Scottish Highlands ... Edinburgh: 1952. 1st edn. 8vo. 64 plates. Orig cloth gilt. Dw (sl torn).
(Hollett) **£30 [≈ $57]**

Holland, G. Calvert
- The Philosophy of Animated Nature; or the Laws and Actions of the Nervous System. London: Churchill, 1848. 8vo. 512 pp. Orig cloth, worn, spotted. *(Goodrich)* **$125 [≈ £65]**

Holland, Henry
- General View of the Agriculture of Cheshire ... for the consideration of the Board of Agriculture and Internal Improvement ... London: 1813. 1st edn. 8vo. xii, 375, [3], [2] pp. 2 fldg maps, fldg section, 5 plates (2 cold, 1 offset). Rec half calf.
(Young's) **£150 [≈ $287]**

Holland, Sir Henry
- Chapters on Mental Physiology. London: 1852. 1st edn. xii,301 pp. New cloth.
(Whitehart) **£18 [≈ $34]**
- Chapters on Mental Physiology. London: Longman ..., 1852. 1st edn. 8vo. Orig cloth, spine faded. *(Ximenes)* **$250 [≈ £130]**
- Chapters on Mental Physiology. London: 1858. 2nd edn. xvi,347 pp. Name label on endpaper. Sl foxing. Spine faded.
(Whitehart) **£25 [≈ $47]**

- Essays on Scientific and Other Subjects. London: 1862. 1st edn. 499 pp. Orig bndg.
(Fye) **$60 [≈ £31]**
- Medical Notes and Reflections. Phila: 1839. 1st Amer edn. 383 pp. Half leather.
(Fye) **$100 [≈ £52]**
- Medical Notes and Reflections. From the Third London Edition. Phila: 1857. 8vo. 493 pp. Orig bndg. *(Goodrich)* **$25 [≈ £13]**
- Recollections of Past Life. New York: 1872. 8vo. 351 pp. Orig bndg.
(Goodrich) **$25 [≈ £13]**

Holland, John
- The History and Description of Fossil Fuel, the Collieries, and Coal Trade of Great Britain. Second Edition. London: Whittaker, 1841. 8vo. xvi,485 pp. 42 text figs. Orig pink cloth, faded, rebacked. Anon.
(Gough) **£45 [≈ $86]**

Holland, Mary
- The Complete Economical Cook and Frugal Housewife ... Fifth Edition. London: Tegg ..., 1824. 12mo. lx,288 pp. Frontis, engvd title, 4 plates. Contemp half calf, rebacked, new endpapers.
(Frew Mackenzie) **£145 [≈ $278]**

Hollander, B.
- The Mental Functions of the Brain ... London: 1901. xviii,512 pp. Frontis, 37 ills. Foxing on page edges. Cloth, sl worn.
(Whitehart) **£25 [≈ $47]**

Hollom, P.A.D.
- The Popular Handbook of British Birds. London: Witherby, 1952. 1st edn. 8vo. xxiii, 424 pp. 152 plates. Dw (sl chipped).
(Gough) **£20 [≈ $38]**

Holly, H.W.
- The Art of Saw-Filing; Scientifically treated and explained on Philosophical Principles ... New York: John Wiley, 1864. 1st edn. 12mo. 56 pp. 44 text figs. Orig cloth gilt.
(Gough) **£40 [≈ $76]**

Holmes, E.M.
- Catalogue of the Hanbury Herbarium in the Museum of the Pharmaceutical Society of Great Britain. London: 1892. 1st edn. 4to. [viii], 136, xiv pp. Endpapers browned. Orig cloth, t.e.g. *(Bow Windows)* **$65 [≈ $124]**

Holmes, T.
- Introductory Address delivered at St. George's Hospital, October 2, 1893, on the

Centenary of John Hunter's Death. London: 1893. 80 pp. Cold pencil name on title. Orig bndg. *(Whitehart)* **£25 [≈ $47]**

Holmes, T.V. & Sherborn, C.D. (eds.)
- A Record of Excursions made between 1860 and 1890. London: 1891. vii,571 pp. 2 fldg plates, 213 text figs. Orig bndg, spine dull, jnts sl weak. *(Whitehart)* **£25 [≈ $47]**

Holt, John
- General View of the Agriculture of the County of Lancaster ... London: J. Nichols, 1794. Large Paper. Sq 4to. 114 pp. Fldg map, 1 plate. Half mor gilt by Fazakerley. *(Hollett)* **£95 [≈ $182]**

Home, Everard
- A Dissertation on the Properties of Pus ... London: John Richardson, 1788. 1st edn. Sm 4to. 63 pp. Lacks half-title. Last 4 pp sl marked. Old half calf, rubbed, sl wear to jnts. *(Bickersteth)* **£65 [≈ $124]**
- Practical Observations on the Treatment of Strictures in the Urethra, and the Esophagus. London: 1805-21. Vol 1 3rd edn, vol 2 2nd edn, vol 3 1st edn. 3 vols. Engvd plates. Orig bds, 1 bd detached. *(Fye)* **$150 [≈ £78]**

Homes, R.C., et al.
- The Birds of the London Area since 1900. London: Collins New Naturalist, 1957. 1st edn. 8vo. x,305,4 advt pp. 24 plates. Ends sl foxed. Orig cloth. *(Henly)* **£22 [≈ $42]**

The Honours of the Table ...
- See Trusler, J.

Hood, P.
- The Successful Treatment of Scarlet Fever: also Observations on the Pathology and Treatment of Crowing Inspiration. London: 1857. iv,200 pp. Orig cloth. *(Whitehart)* **£40 [≈ $76]**

Hooke, Robert
- The Diary of Robert Hooke, 1672-1680. Edited by Henry W. Robinson and Walter Adams ... London: 1935. 8vo. 527 pp. Ills. Orig bndg. *(Goodrich)* **$65 [≈ £33]**

Hooker, Sir William Jackson
- A Century of Ferns: being Figures and Brief Descriptions of One Hundred New or Imperfectly described Ferns from Various Parts of the World. London: 1854. Roy 8vo. 100 hand cold plates. Half mor. *(Wheldon & Wesley)* **£375 [≈ $719]**

- Flora Scotica, or a Description of Scottish Plants ... London: 1821. 2 vols in one. 8vo. Sound ex-lib, somewhat foxed. Cloth, spine label defective. *(Wheldon & Wesley)* **£60 [≈ $115]**
- Garden Ferns, or Coloured Figures and Descriptions of a Selection of Exotic Ferns adapted for Cultivation. London: 1862. Roy 8vo. 64 hand cold plates. Orig cloth. *(Wheldon & Wesley)* **£120 [≈ $230]**
- Niger Flora, or an Enumeration of the Plants of Western Tropical Africa ... London: 1849. 8vo. xvi,587 pp. Map, 2 plates of views & 50 plates of plants on 43 ff. Stamp on title & reverse of plates. Trifle used. Cloth. *(Wheldon & Wesley)* **£100 [≈ $191]**
- Species Filicum: being Descriptions of the Known ferns. London: 1846-64. 1st edn. 5 vols. 8vo. 304 plates. Lib stamps on titles & reverse of plates. 3 vols in old half leather, 2 in orig cloth, 2 vols reprd. *(Wheldon & Wesley)* **£220 [≈ $422]**

Hooker, Sir William Jackson & Baker, John Gilbert
- Synopsis Filicum; or, a Synopsis of all Known Ferns ... London: Hardwicke, [1865]-1868. 1st edn. 8vo. [4],482,[18] pp. 9 hand cold plates. Orig cloth, hinges weakened. *(Rootenberg)* **$350 [≈ £182]**
- Synopsis Filicum, or a Synopsis of all Known Ferns. London: 1874. 2nd edn. 8vo. xiv, 9-559 pp, complete. 9 cold plates. New cloth. *(Wheldon & Wesley)* **£70 [≈ $134]**
- Synopsis Filicum: or a Synopsis of all Known Ferns. London: 1883. 2nd edn, reissue. 8vo. xiv,9-559 pp. 9 hand cold plates. Cloth. *(Wheldon & Wesley)* **£75 [≈ $143]**

Hooker, Sir William Jackson & Taylor, T.
- Muscologia Britannica: containing the Mosses of Great Britain and Ireland. London: 1827. 2nd edn. 8vo. xxxvii,[ii],272 pp. 37 hand cold plates on 36 ff. Title sl foxed. Mod buckram. *(Wheldon & Wesley)* **£120 [≈ $230]**
- Muscologia Britannica: containing the Mosses of Great Britain and Ireland. London: 1827. 2nd edn. 8vo. xxxvii,[ii],272 pp. 37 plain plates on 36 ff. Lower outer crnrs stained. New cloth. *(Wheldon & Wesley)* **£75 [≈ $143]**

Hooper, R.
- Physician's Vade Mecum ... Enlarged by W.A. Guy. London: 1854. xii,326 pp. Contemp half roan, rubbed & dusty, hinges weak. *(Whitehart)* **£40 [≈ $76]**

Hope, James
- A Treatise on the Diseases of the Heart and Great Vessels ... With Notes and a Detail of Recent Experiments by C.W. Pennock. Phila: 1846. 572 pp. Litho plates. Rec half leather.
(Fye) **$300** **[≈ £156]**

Hope, Mrs James
- Memoir of the late James Hope, M.D. Physician to St. George's Hospital ... to which are added Remarks on Classical Education. London: 1842. 8vo. 358 pp. Frontis. Orig bndg, jnt split.   *(Goodrich)* **$95** **[≈ £49]**
- Memoir of the late James Hope, M.D. London: 1848. 4th edn. 367 pp. Port. Orig bndg.   *(Fye)* **$100** **[≈ £52]**

Hopewell-Smith, A.
- An Introduction to Dental Anatomy and Physiology. Descriptive and Applied. Philadelphia & New York: 1913. 372 pp. Frontis, 5 plates, 344 text diags. Spine sl worn. Author's pres copy.
(Whitehart) **£35** **[≈ $67]**

Hopgood, George
- On the Management of the Hair and Scalp. Ryde, Isle of Wight: W. Gabell, 1856. 1st edn. 12mo. [iv],iv,7-78 pp. Orig limp cloth, a.e.g., rubbed.   *(Burmester)* **£90** **[≈ $172]**

Hopkins, B.S.
- Chapters in the Chemistry of the Less Familiar Elements. Illinois: 1939. 2 vols. 266; 286 pp. Tables, a few figs. Stiff wraps, linen spine, spines marked.
(Whitehart) **£25** **[≈ $47]**

Hopkins, G.M.
- Experimental Science. Elementary Practical and Experimental Physics. London: 1891. xiii, 719 pp. 1 plate, 672 text figs. Orig pict cloth, rebacked.   *(Whitehart)* **£28** **[≈ $53]**
- Experimental Science: Elementary Practical and Experimental Physics. New York: Munn & Co, 1895. 17th edn. 8vo. xiii,840 pp. Num ills. Elab dec cloth. *(Gemmary)* **$125** **[≈ £65]**

Hopkinson, J.
- Original Papers by the late John Hopkinson, D.Sc., F.R.S. Edited by B. Hopkinson. Cambridge: 1901. 2 vols. Port frontis, text diags. Orig bndg, partly unopened.
(Whitehart) **£35** **[≈ $67]**

Hopkirk, T.
- Flora Glottiana. A Catalogue of the Indigenous Plants on the Banks of the River Clyde and in the Neighbourhood of the City of Glasgow. Glasgow: 1813. 8vo. [ii],iv, [ii], 6-170 pp. Stamp on title & half-title. New cloth.   *(Wheldon & Wesley)* **£60** **[≈ $115]**

Hoppough, C.I.
- A Treatise upon Wireless Telegraphy and Telephony. 1912. 1st edn. 235 pp. 35 photos, 122 ills. Orig bndg.
(New Wireless) **$95** **[≈ £49]**

Horblit, Harrison D.
- One Hundred Books Famous in Science. New York: The Grolier Club, 1964. 4to. 449 pp. Num plates. Cloth. Slipcase. Sl water spots on spine & slipcase.
(Gemmary) **$475** **[≈ £247]**
- One Hundred Books Famous in Science, based on an Exhibition held at the Grolier Club. New York: 1964. 1st edn. 4to. 464 pp. 220 ills. Orig bndg. Slipcase.
(Fye) **$450** **[≈ £234]**

Horne, Henry
- Essays concerning Iron and Steel ... London: T. Cadell, 1773. 1st edn. 12mo. iii, 223 pp. Later polished calf, backstrip relaid. The Boulton copy. *(Bookpress)* **$2,500** **[≈ £1,302]**

Hornor, S.S.
- The Medical Student's Guide in Extracting Teeth: with Numerous Cases in the Surgical Branch of Dentistry. Phila: 1851. 76 pp. 2 plates. Lib label & lib label removal endpaper, occas sl marg water staining. Cloth sl worn.   *(Whitehart)* **£45** **[≈ $86]**

Horsley, J. Shelton
- Surgery of the Blood Vessels. St. Louis: 1915. 1st edn. 304 pp. 89 ills. Orig bndg.
(Fye) **$250** **[≈ £130]**

Hortator (pseud.)
- Simplicity of Health: exemplified. By Hortator. London: for the author by Effingham Wilson, 1829. 1st edn. Lge 12mo. x,[2],120 pp. Orig bds, uncut, paper label on upper bd, spine sl chipped & worn.
(Fenning) **£35** **[≈ $67]**

Horton, Richard
- Tables for Planting and Valuing Underwood and Woodland; also Lineal, Superficial, Cubical, Wages, Marketing, and Decimal Tables ... London: 1832. 1st edn. 8vo. Tree calf.   *(Young's)* **£25** **[≈ $47]**

Hortus Collinsonianus ...
- See Dillwyn, L.

Horwood, A.R.

- A New British Flora: British Wild Flowers in their Natural Haunts. London: 1919. 6 vols. Lge 8vo. Cold frontis, 3 cold maps, 64 cold plates, num other ills. Orig cloth, sev cvrs marked.   *(Bow Windows)* £40 [≈ $76]

Horwood, A.R. & Noel, C.W.F.

- The Flora of Leicestershire and Rutland ... Oxford: 1933. ccxcvii,687 pp. 5 maps, 31 plates. Orig cloth. Dw.
(Wheldon & Wesley) £60 [≈ $115]

Hosack, David

- Catalogue of the Entire Medical Library of the late Doctor David Hosack ... to be Sold at Auction ... by Bangs, Merwin & Co. New York: 1867. 8vo. 39 pp. Orig wraps.
(Goodrich) $450 [≈ £234]
- An Inaugural Discourse Delivered at the Opening of the Rutgers Medical College ... New York: Seymour, 1826. 8vo. 176 pp. Frontis. Sl foxing. Orig bds, worn.
(Goodrich) $195 [≈ £101]
- An Inaugural Discourse delivered at the Opening of Rutgers Medical College in the City of New York on Monday, the 6th Day of November, 1826. New York: Seymour, 1826. 1st edn. 8vo. 196 pp. Frontis. Orig cloth backed bds, label.
(Offenbacher) $250 [≈ £130]

Hoskins, John

- Observations on that Form of Disease, Nosologically called Dysentery. Phila: for the author, 1804. 1st edn. Sm 4to. [3]-40 pp. Disbound.   *(Bookpress)* $165 [≈ £85]

Hoskins, W.G. & Stamp, L. Dudley

- The Common Lands of England and Wales. London: Collins New Naturalist, 1963. 1st edn. 8vo. xvii,366 pp. Plates, ills. Dw (sl chipped).   *(Gough)* £30 [≈ $57]
- The Common Lands of England and Wales. London: Collins New Naturalist, 1963. 1st edn. 8vo. xvii,366 pp. 4 cold & 24 plain plates. Orig cloth. Dw. *(Henly)* £20 [≈ $38]

Hough, Horatio Gates

- Diving, or an Attempt to Describe upon Hydraulic and Hydrostatic Principles, A Method of Supplying the Diver with Air Underwater. Hartford: John Russell ..., 1871. 1st edn. 8vo. 8 pp. Diag on final page. Folded & unopened as issued. Box.
(Young's) £125 [≈ $239]

Houghton, William

- British Fresh-Water Fishes. London: William Mackenzie, [1879]. 2 vols in one. Folio. xxvi,204 pp. 41 chromolitho plates. Occas sl spotting of text. Contemp red half mor gilt, rubbed.   *(Frew Mackenzie)* £750 [≈ $1,439]
- Country Walks of a Naturalist with his Children. Fifth Edition. London: Groombridge, 1878. Sm 8vo. vi,154 pp. 9 chromolitho plates. Orig blue pict cloth gilt.
(Gough) £25 [≈ $47]

Houlton, C.

- Cage-Bird Hybrids, containing Full Directions for Selection, Breeding, Exhibition and General Management of Canary Mules and British Bird Hybrids. London: n.d. 4to. 128 pp. 16 cold plates. Cloth, rebacked.
(Wheldon & Wesley) £30 [≈ $57]

House, H.D.

- Wild Flowers of New York. Albany: 1923. 2nd printing. 2 vols. 362 pp. 264 cold plates. Endpapers spotted. Cloth gilt.
(Henly) £150 [≈ $286]

The Housekeeper's Receipt Book ...

- The Housekeeper's Receipt Book, or, the Repository of Domestic Knowledge; containing a Complete System of Housekeeping ... London: the editor, 1813. 1st edn. 8vo. iv,376 pp. 2 plates (stained, 1 reprd). Some soiling & marking. Contemp calf, worn.   *(Young's)* £110 [≈ $211]

Houston, Edwin J. & Kennelly, A.E.

- The Electric Motor and the Transmission of Power. 1894. 1st edn. 377 pp. 122 ills. Orig bndg.   *(New Wireless)* $85 [≈ £45]
- Electric Telegraphy. 1897. 1st edn. 448 pp. 163 ills. Orig bndg.
(New Wireless) $40 [≈ £20]
- Recent Types of Dynamo-Electric Machinery. 1898. 1st edn. 612 pp. 435 ills. Orig bndg, front cvr loose, spine worn.
(New Wireless) $45 [≈ £24]

Hovey, O.E.

- Movable Bridges. New York: 1926. 2 vols. Num fldg plates & diags. Orig bndgs.
(Whitehart) £25 [≈ $47]

Howard, H. Eliot

- The British Warblers, with Problems of their Lives. London: 1907-15. 2 vols. 35 cold & 51 plain plates. 2 cold plates sl marked in margs, occas v sl mark, marg notes to 2 pp. Half mor.

(Grayling) **£500 [≈$959]**
- The British Warblers ... London: 1907-15. 9
parts in 11 (1-9, 6 (plates), 9*). Imperial 8vo.
12 maps, 35 cold & 51 gravure plates. Orig
bds, uncut, 2 parts reprd.
(Wheldon & Wesley) **£550 [≈$1,055]**
- An Introduction to the Study of Bird
Behaviour. London: 1929. Folio. Plates by
George Lodge. Orig bndg, sl marked.
(Grayling) **£80 [≈$153]**
- Territory in Bird Life. London: 1920. 1st
edn. 8vo. xiii, 308 pp. 2 plans, 11 plates. Orig
cloth.   *(Wheldon & Wesley)* **£30 [≈$57]**
- Territory in Bird Life. London: 1920. 1st
edn. 8vo. xiii,308 pp. 2 plans, 11 plates. Orig
cloth, sm tear hd of spine.
(Wheldon & Wesley) **£30 [≈$57]**

Howard, M.M.
- Wild Flowers and their Teachings. London:
1845. 8vo. ix,92 pp. 37 actual mtd specimens.
Specimens well preserved. Cloth gilt, trifle
worn. Anon.
(Wheldon & Wesley) **£55 [≈$105]**

Howard, William
- An Essay on the Hydropic State of Fever.
Phila: the author, 1805. 1st edn. Sm 4to. 34
pp. Disbound.   *(Bookpress)* **$150 [≈£78]**

Howell, John W. & Schroeder, Henry
- The History of the Incandescent Lamp. 1927.
1st edn. 208 pp. 98 photos, 25 ills. Orig bndg.
(New Wireless) **$40 [≈£21]**

Howie, C.
- The Moss Flora of Fife and Kinross. Cupar:
[1889]. 8vo. [iv],116,[iv] pp. Good ex-lib.
Cloth.   *(Wheldon & Wesley)* **£25 [≈$47]**

Howitt, R.C.L. & B.M.
- A Flora of Nottinghamshire. Newark:
privately ptd, 1963. 8vo. 252 pp. Cloth.
(Wheldon & Wesley) **£25 [≈$47]**

Howorth, Sir H.H.
- The Glacial Nightmare and the Flood. A
Second Appeal to Common Sense from the
Extravagance of some Recent Geology.
London: 1893. 2 vols. lvi, 536; xi, 377-920
pp. Foxing on page edges. Orig bndg.
(Whitehart) **£25 [≈$47]**
- Ice or Water. Another Appeal to Induction
from the Scholastic Methods of Modern
Geology. London: 1905. 2 vols (all
published). lvi,536; viii,498 pp. Orig cloth,
dust stained.   *(Whitehart)* **£25 [≈$47]**

Howship, John
- Practical Observations on the Symptoms of
Discrimination, and Treatment, of some of
the most Important Diseases of the Lower
Intestines and Anus. Illustrated by Numerous
Cases. London: 1821. 2nd edn. 240 pp.
Leather.   *(Fye)* **$175 [≈£91]**

Huber, Francois
- Observations on the Natural History of Bees.
London: for Thomas Tegg, 1841. 2nd edn.
8vo. 352 pp. Addtnl hand cold vignette title,
5 hand cold plates. Orig pict gilt cloth, spine
ends & crnrs sl rubbed.
(Chapel Hill) **$95 [≈£49]**

Huber, G.L. & Menzi, K.
- The Story of Chemical Industry in Basle.
Lausanne: CIBA, 1959. 233 pp. Num ills.
Orig parchment backed bds. Slipcase (sl
worn).   *(Whitehart)* **£35 [≈$67]**

Hudson, C.T. & Gosse, P.H.
- The Rotifera or Wheel-Animalcules. London:
1886. 2 vols. 30 cold & 4 plain plates. [With]
Supplement. London: 1889. 64 pp. 4 plain
plates. Together 3 vols. 4to. Half calf.
(Wheldon & Wesley) **£200 [≈$383]**

Hudson, N. (ed.)
- An Early English Version of Hortus Sanitatis.
A Recent Bibliographical Discovery ...
London: 1954. One of 550. xvi, 164, xvii-xxxi
pp. Num ills. Orig cloth, sl marked.
(Whitehart) **£25 [≈$47]**

Hudson, W.H.
- Birds of la Plata. London: 1920. 2 vols. Roy
8vo. 22 cold plates. Orig half buckram.
(Wheldon & Wesley) **£100 [≈$191]**

Hues, Robert
- A Learned Treatise of Globes ... now ... made
English ... by John [but Edmund] Chilmead.
London: J.S. for Andrew Kemb, 1659. 2nd
English edn. 8vo. [xxxvii],209, 220-241,
142-186, [1] pp. C4 & U8 blank. Occas sl
water stain. Contemp calf, ft of spine
chipped. Wing H.3298.
(Gaskell) **£1,200 [≈$2,303]**

Huggins, Sir William
- The Royal Society or, Science in the State and
in the Schools. New York: 1906. 4to. 131 pp.
25 ills. Orig bndg, uncut & unopened.
(Goodrich) **$65 [≈£33]**

Hughes, A.J.
- The Book of the Sextant. Glasgow: Brown, Son & Ferguson, 1941. 1st edn. 8vo. 90 pp. 37 text figs. Bds.   *(Gemmary)* **$35 [≈£18]**

Hughes, William
- Geological Notes of Ireland ... Dublin: M'Glashan & Gill, 1876. 1st edn. 12mo. xiii, [2], 67 pp. Rec wraps. *(Fenning)* **£35 [≈$67]**

Hughes, William Carter
- The American Miller, and Mill-Wright's Assistant. Detroit: 1850. 228 pp. 4 plates. Sheep.   *(Reese)* **$450 [≈£234]**

Huish, Robert
- A Treatise on the Nature, Economy, and Practical Management, of Bees, in which the Various Systems of the British and Foreign Apiarians are examined ... London: 1815. 1st edn. 8vo. xxiii,414 pp. 6 plates. Title & plates sl foxed. Mod half calf.
 (Wheldon & Wesley) **£100 [≈$191]**
- A Treatise on the Nature, Economy, and Practical Management, of Bees. London: 1817. 2nd edn. 8vo. xxxix,400 pp. 6 plates. Calf, rebacked.
 (Wheldon & Wesley) **£60 [≈$115]**

Hull, E.
- Volcanoes: Past and Present. London: Contemporary Science Series, 1892. xv,270 pp. 4 plates, 41 text ills. Orig cloth.
 (Whitehart) **£18 [≈$34]**

Hulme, F. Edward
- Butterflies and Moths of the Countryside ... London: Hutchinson, [1904]. Lge 8vo. xx, 300 pp. 312 ills on 35 plates. Orig cloth, extremities sl rubbed.
 (Claude Cox) **£28 [≈$53]**
- Familiar Wild Flowers. London: Cassell, [ca 1882-86]. Series 1-5. 5 vols. 200 cold plates. Occas text spot. Orig pict cloth gilt, a.e.g.
 (Hollett) **£140 [≈$268]**
- Wild Fruits of the Country-Side. London: Hutchinson, Woburn Library of Natural History, 1902. 1st edn. Sm 4to. viii,259 pp. 36 cold plates. Occas sl spotting. Orig pict cloth gilt, t.e.g.   *(Gough)* **£38 [≈$72]**

Humber, William
- A Comprehensive Treatise on the Water Supply of Cities and Towns with Numerous Specifications of Existing Waterworks. London: Crosby Lockwood, 1876. 1st edn. Lge 4to. xiv,378, advt pp. Cold frontis, 51 plates, 258 ills. Sl marg fingering. Rec cloth.

(Fenning) **£135 [≈$259]**
- A Comprehensive Treatise on the Water Supply of Cities and Towns with Numerous Specifications of Existing Waterworks. Chicago: 1879. 1st Amer edn. Lge 4to. xiv,298 pp. Cold frontis, 50 dble-page litho plates, 1 other plate, 258 ills. Orig half mor gilt, sl rubbed.   *(Fenning)* **£125 [≈$239]**

Humble, W.
- Dictionary of Geology and Mineralogy ... London: [1860]. vii,470 pp. Orig cloth, edges sl worn, rebacked. *(Whitehart)* **£65 [≈$124]**
- Dictionary of Geology and Mineralogy. London: Griffin, 1860. 3rd edn. 8vo. viii,470 pp. New endpapers. Cloth, rebacked.
 (Gemmary) **$150 [≈£79]**

Humboldt, Alexander von
- Cosmos: A Sketch of a Physical Description of the Universe. London: Bell & Daldy, 1871-76. 5 vols. Cr 8vo. 369; 370-742; 289; 601; 500 pp. Cloth, all unopened except vol 2.   *(Gemmary)* **$200 [≈£104]**
- Letters ... Written between the Years 1827 and 1858 ... Authorized Translation from the German ... London: Trubner, 1860. 8vo. xxvi, 334 pp. Contemp calf gilt, spine sl faded.   *(Frew Mackenzie)* **£90 [≈$172]**
- Views of Nature ... Translated from the German by E.C. Otte and Henry G. Bohn. London: Bohn's Scientific Library, 1850. 8vo. xxx,452, [8],[40 ctlg] pp. Cold frontis, facs plate. Orig red cloth.
 (Bickersteth) **£25 [≈$47]**

Hume, Edgar E.
- Medical Work of the Knights Hospitallers of Saint John of Jerusalem ... Baltimore: 1940. 8vo. 371 pp. Frontis. Orig bndg.
 (Goodrich) **$65 [≈£33]**

Humelbergius Secundus, Dick (pseud.)
- Apician Morsels; or, Tales of the Table, Kitchen, and Larder ... London: Whittaker, Treacher, 1829. 1st edn. Frontis. Contemp half roan, sl rubbed. *(Jarndyce)* **£60 [≈$115]**

Humphreys, Henry Noel
- The Genera of British Moths ... London: Paul Jerrard & Son, [1860]. 2 vols. Imperial 8vo. 206 pp, continuously paginated. 62 hand cold plates. Sl foxing at starts. Lib stamps on title versos. Lib labels on pastedowns. Orig cloth gilt, a.e.g.
 (Wheldon & Wesley) **£220 [≈$422]**

Humphreys, Henry Noel & Westwood, J.O.
- British Butterflies and Their Transformations. London: William Smith, 1841. 1st edn. 4to. xii,138,[1 index] pp. Hand cold title, 42 hand cold plates. Few v sl marks. Mod half mor. *(Sotheran's)* **£795 [≃$1,526]**

Hunt, Robert
- A Manual of Photography. [From the Encyclopaedia Metropolitana. Applied Sciences. No. 16]. Third Edition, Enlarged. London: Joseph Griffin, 1853. [8 advt], x, 321, [ii advt] pp. Hand cold frontis, 88 w'engvd ills. Orig pict red cloth, spine ends sl worn. *(Gough)* **£175 [≃$335]**
- Researches on Light: an Examination of all the Phenomena connected with the Chemical and Molecular Changes produced by the Influence of the Solar Rays ... London: Longman ..., 1844. 1st edn. 8vo. vii,[1], 303,[1], 32 advt pp. Errata slip. Hand cold frontis. Orig cloth. *(Rootenberg)* **$600 [≃£312]**
- Researches on Light in its Chemical Relations; embracing a Consideration of all the Photographic Processes. Second Edition. London: Longman ..., 1854. xx,396 pp. Fldg cold plate. Rec qtr calf. *(Fenning)* **£165 [≃$316]**

Hunter, Alexander
- Georgical Essays ... York: by A. Ward, for J. Dodsley ..., 1777. All published in this edn. 8vo. [iv], 560, [vii] pp. 3 fldg plates. Contemp calf backed bds, mor label, jnts cracked, spine ends worn, crnrs knocked, sides rubbed. *(Finch)* **£45 [≃$86]**

Hunter, John
- Observations on Certain Parts of the Animal Oeconomy. London: sold at No. 13, Castle-Street, Leicester-Square, 1786. 1st edn. 4to. 18 plates. Orig bds, minor rubbing. Cloth case. *(Ximenes)* **$3,500 [≃£1,822]**
- A Treatise on the Blood, Inflammation, and Gun-Shot Wounds. Phila: 1817. 2nd Amer edn. 514 pp. 8 plates. Leather, lacks label. *(Fye)* **$500 [≃£260]**
- A Treatise on the Blood, Inflammation, and Gun-Shot Wounds. Phila: 1817. 2nd Amer edn. 514 pp. 8 plates. Leather, lacks label. *(Fye)* **$500 [≃£260]**
- A Treatise on the Venereal Disease. With an Introduction and Commentary by Joseph Adams. First American Edition. Phila: 1818. 8vo. xx,367xv pp. 6 plates. Contemp calf, hinges sl rubbed. *(Hemlock)* **$200 [≃£104]**
- A Treatise on the Venereal Disease. With

Copious Additions by Dr. Philip Ricord. Translated and Edited, with Notes, by Freeman Bumstead. Phila: 1859. 2nd edn. 552 pp. Litho plates. Orig bndg, fine. *(Fye)* **$150 [≃£78]**
- Works. Phila: Webb, 1839-40. 2 vols. 8vo. 9 plates. Orig qtr calf, some wear. *(Goodrich)* **$275 [≃£143]**

Hunter, Richard & Macalpine, Ida
- Three Hundred Years of Psychiatry 1535-1860. Oxford: 1963. xxvi,1107 pp. 204 text figs. Dw. *(Whitehart)* **£48 [≃$92]**
- Three Hundred Years of Psychiatry, 1535-1860. London: 1963. 1st edn, 3rd printing. 1107 pp. Dw. *(Fye)* **$125 [≃£65]**

Hunter, William
- Two Introductory Lectures, delivered by Dr. William Hunter, to his Last Course of Anatomical Lectures ... added, Some Papers relating to ... Plan for ... a Museum ... London: J. Johnson, 1784. 4to. 130 pp. Half-title. Fldg plate. Orig qtr calf, uncut. *(Goodrich)* **$1,950 [≃£1,015]**
- See also Teacher, J.H.

Hunter, William
- Historical Account of Charing Cross Hospital and Medical School ... London: 1914. 1st edn. 4to. xxiv,309,[3] pp. 40 plates. A few pen or pencil marginalia. Orig cloth. *(Bow Windows)* **£85 [≃$163]**

Hurd-Mead, Kate Campbell
- A History of Women in Medicine from the Earliest Times to the Beginning of the Nineteenth Century. Haddam: 1938. 1st edn. 569 pp. Ex-lib. *(Fye)* **$225 [≃£117]**

Hurst, A.F. & Stewart, M.J.
- Gastric and Duodenal Ulcer. Oxford: 1929. 4to. xvii,544 pp. Text ills. Orig bndg, hd of spine v sl worn. *(Whitehart)* **£25 [≃$47]**

Hussey, E.L.
- Miscellanea Medico-Chirurgica. Cases in Practice, Reports, Letters and Occasional Papers. Oxford: 1882. vii,418 pp. Lib stamp & discolouration of title. A few pp blank edges sl torn. Orig cloth, spine sl worn. *(Whitehart)* **£25 [≃$47]**

Hutchinson, Revd H.N.
- Creatures of Other Days. Popular Studies in Palaeontology. London: 1896. xxiv,270 pp. 24 plates, 79 text ills. Orig pict cloth, sl dust stained. *(Whitehart)* **£15 [≃$28]**

Hutchinson, R.W.
- Television. Up-To-Date. London: 1935. xii, 184 pp. Frontis, 125 text figs. Orig bndg. Dw.   *(Whitehart)* **£25 [≈$47]**

Hutton, Charles
- A Mathematical and Philosophical Dictionary ... London: J. Davis, 1796-95. 1st edn. 2 vols. 4to. [iii]-viii, 650; [ii],756 pp. 37 plates, text ills. Lacks half-titles. Occas sl marks. Contemp calf, rebacked, crnrs sl worn.
  (Clark) **£225 [≈$431]**
- Miscellanea Mathematica: consisting of a Large Collection of Curious Mathematical Problems ... London: Baldwin, 1775. 1st edn, all published. 12mo. iv, 342, [2 errata & advt] pp. Text diags. Contemp calf backed mrbld bds, bds rubbed.   *(Gaskell)* **£265 [≈$508]**

Hutton, F.W.
- Manual of the New Zealand Mollusca (Marine and Land). Wellington: 1880. 8vo. xvi,iv,224 pp. Cloth.
  (Wheldon & Wesley) **£45 [≈$86]**

Huxley, T.H.
- American Addresses, with a Lecture on the Study of Biology. New York: 1877. 1st edn. 164 pp. Orig bndg.   *(Fye)* **$60 [≈£31]**
- The Crayfish, an Introduction to the Study of Zoology. London: 1880. One of 250 Large Paper. 8vo. xiv,371 pp. 82 ills. Blind stamp on title. New cloth.
  (Wheldon & Wesley) **£35 [≈$67]**
- Essays upon some Controverted Questions. London: 1892. 1st edn. viii,625 pp. Inscrptn on half-title offset. Cloth worn & sl marked.
  (Whitehart) **£25 [≈$47]**
- Evidence as to Man's Place in Nature. London: 1863. 1st edn. 8vo. [v],159 pp. Plate, 82 figs. Orig cloth, rather used.
  (Wheldon & Wesley) **£120 [≈$230]**
- Lay Sermons, Addresses, and Reviews. London: Macmillan, 1870. 1st edn. 8vo. xi, 378, ctlg pp. Orig cloth, discold, slit in jnt.
  (Bickersteth) **£25 [≈$47]**
- Lectures on the Elements of Comparative Anatomy ... On the Classification of Animals and on the Vertebrate Skull. London: John Churchill, 1864. 1st edn. 8vo. 303,31 pp. Ills. V sl foxing. Orig cloth.
  (Chapel Hill) **$300 [≈£156]**
- A Manual of the Anatomy of Invertebrated Animals. London: J. & A. Churchill, 1877. 1st edn. 8vo in 12s. 596,[16 advt dated Feb 1884] pp. 158 figs. Orig brown cloth.
  (Bow Windows) **£85 [≈$163]**
- The Oceanic Hydrozoa; a Description of the Calycophoridae and Psyophoridae observed during the Voyage of H.M.S. Rattlesnake, 1846-1850. London: Ray Society, 1858. Folio. x,143 pp. 12 plates (sl foxed). Orig bds, unopened, backstrip worn at ft.
  (Henly) **£78 [≈$149]**
- On Our Knowledge of the Causes of the Phenomena of Organic Nature. Being Six Lectures to Working Men ... London: Hardwicke, 1863. 8vo. 156 pp. Orig cloth.
  (Frew Mackenzie) **£80 [≈$153]**
- Science and Culture and Other Essays. London: Macmillan, 1881. 1st edn. 8vo. ix, 349, 2 advt pp. Name on title. Orig cloth, sl soiled, ft of spine sl defective.
  (Bickersteth) **£28 [≈$53]**
- The Scientific Memoirs ... Edited by Michael Foster and E. Ray Lankester. London: 1898-1902. 1st edn. 2529 pp. 4 ports, over 100 plates (many fldg). Very good ex-lib. Orig bndg.   *(Fye)* **$400 [≈£208]**

Huygens, Christian
- The Celestial Worlds Discover'd ... The Second Edition, Corrected and Enlarged. London: 1722. Sm 8vo. vi,162 pp. 5 fldg plates (sev foxed or dust marked, 1 reprd on reverse). Old calf, rebacked, crnr tips worn.
  (Bow Windows) **£175 [≈$335]**

Hymers, J.
- A Treatise on Conic Sections and the Application of Algebra to Geometry. Cambridge: 1845. 3rd edn, rvsd & enlgd. 8vo. iv, 228 pp. 4 fldg figs. Orig cloth backed bds.
  (Young's) **£30 [≈$57]**

Hyndman, H.H. Francis
- Radiation. 1898. 1st edn. 307 pp. Orig bndg.
  (New Wireless) **$95 [≈£49]**

Ibbetson, John Holt
- A Practical View of an Invention for Better Protecting Bank-Notes against Forgery ... Second Edition. London: for the author ..., 1821. 8vo. [2],68 pp. 2 titles (1 dated 1820). 19 plates. 72 tipped-in slips. Contemp calf gilt, a.e.g., backstrip relaid.
  (Beech) **£220 [≈$422]**

Iddings, J.P.
- Igneous Rocks. New York: John Wiley & Sons, 1909-13. 2 vols. 8vo. 30 text figs, 140 tables. Cloth.   *(Gemmary)* **$125 [≈£65]**

Iles, George
- Flame, Electricity and the Camera. 1900. 1st edn. 398 pp. 93 ills. Orig bndg.
  (New Wireless) **$35 [≈£18]**

Imison, John
- A Treatise of the Mechanical Powers. I. Of the Lever, II. The Wheel ... VI. The Inclined Plane. To which are added Several Useful Improvements ... London: for the author ..., [1787]. 8vo. [iv],39 pp. 2 fldg plates (1 sm tear, no loss) inc frontis. Mod qtr calf.
(Finch) **£225 [≈ $431]**

Imms, A.D.
- Insect Natural History. London: Collins New Naturalist, 1947. 1st edn. 8vo. xviii,317 pp. 40 cold & 32 plain plates. Orig cloth.
(Henly) **£12 [≈ $23]**

An Improved Method of Opening the Temporal Artery ...
- See Butter, William.

Ingersoll, Ernest
- Dragons and Dragon Lore ... New York: Payson & Clarke, 1928. 1st edn. xii,203 pp. Frontis, plates, ills. Orig half cloth, mrbld bds, spine sl faded, crnrs bumped. Dw (worn). *(Wreden)* **$58.50 [≈ £30]**

Ingold, C.K.
- Structure and Mechanism in Organic Chemistry. Ithaca, New York: 1969. 2nd edn. ix, 1266 pp. Num diags.
(Whitehart) **£25 [≈ $47]**

Ingraham, F.D. & Matson, D.
- Neurosurgery of Infancy and Childhood. Springfield: 1961. 1st edn, 2nd printing. 8vo. 456 pp. Orig bndg, sl rubbed.
(Goodrich) **$45 [≈ £23]**

Ingram, Collingwood
- The Birds of the Riviera. London: Witherby, 1926. 1st edn. 8vo. xv,155 pp. 6 plates. Orig pict cloth gilt, sl faded. *(Gough)* **£28 [≈ $53]**

International Correspondence Schools
- A Treatise on Telegraphy. 1901. 1st edn. 4 vols. 2166 pp. Num ills. Half leather, sl wear to spine & edges. *(New Wireless)* **$80 [≈ £41]**

Iredale, T.
- Birds of New Guinea. Melbourne, 1956. 2 vols. 4to. Map, 35 cold plates by Lillian Medland. Half mor.
(Wheldon & Wesley) **£340 [≈ $652]**

Irwin, Raymond
- British Bird Books. An Index to British Ornithology, A.D. 1481 - A.D. 1948. London: Grafton, 1951. 1st edn. 8vo. xix,398

pp. Orig cloth.   *(Gough)* **£20 [≈ $38]**

Iselin,, Marc
- Surgery of the Hand: Wounds, Infections, and Closed Traumata. London: 1940. 1st English translation. 353 pp. 135 ills. Orig bndg.   *(Fye)* **$300 [≈ £156]**

Jackson, B.D.
- Guide to the Literature of Botany ... London: 1881. Roy 8vo. xl,626 pp. Good ex-lib. Binder's cloth.
(Wheldon & Wesley) **£50 [≈ $95]**

Jackson, Sir Frederick John
- The Birds of Kenya Colony and the Uganda Protectorate. Completed and Edited by W.L. Sclater. London: Gurney & Jackson, 1938. 3 vols. Roy 8vo. Fldg cold map, port frontis, 24 cold plates, 241 text ills. Some foxing. Orig cloth, rubbed, sl worn.
(Sotheran's) **£625 [≈ $1,199]**
- Notes on the Game-Birds of Kenya and Uganda ... London: 1926. 8vo. xvi,258 pp. 13 cold plates. Cloth.
(Wheldon & Wesley) **£70 [≈ $134]**

Jackson, I.W.
- An Elementary Treatise on Optics. New York: A.S. Barnes, 1848. 8vo. vii,259 pp. 10 plates. Cloth, spine torn.
(Gemmary) **$45 [≈ £23]**

Jackson, J.
- Ambidexterity or Two-handedness and Two-brainedness ... London: 1905. 1st edn. 8vo. 24 ills. Orig bndg.
(Bow Windows) **£25 [≈ $47]**

Jackson, J. Hughlings
- Selected Writings. London: 1931. 1st edn. 2 vols. 500; 510 pp. Orig bndg, fine.
(Fye) **£500 [≈ £260]**
- Selected Writings. New York: 1958. Facs of 1931 edn. 2 vols. 500; 510 pp. Orig bndg. Dws.   *(Fye)* **£250 [≈ £130]**

Jackson, J.R.
- Minerals and their Uses. In a Series of Letters to a Lady. London: 1849. 1st edn. Sm 8vo. xvi,464 pp. Cold frontis. Few marks. Orig cloth, hd of spine worn.
(Bow Windows) **£65 [≈ $124]**

Jackson, Robert
- A Sketch (Analytical) of the History and Cure of Contagious Fever. London: 1819. viii, 284 pp. Lib stamp on title & verso of errata leaf.

Mod half mor gilt. *(Whitehart)* **£150** [≈ $287]
- A Systematic View of the Formation, Discipline, and Economy of Armies. London: for the author, 1804. 4to. xxxi,347 pp. Contemp bds, uncut, rebacked.
(Goodrich) **$325** [≈ £169]
- A Treatise on the Fevers of Jamaica ... Phila: Robert Campbell, 1795. 1st Amer edn. 12mo. 276,19,[5] pp. 4 advt pp. Contemp sheep.
(Bookpress) **$250** [≈ £130]
- A Treatise on the Fevers of Jamaica ... Phila: 1795. 8vo. xi,296,19 pp. 5 pp ctlg of Robert Campbell. Sl browning. Contemp tree calf, front hinge cracked. *(Hemlock)* **$275** [≈ £143]

Jacob, W.
- An Historical Inquiry into the Production and Consumption of the Precious Metals. London: Murray, 1831. 2 vols. 8vo. xvi,380; xi,415 pp. Leather backed mrbld bds, rubbed.
(Gemmary) **$250** [≈ £130]

Jacobi, Eduard
- Portfolio of Dermachromes. (English Adaptation of Text by J.J. Pringle). London: Rebman, 1903-06. 1st edn. With Supplement. 3 vols. 4to. viii,82; vi,83-180; iv,72 pp. 117 cold plates. Orig qtr mor gilt, spine ends sl rubbed. *(Gough)* **£50** [≈ $95]
- Portfolio of Dermachromes. New York: 1905. 2nd English edn. 3 vols. 233 cold plates. Leather. *(Fye)* **$150** [≈ £78]

Jaeger, B.
- The Life of North American Insects ... Providence: for the author ..., 1854. 1st edn. Tall 8vo. iv,204 pp. Litho frontis, port, 6 hand cold plates. Sl text foxing. Orig blue cloth, gilt spine. *(Karmiole)* **$250** [≈ £130]

Jakob, Christfried
- Atlas of Methods of Clinical Investigation, with an Epitome of Clinical Diagnosis ... Phila: 1898. 1st English translation. 259 pp. 182 cold ills. Orig bndg. *(Fye)* **$75** [≈ £39]
- Atlas of the Nervous System. New York: 1896. 1st English translation. 232 pp. 78 chromolitho plates, some with fldg flaps. Orig bndg. *(Fye)* **$125** [≈ £65]

James, R. Rutson
- Studies in the History of Ophthalmology in England prior to the Year 1800. Cambridge: UP for the British Journal of Ophthalmology, 1933. Med 8vo. 9 plates. Orig bndg.
(Georges) **£85** [≈ $163]

James, W.
- Wireless Valve Transmitters. 1925. 1st edn. 271 pp. 210 ills. Orig bndg, spine sl worn.
(New Wireless) **$30** [≈ £16]

Jameson, E.
- An Outline of the Mineralogy of the Shetland Islands and of the Island of Arran, with an Appendix ... Edinburgh: 1798. 8vo. xiv, 202 pp. 2 maps, plate. Blind stamp on title. Some browning. Orig bds, rebacked.
(Wheldon & Wesley) **£150** [≈ $287]

Jameson, Edwin
- Gynecology and Obstetrics. New York: 1936. 1st edn. 170 pp. Ink underlining on 3 pp. Orig bndg. *(Fye)* **$75** [≈ £39]

Jamieson, Alexander
- A Treatise on the Construction of Maps ... London: Darton, Harvey ..., 1814. 1st edn. 8vo. 20 maps & plates (12 fldg). Occas foxing. Half calf antique. *(Ximenes)* **$650** [≈ £338]

Janet, Pierre
- The Major Symptoms of Hysteria. New York: 1907. 1st edn. 345 pp. Orig bndg.
(Fye) **$100** [≈ £52]

Jansky, Cyril M.
- Principles of Radio-Telegraphy. 1919. 1st edn. 242 pp. 179 ills. Orig bndg, sl spotted.
(New Wireless) **$40** [≈ £20]

Jardine, Sir William
- The Birds of Western Africa. Edinburgh: Lizars, Naturalist's Library, 1837. 2 vols. 32 + 32 hand cold plates. Orig purple cloth, spines faded. *(Boswell)* **$220** [≈ £114]
- Entomology. Edinburgh: Jardine's Naturalist's Library, 1843. 7 vols (the complete section). Post 8vo. 7 ports, 7 vignettes (6 cold), 222 plates (203 hand cold). New cloth. Introduction; British Butterflies; Beetles; British Moths; Foreign Butterflies; Bees; Foreign Moths.
(Wheldon & Wesley) **$300** [≈ $575]
- Entomology. Edinburgh: Lizars, Naturalist's Library, 1835-40. 2 vols. 331; 269 pp. 35 + 30 hand cold plates. Orig purple cloth, spines faded. *(Boswell)* **$180** [≈ £93]
- The Natural History of Game-Birds. Ornithology Volume 4. Edinburgh: Naturalist's Library, n.d. Cr 8vo. xi, 17-175 pp, complete. Port, cold vignette, 30 cold plates. Half calf, trifle used.
(Wheldon & Wesley) **£40** [≈ $76]
- The Natural History of Humming Birds.

Edinburgh: W.H. Lizars ..., 1834. 2 vols in one. Sm 8vo. [6],6,iii, (5)-147,[1]; [2],iv, 156,[2], 157-166 pp. Addtnl vignette titles, 2 ports, 64 hand cold plates. Orig green cloth, a.e.g., old calf reback.
(Fenning) **£125 [≈ $239]**
- Humming Birds. Part II. Edinburgh: W.H. Lizars, The Naturalists Library Vol VII, Ornithology, [ca 1840]. Sm 8vo. [8],192 pp. Port, engvd title with hand cold vignette, 30 hand cold plates. 1 gathering sl loose. Orig red cloth gilt, spine worn & faded.
(Beech) **£60 [≈ $115]**
- Mammalia. Edinburgh: Lizars, Naturalist's Library, 1843. 13 vols inc Introductory vol. 402 hand cold plates. Qtr green leather, raised bands, red labels, sl shelf wear.
(Boswell) **$750 [≈ £390]**
- The Natural History of Fishes of the Perch Family. Edinburgh: Jardine's Naturalist's Library, 1835. Sm 8vo. 177 pp. Port, cold vignette, 2 plain & 32 cold plates. Orig cloth.
(Wheldon & Wesley) **£45 [≈ $86]**
- The Natural History of the Nectariniadae or Sun-Birds. London: Bohn, 1864. Re-issue. Sm 8vo. v, 17-277 pp. Port, cold vignette, 30 cold plates. Orig red cloth, trifle used.
(Wheldon & Wesley) **£80 [≈ $153]**
- The Naturalist' Library. Edinburgh: Lizars, [1845-46]. 2nd issue. Complete set. 40 vols. Post 8vo. 40 title vignettes (25 hand cold), 40 ports, 1278 plates (1237 hand cold). Dble-page plate Insects 4 counted as 1 plate. Mor, a.e.g., few sm reprs.
(Wheldon & Wesley) **£2,500 [≈ $4,799]**
- The Natural History of the Ordinary Cetacea or Whales. Edinburgh: Lizars, Naturalist's Library Vol VI, 1837. 16mo. xv, 264 pp. Port, addtnl engvd title with cold vignette, 30 plates (28 cold). Orig cloth, a.e.g.
(High Latitude) **$295 [≈ £153]**

Jeafferson, J. Cordy
- A Book about Doctors. London: Hurst & Blackett, 1860. 1st edn. 2 vols. 8vo. viii, 314; iv,311,[i],16 advt pp. 2 frontis. Orig brown cloth, upper hinge of vol 1 cracked but firm.
(Frew Mackenzie) **£65 [≈ $124]**

Jeans, H.W.
- Problems in Astronomy, Surveying, and Navigation; with their Solutions. New Edition. London: 1849. Sm 8vo. iv,239,[3] pp. 2 fldg plates. Orig cloth.
(Bow Windows) **£40 [≈ $76]**

Jeans, J.H.
- The Dynamical Theory of Gases. Cambridge:

1925. 4th edn. viii,444 pp. Orig cloth.
(Whitehart) **£25 [≈ $47]**
- The Mathematical Theory of Electricity and Magnetism. Cambridge: 1915. 3rd edn. vi,627 pp. New cloth.
(Whitehart) **£25 [≈ $47]**
- Problems of Cosmogony and Stellar Dynamics. Cambridge: 1919. 1st edn. viii,293 pp. 4 plates, 44 text figs. New cloth, traces of label removal inside cvrs.
(Whitehart) **£35 [≈ $67]**

Jeffreys, J.
- Views upon the Statics of the Human Chest, Animal Heat and Determination of Blood to the Head. London: 1843. 8vo. xix,233 pp. Occas v sl foxing. Orig cloth.
(Whitehart) **£80 [≈ $153]**

Jeffreys, J.G.
- British Conchology, or an Account of the Mollusca which now inhabit the British Isles and the Surrounding Seas. London: 1862-69. 5 vols. 8vo. 107 hand cold & 40 plain plates. Orig cloth.
(Wheldon & Wesley) **£500 [≈ $959]**

Jeffries, D.
- A Treatise on Diamonds and Pearls. London: for R. Lea, 1800. 8vo. xvi,116,30 pp. 30 pp of figs & tables. Foxed. Qtr leather.
(Gemmary) **$250 [≈ £131]**

Jehl, Francis
- Menlo Park Reminiscences. 1936. 1st edn. 3 vols. 1156 pp. 476 photos, 170 ills. Orig bndg. Sgnd by the author.
(New Wireless) **$140 [≈ £72]**

Jekyll, Gertrude
- Lilies for English Gardens, a Guide for Amateurs. London: 1901. 1st edn. 8vo. xii,72 pp. 72 plates, text figs. Orig cloth.
(Henly) **£50 [≈ $95]**
- Lilies for English Gardens. London: 1901. 1st edn. 8vo. xii,72 pp. 62 ills. Sl foxing. Orig buckram. *(Wheldon & Wesley)* **£35 [≈ $67]**
- Wood and Garden. London: 1899. 3rd edn. 8vo. xvi,286 pp. 71 photos. Orig buckram, spine trifle faded.
(Wheldon & Wesley) **£40 [≈ $76]**
- See also the companion IRBP volume The Arts and Architecture.

Jenkins, C. Francis
- Vision by Radio - Radio Photographs. 1925. 1st edn. 140 pp. 35 photos, 30 ills. Orig bndg.
(New Wireless) **$190 [≈ £98]**

Jenkins, F.A. & White, H.E.
- Fundamentals of Physical Optics. New York: 1937. 1st edn. xiv,453 pp. Num figs. Orig bndg. Pres copy from both authors.
(Whitehart) £25 [≈ $47]

Jenner, Edward
- An Inquiry into the Causes and Effects of the Variolae Vaccinae 1798. London: 1966. Facs reprint. iv,75 pp. 4 plates. Cloth, sl dusty.
(Whitehart) £40 [≈ $76]

Jennings, C.
- The Eggs of British Birds. Bath: Binns & Goodwin, 1853. 2nd edn. Sm 8vo. xxi,[i],266 pp. Cold title, 7 cold plates. Orig black lacquered bds, leather spine gilt, cold onlay, recased, spine ends worn.
(Wheldon & Wesley) £45 [≈ $86]

Jennings, D.
- An Introduction to the Globes and the Orrery: as also the Application of Astronomy to Chronology ... London: 1752. [xii],178 pp. 13 figs on 5 fldg plates. Old leather gilt, crudely rebacked, inner hinge sl cracked.
(Whitehart) £50 [≈ $95]

Jennings, Otto Emery & Avinoff, Andrey
- Wildflowers of Western Pennsylvania and the Upper Ohio River Basin. Pittsburgh: UP, 1953. 2 vols. Folio. Dws (one sl marked).
(Schoyer) $325 [≈ £169]

Jepson, W.L.
- A Flora of California. Berkeley: (1909)-1943. 3 vols in 4. Roy 8vo. Wraps, unopened.
(Wheldon & Wesley) £55 [≈ $105]

Jerdon, T.C.
- The Birds of India. Calcutta: 1862-64. 3 vols (vol 1, vol 2 part 1, vol 3) complete. 8vo. Cloth. Numerous annotations by Andrew Anderson.
(Wheldon & Wesley) £120 [≈ $230]
- The Mammals of India. London: 1874. Roy 8vo. xxxi,335 pp. New cloth.
(Wheldon & Wesley) £40 [≈ $76]

Jervis, Thomas Best
- Records of Ancient Science, exemplified and authenticated ... Calcutta: Baptist Mission Press, 1835. 1st edn. 8vo. vii,97 pp. Lacks front flyleaf. Orig cloth, sl discold, paper label.
(Burmester) £300 [≈ $575]

Jesse, Edward
- Gleanings in Natural History. London: 1838.

5th edn. 2 vols. Cr 8vo. Engvd titles & vignettes, text figs. Sm lib stamps on title versos. Orig cloth.
(Henly) £50 [≈ $95]
- Gleanings in Natural History. London: 1838. New edn. 2 vols. Sm 8vo. Frontis, engvd titles, text figs. Cloth.
(Wheldon & Wesley) £30 [≈ $57]

Jevons, W.S.
- The Principles of Science. A Treatise on Logic and Scientific Method. Second Edition, revised ... London: 1877. 8vo. xliv,786,[2] pp. Frontis. Contemp sgntr on title, few sm tears & folded crnrs, pencil & ink marginalia, marks. Orig cloth, dull, sl worn.
(Bow Windows) £205 [≈ $393]

Johannsen, A.
- A Descriptive Petrography of the Igneous Rocks. Chicago: (1931-38) 1962-63. 4 vols. Roy 8vo. 167 ports, 479 text figs. Cloth.
(Wheldon & Wesley) £50 [≈ $95]

Johns, Revd C.A.
- The Forest Trees of Britain. London: SPCK, 1847-49. 2 vols. 373; 352,ctlg pp. Num engvs by Whymper. Orig cloth, rebacked, cvrs sl stained.
(Willow) £40 [≈ $76]

Johnson, C.W.
- The Farmer's Encyclopaedia and Dictionary of Rural Affairs; embracing all the most Recent Discoveries in Agricultural Chemistry ... London: 1842. [xvi],iv,1320,[16] pp. Figs & tables. Orig cloth, worn, sl stained, spine marked.
(Whitehart) £40 [≈ $76]

Johnson, Charles
- British Poisonous Plants. London: John E. Sowerby, 1856. 1st edn. 8vo. iv,59 pp. 28 hand cold engvd plates. Orig cloth, rebacked.
(Rootenberg) $400 [≈ £208]
- British Poisonous Plants ... see also Sowerby, J.E. & Johnson, C.P.

Johnson, Charles & Johnson, C. Pierpoint
- British Poisonous Plants ... Second Edition. London: Van Voorst, 1861. iv,76,32 pp. 32 cold plates. Name on title. Orig cloth.
(Wreden) $185 [≈ £96]

Johnson, Francis R.
- Astronomical Thought in Renaissance England. Baltimore: John Hopkins Press, 1937. 8vo. 4 ills. Orig bndg.
(Georges) £40 [≈ $76]

Johnson, George W.
- The British Ferns Popularly Described ... London: Cottage Gardener Office, 1857. 1st edn. 8vo. viii,284 pp. Num plates. Orig cloth gilt.   *(Gough)* £18 [≈ $34]

Johnson, James
- The Influence of Tropical Climates on European Constitutions, to which is now added, An Essay on the Morbid Sensibility of the Stomach and Bowels ... London: 1827. 4th edn, enlgd. 8vo. viii,680 pp. Mod cloth.
                          (Bickersteth) £38 [≈ $72]

Johnson, Laurence
- A Manual of the Medical Botany of North America. New York: 1884. 1st edn. 292 pp. Plates. Orig bndg.   *(Fye)* $175 [≈ £91]

Johnson, Robert Wallace
- Friendly Cautions to the Heads of Families and Others ... With Ample Directions to Nurses who attend the Sick, Women in Child-Bed, etc ... Third Edition, with Additions. Phila: James Humphreys, 1804. 1st Amer edn. 8vo. xii,155,[4] pp. Foxed. Orig calf, rebacked.   *(Goodrich)* $175 [≈ £91]

Johnson, Stephen
- The History of Cardiac Surgery. Baltimore: 1970. 1st edn. 210 pp. Orig bndg. Dw.
                              (Fye) $90 [≈ £46]

Johnston, Alexander Keith
- A School Atlas of Astronomy ... Edited by J.R. Hind. Edinburgh & London: Blackwood, 1856. 1st edn. Sm folio. 18 cold plates, finished by hand. Text sl spotted. Orig half mor, sl rubbed.   *(Ximenes)* $175 [≈ £91]

Johnston, G.
- The Botany of the Eastern Borders (Berwick, etc.) ... London: 1853. 8vo. xii, 336 pp. Frontis, 14 plates (1 cold). Ex-lib. Cloth, sm tear in spine.
          (Wheldon & Wesley) £45 [≈ $86]
- A Flora of Berwick-upon-Tweed. Edinburgh: 1829-31. 2 vols in one. Cr 8vo. 8 plates. Lib stamps. New cloth.
          (Wheldon & Wesley) £60 [≈ $115]
- A History of British Sponges and Lithophytes. Edinburgh: 1842. 8vo. xii,264 pp. 25 tinted plates. New cloth.
          (Wheldon & Wesley) £60 [≈ $115]
- A History of the British Zoophytes. London: 1847. 2nd edn. 2 vols. 8vo. 73 plates (1-74, 34*, less 64 & 65 which never appeared). Some offsetting from plates. Half calf gilt.

          (Wheldon & Wesley) £60 [≈ $115]

Johnston, J.F.W.
- Lectures on Agricultural Chemistry and Geology with an Appendix containing Suggestions for Experiments in Practical Agriculture. London: 1844. 1st edn. 911, 116, xx pp. Contemp three qtr roan, gilt spine, leather label, edges sl worn, spine sl rubbed.   *(Whitehart)* £45 [≈ $86]

Johnston, W.J.
- Lightning Flashes and Electric Dashes. 1882. 3rd edn. 160 pp. Orig bndg.
                    (New Wireless) $75 [≈ £40]

Johnston-Lavis, H.J.
- The Eruption of Vesuvius in April, 1906. (Reprinted from the Scientific Transactions of the Royal Dublin Society). Dublin: UP, 1909. 4to. Title,139-200 pp. Plates III to XXIII as called for. Some marks. Contemp cloth, stained, faded, sl worn. Author's inscrptn.   *(Bow Windows)* £60 [≈ $115]

Johnstone, John
- An Account of the Mode of Draining Land, according to the System practised by Mr. Joseph Elkington ... London: for Richard Phillips, 1808. 3rd edn, enlgd. Fldg frontis, plates. Contemp speckled calf, red label.
                    (Jarndyce) £85 [≈ $163]

Johnstone, R.W.
- William Smellie. The Master of British Midwifery. Edinburgh: 1952. viii, 139 pp. Frontis port, 30 figs. Orig bndg.
                    (Whitehart) £25 [≈ $47]

Johnstone, W.G. & Croall, A.
- The Nature-Printed British Sea-Weeds ... Nature Printed by Henry Bradbury. London: 1859-60. 4 vols. 8vo. Half-titles. Engvd titles, 221 cold plates, 1 plain plate. Some foxing. Damp stains affecting a few plates & ff. 2 sm tears reprd. Orig green cloth, recased.
          (Bow Windows) £305 [≈ $585]
- The Nature-Printed British Sea-weeds ... Nature-Printed by Henry Bradbury. London: 1859-60. 4 vols. Roy 8vo. 4 cold title vignettes, 1 plain & 221 cold plates (1-207, 15 bis, 2 unnumbered). Less than usual foxing. Lib b'plates. Contemp half mor.
          (Wheldon & Wesley) £350 [≈ $671]

Jolley, J.B.W., Waldram, J.M., et al.
- The Theory and Design of Illuminating Engineering Equipment. London: [1930]. xxxi, 709 pp. 555 figs, some on plates. Orig

bndg.   *(Whitehart)* **£18 [≈$34]**

Jones, A.B. & Llewellyn, L.J.
- Malingering or the Simulation of Disease ... London: 1917. xxiii,708 pp. 5 plates. Cloth, sl marked, sm nick hd of spine.
    (Whitehart) **£25 [≈$47]**

Jones, C.H. & Sieveking, E.H.
- A Manual of Pathological Anatomy. London: 1854. xii,788 pp. 167 text figs. Orig cloth, rebacked.   *(Whitehart)* **£30 [≈$57]**

Jones, E.P.
- Kielland's Forceps. London: 1952. x,212 pp. Frontis port, 3 dble-sided plates, 111 text figs. Dw.   *(Whitehart)* **£25 [≈$47]**

Jones, F. Wood
- Coral and Atolls. Their History, Description, Theories of their Origin. London: 1910. xxiii,392 pp. Port, map, 27 plates, 79 text figs. Orig bndg.   *(Whitehart)* **£38 [≈$72]**

Jones, F.W.
- Structure and Function as Seen in the Foot. London: 1944. iv,329 pp. 150 figs.
    (Whitehart) **£25 [≈$47]**

Jones, J.P. & Kingston, J.F.
- Flora Devoniensis. London: 1829. 2 parts in one vol. 8vo. New cloth.
    (Wheldon & Wesley) **£50 [≈$95]**
- Flora Devoniensis. London: 1829. 2 parts in 1 vol. 8vo. Some notes. Bds, sl worn.
    (Wheldon & Wesley) **£50 [≈$95]**
- Flora Devoniensis. London: 1829. 8vo. xlvii, 162, lxvii, 217, [1] pp. Bds, worn.
    (Wheldon & Wesley) **£38 [≈$72]**

Jones, J.W.
- The Salmon. London: Collins New Naturalist, 1959. 1st edn. 8vo. xvi,192 pp. 12 plates, 24 text figs. Orig cloth.
    (Henly) **£24 [≈$46]**

Jones, Paul
- Flora Magnifica. Selected and Painted by the Artist. Text by William Blunt. London: 1976. One of 506. 16 cold ills. Half vellum gilt, by Zaehnsdorf. Slipcase.
    (Henly) **£240 [≈$460]**

Jones, Robert (ed.)
- Orthopaedic Surgery of Injuries. By Various Authors. London: 1921. 2 vols. 267 figs. Lib stamps, perf stamps on titles.
    (Whitehart) **£35 [≈$67]**

- Orthopaedic Surgery of Injuries by Various Authors. London: 1921. 1st edn. 2 vols. 540; 692 pp. Orig bndg.   *(Fye)* **£250 [≈£130]**

Jones, Robert & Lovett, Robert
- Orthopedic Surgery. New York: 1924. 1st Amer edn. 699 pp. Orig bndg, fine.
    (Fye) **$250 [≈£130]**

Jones, Stephen
- Rudiments of Reason; or, the Young Experimental Philosopher. A New Edition, carefully revised and enlarged, by the Rev. Thomas Smith. London: J. Harris, 1805. 8vo. xix, [i],386 pp. Half-title. 4 plates. Contemp tree calf, red gilt label. *(Spelman)* **£50 [≈$95]**

Jones, William
- The Gardener's Receipt Book: a Treasury of Interesting Facts and Practical Information ... Third Edition, much enlarged. London: Groombridge, 1858. Sm 8vo. viii,iv,83,24 advt pp. Orig cloth gilt, a.e.g., sl marked.
    (Beech) **£35 [≈$67]**

Jones, Revd William
- An Essay on the First Principles of Natural Philosophy ... Oxford: S. Parker ..., 1762. 1st edn. 4to. [vi],281 pp. 3 plates (2 fldg). Contemp calf, rebacked.
    (Bookpress) **$600 [≈£312]**

Jordan, D.S.
- A Guide to the Study of Fishes. New York: 1905. 2 vols. 4to. 2 cold frontis, 934 text figs. Sl used ex-lib. Orig buckram, vol 2 reprd.
    (Wheldon & Wesley) **£120 [≈$230]**

Jordan, D.S. & Evermann, B.W.
- The Fishes of North and Middle America. Washington: 1896-1900. 4 vols. Roy 8vo. 392 plates. Cloth, worn, recased.
    (Wheldon & Wesley) **£200 [≈$383]**

Jordan, R.J.
- Skin Diseases and their Remedies. London: 1860. xi,283 pp. Heavy pencilling on endpaper, lacks rear f.e.p., front endpaper replaced. Orig cloth, spine ends sl defective.
    (Whitehart) **£35 [≈$67]**

Jordan, W.L.
- The Ocean. A Treatise on Ocean Currents and Tides and their Causes demonstrating the System of the World. London: 1885. xvi,281 pp. 18 plates, 5 text figs. Orig cloth, side of spine sl worn.   *(Whitehart)* **£18 [≈$34]**

The Journal of a Naturalist ...
- See Knapp, J.L.

Judd, John W.
- The Geology of Rutland and the Parts of Lincoln, Leicester, Northampton, Huntingdon, and Cambridge ... Appendix ... London: Longmans & Stanford, 1875. xv,320 pp. 3 fldg hand cold diags, 8 tinted lithos, 19 text ills. 4 ff sl creased. Lib stamp title verso. Orig cloth faded. *(Hollett)* **£120** [≈ $230]

Jukes, J.B.
- The Student's Manual of Geology. Edinburgh: 1872. 3rd edn. xx,778 pp. Frontis, 167 text figs. Half roan, v rubbed, jnts cracked but firm.
 (Whitehart) **£25** [≈ $47]

Justice, J.
- The British Gardener's New Director. Dublin: 1765. 4th edn. 8vo. [xvi],xxvi, 443, [12] pp. 4 plates. Upper crnr of title cut away, sl water stain at end. Tear in 1 plate reprd. New cloth. *(Wheldon & Wesley)* **£60** [≈ $115]

Kanavel, Allen
- Infections of the Hand ... Second Edition ... Illustrated with 147 Engravings. Phila: 1914. 8vo. 463 pp. Orig bndg.
 (Goodrich) **$65** [≈ £33]

Kane, W.F. de Vismes
- European Butterflies. London: Macmillan, 1885. 1st edn. xxxii,184 pp. 15 b/w plates. Orig green cloth, gilt spine.
 (Gough) **£20** [≈ $38]

Kappel, A.W. & Kirby, W. Egmont
- Beetles, Butterflies, Moths and Other Insects ... London: Cassell, 1892. 1st edn. 182 pp. 12 cold plates, num text ills. Orig orange pict cloth, sl rubbed. *(Gough)* **£35** [≈ $67]
- Beetles, Butterflies, Moths, and Other Insects. London: Cassell, 1892. 1st edn. Sm 4to. 182,15 advt pp. 12 cold plates. Orig pict cloth.   *(Gough)* **£30** [≈ $57]
- Sketches of British Insects ... London: Groombridge, 1888. 1st edn. Sm 8vo. viii, 161, 5 advt pp. 6 chromolitho plates. Orig green pict cloth gilt. *(Gough)* **£25** [≈ $47]
- Sketches of British Insects ... London: Groombridge, 1888. 1st edn. Sm 8vo. viii, 161, 5 advt pp. 6 chromolitho plates. Orig green pict cloth gilt. *(Gough)* **£25** [≈ $47]

Kater, Henry & Lardner, D.
- A Treatise on Mechanics (from Lardner's

Cabinet Cyclopaedia). London: 1830. Lge 12mo. ix, 342 pp. Engvd title, 21 plates. Occas spotting. Contemp half mor, rubbed.
 (Bow Windows) **£30** [≈ $57]
- A Treatise on Mechanics. London: Lardner's Cabinet Cyclopaedia, 1830. 1st edn. Sm 8vo. Orig cloth, paper label.
 (Fenning) **£32.50** [≈ $63]

Kato, Genichi
- The Theory of Decrementless Conduction in Narcotised Region of Nerve. Tokyo, Nandoko, 1924. [With] The Further Studies of Decrementless Conduction. Tokyo: 1926. 2 vols. 8vo. [2],3, 166,[2]; [2],2, 4,[2],163 pp. Dws. *(Goodrich)* **$595** [≈ £309]

Kay, John
- A Series of Original Portraits and Caricature Etchings ... With Biographical Sketches and Anecdotes. Edinburgh: 1877. Rvsd edn. 2 vols. Thick folio. viii,445; viii,504 pp. 360 etched plates. Contemp half calf, t.e.g.
 (Hemlock) **$500** [≈ £260]

Kay, William
- Report on the Sanitary Conditions of Bristol and Clifton. Clifton: January 22, 1844. Folio. 32 pp. Half calf. Author's pres copy.
 (Goodrich) **$65** [≈ £33]

Kearton, A. & C.
- Kearton's Nature Pictures. London: 1910. 2 vols. Lge 4to. Cold frontises, num photo plates (sev cold), text ills. Orig cloth, sl rubbed. *(Grayling)* **£50** [≈ $95]

Keating, John (ed.)
- Cyclopedia of the Diseases of Children. Phila: 1890. 4 vols. 8vo. Ex-lib but good. Sheep, rubbed.. *(Goodrich)* **$125** [≈ £65]

Keble Martin, W.
- The Concise British Flora in Colour. London: Ebury Press, [1969]. One of 160 Large Format, sgnd by the author. 4to. 94 cold & 6 plain plates. Orig buckram backed bds. Glassine dw. Slipcase.
 (Georges) **£75** [≈ $143]

Keele, K.D.
- Leonardo Da Vinci on Movement of the Heart and Blood. London: 1952. Ltd edn. 142 pp. 68 ills. Qtr leather.
 (Fye) **$125** [≈ £65]

Keen, R.
- Wireless Direction Finding and Directional

Reception. 1922. 1st edn. 254 ills. Orig bndg.
(New Wireless) **$45 [≈ £24]**

Keen, William W.
- Selected Papers and Addresses. Phila: Jacob, 1923. 8vo. 340 pp. Orig bndg. Author's pres inscrptn.   *(Goodrich)* **$90 [≈ £46]**
- The Surgical Operations on President Cleveland in 1893. Phila: Jacobs, 1917. 8vo. 52 pp. Orig bndg. Author's pres inscrptn.
(Goodrich) **$135 [≈ £70]**
- The Surgical Operations on President Cleveland in 1893. Together with Six Additional Papers of Reminiscences. Phila: 1928. 8vo. 251 pp. Orig bndg.
(Goodrich) **$35 [≈ £18]**

Keen, William W., et al.
- Surgery. Its Principles and Practice. Phila: 1910-26. 8 vols. 8vo. Orig red cloth.
(Goodrich) **$150 [≈ £78]**

Keill, James
- An Account of Animal Secretion ... London: Strahan, 1708. 1st edn. 8vo. xxviii,187,[1] pp. Text ills. Minor staining & soiling. Contemp calf, headcap chipped, spine & crnrs rubbed, lacks label.   *(Gaskell)* **£525 [≈ $1,007]**

Keith, A.
- The Antiquity of Man. London: 1915. 1st edn. xx,519 pp. Frontis, 189 figs. Embossed stamps on title. Orig cloth.
(Whitehart) **£15 [≈ $28]**
- The Antiquity of Man. London: 1925. 2nd edn. 2 vols. xxxii,xiv,753 pp. 266 text figs. Orig cloth, traces of label removal from ft of spines.   *(Whitehart)* **£25 [≈ $47]**

Keith, Thomas
- An Introduction to the Theory and Practice of Plane and Spherical Trigonometry, and the Stereographic Projection of the Sphere ... London: for the author, 1810. 2nd edn. 8vo. xxviii, 410 pp. 5 fldg plates. Contemp calf, rehinged.   *(Young's)* **£48 [≈ $92]**
- An Introduction to the Theory and Practice of Plane and Spherical Geometry, and Stereographic Projection of the Sphere ... Fifth Edition, Corrected and Improved. London: 1826. 8vo. xxviii,442 pp, advt leaf. 5 fldg plates. Orig bds, uncut, rebacked.
(Bickersteth) **£25 [≈ $47]**
- A New Treatise on the Use of the Globes, or a Philosophical View of the Earth and Heavens. New York: Samuel Wood & Sons, 1826. 8vo. 334 pp. 5 plates. Some foxing. Leather, some wear.

(Gemmary) **$150 [≈ £78]**

Kelland, P. & Tait, P.G.
- Introduction to Quaternions, with Numerous Examples. London: 1873. 1st edn. xi,227 pp. A few figs.   *(Whitehart)* **£25 [≈ $47]**
- Introduction to Quaternions, with Numerous Examples. London: 1882. 2nd edn. xiii,232 pp. A few figs. Prelims sl foxed. Cloth sl marked.   *(Whitehart)* **£25 [≈ $47]**

Kelley, S.W.
- Surgical Diseases of Children. A Modern Treatise on Pediatric Surgery. New York: 1909. 765 pp. 293 text ills. A few rough edges to pp. Cloth, sl dust stained.
(Whitehart) **£25 [≈ $47]**

Kelly, H.A. & Burrage, W.
- Dictionary of American Medical Biography. New York: 1928. 1364 pp. Orig bndg.
(Fye) **$200 [≈ £104]**

Kelsall, J.E. & Munn, Philip W.
- The Birds of Hampshire and the Isle of Wight. London: Witherby, 1905. 1st edn. 8vo. xliv, 371 pp. 19 plates (sl spotted). Orig cloth gilt, jnts sl rubbed. *(Gough)* **£40 [≈ $76]**

Kelt, Thomas (compiler)
- The Mechanic's Text-Book and Engineer's Practical Guide. Boston: Phillips, Sampson & Co, 1850. Sm 8vo. 403 pp. Ills. Orig cloth, pict gilt spine.   *(Bookpress)* **$50 [≈ £26]**

Kelvin, William Thomson, 1st Baron
- Baltimore Lectures on Molecular Dynamics and the Wave Theory of Light. London: C.J. Clay & Sons, 1904. 8vo. xxi,703 pp. Cloth.
(Gemmary) **$175 [≈ £91]**
- Reprint of Papers on Electrostatics and Magnetism. London: Macmillan, 1884. 2nd edn. 8vo. xv,592 pp. 3 plates. Ex-lib. Orig cloth, unopened.   *(Gemmary)* **$100 [≈ £52]**

Kendall, P.F. & Wroot, H.E.
- Geology of Yorkshire. Privately Printed: 1924. 8vo. xxii,995 pp. Num ills. Cloth.
(Henly) **£85 [≈ $163]**

Kennedy, Alexander W.M. Clark
- The Birds of Berkshire and Buckinghamshire ... Eton: Ingalton & Drake, & Simpkin, Marshall, 1868. 1st edn. 8vo. xiv,232 pp. 4 tinted photos. Orig blue cloth gilt, partly uncut.   *(Hollett)* **£150 [≈ $287]**

Kennedy, Evory
- Observations on Obstetric Auscultation, with an Analysis of the Evidences of Pregnancy. New York: 1843. 1st Amer edn. 311 pp. Plates. Orig bndg.   *(Fye)* **$200 [≈ £104]**

Kennedy, John
- A Treatise upon Planting, Gardening, and the Management of the Hot-House. Dublin: for W. Wilson, 1784. 1st Dublin edn. 8vo. xiii, [iii], 462,[ii advt] pp. Sl browned, occas spot. Contemp tree calf, mor label, spine worn, sides rubbed, crnrs bumped.
(Finch) **£75 [≈ $143]**

Kennedy, P.G.
- A List of the Birds of Ireland. Dublin: 1961. 8vo. Cloth bds.   *(Emerald Isle)* **£30 [≈ $57]**

Kennedy, R.
- The Book of Electrical Installations: Electric Light, Power, Traction and Industrial Electrical Machinery. London: 1914-15. 3 vols. viii,254; viii,235; viii,259 pp. 1 sectional model in each vol, 24 plates, 912 diags. Orig pict cloth, lower edges sl water stained.
(Whitehart) **£45 [≈ $86]**
- The Book of the Motor Car ... London: [1913]. 3 vols. ix,213; ix,213; ix,216 pp. Each vol with cold movable overslip plate, 23 plates, 781 ills. Orig bndgs.
(Whitehart) **£50 [≈ $95]**
- Modern Engines and Power Generators. A Practical Work on prime Movers and the Transmission of Power, Steam, Electric, Water and Hot Air. London: [1905]. 6 vols. Each vol ca 220 pp. Num plates & ills. Orig cloth.   *(Whitehart)* **£35 [≈ $67]**

Kennelly, A.E.
- Wireless Telegraphy. 1906. 1st edn. 211 pp. 66 ills. Orig bndg.
(New Wireless) **$115 [≈ £59]**
- Wireless Telegraphy and Telephony. 1917. 2nd edn. 279 pp. 84 ills. Some marg staining. Orig bndg, rear cvr water stained.
(New Wireless) **$40 [≈ £20]**

Kennelly, A.E., et al.
- Electricity in Daily Life. 1890. 1st edn. 288 pp. 125 ills. Orig bndg.
(New Wireless) **$65 [≈ £33]**

Kent, Elizabeth
- Flora Domestica, or the Portable Flower-Garden; with Directions for the Treatment of Plants in Pots, and Illustrations from the Works of the Poets. London: 1823. 1st edn.

8vo. xxiv,[ii],396 pp, interleaved. Half calf. Anon.   *(Wheldon & Wesley)* **£50 [≈ $95]**

Kent, Nathaniel
- General View of the Agriculture of the County of Norfolk ... for the Consideration of the Board of Agriculture ... Norwich: at the Norfolk Press ..., 1796. 2nd edn. 8vo. xvi, 236, [i errata] pp. Fldg map, 3 plates. Orig bds, uncut, paper label, spine worn.
(Finch) **£100 [≈ $191]**
- Hints to Gentlemen of Landed Property. London: Dodsley, 1775. 1st edn. 8vo. vii,[i], 268 pp. 10 fldg plates. Tables in text. Contemp calf, mor label, dec gilt spine, spine chipped at hd, crnrs worn, jnts cracked.
(Finch) **£165 [≈ $316]**

Kenyon, G.H.
- The Glass Industry of the Weald. Leicester: UP, 1967. 4to. Fldg map, 22 plates. Cloth. Dw.   *(Ars Libri)* **$100 [≈ £52]**

Kerenyi, C.
- Asklepios. Archetypal Image of the Physician's Existence ... New York: 1959. 8vo. 151 pp. 58 ills. Dw.
(Goodrich) **$45 [≈ £23]**

Kerner von Marilaun, A.
- The Natural History of Plants, their Forms, Growth, Reproduction and Distribution. London: 1894. 2 vols. Imperial 8vo. 16 cold plates (sm water stain on 1 crnr), ca 2000 text figs. Half mor, rubbed. *(Henly)* **£28 [≈ $53]**
- The Natural History of Plants, their Forms, Growth, Reproduction and Distribution. Translated by F.W. Oliver. London: 1895. 2 vols. Imperial 8vo. 16 cold plates, ca 2000 text figs. Half mor.
(Wheldon & Wesley) **£45 [≈ $86]**
- See also Von Marilaun, A.K.

Kerr, Richard
- Wireless Telegraphy Popularly Explained. 1898. 1st edn. 111 pp. 12 ills. Rebound.
(New Wireless) **$225 [≈ £117]**

Keynes, Sir Geoffrey
- A Bibliography of Dr. Robert Hooke. Oxford: Clarendon Press, 1960. 4to. xxiii,115 pp. 12 plates. Cloth. Dw. *(Gemmary)* **$225 [≈ £117]**
- A Bibliography of Dr. Robert Hooke. OUP: 1960. Roy 8vo. 12 plates, ills. Dw.
(Georges) **£100 [≈ $191]**
- A Bibliography of Sir Thomas Browne. Cambridge: UP, 1924. One of 500. Roy 8vo. Plates, ills. Cvrs sl marked & faded.

(Georges) **£75 [≈ $143]**
- A Bibliography of Sir Thomas Browne.
Cambridge: 1924. One of 500. 4to. Ills. Orig
bndg, outer hinges cracked.
(Fye) **$150 [≈ £78]**
- A Bibliography of Sir William Petty F.R.S.
and of Observations on the Bills of Mortality
by John Graunt F.R.S. OUP: 1971. Roy 8vo.
Errata slip. 2 plates, ills. Dw (faded & sl torn).
(Georges) **£45 [≈ $86]**
- A Bibliography of the Writings of William
Harvey. Second Edition, revised. Cambridge:
1953. One of 750. Orig bndg, bds sunned.
Good ex-lib. *(Goodrich)* **$145 [≈ £75]**
- Blood Transfusion. London: 1949. 1st edn.
574 pp. 109 ills. Orig cloth.
(Whitehart) **£25 [≈ $47]**
- Dr. Timothie Bright 1550-1615. A Survey of
his Life with a Bibliography of his Writings.
London: Wellcome Hist Med Lib, 1962. Roy
8vo. 17 ills. *(Georges)* **£20 [≈ $38]**
- The Personality of William Harvey. The
Linacre Lecture. Cambridge: 1949. 8vo. 48
pp. Plates. Dw. *(Goodrich)* **£65 [≈ $33]**
- The Portraiture of William Harvey. With a
Catalogue and Reproductions of the Pictures.
The Thomas Vicary Lecture. London: 1949.
4to. 42 pp. 12 plates. Orig bndg, spine
sunned. *(Goodrich)* **$45 [≈ £23]**

Keys, John
- The Antient Bee-Master's Farewell; or, Full
and Plain Directions for the Management of
Bees. London: 1796. 1st edn. 8vo. xvi,273 pp.
2 plates. Trifle foxed. Calf, reprd.
(Wheldon & Wesley) **£175 [≈ $335]**
- A Treatise on the Breeding and Management
of Bees ... New Edition. London: 1814.
12mo. xvi, 272 pp. 2 plates. Orig tree calf, gilt
spine, mor label. *(Bickersteth)* **£148 [≈ $284]**

Kidd, John
- On the Adaptation of External Nature to the
Physical Condition of Man ... London: 1833.
2nd edn. 8vo. Minor foxing. Contemp calf, sl
scraped & marked.
(Bow Windows) **£35 [≈ $67]**
- On the Adaptation of External Nature to the
Physical Condition of Man. London: 1834.
3rd edn. 8,2, xvi, 375 pp. Cloth, rebacked.
(Henly) **£24 [≈ $46]**

Kinahan, G.A.
- Economic Geology of Ireland. London:
Journal Royal Geog Soc vol 18, 1889. 8vo.
514 pp. Cloth bds.
(Emerald Isle) **£85 [≈ $163]**

- Economic Geology of Ireland. London: 1889.
1st coll edn. 8vo. vii,[2],456, 461-464,
469-514 pp, complete. Contemp half calf,
worn but strong, 1 label defective.
(Fenning) **£75 [≈ $143]**

King, A.G.
- Kelvin the Man. 1925. 1st edn. 142 pp. 12
photos. Orig bndg. Author's pres copy.
(New Wireless) **$85 [≈ £44]**

King, C.W.
- The Natural History of Gems, or Semi-
Precious Stones. London: Bell & Daldy,
1870. Retitled reprinting of The Natural
History of Gems or Decorative Stones. 8vo.
xii, 377 pp. Frontis. rebound in buckram.
(Gemmary) **$40 [≈ £20]**
- The Natural History of Precious Stones and
of the Precious Metals. London: 1867. 8vo.
xii, 364 pp. Frontis, 6 plates. Some marks &
stains. Some sewing strained. Lib b'plates.
Orig cloth, spine ends a little rubbed.
(Bow Windows) **£65 [≈ $124]**

King, H.C.
- The History of the Telescope. London: 1955.
xv,456 pp. 196 text ills. Endpapers marked.
Piece of blank marg of 1 leaf cut away. Orig
bndg. *(Whitehart)* **£40 [≈ $76]**
- The History of the Telescope. London: 1955.
xvi,456 pp. 196 text figs. Stamp on title
recto & verso. Traces of label removal from
endpapers. Cloth, sl faded & worn.
(Whitehart) **£40 [≈ $76]**

King, J.
- American Eclectic Obstetrics. Cincinnati:
1851. 741 pp. Frontis, 79 figs. Occas sl
foxing, sm marg water stain. Soft leather,
spine crnrs & edges rubbed.
(Whitehart) **£25 [≈ $47]**

Kingdon-Ward, Francis
- Assam Adventure. London: 1942. 2nd edn.
304 pp. Map, 16 plates. Orig cloth, sl soiled.
(Henly) **£28 [≈ $53]**
- Burma's Icy Mountains. London: 1949. 1st
edn. 8vo. 287 pp. 2 maps, 16 plates. Orig
cloth. *(Henly)* **£24 [≈ $46]**
- Pilgrimage for Plants. London: 1960. 1st edn.
191 pp. 23 plates. Orig bndg.
(Henly) **£25 [≈ $47]**
- Plant Hunter in Manipur. London: 1952. 1st
edn. 8vo. 254 pp. Map, 12 plates. Orig cloth.
(Henly) **£35 [≈ $67]**
- Plant Hunters Paradise. London: 1937. 1st
edn. 8vo. 347 pp. 2 maps, 12 plates. Lacks

f.e.p. Orig cloth, sl soiled.
.   *(Henly)* **£28 [≈ $53]**
- Plant Hunting on the Edge of the World.
London: 1930. 1st edn. 8vo. 383 pp. 16
plates. Orig cloth.   *(Henly)* **£56 [≈ $107]**
- Return to the Irrawaddy. London: 1956. 1st
edn. 8vo. 224 pp. Map, 31 plates. Orig cloth,
spine a little faded.   *(Henly)* **£38 [≈ $72]**

Kingsley, Charles
- Glaucus; or, the Wonders of the Shore.
London: Macmillan, 1855. 1st edn. Fcap 8vo.
[6], 165, [3], 16 pp. Frontis. Orig cloth,
rebacked. Author's pres inscrptn.
(Spelman) **£25 [≈ $47]**

Kingsley, N.W.
- A Treatise on Oral Deformities as a Branch of
Mechanical Surgery. London: 1891. xii,541
pp. 357 text figs. Ink stamp on title. Cloth, sl
marked.   *(Whitehart)* **£40 [≈ $76]**

Kinns, S.
- Moses and Geology. London: 1882. viii,494
pp. 110 ills. Orig gilt dec cloth, backstrip
relaid.   *(Baldwin)* **£20 [≈ $38]**
- Moses and Geology: or The Harmony of the
Bible with Science ... Twelfth Thousand.
London: 1889. 8vo. xxx,514, [18 advt] pp.
Cold frontis, 16 plates in the text, 94 figs. Sl
spotting & other marks. Orig cloth, sl marked,
spine ends sl worn, inner hinges weak.
(Bow Windows) **£30 [≈ $57]**
- Moses and Geology: or, The Harmony of the
Bible with Science. London: 1895. 14th edn.
8vo. xxxii, 518,[12] pp. Cold frontis, 110 ills.
Orig cloth gilt, t.e.g.
(Bow Windows) **£45 [≈ $86]**

Kipling, John Lockwood
- Beast and Man in India ... London:
Macmillan, 1904. 1st edn. xii,359 pp. Num
b/w ills. Spotted. Orig pict blue cloth gilt.
(Gough) **£28 [≈ $53]**

Kipping, Robert
- Rudimentary Treatise on Masting, Mast-
Making, and Rigging of Ships ... Sixth
Edition. London: John Weale, 1861. 12mo.
Half-title. Ills, tables. Contemp calf,
rebacked.   *(Jarndyce)* **£40 [≈ $76]**

Kirby, William & Spence, William
- An Introduction to Entomology ... London:
Longman, Hurst ..., 1815. 2 vols. 8vo. xxiv,
512; 529, [2] pp. 5 hand cold plates (sl
offsetting). Old calf gilt, rubbed.
(Hollett) **£150 [≈ $287]**

- An Introduction to Entomology ... London:
1858. 7th edn. xxviii,607 pp. Orig pict cloth,
spine sl torn.   *(Whitehart)* **£15 [≈ $28]**

Kirby, William Forsell
- The Butterflies and Moths of Europe.
London: Cassell, 1903. Lge 8vo. lxxii,432 pp.
54 cold & 1 plain plate. Some finger & other
marks. Front fly leaf removed. Sl shaken,
inner hinges torn. Orig pict cloth, crnrs &
spine ends trifle rubbed.
(Bow Windows) **£115 [≈ $220]**
- The Butterflies and Moths of Europe.
London: [1903]. In the orig 32 parts. 4to.
lxxii, 432 pp. 54 cold & 1 plain plate. Orig
wraps, uncut, 1st & last wraps rather worn &
detached. *(Wheldon & Wesley)* **£150 [≈ $287]**
- The Butterflies and Moths of Europe.
London: [1903]. 4to. lxxii, 432 pp. 54 cold &
1 plain plate. Occas sl foxing. Rebound in art
leather, spine faded.
(Wheldon & Wesley) **£100 [≈ $191]**
- Elementary Text-Book of Entomology.
Second Edition, Revised and Augmented.
London: Swan Sonnenschein, 1892. viii,281
pp. 87 steel engvd plates. Orig green cloth,
gilt spine.   *(Gough)* **£40 [≈ $76]**

Kirk, T.
- The Forest Flora of New Zealand.
Wellington: 1889. Sm folio. xv,345 pp. 159
plates. Orig cloth, trifle used.
(Wheldon & Wesley) **£150 [≈ $287]**
- The Forest Flora of New Zealand. London:
1889. Folio. xv,345 pp. 159 plates. Title sl
spotted. Cloth gilt.   *(Henly)* **£220 [≈ $422]**

Kirkman, F.B. (ed.)
- The British Bird Book ... London: 1911-13. 4
vols. 4to. 179 cold plates of birds, 20 cold &
3 plain plates of eggs, 80 plates from photos.
Orig buckram.
(Wheldon & Wesley) **£130 [≈ $249]**

Kirkman, F.B. & Hutchinson, G.
- British Sporting Birds. London: Jack, 1924.
1st edn. 4to. 43 plates (31 cold). Orig cloth, sl
rubbed & shaken.   *(Young's)* **£40 [≈ $76]**

Kirkman, F.B. & Jourdain, F.C.R.
- British Birds. London: 1930. Roy 8vo. 199
cold & 3 plain plates. Cloth.
(Wheldon & Wesley) **£20 [≈ $38]**

Kirwan, Richard
- Elements of Mineralogy. London: 1784. 1st
edn. 8vo. xviii,412,12 pp. Contemp calf,
crnrs sl worn.   *(Henly)* **£720 [≈ $1375]**

- An Essay on the Analysis of Mineral Waters. London: J.W. Myers for D. Bremner, 1799. 1st edn. 8vo. vii,279 pp. Errata slip mtd on last contents page. 7 fldg tables. Sl marg water stain. Orig bds, uncut, lacks most of paper spine. *(Bickersteth)* **£170 [≈$326]**
- An Estimate of the Temperature of Different Latitudes. London: J. Davis, for P. Elmsley, 1787. 1st edn. 8vo. viii,114 pp. Title & last page a little dusty. Disbound.
(Bickersteth) **£120 [≈$230]**
- Geological Essays. London: 1799. 1st edn. 8vo. xvi,502 pp. Some marks. Lib stamp on title verso & last leaf, label on endpaper. Old mrbld bds, rec calf spine.
(Bow Windows) **£305 [≈$585]**
- The Manures most advantageously applicable to the Various Sorts of Soils, and the Causes of their Beneficial Effect ... London: for Vernor & Hood, 1796. 4th edn. 8vo. Title sl soiled. New wraps. *(Stewart)* **£85 [≈$163]**

Kisch, B.
- Scales and Weights. London: Yale UP, 1966. Cr 4to. xxi,297 pp. 10 charts, 98 text figs. Cloth. Dw. *(Gemmary)* **$90 [≈£46]**

Kitchiner, William
- The Cook's Oracle; containing Receipts for Plain Cookery, on the most Economical Plan for Private Families ... New Edition. London: Cadell, 1829. Fcap 8vo. xix,[i],512 pp,2 ff. Occas foxing. Orig cloth, backstrip relaid, label defective. *(Spelman)* **£50 [≈$95]**

Kline, M.
- Mathematics in Western Culture. New York: (1953) 1959. xv,484 pp. 8 dble-sided plates, 88 text figs. *(Whitehart)* **£25 [≈$47]**

Knapp, John Leonard
- The Journal of a Naturalist. London: Murray, 1829. 1st edn. 8vo. 396 pp. 7 plates. Contemp half mor, gilt spine (rubbed). Anon. *(Chapel Hill)* **$150 [≈£78]**

Knight, K.W.
- The Book of the Rabbit. London: 1889. 2nd edn, rvsd & enlgd. 8vo. xvi,484 pp. 8 cold & 6 plain plates. Orig dec cloth, trifle worn.
(Wheldon & Wesley) **£30 [≈$57]**

Knott, C.G. (ed.)
- Napier Tercentenary Memorial Volume. London: Longmans, Green, 1915. Roy 8vo. xi, 441 pp. 15 plates. Dec cloth.
(Gemmary) **$175 [≈£91]**

Knox, A.E.
- Ornithological Rambles in Sussex; with a Systematic Catalogue of the Birds of that County ... Third Edition. London: 1855. 8vo. [xii], 260 pp, advt leaf. 4 tinted litho plates. Orig gilt illust cloth.
(Bow Windows) **£40 [≈$76]**

Koch, Robert
- Investigations into the Etiology of Traumatic Infective Diseases. London: 1880. 1st English translation. 101 pp. Orig bndg.
(Fye) **$250 [≈£130]**

Kocher, T.
- Text-Book of Operative Surgery. Translated by H.J. Stiles and C.B. Paul. London: 1911. 3rd English edn. xxxii,723 pp. 415 ills. Cloth, marked, worn, dusty, inner hinge sl cracked.
(Whitehart) **£25 [≈$47]**

Koehler, R.
- A Contribution to the Study of Ophiurans of the U.S. National Museum. Washington: 1914. 4to. vii,137 pp. 18 plates. Ex-lib. Orig wraps bound in. *(Henly)* **£36 [≈$69]**

Kohler, Wolfgang
- The Mentality of Apes. Translated from the Second Revised Edition by E. Winter. London: Kegan Paul, 1925. 1st English edn. 8vo. viii, 342, [2 blank] pp. 9 plates. Orig cloth. *(Fenning)* **£35 [≈$67]**

Kohlrausch, F.
- An Introduction to Physical Measurements with Appendices on Absolute Electrical Measurement, etc. Translated by T.H. Waller and H.R. Procter. London: 1873. xii,249 pp. 25 figs. Occas foxing on front blank & half title. Prize calf gilt, mrbld edges.
(Whitehart) **£45 [≈$86]**

Kollar, Vincent
- A Treatise on Insects Injurious to Gardeners, Foresters & Farmers. Translated and Illustrated by J. and M. Loudon; With Notes by J.O. Westwood. London: William Smith, 1840. 1st English edn. 8vo. xvi,377 pp. Num text engvs. Orig blue cloth, gilt spine.
(Gough) **£35 [≈$67]**

Kolle, Fredrik
- Plastic and Cosmetic Surgery. New York: 1911. 1st edn. 511 pp. Over 500 text ills. Rec linen. *(Fye)* **$300 [≈£156]**

Krafft-Ebing, R. von
- Psychopathia Sexualis with especial reference to Contrary Sexual Instinct ... Authorized Translation ... by C.G. Chaddock. Phila: 1920. 8vo. xiv,436 pp. Sl use. Orig cloth.
(Bow Windows) **£28 [≈ $53]**

Kramer, E.E.
- The Nature and Growth of Modern Mathematics. New York: 1970. xxiv,758 pp. Text diags. *(Whitehart)* **£25 [≈ $47]**

Krogh, August
- The Anatomy and Physiology of the Capillaries. New Haven: 1924. 1st edn. 276 pp. Orig bndg. *(Fye)* **$125 [≈ £65]**

Kronfeld, P.C., et al.
- The Human Eye in Anatomical Transparencies. Bausch & Lomb: 1943. xi,99 pp. Cold layered transparencies. Text ills.
(Whitehart) **£35 [≈ $67]**

Kuchenmeister, F.
- On Animal and Vegetable Parasites of the Human Body. A Manual of their Natural History, Diagnosis, and Treatment. Translated from the Second German Edition ... London: Sydenham Society, 1857. 2 vols. 8vo. Cloth worn. *(Goodrich)* **$85 [≈ £44]**

Kunz, G.F.
- Gems and Precious Stones of North America. New York: The Scientific Publ Co, 1890. 1st edn. Cr 4to. 336 pp. 8 cold litho plates, 16 photo ills. Orig gilt dec cloth.
(Gemmary) **$375 [≈ £195]**
- Gems and Precious Stones of North America. New York: The Scientific Publ Co, 1890. 1st edn. Cr 4to. 336 pp. 8 cold litho plates, 16 photo ills. Pages loose. Rebound in buckram.
(Gemmary) **$225 [≈ £117]**
- Gems and Precious Stones of North America. New York: The Scientific Publ Co, 1890. 1st edn. Cr 4to. 336 pp. 8 cold litho plates, 16 photo ills. Rebound in buckram.
(Gemmary) **$250 [≈ £130]**
- Precious Stones. Washington: USGS 20th Annual Report, 1899. 4to. 557-601 pp. Cold plate. Disbound. *(Gemmary)* **$50 [≈ £26]**
- Rings for the Finger. Phila: Lippincott, 1917. 1st edn. 8vo. xviii,381 pp. 3 cold & 108 other plates. Orig gilt dec cloth, spine sl worn.
(Gemmary) **$275 [≈ £143]**

Kurr, J.G.
- The Mineral Kingdom ... Edinburgh: 1859. Folio. iii,70 pp. 24 plates (23 cold). Some

offsetting from the plates. Orig half mor, rebacked. *(Wheldon & Wesley)* **£400 [≈ $767]**

Kustel, G.
- A Treatise on Concentration of all Kinds of Ores. San Francisco: Mining & Scientific Press Office, 1868. 8vo. 259 pp. 7 plates, 120 text figs. Cloth. *(Gemmary)* **$200 [≈ £104]**

La Beaume, Michael
- Cases of Indigestion, from Disorders of the Stomach, Liver and Bowels, and Other Complaints ... cured by Galvanism ... London: S. Highley, 1827. 2nd edn. Sm 8vo. [iv], 131, [3] pp. Litho plate. Old wraps.
(Burmester) **£120 [≈ $230]**

Lack, D.
- Darwin's Finches. Cambridge: 1947. 1st edn. 8vo. x,208 pp. 9 plates (4 cold), text figs. Orig cloth, crnr sl bumped. Dw.
(Wheldon & Wesley) **£35 [≈ $67]**

Lacroix, S.F. & Bezout, E.
- An Elementary Treatise on Plane and Spherical Trigonometry; and on the Application of Algebra to Geometry; from the Mathematics of Lacroix and Bezout ... by J. Farrar. Cambridge (US): 1820. v,163 pp. 5 plates. Sl worn & marked.
(Whitehart) **£40 [≈ $76]**

Laennec, R.T.H.
- A Treatise on the Diseases of the Chest and om Mediate Auscultation ... London: 1827. 2nd edn. 723 pp. Port. Rec qtr leather.
(Fye) **$900 [≈ £468]**
- A Treatise on the Diseases of the Chest and on Mediate Auscultation. Translated ... with Notes and a Sketch of the Author's Life by John Forbes. New York: 1830. 736 pp. 8 plates. Sm lib stamp on title. Occas foxing. Rec qtr leather. *(Fye)* **$350 [≈ £182]**

Lagrange, J.B.B.
- A Manual of a Course of Chemistry ... London: 1800. 2 vols. xx,448,[19]; vii,457, [17] pp. Half leather gilt, rebacked.
(Whitehart) **£220 [≈ $422]**

Laing, S.
- Prehistoric Remains of Caithness, with Notes on the Human Remains by T.H. Huxley. London: Williams & Norgate, 1866. 1st edn. 8vo. 160, [1 table, 8 advt] pp. Frontis, 68 figs. Orig cloth gilt, jnts splitting, sl bumped.
(Hollett) **£120 [≈ $230]**

Lamb, H.

- The Dynamical Theory of Sound. London: Edward Arnold, 1931. 2nd edn. 8vo. viii,307 pp. 86 text figs. Ex-lib. Cloth.
(Gemmary) **$65 [≈ £33]**

Lambert, A.B.

- An Illustration of the Genus Cinchona ... London: 1821. 4to. x,181 pp. 5 plates (some sl foxing). New bds.
(Wheldon & Wesley) **£375 [≈ $719]**

Lamouroux, J.V.F.

- Corallina: or, a Classical Arrangement of Flexible Coralline Polypidoms. London: 1824. 8vo. 284 pp. 19 litho plates. 1st 6 ff water stained. Orig bds, worn, front jnt cracked but intact.
(Wheldon & Wesley) **£100 [≈ $191]**

Lancereaux, E.

- A Treatise on Syphilis. Historical and Practical. Translated by G. Whitley. London: New Sydenham Society, 1868-69. 1st edn in English. 2 vols. 8vo. Orig cloth, hd of spines sl worn. *(Bickersteth)* **£40 [≈ $76]**

Landen, John

- Mathematical Memoirs respecting a Variety of Subjects ... London: for the author, & sold by J. Nourse, 1780. [With] Vol. II. London: sold by F. Wingrave, 1789. 1st edn. 2 vols in one. 4to. 11 fldg plates. 1st title sl browned, sl foxing. 19th c bds, later calf spine.
(Ximenes) **$1,000 [≈ £520]**

Landois, L.

- A Text-Book of Human Physiology, including Histology and Microscopical Anatomy; with special reference to the Requirements of Practical Medicine. London: 1886. 2nd edn. 2 vols. Num ills. Cloth, dust stained, sl worn, inner hinge vol 2 cracked but firm. *(Whitehart)* **£25 [≈ $47]**

Landolt, H.

- Handbook of the Polariscope and its Practical Applications. Translated by D.C. Robb and V.H. Veley. London: 1882. 1st edn. xvi, 262 pp. 57 ills. Endpaper & half-title sl holed. Orig cloth. *(Whitehart)* **£38 [≈ $72]**

Landsborough, D.

- A Popular History of British Zoophytes or Corallines. London: 1852. Cr 8vo. xii,404 pp. 20 hand cold plates. A few lib blind stamps on title & some plates. Orig cloth gilt, partly unopened. *(Henly)* **£28 [≈ $53]**

- A Popular History of British Seaweeds. London: 1849. 1st edn. 8vo. xx,368 pp. 20 hand cold cold & 2 plain plates. Half calf, sl rubbed. *(Henly)* **£40 [≈ $76]**

- A Popular History of British Seaweeds ... London: Reeve, Benham & Reeve, 1849. 1st edn. Sm sq 8vo. xx,368 pp. 20 hand cold cold plates. Contemp cloth, spine sl faded.
(Gough) **£25 [≈ $47]**

- A Popular History of British Sea-Weeds ... Second Edition. London: Reeve & Benham, 1851. 12mo. xx,400,8 advt pp. 20 hand finished cold & 2 plain plates. Orig pict cloth, spine faded & sl chipped at hd.
(Gough) **£35 [≈ $67]**

- A Popular History of British Seaweeds ... London: 1857. 3rd edn. Sm 8vo. 400 pp. 20 cold & 2 other plates. New cloth.
(Whitehart) **£25 [≈ $47]**

Lane, Levi

- The Surgery of the Head and Neck. Phila: 1898. 2nd edn. 1180 pp. Orig bndg.
(Fye) **$200 [≈ £104]**

Lane, W. Arbuthnot

- Cleft Palate; Treatment of Simple Fractures by Operation; Diseases of Joints ... London: 1897. 1st edn. 278 pp. Orig bndg.
(Fye) **$150 [≈ £78]**

Lang, H.C.

- Rhopalocera Europae Descriptae. The Butterflies of Europe Described and Figured. London: 1884. 2 vols. Roy 8vo. 82 cold plates. 2 plates sl foxed. Half calf, worn.
(Henly) **£260 [≈ $499]**

Langford-Smith, F.

- Radiotron Designer's Handbook. 1953. 4th edn. 1482 pp. Num ills. Orig bndg.
(New Wireless) **$45 [≈ £23]**

Lankester, Sir E. Ray

- Extinct Animals. London: Constable, 1905. 1st edn. 8vo. 331 pp. Frontis, maps, ills. Piece lacking from front free endpaper. Orig maroon cloth gilt. *(Chapel Hill)* **$110 [≈ £57]**

- Extinct Animals. Second Impression. London: 1906. 8vo. xxiv,331 pp. Port, num text ills. Sl spotting. Orig cloth.
(Bow Windows) **£35 [≈ $67]**

- Extinct Animals. London: 1909. New edn. xxiii, 331 pp. 218 ills. Orig pict cloth, bottom edge sl worn. *(Whitehart)* **£15 [≈ $28]**

- Monograph of the Okapi. London: BM, 1910. Folio. Atlas of 48 plates, many cold & other plates. Orig cloth, mint.

(Grayling) £180 [≈ $345]

Lankester, Phebe, Mrs Edwin (ed.)
- A Plain and Easy Account of the British Ferns ... London: Robert Hardwicke, (1859). 12mo. xvi,108,4 advt pp. 42 ills on 9 chromolitho plates (hand-finished?). Orig cloth gilt.   *(Claude Cox)* £18 [≈ $34]

Lanning, George
- Wild Life in China; or, Chats on Chinese Birds and Beasts. Shanghai: The National Review Office, 1911. 1st edn. xvi,255 pp. Orig green cloth, gilt spine.
(Gough) £40 [≈ $76]

Lardner, Dionysius
- Common Things Explained. London: Walton & Maberly, 1856. Cr 8vo. Num text figs. Cloth.   *(Gemmary)* £45 [≈ £23]
- Hand-Book of Astronomy. London: 1853-56. 2 vols. xxvii,872 pp. 37 plates, 200 text figs. Orig cloth.   *(Whitehart)* £35 [≈ $67]
- Hand-Book of Astronomy. Edited by E. Dunkin. London: 1860. 2nd rvsd edn. xxii,496 pp. 37 plates, 109 text figs. Orig cloth, v sl worn.   *(Whitehart)* £35 [≈ $67]
- The Museum of Science & Art. London: Walton & Maberly, 1854-56. 12 vols in 6. Cr 8vo. Num ills. Late 19th c red half calf, gilt spines, green labels. *(Fenning)* £110 [≈ $211]
- The Museum of Science and Art. New Edition. London: Walton & Maberly, 1854-56. 12 vols in 6. 8vo. Num ills. Orig pict cloth gilt.   *(Gough)* £90 [≈ $172]
- Popular Geology. Containing: Earthquakes and Volcanoes. The Crust of the Earth. The Pre-Adamite Earth. London: 1856. Cr 8vo. ii advt, [xii], 145-176, 33-136, 1-160, 8 advt pp. 211 w'engvs in text. Sm stamp on pastedown, crnr missing from endpaper. Orig pict cloth gilt.   *(Henly)* £32 [≈ $61]
- Railway Economy: A Treatise on the New Art of Transport ... London: Taylor, Walton & Maberly, 1850. 12mo. xxiii,528 pp. Orig cloth, backstrip relaid.
(Schoyer) $100 [≈ £52]
- A Treatise on Heat. London: Lardner's Cabinet Cyclopaedia, 1833. 1st edn. Sm 8vo. Orig cloth, ptd label.
(Fenning) £24.50 [≈ $47]
- A Treatise on Hydrostatics and Pneumatics. (From Lardner's Cabinet Cyclopaedia). London: 1831. Lge 12mo. viii,353 pp. Engvd title, 130 figs. Some foxing of outer ff. Contemp half mor, rubbed.
(Bow Windows) £25 [≈ $47]

Large, E.C.
- The Advance of the Fungi. London: 1940. 8vo. 488 pp. 6 plates. Orig cloth.
(Henly) £18 [≈ $34]
- The Advance of the Fungi. London: 1940. 8vo. 488 pp. 6 plates, 58 text figs. Cloth.
(Wheldon & Wesley) £25 [≈ $47]

Larmor, J.
- Aether and Matter. Cambridge: UP, 1900. 8vo. xxx,365 pp. Ex-lib. Cloth, unopened.
(Gemmary) $150 [≈ £78]

Larner, Edgar T.
- Practical Television. 1928. 1st edn. 175 pp. 13 photos, 84 ills. Orig bndg.
(New Wireless) $155 [≈ £80]
- Practical Television. With a Foreword by John L. Baird. London: 1928. 1st edn. 8vo. 175, [4 advt] pp. 13 plates, 85 ills. Orig cloth.
(Fenning) £65 [≈ $124]

Latham, Peter M.
- The Collected Works ... with Memoir by Sir Thomas Watson. Edited by R. Martin. London: New Sydenham Soc, 1876-88. 2 vols. Occas sl foxing. Orig cloth, spine ends sl worn.   *(Whitehart)* £35 [≈ $67]
- The Collected Works ... with Memoir by Sir Thomas Watson. London: 1876-78. 1st edn. 2 vols. 480; 575 pp. Orig bndg.
(Fye) $225 [≈ £117]
- Lectures on Subjects connected with Clinical Medicine: comprising Diseases of the Heart. Phila: 1847. 1st Amer edn. 365 pp. Leather, rear hinge cracked, front hinge weak.
(Fye) $150 [≈ £78]

Latham, R.G.
- The Natural History of the Varieties of Man. London: 1850. 1st edn. 8vo. xviii, 574, [2] pp. Figs. Occas spotting. Orig cloth.
(Bow Windows) £45 [≈ $86]

Lathrop, Leonard E.
- The Farmers' Library: or Essays designed to Encourage the Pursuits and Promote the Science of Agriculture. Third Edition, corrected and enlarged. Rochester: 1828. 12mo. 344 pp. Occas sl foxing. Mod half cloth.   *(Reese)* $150 [≈ £78]

Lauder, Sir Thomas & Brown, Thomas
- The Miscellany of Natural History. Volume I. Parrots. Edinburgh: 1833. 1st edn. Sm 8vo. 170, [1,22,2 advt] pp. Addtnl engvd title, port of Audubon, 1 uncold plate, 35 hand cold plates. Orig cloth, spine faded.

(Fenning) £165 [≈ $316]

Laughter, Victor H.

- Operator's Wireless Telegraph and Telephone Hand-Book. 1909. 1st edn. 180 pp. 30 photos, 56 ills. Orig bndg.
(New Wireless) $35 [≈ £18]

Laurence, Edward

- A Dissertation on Estates upon Lives and Years whether in Lay or Church-Hands. With an Exact Calculation of their Real Worth, by Proper Tables ... London: Knapton, 1730. 64 pp. Rebound in bds.
(C.R. Johnson) £285 [≈ $547]

Laurence, John

- The Fruit-Garden Kalendar; or, a Summary of the Art of Managing the Fruit-Garden ... Appendix of the usefulness of the Barometer. London: for Bernard Lintot, 1718. 1st edn. 8vo. Half-title. 3 ctlg pp. Fldg frontis, 1 text ill. Mod bds. *(Stewart)* £100 [≈ $191]

Lavater, Johann Caspar

- Essays on Physiognomy ... Abridged from Mr. Holcroft's Translation. Boston: William Spotswood & David West, (1794). 1st Amer edn. 12mo. [6],272 pp. Engvd title, 7 plates. Minor foxing. Contemp calf.
(Karmiole) $300 [≈ £156]
- Essays on Physiognomy ... also One Hundred Physiognomical Rules ... and a Memoir of the Author. London: [ca 1886]. 19th edn. cxxviii, 507, [4] pp. Port, num ills. Orig cloth, v sl worn & dust stained. *(Whitehart)* £35 [≈ $67]
- Lavater's Looking-Glass; or, Essays on the Face of Animated Nature, from man to Plants. By Lavater, Sue & Co. London: Millar Ritchie, 1800. xii,216 pp. Frontis. Half-title. Old calf, rebacked.
(Karmiole) $100 [≈ £52]

Laveran, A.

- Paludism. London: New Sydenham Society, 1893. 1st edn in English. 8vo. 197 pp. 4 chromolitho plates, 2 photo plates. Orig cloth gilt. *(Gough)* £25 [≈ $47]
- Paludism. Translated by J.W. Martin. London: Sydenham Society, 1893. 1st English edn. 8vo. 197 pp. 6 plates. Orig cloth, a bit worn. *(Goodrich)* $95 [≈ £49]

Laveran, Charles L. Alphonse & Mesnil, F.

- Trypanosomes and Trypanosomases. Translated and much enlarged by David Nabarro. London: 1907. 1st edn of this translation. Roy 8vo. xix,538,[1] pp. Cold

plate, 81 ills. Orig cloth gilt, inner hinges weak or cracked. *(Fenning)* £65 [≈ $124]

Lavoisier, A.

- Elements of Chemistry. Translated from the French by Robert Kerr. Edinburgh: William Creech, 1796. 2nd edn. 8vo. 592 pp. 2 fldg tables, 13 fldg plates. Contemp calf, gilt spine. *(Gemmary)* $650 [≈ £338]
- Elements of Chemistry. Translated from the French by Robert Kerr. Edinburgh: William Creech, 1799. 4th edn. 8vo. 592 pp. 2 fldg tables, 13 fldg plates (foxed). Contemp calf, sl shaken & worn. *(Gemmary)* $450 [≈ £234]

Lawrence, John

- A Practical Treatise on Breeding, Rearing, and Fattening all Kinds of Domestic Poultry, Pheasants, Pigeons, and Rabbits ... Second Edition, with Additions ... By Bonington Moubray ... London: Sherwood, Neely ..., 1816. Cr 8vo. Contemp bds, new spine.
(Stewart) £60 [≈ $115]

Lawrence, Sir William

- Lectures on Physiology, Zoology, and the Natural History of Man, delivered in the Royal College of Surgeons. London: 1823. 3rd edn. 8vo. xix,496 pp. 13 plates. Sl foxing & soiling, sm tear in 1 plate without loss of image. Contemp half calf, sl rubbed.
(Wheldon & Wesley) £60 [≈ $115]
- A Treatise on the Diseases of the Eye. Third Edition, revised, corrected and enlarged. London: Bohn, 1844. 8vo. xv,820 pp. Faint lib stamp on title. Half mor.
(Hemlock) $225 [≈ £117]

Lawson, George

- Injuries of the Eye, Orbit, and Eyelids: their Immediate and Remote Effects. London: Longmans, Green, 1867. 1st edn. 8vo. xiv,430 pp. 92 w'cut text ills, test types. Some foxing. Contemp three qtr shagreen gilt.
(Offenbacher) $350 [≈ £182]
- The Royal Water-Lily of South America, and the Water-Lilies of Our Own Land, their History and Cultivation. Edinburgh: James Hogg, 1851. Lge 16mo. 108 pp. 2 cold lithos. Orig red cloth gilt, a.e.g., v sl wear.
(Beech) £38 [≈ $72]

Lawson, William

- A New Orchard and Garden, or the Best Way of Planting ... With The Country Housewifes Garden for Hearbes ... London: Edward Griffin, 1638. 3rd edn, enlgd. Sm 8vo. [viii], 123 pp. Ills. Old reprs to last 12 ff. Disbound.
(Bookpress) $450 [≈ £234]

Layard, E.L.
- The Birds of South Africa ... Cape Town: 1867. 1st edn. 8vo. xvi,192, 197-382, xxi pp. Ptd slip at p 197 explaining mispagination. Frontis. Mod half mor.
(Wheldon & Wesley) £120 [≈ $230]

Leach, D.G.
- Rhododendrons of the World. London: 1962. 4to. 544 pp. Lge fldg cold plate, 8 other plates, map endpapers, num text figs. Orig cloth. *(Henly)* £60 [≈ $115]

Le Blanc, V. & Armengaud, J.E. & C.
- The Engineer and Machinist's Drawing Book, a Complete Course of Instruction for the Practical Engineer ... Glasgow: Blackie, 1855. viii,116 pp. Engvd title, frontis, 70 plates, 246 text figs. Occas sl foxing & marg water stain. Contemp calf, gilt spine.
(Spelman) £140 [≈ $268]

Lee, A.B.
- The Microtomist's Vade-Mecum. London: Churchill, 1905. 6th edn. 8vo. x,538 pp. Cloth. *(Gemmary)* $60 [≈ £31]

Lee, Henry
- The Vegetable Lamb of Tartary; a Curious Fable of the Cotton Plant ... Sketch of the History of Cotton and the Cotton Trade. London: Sampson, Low ..., 1887. 1st edn. xi, 112 pp. Frontis, ills. Orig pict gilt cloth, shaken, extremities rubbed, rear cvr sl soiled.
(Wreden) $95 [≈ £49]
- The White Whale. London: [1878]. 8vo. 16 pp. Orig ptd wraps. *(Bickersteth)* £25 [≈ $47]

Lee, James
- An Introduction to Botany. Containing an Explanation of the Theory of that Science; extracted from the Works of Dr. Linnaeus ... Third Edition, corrected, with large Additions. London: 1776. 8vo. xxiv,432 pp. 12 plates. Contemp calf, hinges cracking but sound. *(Claude Cox)* £55 [≈ $105]

Lee, John Edward
- Note-Book of an Amateur Geologist. London: Longmans, Green, 1881. 1st edn. 8vo. v,90 pp. 208 litho plates, 17 text ills. Orig pict cloth gilt. *(Gough)* £35 [≈ $67]

Lee, Rawdon B.
- A History and Description of the Modern Dogs of Great Britain and Ireland. The Terriers. London: Horace Cox, 1903. 3rd edn. 8vo. xiv,492,[8 advt] pp. 21 plates. Occas

sl marg water stain. Orig cloth gilt, sl marked.
(Fenning) £55 [≈ $105]

Leech, J.H.
- British Pyralides, including the Pterophidae. London: 1886. Cr 8vo. viii,122 pp. 18 hand cold plates. Neat ink notes. Cloth, trifle used.
(Wheldon & Wesley) £50 [≈ $95]

Lees, Edwin
- The Botany of Worcestershire. Worcester: 1867. 8vo. xcii,145,51 pp. Cold map, ills. Endpapers & a few pp foxed. Cloth.
(Wheldon & Wesley) £38 [≈ $72]
- Pictures of Nature in the Silurian Region around the Malvern Hills and Vale of Severn ... Malvern: H.W. Lamb; London: D. Bogue, 1856. 1st edn. 8vo. 336 pp. Plate, text diags. Orig cloth, some fading.
(Chapel Hill) $75 [≈ £39]

Lees, F.A.
- The Flora of West Yorkshire. London: 1888. 8vo. xii,843 pp. Cold map. Sgntrs on title. Buckram. *(Wheldon & Wesley)* £45 [≈ $86]
- The Flora of West Yorkshire. London: 1888. 8vo. xii,843 pp. Cold map. Orig cloth, spine faded, jnts loose.
(Wheldon & Wesley) £45 [≈ $86]

Lefanu, W.R.
- A Bio-bibliography of Edward Jenner 1749-1923. Phila: 1951. 1st edn. One of 500. 8vo. xx,176 pp. Frontis, 28 ills. Orig bndg.
(Goodrich) $45 [≈ £23]

Legallois, Julien Jean Cesar
- Experiments on the Principle of Life, and particularly on the Principle of the Motions of the Heart, and on the Seat of this Principle. Phila: 1813. 1st English translation. 328 pp. Leather. *(Fye)* $500 [≈ £260]
- Experiments on the Principle of Life, and particularly on the Principle of the Motions of the Heart ... Translated by N.C. and J.G. Nancrede. Phila: 1813. 1st edn in English. Fldg frontis. Sm stamp on title. Ends sl spotted. Old leather, cvrs loose.
(Hemlock) $475 [≈ £247]

Leibowitz, J.O.
- The History of Coronary Heart Disease. London: 1970. 1st edn. 227 pp. Orig bndg. Dw. *(Fye)* $60 [≈ £31]

Leigh, Charles
- The Natural History of Lancashire, Cheshire and the Peak in Derbyshire ... Oxford: 1700.

Folio. Engvd port, title, imprimatur, dble page map, 24 plates. Occas offsetting. Half calf, rebacked, crnrs reprd.
(Henly) **£315 [≈ $604]**

Leighton, Gerald R.
- The Life History of British Lizards ... Edinburgh: George A. Morton, 1903. 1st edn. xiv, 214 pp. 29 photo plates, 3 diags. Orig green pict cloth gilt.
(Gough) **£35 [≈ $67]**
- The Life History of British Serpents ... London: William Blackwood, 1901. 1st edn. xvi, 383,32 ctlg pp. 50 photo plates & ills. Orig green pict cloth gilt.
(Gough) **£35 [≈ $67]**

Leighton, W.A.
- The British Species of Angiocarpous Lichens; elucidated by their Sporidia. London: Ray Society, 1851. 8vo. 101 pp. 30 hand cold plates. Ex-lib. Orig cloth, rebacked.
(Wheldon & Wesley) **£40 [≈ $76]**
- The British Species of Angiocarpous Lichens; Elucidated by their Sporidia. London: Ray Society, 1851. 1st edn. 101,21 pp. 30 hand cold plates. Orig blue cloth, faded, spine sl worn at hd. *(Gough)* **£40 [≈ $76]**
- A Flora of Shropshire. Shrewsbury: 1841. 8vo. xii,573 pp. 20 plates. Half mor gilt.
(Wheldon & Wesley) **£50 [≈ $95]**
- A Flora of Shropshire. Shrewsbury: 1841. 8vo. xii,573 pp. New cloth.
(Wheldon & Wesley) **£50 [≈ $95]**
- The Lichen-Flora of Great Britain, Ireland, and the Channel Islands. Shrewsbury: Privately Printed, 1879. 3rd edn. 8vo. xvii, 547 pp. Cloth, trifle used.
(Wheldon & Wesley) **£45 [≈ $86]**

Leishman, William
- Systems of Midwifery ... Second American from the Second and Revised English Edition. Phila: Henry C. Lea, 1875. 8vo. xxiv,766,32 ctlg pp. Some pencil notes. Leather, spine rubbed. *(Schoyer)* **$65 [≈ £33]**

Le Lievre, -
- Observations on the Baume de Vie, first Discovered by Mr Le Lievre, the King's Apothecary at Paris ... London: ptd by W. Griffin ..., 1765. 8vo. Title, 49, [iii] pp. 2 sm tears reprd. Mod wraps.
(Bickersteth) **£145 [≈ $278]**

Lemery, Nicolas
- A Course of Chymistry. Containing an easie Method of preparing those Chymical

Medicins which are used in Physick ... Translated by Walter Harris, M.D. London: 1686. 2nd edn in English. 8vo. [28],548, [14],2 advt pp. Imprimatur leaf. 3 plates. Prelims browned. Half calf.
(Rootenberg) **$650 [≈ £338]**

Lemery, Nicolas (attributed author)
- Modern Curiosities of Art & Nature ... London: for Matthew Gilliflower, & James Partridge, 1685. 1st edn in English. 12mo. Engvd title with facing leaf of explanation. Contemp calf, rebacked, edges rubbed, inner hinges strengthened. Wing L.1041.
(Ximenes) **$1,750 [≈ £911]**

Lemnius, Levinus
- An Herbal for the Bible ... Drawen into English by Thomas Newton. London: Edmund Bollifant, 1587. 8vo. [6],287,[9] pp, last page blank. With 1st & last blank ff. Q8 in photostat facs. Contemp limp vellum, browned. STC 15454.
(Hemlock) **$750 [≈ £390]**

Leonardo, Richard
- History of Surgery. New York: 1943. 1st edn. 504 pp. 100 plates. Ex-lib. Orig bndg.
(Fye) **$200 [≈ £104]**

Leslie, Eliza
- Domestic French Cookery, chiefly translated from Sulpice Barue. Phila: Carey & Hart, 1832. 1st edn. 12mo. Orig purple cloth (faded), paper label. *(Ximenes)* **$400 [≈ £208]**

Leslie, J.
- Geometrical Analysis, and Geometry of Curve Lines, being Volume Second of a Course of Mathematics ... Edinburgh: 1821. ix,448 pp. 219 figs on 24 fldg plates. Lib label on endpaper. Soft half leather, rubbed.
(Whitehart) **£40 [≈ $76]**

Leslie, Sir John
- An Experimental Inquiry into the Nature, and Propagation, of Heat. London: Mawman, 1804. 1st edn. 8vo. xv,[1],562 pp. Fldg frontis, 8 plates (4 fldg). Browned at ends. Contemp half calf, mrbld bds, somewhat worn. *(Rootenberg)* **$950 [≈ £494]**

Le Souef, A.S. & Burrell, H.
- The Wild Animals of Australia ... London: Harrap, 1926. 1st edn. 8vo. 387 pp. Over 100 ills. Orig cloth. Dw (worn).
(Fenning) **£55 [≈ $105]**

Lettsom, John Coakley
- The Naturalist's and Traveller's Companion, containing Instructions for Collecting and Preserving Objects of Natural History. London: 1774. 2nd edn. 8vo. xvi,89, [8] pp. Cold frontis, cold title vignette. Half calf. *(Wheldon & Wesley)* **£85 [≈ $163]**
- Observations on the Cow-Pock. [London]: Nichols & Son for Joseph Mawman, 1801. 1st edn. [One of 100]. Lge 4to. vi,88 pp. Lib stamp on title verso. Title sl spotted. Lacks half-title. Contemp calf, inner hinge strengthened. *(Hemlock)* **$750 [≈ £390]**

Leutz, Charles R.
- Modern Radio Reception. 1925. 1st edn. 337 pp. 254 ills. *(New Wireless)* **$55 [≈ £28]**
- Short Waves. 1930. 1st edn. 384 pp. 185 ills. *(New Wireless)* **$55 [≈ £28]**

Levi-Civita, T.
- The Absolute Differential Calculus. London: Blackie, 1929. 8vo. xvi,452 pp. Cloth. *(Gemmary)* **$60 [≈ £31]**

Levine, Samuel
- Coronary Thrombosis: Its Various Clinical Features. Baltimore: 1931. 1st edn. 178 pp. Orig bndg. *(Fye)* **$125 [≈ £65]**

Levy, H. & Roth, L.
- Elements of Probability. Oxford: Clarendon Press, 1936. 1st edn. 8vo. x,200 pp. Figs. Orig cloth. *(Bow Windows)* **£36 [≈ $69]**

Levy, S.I.
- The Rare Earths: Their Occurrence, Chemistry and technology. London: Edward Arnold, 1915. 8vo. xiv,345 pp. 8 text figs. Cloth. *(Gemmary)* **$60 [≈ £31]**

Lewis, Henry Carvill
- Papers and Notes on the Glacial Geology of Great Britain and Ireland. London: 1894. lxxxi, 469 pp. 10 maps, 82 text figs. New cloth. *(Whitehart)* **£28 [≈ $53]**
- Papers and Notes on the Glacial Geology of Great Britain and Ireland. London: Longman, Green, 1894. 1st edn. 8vo. lxxxi,469,32 advt pp. 10 fldg cold maps, 82 text figs. Orig cloth. *(Gough)* **£30 [≈ $57]**

Lewis, Thomas
- Clinical Disorders of the Heartbeat. London: 1912. 1st edn. 104 pp. Ex-lib. Orig bndg. *(Fye)* **$200 [≈ £104]**
- Clinical Electrocardiography. London: 1913. 1st edn. 120 pp. Ills. B'plate. Orig bndg,

white ink call number on spine. *(Fye)* **$350 [≈ £182]**
- Clinical Electrocardiography. New York: 1919. 2nd edn. 120 pp. Orig bndg. *(Fye)* **$100 [≈ £52]**
- Clinical Electrocardiography. Chicago: 1931. 5th edn. 128 pp. Orig bndg. *(Fye)* **$25 [≈ £13]**
- Diseases of the Heart for the Practitioner. New York: 1933. 1st Amer edn. 8vo. xx,297 pp. Some pencil annotations. Orig bndg. *(Goodrich)* **$35 [≈ £18]**
- Diseases of the Heart. New York: 1933. 1st edn. 297 pp. Orig bndg. *(Fye)* **$50 [≈ £26]**
- Lectures on the Heart. New York: 1915. 1st edn. 124 pp. Orig bndg. *(Fye)* **$100 [≈ £52]**
- The Mechanism and Graphic Registration of the Heart-Beat. London: 1925. 3rd edn. 529 pp. Orig bndg, hinges & backstrip worn. *(Fye)* **$150 [≈ £78]**
- The Soldier's Heart and the Effort Syndrome. London: 1918. 1st edn. 8vo. 144 pp. Orig bndg, some rubbing. *(Goodrich)* **$150 [≈ £78]**
- The Soldier's Heart and the Effort Syndrome. New York: 1919. 1st Amer edn. 144 pp. Orig bndg. *(Fye)* **$150 [≈ £78]**

Lewis, William
- The New Dispensatory: containing I. The Elements of Pharmacy. II. The Materia Medica. III. The Preparations and Compositions of the new London and Edinburgh Pharmacopoeias ... London: Nourse, 1785. 5th edn. 8vo. x,[v],688 pp. Sl marg water stain. Orig calf, sl rubbed. *(Bickersteth)* **£65 [≈ $124]**

Leybourn, William
- The Complete Surveyor: Containing the whole Art of Surveying of Land ... London: 1653. 1st edn. Sm folio. [xii],279 pp. Port frontis, num w'cut ills. Sm burn hole in A4. Orig vellum, top edge front cvr sl damaged. Wing L.1907. *(Vanbrugh)* **£525 [≈ $1,007]**
- Compleat Surveyor: or, the Whole Art of Surveying of Land. London: Samuel Ballard, 1722. 5th edn. Folio. Frontis, 14 fldg plates. Lib stamp & b'plate. Contemp calf, rebacked. *(Bookpress)* **$575 [≈ £299]**
- An Introduction to Astronomy and Geography ... London: J.C. for Modern & Berry, 1675. 8vo. Fldg plate. Occas headline shaved. Contemp calf, rebacked. Wing L. 1915. *(Waterfield's)* **£125 [≈ $239]**

Library of Useful Knowledge ...
- Library of Useful Knowledge. London:

1829-38. 1st edn. 4 vols. Approx 250-300 pp each. Over 1000 text ills. Contemp leather, cloth reback, orig labels preserved.
(Whitehart) £120 [≈ $230]

Liddell, E.G.T.
- Discovery of Reflexes. Oxford: 1960. 1st edn. 174 pp. Dw.   *(Fye)* $100 [≈ £52]

Lieber, O.M.
- The Assayer's Guide; or, Practical Directions to Assayers, Miners, and Smelters. Phila: H.C. Baird, (1852) 1888. Cr 8vo. 133,32 ctlg pp. 5 w'cut plates. Cloth.
(Gemmary) $45 [≈ £24]

Liebig, Justus von
- Animal Chemistry, or Organic Chemistry in its Application to Physiology and Pathology. Edited from the Author's Manuscript by William Gregory. London: 1842. 1st edn in English. 8vo. xxiv, 354, [2,8 advt] pp. Rec bds.   *(Fenning)* £58.50 [≈ $113]
- Familiar Letters on Chemistry, and its relation to Commerce, Physiology, and Agriculture. London: 1843. 1st edn. xii,179 pp. Lacks front endpaper. Spine defective.
(Whitehart) £35 [≈ $67]
- Familiar Letters on Chemistry, in its relations to Physiology, Dietetics, Agriculture, Commerce and Political Economy. London: 1851. 3rd edn. Sm 8vo. xx,536 pp. Occas sl foxing. Ink notes on f.e.p. New cloth, sl marked.   *(Whitehart)* £25 [≈ $47]
- Letters on Modern Agriculture. Edited by J. Blyth. London: 1859. 1st English edn. xxviii, 284 pp. Occas foxing. Orig cloth, dust stained & sl worn, front inner hinge sl cracked.
(Whitehart) £40 [≈ $76]

Lilford, Lady
- Lord Lilford; Thomas Littleton, Fourth Baron, F.Z.S., President of the British Ornithologists' Union. London: Smith, Elder, 1900. 1st edn. xxiii,290,6 advt pp. 18 plates after Thorburn & others, 4 sketches. Orig pict green cloth. *(Gough)* £45 [≈ $86]

Lilford, Lord
- Coloured Figures of the Birds of the British Islands. London: 1885-97. 1st edn. 7 vols. Roy 8vo. Port, 421 cold plates. Somewhat foxed, mainly on the text. Half mor, t.e.g., jnts tender.
(Wheldon & Wesley) £1,850 [≈ $3,551]
- Notes on the Birds of Northamptonshire and Neighbourhood. London: R.H. Porter, 1895. Large Paper. 2 vols. Lge 4to. xvi,367; viii,

339 pp. Frontis, fldg map, 67 ills. Three qtr levant mor gilt, rubbed, jnts cracking, 1 jnt split but holding, orig wraps bound in.
(Hollett) £150 [≈ $287]

Lind, J.
- An Essay on Diseases incidental to Europeans in Hot Climates with the Methods of preventing their Fatal Consequences. London: 1792. 5th edn. xvi,366 pp. Leather, new label, spine sl rubbed.
(Whitehart) £190 [≈ $364]

Lindeboom, G.A.
- Bibliographia Boerhaaviana. List of Publications written or provided by H. Boerhaave or based upon his Works and Teachings. Leiden: Brill, 1959. 1st edn. 105 pp. 4 plates.   *(Robertshaw)* £20 [≈ $38]

Lindgren, W.
- Mineral Deposits. New York: McGraw Hill, 1919. 2nd edn. 8vo. xviii,957 pp. 284 ills. Cloth.   *(Gemmary)* $40 [≈ £20]

Lindley, J.
- Ladies Botany; or a Familiar Introduction to the Study of the Natural System of Botany. London: 1841. 2nd edn. 8vo. 50 hand cold text figs. Cloth.   *(Henly)* £75 [≈ $143]
- Medical and Oeconomical Botany. London: 1856. 2nd edn. 8vo. 274 pp. 363 figs. Cloth, reprd.   *(Wheldon & Wesley)* £45 [≈ $86]
- School Botany; or the Rudiments of Botanical Science. London: [1880]. 14th edn. viii, 212 pp. Num text figs. Orig cloth.
(Henly) £18 [≈ $34]
- The Theory and Practice of Horticulture; or an Attempt to Explain the Chief Operations of Gardening upon Physiological Grounds. London: 1855. 2nd edn of Theory of Horticulture, 1840. 8vo. xvi,606 pp. Orig cloth, sl faded, sm tear in jnt.
(Wheldon & Wesley) £35 [≈ $67]
- The Vegetable Kingdom ... London: 1853. 3rd edn. 8vo. lxviii,908,[10] pp. Over 500 text figs. Sound ex-lib. Half calf.
(Wheldon & Wesley) £45 [≈ $86]

Lindley, J. & Moore, T.
- The Treasury of Botany ... London: 1884. 4th edn. 2 vols. Cr 8vo. 20 plates, num text figs. Cloth, backstrips relaid.
(Henly) £38 [≈ $72]

Lindsay, W.L.
- Mind in the Lower Animals in Health and Disease. London: 1879. 2 vols. 8vo. Cloth, sl

used.   *(Wheldon & Wesley)* **£36 [≈ $69]**
- A Popular History of British Lichens. London: 1856. Post 8vo. xxxii,351 pp. 22 hand cold plates. Orig cloth, trifle loose.
    (Wheldon & Wesley) **£40 [≈ $76]**

Linnaeus, C.
- Miscellaneous Tracts relating to Natural History, Husbandry, and Physick, to which is added the Calendar of Flora, by B. Stillingfleet. London: 1762. 2nd edn. 8vo. [xxxii], 391 pp. 11 plates. Contemp calf.
    (Wheldon & Wesley) **£75 [≈ $143]**
- Miscellaneous Tracts ... see also Stillingfleet, B.

Linton, W.J.
- The Ferns of the English Lake Country. London: 1865. 12mo. iv,124 pp. Cold plate, w'cuts. Trifle foxed. Cloth gilt.
    (Wheldon & Wesley) **£18 [≈ $34]**
- The Ferns of the English Lake Country; with Tables of Varieties. Windermere: J. Garnett, 1878. 2nd edn. Sm 8vo. ii,179,[8 advt] pp. Ills. Orig dec green cloth gilt.
    (Hollett) **£25 [≈ $47]**

Lipscomb, William
- Verses on the Beneficial Effects of Inoculation, which obtained One of the Chancellor's Prizes at the University of Oxford in the Year 1772. Now republished ... London: J. Davis, 1793. 4to. 8 pp. Disbound.
    (C.R. Johnson) **£275 [≈ $527]**

Lister, A.
- A Monograph of the Mycetozoa. London: BM, 1894. 1st edn. 8vo. 224 pp. 78 plates, 51 text figs. Good ex-lib. Cloth.
    (Wheldon & Wesley) **£30 [≈ $57]**
- A Monograph of the Mycetozoa. London: BM, 1911. 2nd edn. 8vo. [v],302 pp. 202 ills on 101 plates (many cold), 56 w'cuts. Sm lib stamp on title & endpaper. Cloth.
    (Wheldon & Wesley) **£60 [≈ $115]**

Lister, Joseph, Baron
- The Collected Papers of Joseph, Baron Lister. Oxford: 1909. 1st edn. 2 vols. Lge 4to. Port, 14 plates, text figs. Orig cloth, spines faded, sl marked. *(Whitehart)* **£170 [≈ $326]**
- "On the Early Stages of Inflammation". Extracted from Phil Trans RS Lond 148: 645-702. London: 1859. 4to. 2 cold plates. New bds.   *(Goodrich)* **£275 [≈ £143]**

Liston, Robert
- Elements of Surgery. Phila: 1837. 1st Amer

edn. 540 pp. Leather.   *(Fye)* **$150 [≈ £78]**
- Elements of Surgery. Second Edition, illustrated with Engravings ... London: 1840. 8vo. xvi,800 pp. 3 engvd plates, num w'engvd text figs. 2 lib stamps. Contemp half calf, rebacked.   *(Bickersteth)* **£90 [≈ $172]**
- Memoir on the Formation and Connexions of the Crural Arch, and other Parts concerned in Inguinal and Femoral Hernia. Edinburgh: 1819. 22 pp. 3 plates. Sl foxing. Later calf backed mrbld bds. *(Whitehart)* **£55 [≈ $105]**

Little, E.M.
- History of the British Medical Association. London: 1932. 8vo. 341 pp. Plates. Orig cloth, faded.   *(Goodrich)* **$75 [≈ £39]**

Littlewood, J.E.
- [Lectures on the Theory of Functions]. [Oxford 1931?]. 151 pp. No title-page & no title. Plain cloth.   *(Whitehart)* **£35 [≈ $67]**

Liversidge, A.
- The Minerals of New South Wales, etc. London: 1888. 3rd edn, enlgd. 8vo. viii, 326, [2 advt] pp. Fldg cold map, 2 fldg charts, 1 plate, ills. Minor marks. Orig cloth, t.e.g., sl marked.   *(Bow Windows)* **£175 [≈ $335]**

Lives of British Physicians ...
- See MacMichael, William.

Livingston, R.R.
- Essay on Sheep; their Varieties - Account of the Merinoes of Spain, France ... New York: 1809. 8vo. 186 pp. Blind stamp on title, sl stained at ends. New bds.
    (Wheldon & Wesley) **£45 [≈ $86]**

Lloyd, H.
- Elementary Treatise on the Wave Theory of Light. London: 1873. 3rd edn. xi,247 pp. Lib stamp on title verso, lib number on title, label inside front cvr. Cloth, spine faded & worn.
    (Whitehart) **£35 [≈ $67]**

Lloyd, R.E.
- A Syllabus of a Course of Lectures on Astronomy; illustrated by that magnificent and highly improved Apparatus the new Dioastrodoxon: or, Grand Transparent Orrery ... Oxford: 1811. Sm 8vo. 35 pp. Pages discold. Wraps.   *(Whitehart)* **£25 [≈ $47]**

Lobb, T.
- A Practical Treatise of Painful Distempers, with some Effectual Methods of curing them, exemplified in a great Variety of suitable

Histories. London: 1739. xxx,[2], 320, [14] pp. Contemp calf, rebacked, edges & crnrs worn. *(Whitehart)* **£120 [≈$230]**

Locket, G.H., Millidge, A.F., & Merrett, P.
- British Spiders. London: Ray Society, 1951-74. 3 vols. 8vo. 612 maps, 471 text figs. Cloth. *(Wheldon & Wesley)* **£35 [≈$67]**

Lockley, R.M.
- Sea-Birds ... London: Collins New Naturalist, 1954. Ills. Orig cloth, sl marked. *(Grayling)* **£30 [≈$57]**
- Shearwaters. London: 1942. 1st edn. 8vo. xii, 238 pp. 20 plates, text ills. Orig cloth. *(Henly)* **£16 [≈$30]**

Lockyer, Sir Joseph Norman
- The Chemistry of the Sun. London: 1887. 1st edn. xix,457 pp. 134 ills. Orig cloth, spine sl marked. *(Whitehart)* **£35 [≈$67]**
- Inorganic Evolution as Studied by Spectrum Analysis. London: 1900. x,198 pp. 43 text ills. Orig cloth. *(Whitehart)* **£18 [≈$34]**
- The Meteoritic Hypothesis. A Statement of the Results of a Spectroscopic Inquiry into the Origin of the Cosmical Systems. London: 1879. 1st edn. 560 pp. 7 plates, 101 text figs. Orig cloth, spine sl marked at hd. *(Whitehart)* **£38 [≈$72]**
- Studies in Spectrum Analysis. London: Kegan Paul ..., 1894. 5th edn. Cr 8vo. xii, 258 pp. 8 plates, 51 text figs. Cloth. *(Gemmary)* **$45 [≈£23]**
- Studies in Spectrum Analysis. London: Kegan Paul ..., 1904. 6th edn. Cr 8vo. xii, 258 pp. 8 plates, 51 text figs. Cloth. *(Gemmary)* **$45 [≈£23]**

Locy, W.A.
- The Growth of Biology. Zoology from Aristotle to Cuvier, Botany from Theophrastus to Hofmeister, Physiology from Harvey to Claude Bernard. London: [1925]. xiv,481 pp. 140 ills. Orig cloth, sl marked. *(Whitehart)* **£35 [≈$67]**

Lodge, Sir Oliver
- Atoms and Rays. London: 1924. 1st edn. 208 pp. Orig bndg. *(New Wireless)* **$35 [≈£18]**
- Atoms and Rays. New York: Doran, 1924. 8vo. 208 pp. Cloth. Dw. *(Gemmary)* **$35 [≈£18]**
- Electrons. London: George Bell & Sons, 1907. 2nd edn. 8vo. xv,230 pp. 25 text figs. Cloth. *(Gemmary)* **$65 [≈£33]**
- The Ether of Space. London: Harper, 1909.

Cr 8vo. xvi,156 pp. 18 text figs. Cloth, spine worn. *(Gemmary)* **$25 [≈£13]**
- Modern Views of Electricity. London: Macmillan, 1889. Cr 8vo. xvi,422 pp. 54 text figs. Ex-lib. Cloth. *(Gemmary)* **$35 [≈£18]**
- Pioneers of Science. London: Macmillan, 1893. Cr 8vo. xv,404 pp. 120 text figs. Cloth. *(Gemmary)* **$30 [≈£15]**
- Signalling through Space without Wires. 1898. 3rd edn of "The Work of Hertz". 72,32 ctlg pp. 32 ills. Orig bndg. *(New Wireless)* **$185 [≈£96]**
- Talks about Wireless. London: 1925. 1st edn. 251 pp. Orig bndg. *(New Wireless)* **$35 [≈£18]**
- The Work of Hertz and some of his Successors. 1894. 1st edn. 58 pp. 32 ills. Orig bndg. *(New Wireless)* **$270 [≈£140]**

Lodge, Sir Oliver, et al.
- Harmsworth's Wireless Encyclopaedia. London: 1923. 1st edn. 3 vols. 2272 pp. Over 5000 ills. Orig bndg. *(New Wireless)* **$175 [≈£91]**

Lodge, R.B.
- Pictures of Bird Life. Woodland, Meadow, Mountain and Marsh. London: 1903. 8 cold plates, num ills. Orig bndg, sl worn. *(Grayling)* **£35 [≈$67]**

Loeb, L.B.
- Atomic Structure. New York: John Wiley & Sons, 1938. 1st edn. 8vo. xvi,444 pp. Cloth. *(Gemmary)* **$35 [≈£18]**

Longfield, C.
- The Dragonflies of the British Isles. L: 1949. 2nd edn. 256 pp. 58 plates (16 cold). Cloth gilt. *(Henly)* **£30 [≈$57]**

Longmore, Thomas
- A Treatise on Gunshot Wounds. Phila: 1862. 1st edn. 132 pp. Orig bndg, fine. *(Fye)* **$400 [≈£208]**

Longridge, C.C.
- Gold Dredging. London: The Mining Journal, 1905. 1st edn. 8vo. 195,[27 advt] pp. Num ills, some fldg. Rebound in cloth. *(Gemmary)* **$90 [≈£46]**
- Gold Dredging and Mechanical Excavators. London: The Mining Journal, 1907. 2nd edn. Roy 8vo. xiii,339,[44 advt] pp. Num plates & figs, some fldg. Orig yellow cloth, soiled, sl loose. *(Gemmary)* **$125 [≈£65]**

Lonsdale, Henry
- A Sketch of the Life and Writings of Robert Knox the Anatomist. London: Macmillan, 1870. 8vo. 420 pp. Frontis port. Orig bndg.
(Goodrich) **$85 [≈ £44]**

Loomis, Alfred
- Lectures on Diseases of the Respiratory Organs, Heart and Kidneys. New York: 1878. 1st edn. 549 pp. Orig bndg. *(Fye)* **$75 [≈ £39]**

Lord, John
- Memoir of John Kay of Bury, County of Lancaster, Inventor of the Fly-Shuttle, Metal Reeds, etc., etc., with a Review of the Textile Trade and Manufacture ... Rochdale: Aldine Press, 1903. One of 300. Sm 4to. xix, 171, 1 pp. 24 ills. Orig cloth gilt, sl dulled.
(Hollett) **£95 [≈ $182]**

Lorgna, A.M.
- A Dissertation on the Summation of Infinite Converging Series with Algebraic Divisors ... [Translated by H. Clarke]. London: for the author, 1779. 4to. xx,222 pp. 2 fldg plates. Contemp roan backed bds, v sl rubbed, sl worn. *(Whitehart)* **£60 [≈ $115]**

Lothian, J.
- Practical Hints on the Culture and General Management of Alpine or Rock Plants. Edinburgh: [1845]. Post 8vo. 84 pp. Engvd title, 4 cold & 2 plain plates. Orig cloth gilt.
(Wheldon & Wesley) **£60 [≈ $115]**

Loudon, Jane
- Facts from the World of Nature, Animate and Inanimate. London: Grant & Griffith, 1848. 1st edn. Sm 8vo. x,390,20 ctlg pp. Frontis, num w'engvd text ills. Marg stain to prelims. Orig cloth gilt, a.e.g., inner hinges cracked but firm. *(de Beaumont)* **£48 [≈ $92]**
- The Ladies' Companion to the Flower Garden ... Third Edition, with considerable additions and corrections. London: William Smith, 1844. Sm 8vo. Advt leaf, viii,346 pp. Cold frontis, 70 ills. Orig cloth gilt, headband v sl worn. *(Fenning)* **£38.50 [≈ $74]**
- The Ladies Companion to the Flower Garden ... Eighth Edition, considerably enlarged ... by Charles Edmonds. London: Bradbury, Evans, [1864]. Sm 8vo. viii,382,2 advt pp. Hand cold frontis, w'engvs in text. Orig green cloth gilt, a.e.g., recased. *(Beech)* **£30 [≈ $57]**
- The Lady's Country Companion ... London: Longman, 1845. 1st edn. 8vo. xi,396,32 ctlg pp. Frontis. Orig cloth, spine sunned.
(Bookpress) **$250 [≈ £130]**

- The Year-Book of Natural History, for Young Persons. London: Murray, 1842. 1st edn. Sm sq 8vo. xvi,264 pp. text ills. Lacks front free endpaper. Orig cloth gilt.
(Bickersteth) **£22 [≈ $42]**

Loudon, John C.
- Arboretum et Fruticetum Britannicum, or the Trees and Shrubs of Britain, Native and Foreign, Hardy and Half Hardy. London: 1838. 1st edn. 8 vols. 8vo. 412 plates, 2546 text figs. Sm sections cut from titles. Unfoxed. Orig cloth, backstrips relaid, vol 1 spine faded. *(Henly)* **£150 [≈ $287]**
- Arboretum et Fruticetum Britannicum; or the Trees and Shrubs of Britain ... London: 1844. 2nd edn. 8 vols. 8vo. 412 plates, ca 2500 text figs. A fair amount of foxing. Orig cloth.
(Wheldon & Wesley) **£150 [≈ $287]**
- An Encyclopaedia of Gardening ... Fifth Edition. London: Longman ..., 1828. Thick 8vo. [16 inserted ctlg dated March 1829], [2], xii, 1234 pp. Text w'engvs. Contemp green parchment, paper label, mrbld bds, largely unopened, worn at extremities.
(Beech) **£110 [≈ $211]**
- An Encyclopaedia of Gardening ... New Edition. Edited by Mrs Loudon. London: Longman, 1860. Thick 8vo. xl,1278,40 advt pp. Orig green cloth, sm reprs to jnts.
(Spelman) **£75 [≈ $143]**
- An Encyclopaedia of Gardening ... New Edition. Edited by Mrs Loudon. London: 1878. 8vo. xl, 1278, [2,24 advt dated July 1879] pp. 1020 ills. 2 sm marg reprs. Orig cloth, inside jnts reprd.
(Fenning) **£125 [≈ $239]**
- An Encyclopaedia of Plants ... London: 1829. 8vo. xx,2,1159 pp. Text figs. Few pp at end taped in. Calf, rebacked.
(Wheldon & Wesley) **£55 [≈ $105]**
- An Encyclopaedia of Plants ... London: 1836. 8vo. xx,2,1159 pp. Num ills. Rec bds.
(Fenning) **£65 [≈ $124]**
- The Green-House Companion; comprising a General Course of Green-House and Conservatory Practice throughout the Year ... London: 1825. 2nd edn. 8vo. xii,256,204 pp. Cold plate. Orig cloth, reprd. Anon.
(Wheldon & Wesley) **£65 [≈ $124]**
- Hortus Britannicus ... London: 1832. 2nd edn, with Supplement. 8vo. xxiv,602 pp. Mod half calf.
(Wheldon & Wesley) **£30 [≈ $57]**
- The Suburban Gardener, and Villa Companion ... London: for the author, & sold by Longman ..., 1838. 1st edn. 8vo. xvi,752,32 ctlg pp. 343 w'engvs. Orig cloth, 2

sm tears on spine. *(Bookpress)* **$425 [≈£221]**
- The Suburban Horticulturalist; or, an Attempt to teach the Science and Practice of the Culture and Management of the Kitchen, Fruit and Forcing Garden ... London: for the author, 1842. 1st edn. Lge 8vo. 32, 732 pp. Ills. Orig cloth, recased.
(Spelman) **£140 [≈$268]**

Louis, P.C.A.
- Pathological Researches on Phthisis. London: 1835. li,388 pp. Orig cloth, rebacked, sl worn.   *(Whitehart)* **£40 [≈$76]**
- Researches on Phthisis. Anatomical, Pathological and Therapeutical. Translated by W.H. Walshe. London: 1844. xxxv,571 pp. Some lib marks. Cloth, dusty & worn, spine edges partly split.
(Whitehart) **£35 [≈$67]**

Lousley, J.E.
- Flora of the Isles of Scilly. Newton Abbot: David & Charles, 1971. 1st edn. 8vo. x, 336 pp. 16 plates, 28 figs & maps. Orig bndg. Dw.
(Claude Cox) **£15 [≈$28]**
- Wild Flowers of the Chalk and Limestone. London: Collins New Naturalist, 1950. 1st edn. 8vo. xvii,254 pp. 48 cold & 24 plain plates. Orig cloth.   *(Henly)* **£18 [≈$34]**

Love, James K.
- Diseases of the Ear: for Practitioners and Students of Medicine. London: 1904. xvi,339 pp. 2 cold plates, 54 stereoscopic photos, 63 text ills. Orig bndg. *(Whitehart)* **£38 [≈$72]**
- Diseases of the Ear. With 54 Stereoscopic Photographs. Bristol: 1904. 1st edn. 339 pp. 54 actual photo plates. Orig bndg.
(Fye) **$250 [≈£130]**

Low, A.M.
- Wireless Possibilities. 1924. 1st edn. 77 pp. Orig bndg.   *(New Wireless)* **$35 [≈£18]**

Lowe, Edward J.
- Ferns: British and Exotic. London: (1856-60). 8 vols. Roy 8vo. 479 cold plates. Occas foxing. Orig cloth, trifle used & frayed at spine ends.
(Wheldon & Wesley) **£180 [≈$345]**
- A Natural History of British Grasses. London: 1858. 1st edn. Roy 8vo. vi,245 pp. 74 cold plates. Orig cloth gilt, fine.
(Henly) **£85 [≈$163]**
- A Natural History of British Grasses. London: 1862. Roy 8vo. 245 pp. 74 cold plates. Orig cloth, spine faded.
(Wheldon & Wesley) **£35 [≈$67]**

- A Natural History of New and Rare Ferns ... London: 1868. Roy 8vo. viii,192 pp. 72 cold plates. Ex-lib. Orig cloth.
(Wheldon & Wesley) **£35 [≈$67]**
- Fern Growing, Fifty Years Experience ... New York: 1898. Roy 8vo. xi,196 pp. Cold plate, 6 ports, 59 text figs. Cloth, sound ex-lib.   *(Wheldon & Wesley)* **£50 [≈$95]**
- Ferns, British and Exotic. London: 1872. 8 vols. Roy 8vo. 479 cold plates. Sl water stain to 1 plate. Orig gilt dec cloth.
(Baldwin) **£200 [≈$383]**
- Ferns: British and Exotic. London: George Bell, 1872. Half-titles lettered "New Edition". 8 vols. Roy 8vo. Advts dated 1881. 479 cold plates, num text ills. Orig purple cloth gilt.
(Fenning) **£165 [≈$316]**
- A Natural History of New and Rare Ferns. London: 1871. Roy 8vo. viii,192 pp. 72 cold plates. Orig green cloth gilt, sm water mark on rear cvr.   *(Baldwin)* **£55 [≈$105]**
- Our Native Ferns or a History of the British Species and their Varieties. London: 1874. 2 vols. 79 cold plates, 909 w'cuts. Orig cloth gilt, sl soiled.   *(Baldwin)* **£45 [≈$86]**

Lowe, Edward J. & Howard, W.
- Beautiful Leaved Plants. London: 1864. Roy 8vo. 60 cold plates (some finished by hand). Text & 2 plates sl foxed. Orig cloth, spine faded.   *(Henly)* **£85 [≈$163]**

Lowe, Frank A.
- The Heron. London: Collins New Naturalist, 1954. 1st edn. 8vo. xiii,177 pp. 1 cold & 8 plain plates. Orig cloth. *(Henly)* **£60 [≈$115]**
- The Heron. London: Collins New naturalist, 1954. 1st edn. 8vo. 177 pp. Cold frontis, maps, ills. Orig cloth gilt (2 sm dents lower bd). Dw (sm tear spine).
(Hollett) **£75 [≈$143]**

Lowe, John
- The Yew-Trees of Great Britain and Ireland. London: Macmillan, 1897. 1st edn. 8vo. xiv,270 pp. 23 plates, 16 text ills. Orig pict cloth gilt.   *(Gough)* **£55 [≈$105]**

Lowe, Percy R.
- A Naturalist on Desert Islands. London: Witherby, 1911. 1st edn. 8vo. xii,230 pp. 3 cold maps, 32 plates. Orig blue cloth.
(Gough) **£24 [≈$46]**

Lowe, R.T.
- A History of the Fishes of Madeira. [Vol. 1 all published]. London: Van Voorst 1843-44 [Parts 1-4], Quaritch 1860 [Part 5]. Roy 8vo.

xvi,196 pp. 28 plates (numbered 1-27 with an unnumbered introductory plate). Sl foxing. Half roan, sl worn.
(Wheldon & Wesley) **£385 [≈ $739]**

- A Manual Flora of Madeira and the Adjacent Islands of Porto Santo and the Desertas. London: [1857-] 1868 [-1872]. Vol 1 & vol 2 part 1, all published. 8vo. xii,618,113 pp. New cloth. *(Wheldon & Wesley)* **£75 [≈ $143]**

Lower, R.
- Vindicatio. A Defence of the Experimental Method. Oxford: 1983. One of 250. xxxiv,314 pp. Orig bndg.
(Whitehart) **£38 [≈ $72]**

Lowry, D.
- Conversations on Mineralogy. London: Longman ..., 1826. 2nd edn. 2 vols. Cr 8vo. xv, 270; iv,297 pp. 12 fldg plates (1 hand cold). Leather, rebacked.
(Gemmary) **$350 [≈ £182]**

Lubbock, Sir John
- Monograph of the Collembola and Thysanura. London: Ray Society, 1873. 1st edn. x,276 pp. 31 hand cold & 47 plain plates. Occas mostly sl spotting, plate 36 browned. Orig blue cloth gilt, t.e.g., spine faded.
(Gough) **£90 [≈ $172]**

Lubbock, Richard
- Observations on the Fauna of Norfolk, and More Particularly on the District of the Broads. Norwich: 1845. 1st edn. 8vo. viii,156 pp. Map, 2 plates. Occas spotting. Lib label. Orig cloth, backstrip relaid. Interesting MS notes. *(Bow Windows)* **£45 [≈ $86]**
- Observations on the Fauna of Norfolk, and More Particularly on the District of the Broads. Norwich: 1848. 8vo. viii,156 pp. Map, 2 plates. Map rather foxed. Orig cloth.
(Wheldon & Wesley) **£50 [≈ $95]**
- Observations on the Fauna of Norfolk, and More Particularly on the District of the Broads ... Norwich: Jarrold, 1879. 2nd edn. 8vo. xxxvi,239 pp. Map (reprd), 2 plates. Orig cloth, recased. *(Gough)* **£24 [≈ $46]**
- Observations on the Fauna of Norfolk, and More Particularly on the District of the Broads ... New Edition, with Additions ... . Norwich: 1879. 8vo. xxxvi,239 pp. Map, 2 plates. Occas spotting. Orig cloth, sl rubbed, new endpapers. *(Bow Windows)* **£52 [≈ $99]**

Lucas, W.J.
- British Dragonflies: Odonata. London: Upcott Gill, 1900. 1st edn. xiv,356 pp. 27 cold plates, 57 text figs. Occas sl spotting. Orig pict brown cloth gilt.
(Gough) **£90 [≈ $172]**

Lummer, Otto
- Contributions to Photographic Optics. London: 1900. xi,135 pp. 55 text figs. Orig cloth. *(Whitehart)* **£35 [≈ $67]**
- Contributions to Photographic Optics. Translated and augmented by Silvanus P. Thompson. London: Macmillan, 1900. 1st edn. 8vo. Ills, diags. Orig cloth, trifle shaken.
(Young's) **£60 [≈ $115]**

Lupton, Thomas
- A Thousand Memorable Things. Containing Modern Curiosities ... London: for G. Conyers, [?early 1700s]. 12mo. [ii],264,[x] pp. Some wear & tear, marg worm in 3 prelims. New qtr calf. Anon. *(Rankin)* **£85 [≈ $163]**

Lydekker, Richard
- The Game Animals of Africa. London: 1926. 2nd edn, rvsd. 488 pp. Ills. Orig bndg, fine.
(Trophy Room) **$325 [≈ £169]**
- The Game Animals of Africa. Second Edition, edited by J.G. Dollman. London: 1926. 8vo. Num ills. Orig cloth, v sl marked.
(Grayling) **£150 [≈ $287]**
- The Game Animals of Africa. Second Edition, edited by J.G. Dollman. London: 1926. 8vo. Num ills. Some foxing & damp marking to margs. Orig cloth, upper cvr damaged on foredge, hinges sprung.
(Grayling) **£60 [≈ $115]**
- The Game Animals of India, Burma, Malaya and Tibet. Second Edition, revised by J.G. Dollman. London: 1924. 8vo. Ills. Orig bndg, v sl bumped. *(Grayling)* **£110 [≈ $211]**
- The Game Animals of India, Burma, Malaya and Tibet. Second Edition, revised by J.G. Dollman. London: 1924. 8vo. Sl affected by damp. Ills. Orig buckram, v faded.
(Grayling) **£55 [≈ $105]**
- Handbook to the Carnivora. Cats, Civets and Mongooses. London: 1896. 8vo. Cold plates. Frontis reprd. Orig bndg, sl worn.
(Grayling) **£20 [≈ $38]**
- A Handbook to the Marsupialia and Monotremata. London: 1896. Cr 8vo. xvi,320 pp. 38 cold plates. Cloth.
(Wheldon & Wesley) **£35 [≈ $67]**
- Mostly Mammals. Zoological Essays. London: 1903. 8vo. Ills. Orig bndg, v sl rubbed. *(Grayling)* **£30 [≈ $57]**
- The Royal Natural History. London: 1893-94. 6 vols. Num cold & other plates, text ills. Orig pict gilt & silver cloth, sl rubbed,

stitching of 1 vol sl weak.
(Grayling) **£110 [≈ $211]**
- The Royal Natural History. London: Warne,
1893-96. 1st edn. 6 vols. 72 chromolithos, ca
1600 engvd plates & text ills. Some general,
mostly light foxing. Contemp red half mor,
gilt dec spines, t.e.g., fine.
(Gough) **£250 [≈ $479]**
- The Royal Natural History. London:
1893-94. 6 vols. Num cold & other plates, text
ills. Occas foxing. Orig pict cloth.
(Grayling) **£120 [≈ $230]**

Lyell, Sir Charles
- The Geological Evidence of the Antiquity of
Man, with Remarks on Theories of the Origin
of Species by Variation. London: Murray,
1863. 1st edn. xii,520,[32 advts dated Jan
1863] pp. 2 plates, 58 ills. Sl pencil marks.
Rec cloth. Inc Appendix pp 507-513, [1].
(Fenning) **£85 [≈ $163]**
- The Geological Evidences of the Antiquity of
Man with Remarks on Theories of the Origin
of Species by Variation. London: Murray,
1863. 1st edn. 8vo. 520,32 advt pp. Frontis,
plate, maps, ills. Orig green cloth gilt.
(Chapel Hill) **£350 [≈ $182]**
- The Geological Evidences of the Antiquity of
Man ... London: Murray, 1863. 1st edn. 8vo.
xii,520 pp. 32 pp ctlg at end dated Jan 1863.
2 plates, num text figs. Orig green cloth gilt,
recased, sm stain ft of upper cvr.
(Bickersteth) **£120 [≈ $230]**
- The Geological Evidences of the Antiquity of
Man, with Remarks on Theories of the Origin
of Species by Variation. London: 1863. 1st
edn. 8vo. xii,520 pp. 2 plates, text figs. Sm
stain in marg of plates & a few other ff. Lacks
half-title & advts. Mod qtr mor.
(Wheldon & Wesley) **£100 [≈ $191]**
- The Geological Evidences of the Antiquity of
Man ... Second Edition, revised. London:
Murray, 1863. 8vo. xvi,528 pp. 2 plates, num
text ills. Orig cloth.
(Bickersteth) **£80 [≈ $153]**
- The Geological Evidences of the Antiquity of
Man ... London: 1863. 2nd edn. 8vo. xvi, 528
pp. Cloth, recased.
(Wheldon & Wesley) **£90 [≈ $172]**
- The Geological Evidences of the Antiquity of
Man. London: 1873. 4th edn. 8vo. xix,572
pp. 2 plates, 56 text figs. Orig cloth gilt.
(Henly) **£52 [≈ $99]**
- The Geological Evidences of the Antiquity of
man. London: 1873. 4th edn. 8vo. xix,572
pp. 2 plates, 56 text figs. Cloth gilt, sl worn.
(Henly) **£48 [≈ $92]**
- The Geological Evidences of the Antiquity of

Man ... London: 1873. 4th edn, rvsd. 8vo.
xix,572 pp. 2 plates, 56 text figs. Cloth, sl
used.
(Wheldon & Wesley) **£60 [≈ $115]**
- Life, Letters and Journals of Sir Charles
Lyell, Bart. Edited by Mrs. Lyell. London:
1881. 2 vols. New cloth.
(Baldwin) **£140 [≈ $268]**
- A Manual of Elementary Geology ... Fifth
Edition, greatly enlarged, and illustrated with
750 Woodcuts. London: Murray, 1855. 8vo.
xvi, 655 pp. Frontis, ills. Stain on crnr of 1st
few ff. Rec bds.   *(Fenning)* **£38.50 [≈ $74]**
- Principles of Geology ... London: 1847. 7th
edn. 8vo. xvii,810,16 pp. 7 maps, 5 plates.
Cloth gilt, backstrip relaid.
(Henly) **£85 [≈ $163]**
- Principles of Geology of the Modern Changes
of Earth and its Inhabitants considered as
Illustrative of Geology. London: 1867-68.
10th edn, rvsd. 2 vols. 8vo. xvi, 671, [32
advt]; xvi,[1], 649,[2 advt] pp. Fldg map, 7
plates, num w'cuts. Rec bds, uncut.
(Fenning) **£55 [≈ $105]**
- Principles of Geology. London: Murray,
1872. 11th edn. 2 vols. 8vo. 7 plates, 164 text
figs. Cloth, worn.   *(Gemmary)* **$50 [≈ £26]**
- The Students Elements of Geology. London:
1874. 2nd edn. 12mo. xix,672 pp. Frontis,
645 text figs. Orig cloth gilt.
(Henly) **£25 [≈ $47]**

Lyell, D.
- The African Elephant and its Hunters.
London: 1924. 1st edn. 221 pp. Orig bndg.
(Trophy Room) **$750 [≈ £390]**

Lyell, K.M.
- A Geographical Handbook of all the Known
Ferns with Tables to show their Distribution.
London: 1870. Cr 8vo. x,[ii],225 pp. Engvd
title. Sl foxed at ends. Orig cloth, trifle used.
(Wheldon & Wesley) **£20 [≈ $38]**

Lynch, Bernard
- A Guide to Health through the Various
Stages of Life. London: for the author, & sold
by Mrs. Cooper ..., 1744. 8vo. 5 pp
subscribers. Contemp calf, gilt borders, spine
rubbed & chipped at hd.
(Jarndyce) **£140 [≈ $268]**

Lyon, P.
- Observations of the Barrenness of Fruit
Trees, and of the means of Preventions and
Cure. Edinburgh: C. Stewart, for William
Blackwood ..., 1813. 1st edn. 8vo. [iv],80, [16
advt] pp. Frontis. Orig bds, ptd label.
(Burmester) **£110 [≈ $211]**

M., G.

- The English House-Wife ... see Markham, Gervase.

M'Alpine, D.

- The Botanical Atlas ... Edinburgh: 1883. 2 vols. Imperial 4to. Addtnl cold titles, 52 cold plates. Sl foxed at ends. Orig dec cloth gilt.
(Henly) **£85 [≈ $163]**

M'Alpine, D. & A.N.

- Biological Atlas, a Guide to the Practical Study of Plants and Animals ... London: 1880. 1st edn. 4to. ix,49,4 pp. 423 cold figs on 24 plates. Sm lib stamp on title. Dec green cloth, fine.
(Henly) **£48 [≈ $92]**

Macan, T.T. & Worthington, E.B.

- Life in Lakes and Rivers. London: Collins New Naturalist, 1951. 1st edn. 8vo. xvi,272 pp. 40 cold & 32 plain plates. Orig cloth.
(Henly) **£12 [≈ $23]**

Macaulay, J. (ed.)

- Modern Railway Working. A Practical Treatise by Engineering and Administrative Experts. London: 1912-14. 8 vols. (1739) pp. 87 plates (4 cold), 723 text figs. Orig pict cloth gilt.
(Whitehart) **£50 [≈ $95]**

MacCallum, William G.

- William Stewart Halsted, Surgeon. Baltimore: 1931. 1st edn, 2nd printing. 241 pp. Orig bndg.
(Fye) **$140 [≈ £72]**

McCarthy, L.

- Histopathology of Skin Diseases. London: 1931. Lge 4to. 513 pp. 250 ills (54 cold). Obtrusive MS notes. Orig bndg.
(Whitehart) **£25 [≈ $47]**

McClellan, George

- Regional Anatomy in its relation to Medicine and Surgery. Phila: 1892. 2 vols. 4to. 436; 414 pp. Cold ills. Half leather.
(Fye) **$250 [≈ £130]**

McClung, C.E.

- Handbook of Microscopical Technique. New York: Hoeber, 1929. 1st edn. Med 8vo. 495 pp. 43 ills. Orig cloth, front inner hinge sl loose.
(Savona) **£25 [≈ $47]**

McClure, J.B.

- Edison and his Inventions. 1891. 1st edn. 286 pp. 103 ills. Orig bndg, cvrs soiled.
(New Wireless) **$75 [≈ £39]**

MacCormac, W.

- Antiseptic Surgery. An Address ... London: 1880. xi,286 pp. 60 figs. Page edges sl foxed. Cloth, sl worn & dusty.
(Whitehart) **£38 [≈ $72]**

MacCulloch, J.

- The Highlands and Western Isles of Scotland ... London: 1824. 4 vols. Half calf, crnrs sl rubbed.
(Baldwin) **£240 [≈ $460]**

MacCulloch, John

- An Essay on the Remittent and Intermittent Diseases including generically Marsh Fever and Neurologia ... Tic Doloureux, Sciatica, Headache, Ophthalmia, Toothache, Palsy ... Phila: 1830. 8vo. xiv,474 pp. Foredge cut from front blank. Sheep, worn.
(Goodrich) **$65 [≈ £33]**
- Remarks on the Art of Making Wine ... London: Longman ..., 1816. 1st edn. 12mo. [2],vi, 261,[1] pp, inc errata leaf. Rec half calf. Anon.
(Rootenberg) **$550 [≈ £286]**

McCusick, Victor

- Cardiovascular Sound in Health and Disease. Baltimore: 1958. 1st edn. 570 pp. Ex-lib. Orig bndg.
(Fye) **$150 [≈ £78]**

McDonald, A.

- A Complete Dictionary of Practical Gardening ... London: 1807. 2 vols. 4to. 61 plain plates (61 by Sydenham Edwards). Vol 2 title & 1 plate creased. Sl foxing & offsetting. New cloth. Also appears under the name of R.W. Dickson.
(Wheldon & Wesley) **£200 [≈ $383]**

MacDonald, Arthur

- Abnormal Man; Being Essays on Education and Crime and Related Subjects ... Washington: W.H. Lowdermilk, 1895. 1st edn. 8vo. 445 pp. Contemp cloth.
(Gough) **£35 [≈ $67]**

McDonald, D.

- Percival Norton Johnson. The Biography of a Pioneer Metallurgist. London: 1951. 224 pp. 7 plates. Three qtr mor, uncut, rubbed.
(Whitehart) **£18 [≈ $34]**

Macdonald, J.D.

- Birds of Australia. London: 1973. 4to. 552 pp. 24 cold plates, other ills. Dw.
(Wheldon & Wesley) **£30 [≈ $57]**

McDowall, R.J.S.

- The Control of the Circulation of the Blood.

With Supplemental Volume. London: 1938-56. xv,619; [vii],257 pp. Figs. Orig bndg. *(Whitehart)* **£65 [≈ $124]**

MacEwen, William
- The Growth of Bone. Observations on Osteogenesis. An Experimental Inquiry ... Glasgow: 1912. 8vo. 210 pp. 61 photo plates. Orig cloth, sl worn. *(Goodrich)* **$195 [≈ £101]**

Mac Fadyean, Sir John
- The Anatomy of the Horse: a Dissection Guide. London: [1884]. 1st edn. 8vo. xx,375 pp. 48 plates (43 cold), 48 ills. Orig cloth gilt. *(Fenning)* **£55 [≈ $105]**

Macfadyen, J.
- The Flora of Jamaica; a Description of the Plants of that Island. Vol 1, Ranunculaceae - Leguminosae. London: 1837. All published. 8vo. xiv,351 pp. Rather used ex-lib. Some foxing. Orig cloth.
(Wheldon & Wesley) **£225 [≈ $431]**

Macgillivray, W.
- A History of British Birds Indigenous and Migratory. London: 1837-52. 5 vols. 8vo. 29 plates (unfoxed), 378 text figs. Half mor, rubbed, jnts reprd.
(Wheldon & Wesley) **£100 [≈ $191]**

McGregor-Morris, J.T. & Henley, J.A.
- Cathode Ray Oscillography. 1936. 1st edn. 249 pp. 151 ills. Orig bndg.
(New Wireless) **$35 [≈ £18]**

Mach, E.
- The Science of Mathematics. A Critical and Historical Account of its Development. Translated by T.J. McCormack. Chicago: 1919. 4th edn. xiv,605 pp. Port, 250 diags & ills. Top half of pp v-vi loose.
(Whitehart) **£25 [≈ $47]**

McHenry, Lawrence
- Garrison's History of Neurology Revised and Enlarged with a Bibliography of Classical, Original, and Standard Works in Neurology. Springfield: 1969. 552 pp. Dw.
(Fye) **$125 [≈ £65]**

Macilwain, G.
- Memoirs of John Abernethy, with a View of his Lectures, his Writings and Character; with Additional Extracts from Original Documents. London: 1856. 3rd edn. xiv,396 pp. Frontis, 1 plate, facs letter. Orig cloth, backstrip relaid. *(Whitehart)* **£45 [≈ $86]**

McIlwraith, T.
- The Birds of Ontario with a Description of their Nests and Eggs. Toronto: 1894. 2nd edn, enlgd & rvsd. 8vo. 426 pp. Port, text figs. Cloth. *(Wheldon & Wesley)* **£35 [≈ $67]**

McInnes, W., et al.
- The Coal Resources of the World. Toronto: 1913. Folio. 48 mps. Sm lib stamps on cvr, endpaper & title. Wraps, upper cvr soiled.
(Henly) **£48 [≈ $92]**

M'Intosh, Charles
- The Flower Garden, Its Cultivation, Arrangement, and General Management. A New Edition carefully revised. London: Wm. S. Orr, 1839. Sm 8vo. iv,515 pp. Hand cold title vignette, 10 hand cold plates. Few spots. Contemp half mor gilt. Anon.
(Hollett) **£120 [≈ $230]**
- The New and Improved Practical Gardener, and Modern Horticulturist ... London: Thomas Kelly, 1851. 1st edn. Thick 8vo. [15],[1],972 pp. Port frontis, 10 hand cold plates, num text engvs. Rec period style half mor. *(Spelman)* **£110 [≈ $211]**

Mackay, James T.
- Flora Hibernica, comprising Flowering Plants, Ferns ... Lichens and Algae of Ireland ... Dublin: Curry, 1836. 8vo. 279 pp. Cloth bds. *(Emerald Isle)* **£75 [≈ $143]**

McKay, Robert
- Potato Diseases. Dublin: Irish Potato Marketing Board, 1955. 1st edn. Roy 8vo. x, 126 pp. 64 plates (4 cold). Orig cloth.
(Fenning) **£24.50 [≈ $47]**

McKay, W.J. Stewart
- The History of Ancient Gynaecology. New York: 1901. 1st Amer edn. 302 pp. Orig bndg. *(Fye)* **$200 [≈ £104]**

Mackenzie, J.
- The History of Health and the Art of Preserving It ... Edinburgh: 1759. 2nd edn. xii, 436 pp. Leather, hd of spine sl chipped.
(Whitehart) **£180 [≈ $345]**

Mackenzie, Sir James
- Angina Pectoris. London: 1923. 1st edn. 253 pp. Orig bndg, outer hinges weak.
(Fye) **$300 [≈ £156]**
- Diseases of the Heart. London: 1910. 2nd edn. 419 pp. Orig bndg, cvrs water stained. *(Fye)* **$100 [≈ £52]**
- Diseases of the Heart. New York: 1910. 2nd

edn. 419 pp. Orig bndg. *(Fye)* **$150** [≈ £78]
- Diseases of the Heart. London: 1918. 3rd edn, rvsd. 502 pp. Orig bndg, fine.
(Fye) **$125** [≈ £65]
- The Study of the Pulse ... Edinburgh: 1902. 1st edn. 325 pp. Ills. Orig bndg.
(Fye) **$500** [≈ £260]
- The Study of the Pulse: Arterial, Venous and Hepatic and of the Movements of the Heart. Edinburgh: 1902. 1st edn. 325 pp. Ills. Orig bndg. *(Fye)* **$500** [≈ £260]

Mackenzie, Morell
- Diseases of the Pharynx, Larynx, and Trachea. New York: 1880. 440 pp. [With his] Diseases of the Oesophagus, Nose and Naso-Pharynx. New York: 1884. 550 pp. 1st Amer edns. Orig green & yellow cloth.
(Fye) **$150** [≈ £78]
- Diseases of the Throat and Nose. Phila: 1880-84. 1st Amer edn. 570; 550 pp. Orig bndgs. damp stained. *(Fye)* **$100** [≈ £52]
- The Use of the Laryngoscope in Diseases of the Throat. With an Appendix on Rhinoscopy. Phila: 1865. 1st Amer edn. 160 pp. W'cut ills. Orig bndg.
(Fye) **$350** [≈ £182]

Mackenzie, P.
- Practical Observations on the Medical Powers of the most celebrated Mineral Waters and of the Various Modes of Bathing. Intended for the Use of Invalids. London: 1819. iii, 151 pp. Orig bds, rebacked.
(Whitehart) **£40** [≈ $76]

Mackenzie, W. (publisher)
- Chemistry, Theoretical, Practical, and Analytical, as applied to the Arts and Manufacturers. By Writers of Eminence. London: n.d. 2 vols. Lge 4to. [v],1048; [v], 1008 pp. 53 plates. Orig cloth gilt, a.e.g., rubbed, edges worn, vol 1 inner hinge cracked but firm. *(Whitehart)* **£30** [≈ $57]
- Chemistry, Theoretical, Practical, and Analytical, as applied to the Arts and Manufacturers. By Writers of Eminence. London: [ca 1876]. 2 vols in 8. Lge 8vo. 1048, 1008 pp. 53 plates. Few v sl tears. Orig cloth gilt, few spine ends v sl fingered.
(Bow Windows) **£120** [≈ $230]

Mackenzie, William
- A Practical Treatise on the Diseases of the Eye ... Phila: 1855. 1027 pp. 175 w'cut ills. Orig bndg, fine. *(Fye)* **$100** [≈ £52]

M'Keown, William A.
- A Treatise on Unripe Cataract. London: H.K. Lewis (Belfast ptd), 1898. 1st edn. Roy 8vo. 202,advt pp. 9 plates. Cloth bds.
(Emerald Isle) **£75** [≈ $143]

MacKinney, Loren
- Medical Illustrations in Medieval Manuscripts. London: 1965. 1st edn. 263 pp. Cold plates. Orig bndg. *(Fye)* **$100** [≈ £52]

Mackintosh, John
- Principles of Pathology and Practice of Physic. From the last London Edition with Notes and Additions by Samuel George Morton. Phila: 1836. 2 vols. 8vo. Foxed. Orig calf. *(Goodrich)* **$75** [≈ £39]

Maclaurin, Colin
- An Account of Sir Isaac Newton's Philosophical Discoveries, in Four Books. London: A. Millar, 1750. 2nd edn. 8vo. xxvi, 412 pp. 6 fldg plates. Sl foxed. New leather.
(Gemmary) **$400** [≈ £208]
- A Treatise of Algebra, in Three Parts ... added an Appendix ... London: Millar & Nourse, 1748. 1st edn. 8vo. xiv,366,[2], 65, [1] pp. 12 fldg plates. Contemp sprinkled calf, mor label, hd of spine worn & chipped, jnts cracked but sound. *(Gaskell)* **£400** [≈ $767]

MacLaurin, W. Rupert
- Invention and Innovation in the Radio Industry. 1949. 1st edn. 304 pp. Dw.
(New Wireless) **$45** [≈ £23]

Macleod, George
- Notes on the Surgery of the War in the Crimea, with Remarks on the Treatment of Gunshot Wounds. Phila: Lippincott, 1862. 1st Amer edn. 403 pp. Orig bndg.
(Fye) **$300** [≈ £156]

Macleod, George H.
- Outlines of Surgical Diagnosis. First American Edition, reprinted from Advance Sheets. New York: Bailliere, 1864. 8vo. 505 pp. Water stain to lower margs. Orig cloth, faded. *(Goodrich)* **$125** [≈ £65]

Maclise, Joseph
- Surgical Anatomy. London: Churchill, 1851. 1st edn. Royal folio (text & atlas). [10], [70], [4] pp. 35 lithos, mostly hand cold. Title reprd. A few stains on intl ff. Red half mor.
(Rootenberg) **$1,600** [≈ £833]
- Surgical Anatomy. Phila: 1851. 1st Amer edn. Folio. 156 pp. Ills. Orig leather.

(Fye) **$600 [≈ £312]**

McMenemey, W.H.
- The Life and Times of Sir Charles Hastings Founder of the British Medical Association. Edinburgh: 1959. xii,516 pp. Frontis, 32 plates. Orig bndg. *(Whitehart)* **£25 [≈ $47]**

MacMichael, William
- Lives of British Physicians. London: Murray, 1830. Sm 8vo. ix,341 pp. Title vignette, 4 engvd ports. Polished calf gilt, recased. Anon. *(Hollett)* **£50 [≈ $95]**

Macmillan, H.
- Holidays on High Lands; or, Rambles and Incidents in Search of Alpine Plants. London: 1869. Post 8vo. vii,300 pp. Cloth. *(Wheldon & Wesley)* **£35 [≈ $67]**

McMurrich, J. Playfair
- Leonardo Da Vinci, the Anatomist. Baltimore: 1930. 8vo. 265 pp. Ills. Orig gilt dec bds, uncut. *(Goodrich)* **$125 [≈ £65]**

MacNair, P. & Mort, F.
- History of the Geological Society of Glasgow 1858-1908 ... Glasgow: the Society, 1908. 1st edn. 8vo. [viii],303,[1] pp. 24 ports, 2 ills. Orig cloth. *(Bow Windows)* **£65 [≈ $124]**

Macnamara, N.C.
- Asiatic Cholera: History up to July 15 1892, Causes and Treatment. London: 1892. 1st edn. 8vo. [iv],71,[1] pp. Orig cloth. *(Bow Windows)* **£45 [≈ $86]**

McNicol, Donald
- Radio's Conquest of Space. 1946. 1st edn. 374 pp. 53 ills. Orig bndg. *(New Wireless)* **$50 [≈ £26]**

MacNish, Robert
- The Philosophy of Sleep. Glasgow: W.R. M'Phun, 1830. 1st edn. 12mo. xi,[i],268 pp. Lacks half-title. Contemp half calf, gilt spine, sl scuffed. *(Burmester)* **£80 [≈ $153]**

Macoun, J. & J.M.
- Catalogue of Canadian Birds. Ottawa: 1909. 8vo. viii,761,xviii pp. Orig cloth. *(Bow Windows)* **£20 [≈ $38]**
- Catalogue of Canadian Birds. Ottawa: 1909. Rvsd edn. Roy 8vo. 761 pp. Half leather. *(Wheldon & Wesley)* **£35 [≈ $67]**

MacPherson, H.A. & Ferguson, R.S.
- A Vertebrate Fauna of Lakeland including

Cumberland and Westmorland, with Lancashire North of the Sands. Edinburgh: David Douglas, 1892. 1st edn. Lge 8vo. civ,552,[20 advt] pp. Fldg map, 8 plates, 9 text w'cuts. Orig cloth gilt, spine ends chipped, faded & stained. *(Hollett)* **£95 [≈ $182]**
- A Vertebrate Fauna of Lakeland (Edinburgh, 1892). Paul Minet: 1972. Facs reprint. Orig cloth gilt. *(Hollett)* **£25 [≈ $47]**

MacPike, E.F.
- Hevelius, Flamsteed and Halley. Three Contemporary Astronomers and their Mutual Relations. London: 1937. ix,140 pp. 5 plates. Spine sl faded. *(Whitehart)* **£38 [≈ $72]**

McWatt, J.
- The Primulas of Europe. London: 1923. Cr 8vo. xvi,208 pp. 49 ills (8 cold). Bds, sl soiled. *(Wheldon & Wesley)* **£40 [≈ $76]**

McWilliam, John Morell
- The Birds of the Island of Bute. London: Witherby, 1927. 1st edn. 128 pp. Map, 9 plates. Dw (sl chipped). *(Gough)* **£35 [≈ $67]**

Maddison, R.E.W.
- The Life of the Honourable Robert Boyle. London: 1969. xxii,332 pp. 40 plates. Dw. *(Whitehart)* **£35 [≈ $67]**

Magendie, Francois
- An Elementary Compendium of Physiology. Translated from the French, with copious Notes and Illustrations, by E. Milligan ... Revised and Corrected by a Physician of Philadelphia ... Phila: 1824. 496 pp. Leather, backstrip worn. *(Fye)* **$200 [≈ £104]**
- Physiological and Chemical Research on the Use of the Prussic or Hydro-Cyanic Acid in the Treatment of the Breast and particularly in Phthisic Pulmonale. New Haven: 1820. 1st Amer edn. 8vo. xv,89 pp. Old bds, rebacked. *(Goodrich)* **$135 [≈ £70]**

Magnus, Hugo
- Superstition in Medicine. New York: 1905. 1st English translation. 205 pp. Orig bndg. *(Fye)* **$65 [≈ £33]**

Maham, D.H.
- An Elementary Course of Civil Engineering. London: Fullarton & Co, 1859. 2nd edn. 4to. xiii, [ii],211 pp. 15 plates. Orig cloth, spine damaged. *(Young's)* **£75 [≈ $143]**

Maillet, Benoit de
- Telliamed; or, the World Explain'd: containing Discourses between an Indian Philosopher and a Missionary ... A Very Curious Work. Baltimore: W. Pechelin for D. Porter, 1797. 1st Amer edn. 8vo. 268 pp. Sl browned. Contemp calf. Anon.
(*Rootenberg*) **$600 [≈ £312]**

Major, Ralph Hermon
- Classic Descriptions of Disease. Springfield: (1945) 1978. 3rd edn, reprint. xxxii, 679 pp. 158 ills. Orig bndg. (*Whitehart*) **£35 [≈ $67]**
- Classic Descriptions of Disease. With Biographical Sketches of the Authors. Third Edition. London: Bailliere, Tindall & Cox, 1945. Med 8vo. Num ills. Cvrs a trifle soiled.
(*Georges*) **£35 [≈ $67]**
- Classic Descriptions of Disease. With Biographical Sketches of the Authors. Third Edition. Third Printing. Oxford: 1948. Lge 8vo. xxxii,679 pp. Ills. Orig cloth. Dw.
(*Bickersteth*) **£40 [≈ $76]**
- A History of Medicine. Springfield: 1954. 1st edn. 2 vols. 1155 pp. Orig bndg.
(*Fye*) **$175 [≈ £91]**
- A History of Medicine. Springfield: 1954. 2 vols. 8vo. Dws. (*Goodrich*) **$125 [≈ £65]**

Malcolm, William, James, & Jacob
- General View of the Agriculture of the County of Buckingham ... Drawn up for the consideration of the Board of Agriculture and Internal Improvement. London: Colin Macrae, 1794. 1st edn. 4to. 63 pp. Disbound, sewing defective. (*Bickersteth*) **£45 [≈ $86]**

Malgaigne, J.F.
- A Treatise on Fractures. Phila: 1859. 675 pp. 106 ills. Sm ink name stamp on a few pp. Back pp loose, page edges rather dusty. Leather, v worn. (*Whitehart*) **£35 [≈ $67]**

Mallet, Robert
- Great Neapolitan Earth Quake of 1857 ... Observational Seismology ... London: Chapman & Hall, 1862. 1st edn. 2 vols. 8vo. 431; 399, 8 advt pp. Errata slip. 2 maps in pocket, litho plates & maps, text ills. Orig cloth, sl soiled, 2 sm damp stains.
(*Chapel Hill*) **$275 [≈ £143]**

Malloch, P.D.
- Life History and Habits of the Salmon, Sea Trout, and other Freshwater Fish. London: 1910. Roy 8vo. xvi,264 pp. 239 ills. Cloth.
(*Wheldon & Wesley*) **£35 [≈ $67]**

Manchester University Library
- Catalogue of Medical Books in Manchester University Library 1480-1700. Manchester: 1972. 8vo. [5],399 pp. Dw.
(*Goodrich*) **$165 [≈ £85]**

Manley, G.
- Climate and the British Scene. London: Collins New Naturalist, 1952. 1st edn. 8vo. xviii, 314,4 advt pp. 32 cold & 24 plain plates. Orig cloth. (*Henly*) **£15 [≈ $28]**

Mann, Ida
- Developmental Abnormalities of the Eye. Cambridge: 1937. 1st edn. 444 pp. 284 ills. Dw. (*Fye*) **$100 [≈ £52]**

Mann, James
- Medical Sketches of the Campaigns of 1812, 13, 14 ... Dedham: 1816. 1st edn. 318 pp. Rec cloth, new endpapers. (*Fye*) **$700 [≈ £364]**

Manning, Henry
- Modern Improvements in the Practice of Physic. London: Robinson, Murray, 1780. 1st edn. 8vo. [viii], "240" [ie 440] pp. Sl dust soiled. Contemp half calf, worn, label defective. (*Gaskell*) **£180 [≈ $345]**

Mansfield, Edward D.
- Memoirs of the Life and Services of Daniel Drake, M.D., Physician, Professor, and Author; with Notices of the Early Settlement of Cincinnati ... Cincinnati: 1855. x,11-408, advt pp. Port. Occas foxing & spotting. 2 sgntrs starting. Orig cloth, extremities worn
(*Reese*) **$150 [≈ £78]**

Manson-Bahr, Sir Philip
- History of the School of Tropical Medicine in London (1899-1949). London: 1956. 1st edn. Lge 8vo. [xiv],328 pp. Num ills. Orig cloth.
(*Bow Windows*) **£22 [≈ $42]**

Mantell, Gideon Algernon
- The Fossils of the South Downs; or Illustrations of the Geology of Sussex. London: 1822. 1st edn. 4to. (iii-xvi),327,[1 advt] pp. 42 hand cold plates. Some offsetting of frontis onto title. Lacks half-title. Contemp half calf, backstrip relaid, crnrs worn.
(*Bow Windows*) **£575 [≈ $1,103]**
- The Fossils of the South Downs; or Illustrations of the Geology of Sussex. London: 1822. 4to. xvi,327 pp. Cold map, 41 plates (5 hand cold). Sm piece cut from dedic leaf. Water stains on plates. Half calf, backstrip relaid. (*Henly*) **£180 [≈ $345]**

- Geological Excursions round the Isle of Wight, and along the Adjacent Coast of Dorsetshire ... London: 1847. 1st edn. Sm 8vo. 430 pp, inc half-title & advt leaf. Hand cold fldg map, 19 plates, 1 fldg table, ills. Orig cloth, edges & hd of spine sl worn.
  (Bow Windows) **£145 [≈ $278]**
- Geological Excursions round the Isle of Wight, and along the Adjacent Coast of Dorsetshire ... London: 1854. 3rd edn. Sm 8vo. Fldg map (laid down on endpaper), 19 plates, 1 fldg ·.able, ills. Some stains. Lacks half-title. Contemp calf gilt.
  (Bow Windows) **£125 [≈ $239]**
- Geological Excursions round the Isle of Wight. London: Bohn, 1854. 3rd edn. Cr 8vo. xxxi, 356 pp. 20 plates (some cold), 45 text figs. Cloth.   *(Gemmary)* **$50 [≈ £26]**
- The Geology of the South-East of England. London: 1833. 1st edn. 8vo. xvi,[1 blank], 415, [1 blank] pp. Frontis & 5 other litho plates, cold fldg map (torn), num figs. Some marks. Rec cloth.
  (Bow Windows) **£145 [≈ $278]**
- The Journal ... covering the years 1818-1852. Edited with an Introduction and Notes by E.C. Curwen. London: OUP, 1940. 1st edn. 8vo. xii,316 pp. 4 plates. Orig cloth. Dw.
  (Bow Windows) **£50 [≈ $95]**
- The Journal ... covering the years 1818-1852. Edited with an Introduction and Notes by E.C. Curwen. London: OUP, 1940. 1st edn. 8vo. xii,316 pp. 4 plates. Inscrptn on fly leaf. Orig cloth.   *(Bow Windows)* **£40 [≈ $76]**
- The Medals of Creation; or, First Lessons in Geology ... London: 1844. 1st edn. 2 vols. Sm 8vo. 4 cold & 2 plain plates, 1 fldg diag, num figs. Plates & adjacent ff foxed. Contemp half calf, trifle rubbed.
  (Bow Windows) **£175 [≈ $335]**
- Petrifactions and their Teachings ... London: 1851. 1st edn. Cr 8vo. xi,496 pp. Frontis, 115 ills. Cloth, backstrip relaid.
  (Henly) **£40 [≈ $76]**
- Petrifactions and their Teachings; or, A Hand-book to the Gallery of Organic Remains of The British Museum. London: 1851. 1st edn. 8vo. xi, [1 blank],496 pp. Frontis, 115 figs. Few sl marks. Orig cloth, sl dull, crnr tips & spine ends trifle rubbed.
  (Bow Windows) **£105 [≈ $201]**
- Petrifactions and their Teachings. London: 1851. xi,496 pp. 115 ills. Frontis sl stained. Orig cloth.   *(Baldwin)* **£45 [≈ $86]**
- A Pictorial Atlas of Fossil Remains ... London: 1850. 4to. 207 pp. Title vignette, 74 cold plates. Orig cloth gilt, 2 sm splits in hinges reprd.   *(Baldwin)* **£200 [≈ $383]**

- A Pictorial Atlas of Fossil Remains ... London: 1850. 4to. 207 pp. Cold frontis, 74 cold plates. Blind stamps on title & plates. Lib b'plates. Orig cloth, rebacked.
  (Wheldon & Wesley) **£250 [≈ $479]**
- A Pictorial Atlas of Fossil Remains ... London: 1850. 1st edn. 4to. 207,[1 blank] pp. 75 cold plates. 3 sm marg reprs. Minor marks. Old qtr calf.   *(Bow Windows)* **£350 [≈ $671]**
- A Pictorial Atlas of Fossil Remains ... 'London: 1850. 1st edn. 4to. 207,[1 blank] pp. 75 cold plates. 3 sm marg reprs. Marg damp stain frontis, sm tear in dedic reprd, some marks. Later half calf.
  (Bow Windows) **£300 [≈ $575]**
- Thoughts on a Pebble, A First Lesson in Geology ... Eighth Edition. London: 1849. Sq 12mo. xiv, (5)-102, [8 advt] pp, complete. Port, 4 hand cold plates, ills. Orig cloth, t.e.g., sl marked & dull.
  (Bow Windows) **£150 [≈ $287]**
- Thoughts on Animalcules ... London: 1846. 8vo. xvi,144, 3,8 pp. 12 hand cold plates (6 sl foxed). Sm lib stamp on title. Cloth, spine faded & worn.   *(Henly)* **£80 [≈ $153]**
- Thoughts on Animalcules. London: Murray, 1846. 1st edn. Dble fcap 8vo. xvi,[148],viii pp. 12 hand cold lithos. Orig elab blind stamped cloth.   *(Ash)* **£100 [≈ $191]**
- Thoughts on Animalcules; or, A Glimpse of the Invisible World revealed by the Microscope. London: 1846. 1st edn. 8vo. xvi, 144, [12 advt] pp. 12 cold plates, text figs. Some marks. Orig cloth, marked, sl shaken, spine ends worn.
  (Bow Windows) **£120 [≈ $230]**
- The Wonders of Geology. London: 1838. 2 vols. Cr 8vo. Addtnl engvd titles, 7 plates (6 hand cold), 80 text figs. Cloth, vol 1 backstrip relaid, vol 2 recased.   *(Henly)* **£65 [≈ $124]**
- The Wonders of Geology; or, A Familiar Exposition of Geological Phenomena ... Seventh Edition, revised and augmented by T. Rupert Jones. London: Bohn, 1857/8. 2 vols. Sm 8vo. Frontis, 6 plates (3 cold), 2 tables, figs. Few marks. Contemp half calf gilt.   *(Bow Windows)* **£135 [≈ $259]**

Marcet, William

- A Contribution to the History of the Respiration of Man; Being the Croonian Lectures ... London: Churchill, 1897. 1st book edn. 4to. 116 pp. 34 plates & charts. Faint lib stamp on title.
  (Gough) **£60 [≈ $115]**
- A Contribution to the History of the Respiration of Man ... London: 1897. 4to. 116 pp. Num charts & few figs in text. Lib

blind stamp on title. Orig cloth, lib mark on spine. *(Whitehart)* **£180 [≈ $345]**

Marconi Wireless Telegraph Co
- The Marconigraph. Volume I. 1911. 1st edn. Issues 1-12. 594 pp. Num ills. Orig red cloth. *(New Wireless)* **$490 [≈ £255]**
- The Marconigraph. Volume II. 1912. 1st edn. Issues 13-24. 594 pp. Num ills. Orig red cloth. *(New Wireless)* **$390 [≈ £203]**
- Traffic Rules and Regulations. 1917. 1st edn. 155 pp. Orig bndg. *(New Wireless)* **$110 [≈ £58]**
- The Yearbook of Wireless Telegraphy. 1914. 1st edn. 734 pp. Num ills. Orig bndg. *(New Wireless)* **$85 [≈ £44]**
- The Yearbook of Wireless Telegraphy. 1915. 1st edn. 800 pp. Fldg map, num ills. Orig bndg. *(New Wireless)* **$90 [≈ £46]**
- The Yearbook of Wireless Telegraphy. 1916. 1st edn. 876 pp. Fldg map, num ills. Orig bndg. *(New Wireless)* **$90 [≈ £46]**

The Marconiphone Co. Ltd.
- The Marconi Book of Wireless. 1936. 1st edn. 223 pp. 56 photos, 14 ills. Orig bndg. *(New Wireless)* **$45 [≈ £24]**

Marcy, Henry
- The Anatomy and Surgical Treatment of Hernia. New York: 1892. 1st edn. 4to. 412 pp. 66 plates (6 cold). Half leather, extremities rubbed & worn. *(Fye)* **$250 [≈ £130]**

Marie, Pierre
- Lectures on Diseases of the Spinal Cord. London: 1895. 1st English translation. 511 pp. 244 ills. Orig bndg. *(Fye)* **$200 [≈ £104]**

Markham, Gervase
- The English House-Wife. Containing the inward and outward Vertues which ought to be in a compleat Woman ... By G.M. Now the fourth time much augmented ... London: Nicholas Oak for John Harison, 1631. Sm 4to. [x],252 pp. Lacks A1 blank. Old calf, backstrip relaid. *(Bickersteth)* **£420 [≈ $806]**
- Markham's Farewell to Husbandry: or, the Enriching of all Sorts of Barren and Sterile Grounds in our Nation. London: 1653. Sm 4to. [vi],126,[4] pp. W'cuts in text. New calf. *(Wheldon & Wesley)* **£120 [≈ $230]**

Marks, E.C.R.
- Notes on the Construction of Cranes and Lifting Machinery. Manchester: 1899. xi,183 pp. 155 text figs. Orig cloth, inner hinges

cracked but firm.   *(Whitehart)* **£25 [≈ $47]**

Marmelzadt, Willard
- Musical Sons of Aesculapius. New York: Froben Press, 1946. Sole edn. 8vo. 112,[4] pp. 16 pp of plates. Orig cloth. Dw. Inscrbd by the author. *(Bickersteth)* **£150 [≈ $287]**

Marr, J.E.
- The Geology of the Lake District and the Scenery as influenced by Geological Structure. Cambridge: 1916. xii,220 pp. Frontis port, map in pocket, 3 other maps, text ills. Orig bndg. *(Whitehart)* **£18 [≈ $34]**

Marshall, A.
- Explosives. Their Manufacture, Properties, Tests and History. London: 1915. xv,624 pp. 137 ills. Orig cloth, spine faded. *(Whitehart)* **£40 [≈ $76]**

Marshall, A.J.
- Bower-Birds, their Displays and Breeding Cycles: a Preliminary Statement. London: 1954. Roy 8vo. 212 pp. 26 plates, 21 text figs. Sl foxing. Cloth. Dw (sl worn). *(Wheldon & Wesley)* **£50 [≈ $95]**

Marshall, C.
- A Plain and Easy Introduction to the Knowledge and Practice of Gardening, with Hints on Fish-Ponds. London: 1813. 5th edn. 8vo. iv,448 pp. New cloth. *(Wheldon & Wesley)* **£28 [≈ $53]**

Marshall, Mark
- The King of Fowls. Sydney, Australia: Federal Society of Game-Fanciers, (1958). 1st edn. One of 200. 8vo. 58 pp. Cold plates, ills. Orig cloth, tape marks on endpapers. *(Respess)* **$100 [≈ £52]**

Marshall, William
- Planting and Ornamental Gardening: a Practical Treatise. London: Dodsley, 1785. 1st edn. 8vo. xi,[5],638 pp. Half-title. Some browning. Full leather, orig label preserved. *(Spelman)* **£120 [≈ $230]**
- Planting and Ornamental Gardening: a Practical Treatise. London: 1785. 1st edn. 8vo. xv,638 pp. Mod bds. Anon. *(Wheldon & Wesley)* **£75 [≈ $143]**
- Planting and Rural Ornament ... London: G. Nicol, 1796. 2nd edn. 2 vols. 8vo. xxxii, 408, [8]; xx,454,[6] pp. Sl marg water stain few ff. Contemp sheep, some wear. *(Bookpress)* **$450 [≈ £234]**
- Planting and Rural Ornament. Being a

Second Edition, with Large Additions, of Planting and Ornamental Gardening. London: 1796. 2 vols. 8vo. xxxii,408,[8]; xx,454,[6] pp. Contemp tree calf, 1 label defective. *(Henly)* **£152 [≈ $291]**

- The Review and Abstract of the County Reports to the Board of Agriculture. 1818. London: Kelley, 1968. Facs reprint. 5 vols. Dws. *(Moon)* **£65 [≈ $124]**

- The Review and the Abstracts of the County Reports to the Board of Agriculture, from several Agricultural Departments of England. York, 1808-1818. London: [ca 1970]. Facs reprint. 5 vols. 8vo. Orig cloth. Dws. *(Sotheran's)* **£60 [≈ $115]**

Martin, Benjamin
- Biographica Philosophica. Being an Account of the Lives, Writings, and Inventions of the most eminent Philosophers and Mathematicians ... to the Present Time. London: W. Owen & the author, 1764. 1st edn. 8vo. [iv],565,[3] pp. Port. Some margs cut close. Rec qtr calf. *(Burmester)* **£180 [≈ $345]**

- The Description and Use of a Case of Mathematical Instruments ... London: the author ..., 1771. 8vo. [ii],18 pp. New bds. *(Georges)* **£150 [≈ $287]**

- Logarithmologia or the Whole Doctrine of Logarithms, Common and Logistical, in Theory and Practice. London: J. Hodges, 1740. 8vo. xii, 248, 64 pp. Calf. *(Gemmary)* **$650 [≈ £338]**

Martin, E.A.
- Bibliography of Gilbert White. London: 1934. vii,194 pp. Ills. Cloth. *(Henly)* **£32 [≈ $61]**

Martin, T.C.
- The Inventions, Researches and Writings of Nikola Tesla. New York: The Electrical Engineer, 1894. 2nd edn. 8vo. xi,496 pp. 313 text figs. Cloth, worn. *(Gemmary)* **$150 [≈ £78]**

Martin, Thomas
- The Circle of the Mechanical Arts; containing Practical Treatises on the Various Manual Arts, Trades, and Manufactures. London: for Richard Rees, 1813. 1st edn. 4to. 616 pp. 38 plates. Later suede, mor label. *(Chapel Hill)* **$275 [≈ £143]**

Martin, Thomas Commerford
- Forty Years of Edison Service 1882-1922. New York: 1922. 1st edn. 181 pp. 43 photos.

Orig bndg. *(New Wireless)* **$45 [≈ £23]**
- Inventions, Researches and Writings of Nikola Tesla. 1894. 1st edn. 496 pp. 313 ills. Orig bndg. *(New Wireless)* **$195 [≈ £101]**
- Inventions, Researches and Writings of Nikola Tesla. (1894), reprint 1977. 496 pp. 313 ills. Orig bndg.
(New Wireless) **$25 [≈ £13]**

Martineau, Harriet
- Letters on Mesmerism. London: Moxon, 1845. 1st edn. 8vo. xii,70 pp,advt leaf. Later calf backed bds. *(Bickersteth)* **£130 [≈ $249]**

Martyn, J.
- The Bucolicks of Virgil with an English Translation and Notes by J. Martyn. London: 1749. 2nd edn. xcix,[i],390, 7,[11] pp. Port, 2 maps, 2 plates. Calf, jnts cracked. *(Wheldon & Wesley)* **£50 [≈ $95]**

Martyn, Thomas
- The English Entomologist exhibiting all the Coleopterous Insects found in England. London: 1792. Text in English & French. Roy 4to. [v],33,[vi], 41,[4] pp. 2 engvd titles, 2 plates of medals, 42 hand cold plates. Contemp half russia, rebacked, crnrs reprd. *(Wheldon & Wesley)* **£750 [≈ $1,439]**

- Flora Rustica: exhibiting Accurate Figures of such Plants as are either Useful or Injurious in Husbandry, drawn and engraved by Frederick P. Nodder ... London: 1792-94. 4 vols. 8vo. 144 hand cold plates. Occas sl browning. Qtr calf, uncut, rebacked. *(Henly)* **£580 [≈ $1,113]**

- Thirty-Eight Plates ... to illustrate Linnaeus's System of Vegetables. London: 1799. 8vo. 38 plain plates. Half mor. *(Wheldon & Wesley)* **£20 [≈ $38]**

- Thirty-Eight Plates ... to illustrate Linnaeus's System of Vegetables ... London: 1799. 8vo. vi,72 pp. 38 hand cold plates. Calf, worn & broken. *(Wheldon & Wesley)* **£80 [≈ $153]**

Maryan, William
- A Treatise explaining the Impossibility of the Disease termed Hydrophobia; being caused by the Bite of any Rabid Animal. London: E. Cox, 1809. Sole edn. 8vo. 60 pp, errata leaf. A2 apparently sgnd A3 in error. 2 lib stamps. Old half calf. *(Bickersteth)* **£220 [≈ $422]**

Mason, Richard
- The Gentleman's New Pocket Farrier ... Also, Annals of the Turf, or Virginia Stud Book. Fourth Edition, enlarged and improved. Richmond: Peter Cotton ..., 1828.

300 pp. 5 plates inc frontis. Foxed, 1 plate chipped affecting caption. Later half calf antique.   *(Reese)* **$3,000 [≈ £1,562]**

Massee, G.
- British Fungi, with a Chapter on Lichens. London: [1911]. 8vo. 551 pp. 2 plain & 40 cold plates. Cloth.
        (Wheldon & Wesley) **£25 [≈ $47]**

Masters, Maxwell Tylden
- Vegetable Teratology, an Account of the Principal Deviations from the Usual Construction of Plants ... London: Ray Society, 1869. 1st edn. 8vo. xxxviii,534 pp. text ills. Orig cloth gilt, uncut.
        (Claude Cox) **£30 [≈ $57]**

Mather, G.M.
- Two Great Scotsmen. The Brothers William & John Hunter. Glasgow: 1893. 1st edn. x,[1], 251 pp. 17 ills inc etched title & 4 etchings by D.Y. Cameron. Orig half cloth, sl worn.
        (Whitehart) **£80 [≈ $153]**

Mather, K.F. & Mason, S.L.
- A Source Book in Geology. New York & London: 1939. 1st edn, 3rd imp. 8vo. xxii,702 pp. Sev figs. Erasure mark on fly leaf. Orig cloth. *(Bow Windows)* **£25 [≈ $47]**

Mathews, G.M.
- The Birds of Norfolk and Lord Howe Islands and the Australasian South Polar Quadrant, with Additions to the 'Birds of Australia'. London: 1928. One of 225. Roy 4to. xiii,139 pp. 38 hand cold & 7 plain plates. Half mor gilt, orig wraps bound in.
        (Wheldon & Wesley) **£750 [≈ $1,439]**

Mathews, L.H.
- British Mammals. London: Collins New Naturalist, 1952. 1st edn. 8vo. xii,410 pp. 16 cold & 48 plain plates. Orig cloth.
        (Henly) **£15 [≈ $28]**

Matland, G.R. & T.C.
- The Teeth in Health and Disease. London: Ward, Lock, 1904. 1st edn. 8vo. 174 pp. 90 w'cut ills. Crnr cut from endpaper. Orig cloth gilt.   *(Gough)* **£20 [≈ $38]**

Matthews, C.G. & Lott, F.E.
- The Microscope in the Brewery and Malthouse. London: Bemrose, 1889. 8vo. xxi, 198 pp. 21 plates, 30 text figs. Ex-lib. Cloth.
        (Gemmary) **$125 [≈ £65]**

Matthews, L.G.
- History of Pharmacy in Britain. Edinburgh: 1962. xiv,427 pp. Frontis, 21 plates. Trace of lib label on endpaper, lib stamps on endpapers. Ft of spine torn.
        (Whitehart) **£25 [≈ $47]**

Matthews, L.H.
- Sea Elephant: The Life and Death of the Elephant Seal. London: 1952. 8vo. 187 pp. Map, 14 plates. Cloth.
        (Wheldon & Wesley) **£25 [≈ $47]**

Mauborgne, J.O.
- Practical Uses of the Wave Meter in Wireless Telegraphy. 1913. 1st edn. 74 pp. 42 ills. Orig bndg, cvrs stained.
        (New Wireless) **$40 [≈ £20]**

Maupertius, Pierre Louis Moreau de
- The Figure of the Earth, determined from Observations ... at the Polar Circle ... London: Cox, Davis ..., 1738. 1st edn in English. 8vo. vii,[i],232 pp. Fldg map, 9 fldg plates. Title backed. Contemp calf, sl later mor label.   *(Burmester)* **£200 [≈ $383]**

Maury, J.C.F.
- Treatise on the Dental Art, founded on Actual Experience. Translated from the French, with Notes and Additions, by J.B. Savier. Phila: Lea & Blanchard, 1843. 1st Amer edn. 324,18,16 ctlg pp. 20 plates, 56 text ills. Some marg staining. Contemp calf.
        (Hemlock) **$675 [≈ £351]**

Maury, M.F.
- The Physical Geography of the Sea. New York: Harper, 1855. 1st edn. Imperial 8vo. xxiv,274 pp. 12 plates (8 fldg) Orig pict brown cloth gilt.   *(Gough)* **£95 [≈ $182]**
- The Physical Geography of the Sea. New York: Harper, 1855. 3rd edn. xxiv,25-287 pp. 12 plates (8 fldg). Some foxing to endpapers. Orig blue cloth with gilt vignette, spine faded, bds rubbed.   *(Parmer)* **$175 [≈ £91]**
- The Physical Geography of the Sea. London: 1857. 6th edn. 360 pp. 13 plates (9 fldg). Occas foxing. Label removed from f.e.p. Orig cloth, dust stained & worn, spine sl defective.
        (Whitehart) **£18 [≈ $34]**
- The Physical Geography of the Sea, and its Meteorology. Fifteenth Edition ... London: 1874. 8vo. xx,487 pp. 15 plates & other diags. Contemp polished calf, gilt spine.
        (Bow Windows) **£40 [≈ $76]**

Maver, William
- American Telegraphy: Systems Apparatus Operation. 1912. 5th edn. 695 pp. 544 ills. Orig bndg, sl wear at hd of spine.
(New Wireless) **$60** [≈ £31]

Mawe, John
- Familiar Lessons on Mineralogy and Geology. London: 1822. 4th edn. Cr 8vo. viii,108, iii,i pp. 4 hand cold plates. Contemp half calf. *(Henly)* **£85** [≈ $163]
- The Linnaean System of Conchology. London: 1823. 8vo. xv,207 pp. 37 plates (1 cold). Sl soiled. Half mor, trifle used.
(Wheldon & Wesley) **£45** [≈ $86]

Mawe, Thomas & Abercrombie, John
- Every Man His Own Gardener ... The Twelfth Edition ... London: 1788. 12mo. [iv],616, [xix] pp. Frontis. Orig calf, rubbed, hd of spine sl worn, upper jnt cracked but firm. *(Bickersteth)* **£56** [≈ $107]
- Every Man his Own Gardener ... Dublin: for P. Byrne, 1798. 14th edn. 8vo. [iv],626,[19] pp. Old sheep, rubbed. *(Young's)* **£42** [≈ $80]
- Every Man His Own Gardener ... The Twenty-First Edition ... London: Rivington ..., 1818. Lge 12mo. viii,727 pp. Port frontis. Orig sheep, rebacked to style.
(Beech) **£50** [≈ $95]
- Every Man his Own Gardener ... The Twenty-Second Edition, with great Improvements ..., London: 1822. Lge 12mo. vii, [1], 726 pp. Frontis, text ills. Orig sheep, jnts cracking but holding.
(Fenning) **£35** [≈ $67]

Maxwell, James Clerk
- Electricity and Magnetism. 1881. 2nd edn. 2 vols. 920 pp. 105 ills. Orig bndg.
(New Wireless) **$425** [≈ £221]
- Electricity and Magnetism. 1881. 2nd edn. 2 vols. 920 pp. 105 ills. Orig bndg, vol 2 spine reprd. *(New Wireless)* **$325** [≈ £170]
- An Elementary Treatise on Electricity. Oxford: Clarendon Press, 1881. 8vo. xvi,208, [44 ctlg] pp. 6 plates, 53 text figs. Ex-lib. Cloth. *(Gemmary)* **$350** [≈ £182]
- Theory of Heat. London: Longmans, Green, 1904. Cr 8vo. xiv,348 pp. 39 text figs. Ex-lib. Cloth. *(Gemmary)* **$75** [≈ £39]
- A Treatise on Electricity and Magnetism. Oxford: Clarendon Press, 1873. 1st edn. 2 vols. 8vo. xxix,[3],425,[5]; xxiii,[1], 444,[2] pp. 2 errata slips, 15 advt pp. 20 plates. A few sm reprs. Orig cloth, rebacked, new endpapers. Half mor slipcase.
(Rootenberg) **$2,500** [≈ £1,302]

- A Treatise on Electricity and Magnetism. Oxford: Clarendon Press, 1881. 2nd edn. 2 vols. 8vo. xxxi,464,13; xxiii,456,7 pp. 20 plates. Ex-lib. Orig gilt dec cloth.
(Gemmary) **$250** [≈ £130]
- A Treatise on Electricity and Magnetism. Oxford: UP, 1904. 3rd edn. 2 vols. 8vo. xxxii, 506,13; xxiv, 500,7 pp. 20 plates. Ex-lib. Orig gilt dec cloth. *(Gemmary)* **$250** [≈ £130]
- A Treatise on Electricity and Magnetism. Third Edition. Oxford: 1904. 2 vols. 8vo. 20 plates, num figs. Some pencilled marginalia & finger marks. Orig cloth.
(Bow Windows) **£185** [≈ $355]

Maxwell, M.
- Elephants and other Big Game Studies from The Times. Camera Studies of Elephants at Home. London: 1930. Oblong 4to. 28 plates. Orig cloth. *(Henly)* **£30** [≈ $57]

Maxwell, Robert
- The Practical Husbandman: being a Collection of Miscellaneous Papers on Husbandry. Edinburgh: 1757. 8vo. xii,432,4 pp. Verso of title sgnd by the author. Half calf, backstrip relaid. *(Henly)* **£60** [≈ $115]
- The Practical Husbandman ... Edinburgh: the author, 1757. 1st edn. 8vo. xii,432,[6] pp. 1 plate. Contemp calf.
(Bookpress) **$475** [≈ £247]

Maxwell-Lefroy, H.
- Indian Insect Life. A Manual of the Insects of the Plains (Tropical India). Calcutta: 1909. Sm 4to. Map, 69 cold & 15 plain plates. Last few ff sl stained, a few worm holes. Mod cloth. *(Wheldon & Wesley)* **£75** [≈ $143]

Maydon, H.
- Big Game of India. London: 1937. 253 pp. Ills. Orig bndg. *(Trophy Room)* **$125** [≈ £65]

Mayer, L.A.
- Islamic Astrolabists and their Work. Geneve: Albert Kundig, 1956. Roy 8vo. 123 pp. 26 plates. Cloth. *(Gemmary)* **$125** [≈ £65]

Mayne, Xavier (ie Edward P. Stevenson)
- The Intersexes: A History of Similisexualism, as a Problem in Social Life ... Privately Printed: [1908]. One of 125. [ii],xii, 641,[iv] pp. Yellowed. Contemp half cloth, partly unopened. *(Buccleuch)* **£75** [≈ $143]

Mayo, Herbert
- Observations on Injuries and Diseases of the Rectum. London: 1833. 1st edn. 220 pp. Qtr

leather, 1-inch missing from hd of spine.
(Fye) **$100 [≃ £52]**
- Popular Superstitions, and the Truths contained therein,· with an Account of Mesmerism. From the Third London Edition. Phila: Lindsay & Blakiston, 1852. Lge 12mo. 260 pp. text figs. Orig cloth, rebacked.   *(Bickersteth)* **£38 [≃ $72]**

Mazzotto, Domenico
- Wireless telegraphy and Telephony. 1906. 1st edn. 416 pp. 253 ills. Orig bndg, sl stained.
(New Wireless) **$125 [≃ £65]**

Mead, Richard
- A Discourse on the Plague. The Ninth Edition corrected and enlarged. London: 1744. 8vo. [viii],164 pp. Strip cut from top of title. Old lib stamp on 2 pp. Old half calf, upper jnt cracked. *(Bickersteth)* **£45 [≃ $86]**
- A Mechanical Account of Poisons in Several Essays. The Second Edition, revised, with Additions. London: J.M. for Ralph Smith, 1708. 8vo. [16],189,[2] pp. Half-title. Fldg engvd plate. Sl worming in inner blank marg. Rec qtr calf.   *(Fenning)* **£85 [≃ $163]**
- A Mechanical Account of Poisons, in Several Essays ... London: J. Brindley, 1745. 3rd edn. 8vo. xlviii,319,[1] pp. 4 plates (1 fldg). Contemp calf, rear hinge cracked.
(Bookpress) **$300 [≃ £156]**
- Medica Sacra; or, a Commentary on the most Remarkable Diseases, mentioned in the Holy Scriptures. London: 1755. 120 pp. Contemp panelled calf, rebacked.
(Whitehart) **£295 [≃ $566]**
- Medical Precepts and Cautions ... London: J. brindley, 1755. 2nd edn. 8vo. xvi,311,[1] pp. Contemp calf, hinges cracked.
(Bookpress) **$185 [≃ £96]**
- Monita et Precepta Medica. London: Brindley, 1751. 1st edn. 8vo. [xii],272 pp. Later half calf.   *(Bookpress)* **$225 [≃ £117]**
- A Treatise concerning the Influence of the Sun and Moon upon Human Bodies and the Diseases thereby produced. Translated from the Latin by Thomas Stack. London: Brindley, 1748. 2 vols in one. 8vo. 130,204 pp. Title dusty & chipped at foredge. New antique style bds.   *(Goodrich)* **$145 [≃ £75]**
- A Treatise on the Small Pox and Measles ... London: for the translator, & sold by R. Griffiths, 1747. 1st edn in English. 8vo. Errata leaf. Old wraps.
(Ximenes) **$250 [≃ £130]**

Meade, Richard
- A History of Thoracic Surgery. Springfield:

1961. 1st edn. 933 pp. Dw.
(Fye) **$200 [≃ £104]**

Mease, James
- Observations on the Arguments of Professor Rush, in favour of the Inflammatory Nature of the Disease produced by the Bite of a Mad Dog. Whitehall (PA): ptd by William Young (Philadelphia), 1801. 1st edn. 8vo. Some damp stains. Stitched as issued.
(Ximenes) **$400 [≃ £208]**

Medical Botany ...
- See Cox, E., & Son, publishers.

Meehan, Thomas
- The Native Flowers and Ferns of the United States. Boston: L. Prang, 1878-80. 1st edns. 4 vols. 4to. 196 chromolitho plates. Some offsetting from plates. Half mor, sl rubbed.
(Bookpress) **$650 [≃ £338]**

Meigs, Arthur
- A Study of the Human Blood-Vessels in Health and Disease. Phila: 1907. 1st edn. 136 pp. 103 ills. Orig bndg. *(Fye)* **$150 [≃ £78]**

Meigs, Charles
- Obstetrics: The Science and the Art. Phila: 1849. 1st edn. 685 pp. Leather.
(Fye) **$150 [≃ £78]**
- On the Nature, Signs, and Treatment of Childbed Fevers. Phila: 1854. 1st edn. 362 pp. Orig bndg.   *(Fye)* **$300 [≃ £156]**
- A Treatise on the Acute and Chronic Diseases of the Neck of the Uterus. Phila: 1854. 1st edn. 116 pp. 22 lithos (mostly cold). Orig bndg, fine.   *(Fye)* **$300 [≃ £156]**

Meiklejohn, A.
- The Life, Work and Times of Charles Turner Thackrah, Surgeon and Apothecary of Leeds (1795-1833). Edinburgh & London: 1957. [v], 238 pp. Port, 3 dble-sided plates. Ink name on title. Dw. Author's inscrptn.
(Whitehart) **£25 [≃ $47]**

Meinertzhagen, Dan & Hornby, R.P.
- Bird Life in an Arctic Spring; The Diaries ... London: R.H. Porter, 1899. 1st edn. 150 pp. Port, 47 plates, sev sketches. Orig pict green cloth gilt, fine.   *(Gough)* **£90 [≃ $172]**

Meinertzhagen, R.
- Birds of Arabia. London: 1954. Orig edn. Roy 8vo. xiii,624 pp. Fldg map, 19 cold & 10 plain plates, 35 text-maps, 53 text figs. Orig cloth.   *(Wheldon & Wesley)* **£450 [≃ $863]**

- Pirates and Predators. London: 1959. Cr 4to. ix,230 pp. 18 cold & 26 plain plates. Orig cloth.   *(Wheldon & Wesley)* **£160 [≈$307]**

Meldrum, A.N.
- Avogadro and Dalton. The Standing in Chemistry of their Hypotheses. Edinburgh: 1904. 113 pp. Cloth, sl worn.
(Whitehart) **£25 [≈$47]**

Mellanby, K.
- Farming and Wildlife. London: Collins New Naturalist, 1981. 1st edn. 8vo. 178 pp. 24 plates. Orig cloth. Dw.   *(Henly)* **£20 [≈$38]**
- The Mole. London: Collins New Naturalist, 1971. 1st edn. 8vo. 159 pp. 12 plates, 24 text figs. Orig cloth. Dw.   *(Henly)* **£20 [≈$38]**
- Pesticides and Pollution. London: Collins New Naturalist, 1967. 1st edn. 8vo. 221 pp. 2 cold & 12 plain plates. Orig cloth. Dw.
(Henly) **£20 [≈$38]**

Memoirs on Diphtheria ...
- Memoirs on Diphtheria. From the Writings of Bretonneau, Guersant, Trousseau ... Translated by Robert Hunter Semple ... London: New Sydenham Society, 1859. 8vo. 407 pp. Lib stamp on front flies. Orig cloth, hd of spine v sl worn.
(Bickersteth) **£30 [≈$57]**

Memoranda on Noses ...
- See Campbell, Frank.

Mernagh, L.R.
- Enamels: their Manufacture and Application to Iron and Steel Ware. London: Charles Griffin, 1928. 8vo. xiii,234 pp. Fldg plates, 19 ills. Cloth.   *(Gemmary)* **$50 [≈£26]**

Merrett, H.S.
- A Practical Treatise on the Science of Land and Engineering Surveying ... Fourth Edition, Revised and Corrected, with an Appendix ... London: Spon, 1890. Imperial 8vo. xiv,346 pp. 42 plates. Orig blue cloth, hd of spine reprd.   *(Gough)* **£38 [≈$72]**

Merrifield, M.P.
- A Sketch of the Natural History of Brighton and Its Vicinity. Brighton: 1864. 2nd edn. 8vo. xi,227 pp. Fldg map. Orig cloth, sl worn.
(Henly) **£36 [≈$69]**

Merrill, G.P.
- Handbook and Descriptive Catalog of the Collection of Gems and Precious Stones in the United States National Museum.

Washington: 1922. 8vo. 255 pp. 2 cold & 14 b/w plates, 26 text figs. Wraps (worn).
(Gemmary) **$45 [≈£23]**

Merritt, Houston & Fremont-Smith, F.
- The Cerebrospinal Fluid. Oxford: 1934. Reprint. 8vo. 58 pp. 3 tables. Orig bndg.
(Goodrich) **$65 [≈£33]**

Metchnikoff, Elias
- Immunity in Infective Diseases. Cambridge: 1905. 1st edn. 591 pp. Orig bndg, crnr of front bd bent.   *(Fye)* **$250 [≈£130]**
- Lectures on the Comparative Pathology of Inflammation. London: 1893. 1st English translation. 218 pp. Orig bndg, fine.
(Fye) **$500 [≈£260]**
- The Nature of Man. Studies in Optimistic Philosophy. London: 1903. 1st English translation. 309 pp. Orig bndg.
(Fye) **$100 [≈£52]**

Mettler, Cecilia
- History of Medicine. Phila: 1947. 1st edn. 1215 pp. Orig bndg.   *(Fye)* **$150 [≈£78]**

Meyer de Schaunsee, R.
- A Guide to the Birds of South America. London: 1971. 8vo. xiv,470 pp. 50 plates (31 cold) & line drawings. Cloth.
(Wheldon & Wesley) **£70 [≈$134]**

Meyer, E. von
- A History of Chemistry from the Earliest Times to the Present Day being also an Introduction to the Study of the Science. Translated by C. McGowan. London: 1898. 2nd English edn. xxiv,631 pp. Cloth sl marked.   *(Whitehart)* **£25 [≈$47]**

Meyer, W. & Schmieden, V.
- Bier's Hyperemic Treatment in Surgery, Medicine, and the Specialities. A Manual of its Practical Application. Phila: 1908. 209 pp. 95 text ills. Occas sl foxing on endpapers. Orig bndg, spine ends sl worn.
(Whitehart) **£25 [≈$47]**

Michaux, F.A. & Nutall, Thomas
- The North American Sylva, or a Description of the Forest Trees of the United States, Canada, and Nova Scotia. Phila: 1871. 5th edn. 5 vols inc Nuttall's supplement. Roy 8vo. Port, 277 hand cold plates. Mor, a.e.g.
(Henly) **£2,200 [≈$4,223]**

Michelet, J.
- The Sea. London: 1875. xvi,334 pp. Frontis,

engvd title, num full-page plates. Orig pict cloth gilt, sl dust stained, inner hinges cracked but firm.   *(Whitehart)* **£15 [≈ $28]**

Michell, William
- On Difficult Cases of Parturition; and the Use of Ergot of Rye. London: 1828. 1st edn. Tall 8vo. 8 ctlg,[2 blank],xv,[1 errata],128 pp. Orig bds, paper label, defects to spine.
     (Hemlock) **$250 [≈ £130]**
- On Difficult Cases of Parturition; and the Use of Ergot of Rye. London: for Thomas & George Underwood, 1828. Sole edn. 8vo. xv, [i], 128 pp. Early pp sl spotted. Lib stamp. Contemp half calf. *(Bickersteth)* **£55 [≈ $105]**

Michelson, A.A.
- Studies in Optics. Chicago: UP, 1928. Cr 8vo. ix,176 pp. Cold plate, 92 text figs. Cloth.
     (Gemmary) **$50 [≈ £26]**

Middleton, R.E. & Chadwick, O.
- A Treatise on Surveying. London: Spon, 1899-1902. 2 vols. 8vo. 162 + 143 text figs. Cloth, sl loose, sl damp marked.
     (Gemmary) **$50 [≈ £26]**

Middleton, W.E.K.
- A History of the Thermometer and its Use in Meteorology. Baltimore: 1966. xiii,249 pp. Frontis, num text diags. Orig bndg.
     (Whitehart) **£18 [≈ $34]**
- A History of the Thermometer and Its Use in Meteorology. Baltimore: The Johns Hopkins Press, 1966. 8vo. xiii,249 pp. Num text figs. Cloth. Dw.   *(Gemmary)* **$50 [≈ £26]**

Miers, H.A.
- Minerals. An Introduction to the Scientific Study of Minerals. London: Macmillan, 1929. 2nd edn. 8vo. xx,658 pp. 761 ills. Cloth gilt.   *(Gemmary)* **$75 [≈ £40]**

Miers, J.
- The Apocynaceae of South America, with Some Preliminary Remarks on the Whole Family. London: 1878. Roy 4to. 277 pp. 35 plates. Lib stamps. Cloth, rebacked.
     (Wheldon & Wesley) **£60 [≈ $115]**

Mihles, Samuel
- The Elements of Surgery ... Adapted to the Use of the Camp and Navy, as well as of the Domestic Surgeon. London: Knapton, 1746. 1st edn. 8vo. [vi],324,[12] pp & inserted leaf after p 271. 25 plates (I-III, A-Y). Contemp polished calf, mor label, fine.
     (Gaskell) **£850 [≈ $1,631]**

Miles, W.G.H.
- Admiralty   Handbook   of   Wireless Telegraphy. London: HMSO, 1925. 8vo. viii,547 pp. 373 text figs. Cloth, split in jnt.
     (Gemmary) **$40 [≈ £20]**

Milham, W.I.
- Meteorology. A Text-Book on the Weather, the Causes of its Changes, and Weather Forecasting. New York: 1912. xvi,549 pp. 50 charts & 157 figs in text. Cloth sl dust stained.
     (Whitehart) **£18 [≈ $34]**

Mill, J.S.
- Autobiography. London: 1873. 1st edn. vi, 313 pp. Inscrptn on half-title. New cloth.
     (Whitehart) **£45 [≈ $86]**

Millais, J.G.
- British Deer and their Horns. London: 1897. Folio. xviii,224 pp. Cold frontis, num ills. Lib b'plate. V sl foxing. Orig buckram, rebacked, trifle used.
     (Wheldon & Wesley) **£200 [≈ $383]**
- British Diving Ducks. London: Longmans, Green, 1913. 1st edn. One of 450. 2 vols. 4to. 74 plates (39 cold). Orig maroon cloth, t.e.g., spines faded, lower cvr vol 1 stained.
     (Sotheran's) **£1,195 [≈ $2,294]**
- Game Birds and Shooting Sketches. London: Sotheran, 1892. 1st edn. Imperial 4to. xii,72 pp. 15 cold litho plates, 18 autotypes, w'engvs in text. Occas sl foxing. Orig half mor, sl rubbed & worn.   *(Ash)* **£500 [≈ $959]**
- The Mammals of Great Britain and Ireland. London: 1904-06. One of 1025. 3 vols. Imperial 4to. 62 cold & 62 gravure plates by the author & others, 125 other plates. Some cold plates foxed. Orig blue half buckram, trifle used.
     (Wheldon & Wesley) **£345 [≈ $662]**
- The Natural History of Surface-Feeding Ducks. London: Longmans, Green, 1902. 1st edn. Large Paper. One of 600. 41 cold plates, 6 gravures, 25 other ills. Orig 2-tone cloth, t.e.g.   *(Claude Cox)* **£485 [≈ $931]**
- The Natural History of the British Surface-Feeding Ducks. London: 1902. One of 600, all Large Paper. Roy 4to. 6 gravures, 41 cold plates, 25 ills. Orig cloth, trifle used & spotted.
     (Wheldon & Wesley) **£550 [≈ $1,055]**
- The Wildfowler in Scotland. London: Longmans, Green, 1901. 1st edn. 8vo. xv,167 pp. 21 plates, num ills. Orig half vellum, t.e.g., marked.   *(Gough)* **£150 [≈ $287]**
- The Wildfowler in Scotland. London: 1901. Roy 8vo. xv,167 pp. 2 cold & 19 other plates,

40 text ills. Orig half parchment, discold, trifle worn.
(*Wheldon & Wesley*) £90 [≈ $172]

Millar, G.H.
- A New ... Body or System of Natural History. London: [1785]. Folio. [iv],5-618, [2] pp. Frontis, 85 plates. Frontis mtd, title creased. Mod bds. (*Wheldon & Wesley*) £225 [≈ $431]

Miller, Charles
- The Correction of Featural Imperfections. Chicago: 1907. 1st edn. 136 pp. 73 ills. Orig bndg. (*Fye*) $300 [≈ £156]
- Cosmetic Surgery; the Correction of Featural Imperfections. Phila: 1924. 1st edn. 263 pp. Orig bndg, inner hinges cracked.
(*Fye*) $250 [≈ £130]

Miller, Edward
- The Medical Works ... New York: 1814. 1st edn. 384 pp. Leather, spine rubbed, hinges cracked. (*Fye*) $150 [≈ £78]
- The Medical Works of Edward Miller, MD. Later Professor of the Practice of Physic in the University of New York ... Collected ... by Samuel Miller. New York: 1814. 1st edn. 2nd issue, with reset prelims & ports added. 8vo. 392 pp. 2 ports. Ex-lib. Orig bds, rebacked in cloth. (*Goodrich*) $195 [≈ £101]

Miller, Gerrit S.
- Catalogue of the Mammals of Western Europe ... in the Collection of the British Museum. London: 1912. 8vo. xv,1019 pp. 213 ills. Orig cloth gilt, sl worn, v sl stained.
(*Fenning*) £45 [≈ $86]
- The Families and Genera of Bats. London: (1907) 1967. xviii,282 pp. 14 plates.
(*Wheldon & Wesley*) £37 [≈ $71]

Miller, Hugh
- The Cruise of the Betsey. London: 1858. 1st edn. [iv],486 pp. Orig cloth, spine sl soiled.
(*Baldwin*) £45 [≈ $86]
- The Testimony of the Rocks ... Edinburgh: Shepherd & Elliot, 1857. 1st edn. The issue with photo frontis. 8vo. xii,500 pp. Port photo frontis, fern w'engv, 152 text figs. Orig red cloth, spine extremities worn, crude repr to ft, hinges reprd.
(*de Beaumont*) £110 [≈ $211]
- The Testimony of the Rocks. London: 1857. 1st edn. 8vo. xii,500 pp. Frontis, 152 text figs. Half mor. (*Henly*) £25 [≈ $47]
- Testimony of the Rocks. London: 1857. 1st edn. xi,500 pp. Orig cloth, sl soiled.
(*Baldwin*) £40 [≈ $76]

Miller, J.S.
- A Natural History of the Crinoidea, or Lily-shaped Animals ... Bristol: 1821. 4to. viii, [ii], 150 pp. 50 tinted plates. Sm blind stamp on title & each plate. Half calf, rebacked.
(*Wheldon & Wesley*) £300 [≈ $575]

Miller, James
- The Practice of Surgery. Phila: 1846. 1st Amer edn. 496 pp. Leather.
(*Fye*) $100 [≈ £52]

Miller, Philip
- The Abridgement of the Gardeners Dictionary ... London: 1771. 6th edn, crrctd & enlgd. 4to. [A4, A-Zzz4, 4A-5Z2] pp. Frontis, 12 plates. Contemp calf, worn, rebacked. (*Henly*) £120 [≈ $230]
- The Gardener's Dictionary ... London: for the author, & sold by C. Rivington, 1731. 1st edn. Folio. xvi,[iv], (B1-8D2, a1-zz2 in 2s) pp. Frontis, 4 fldg plates. Occas minor staining, sl marg worm. Sm hole affecting a few lines. Contemp calf, rebacked, crnrs reprd.
(*Clark*) £280 [≈ $537]
- The Gardeners Dictionary ... abridged from the last folio edition. London: 1754. 4th edn. 3 vols. 8vo. Frontis, 3 plates. Contemp calf, rebacked with mor.
(*Wheldon & Wesley*) £160 [≈ $307]
- The Gardener's Dictionary ... London: the author, (1756)-1759. 7th edn. Folio. Unpaginated. Contemp calf.
(*Bookpress*) $1,500 [≈ £781]
- The Gardener's Kalendar ... The Eighth Edition ... added a List of the Medicinal Plants ... London: Rivington, 1748. 8vo. [2],xvi, 343,10,1 advt pp. Frontis. No intl blank. Tear in dedic. Final blank defective. Contemp calf gilt, short crack in upper jnt.
(*Beech*) £70 [≈ $134]
- The Gardeners Kalendar; directing what works are necessary to be performed every Month in the Kitchen, Fruit, and Pleasure-Gardens. London: 1760. 12th edn. 8vo. xiv,429,1 advt pp. Frontis, 5 fldg plates. Addtnl MS index inserted. Calf, sl worn.
(*Henly*) £65 [≈ $124]
- The Gardeners Kalendar. London: 1769. 15th edn. 8vo. lxvi, 382,[21] pp. Frontis, 5 plates. Contemp calf, jnts cracking.
(*Wheldon & Wesley*) £45 [≈ $86]
- The Practical Gardener ... Compiled and Arranged ... by William Shaw ... London: W. Day for M. Jones, 1810. New edn. 8vo. 679,[5] pp. Orig half calf & bds, blue label, fine. (*Vanbrugh*) £95 [≈ $182]

Millingen, J.G.
- Curiosities of Medical Experience. Phila: 1838. 372 pp. Occas foxing. New cloth.
(Whitehart) **£45 [≈ $86]**

Mills, F.W.
- An Introduction to the Study of the Diatomaceae ... London: 1893. 1st edn. 8vo. 243 pp. Sev figs. Name stamp on title & edges. Orig cloth, dull, spine ends & crnr tips a little worn. *(Bow Windows)* **£36 [≈ $69]**

Mills, J.F.
- Encyclopedia of Antique Scientific Instruments. London: Aurum Press, 1983. 8vo. 255 pp. 16 cold plates, num text ills. Cloth. Dw. *(Gemmary)* **$37.50 [≈ £19]**

Milne, J.
- Earthquakes and other Earth Movements. New York: Intl Scientific Series, 1886. xiv,362 pp. 38 text figs. Orig cloth, dull, sl dust stained, spine sl marked.
(Whitehart) **£15 [≈ $28]**

Minerals and Metals ...
- Minerals and Metals. Their Natural History and Uses in the Arts; with Incidental Accounts of Mines and Mining. London: John W. Parker, 1847. 5th edn. 12mo. xii,255 pp. 9 plates. Qtr leather.
(Gemmary) **$100 [≈ £52]**

Mitchell, Edward, engraver
- A Series of Engravings, representing the Bones of the Human Skeleton ... see Barclay, John.

Mitchell, F.S.
- The Birds of Lancashire. London: Van Voorst, 1885. 1st edn. 8vo. 224,[6 subscribers] pp. 2 cold lithos by Keulemans, fldg map, 9 plates, 3 vignettes. Orig cloth gilt, sm spot on upper bd.
(Hollett) **£67.50 [≈ $130]**

Mitchell, John
- A Manual of Practical Assaying. London: 1888. 6th edn. xxxii,896,lxii pp. 201 w'cuts. Orig cloth, sl worn, inner hinge sl cracked but firm, sl dusty. *(Whitehart)* **£40 [≈ $76]**

Mitchell, John Kearsley
- Five Essays ... Edited by S. Weir Mitchell. Phila: 1859. 1st edn. 371 pp. 1 section starting. Spine rubbed, hinges reinforced.
(Fye) **$200 [≈ £104]**

Mitchell, S. Weir
- The Autobiography of a Quack and the Case of George Dedlow. New York: 1900. 1st edn. 149 pp. Orig bndg. *(Fye)* **$50 [≈ £26]**
- Fat and Blood: and How to Make Them. Phila: 1879. 2nd edn. 109 pp. Orig bndg, fine. *(Fye)* **$175 [≈ £91]**
- Injuries of Nerves and their Consequences. Phila: 1872. 1st edn. Private impression stamp on title. Orig bndg, front outer hinge torn, spine dull & faded with minor tears at ends. *(Fye)* **$600 [≈ £312]**
- Lectures on the Diseases of the Nervous System, especially in Women. Phila: 1881. 1st edn. 238 pp. Orig bndg, cvrs spotted.
(Fye) **$450 [≈ £234]**
- Lectures on the Diseases of the Nervous System, especially in Women. Phila: 1885. 2nd edn. 287 pp. Orig bndg, fine.
(Fye) **$300 [≈ £156]**
- Some Recently Discovered Letters of William Harvey with Other Miscellanea with a Bibliography of Harvey's Works by Charles Perry Fisher. Phila: 1912. 1st edn. 59 pp. Orig wraps. *(Fye)* **$100 [≈ £52]**
- The Wager and Other Poems. New York: 1900. 1st edn. Orig bndg. Inscrbd by the author with sm MS notation p.47.
(Fye) **$150 [≈ £78]**

Mjoberg, Eric
- Forest Life and Adventures in the Malay Archipelago. London: Allen & Unwin, 1930. 1st edn in English. 8vo. 201 pp. Cold frontis, fldg map, 83 photo plates. Orig cloth, sl faded. *(Gough)* **£40 [≈ $76]**

The Modern Practice ...
- The Modern Practice of the London Hospitals ... A New Edition. With an useful Index of Diseases, and their Remedies. London: for G. Lister, [1785]. 121 pp. Engvd frontis. Rec bds.
(C.R. Johnson) **£225 [≈ $431]**

Moellenbrock, Andreas Valentin
- Cochleariae Curiosa: or the Curiosities of Scurvygrass ... London: S. & B. Griffin for William Cademan, 1676. 1st edn in English. Trans by Thomas Sherley. 8vo. [16],[29] pp. 4 fldg plates. Sl browning. Calf, rebacked. Wing M.2381. *(Rootenberg)* **$950 [≈ £494]**

Moggridge, J.T.
- Harvesting Ants and Trap-Door Spiders. Notes and Observations on their Habits and Dwellings. London: 1873. 8vo. xi,156,16 advt pp. 4 dble page cold & 8 plain plates.

Orig cloth.   *(Henly)* £25 [≈ $47]

Moller, F.P.
- Cod-Liver Oil and Chemistry. London: 1895. 4to. cxxiii,508 pp. 2 fldg tables, text diags. Some marg ink & pencil notes. New cloth.
(Whitehart) £35 [≈ $67]

Molloy, Edward (ed.)
- Practical Electrical Engineering. London: [1928]. 5 vols. viii,1928 pp. Num ills & diags.
(Whitehart) £25 [≈ $47]
- Newnes' Complete Wireless. London: 1930. 1st edn. 4 vols. 1544 pp. Num ills. Leather.
(New Wireless) $95 [≈ £49]

Monckton, C.C.F.
- Radio-Telegraphy. 1908. 1st edn. 272 pp. 173 ills. Orig bndg.
(New Wireless) $160 [≈ £83]

Monell, S.H.
- High Frequency Electric Currents. 1910. 1st edn. 24 photos. Orig bndg.
(New Wireless) $45 [≈ £23]
- A System of Instruction in X-Ray Methods and Medical Uses of Light, Hot-Air, Vibration and High-Frequency Currents. New York: 1902. 1st edn. 1010 pp. 314 ills. Damp stain in lower outer blank marg. Orig bndg, inner hinges cracked.
(Fye) $400 [≈ £208]
- The Treatment of Disease by Electric Current. New York: 1900. 2nd edn. 1100 pp. Num ills. Orig bndg, fine. *(Fye)* $150 [≈ £78]

Monge, Gaspard
- An Elementary Treatise on Descriptive Geometry ... London: John Weale, 1851. 1st edn in English. 12mo. [vi],137 pp, advt leaf. 14 plates. Orig cloth, paper label, spine ends sl defective, spine faded.
(Bickersteth) £80 [≈ $153]

Mongredien, A.
- Trees and Shrubs for English Plantations: a Selection and Description of the most Ornamental Trees and Shrubs, Native and Foreign, which will flourish in the Open Air in Our Climate ... London: 1870. xi,388 pp. Cold frontis, 29 ills. Cloth, backstrip relaid, sl worn.   *(Whitehart)* £25 [≈ $47]

Monk, John (ed.)
- An Agricultural Dictionary, consisting of Extracts from the most Celebrated Authors and Papers. London: G. Woodfall, 1794. 3 vols. 384; 372; 374 pp. Contemp qtr calf,

mrbld bds. Matthew Boulton's copy.
(C.R. Johnson) £225 [≈ $431]
- An Agricultural Dictionary, consisting of Extracts from the most celebrated Authors and Papers. London: Woodfall for the author ..., 1794. 1st edn. 3 vols. 8vo. 384; 372; 374 pp. Contemp qtr calf, sl rubbed.
(Burmester) £225 [≈ $431]

Monro, A.
- The Morbid Anatomy of the Human Gullet, Stomach, and Intestines. Edinburgh: 1811. xxv, 567 pp. 20 plates (some cold). Occas sl foxing. Orig half leather, backstrip relaid, sl rubbed & worn.   *(Whitehart)* £120 [≈ $230]
- The Structure and Physiology of Fishes explained ... Edinburgh: 1785. Large Paper. Folio (455 x 285 mm). 128 pp. 50 engvd plates on 44 ff (numbered 1-44, 3*, 9*,10*,14*, 15*, 40*). Occas minor foxing. 2 marg tears reprd. Contemp bds, rebacked in calf.   *(Wheldon & Wesley)* £400 [≈ $767]

Montagu, M.F.A.
- Edward Tyson, M.D., F.R.S. 1650-1708 and the Rise of Human and Comparative Anatomy in England. A Study in the History of Science. Phila: 1943. xxix,488 pp. Frontis, 56 ills. Cloth, sl dusty.
(Whitehart) £35 [≈ $67]

Monteath, Robert
- The Forester's Guide ... Stirling: 1820. 1st edn. 12mo. xxiv,212 pp. 2 fldg plates. New bds.   *(Henly)* £48 [≈ $92]
- The Forester's Guide ... London: 1824. 2nd edn. 8vo. xii,lvi,395 pp. 15 plates. Some spotting & offsetting. Rec bds, uncut.
(Henly) £60 [≈ $115]
- The Forester's Guide and Profitable Planter ... Second Edition, with Important Additions ... Edinburgh & London: 1824. 8vo. lvi, 395 pp. 15 plates inc frontis. Occas sl spotting. Contemp paper bds, ptd paper label, sl wear, jnts cracked but holding. *(Finch)* £48 [≈ $92]
- The Forester's Guide and Profitable Planter ... Third Edition, greatly enlarged and improved ... London: Tegg ..., 1836. 8vo. [ii], xii,500 pp. Half-title. Lge fldg appendix, 16 plates. Occas sl spotting. Orig leather backed bds, ptd paper label, sl wear.
(Finch) £45 [≈ $86]

Montgomery, W.F.
- An Exposition of the Signs and Symptoms of Pregnancy: with Some Other Papers on Subjects connected with Midwifery. From the Second London Edition. Phila: 1857. 8vo.

568 pp. Ills. Cloth, rebacked, orig backstrip relaid.   *(Goodrich)* **$125 [≈ £65]**

Moorat, S.A.J.
- Catalogue of Western Manuscripts on Medicine and Science in the Wellcome Historical Medical Library. I. MSS. Written before 1650 A.D. London: Wellcome, 1962. 4to. Cold frontis. Orig bndg.
    (Georges) **£100 [≈ $191]**

Moore, Arthur
- How to Make a Wireless Set. 1911. 1st edn. 84 pp. Orig bndg, front cvr sl stained.
    (New Wireless) **$55 [≈ £28]**

Moore, Edward Crozier Sibbald
- Sanitary Engineering ... London: Batsford, 1898. 1st edn. 8vo. xxvii,[1],621,[1] pp. Half-title. 74 fldg plates (1 cold), over 500 text figs, diags, tables, errata. Minor marg foxing. Orig cloth.   *(Rootenberg)* **$185 [≈ £96]**

Moore, George
- Health, Disease and Remedy, Familiarly & Practically Considered, in a few of their Relations to the Blood. London: 1850. 1st edn. Lge 12mo. xi,372 pp. Orig cloth, uncut & largely unopened, faded.
    (Bickersteth) **£40 [≈ $76]**
- The Use of the Body in Relation to the Mind. London: Longman ..., 1846. 1st edn. 8vo. x,431 pp. Orig cloth, spine ends sl worn.
    (Gough) **£40 [≈ $76]**
- The Use of the Body in relation to the Mind. London: 1847. 2nd edn. viii,433 pp. Orig cloth, faded & worn, crnrs worn, rear inner hinge cracked.   *(Whitehart)* **£25 [≈ $47]**

Moore, Isabella
- The Useful and Entertaining Family Miscellany ... The Complete English Housekeeper's Companion ... near Five Hundred Receipts ... London: for Thomas Palmer, 1766. 1st edn. Post 8vo. vii,[i],112 pp. A few sl marks & creases. Mod half mor.
    (Ash) **£500 [≈ $959]**

Moore, N.F.
- Ancient Mineralogy: or, an Inquiry respecting Mineral Substances mentioned by the Ancients. New York: 1834. Sm 8vo. 192 pp. Blind stamp on title. New bds.
    (Wheldon & Wesley) **£35 [≈ $67]**

Moore, Norman
- The History of the Study of Medicine in the British Isles. Oxford: 1908. 8vo. 202 pp. Orig

bndg.   *(Goodrich)* **$60 [≈ £31]**

Moore, Thomas
- British Wild Flowers. Familiarly Described ... A New Edition of "The Field Botanist's Companion". London: Reeve & Co, 1867. 8vo. xxvii, 424, [16 advt] pp. 24 hand cold plates. B'plate partly removed. Orig green cloth gilt.   *(Hollett)* **£95 [≈ $182]**
- British Wild Flowers. Familiarly described in the Four Seasons. London: 1867. 4th edn. xxvii, 424, 16 advt pp. 24 hand cold plates. Cloth gilt.   *(Henly)* **£42 [≈ $80]**
- Nature Printed British Ferns ... London: 1859 [-60]. 2 vols. 8vo. 122 cold plates nature ptd by Henry Bradbury. Sl foxing. Prelims of vol 2 sl stained. Half mor.
    (Wheldon & Wesley) **£150 [≈ $287]**
- A Popular History of the British Ferns ... Second Edition. London: Lovell Reeve, 1855. Sm sq 8vo. xii,379 pp. 22 hand cold plates. Orig pict cloth gilt.   *(Gough)* **£20 [≈ $38]**
- A Popular History of the British Ferns ... Third and Revised Edition. London: Routledge, 1859. Sm sq 8vo. xvi,394,6 advt pp. 22 cold plates. Orig cloth gilt, resewn, foredges rubbed, backstrip relaid.
    (Beech) **£18 [≈ $34]**

Moorepark, Carton
- A Book of Birds. London: Blackie & Son, 1900. 1st edn. Sm folio. 28 ff. Ills. Orig pict bds. Dw (spotted, soiled, few tears & some chipping edges).   *(Chapel Hill)* **$75 [≈ £39]**

Moran, James
- Printing Presses. History and Development from the Fifteenth Century to Modern Times. London: Faber, 1973. 4to. 263,[1] pp. 109 ills. Orig cloth. Dw.
    (Sotheran's) **£25 [≈ $47]**
- Printing Presses: History and development from the Fifteenth Century to Modern Times. London: Faber, (1973). 1st edn. Lge 4to. 263 pp. 64 plates, 109 text ills. Orig cloth. Dw.   *(Bookpress)* **$110 [≈ £57]**

Moreau, F.J.
- A Practical Treatise on Midwifery ... Translated from the French by Thomas Forrest Betton and Edited by Paul B. Goddard. Phila: 1844. Folio. 235 pp. 80 hand cold plates. Occas foxing of text. Leather, rubbed, scuffed, front bd nearly detached.
    (Fye) **$1,000 [≈ £520]**

Moreau, R.E.
- The Bird Faunas of Africa and Its Islands.

London: 1966. Roy 8vo. ix,424 pp. Map, 65 text figs. Cloth.
(Wheldon & Wesley) **£60 [≈ $115]**

Morell, J.D.
- Elements of Psychology. Part I. London: William Pickering, 1853. Sole edn, all published. 8vo. xx,309 pp, advt leaf. Few inoffensive lib marks. Orig cloth, v sm hole in cloth at hd of spine. *(Bickersteth)* **£38 [≈ $72]**

Morgagni, Giovanni Baptista
- The Seats and Causes of Diseases investigated by Anatomy ... Translated ... by Benjamin Alexander ... New York: Hafner, 1960. 3 vols. 4to. Slipcase. *(Goodrich)* **$125 [≈ £65]**

Morgan, Alfred P.
- Wireless Telegraph Construction for Amateurs. 1911. 3rd edn. 188 pp. 147 ills. Orig bndg. *(New Wireless)* **$40 [≈ £21]**
- Wireless Telegraph Construction for Amateurs. 1914. 3rd edn. 222 pp. 167 ills. Orig bndg. *(New Wireless)* **$65 [≈ £33]**
- Wireless Telegraphy and Telephony. 1922. 5th edn. 154 pp. 100 photos, 56 ills. Orig bndg. *(New Wireless)* **$25 [≈ £13]**

Morgan, Sir Thomas Charles
- Sketches of the Philosophy of Life. London: Colburn, 1819. 1st edn. 8vo. Evidently lacks half-title. Contemp calf, minor rubbing. *(Ximenes)* **$325 [≈ £169]**

Morgan, Thomas H.
- Evolution and Adaptation. New York: 1903. 8vo. xiii,470 pp. 7 text figs. Cloth, sl used. *(Wheldon & Wesley)* **£65 [≈ $124]**
- The Physical Basis of Heredity. Philadelphia & London: Lippincott, 1919. 1st edn. Cr 8vo. 305 pp. 117 ills. Orig cloth, sl marked & worn. *(Fenning)* **£32.50 [≈ $63]**

Mori, T.
- An Enumeration of Plants hitherto known from Corea. Seoul: 1922. 8vo. 10,3,3,vii, vii, 372, 175 pp. 6 plates. Good ex-lib. Cloth. *(Wheldon & Wesley)* **£50 [≈ $95]**

Morison, A.
- The Sensory and Motor Disorders of the Heart. Their Nature and Treatment. London: 1914. viii,261 pp. 51 text diags. New endpapers. Occas sl foxing. Orig bndg, sm nick on spine. *(Whitehart)* **£25 [≈ $47]**

Morley, C.
- Ichneumonologia Britannica. The

Ichneumons of Great Britain. Plymouth & London: 1903-14. 5 vols. 8vo. 9 plates, num text figs. Good ex-lib. Orig green cloth, trifle used, labels on cvrs.
(Wheldon & Wesley) **£150 [≈ $287]**
- A Revision of the Ichneumonidae, based on the Collection in the British Museum. London: BM, 1912-15. 4 vols. 8vo. 4 cold plates. Cancelled lib labels. Cloth.
(Wheldon & Wesley) **£45 [≈ $86]**

Morley, Derek Wragge
- Ants. London: Collins New Naturalist, 1953. 1st edn. 8vo. xii,179 pp. Maps, ills. Orig cloth gilt. Dw (v sm tear top edge upper panel). *(Hollett)* **£80 [≈ $153]**

Morrice, Alexander
- A Treatise on Brewing; wherein is exhibited the whole Process of the Art and Mystery of Brewing ... Fifth Edition. London: 1815. 8vo. [xxiv],179 pp. Orig half calf, rebacked.
(Bickersteth) **£120 [≈ $230]**

Morris, A.J.T.
- Treatise on Meteorology: The Barometer, Thermometer, Hygrometer, Rain-Gauge and Ozonometer ... Edinburgh: 1866. viii,98 pp. Spine defective. *(Whitehart)* **£25 [≈ $47]**

Morris, Francis Orpen
- A History of British Birds. London: 1851-57. 1st edn. 6 vols. Roy 8vo. 358 hand cold plates. Some ltd foxing but most plates clean. Orig cloth, faded.
(Wheldon & Wesley) **£500 [≈ $959]**
- A History of British Birds. London: [1863-67]. Cabinet edn. 8 vols. Cr 8vo. 358 hand cold plates. Orig red dec cloth t.e.g., spines a little faded. *(Henly)* **£420 [≈ $806]**
- A History of British Birds. Leeds & London: n.d.. Cabinet edn. 8 vols. Cr 8vo. 358 hand cold plates. Some foxing, mostly to text. Labels removed from endpapers. Vols 1-4 half mor, vols 5-8 cloth, cloth bndgs worn, leather bndgs rubbed.
(Wheldon & Wesley) **£300 [≈ $575]**
- A History of British Butterflies. London: Groombridge, 1853. 1st edn. 8vo. vi,168,29 pp. 71 hand cold & 2 plain plates. The 2 b/w plates water stained as usual. Contemp diced black calf, gilt dec spine sl rubbed.
(Gough) **£135 [≈ $259]**
- A History of British Butterflies. London: Groombridge, 1853. 1st edn. Lge 8vo. vi, 168, 29 pp. 71 hand cold plates, 2 uncold engvs. Sl spotting. Contemp rose half calf, gilt spine, mor label.

(Claude Cox) **£135 [≈ $259]**
- A History of British Butterflies. London: 1872. 4th edn. Roy 8vo. 72 cold & 2 plain plates. Orig cloth, spine reprd.
(Wheldon & Wesley) **£85 [≈ $163]**
- A History of British Butterflies. London: 1890. 6th edn. Roy 8vo. viii,184 pp. 72 hand cold & 2 plain plates. Orig cloth.
(Wheldon & Wesley) **£90 [≈ £172]**
- A History of British Butterflies. London: 1891. 6th edn. Roy 8vo. 184 pp. 72 hand cold & 2 plain plates. Trifle soiled. Orig cloth, recased. *(Wheldon & Wesley)* **£75 [≈ $143]**
- A History of British Butterflies. London: 1904. 9th edn. Roy 8vo. viii,234,[1] pp. 79 hand cold plates. Tears in 1 plate & 1 leaf reprd. Orig dec cloth.
(Wheldon & Wesley) **£60 [≈ $115]**
- A History of British Butterflies. London: 1904. Roy 8vo. viii,235 pp. 79 hand cold & 2 plain plates. Foxing at ends of text. Cloth.
(Henly) **£80 [≈ $153]**
- A History of British Butterflies. London: 1908. 10th edn. Roy 8vo. viii,234 pp. 79 cold & 2 plain plates. Orig cloth, recased.
(Wheldon & Wesley) **£50 [≈ $95]**
- A History of British Moths. London: 1896. 5th edn. 4 vols. Imperial 8vo. 132 hand cold plates. Orig cloth gilt. *(Henly)* **£160 [≈ $307]**
- A History of British Moths. London: 1896. 5th edn. 4 vols. Roy 8vo. 133 hand cold plates of 1953 figs. Cloth.
(Wheldon & Wesley) **£120 [≈ $230]**
- A History of British Moths. London: 1903. 5th edn. 4 vols. Roy 8vo. 132 hand cold plates. Cloth.
(Wheldon & Wesley) **£100 [≈ $191]**
- A Natural History of the Nests and Eggs of British Birds. London: Groombridge, 1861. 1st edn. 3 vols. Roy 8vo. 232 cold plates. Occas foxing. Orig pict green cloth gilt, sl rubbed. *(Gough)* **£65 [≈ $124]**
- A Natural History of the Nests and Eggs of British Birds. London: 1866. 3 vols. Roy 8vo. 225 cold plates (numbered 1-232 but plates 11, 55, 56, 60, 69, 94, 119 were not published). Occas sl foxing. Cloth, trifle worn. *(Wheldon & Wesley)* **£60 [≈ $115]**
- A Natural History of the Nests and Eggs of British Birds. London: 1875. 3 vols. Roy 8vo. 233 cold plates. Text at ends foxed, some plates sl foxed. Lib stamp on titles. Calf.
(Henly) **£85 [≈ $163]**
- A Natural History of the Nests and Eggs of British Birds. Fourth Edition. Revised and Corrected by W.B. Tegetmeier. London: Nimmo, 1896. 3 vols. Roy 8vo. 248 plates

'chiefly coloured by hand'. Orig pict cloth gilt, fine. *(Gough)* **£120 [≈ $230]**

Morris, Henry
- Surgical Diseases of the Kidney and Ureter including Injuries, Malformations and Misplacements. London: 1901. 1st edn. 2 vols. 682; 670 pp. Over 200 ills (1 taped). Orig bndg. *(Fye)* **$200 [≈ £104]**

Morris, J. & Lycett, J.
- A Monograph of the Mollusca from the Great Oolite, chiefly from Minchinhampton and the Coast of Yorkshire [with] Lycett's Supplementary Monograph ... London: 1850-53, 1863. 4to. viii,130; [ii],148; [ii],130 pp. 45 litho plates (lib stamps). Calf, backstrip relaid.
(Bow Windows) **£130 [≈ $249]**

Morse, Edward Lind
- Samuel F.B. Morse: His Letters and Journals. 1914. 1st edn. 2 vols. 988 pp. 26 photos. Orig bndg, some wear.
(New Wireless) **$115 [≈ £60]**

Morse, P.M. & Feshbach, H.
- Methods of Theoretical Physics. New York: 1953. 2 vols. A few text diags. Ink name stamps on endpapers.
(Whitehart) **£45 [≈ $86]**

Morton, G.H.
- The Geology of the Country around Liverpool, including the North of Flintshire. London: George Philip & Son, 1891. 2nd edn. 8vo. [ix],287 pp. 20 plates. Few spots. Orig cloth gilt. *(Hollett)* **£40 [≈ $76]**

Morton, William J.
- The X-Ray, or, Photography of the Invisible and its Value in Surgery. 1896. 1st edn. 196 pp. 38 photos, 91 ills. Orig silver pict green cloth, spine & crnrs sl worn.
(New Wireless) **$225 [≈ £118]**
- The X Ray or Photography of the Invisible and its Value in Surgery. New York: 1896. 1st edn. 196 pp. 91 ills. Orig bndg, cvrs v spotted. *(Fye)* **$250 [≈ £130]**

Moseley, Henry
- The Mechanical Principles of Engineering and Architecture. New York: Wiley, 1860. 1st Amer from the 2nd London edn. No. xxi,699 pp. Ills. Half mor, rubbed, piece missing from hd of spine.
(Bookpress) **$50 [≈ £26]**

Moseley, Maboth
- Irascible Genius. A Life of Charles Babbage, Inventor. London: Hutchinson, 1964. 8vo. Ills. Dw.　　　*(Georges)* **£20 [≃ $38]**

Moseley, Sydney A.
- John Baird. 1952. 1st edn. 256 pp. 11 photos. Dw.　　*(New Wireless)* **$35 [≃ £18]**

Moseley, Sydney A. & Chapple, Barton H.J.
- Television - Today & Tomorrow. 1930. 1st edn. 130 pp. 48 photos, 38 ills. Orig bndg.
　　　　　　(New Wireless) **$90 [≃ £46]**

Moseley, Sydney A. & McKay, Herbert H.
- Television: A Guide for the Amateur. 1936. 1st edn. 144 pp. 31 photos, 50 ills. Orig bndg.
　　　　　　(New Wireless) **$45 [≃ £23]**

Mosenthal, J. de & Harting, J.E.
- Ostriches and Ostrich Farming. London: 1877. 8vo. xxii,246 pp. 28 ills. Cloth, used, jnts worn.　　*(Wheldon & Wesley)* **£50 [≃ $95]**

Mosso, Angelo
- Fatigue. Translated by Margaret Drummond and W.B. Drummond. London: 1915. 3rd edn in English. 8vo. xiv,334 pp. Orig cloth.
　　　　　　(Bickersteth) **£40 [≃ $76]**

Motherby, George
- A New Medical Dictionary; or General Repository of Physic ... Second Edition, considerably enlarged and improved ... London: for J. Johnson ..., 1785. Folio. Ms notes. 26 plates. Contemp calf, rebacked, orig label preserved.
　　　　(Frew Mackenzie) **£265 [≃ $508]**

Mott, F.T., et al.
- The Flora of Leicestershire including the Cryptogams. London: 1886. 8vo. xxvi,372,[3] pp. 2 cold maps. Cloth, cvrs damp stained.
　　　　(Wheldon & Wesley) **£35 [≃ $67]**

Mott, Valentine
- Reminiscences of Medical Teaching and Teachers in New York. An Address introductory to a Course of Lectures ... New York: 1850. 8vo. 32 pp. New wraps.
　　　　　　(Goodrich) **$75 [≃ £39]**

Mott, Valentine, Jr.
- Rabies and How to Prevent It. A Paper ... Boston: 1887. 8vo. 14 pp. Orig bndg.
　　　　　　(Goodrich) **$65 [≃ £33]**

Motte, Andrew
- A Treatise of the Mechanical Powers, wherein the Laws of Motion, and the Properties of those Powers are Explained and Demonstrated ... London: Motte, 1727. 1st edn. 8vo. [8],222,[2] pp, inc errata & advt leaf. 3 plates, text w'cuts (1 full page). Contemp calf, rebacked.　　*(Rootenberg)* **$950 [≃ £494]**

Mottelay, P.F.
- Bibliographical History of Electricity and Magnetism. London: Charles Griffin, 1922. Roy 8vo. xx,673 pp. 14 plates. Cloth.
　　　　　　(Gemmary) **$450 [≃ £234]**

Moubray, Bonington
- See Lawrence, John.

Mountfort, G.
- The Hawfinch. London: Collins New Naturalist, 1957. 1st edn. 8vo. 192 pp. 8 plates. Dw.
　　　　(Wheldon & Wesley) **£60 [≃ $115]**
- The Hawfinch. London: Collins New Naturalist, 1957. 1st edn. 8vo. xii,176,4 pp. 8 plates. Orig cloth. Dw. *(Henly)* **£72 [≃ $138]**

Moynihan, B.G.A.
- Abdominal Operations. Philadelphia & London: 1914. 3rd edn. 2 vols. 371 figs. Occas sl foxing. Cloth, sl rubbed.
　　　　　　(Whitehart) **£40 [≃ $76]**
- Gall-Stones and their Surgical Treatment. Phila: 1905. 1st edn, 2nd issue. 8vo. 386 pp. Orig bndg.　　　*(Goodrich)* **$50 [≃ £26]**
- The Spleen and Some of Its Diseases. Phila: 1921. 1st Amer edn. 8vo. 129 pp. 13 ills. Orig bndg.　　　*(Goodrich)* **$35 [≃ £18]**

Mudie, R.
- The Feathered Tribes of the British Islands. London: 1878. 4th edn. 2 vols. 8vo. 2 engvd titles with hand cold vignettes, 19 plates of birds & 7 of eggs, all hand cold. Orig cloth, backstrips relaid.　　*(Henly)* **£60 [≃ $115]**

Mueller, F. von
- Eucalyptographia. A Descriptive Atlas of the Eucalypts of Australia and the adjoining Islands ... Melbourne: 1879-84. 4to. 110 plates. Stamps on title & reverse of plates. New cloth.
　　　　(Wheldon & Wesley) **£240 [≃ $460]**

Muirhead, James Patrick
- The Life of James Watt, with Selections from his Correspondence. London: Murray, 1858. 1st edn. Half-title. 32 pp ctlg dated May

1858. Frontis (sl foxed). Orig green cloth, spine sl faded, sm lib label & stamps.
(Jarndyce) £120 [≈ $230]

Mullins, John, & Sons
- The Divining Rod: Its History, Truthfulness, and Practical Utility. London: J. & H.W. Mullins, 1893. 1st edn. 8vo. 2 ports. Orig cloth.   *(Young's)* £35 [≈ $67]

Mummery, J.H.
- The Microscopic Anatomy of the Teeth. Oxford: 1919. 1st edn. viii,382 pp. 243 text figs. New cloth.   *(Whitehart)* £25 [≈ $47]

Munk, William
- The Roll of the Royal College of Physicians of London; comprising Biographical Sketches. London: 1878. 2nd edn. 3 vols. Orig bndgs, worn & shaken.
(Fye) $75 [≈ £39]
- The Roll of the Royal College of Physicians of London; comprising Biographical Sketches ... London: 1878. 2nd edn. 3 vols. Orig bndgs.   *(Whitehart)* £50 [≈ $95]

Munro, Hugh
- A Compendious System of the Theory and Practice of Modern Surgery ... in the Form of a Dialogue. London: Hodson, 1792. 8vo. 352, [10] pp. Fldg table (reprd). Blank hd of title reprd. New qtr calf, mrbld bds, uncut.
(Goodrich) $250 [≈ £130]

Murchison, Charles
- Functional Derangements of the Liver. London: 1874. xvi,182 pp. 6 text figs. Orig cloth, worn & stained.
(Whitehart) £30 [≈ $57]
- A Treatise on the Continued Fevers of Great Britain. London: 1873. 2nd edn. 729 pp. Cold plates. 2 stamps erased from title. Lacks free endpapers. Orig bndg.
(Fye) $100 [≈ £52]

Murchison, R.I.
- Outline of the Geology of the Neighbourhood of Cheltenham. New Edition, Revised by J. Buckman and H.E. Strickland. London: 1845. 110 pp. Map, 13 plates. Orig cloth.
(Baldwin) £70 [≈ $134]
- Siluria. The History of the Oldest Known Rocks containing Organic Remains. London: 1854. 8vo. xvi,523 pp. Fldg cold geological map, map of formations, 37 plates. Sm blind stamps. Orig cloth, rebacked.
(Wheldon & Wesley) £135 [≈ $259]
- Siluria. The History of the Oldest Known

Rocks containing Organic Remains ... London: 1872. 5th edn. 2 vols. Map, 41 plates. Orig cloth.   *(Baldwin)* £75 [≈ $143]

Murdoch, Patrick
- Mercator's Sailing applied to the Time Figure of the Earth with an Introduction concerning the Discovery and Determination of that Figure. London: for A. Millar, 1741. 4to. xxvii,38,[2 advt] pp. 3 fldg plans & diags. Bds.   *(Lamb)* £125 [≈ $239]

Murphy, John
- A Treatise on the Art of Weaving, with Calculations and Tables for the Use of Manufacturers. Tenth Edition, revised and enlarged. Glasgow: Blackie, 1852. 8vo. [2], xiv, 518 pp. Frontis, 14 fldg plates. Sl used. Contemp half calf. *(Fenning)* £125 [≈ $239]

Murphy, Robert Cushman
- Oceanic Birds of South America. New York: Amer Mus Nat Hist, 1936. 1st edn. 2 vols. 4to. 88 plates (16 cold), 80 text ills. Some foxing. Orig buckram, edges trifle stained.
(Wheldon & Wesley) £200 [≈ $383]
- Oceanic Birds of South America ... New York: Macmillan, [ca 1936]. 2 vols. 4to. xx, [2], 640; vii, 641-1245 pp. 16 cold & 72 b/w plates. Orig cloth.
(High Latitude) $225 [≈ £117]
- Oceanic Birds of South America ... New York: Macmillan, Amer Museum of Nat Hist, [1936]. 2 vols. [xxii],1245 pp. 16 cold & 72 b/w plates. Some mustiness. Orig cloth, spines sl faded. Slipcase (sl scuffed).
(Schoyer) $175 [≈ £91]

Murray, A.
- The Northern Flora; or, a Description of the Wild Plants belonging to the North and East of Scotland. Part 1 [all published]. Edinburgh: 1836. 8vo. xvii,150,xvi pp. 2 plates. Orig ptd bds, cloth spine.
(Wheldon & Wesley) £50 [≈ $95]

Murray, Andrew
- Economic Entomology; Aptera [all published]. London: South Kensington Museum Handbooks, Chapman & Hall, [1877]. 1st edn. 8vo. xxiii,433,9 advt pp. 450 text figs. Orig cloth gilt, orig ptd wraps bound in.   *(Gough)* £35 [≈ $67]

Murray, George
- An Introduction to the Study of Seaweeds. London: Macmillan, 1895. 1st edn. xvi,271 pp. 8 cold plates, 88 other plates & text ills. Orig cloth, spine faded. *(Gough)* £25 [≈ $47]

Murray, J.A.
- The Plants and Drugs of Sind: being a Systematic Account, with Descriptions, of the Indigenous Flora. London: 1881. 8vo. xxxv,219 pp. Cloth, sound ex-lib.
(Wheldon & Wesley) £35 [≈ $67]

Murray, John
- Experimental Researches on The Light and Luminous Matter of the Glow-Worm, the Luminosity of the Sea, the Phenomena of the Chamaeleon ... Glasgow: McPhun, 1826. 1st edn. 177, [3 advt] pp. Orig bds, uncut.
(Gough) £85 [≈ $163]
- A Memoir on the Diamond; including its Economical and Political History. London: Relfe & Fletcher, 1839. 2nd edn, enlgd. 12mo. 2 plates. Orig cloth, sl rubbed.
(Ximenes) $200 [≈ £104]

Murray, Mungo
- A Treatise on Ship-Building and Navigation. In Three Parts ... London: Henry & Cave, for the author ..., 1754. 1st edn. 4to. 18 fldg plates & lge volvelle (1 fold strengthened on verso). Contemp mottled calf gilt, gilt spine, mor label.
(Ximenes) $3,500 [≈ £1,822]

Murrell, William
- Nitro-Glycerine as a Remedy for Angina Pectoris. Detroit: 1882. 1st Amer edn. 78 pp. Orig bndg.
(Fye) $300 [≈ £156]

Murton, R.K.
- Man and Birds. London: Collins New Naturalist, 1971. 1st edn. 8vo. xx,364 pp. 32 plates. Orig cloth. Dw.
(Henly) £30 [≈ $57]
- The Wood Pigeon. London: Collins New Naturalist, 1965. 1st edn. 8vo. 256 pp. Cold plate, 39 ills. Cloth. Dw.
(Wheldon & Wesley) £30 [≈ $57]

Museum Rusticum et Commerciale ...
- Museum Rusticum et Commerciale: or, Select Papers on Agriculture, Commerce, Arts, and Manufactures ... London: 1766-64-66. 3rd edn vol 1, 1st edn vols 2-6. 6 vols. 8vo. 11 plates, plans & tables. Orig calf, sl wear to hd of spines.
(Bickersteth) £280 [≈ $537]

Mushin, W. & Rendell-Baker, I.
- The Principles of Thoracic Anaesthesia. Past and Present. Oxford: 1953. xviii,172 pp. 193 text figs. Trace of label removal from front endpaper. Orig bndg.
(Whitehart) £25 [≈ $47]

Mutter, Thomas
- A Lecture on Loxarthrus, or Club-Foot. Phila: 1839. 1st edn. 104 pp. Sev w'cuts. Foxed & stained. Orig bndg.
(Fye) $200 [≈ £104]

Muybridge, Eadweard
- Animals in Motion ... Fifth Impression. London: 1925. Oblong lge 8vo. x,264 pp. Num ills. 1 or 2 sm tears, a few sl marks. Orig cloth.
(Bow Windows) £48 [≈ $92]
- The Human Figure in Motion ... Fourth Impression. London: Chapman & Hall, 1913. Oblong folio. 277 pp. Frontis port, 128 plates. Orig maroon cloth, sl faded.
(Claude Cox) £65 [≈ $124]

Nadkarni, K.M.
- Indian Plants and Drugs with their Medical Properties and Uses. Madras: 1910. 2nd thousand. iv,450,xxi pp. Cloth, marked, dusty, spine faded, inner hinge sl worn.
(Whitehart) £35 [≈ $67]

Nairne, A.K.
- The Flowering Plants of Western India. London: [1894]. Cr 8vo. xlvii,401 pp. Inscrptn & stamp on half-title, annotations on rear endpaper. Cloth.
(Wheldon & Wesley) £20 [≈ $38]

Nall, G.H.
- The Life of the Sea Trout, especially in Scottish Waters; with Chapters on the Reading and Measurement of Scales. London: 1930. 8vo. 335 pp. 95 plates, 15 diags. V occas foxing. Cloth.
(Wheldon & Wesley) £36 [≈ $69]

Napier, J.
- A Manual of Dyeing and Dyeing Receipts, comprising a System of Elementary Chemistry, as applied to Dyeing ... London: 1875. 3rd edn. xxviii, 420 pp. Num cloth samples. Cloth sl worn, inner hinge sl cracked but bndg firm.
(Whitehart) £25 [≈ $47]

Narrien, J.
- An Historical Account of the Origin and Progress of Astronomy. With Plates illustrating chiefly the Ancient Systems. London: [1833]. xiv,520 pp. Advts at end dated 1850. 5 fldg plates. Orig cloth, new endpapers, hd of spine sl worn.
(Whitehart) £50 [≈ $95]
- An Historical Account of the Origin and Progress of Astronomy. London: 1850. xv,520 pp. 5 fldg plates (sl foxed). Amateur

three qtr roan, paper label, rubbed.
(Whitehart) **£45 [≈ $86]**

Nasmith, Joseph
- Modern Cotton Spinning Machinery, Its principles and Construction. Manchester: John Nasmith, 1890. 1st edn. 4to. 322 pp. Illust advts at ends. 232 w'engvd ills. Orig cloth, gilt spine.   *(Gough)* **£35 [≈ $67]**

Natural History ...
- The Natural History of Bees ... see Bazin, G.A.
- The Natural History of Insects ... see Rennie, J. & Westwood, J.O.

Neal, E.
- The Badger. London: Collins New Naturalist, 1948. 1st edn. 8vo. xv,158 pp. 1 cold & 24 other plates. Orig cloth.
(Henly) **£12 [≈ $23]**

Neale, George
- Some Observations on the Use of the Agaric ... London: for Jacob Robinson, 1757. 1st edn. 8vo. Mod bds. *(Ximenes)* **$275 [≈ £143]**

Neale, R.
- The Medical Digest, or Busy Practitioner's Vade-Mecum ... London: 1882. 2nd edn. [xi], 643, lxxxii pp. Oblong 4to. Orig cloth, sl worn.   *(Whitehart)* **£38 [≈ $72]**
- The Medical Digest. Being a means of ready reference to the Principal Contributions to Medical Science during the last Thirty Years. London: New Sydenham Soc, 1877. xiii,650 pp. Orig cloth.   *(Whitehart)* **£25 [≈ $47]**
- The Medical Digest, or Busy Practitioner's Vade-Mecum ... [with Appendix]. London: 1891. 3rd edn. xi,794, cxxxii, 206, xxi pp. Orig cloth.   *(Whitehart)* **£25 [≈ $47]**

Needham, Joseph
- Biochemistry   and   Morphogenesis. Cambridge: UP, 1942. 1st edn. 8vo. xvi,785,[ii] pp. 35 plates (4 cold), num text figs. Orig cloth.   *(Bickersteth)* **£55 [≈ $105]**
- Biochemistry   and   Morphogenesis. Cambridge: 1942. 1st edn. Roy 8vo. xvi,785,[2] pp. 35 plates. Cloth, trifle used & loose.   *(Wheldon & Wesley)* **£30 [≈ $57]**
- Biochemistry   and   Morphogenesis. Cambridge: (1942) 1950. Roy 8vo. xvi,787 pp. 35 plates (4 cold), num text figs. Orig cloth.   *(Wheldon & Wesley)* **£25 [≈ $47]**
- Clerks and Craftsmen in China and the West ... Cambridge: 1970. Sm 4to. xix,470 pp. 100 plates. Orig cloth gilt. *(Hollett)* **£75 [≈ $143]**

- A History of Embryology. Cambridge: UP, 1934. 8vo. 16 plates, ills. Cvrs sl soiled & faded.   *(Georges)* **£50 [≈ $95]**
- Science   and   Civilisation   in   China. Cambridge: UP, 1965-76. 8 vols (of 11). Vols 1-4 & 5 parts 2 & 3. Sm 4to. Maps, ills. Orig cloth gilt. Dws.   *(Hollett)* **£220 [≈ $422]**

Needham, Joseph (ed.)
- Science Religion and Reality. London: 1925. 1st edn. 8vo. [x],396 pp. Endpapers spotted. Orig cloth. Dw (worn).
(Bow Windows) **£25 [≈ $47]**

Neighbour, Alfred
- The Apiary; or, Bees, Beehives, and Bee Culture ... Third Edition, greatly enlarged ... London: Kent & Co, 1878. 8vo. 2 advt, xxvi, 359, 4 advt pp. Fldg cold litho plate, 2 plates (1 with some hand colouring), w'engvs in text. 1 sm marg tear. Orig cloth gilt.
(Beech) **£45 [≈ $86]**

Nelson, T.H. & Clarke, W.E.
- The Birds of Yorkshire ... London: A Brown & Sons, 1907. Large Paper. 2 vols. Thick 4to. Cold frontis & title to each vol, num ills. Sl spotting. Orig cloth gilt, vol 1 hinges strained.
(Hollett) **£150 [≈ $287]**
- The Birds of Yorkshire. London: 1907. 2 vols. 8vo. 2 cold frontis, 74 plates. Orig green cloth, trifle used & faded.
(Wheldon & Wesley) **£65 [≈ $124]**

Nesbit, J.C.
- On Agricultural Chemistry, and the Nature and Properties of Peruvian Guano. London: [ca 1856]. 8vo. [iv],128 pp. 4 vignettes. Num marg pencil notes. Orig bndg, ft of spine sl worn, sm stain ft of lower cvr penetrating to rear endpaper. *(Bow Windows)* **£35 [≈ $67]**

Nethersole-Thompson, Desmond
- The Greenshank. London: Collins New Naturalist, 1951. 1st edn. 8vo. xii,244 pp. 4 cold & 24 other plates. Orig cloth.
(Henly) **£36 [≈ $69]**
- The Greenshank. London: Collins New Naturalist, 1951. 1st edn. 8vo. 244 pp. Cold & other ills. Orig cloth gilt. Dw (hd of spine internally strengthened).
(Hollett) **£65 [≈ $124]**

Neubauer, C. & Vogel, J.
- A Guide to the Qualitative and Quantitative Analysis of the Urine, designed especially for the use of Medical Men. Translated by W.O. Markham. London: New Sydenham Society,

1863. xv,439 pp. 4 plates, 28 text figs. Orig cloth, marked.   *(Whitehart)* **£25 [≃ $47]**

Neuberger, Max
- History of Medicine. Translated by Ernest Playfair. London: 1910-25. Vols 1 & 2 (part 1 only), all published. 2 vols. 403; 135 pp. New cloth.   *(Goodrich)* **$275 [≃ £143]**

Neugebauer, O.
- A History of Ancient Mathematical Astronomy ... Berlin: 1975. 3 vols. Lib stamps on title versos. Orig bndgs, sm lib mark on spines.   *(Waterfield's)* **£50 [≃ $95]**

Neugebauer, O. & Sachs, A. (eds.)
- Mathematical Cuneiform Texts. New Haven: Amer Oriental Society ..., 1945. 4to. x,178 pp. 49 plates, text figs, charts. Cloth.
                              (Karmiole) **$85 [≃ £44]**

New ...
- The New Female Instructor; or Young Woman's Guide to Domestic happiness ... Elements of Science ... A Complete Art of Cookery ... Medicinal and other useful Receipts ... London: Kelly, [1834]. 8vo. viii, 672 pp. Frontis, 7 plates. Half calf, gilt spine.
                              (Gough) **£110 [≃ $211]**
- The New Handmaid to Arts, Sciences, Agriculture, &c. London: Clements & Sadler, 1790. 1st edn. Sm 8vo. [ii],118 pp. Contemp qtr calf, rubbed. *(Bookpress)* **$850 [≃ £442]**
- New Naturalist. A Journal of British Natural History ... see Fisher, J. (ed.).
                              (Henly) **£25 [≃ $47]**
- A New System of Domestic Cookery ... see Rundell, Maria.

Newman, Edward
- A Familiar Introduction to the History of Insects; Being a New and greatly Improved Edition of 'The Grammar of Entomology'. London: Van Voorst, 1841. 1st edn thus. xiv, 288 pp. Num w'engvd text ills. Contemp green half mor, gilt spine (faded), t.e.g.
                              (Gough) **£60 [≃ $115]**
- A History of British Ferns. London: Van Voorst, 1840. 1st edn. 8vo. xxxvi,[ii],104 pp. Errata slip. W'engvd text figs & vignettes. Orig cloth, sl faded & spotted.
                              (Bickersteth) **£24 [≃ $46]**
- A History of British Ferns. London: Van Voorst, 1854. 1st edn. xiv,344 pp. Num text engvs. Prelims spotted. Contemp green half mor, t.e.g., spine faded. *(Gough)* **£48 [≃ $92]**
- An Illustrated Natural History of British Butterflies. London: W.H. Allen, [1884]. Roy

8vo. xvi,176 pp. Num engvs. Orig cloth.
                    (Wheldon & Wesley) **£25 [≃ $47]**

Newman, George
- The Rise of Preventive Medicine. London: 1932. 1st edn. 270 pp. Orig bndg.
                              (Fye) **$90 [≃ £46]**

Newman, J.R.
- The World of Mathematics. New York: Simon & Schuster, 1956. 2 vols. 8vo. Num ills. Cloth.   *(Gemmary)* **$45 [≃ £23]**

Newnham, William
- Some Observations on the Medicinal and Diuretic Properties of Green Tea ... London: Hatchard, 1827. Only edn. 8vo. 82 pp. Disbound.   *(Georges)* **£150 [≃ $287]**

Newsholme, A.
- Epidemic Diphtheria. A Research on the Origin and Spread of the Disease from an International Standpoint. London: 1900. 2nd edn. iv,196 pp. 60 text figs. Orig cloth.
                              (Whitehart) **£25 [≃ $47]**
- The Last Thirty Years in Public Health. Recollections and Reflections ... London: [1936]. 410 pp. Frontis port, 13 plates, 7 diags. Lib label. Cloth, sl marked & worn. Author's inscrptn. *(Whitehart)* **£20 [≃ $38]**

Newton, Alfred & Gadow, Hans
- A Dictionary of Birds. London: Adam & Charles Black, 1893-96. 1st edn, in 4 parts. 8vo. 1088,xii,124 pp. Num ills. Orig qtr roan gilt, ptd bds.   *(Gough)* **£55 [≃ $105]**
- A Dictionary of Birds. London: 1896. 8vo. xii, 1088 pp. Text figs. Cloth.
                    (Wheldon & Wesley) **£35 [≃ $67]**

Newton, I.
- Finches. London: Collins New Naturalist, 1972. 1st edn. 8vo. 288 pp. 4 cold & 24 plain plates. Orig cloth. Dw. *(Henly)* **£30 [≃ $57]**

Newton, Sir Isaac
- Isaac Newton's Papers and Letters on Natural Philosophy: and Related Documents. Edited by I.B. Cohen. Harvard: 1958. xiii,501 pp. Frontis port. Orig bndg.
                              (Whitehart) **£35 [≃ $67]**
- Mathematical Papers (1664-1684). Edited by D.T. Whiteside. Cambridge: UP, 1967-71. Vols 1-4 (of 6). 4to. 4 frontis, ills. Orig buckram gilt.   *(Hollett)* **£95 [≃ $182]**
- Mathematical Principles of Natural Philosophy ... Translated into English, and illustrated with a Commentary, by Robert

Thorp, M.A. Volume I [all published]
London: 1777. 1st edn. 4to. xlviii, [1], 360
pp. 22 fldg plates. Lacks half-title. Occas sl
foxing. Contemp half roan, sl worn.
(Whitehart) **£1,500 [≈ $2,879]**
- Opticks ... London: Smith & Walford, 1704.
1st edn, 1st issue. 4to. 2 ff, 144,211 pp. Red
& black title. 19 fldg plates. Contemp calf,
backstrip relaid, new endpapers.
(Offenbacher) **$7,500 [≈ £3,906]**
- Opticks ... The Fourth Edition, Corrected.
London: for William Innys, 1730. 8vo. viii,
382, [2 advt] pp. 12 fldg plates (numbered
1-5, 1-2, 1-4, 1). Contemp sprinkled polished
calf, gilt ruled sides & spine, crnrs worn.
(Gaskell) **£800 [≈ $1,535]**
- Opticks: or, a Treatise of the Reflections,
Refractions, Inflections and Colours of Light.
London: Innys, 1718. 2nd edn, 2nd issue.
8vo. [6],382,[2 ctlg] pp. 12 fldg plates. Minor
foxing. Mod leather.
(Gemmary) **$1,000 [≈ £520]**
- Opticks ... London: 1730, reprint 1931. xxx,
414 pp. Figs.   *(Whitehart)* **£35 [≈ $67]**
- The System of the World Demonstrated in an
Easy and Popular Manner ... Second Edition,
Corrected and Improved. London: for J.
Robinson, 1740. Reissue of 1st edn of 1731.
8vo. 2 plates. Title-page is a cancel. Contemp
calf, jnt cracked, lacks label.
(Waterfield's) **£400 [≈ $767]**

Newton, J.
- A Complete Herbal ... London: 1798. 8vo.
176 plates inc port. Sm but rather heavy stain
on text & 1st 12 plates. Mod calf antique
style.   *(Wheldon & Wesley)* **£180 [≈ $345]**
- A Complete Herball ... New Edition.
London: 1805. 8vo. [xvi] pp. Port, 175 engvd
plates. Mod calf.
(Wheldon & Wesley) **£225 [≈ $431]**

Nice, M.M.
- Studies in the Life History of the Song
Sparrow. New York: 1937-43. 1st edn. 2 vols
in one. 8vo. 4 plates (1 cold). Cloth.
(Wheldon & Wesley) **£50 [≈ $95]**

Nichol, John Philip
- Thoughts on some Important Points relating
to the System of the World. Edinburgh:
William Tait, 1846. 1st edn. 8vo. 14 plates (1
with closed tear). Contemp prize calf,
extremities sl worn.   *(Clark)* **£65 [≈ $124]**

Nichols, Thomas
- Observations on the Propagation and
Management of Oak Trees in general; but

more immediately applying to His Majesty's
New-Forest, in Hampshire ... Southampton:
T. Baker, [1791]. Mrbld wraps.
(C.R. Johnson) **£120 [≈ $230]**

Nicholson, A. & Lydekker, R.
- Manual of Palaeontology. London: 1889. 3rd
edn. 2 vols. 8vo. Over 1400 text figs. Sl
foxing. Orig cloth, vol 2 damp stained &
backstrip relaid.   *(Henly)* **£48 [≈ $92]**

Nicholson, E.M.
- Birds and Men. London: Collins New
Naturalist, 1951. 1st edn. 8vo. xvi,256 pp. 40
cold & 32 plain plates. Ends foxed. Orig
cloth. Dw (sl damp stain).
(Henly) **£12 [≈ $23]**

Nicholson, G.
- The Illustrated Dictionary of Gardening.
London: 1884-88. 4 vols. 4to. 4 cold plates,
2377 text ills. Green half mor gilt, sl rubbed.
(Henly) **£48 [≈ $92]**
- The Illustrated Dictionary of Gardening
[with] Century Supplement. London:
[1884-88, 1901]. 5 vols. 4to. Cold & other ills.
Vol 1 half-title creased. Orig dec cloth.
(Wheldon & Wesley) **£50 [≈ $95]**

Nicholson, H.A.
- Lives and Labours of Leading Naturalists.
London: 1894. vi,312 pp. 17 ills. New cloth.
(Whitehart) **£18 [≈ $34]**
- A Manual of Palaeontology ... Second Edition
Revised and Enlarged. Edinburgh: 1879. 2
vols. 8vo. 722 figs. Erratum slip vol 2. Sl
shaken. Orig cloth, sl rubbed & dull.
(Bow Windows) **£55 [≈ $105]**
- A Manual of Palaeontology for the Use of
Students ... London: 1879. 2nd edn. 2 vols.
722 text figs. Orig pict cloth.
(Whitehart) **£35 [≈ $67]**
- A Manual of Palaeontology. London: 1879.
2nd edn. 2 vols. Orig pict gilt blue cloth,
spine sl dull & worn. *(Baldwin)* **£35 [≈ $67]**

Nicholson, H.A. & Etheridge, R.
- A Monograph of the Silurian Fossils of the
Girvan District in Ayrshire ... Vol 1 [all
published]. London: 1878-80. 3 orig parts.
Roy 8vo. ix,vi,vi,341 pp. Fldg table, 24
plates. Bds. *(Wheldon & Wesley)* **£50 [≈ $95]**

Nicholson, W.A.
- A Flora of Norfolk ... London: 1914. 1st edn.
8vo. [viii],214 pp. 2 maps (1 fldg). Some
finger marks. Orig cloth, cvrs soiled.
(Bow Windows) **£30 [≈ $57]**

- A Flora of Norfolk ... London: 1914. 8vo. 214 pp. 2 maps. Cloth.
(Wheldon & Wesley) £27 [≈ $51]

Nicholson, William (ed.)
- A Journal of Natural Philosophy, Chemistry, and the Arts: illustrated with Engravings. London: Robinson, 1797-1801. 1st edn, 1st series. 4 vols. 4to. xxviii, 600; xxiii, [1], 285-564; xix,[1], 552; xvi,562 pp. 85 plates. Few ff damp stained. Contemp calf & half calf, 1 vol rebacked.
(Rootenberg) $1,250 [≈ £651]

Nicol, J.
- Guide to the Geology of Scotland. Edinburgh: 1844. Cr 8vo. 272 pp. Cold fldg map (reprd at folds), frontis, 9 cold plates. Sl foxed, few notes. Cloth, trifle worn, inscrptn on cvr.
(Wheldon & Wesley) £45 [≈ $86]

Nicol, Walter
- The Scotch Forcing and Kitchen Gardener; being a Second Edition with Extensive Additions of The Scotch Forcing Gardener. Edinburgh: for the author, 1798. [ii],9, [vii]-xii, [ii],248 pp. 5 fldg plates (foxed). Half calf, rubbed.
(Wheldon & Wesley) £40 [≈ $76]
- The Villa Garden Directory, or Monthly Index of Work ... Edinburgh: Constable, 1810. 2nd edn. Sm 8vo. xvi,398,[2] pp. Contemp half calf, cvr wear.
(Bookpress) $110 [≈ £57]

Nicoll, M.J.
- Handlist of the Birds of Egypt. Cairo: 1919. 1st edn. Fldg map, 31 plates (24-31 cold). Orig cloth backed ptd bds.
(Trophy Room) $250 [≈ £130]

Nicoll, M.J. & Meinertzhagen, D.
- Nicoll's Birds of Egypt. London: Hugh Rees, 1930. 1st edn. 2 vols. Folio. Frontis port, 37 plates (31 cold), 3 fldg maps. Orig gilt dec cloth.
(Terramedia) $800 [≈ £416]
- See also under Meinertzhagen, D.

Nicols, Thomas
- A Lapidary: or, The History of Pretious Stones: With Cautions for the Undeceiving of all those that deal with Pretious Stones. Cambridge: Thomas Buck, 1652. 1st edn. 8vo. 239 pp. Lacks the fldg key. Some browning. Half leather.
(Gemmary) $1,200 [≈ £628]

Nierenstein, M.
- Incunabula of Tannin Chemistry. A

Collection of some Early Papers on the Chemistry of the Tannins. Reproduced in Facsimile and Published with Annotations. London: 1932. 167 pp. Fldg frontis. Cloth worn, spine defective.
(Whitehart) £15 [≈ $28]
- Incunabula of Tannin Chemistry. A Collection of some Early Papers on the Chemistry of the Tannins. Reproduced in Facsimile and Published with Annotations. London: Arnold, 1932. 1st edn. 4to. [viii], 167 pp. Fldg map. Orig cloth, gilt spine.
(Gough) £50 [≈ $95]

Nightingale, Florence
- Introductory Notes on Lying-in Institutions. Together with a Proposal for Organising an Institution for Training Midwives and Midwifery Nurses. London: 1871. 1st edn. Ills. Tear in marg of title & prelims from careless opening. Rebound in cloth, new endpapers.
(Fye) $200 [≈ £104]
- Notes on Nursing ... London: Harrison, [1860]. 1st edn. 8vo. 79 pp. Strip cut from hd of title. Yellow endpapers & pastedowns (sl defective) with advts. With advts on endpapers & "The right of Translation in reserved" on title but with the uncrrctd text. Orig cloth.
(Bickersteth) £45 [≈ $86]
- Notes on Nursing: What It Is, and What It Is Not. London: Harrison, [1859]. 1st edn, early issue. 8vo. 79 pp. Orig black limp pebbled cloth, yellow endpapers advertising Burke's Peerage for 1860, "Summer search" on rear endpaper. Boxed. *(Rootenberg)* $400 [≈ £208]
- Notes on Nursing: What It Is, and What It Is Not. New York: 1860. 1st Amer edn. 140 pp. Orig bndg.
(Fye) $175 [≈ £91]

Nisbet, J.
- Our Forests and Woodlands. London: 1900. 8vo. x,340 pp. 12 plates, head & tail pieces by Arthur Rackham. Orig cloth gilt, unopened.
(Henly) £45 [≈ $86]

Nisbet, J.F.
- The Insanity of Genius and the General Inequality of Human Faculty Physiologically considered. London: 1891. xxiv,340 pp. Half-title reprd. Orig cloth, backstrip relaid.
(Whitehart) £25 [≈ $47]

Noad, H.M.
- A Manual of Electricity; including Galvanism, Magnetism, Diamagnetism ... and the Electric Telegraph. London: 1855-57. 2 vols. viii,522; xi,523-910 pp. Frontis, 497 text figs. Orig cloth, edges worn, rebacked.
(Whitehart) £90 [≈ $172]

Norman, M.W.
- A Popular Guide to the Geology of the Isle of Wight ... Ventnor: for the author ..., (1887). 1st edn. 8vo. vi,240 pp. Map, 22 plates, sev text figs. Orig cloth.
(Bow Windows) £50 [≈ $95]

Norrie, H.S.
- Induction Coils. 1901. 2nd edn. 269 pp. 78 ills. Orig pict gilt bndg.
(New Wireless) $115 [≈ £60]
- Induction Coils. 1907. 4th edn. 269 pp. 79 ills. Orig pict gilt bndg.
(New Wireless) $95 [≈ £49]

Norris, Richard (ed.)
- An American Text-Book of Obstetrics. Phila: 1895. 1st edn. 1009 pp. Ills. Leather.
(Fye) $100 [≈ £52]

North, F.J., Campbell, B. & Scott, R.
- Snowdonia. London: Collins New Naturalist, 1949. 1st edn. 8vo. xiii,469 pp. 6 maps, 40 cold & 32 plain plates. Orig cloth.
(Henly) £24 [≈ $46]

North, Roger
- A Discourse of Fish and Fish-Ponds ... Dome by a Person of Honour. London: for E. Curll, 1713. 1st edn. 8vo. viii,79,[1] pp. Some worming in lower blank margs. Contemp sheep.
(Gaskell) £250 [≈ $479]

Nott, John
- The Cooks and Confectioners Dictionary: Or, The Accomplish'd Housewifes Companion ... The Third Edition with Additions. London: Rivington, 1726. Engvd frontis. Contemp panelled calf, hinges cracking, spine ends sl worn.
(C.R. Johnson) £475 [≈ $911]

Nutt, Frederic
- The Complete Confectioner... Fourth Edition, with Considerable Additions. New York: for Richard Scott, 1807. 1st Amer edn. 12mo. 92, index pp. Frontis. Some foxing. Contemp tree calf, spine chipped.
(Karmiole) $150 [≈ £78]

Nutt, Thomas
- Humanity to Honey Bees: or, Practical Directions for the Management of Honey Bees ... Wisbech: Leach, 1832. 1st edn. 8vo. xxvi, 240, 1 errata pp. 9 pp subscribers. Advt slip. Fldg plate, 9 text engvs. Orig blue bds, uncut, rebacked to style.
(Beech) £90 [≈ $172]
- Humanity to Honey Bees ... Fourth Edition,

revised, enlarged, and edited by the Rev. Thomas Clark. Wisbech: John Leach, for the author ... , 1837. 8vo. xxx,281 pp. Frontis, fldg plate, 10 w'engvd text ills. Few blank margs torn. Binder's cloth.
(Burmester) £60 [≈ $115]
- Humanity to Honey Bees: or, Practical Directions for the Management of Honey Bees ... Wisbech: 1839. 5th edn. 8vo. xxx,281 pp. Frontis, text figs. Somewhat used. Cloth, worn.
(Wheldon & Wesley) £50 [≈ $95]

Nuttall, G.C.
- Wild Flowers as They Grow. London: [1914]. 7 vols. 175 cold photo plates. Orig cloth, spines a little faded.
(Henly) £35 [≈ $67]

O'Connor, Andy
- Forty Years with Fighting Cocks. Goshen, New York: E.W. Rogers, 1929. 1st edn. 8vo. 327 pp. Ills. Orig bndg.
(Respess) $85 [≈ £44]

O'Dea, W.T.
- Handbook of the Collections illustrating Radio Communication - Its History and Development. London: HMSO, 1934. 8vo. 95 pp. 58 ills. Ex-lib.
(Gemmary) $60 [≈ £31]
- The Social History of Lighting. London: 1958. xiii,254 pp. 32 plates, 59 figs. Orig bndg.
(Whitehart) £25 [≈ $47]

O'Malley, C.D.
- Andreas Vesalius of Brussels, 1514-1564. Los Angeles: 1964. 8vo. 480 pp. Dw (worn).
(Goodrich) $85 [≈ £44]

O'Neil, John J.
- Prodigal Genius: The Life of Nikola Tesla. 1944. 1st edn. 326 pp. Orig bndg.
(New Wireless) $55 [≈ £29]

Oakley, Violet
- Samuel F.B. Morse. 1939. 1st edn. One of 500. 98 pp. 9 ills. Orig bndg.
(New Wireless) $55 [≈ £29]

Oestrelen, F.
- Medical Logic. Translated and Edited by G. Whitley. London: Sydenham Society, 1855. 8vo. 437 pp. Orig cloth, sunned & faded.
(Goodrich) $45 [≈ £23]

Ogilvie, Fergus Monteith
- Field Observations on British Birds. London: Selwyn & Blount, 1920. 1st edn. Cr 8vo. xvi,223 pp. 3 maps, 6 plates, 14 text ills. Orig qtr linen, trifle spotted. *(Gough)* £28 [≈ $53]

Ogle, John
- The Harveian Oration 1880. London: 1881. 8vo. 209 pp. Frontis. Orig bndg, front jnt split. Author's ALS inserted.
(Goodrich) **$95 [≈ £49]**
- The Harveian Oration 1880. London: 1881. 8vo. 209 pp. Frontis. Orig bndg, bd v stained.
(Goodrich) **$50 [≈ £26]**

Oliver, C.P.
- Meteors. Baltimore: Williams & Wilkins, 1925. 8vo. xvii,276 pp. 22 plates. Cloth. Dw.
(Gemmary) **$65 [≈ £34]**

Oliver, D., et al.
- Flora of Tropical Africa. London: 1868-1902. Vols 1-8 in 10 vols, all published except for vol 9 & part of vol 10 which were withdrawn by the publishers. 8vo. Cloth.
(Wheldon & Wesley) **£150 [≈ $287]**

Olmsted, J.M.D.
- Charles-Edouard Brown-Sequard. A Nineteenth Century Neurologist and Endocrinologist. Baltimore: 1946. 8vo. 253 pp. Frontis. Orig bndg.
(Goodrich) **$65 [≈ £33]**

Olson, Harry F.
- Dynamical Analogies. 1948. 1st edn, 5th printing. 196 pp. Orig bndg.
(New Wireless) **$55 [≈ £29]**
- Elements of Acoustical Engineering. 1949. 2nd edn. 539 pp. Orig bndg.
(New Wireless) **$80 [≈ £42]**

The Origin of Printing ...
- See Bowyer, William & Nichols, John (eds.).

Ornithologia Nova ...
- Ornithologia Nova; or a New General History of Birds, Extracted from the Best Authorities ... Birmingham: T. Warren, 1743-45. 1st edn. 2 vols. 12mo. 340; viii, 314, 6 pp. 2-cold titles. 347 w'engvd plates. Contemp tree sheep, jnts reprd.
(Gough) **£395 [≈ $758]**

Osler, Sir William
- Aequanimatis and Other Papers that have stood the Test of Time. Phila: 1906. 2nd edn. 475 pp. Orig bndg.
(Fye) **$200 [≈ £104]**
- An Alabama Student and other Biographical Essays. London: 1908. 1st edn, 1st printing. 334 pp. Orig cloth, fine. *(Fye)* **$225 [≈ £117]**
- An Alabama Student and other Biographical Essays. Oxford: 1908. 1st edn. 8vo. Orig cloth, some wear. *(Goodrich)* **$95 [≈ £49]**

- An Alabama Student and Other Biographical Addresses. London: 1909. 1st edn, 2nd printing. 334 pp. Orig bndg.
(Fye) **$100 [≈ £52]**
- An Alabama Student and other Biographical Essays. Oxford: 1929. [ix],334 pp. Frontis, plates. Dw. *(Whitehart)* **£45 [≈ $86]**
- Bibliotheca Osleriana. A Catalogue of Books illustrating the History of Medicine ... Oxford: 1929. 1st edn. Thick 4to. Stamp on title verso. Orig blue cloth, rubbed, inner front jnt taped. *(Goodrich)* **$495 [≈ £257]**
- Bibliotheca Osleriana. A Catalogue of Books illustrating the History of Medicine and Science ... Montreal: 1969. Reprint of the Oxford 1929 edn. Lge 4to. xli,792 pp. Orig bndg. *(Whitehart)* **£150 [≈ $287]**
- Counsels and Ideas ... Second Edition. OUP: 1929. 8vo. xxiv,355,[1] pp. Port, 1 plate. Orig cloth. Dw (internally reprd).
(Bow Windows) **£28 [≈ $53]**
- The Evolution of Modern Medicine. A Series of Lectures delivered at Yale University ... New Haven: 1921. 4to. 243 pp. Ex-lib. New cloth. *(Goodrich)* **$115 [≈ £59]**
- The Evolution of Modern Medicine. New Haven: 1921. 1st edn. 243 pp. Orig bndg.
(Fye) **$250 [≈ £130]**
- The Evolution of Modern Medicine. A Series of Lectures delivered at Yale University ... New Haven: 1921. 5th printing. 4to. xiv,[1], 243 pp. 107 text ills. Orig bndg.
(Whitehart) **£35 [≈ $67]**
- The Growth of Truth as Illustrated in the Discovery of the Circulation of the Blood. (Harveian Oration 1906). London: 1907. 8vo. 44 pp. Orig ptd wraps.
(Goodrich) **$145 [≈ £75]**
- The Growth of Truth as illustrated in the Discovery of the Circulation of the Blood. London: 1906. 44 pp. Orig ptd wraps, front wrapper almost detached, rear wrapper missing. *(Whitehart)* **£30 [≈ $57]**
- Lectures on Angina Pectoris and Allied States. New York: 1897. 1st edn. 160 pp. Sev lib stamps on title & verso. B'plate removed. Orig bndg, lib label on spine.
(Fye) **$400 [≈ £208]**
- Man's Redemption of Man. New York: 1913. 1st edn. 63 pp. Orig bndg. *(Fye)* **$90 [≈ £46]**
- The Old Humanities and New Sciences. London: 1919. 1st edn. 8vo. 32 pp. Orig red ptd wraps. *(Goodrich)* **$95 [≈ £49]**
- The Old Humanities and the New Science. Boston: 1920. 1st edn in book form. 64 pp. Orig bndg. *(Fye)* **$100 [≈ £52]**
- The Principles and Practice of Medicine.

New York: 1892. 1st edn. 1079 pp. Orig half leather, minor rubbing to spine extremities.
(Fye) **$1,000 [≈ £520]**
- The Principles and Practice of Medicine ... New York: Appleton, 1892. 1st edn, 2nd issue. Rebound in blue panelled calf gilt.
(Goodrich) **$595 [≈ £309]**
- The Principles and Practice of Medicine. Edinburgh: 1894. 1st British edn. 1079 pp. Ex-lib. Orig bndg, label removed from spine, some rubbing of extremities.
(Fye) **$400 [≈ £208]**
- The Principles and Practice of Medicine. New York: 1896. 2nd edn. 1143 pp. Half leather.
(Fye) **$250 [≈ £130]**
- The Principles and Practice of Medicine ... New York: Appleton, 1899. 3rd edn. Three qtr calf, worn, jnts weak.
(Goodrich) **$95 [≈ £49]**
- The Principles and Practice of Medicine. New York: 1899. 3rd edn. 1181 pp. Orig half leather, hd of spine chipped, moderate wear.
(Fye) **$100 [≈ £52]**
- The Principles and Practice of Medicine. Designed for the Use of Practitioners and Students of Medicine. Edinburgh & London: 1901. 4th edn. xviii,1182 pp. 21 charts, 11 ills. Cloth, sl worn, inner hinge split.
(Whitehart) **£38 [≈ $72]**
- The Principles and Practice of Medicine. New York: 1902. 4th edn. 1182 pp. Orig green cloth.
(Fye) **$150 [≈ £78]**
- The Principles and Practice of Medicine ... New York: Appleton, 1909. 7th edn. Orig cloth, recased, orig backstrip preserved.
(Goodrich) **$125 [≈ £65]**
- The Principles and Practice of Medicine. New York: 1910. 7th edn. 1143 pp. B'plate removed. Orig red cloth, gilt lib mark at ft of spine.
(Fye) **$150 [≈ £78]**
- The Principles and Practice of Medicine. London: 1917. 8th edn (with T. McCrael). xxiv, 1225 pp. Orig cloth, marked, sl worn, new endpapers.
(Whitehart) **£25 [≈ $47]**
- Records of the Lives of Ellen Free Pickton and Featherstone Lake Osler. Oxford: 1915. 4to. 275 pp. Ports, facss of letters. Water stains affecting outer margs of most ff. Minor rubbing.
(Fye) **$1,250 [≈ £651]**
- Science and Immorality. London: 1904. 12mo. 94 pp. Bds worn.
(Goodrich) **$45 [≈ £23]**
- Thomas Linacre. Cambridge: 1908. 1st edn. 64 pp. Plates. Orig bndg. *(Fye)* **£225 [≈ £117]**
- Thomas Linacre. Cambridge: UP, 1908. 1st edn. Sm 8vo. [vi],64 pp. 11 plates. Orig bds, spine sunned.
(Bookpress) **$300 [≈ £156]**

- A Way of Life. New York: 1914. 1st Amer edn. 62 pp. Orig bndg.   *(Fye)* **$100 [≈ £52]**

Osler, Sir William & McCrae, T.
- The Principles and Practice of Medicine designed for the Use of Practitioners and Students of Medicine. London: 1920. 9th edn. xxiv, 1168 pp. Port frontis. Cloth, sl worn.   *(Whitehart)* **£30 [≈ $57]**

Osler, Sir William & McCrae, T. (eds.)
- A System of Medicine. London: 1907-10. 1st edn. 7 vols. Ills. A few pp loose. Orig cloth, mrbld endpapers, 1 hinge sl cracked but firm, vol 7 cvr & page crnrs water stained.
(Whitehart) **£120 [≈ $230]**

Osmond, Floris
- Microscopic Analysis of Metals. Edited by J.E. Stead. London: 1904. 1st English edn. Cr 8vo. x,178 pp. 3 fldg plates, 90 ills. Sm stamp on title. Orig cloth gilt. *(Fenning)* **£45 [≈ $86]**

Ottley, D. (ed.)
- Observations on Surgical Diseases of the Head and Neck. Selected from the Memoirs of the Royal Academy of Surgery of France. London: Sydenham Society, 1848. x,293 pp. Occas foxing, sl dust staining. Orig cloth, dust stained & worn. *(Whitehart)* **£40 [≈ $76]**

Outlines of British Geology ...
- Outlines of British Geology, chiefly intended to illustrate the geology of England and Wales ... London: SPCK, 1850. 8vo. xii, 305 pp. Fldg hand cold map, fldg hand cold chart. Orig green cloth.   *(Claude Cox)* **£25 [≈ $47]**

Owen, Charles
- An Essay towards a Natural History of Serpents: In two Parts. London: for the author, 1742. 1st edn. 4to. xxiii,240,[12] pp. 7 full page ills. Errata, directions to binder, 15 pp subscribers. Rec half calf.
(Rootenberg) **$550 [≈ £286]**
- An Essay towards a Natural History of Serpents ... London: the author, 1742. 1st edn. 4to. xxiii, 240, [12] pp. Subscribers. 7 plates. Sev reprs, name clipped from title. Half calf.   *(Bookpress)* **$600 [≈ £312]**

Owen, G.A.
- A Treatise on Weighing Machines. London: Charles Griffin, 1922. 8vo. xii,202 pp. Plates, ills. Cloth.   *(Gemmary)* **$50 [≈ £26]**

Owen, J.A. (ed.)
- The Wild-Fowl and Sea-Fowl of Great

Britain. By a Son of the Marshes. London: Chapman & Hall, 1895. 1st edn. 326 pp. 12 plates. 1st few pp foxed. Orig pict cloth, sl bumped & faded.   *(Gough)* £30 [≃ $57]

Owen, Sir Richard

- Description of the Fossil Reptilia of South Africa in the Collection of the British Museum. London: BM, 1876. 4to. xii,88 pp. 70 plates (many fldg). Cloth.
  (Wheldon & Wesley) £360 [≃ $691]
- Description of the Skeleton of an Extinct Gigantic Sloth, Mylodon Robustus ... London: 1842. 4to. 176 pp. 24 plates. 1 plate spotted, tear in 1 plate reprd. Cloth, rebacked.   *(Baldwin)* £100 [≃ $191]
- A History of British Fossil Mammals and Birds. London: 1846. xliv,560 pp. 237 w'cuts. Half calf, sl rubbed.   *(Baldwin)* £48 [≃ $92]
- A History of British Fossil Reptiles. London: 1849-84. 4 vols. 4to. 286 plates. Sl foxing. Good ex-lib. Buckram, reprd.
  (Wheldon & Wesley) £650 [≃ $1,247]
- The Life of Richard Owen ... With an Essay ... by T.H. Huxley. London: Murray, 1894. 1st edn. 2 vols. 21 plates. Occas sl spotting. Orig green cloth gilt. *(Gough)* £65 [≃ $124]
- Odontography; or, a Treatise on the Comparative Anatomy of the Teeth ... London: 1840-45. 2 vols (text & atlas). xix, lxxiv, 655; 37 pp. 168 plates. Sm ink stamp on titles. Half mor, rather worn, cloth bds sl dust stained.   *(Whitehart)* £280 [≃ $537]
- On Parthenogenesis ... London: Van Voorst, 1849. 1st edn. 8vo. 76 pp. Minor foxing. Orig blue cloth, rebacked. Author's unsigned pres inscrptn to Henry Hallam.
  (Rootenberg) £300 [≃ £156]
- Palaeontology or a Systematic Summary of Extinct Animals and their Geological Relations. Edinburgh: 1860. 1st edn. xv,420 pp. 142 figs. Orig cloth
  (Baldwin) £50 [≃ $95]
- Palaeontology or a Systematic Summary of Extinct Animals and their Geological Relations. Edinburgh: 1860. 1st edn. xv,420 pp. 142 figs. Half calf.
  (Baldwin) £65 [≃ $124]
- Palaeontology or A Systematic Summary of Extinct Animals. Edinburgh: 1861. 2nd edn. xvi, 463 pp. Orig cloth, dull & dust stained, inner hinge cracked but firm.
  (Whitehart) £35 [≃ $67]

Ozanam, Jacques

- Recreations in Mathematics and Natural Philosophy ... Now Translated into English, and improved ... by Charles Hutton ...

London: Kearsley, 1803. 1st Hutton edn. 4 vols. 8vo. 97 fldg plates on 96 sheets. Contemp speckled calf, gilt spines. Earl of Stradbroke b'plate.
  (Bickersteth) £450 [≃ $863]

Packard, Francis

- History of Medicine in the United States. New York: Hoeber, 1931. 2 vols. 8vo. Lib stamp on titles. New cloth.
  (Goodrich) $185 [≃ £96]
- History of Medicine in the United States. New York: 1931. 1st edn. 2 vols. Orig bndg.
  (Fye) $350 [≃ £182]

Paddock, G.H.

- Catalogue of Shropshire Birds. Newport: 1897. 1st edn. [ii MS index],[vi], 104,[3 MS index] pp. 2 plates. Stamp on title. Orig green cloth gilt.   *(Gough)* £75 [≃ £143]

Padgett, Earl

- Plastic and Reconstructive Surgery. Springfield: 1948. 1st edn. 4to. 945 pp. Num ills. Orig bndg.   *(Fye)* $150 [≃ £78]

Page, John

- Receipts for Preparing and Compounding the Principal Medicines made Use of by the late Mr. Ward ... London: Henry Whitridge ..., 1763. 1st edn. 8vo. [2],33 pp. Disbound.
  (Young's) £200 [≃ $383]

Paget, Sir James

- Selected Essays and Addresses. Edited by Stephen Paget. London: 1902. 1st edn. 8vo. viii,445 pp. Few pale lib stamps. Orig cloth, lib label on upper cvr.
  (Bickersteth) £20 [≃ $38]

Paget, Stephen

- John Hunter, Man of Science and Surgeon (1728-1793). With an Introduction by Sir James Paget. London: 1897. 8vo. 272 pp. Red & black title. Frontis port. Orig bndg, uncut, sl rubbed.   *(Goodrich)* $45 [≃ £23]

Palmeiri, Luigi

- The Eruption of Vesuvius in 1872 ... With Notes ... by Robert Mallet. London: 1873. 1st edn. 8vo. [iv],148 pp. 8 plates. Orig cloth, recased, reprd, title inked on head & tail edges of leaves.   *(Bow Windows)* £60 [≃ $115]

Pancoast, Joseph

- A Treatise on Operative Surgery ... Phila: 1844. 1st edn. 4to. 380 pp. 80 plates. Occas foxing. Orig bndg, cvrs stained.
  (Fye) $1,250 [≃ £651]

Papaspyros, N.S.
- The History of Diabetes Mellitus. London: 1952. xv,100 pp. Sl foxing. Cloth, sl dusty.
(Whitehart) **£25 [≈ $47]**

Pare, Ambroise
- The Apologie and Treatise of ... Containing the Voyages made into Divers Places. With many of his Writings upon Surgery. Edited by Geoffrey Keynes. London: Falcon Books, 1951. 8vo. 4 plates. Orig cloth.
(Stewart) **£20 [≈ $38]**

Paris, John Ayrton
- The Life of Sir Humphry Davy .... London: 1831. 1st edn. 2 vols. 8vo. Port, facs MS. Stain in upper crnr vol 2. Old half calf, rebacked, crnrs worn.
(Bow Windows) **£105 [≈ $201]**
- The Life of Sir Humphry Davy. London: 1831. Large Paper. xv,547 pp. Frontis. Sm lib stamps on title verso. Occas sl marg foxing. Later half leather.
(Whitehart) **£125 [≈ $239]**
- Memoir of the Life and Scientific Labours of the late Rev. William Gregor ... London: 1818. 8vo. 37 pp. Disbound. Author's pres copy.
(Goodrich) **$65 [≈ £33]**
- Pharmacologia ... London: 1820. 3rd edn. lxx, 429 pp. Half roan & bds, sl rubbed.
(Whitehart) **£40 [≈ $76]**
- Pharmacologia ... London: 1820. 4th edn. lxx, 429 pp. New half leather gilt.
(Whitehart) **£50 [≈ $95]**
- Pharmacologia; Comprehending the Art of Prescribing upon Fixed and Scientific Principles; together with the History of Medicinal Substances. Fifth Edition, Enlarged. London: W. Phillips, 1822. 2 vols. 8vo. Occas foxing, damp stain end of vol 2. Orig bds, uncut.
(Gough) **£90 [≈ $172]**
- Pharmacologia. New York: 1828. 3rd Amer edn. 544 pp. Hand cold "dynameter". Orig bndg, front bd nearly detached.
(Fye) **$100 [≈ £52]**
- Pharmacologia ... London: 1843. 9th edn. xvi, 622 pp. Orig cloth, sl stained & worn.
(Whitehart) **£40 [≈ $76]**
- A Treatise on Diet ... London: Underwood, 1826. 1st edn. 8vo. vii,307 pp. 2 intl advt ff. Orig blue bds, paper spine, uncut, jnts cracked, lengthwise crack on spine, label chipped.
(Bickersteth) **£160 [≈ $307]**

Parker, George
- The Elementary Nervous System. Phila: 1919. 8vo. 229 pp. Ills. Orig bndg.
(Goodrich) **$95 [≈ £49]**

Parkes, Samuel
- The Chemical Catechism ... Tenth Edition, Carefully Corrected. London: for the author, & publ by Baldwin, Cradock & Joy, 1822. 8vo. Final advt leaf. Fldg frontis, 2 plates. Contemp half calf, worn but sound.
(Sanders) **£40 [≈ $76]**

Parkhurst, C.D.
- Dynamo and Motor Building for Amateurs. 1892. 1st edn. 163 pp. 71 ills. Orig bndg.
(New Wireless) **$65 [≈ £34]**

Parkin, John
- The Utilisation of the Sewage of Towns. London: John Churchill, 1862. viii,60,[7 advt] pp. Errata slip. Disbound.
(Wreden) **$55 [≈ £28]**

Parkinson, James
- Fossil Organic Remains. London: 1830. 2nd edn. viii,350 pp. 10 plates. Orig cloth.
(Baldwin) **£60 [≈ $115]**
- Organic Remains of a Former World. London: 1833. 2nd edn. 3 vols. 4to. 3 frontis (2 cold), 50 plates (49 hand cold). Vols 1 & 3 lack half-titles. Blind stamp on frontises & titles. Buckram. *(Baldwin)* **£600 [≈ $1,151]**

Parkinson, John
- Theatrum Botanicum, The Theater of Plants, or An Universall and Compleate Herball. London: 1640. Folio. xviii,1755 pp, errata leaf. Addtnl engvd title, over 2700 w'cut ills. A few edges strengthened. Some marginalia. 18th c calf, rebacked, new endpapers.
(Henly) **£1,250 [≈ $2,399]**
- Theatrum Botanicum. London: Thomas Cotes, 1640. 1st edn. Folio. [xx],1746,[2] pp. Water stain to last few ff. Contemp calf bds, rebacked. *(Bookpress)* **$2,750 [≈ £1,432]**

Parnell, E.A. (ed.)
- Applied Chemistry in Manufactures, Arts, and Domestic Economy. Volume I [only, of 2]. London: 1844. xvi,453 pp. 23 fabric samples, 40 figs. Occas sl foxing. Half leather, backstrip relaid on cloth reback.
(Whitehart) **£60 [≈ $115]**

Parnell, R.
- The Grasses of Britain. London: [1842-] 1845. 2 vols. Roy 8vo. xxvii,xxi,311 pp. 142 plates. Orig cloth, reprd. Comprises Grasses of Scotland 1842; Grasses of Britain 1845.
(Wheldon & Wesley) **£60 [≈ $115]**

Parry, Thomas
- On Diet, with Its Influence on Man. London: 1844. 1st edn. 119 pp. Orig bndg.
(Fye) **$100 [≈ £52]**

Parsons, William Barclay
- Robert Fulton and the Submarine. New York: Columbia UP, 1922. 1st edn. xiii,154 pp. 20 ills. Orig dec cloth gilt.
(Parmer) **$95 [≈ £49]**

Partington, Charles Frederick
- An Historical and Descriptive Account of the Steam Engine ... London: 1822. xvi,187,90 pp. 8 fldg plates inc frontis. Sl dust staining & browning. Orig bds, new cloth spine.
(Whitehart) **£80 [≈ $153]**
- A Manual of Natural and Experimental Philosophy ... London: for J. taylor, 1828. 1st edn. 2 vols. 8vo. 304; 432 pp. 2 frontis, 2 fldg plates, num text ills. Contemp half mor, extremities rubbed, sl damp stains.
(Chapel Hill) **$175 [≈ £91]**

Partington, J.R.
- A History of Chemistry. Volume Three. London: Macmillan, 1962. Med 8vo. Text ills. Orig bndg. *(Georges)* **£40 [≈ $76]**

Pasteur, L.
- Studies on Fermentation. The Diseases of Beer, their Causes, and the means of preventing them. London: 1879. 1st English edn. xv,418 pp. 12 plates, 85 text ills. Sl damp staining of a few pp at ends, mostly marginal. New cloth, incorrectly titled.
(Whitehart) **£85 [≈ $163]**

Patten, C.J.
- The Aquatic Birds of Great Britain and Ireland. London: 1906. Plates, num text ills. Orig cloth, sl rubbed, inner hinge sprung.
(Grayling) **£60 [≈ $115]**

Patterson, Arthur H.
- Norfolk Bird Haunts in A.D. 1755. Holt: Rounce & Wortley, 1930. 1st edn. 8vo. 103 pp. 18 ills. Orig dec cloth.
(Gough) **£35 [≈ $67]**

Patton, W.S. & Evans, A.M.
- Insects, Ticks, Mites and Venomous Animals of Medical and Veterinary Importance. Croydon: 1929-31. 2 vols. 117 plates, 761 figs. Orig pict cloth. *(Whitehart)* **£40 [≈ $76]**

Paul, Constantin
- Diagnosis and Treatment of Diseases of the Heart. New York: 1884. 1st English translation. 335 pp. Orig bndg.
(Fye) **$50 [≈ £26]**

Pavlov, Ivan P.
- Conditioned Reflexes. An Investigation of the Physiological Activity of the Cerebral Cortex. Translated and Edited by G.V. Anrep. Oxford: 1928. 2nd imp. 8vo. 430 pp. Ills. Orig bndg. *(Goodrich)* **$75 [≈ £39]**
- Conditioned Reflexes. London: (1927) 1940. xv, 430 pp. 18 figs. Name stamp on title. Orig bndg. *(Whitehart)* **£40 [≈ $76]**
- Lectures on Conditioned Reflexes ... Translated from the Russian by W. Horsley Gantt. New York: 1928. 1st English translation. 414 pp. Orig bndg.
(Fye) **$100 [≈ £52]**
- The Work of the Digestive Glands. London: 1910. 2nd English edn. 266 pp. Orig bndg, fine. *(Fye)* **$150 [≈ £78]**

Paxton's Flower Garden ...
- Paxton's Flower Garden. By J. Lindley and J. Paxton. Second Edition by T. Baines. London: 1882-84. 3 vols. 4to. 108 colour-printed plates. Sl foxing of text. Stamps on endpapers. Marg of 1 plate sl defective. Orig dec cloth, minor wear to 1 jnt.
(Wheldon & Wesley) **£500 [≈ $959]**

Paxton, Sir Joseph & Lindley, Professor
- Paxton's Flower Garden. [Revised by Thomas Baines]. Second Edition. London: Cassell, Petter & Galpin, 1882-84. 3 vols. 108 chromolitho plates. Foredges & prelims sl spotted. Orig pict blue cloth gilt, t.e.g., fine.
(Gough) **£1,100 [≈ $2,111]**

Payne, Joseph
- English Medicine in the Anglo-Saxon Times. Oxford: 1904. 1st edn. 162 pp. Plates. Orig bndg. *(Fye)* **$100 [≈ £52]**

Peach, B.N. & Horne, J.
- Chapters on the Geology of Scotland. London: 1930. xvi,232 pp. Map, 18 plates, 27 figs. Orig cloth. *(Baldwin)* **£45 [≈ $86]**
- The Silurian Rocks of Britain. Volume I, Scotland. London: 1899. xviii,749 pp. 3 maps, 27 plates, 121 figs. Orig cloth.
(Baldwin) **£95 [≈ $182]**

Pearsall, W.H.
- Mountains and Moorlands. London: Collins New Naturalist, 1950. 1st edn. 8vo. xv,312 pp. 32 cold & 32 plain plates. Orig cloth.
(Henly) **£12 [≈ $23]**

Pearsall, W.H. & Pennington, Winifred
- The Lake District. London: Collins New Naturalist, 1973. 1st edn. 8vo. 320 pp. 32 plates. Orig cloth. Dw. *(Henly)* £32 [≈ $61]
- The Lake District. A Landscape History. London: Collins New Naturalist, 1973. 1st edn. 8vo. 320 pp. 32 plates. B'plate. Orig cloth gilt. Dw, mint. *(Hollett)* £45 [≈ $86]

Pearson, Karl
- The Chances of Death and Other Studies in Evolution. London: 1897. 2 vols. Figs. Top marg of both frontises & titles water stained. Cloth, partly unopened, faded, sl marked. *(Whitehart)* £60 [≈ $115]
- The Life, Letters and Labours of Francis Galton. Cambridge: 1914. 1st edn. 3 vols in 4. Rebound in buckram. *(Fye)* $200 [≈ £104]
- Life, Letters and Labours of Francis Galton. Volume I. Birth 1822 to Marriage 1853. Cambridge: 1914. Lge 4to. xxiv,242 pp. Port frontis, 66 plates. 5 pedigrees missing from back pocket & replaced by Fingerprint plate. Cloth, marked. *(Whitehart)* £60 [≈ $115]

Pearson, W.H.
- The Hepaticae of the British Isles, being Figures and Descriptions of all the known Species. London: 1902. 2 vols. Roy 8vo. 228 plain plates. Orig cloth. *(Wheldon & Wesley)* £100 [≈ $191]

Pease, A.E.
- The Book of the Lion. London: 1914. 2nd printing. 293 pp. Illust. Orig bndg. *(Trophy Room)* $200 [≈ £104]

Peasonton, Augustus J.
- Influence of the Blue Ray of the Sunlight and of the Blue Colour of the Sky in Developing Animal and Vegetable Life ... Phila: 1877. 8vo. 38,185 pp. Frontis. Orig dark blue cloth gilt, spine discold. *(Schoyer)* $65 [≈ £33]

Pechey, J.
- The Complete Herbal of Physical Plants ... London: 1707. 2nd edn. Sm 8vo. [viii],1-248, 193-336, 331-349, [29] pp, complete. Some mostly marg worm of 1st 20 ff, loss of a few letters. Few sl stains, few blank crnrs sl defective. Mod calf. *(Wheldon & Wesley)* £180 [≈ $345]

Peddie, Alexander
- The Manufacturer, Weaver and Warper's Assistant, containing a New and Correct Set of Tables, Drafts, Cordings, Arithmetical Rules and Examples ... Glasgow: for W.

Sommerville, 1818. 5th edn. 24mo. 292 pp. Frontis, ills. New half calf. *(Bookpress)* $235 [≈ £122]

Peirce, Benjamin
- Physical and Celestial Mathematics; A System of Analytic Mechanics. Boston: Little & Brown, 1855. 1st edn. 4to. xxxix,[1],496 pp. 2 title pages. Errata. Subscribers. Fldg plate, num text diags. Orig cloth, rubbed. Thomas Hill b'plate. *(Rootenberg)* $400 [≈ £208]

Pemberton, Christopher Robert
- A Practical Treatise on Various Diseases of the Abdominal Viscera. First American Edition. Worcester: George A. Trumball ..., 1815. 8vo. xi,[i],202 pp. 2 plates. Few ff sl browned. Contemp calf, dull, front hinge cracked. *(Hemlock)* $175 [≈ £91]

Pemberton, Henry
- The Dispensatory of the Royal College of Physicians, London ... London: 1748. 2nd edn. x, 414 pp. Contemp calf, gilt borders, mor label, edges of crnrs worn. *(Whitehart)* £135 [≈ $259]
- A View of Sir Isaac Newton's Philosophy. London: S. Palmer, 1728. 1st edn. 4to. [48], 407 pp. 12 fldg plates. Qtr leather, rebacked. *(Gemmary)* $750 [≈ £390]
- A View of Sir Isaac Newton's Philosophy. London: S. Palmer, 1728. 4to. Subscribers. 12 plates, num text decs by Pine. Few sm marg worm holes. Contemp calf, rebacked. Anon. *(Waterfield's)* £450 [≈ $863]
- A View of Sir Isaac Newton's Philosophy. Dublin: re-printed by & for John Hyde, 1728. 44, 333 pp. 12 fldg plates. Contemp calf, red label. *(C.R. Johnson)* £425 [≈ $815]

Penfield, Wilder
- The Second Career with Other Essays and Addresses. Boston: 1963. 8vo. 189 pp. Dw. *(Goodrich)* $35 [≈ £18]

Penfield, Wilder & Erickson, Theodore
- Epilepsy and Cerebral Localization. Springfield: 1941. 1st edn. 623 pp. Orig bndg. *(Fye)* $250 [≈ £130]

Penfield, Wilder & Jasper, Herbert
- Epilepsy and the Functional Anatomy of the Human Brain. Boston: 1954. 8vo. 896 pp. Ex-lib. Orig bndg, some wear. *(Goodrich)* $75 [≈ £39]
- Epilepsy and the Functional Anatomy of the Human Brain. Boston: 1954. 1st edn. 896 pp.

Orig bndg. *(Fye)* **$175 [≈£91]**

Penfield, Wilder & Kristiansen, K.
- Epileptic Seizure Patterns. A Study of the Localizing Value of Initial Phenomena in Focal Cortical Seizures. Springfield: 1951. 8vo. 103 pp. Ills. Dw. *(Goodrich)* **$75 [≈£39]**

Penfield, Wilder & Roberts, L.
- Speech and Brain Mechanisms. Princeton: 1959. 8vo. 286 pp. Ills. Dw (worn & chipped).
 (Goodrich) **$65 [≈£33]**

Pengelly, William
- A Memoir of William Pengelly of Torquay, F.R.S. Geologist, with a Selection from his Correspondence. Edited by his Daughter Hester Pengelly ... London: 1897. 1st edn. 8vo. x, 341 pp. Port (spotted, sm tear), 10 ills. Orig cloth, marked. Editor's pres inscrptn.
 (Bow Windows) **£60 [≈$115]**

Pennant, Thomas
- Arctic Zoology. London: 1792. 2nd edn. 3 vols. 4to. Frontis, 2 title vignettes, 23 plates. Lacks the 2 fldg maps. Without the 2 unnumbered plates sometimes found. Some offsetting from plates. 2 sm tears reprd. Contemp calf, worn, rebacked, jnts sl weak.
 (Wheldon & Wesley) **£400 [≈$767]**
- British Zoology. Warrington & London: 1776-77. 4th edn. 4 vols. 8vo. Engvd titles (vol 2 title comprises plate 60 of Birds), fldg music plate, 280 plates. Contemp calf, jnts beginning to crack.
 (Wheldon & Wesley) **£180 [≈$345]**
- British Zoology. London: 1812. 4 vols. Num engvd plates. Sl foxing. Contemp diced calf gilt, 2 hinges weakening.
 (Grayling) **£220 [≈$422]**
- British Zoology. A New Edition. London: 1812. 4 vols. 8vo. 4 addtnl engvd titles, 293 plates. Calf, rebacked. *(Henly)* **£200 [≈$383]**
- Genera of Birds. London: for B. White, 1781. 2nd (1st 4to) edn. Post 4to. [iv], [xxvi], (70) pp. Engvd title & 15 plates, all hand cold in a later hand. Washed & reprd, new tissue guards. Rec 18th c style mor.
 (Ash) **£300 [≈$575]**

Penning, W.H.
- A Text Book of Field Geology ... Second Edition, Revised and Enlarged. London: 1879. 8vo. [xii],319,[1] pp. Cold plate, text figs. Few marks. Orig cloth, hd spine v sl fingered, upper cvr trifle marked.
 (Bow Windows) **£35 [≈$67]**

Pepper, J.H.
- The Boy's Playbook of Science ... New Edition. London: 1864. 8vo. viii,440 pp. 4 plates, ca 400 text engvs. Pres inscrptn on flyleaf. Orig cloth gilt, hd of spine v sl rubbed. *(Bow Windows)* **£25 [≈$47]**
- The Playbook of Metals. London: Routledge, 1866. Cr 8vo. viii,504 pp. Frontis, 300 w'cut ills. Cloth, sl worn. *(Gemmary)* **$75 [≈£39]**

Pepper, William, et al.
- An American Text-Book of the Theory and Practice of Medicine. Phila: 1893. 2 vols. 8vo. Orig cloth. *(Goodrich)* **$95 [≈£49]**
- A System of Practical Medicine by American Authors. Phila: 1885-86. 5 vols. 8vo. Orig sheep, worn. *(Goodrich)* **$125 [≈£65]**
- A System of Practical Medicine by American Authors. Phila: 1885. 1st edn. 5 vols. Orig leather. *(Fye)* **$250 [≈£130]**

Percival, A.S.
- The Prescribing of Spectacles. Bristol: 1910. 159 pp. 24 figs. Cloth, sl marked.
 (Whitehart) **£25 [≈$47]**

Percivall, W.
- A Series of Elementary Lectures on the Veterinary Art ... London: 1823. xxxvi,377 pp. Occas foxing. Orig three qtr sheep & mrbld bds, sl worn. *(Whitehart)* **£50 [≈$95]**

Percy, J.
- The Metallurgy of Lead. London: Murray, 1870. 8vo. xvi,567 pp. 155 text figs. Fine ex-lib. Half leather. Sl worn.
 (Gemmary) **$150 [≈£78]**

Pereira, Jonathan
- Lectures on Polarized Light; delivered before the Pharmaceutical Society ... London: Longman ..., 1843. 1st edn. 8vo. 110,30 advt pp. Orig cloth. *(Chapel Hill)* **$250 [≈£130]**
- A Treatise on Food and Diet: with Observations on the Dietetical Regimen suited for Disordered States of the Digestive Organs ... London: Longmans, 1843. 1st edn. 32 pp ctlg dated June 1843. Contemp cloth, sl rubbed & marked. *(Jarndyce)* **£95 [≈$182]**

Perkins, Walter Frank
- Southampton University Library. Catalogue of the Walter Frank Perkins Agricultural Library. Southampton: 1961. One of 500. Med 8vo. Port. Orig bndg.
 (Georges) **£50 [≈$95]**

Perrault, C.
- The Natural History of Animals ... Done into English by a Fellow of the Royal Society [A. Pitfield] ... London: 1702. 3rd English edn of the 'Parisian Memoirs'. Folio. [x], 3-267, [13], 40 pp. Frontis, 35 plates. Some wear & tear. Calf, rebacked.
(Wheldon & Wesley) **£180 [≈ $345]**

Perrin, Mrs H. & Boulger, G.S.
- British Flowering Plants. London: 1914. One of 1000. 4 vols. Roy 4to. 300 cold plates. Buckram gilt.   *(Henly)* **£150 [≈ $287]**

Perring, F.H. & Walters, S.M. (eds.)
- Atlas of the British Flora. London: 1962. 4to. 432 pp. Overlays. Cloth, used, rather crudely rebacked.   *(Wheldon & Wesley)* **£30 [≈ $57]**

Perring, F.H., Sell, P.D. & Walters, S.M.
- A Flora of Cambridgeshire. London: 1964. Cr 8vo. xvi,366 pp. 9 plates, 5 charts, 4 tables. Cloth.
(Wheldon & Wesley) **£20 [≈ $38]**

Perrins, C.M.
- British Tits. London: Collins New naturalist, 1980. 2nd edn. 8vo. 304 pp. 16 plates. Orig cloth. Dw.   *(Henly)* **£15 [≈ $28]**

Perry, J.
- Spinning Tops. London: SPCK, 1901. Cr 8vo. 136 pp. 58 text figs. Cloth.
(Gemmary) **$25 [≈ £13]**

Petch, C.P. & Swann, E.L.
- Flora of Norfolk. London: 1968. 8vo. 288 pp. Cold ills. Orig cloth. Dw.
(Henly) **£28 [≈ $53]**

Petersen, W.
- The Patient and the Weather. Ann Arbor: 1934-38. 7 vols. Num figs. Names & b'plates. Cloth, sl dull.   *(Whitehart)* **£65 [≈ $124]**

Peterson, Frederick & Haines, Walter
- A Text-Book of Legal Medicine and Toxicology. Phila: 1903. 1st edn. 2 vols. 730; 825 pp. Chromolitho & other plates. Orig bndgs.   *(Fye)* **$100 [≈ £52]**

Pettey, George
- The Narcotic Drug Diseases and Allied Ailments: Pathology, Pathogenesis, and Treatment. Phila: 1913. 1st edn. 516 pp. Orig bndg.   *(Fye)* **$75 [≈ £39]**

Pettigrew, Thomas
- On Superstitions connected with the History and Practice of Medicine and Surgery. London: 1844. 1st edn. 167 pp. Orig bndg.
(Fye) **$200 [≈ £104]**

Pfaundler, M. & Schlossmann, A.
- The Diseases of Children. Phila: 1908. 1st English translation. 4 vols. 440; 619; 552; 543 pp. Num cold & photo plates. Orig bndg, fine.   *(Fye)* **$150 [≈ £78]**

Pharmacopoeia ...
- Pharmacopoeia Londinensis of 1618. Reproduced in Facsimile with an Historical Introduction by G. Urdang. Madison: 1944. vii, 299 pp. Binder's cloth.
(Whitehart) **£40 [≈ $76]**
- The Pharmacopoeia of the United States of America. Boston: 1820. 1st edn. 272 pp. Orig leather, rebacked, front bd detached.
(Fye) **$350 [≈ £182]**
- Pharmacopoeias .... see also under British Pharmacopoeia; Culpeper, N.; Healde, T.; Phillips, R.; Radcliffe, J.; Waring, E.

Phelps, Charles
- Injuries of the Brain and its Membrane from External Violence. With a Special Study of Pistol-Shot Wounds of the Head ... New York: 1900. 2nd edn. 8vo. 602 pp. 49 ills. Orig bndg.   *(Goodrich)* **$75 [≈ £39]**

Philip, A.P.W.
- A Treatise on Indigestion, and its Consequences, called Nervous and Bilious Complaints ... London: 1821. xiv,363 pp. Interleaved with contemp notes. Orig half calf, backstrip relaid. Author's inscrptn.
(Whitehart) **£85 [≈ $163]**

Phillips, H.J.
- Gold Assaying - A Practical Handbook. London: Crosby Lockwood, 1904. 8vo. xii,138 pp. 62 text figs. Cloth.
(Gemmary) **$65 [≈ £33]**

Phillips, J.
- Geology of Oxford and the Valley of the Thames. London: 1871. 8vo. xxiv,523,15 advt pp. 2 geological maps, 2 hand cold sections, 2 vertical sections, 11 plates, 210 text ills. Cloth, backstrip relaid.
(Henly) **£85 [≈ $16,412]**
- Memoirs of William Smith, LL.D. Author of the "Map of the Strata of England and Wales". London: 1844. viii,150,8 advt pp. 18 plates & w'cuts, frontis port. Lib stamp on

title. Lacks part of rear endpaper. Orig cloth, uncut, backstrip relaid.
(Baldwin) **£150 [≈ $287]**
- A Treatise on Geology, forming the Article under that head in the Seventh Edition of the Encyclopaedia Britannica. London: 1837. 8vo. vi,295,4 pp. 2 fldg plates, text figs. Cloth, rebacked.   *(Henly)* **£48 [≈ $92]**

Phillips, J.A.
- The Mining and Metallurgy of Gold and Silver. London: 1867. xix,532 pp. Frontis & 8 plates, 84 text figs. Ink sgntr on title. Cloth, rather marked & sl worn, orig backstrip relaid.   *(Whitehart)* **£45 [≈ $86]**
- A Treatise on Ore Deposits. London: Macmillan, 1884. 8vo. xvi,651 pp. 95 text figs. Cloth.   *(Gemmary)* **$60 [≈ £31]**

Phillips, John
- The Geology of Oxford. London: 1871. xxiv, 523 pp. Cold map, 6 plates, 207 figs. Few plates sl stained in 1 crnr. Orig cloth.
(Baldwin) **£65 [≈ $124]**
- A Guide to Geology. Third Edition. London: 1836. Sm 8vo. xiv,186 pp, advt leaf. 3 plates (rather foxed). Sm marks. Orig cloth, sl marked.   *(Bow Windows)* **£40 [≈ $76]**
- Illustrations of the Geology of Yorkshire ... [Part I] The Yorkshire Coast ... Part II. The Mountain Limestone District. London: 1829-36. 1st edn. 2 vols. 4to. xvi, 192; xx, 253 pp. 2 maps, 11 sections, 36 plates (sl foxed). Contemp calf gilt, a.e.g., rebacked.
(Baldwin) **£475 [≈ $911]**
- Illustrations of the Geology of Yorkshire ... [Part I] The Yorkshire Coast. London: 1829. 1st edn. 4to. Map, 9 sections, 14 plates. Title sl soiled, plates sl foxed. Half calf.
(Baldwin) **£240 [≈ $460]**
- Illustrations of the Geology of Yorkshire ... London: 1835-36. 2nd edn Part I, 1st edn Part II. 2 vols. 4to. xvi,192; xx,253 pp. 2 maps, 11 sections, 36 plates. Contemp half calf & mrbld bds.   *(Baldwin)* **£400 [≈ $767]**
- Illustrations of the Geology of Yorkshire ... Part II. The Mountain Limestone District. London: Murray, 1836. 1st edn. 4to. xx,253 pp. 25 plates. Rather fingered, soiled & spotted, some reprs. New polished half calf gilt.   *(Hollett)* **£95 [≈ $182]**
- The Rivers, Mountains and Sea-Coast of Yorkshire. London: 1855. 2nd edn. xv,316 pp. 36 plates inc map. Orig cloth.
(Baldwin) **£80 [≈ $153]**

Phillips, R.
- Translation of the Pharmacopoeia of the

Royal College of Physicians of London 1836. London: 1837. 2nd edn. xxiii,421 pp. Occas foxing. Half leather, v worn.
(Whitehart) **£35 [≈ $67]**
- Translation of the Pharmacopoeia of the Royal College of Physicians of London 1836. London: 1837. 2nd edn. xxiii,421 pp. New cloth.   *(Whitehart)* **£40 [≈ $76]**

Phillips, Sir Richard
- Essays on the Proximate Mechanical Causes of the General Phenomena of the Universe. London: Jas. Adlard, sold by J. Souter, 1818. 1st edn. 12mo. viii,96 pp. Orig grey wraps, ptd side-label, backstrip worn.
(Burmester) **£36 [≈ $69]**

Phillips, William
- An Elementary Introduction to the Knowledge of Mineralogy. New York: Collins & Co, 1818. 8vo. x,xxxiv,246 pp. Rebound in buckram.
(Gemmary) **$150 [≈ £78]**
- An Elementary Introduction to the Knowledge of Mineralogy. London: W. Phillips, 1823. 3rd edn. Cr 8vo. cxx,409 pp. Fldg plate, ills. Half leather.
(Gemmary) **$150 [≈ £78]**
- An Elementary Introduction to Mineralogy. London: Longman ..., 1852. 8vo. xii,700 pp. 647 text figs. Cloth. *(Gemmary)* **$175 [≈ £91]**
- An Outline of Mineralogy and Geology ... London: 1815. 1st edn. Sm 8vo. [xii],193,[1 blank] pp. 4 plates (2 hand cold). Stain at ft of frontis, some foxing. Old half calf, jnts cracked, spine ends chipped.
(Bow Windows) **£165 [≈ $316]**

Phillips, William W.A.
- Manual of the Mammals of Ceylon. Ceylon & London: Ceylon Journal of Science, 1935. Only edn. 4to. xxviii,373 pp. Fldg map, 38 plates, 55 ills. Orig cloth.
(Fenning) **£95 [≈ $182]**

Pickering, W.H.
- A Popular Atlas of the Moon. Cambridge, MA: 1903. 1st edn. Lge 4to. v,39 pp. 86 photo & 4 other plates. Half cloth & bds, sl worn.   *(Whitehart)* **£120 [≈ $230]**

Piesse, G.W. Septimus
- The Art of Perfumery. London: Longman ..., 1855. 1st edn. Cr 8vo. xiv,[288],24 pp. Plates, w'engvs in text. Sl foxing at extremities, a few faint marks. Orig pict cloth gilt.
(Ash) **£150 [≈ $287]**
- The Art of Perfumery ... Second Edition.

London: Longman ..., 1856. 8vo. xvi,352 pp.
W'engvs. Advt endpapers. Orig blue cloth
gilt, recased.   (Beech) £50 [≈ $95]

Pike, W.T. (ed.)

- British Engineers and Allied Professions in
the Twentieth Century: Contemporary
Biographies. Brighton: W.T. Pike, 1910.
Thick 4to. 348,3 pp. Num ills. Orig elab gilt
mor.   (Bell) £50 [≈ $95]

Pilcher, Lewis Stephen

- A List of Books by Some of the Old Masters
of Medicine and Surgery together with Books
on the History of Medicine and on Medical
Biography in the Possession of ... Brooklyn:
1918. One of 250. 8vo. 201 pp. Ills. Orig
bndg.   (Goodrich) $145 [≈ £75]

Pilkington, James

- The Artist's Guide and Mechanic's Own
Book, embracing the Portion of Chemistry
applicable to the Mechanic Arts ... Boston:
Sanborn, Carter & Bazin, 1856. 1st edn. 8vo.
490 pp. Frontis, sev text ills. Orig cloth, hd of
spine sl worn.   (Gough) £35 [≈ $67]

Pinches, T.G. & Strassmaier, J.N.

- Late Babylonian Astronomical and Related
Texts ... Providence: Brown UP, 1955.
Oblong 4to. lvi,272 pp. Orig cloth. Dw (sl
soiled).   (Karmiole) $65 [≈ £33]

Pirrie, William

- The Principles and Practice of Surgery.
London: 1852. 1st edn. 952 pp. 248 ills. Orig
bndg.   (Fye) $150 [≈ £78]

Planck, M.

- Theory of Heat. Being Volume V of
"Introduction to Theoretical Physics".
Translated by H.L. Brose. London: 1932. 1st
English edn. viii,301 pp. A few figs. Dw.
                  (Whitehart) £48 [≈ $92]

- Theory of Light. Being Volume IV of
"Introduction to Theoretical Physics".
Translated by H.L. Brose. London: 1932. 1st
English edn. vii,216 pp. A few figs. Dw.
                  (Whitehart) £35 [≈ $67]

- Treatise on Thermodynamics. New York:
Longmans, Green, 1903. 8vo. xii,272 pp. Ex-
lib. Cloth.   (Gemmary) $125 [≈ £65]

Planting ...

- Planting and Ornamental Gardening,
Planting and Rural Ornament ... see
Marshall, William.

Plat, Hugh

- The Garden of Eden: or, an Accurate
Description of all Flowers and Fruits now
growing in England ... London: Leake, 1675.
6th edn. 2 parts in one vol. Sm 8vo. [xxvi],
148, [xvi], 159 pp. Contemp sheep, rebacked
& recrnrd.   (Bookpress) $650 [≈ £338]

Pluche, Noel Antoine

- The History of the Heavens, considered
according to the Notions of the Poets and
Philosophers, compared with the Doctrines of
Moses. Translated ... by J.B. De Freval.
London: 1740. 1st edn in English. 2 vols. 8vo.
25 plates. Orig calf, rubbed, jnt cracked.
                  (Bickersteth) £110 [≈ $211]

- Spectacle de la Nature: or, Nature Display'd
... Translated from the Original French, By
Mr. Humphreys. The Fourth Edition.
London: L. Francklin, Davis ..., 1740. 7 vols.
8vo. 7 frontis, num plates. Contemp calf, sl
worn. Anon.   (Finch) £325 [≈ $623]

- Spectacle de la Nature: or, Nature Display'd.
London: L. Davis ..., 1770. 7 vols. Num fldg
plates. Contemp calf.
                  (Bookpress) $850 [≈ £442]

Plues, Margaret

- British Ferns; An Introduction to the Study
of the Ferns, Lycopods and Equiseta
indigenous to the British Isles... London:
Reeve, [ca 1870]. x,281,16 advt pp. 16 hand
cold plates. Orig pict green cloth gilt.
                  (Gough) £35 [≈ $67]

- British Grasses. London: 1867. Cr 8vo. viii,
307 pp. 16 cold plates. Cloth, trifle used.
              (Wheldon & Wesley) £20 [≈ $38]

- British Grasses; An Introduction to the Study
of the Gramineae of Great Britain and
Ireland. London: Reeve, [1867]. 1st edn. viii,
307,16 advt pp. 16 hand cold plates. Occas sl
foxing. Orig pict green cloth gilt.
                  (Gough) £35 [≈ $67]

- Rambles in Search of Flowerless Plants.
London: Journal of Horticulture, 1864. 1st
edn. viii,317 pp. 20 plates (some cold by
hand). Orig green cloth, gilt spine, sl rubbed.
                  (Gough) £40 [≈ $76]

- Rambles in Search of Wild Flowers. London:
1879. 3rd edn. 8vo. xii,364 pp. 16 cold plates.
Cloth.   (Wheldon & Wesley) £18 [≈ $34]

Plummer, H.C.

- An Introductory Treatise on Dynamical
Astronomy. Cambridge: 1918. xix,343 pp.
Orig cloth.   (Whitehart) £25 [≈ $47]

Poincare, H.
- Science and Hypothesis. London: Walter Scott, 1907. Cr 8vo. xxxvii,244 pp. Cloth, sl shaken.   *(Gemmary)* **$60 [≈ £31]**

Poinsot, Louis
- Outlines of a New Theory of Rotary Motion. Translated by C. Whitley. Cambridge: 1834. iv,96 pp. 28 figs on fldg plates. Lib stamp on title, b'plate on verso. Sl foxing. Orig cloth, rebacked.   *(Whitehart)* **£40 [≈ $76]**

Pointer, John
- A Rational Account of the Weather ... Second Edition corrected and much enlarg'd ... added, Three Essays ... London: for Aaron Ward, 1738. 8vo. Half-title. Contemp calf, rebacked, crnrs reprd.
                    (Georges) **£200 [≈ $383]**

Pole, Thomas
- The Anatomical Instructor ... Preparing and Preserving the different Parts of the Human Body, and of Quadrupeds ... London: the author, Darton & Co, 1790. 1st edn. 8vo. lxxx, [xii],304, [xv] pp, errata leaf. 10 plates (spotted). 19th c half mor, rubbed.
                    (Bickersteth) **£110 [≈ $211]**
- The Anatomical Instructor. London: the author & W. Darton, 1790. 1st edn. 8vo. lxxx, [xii], 304,[15] pp. 10 plates. 1 index leaf defective. Contemp tree calf, hinges starting to crack.   *(Bookpress)* **$450 [≈ £234]**
- The Anatomical Instructor; or, an Illustration of the Modern and Most Approved Methods of Preparing and Preserving the Different Parts of the Human Body and of Quadrupeds ... London: 1790. 8vo. lxxx, [6],304,[7] pp. 10 plates. Calf, jnts split.
                    (Goodrich) **$125 [≈ £65]**

Pollard, E., Hopper, M.D. & Moore, N.W.
- Hedges. London: Collins New Naturalist, 1974. 1st edn. 8vo. 256 pp. 20 plates. Orig cloth. Dw.   *(Henly)* **£45 [≈ $86]**

Pollard, H.B.C. & Barclay-Smith, Phyllis
- British and American Game-Birds. London: Eyre & Spottiswoode, 1945. 1st edn. Sm 4to. x,48 pp. 20 cold plates by Philip Rickman. Orig cloth, bumped & marked. Dw (sl chipped).   *(Gough)* **£50 [≈ $95]**

Pontey, William
- The Forest Pruner; or, Timber Owner's Assistant: a Treatise on the Training or Management of British Timber Trees ... Fourth Edition. Leeds: 1826. xxiii,248,

viii,[i], [3 advt] pp. 9 plates. Orig bds, uncut, rebacked.   *(Spelman)* **£45 [≈ $86]**

Poor, C.L.
- The Solar System. A Study of Recent Observations. London: 1908. x,310 pp. Frontis, 32 ills. Title sl foxed.
                    (Whitehart) **£18 [≈ $34]**

Pope, Franklin Leonard
- Evolution of the Electric Incandescent Lamp. 1889. 1st edn. 91 pp. 20 ills. Orig bndg.
                    (New Wireless) **$85 [≈ £44]**
- Evolution of the Electric Incandescent Lamp. 1894. 2nd edn. 91 pp. 21 ills. Orig bndg, ex-lib, cvrs worn. *(New Wireless)* **$50 [≈ £26]**
- Modern Practice of the Electric Telegraph. 1872. 6th edn. 160 pp. 65 ills. Orig bndg.
                    (New Wireless) **$75 [≈ £40]**

Popovic, Vojin
- Tribute to Nikola Tesla. Beograd: 1961. 1st edn. 571 pp. Num ills. Orig bndg.
                    (New Wireless) **$190 [≈ £98]**

Popular Flowers ...
- See Tyas, Robert.

Porter, George Richardson
- The Nature and Properties of the Sugar Cane ... Second Edition, with an Additional Chapter on the Manufacture of Sugar from Beetroot. London: Smith, Elder, 1843. ii,xv, 240,32 advt pp. 9 fldg plates (1 foxed). Orig green pict cloth, gilt spine.
                    (Gough) **£150 [≈ $287]**

Portlock, J.E.
- Report on the Geology of the County of Londonderry and Parts of Tyrone and Fermanagh. Dublin: Milliken, 1843. 8vo. 784 pp. Fldg maps, plates. Cloth bds.
                    (Emerald Isle) **£75 [≈ $143]**
- Report on the Geology of the County of Londonderry, and Parts of Tyrone and Fermanagh. Dublin: 1843. 8vo. xxxii,784 pp. Fldg cold map, 54 plates (5 cold). Orig cloth, trifle used.
                    (Wheldon & Wesley) **£120 [≈ $230]**

Postlethwaite, John
- Mines and Mining in the Lake District ... Leeds: Samuel Moxon, 1877. 1st edn. viii,51, [8 advt] pp. Fldg map, plans. Orig ptd wraps, sl used, lacks lower panel.
                    (Hollett) **£45 [≈ $86]**
- Mines and Mining in the Lake District. Leeds: Samuel Moxon, 1889. 2nd edn. 8vo.

Map, 22 ills. Orig cloth, trifle rubbed.
(Hollett) **£65** **[≈$124]**

Pott, Percival
- An Account of the Method of obtaining a Perfect or Radical Cure of the Hydrocele, or Watry Rupture, by means of a Seton. The Second Edition. London: Hawes, Clarke, Collins, 1772. 8vo. [iv],43 pp. 1 plate. Old half calf, rebacked. *(Bickersteth)* **£85** **[≈$163]**
- Chirurgical Observations relative to the Cataract, the Polypus of the Nose, the Cancer of the Scrotum ... London: Carnegy, 1775. 8vo. [iv],xi, [i],208 pp. Later half calf. Bound with Thomas Percival's Essays Medical and Experimental, Vol II, London, 1773.
(Goodrich) **$3,750** **[≈£1,953]**
- A Treatise on the Hydrocele, or Watry Rupture, and other Diseases of the Testicle ... Third Edition, improved with very considerable Additions. London: Hawes, Clarke, Collins, 1773. 8vo. vii,[iii],372 pp. 2 plates. Title sl marked. Orig calf, rebacked.
(Bickersteth) **£180** **[≈$345]**

Potter, Stephen & Sargent, Laurens
- Pedigree: Essays on the Etymology of Words from Nature. London: Collins New Naturalist, 1973. 1st edn. 8vo. 322 pp. Orig cloth. Dw. *(Henly)* **£68** **[≈$130]**
- Pedigree: Words from Nature ... London: Collins New Naturalist Series, 1973. 1st edn. 8vo. Orig cloth gilt. Dw, mint.
(Hollett) **£95** **[≈$182]**

Power, Sir D'Arcy
- Portraits of Dr. William Harvey. Oxford: 1913. Folio. 49 pp. 20 plates. Orig bndg, bds showing some wear. *(Goodrich)* **$135** **[≈£70]**
- Selected Writings 1877-1930. Oxford: 1931. x,368 pp. Frontis, 16 plates, fldg map, 9 text figs. *(Whitehart)* **£35** **[≈$67]**
- Selected Writings, 1877-1930. Oxford: 1931. 8vo. 368 pp. Orig bndg..
(Goodrich) **$50** **[≈£26]**

Power, Sir D'Arcy & Thompson, C.J.S.
- Chronologia Medica. A Handlist of Persons, Periods and Events in the History of Medicine. London: 1923. Sm 8vo. iv,278 pp. Ills. Cloth, marked. *(Whitehart)* **£38** **[≈$72]**

Poynter, F.N.L.
- A Bibliography of Gervase Markham 1568?-1637. Oxford: Oxford Bibl Soc, 1962. Med 8vo. 4 plates. Orig linen backed bds.
(Georges) **£75** **[≈$143]**
- A Catalogue of Incunabula in the Wellcome

Historical Museum. London: 1954. 4to. 159 pp. Dw (torn). *(Goodrich)* **$85** **[≈£44]**

Poynter, F.N.L. (ed.)
- The History and Philosophy of Knowledge of the Brain and its Functions. Oxford: 1958. 278 pp. Dw. *(Goodrich)* **$75** **[≈£39]**

Poynting, F.
- Eggs of British Birds with an Account of their Breeding Habits: Limicolae. London: 1895-96. 4to. 54 cold plates. Almost free from usual foxing. Contemp half mor, t.e.g.
(Wheldon & Wesley) **£200** **[≈$383]**

Poynton, F.J. & Paine, A.
- Researches on Rheumatism. New York: 1914. 1st Amer edn. 461 pp. Orig bndg.
(Fye) **$150** **[≈£78]**

Practical ...
- The Practical Housewife, Forming a Complete Encyclopaedia of Domestic Economy ... London: Ward & Lock, [inscrptn dated 1858]. 1st edn (?). 8vo. xxix,192 pp. W'engvd frontis & title, num text ills. Orig blue cloth gilt. *(Gough)* **£48** **[≈$92]**
- A Practical Treatise on Breeding ... Poultry ... see Lawrence, John.

Praeger, R.L.
- The Botanist in Ireland. Dublin: 1934. 1st edn. 8vo. xii,587 pp. 6 cold maps, 44 plates, 29 text ills. Orig cloth.
(Wheldon & Wesley) **£45** **[≈$86]**
- Irish Topographical Botany. Dublin: RIA, 1901. 8vo. 410 pp. Maps. Orig cloth bds.
(Emerald Isle) **£75** **[≈$143]**
- A Tourist's Flora of the West of Ireland. Dublin: 1909. 1st edn. Cr 8vo. xii,243 pp. 5 fldg maps, 27 plates, ills. Orig cloth.
(Fenning) **£65** **[≈$124]**

Pratt, Anne
- The British Grasses and Sedges. London: [1861]. 8vo. viii,136 pp. 35 cold plates (numbered 238*, 239-272). Orig cloth, faded. *(Wheldon & Wesley)* **£25** **[≈$47]**
- The British Grasses and Sedges. London: SPCK, [ca 1864]. 8vo. xviii,136 pp. 35 cold plates. Cloth, faded.
(Wheldon & Wesley) **£20** **[≈$38]**
- Chapters on the Common Things of the Sea-Coast. London: SPCK, 1853. 1st edn. 12mo. x,345 pp. Frontis, w'engvd vignettes. Orig cloth. *(Claude Cox)* **£18** **[≈$34]**
- The Ferns of Great Britain. London: n.d. 3rd edn. 8vo. iv,164 pp. 41 cold plates. Orig

cloth, trifle faded, worn.
(Wheldon & Wesley) **£20 [≈ $38]**
- The Grasses, Sedges and Ferns of Great
Britain. London: SPCK, [ca 1867]. 2 parts in
one vol. 8vo. 76 cold plates. Orig dec cloth.
(Wheldon & Wesley) **£25 [≈ $47]**
- The Grasses, Sedges and Ferns of Great
Britain. London: n.d. 8vo. x,140,4 advt pp.
75 cold plates. Orig cloth gilt.
(Henly) **£30 [≈ $57]**
- The Poisonous, Noxious, and Suspected
Plants of Our Fields and Woods. London:
SPCK, [1856]. 1st edn (?). 12mo. 44
chromolithos. Contemp red half mor.
(Gough) **£40 [≈ $76]**
- Poisonous, Noxious, and Suspected Plants of
Our Fields and Woods. London: SPCK, [ca
1860]. Tall 8vo (10 x 7 1/8 ins). 44
chromolitho plates. Contemp gilt dec mor.
(Book Block) **$450 [≈ £234]**
- Wild Flowers. London: SPCK, 1857. 2 vols.
12mo. 192 cold plates. Orig cloth gilt, sl
marked, 1 vol recased.
(Hollett) **£120 [≈ $230]**

Pratt, J.H.
- The Mathematical Principles of Mechanical
Philosophy and their Application to the
Theory of Universal Gravitation. Cambridge:
1836. xxvi,[1],616 pp. 5 fldg plates. Occas sl
foxing. Half calf, edges sl worn.
(Whitehart) **£35 [≈ $67]**

Prentiss, Henry M.
- The Great Polar Current. Polar Papers
DeLong - Nansen - Peary. New York: Stokes,
1897. [viii],153 pp. Orig dec cloth, t.e.g.,
some minor soil & wear.
(High Latitude) **$45 [≈ £23]**

Prescott, George B.
- Electricity and the Electric Telegraph. 1892.
8th edn. 2 vols. 1221 pp. 722 ills. Orig bndg.
(New Wireless) **$110 [≈ £57]**
- History, Theory, and Practice of the Electric
Telegraph. 1860. 1st edn. 468 pp. 98 ills.
Orig bndg. *(New Wireless)* **$110 [≈ £58]**
- History, Theory, and Practice of the Electric
Telegraph. 1866. 3rd edn. 508 pp. 111 ills.
Orig bndg, spine ends sl defective.
(New Wireless) **$65 [≈ £33]**
- The Speaking Telephone, Talking
Phonograph, and Other Novelties. 1878. 1st
edn. 431 pp. 208 ills. Orig bndg, sl worn.
(New Wireless) **$165 [≈ £85]**

Preston, T.
- The Theory of Heat. London: Macmillan,

1894. 8vo. xvi,719 pp. 190 text figs. Ex-lib.
Cloth. *(Gemmary)* **$75 [≈ £39]**
- The Theory of Light. London: Macmillan,
1895. 2nd edn. 8vo. xvii,574 pp. 251 text figs.
Cloth. *(Gemmary)* **$50 [≈ £26]**

Preston, T.A.
- The Flowering Plants of Wilts. London:
1888. 8vo. lxix,436 pp. Cold map. Orig cloth,
sl stained, front jnt torn.
(Wheldon & Wesley) **£27 [≈ $51]**

Prestwich, Sir Joseph
- Geology. Chemical, Physical and
Stratigraphical. London: 1886. 2 vols. Roy
8vo. 2 cold geological & 3 other maps, 3
sections, 16 plates of fossils, 474 text figs.
Half calf, rebacked. *(Henly)* **£42 [≈ $80]**
- Life and Letters of Sir Joseph Prestwich. By
Mrs. Prestwich. London: 1899. xiv,444 pp.
24 ills. Orig cloth. *(Baldwin)* **£35 [≈ $67]**

Price, Sarah
- Illustrations of the Fungi of our Fields and
Woods ... London: for the author by Lovell
Reeve, 1864-65. 1st edn. 1st & 2nd Series. 2
vols in one. 4to. 20 hand cold lithos. Occas v
sl soiling. Contemp cloth, soiled & worn.
(Frew Mackenzie) **£650 [≈ $1,247]**

Priest, C.D.
- The Birds of Southern Rhodesia. London:
1933-36. 4 vols. Roy 8vo. Map, 40 cold
plates, 521 text figs. Cloth.
(Wheldon & Wesley) **£300 [≈ $575]**

Priestley, Joseph
- Experiments and Observations on Different
Kinds of Air. London: 1775-76. 2nd edn. 2
vols (only, of 3). xxiii, [2],324; xliv, 399,[8]
pp. 4 plates. Contemp leather, rebacked.
(Whitehart) **£180 [≈ $345]**
- The History and Present State of Discoveries
relating to Vision, Light, and Colours.
London: J. Johnson, 1772. 1st edn. 2 vols.
4to. v,[1], xvi,422; [2], 423-812, [20] pp.
Subscribers. Errata leaf. Frontis, 24 plates.
Some browning & offsetting to plates.
Contemp calf, rehinged.
(Rootenberg) **$1,600 [≈ £833]**
- The History and Present State of Electricity
... Third Edition, corrected and enlarged.
London: for C. Bathurst ..., 1775. 2 vols. 8vo.
Usual mispaginations. Ctlg inserted in vol 2.
8 fldg plates. Contemp calf, sl worn at ft of
spine, new label. *(Waterfield's)* **£220 [≈ $422]**

Prime, C.T.
- Lords and Ladies. London: Collins New Naturalist, 1960. 1st edn. 8vo. xiv,241 pp. 1 cold & 4 other plates. Orig cloth. Dw.
(*Henly*) **£32 [≈ $61]**

Prince, William
- A Short Treatise on Horticulture ... New York: 1828. ix,196 pp. Light to moderate foxing. Orig cloth backed paper bds, paper label, some wear & soiling.
(*Reese*) **$300 [≈ £156]**

Pringle, John
- Observations on the Diseases of the Army ... Fourth Edition enlarged. London: Millar, Wilson ..., 1764. xxvii,355, cxxviii,[30] pp. Engvd title. Ex-lib. Lacks half-title. Calf gilt, scuffed, front jnt cracked but holding.
(*Wreden*) **$50 [≈ £26]**

Prinzing, Friedrich
- Epidemics resulting from Wars. Edited by H. Westergaard. Oxford: 1916. xii,340,6 pp. Cloth, sl worn & faded.
(*Whitehart*) **£25 [≈ $47]**
- Epidemics resulting from Wars. Oxford: 1916. 340 pp. Orig bndg. (*Fye*) **$100 [≈ £52]**

Prior, Thomas
- An Authentic Narrative of the Success of Tar-Water, In curing a great Number and Variety of Distempers ... New Edition, Complete. London: Dublin ptd, London reptd, for W. Innys ..., 1746. 8vo. 88 pp. Orig wraps, uncut,wraps detached, edges sl frayed.
(*Finch*) **£180 [≈ $345]**

Pritchard, Andrew
- The Natural History of Animalcules. London: Whittaker, 1834. 8vo. 194 pp. 301 ills on 7 plates (crnr of 1 plate water stained). Bds. (*Gemmary*) **$350 [≈ £182]**
- A History of Infusiora, including the Desmidiaceae and Diatomaceae, British and Foreign. London: 1861. 4th edn. 8vo. xii,968 pp. 40 plates. Orig cloth, faded, trifle used.
(*Wheldon & Wesley*) **£50 [≈ $95]**
- The Microscopic Cabinet of Select Animated Objects. London: Whittaker, Treacher & Arnot, 1832. 1st edn. Demy 8vo. 246 pp. Hand cold etched & engvd plates. Some annotations. Contemp half calf gilt, v sl rubbed. (*Ash*) **£100 [≈ $191]**

Pritchard, James C.
- The Natural History of Man ... Third Edition, enlarged. London: 1848. Thick 8vo.

xvii, 677 pp. 50 cold & 5 plain plates, 97 w'engvs. Some soiling, occas foxing. Later three qtr mor & cloth. (*Reese*) **$600 [≈ £312]**

Proctor, Michael & Yeo, Peter
- The Pollination of Flowers. London: Collins New Naturalist, 1973. 1st edn. 8vo. 418 pp. Ills. Orig cloth gilt. Dw (plastic cvr lightly adhered to verso of wraps at edges, as issued), mint. (*Hollett*) **£50 [≈ $95]**
- The Pollination of Flowers. London: Collins New Naturalist, 1973. 1st edn. 8vo. 418 pp. 4 cold & 48 plain plates. Orig cloth. Dw.
(*Henly*) **£48 [≈ $92]**

Proctor, R.A.
- Myths and Marvels of Astronomy. London: 1878. 1st edn. vii,363 pp. A few ills. Sl foxing. Cloth dust stained.
(*Whitehart*) **£25 [≈ $47]**
- A New Star Atlas. London: Longmans, Green, 1891. 16th edn. 8vo. xii,27 pp. 14 maps. Cloth. (*Gemmary*) **$50 [≈ £26]**

Prout, William
- Chemistry, Meteorology and the Function of Digestion considered with reference to Natural Theology. London: W. Pickering, Bridgewater Treatises VIII, 1834. 1st edn. 8vo. 8 advt, xxiii,[5], 564,[2] pp. Fldg map. Orig cloth, sl discold, lacks paper label.
(*Fenning*) **£45 [≈ $86]**
- An Inquiry into the Nature and Treatment of Gravel, Calculus, and Other Diseases connected with a Deranged Operation of the Urinary organs. London: 1821. 1st edn. 227 pp. Leaf with 9 colour samples. Orig bndg, bds detached. (*Fye*) **$250 [≈ £130]**
- On the Nature and Treatment of Stomach and Urinary Diseases ... London: 1840. 3rd edn. xvi,cxi,483 pp. 6 plates. Contemp prize leather, rebacked. (*Whitehart*) **£40 [≈ $76]**

Pryce, William
- Mineralogia Cornubiensis; a Treatise on Minerals, Mines, and Mining ... London: for the author, by James Phillips, 1778. 1st edn. Folio. [36],xiv, [2],331, [1] pp. Frontis port, 7 plates (3 fldg), 2 fldg tables. Few sl marks. Orig bds, backed in cloth, worn.
(*Rootenberg*) **$1,200 [≈ £625]**

Pryor, A.R.
- A Flora of Hertfordshire. Edited by B.D. Jackson. London: 1887. 8vo. viii,588 pp. 3 maps. V sl foxing. Cloth, jnts loose.
(*Wheldon & Wesley*) **£40 [≈ $76]**

Przibaum, H.
- Experimental Zoology. Part I [all published].
Embryogeny ... Cambridge: 1908. viii, 124
pp. 16 fldg plates. Orig cloth.
(Whitehart) **£18 [≈ $34]**

Pugsley, A.J.
- Dewponds in Fable and Fact. London:
(1939). 1st edn. Sm 8vo. x,62 pp. Ills. Orig
bds, dull.   *(Bow Windows)* **£24 [≈ $46]**

Pulteney, Richard
- A General View of the Writings of Linnaeus.
London: 1781. 1st edn. 8vo. iv,425, [1] pp.
Contemp calf.
(Wheldon & Wesley) **£175 [≈ $335]**

Pumpelly, Raphael
- My Reminiscences. New York: Henry Holt,
1918. 2 vols. 8vo. xiii,438; xi,439-844 pp. 13
maps, 65 plates. Cloth.
(Gemmary) **$100 [≈ £52]**

Purcell, John
- A Treatise of the Cholick; containing
Analytical Proof of its Many Causes ...
London: J. Morphew, 1715. 2nd edn. Sm
8vo. [xvi], 188, [12] pp. Contemp calf,
rebacked.   *(Bookpress)* **$300 [≈ £156]**

Purchon, R.D.
- The Biology of the Mollusca. Oxford: 1977.
2nd edn. 8vo. xxv,560 pp. 185 text figs.
Cloth.   *(Wheldon & Wesley)* **£55 [≈ $105]**

Purple, S.S.
- A Literary and Practical Sketch of Acrania,
Brainless or Pseudencephalous Monsters.
New York: 1850. 32 pp. Frontis. New qtr
calf.   *(Goodrich)* **$125 [≈ £65]**

Pusey, W.A.
- The Principles and Practice of Dermatology
designed for Students and Practitioners.
London: 1907. xxiv,1021 pp. 1 cold plate,
367 text ills. Lib stamp on title verso. Orig
cloth, lib mark on spine.
(Whitehart) **£25 [≈ $47]**

Pusey, William & Caudwell, Eugene
- The Practical Application of the Roentgen
Rays in Therapeutics and Diagnosis. Phila:
1903. 1st edn. 591 pp. 176 ills. Orig bndg.
(Fye) **$250 [≈ £130]**

Quain, Richard
- The Diseases of the Rectum. London: 1854.
1st edn. 285 pp. 4 hand cold plates. Occas ink

notes. Orig bndg.   *(Fye)* **$150 [≈ £78]**

Quain, Richard (ed.)
- A Dictionary of Medicine including General
Pathology, General Therapeutics, Hygiene,
and the Diseases peculiar to Women and
Children. By Various Authors. New York:
Appleton, 1884. 7th edn. Thick 4to. 1816 pp.
Qtr mor, mrbld bds, worn.
(Goodrich) **$125 [≈ £65]**

Quarrington, C.A.
- Modern Practical Radio and Television.
London: Caxton Publ Co, 1955. 4 vols. Lge
8vo. 17 plates, 7 fldg diags, num text figs.
Orig blue cloth.   *(Claude Cox)* **£20 [≈ $38]**

Quekett, J.
- Practical Treatise on the Use of the
Microscope. London: H. Bailliere, 1855. 3rd
edn. 8vo. xii,556 pp. 11 plates, num w'engvs.
Some foxing. Cloth, shaken.
(Gemmary) **$150 [≈ £78]**
- Practical Treatise on the Use of the
Microscope. London: H. Bailliere, 1855. 3rd
edn. 8vo. xii,556 pp. 11 plates, num w'engvs.
New qtr leather.   *(Gemmary)* **$225 [≈ £117]**

Quincy, John
- The Dispensatory of the Royal College of
Physicians in London. London: R. Knaplock
..., 1721. 1st edn. 8vo. xvi,362,[15] pp.
Frontis. Contemp calf, rebacked.
(Bookpress) **$475 [≈ £247]**
- Lexicon Physico-Medicum; or, a New
Physical Dictionary ... London: Andrew Bell,
1719. 1st edn. 8vo. xvi,462,[2 advt] pp.
Contemp sheep, rebacked.
(Gough) **£100 [≈ $191]**
- See also under Sanctorius, Sanctorius

Radbill, Samuel X.
- Bibliography of Medical Ex Libris
Literature. Hilprand Press: 1951. 8vo. 40 pp.
8 plates. Orig bndg. *(Goodrich)* **$85 [≈ £44]**

Radcliffe, John
- Pharmacopoeia Radcliffeana: or, Dr.
Radcliff's Prescriptions, faithfully gathered
from his Original Recipe's ... by Edward
Strother. London: Rivington, 1716. 1st edn.
12mo. xii,166,2 advt pp. Possibly lacks a
port. Marg browning. Half calf.
(Rootenberg) **$400 [≈ £208]**

Radcliffe-Crocker, H.
- Diseases of the Skin ... London: 1903. 3rd
edn. 2 vols. xxxii,1387 pp. 4 plates, 112 ills.

Sm lib stamp on title & a few margs. Inner hinge of vol 2 cracked but firm.
(Whitehart) £25 [≈ $47]

Raffald, Elizabeth
- The Experienced English Housekeeper, for the use of Ladies, Housekeepers, Cooks ... New Edition ... London: Millar, Law & Cater [ie York: Wilson, Spence & Mawman], 1791. W'cut frontis, 3 fldg plates. Mod buckram.
(Waterfield's) £150 [≈ $287]

Ralfs, John
- The British Desmidieae. The Drawings by Edward Jenner. London: 1848. 1st edn. Lge 8vo. [xxiv],226, [2],16 advt pp. 35 cold plates. Some sl marks. Orig cloth, dull, backstrip repaid, crnr tips worn. Author's sgntr on title.
(Bow Windows) £185 [≈ $355]

Ralph, T.S.
- Icones Carpologicae, or Figures and Descriptions of Fruit and Seeds - Leguminosae [all published]. London: 1849. 4to. 48,[4] pp. 40 plates. Ex-lib. Orig bds, rebacked. *(Wheldon & Wesley)* £50 [≈ $95]

Ramsay, A.C.
- Geological Map of the British Isles ... London: Geological Survey, 1878. Lge fldg cold map. 54 x 61 inches. Dissected on linen. Fldg into lge 8vo slipcase (rather worn).
(Bow Windows) £60 [≈ $115]

Ramsay, Sir William
- Elements and Electrons. London: Harper & Bros, 1912. Sm 8vo. ix,173 pp. Cloth gilt.
(Gemmary) $35 [≈ £18]
- The Gases of the Atmosphere, the History of their Discovery. Third Edition. London: 1905. 8vo. xiv,296 pp. 9 ports, sev figs. Outer blanks sl foxed. Contemp polished prize tree calf gilt, a.e.g., 1 jnt trifle rubbed.
(Bow Windows) £55 [≈ $105]
- The Gases of the Atmosphere. The History of their Discovery. London: 1905. 3rd edn. xiii, 296 pp. Frontis port, 8 plates, 8 figs.
(Whitehart) £25 [≈ $47]

Ramsbottom, J.
- Mushrooms and Toadstools. London: Collins New Naturalist, 1953. 1st edn. 8vo. xiv,306 pp. 46 cold & 24 plain plates. Orig cloth, spine sl faded. *(Henly)* £22 [≈ $42]

Randolph, Mrs Mary
- The Virginia Housewife, or Methodical Cook. Washington: P. Thompson, 1830. 4th

edn. 12mo. 186 pp. Some foxing, sm hole through 1st few ff. Contemp sheep, rebacked.
(Bookpress) $485 [≈ £252]
- The Virginia Housewife: or, Methodical Cook. Phila: E.H. Butler, 1854. 8vo. 180 pp. Occas sl foxing. Orig mor backed bds, spine ends worn away, jnts reprd, rear hinge reinforced with bndg tape.
(Chapel Hill) $200 [≈ £104]

Ranshoff, Joseph
- Under the Northern Lights and Other Stories. Cincinnati: 1921. 8vo. 166 pp. Ex-lib. Orig bndg. *(Goodrich)* $50 [≈ £26]

Raspe, Rudolph Eric
- An Account of some German Volcanos, and their Productions ... London: Lockyer Davis, 1776. 1st edn. 8vo. xix,[1],140 pp, inc 4 advt pp. Half-title. 2 fldg plates. Contemp calf, rebacked. *(Rootenberg)* $500 [≈ £260]

Ratcliffe, H.
- Observations on the Rate of Mortality & Sickness existing among Friendly Societies ... Manchester: 1850. 168 pp. Lib stamp on title. Cloth, sl bumped, new endpapers.
(Whitehart) £40 [≈ $76]

Ratzel, Fr.
- The History of Mankind. Translated from the Second German Edition by A.J. Butler ... London: 1896-98. 3 vols. Lge 8vo. 5 cold maps, 30 cold plates, over 1100 text ills. Minor spotting. Orig gilt illust cloth, t.e.g.
(Bow Windows) £165 [≈ $316]

Raven, C.E.
- English Naturalists from Neckham to Ray. Cambridge: 1947. Orig printing. 8vo. x,379 pp. Cloth. *(Wheldon & Wesley)* £60 [≈ $115]

Raven, J. & Walters, M.
- Mountain Flowers. London: Collins New Naturalist, 1956. 1st edn. 8vo. xv,240 pp. 16 cold & 24 plain plates. Orig cloth.
(Henly) £25 [≈ $47]

Ray, A.P.C.
- History of Chemistry in Ancient and Medieval India incorporating the History of Hindu Chemistry. Edited by P. Ray. Calcutta: 1956. [xix],ii,494 pp. Fldg table, sev plates. Sm worm hole through front cvr to p 24. *(Whitehart)* £25 [≈ $47]

Ray, John
- A Collection of English Words Not Generally

used ... with ... an Account of the preparing and refining such Metals and Minerals as are gotten in England. London: 1674. 1st edn. 8vo. [xiv],178 pp. Lacks A1 (blank). Contemp sheep, sometime reprd, worn. Wing R.388.
(Gaskell) £525 [≈ $1,007]
- Philosophical Letters between the late learned Mr. Ray and several of his Ingenious Correspondents ... Published by W. Derham. London: 1718. 1st edn. 8vo. [viii], 376, [10], [2] pp. Contemp calf, rebacked.
(Wheldon & Wesley) £150 [≈ $287]
- Three Physico-Theological Discourses ... Second Edition Corrected, very much enlarged ... London: Sam. Smith, 1693. 8vo. [xxiv], 1-160, [viii], 161-406, [ii] pp. Final advt leaf. 4 plates. Some browning, occas marg staining. Rec half calf. Wing R.409.
(Clark) £285 [≈ $547]
- The Wisdom of God, manifested in the Works of the Creation. London: 1717. 7th edn. 8vo. [xxvi], 17-405, [3] pp. Port. Endpapers & last 2 ff v sl foxed. Contemp calf, rebacked.
(Wheldon & Wesley) £175 [≈ $335]

Rayer, P.F.
- A Theoretical and Practical Treatise on the Diseases of the Skin, from the Second Edition, entirely remodelled ... by John Bell. Phila: 1845. 1st Amer edn. 4to. 449 pp. 40 hand cold plates. Occas foxing. Rec leatherette. *(Fye)* $300 [≈ £156]

Rayleigh, J.W. Strutt, 3rd Baron
- The Theory of Sound. London: Macmillan, 1877. 1st edn. 2 vols. 8vo. xi,326; x,302 pp. Ex-lib. Orig cloth. *(Gemmary)* $400 [≈ £208]
- The Theory of Sound. London: Macmillan, 1929. 2nd edn. 2 vols. 8vo. xiv,480; xvi,504 pp. Orig cloth. *(Gemmary)* $100 [≈ £52]

Rayleigh, J.W. Strutt, 3rd Baron & Ramsay, William
- Argon: A New Constituent of the Atmosphere. Washington: Smithsonian, 1896. 1st edn. Folio. iv,43 pp. Orig cloth.
(Whitehart) £65 [≈ $124]

Raynaud, Maurice
- On Local Asphyxia and Symmetrical Gangrene of the Extremities. London: 1888. 1st English translation. 199 pp. Orig bndg.
(Fye) $100 [≈ £52]

Rea, R.L.
- Chest Radiography at a Casualty Clearing Station with Atlas. Belfast: 1919. 24 pp.

Plates. Occas sl text foxing. Cloth, stained.
(Whitehart) £40 [≈ $76]

Read, J.
- Humour and Humanism in Chemistry. London: 1947. xxiii,388 pp. 90 ills inc cold plates. *(Whitehart)* £28 [≈ $53]

Reader, W.J.
- Imperial Chemical Industries. A History. Oxford: 1970-75. 2 vols. 80 plates, 12 text figs. Orig bndgs. *(Whitehart)* £38 [≈ $72]

Reclus, Elisee
- The Earth. A Descriptive History of the Phenomena of the Life of the Globe. Translated by B.B. Woodward .v. London: Chapman & Hall, 1871. 1st edn in English. 2 vols. 8vo. vii,573 pp. 24 cold maps, num w'engvd ills. Orig green cloth, sl rubbed.
(Ximenes) $275 [≈ £143]
- The Earth. A Descriptive History of the Phenomena of the Life on the Globe. Translated by B.B. Woodward ... New York: Harper, 1872. 8vo. vii,573 pp. 23 cold maps, 230 maps in text. Orig gilt dec cloth.
(Gemmary) $50 [≈ £26]

Redhead, William, et al.
- Observations on the Different Breeds of Sheep, and the State of Sheep Farming in some of the Principal Counties of England ... Edinburgh: ptd by W. Smellie ..., 1792. 1st edn. 8vo. 7, [i], xviii, 99 pp. Half-title stained. 1 sm repr. Old wraps.
(Burmester) £250 [≈ $479]

Redoute, P.J.
- The Best of Redoute's Roses. Selected and Edited by Eva Mannering. London: 1959. Folio. 30 cold plates. Cloth.
(Wheldon & Wesley) £45 [≈ $86]

Redwood, Sir B.
- Petroleum: A Treatise on the Geographical Distribution and Geological Occurrence of Petroleum and Natural Gas ... London: 1913. 3rd edn. 3 vols. 3 frontis, 29 plates, 345 text figs. 1 half-title damaged. Orig cloth, dust stained. *(Whitehart)* £35 [≈ $67]

Reed, Walter
- Yellow Fever, A Compilation of Various Publications. Washington: GPO, 1911. 1st edn. One of 1000. 8vo. 250 pp. frontis, 4 plates. Stain in upper crnr of front wrapper & a few pp. New sheep, orig wraps bound in.
(Bookpress) $225 [≈ £117]

Reed, Walter, et al.
- The Etiology of Yellow Fever. A Preliminary Note. [In] The Philadelphia Medical Journal (pp 790-796). Phila: 1900. 4to. Orig half mor, sl rubbed.   *(Bookpress)* **$900 [≈ £468]**

Reemelin, Charles
- The Wine-Maker's Manual. Cincinnati: Robert Clarke, 1868. 1st edn. 8vo. 123 pp. Ills. Few marg pencil marks. Orig cloth.
        (Respess) **$85 [≈ £44]**

Rees, Abraham
- Rees's Manufacturing Industry (1819-20). A Selection from the Cyclopaedia; or Universal Dictionary of Arts, Sciences and Literature ... Edited by Neil Cossons. Newton Abbot: 1972. 5 vols. 4to. Num plates, text ills. Orig cloth. Dws. Boxed. *(Sotheran's)* **£95 [≈ $182]**

Regimen Sanitatis Salerni ...
- Regimen Sanitatis Salerni: or, The Schoole of Salernes Regiment of Health ... London: B. Alsop, 1649. 1st edn of this transl. Sm 4to. [iv], 220, [3] pp. Lib stamps on title & 2nd leaf. New qtr mor. *(Bookpress)* **$785 [≈ £408]**

Regnault, Noel
- Philosophical Conversations: or, a New System of Physics, by Way of Dialogue. Translated into English and Illustrated with Notes by Thomas Dale, M.D. London: 1731. 1st edn in English. 3 vols. 8vo. 89 plates. Contemp calf, spine sl rubbed with some wear at ends.   *(Burmester)* **£600 [≈ $1,151]**

Reichenbach, Charles von, Baron
- Physio-Physiological Researches of the Dynamics of Magnetism, Electricity, Heat, Light, Crystallization, and Chemism ... Notes by John Ashburner. London: 1850. 1st edn of this translation. 8vo. xx,609 pp. Plate, ills. Orig black cloth.   *(Burmester)* **£45 [≈ $86]**
- Researches on Magnetism, Electricity, Heat, Light, Crystallization, and Chemical Attraction ... Translated ... by William Gregory. London: 1850. 1st English edn. Parts I & II (all published) inc 2nd edn of 1st part. 8vo. 3 fldg plates. Orig cloth, sl worn & used   *(Bow Windows)* **£90 [≈ $172]**
- Researches on Magnetism, Electricity, Heat, Light, Crystallization and Chemical Attraction ... Notes ... by William Gregory. London: 1850. xlv,463 pp. 3 fldg plates, 23 text ills. Orig cloth, spine sl worn, inner hinge cracked.   *(Whitehart)* **£50 [≈ $95]**

Remarks on the Art of Making Wine ...
- See MacCulloch, John.

Remington, Joseph P.
- Practice of Pharmacy ... Third Edition, enlarged and thoroughly revised. Phila: Lippincott, (1894). 8vo. 1497 pp. 600 text ills. Some soil. Sheep, jnts shaken but sound.
        (Schoyer) **$45 [≈ £23]**

Remondino, P.C.
- A History of Circumcision from the Earliest Times to the Present with a History of Eunuchism, Hermaphroditism, etc. Phila: 1891. 1st edn. 346 pp. Orig bndg, cvrs spotted. Author's pres copy.
        (Fye) **$100 [≈ £52]**

Rennie, J.
- Insect Architecture. London: Library of Entertaining Knowledge, 1830. 2nd edn. Orig cloth, rebacked. *(Whitehart)* **£18 [≈ $34]**

Rennie, J. & Westwood, J.O.
- The Natural History of Insects. London: 1830-38. 2 vols. 12mo. Num text figs. Half vellum. Anon.
        (Wheldon & Wesley) **£30 [≈ $57]**

Rennie, R.
- Essays on the Natural History and Origin of Peat Moss ... Edinburgh: for Constable, & Murray, 1807. 1st edn. viii,233,[i] pp. Prelim lower margs sl marked. Orig cloth gilt, sl marked.   *(Hollett)* **£85 [≈ £163]**

Renouard, P.-V.
- History of Medicine ... to the Nineteenth Century. Translated ... by C.G. Comegys. Cincinnati: 1856. 8vo. 719 pp. Sheep, worn. Translator's pres copy.
        (Goodrich) **$125 [≈ £65]**

Renshaw, S.A.
- The Cone and its Sections treated Geometrically. London: Hamilton, Adams ..., 1875. 1st edn. Roy 8vo. [2],148 pp. Errata slip. Frontis, 22 fldg plates, text diags. Orig cloth gilt, inside rear jnt cracked but strong.
        (Fenning) **£45 [≈ $86]**

Reuleaux, F.
- The Constructor. A Hand-Book of Machine Design. Translated by H.H. Suplee. Phila: 1893. Lge 4to. xviii,312 pp. Port, over 1200 ills. Lacks f.e.p. Orig bndg, inner hinges cracked but firm. *(Whitehart)* **£55 [≈ $105]**
- The Kinematics of Machinery. Outlines of a Theory of Machines. Translated and edited by A.B.W. Kennedy. London: 1876. 1st edn. xvi, 622 pp. 451 ills. Cloth worn & marked.

(Whitehart) **£40 [≈ $76]**

Reynolds, Michael
- Locomotive Engine Driving; A Practical Manual for Engineers in Charge of Locomotive Engines. Ninth Edition. London: Crosby Lockwood, 1892. xiii,258,[40,16 advt] pp. Port, 35 w'engvd plates & ills. Prelims sl spotted. Orig pict cloth gilt.   *(Gough)* **£55 [≈ $105]**

Reynoldson, John
- Practical and Philosophical Principles of Making Malt ... Second Edition. Newark: M. Hage; London: for Gale & Curtis, 1809. 8vo. xxxi, [3], 293,[1 errata] pp. Orig bds, uncut, rebacked, wear to edges of bds.
          (Spelman) **£90 [≈ $172]**

Rhazes
- A Treatise on the Small-Pox and Measles. Translated from the Original Arabic by William Alexander Greenhill. London: Sydenham Society, 1848. 1st edn thus. 8vo. viii,212,40 pp. Lib stamp on title & 3 pp, name cut from hd of title. Orig cloth gilt.
          (Gough) **£25 [≈ $47]**

Rhees, William
- The Smithsonian Institution Documents relative to its Origin and History, 1835-1899. Washington: 1901. 1st edn. 2 vols. 1983 pp. Orig bndg.   *(Fye)* **$100 [≈ £52]**

Rhind, William
- A History of the Vegetable Kingdom ... Revised Edition, with Supplement. London: Blackie & Son, 1868. Sm 4to. xvi,744 pp. Port, hand cold title vignette, 22 hand & 22 other plates. Contemp half calf, recased, crnrs a trifle bumped.   *(Gough)* **£80 [≈ $153]**
- A History of the Vegetable Kingdom. London: Blackie & Son, 1877. Thick 8vo. 744 pp. Num hand cold plates. Orig half mor, some rubbing of spine & crnrs.
          (Chapel Hill) **$150 [≈ £78]**

Rhododendron Society
- The Species of Rhododendron. London: 1947. 2nd edn. 8vo. ix,861 pp. Text ills. Orig cloth.   *(Henly)* **£68 [≈ $130]**

Ribbands, C.R.
- The Behaviour and Social Life of Honeybees. L: 1953. 1st edn. 8vo. 352 pp. 9 plates, 66 text figs. Cloth.   *(Henly)* **£18 [≈ $34]**

Ribot, Theodule A.
- Heredity: a Psychological Study of its Phenomena, Laws, Causes and Consequences. From the French ... London: Henry S. King, 1875. 1st edn in English. 8vo. x,393 pp. Orig cloth gilt.
          (Fenning) **£32.50 [≈ $63]**

Richard, Louis-Claude
- Observations on the Structure of Fruits and Seeds; translated from the Analyse du Fruit ... Original Notes by John Lindley. London: Harding; Norwich: Wilkin & Youngman, 1819. 1st edn in English. 8vo. xx,100 pp. 6 plates (sl foxed). Orig blue bds, uncut, spine worn.   *(Burmester)* **£75 [≈ $143]**

Richards, V.
- The Land-marks of Snake Poison Literature being a Review of the more Important Researches into the Nature of Snake Poisons. Calcutta: 1885. Post 8vo. [iii],x,[i],176,v pp. Sl used. Cloth, spine reprd.
          (Wheldon & Wesley) **£45 [≈ $86]**

Richards, Vyvyan
- From Crystal to Television. 1928. 1st edn. 116 pp. Orig bndg.
          (New Wireless) **$45 [≈ £23]**

Richardson, Sir B.W.
- Vita Medica: Chapters of Medical Life and Work. London: 1897. 1st edn. 8vo. xvi, 495, [1], [16 advt] pp. Rec bds.
          (Fenning) **£45 [≈ $86]**

Richardson, G.F.
- An Introduction to Geology, and its Associate Sciences ... London: 1851. New edn. Cr 8vo. xvi,508 pp. Frontis, 304 text ills. New cloth.   *(Henly)* **£18 [≈ $34]**

Richardson, John
- Fauna Boreali-Americana: or the Zoology of the Northern Parts of British America ... [Quadrupeds]. London: 1829. 300 pp. 28 plates. Half calf, spine somewhat worn.
          (Reese) **$1,000 [≈ £520]**

Richardson, O.W.
- The Electron Theory of Matter. Cambridge: UP, 1916. 2nd edn. 8vo. viii,631 pp. 58 text figs. Cloth.   *(Gemmary)* **$85 [≈ £44]**
- The Emission of Electricity from Hot Bodies. London: 1916. 1st edn. vii,304 pp. 34 figs. Cloth sl dusty & damp stained.
          (Whitehart) **£30 [≈ $57]**

Richardson, W.H. (compiler)
- The Boot and Shoe Manufacturers' Assistant and Guide ... Boston: Higgins, Bradley & Dayton, 1858. xxvi,346,18 pp. Text ills. Orig dec cloth.   *(Karmiole)* **$150 [≈£78]**

Ricketson, Shradah
- Means of Preserving Health and Preventing Diseases founded principally on Attention to Air and Climates ... with an Appendix for Cleanliness, Ventilation, and Medical Electricity. New York: 1806. 8vo. xi,298 pp. Hosack letter present. Foxing. Orig sheep, worn.   *(Goodrich)* **$295 [≈£153]**

Rickett, H.W.
- Wild Flowers of the United States ... New York: 1966-73. 6 vols & index, in 15 vols. 4to. 1306 cold plates. Orig cloth. Slipcases.
          (Wheldon & Wesley) **£500 [≈$959]**

Ricketts, Benjamin
- The Surgery of the Heart and Lungs: a History and resume of Surgical Conditions ... New York: 1904. 1st edn. 510 pp. 87 plates. Lib perf stamp on title, b'plate. Orig bndg, lib number on spine.   *(Fye)* **$400 [≈£208]**

Ricord, Philip
- Illustrations of Syphilitic Disease. Translated from the French by Thomas F. Betton with the Addition of a History of Syphilis ... Phila: 1852. 1st edn. Folio. 359 pp. 50 hand cold plates (browned). Leather, rubbed, hinges weak.   *(Fye)* **$400 [≈£208]**
- Lectures on Venereal and Other Diseases arising from Sexual Intercourse ... Reported and Translated by Victor De Meric. Phila: Barrington & Haswell, 1849. 1st Amer edn. 12mo. 298,[2 advt] pp. Foxing. Contemp calf, worn but sound.   *(Karmiole)* **$75 [≈£39]**
- A Practical Treatise on Venereal Diseases ... New York: 1842. 1st Amer edn. 339 pp. Orig bndg.   *(Fye)* **$175 [≈£91]**

Riddell, Colonel John (i.e. Robert)
- Riddellian System; or, New Medical Improvements ... London: J. Ridgway, 1808. 1st edn. 8vo. [ii],iv,113 pp. New wraps.
          (Bookpress) **$225 [≈£117]**

Ridenour, L.N.
- Radar System Engineering. New York: McGraw-Hill, MIT Rad Lab Series Vol 1, 1947. 8vo. xviii,748 pp. Ex-lib. Cloth.
          (Gemmary) **$35 [≈£18]**

Ridgway, R. & Friedmann, H.
- The Birds of North and Middle America, a Descriptive Catalogue ... Washington: 1901-50. Vols 1-11, all so far published. 11 vols. 222 plates. Vols 1-8 cloth (vol 8 spine faded), the rest in orig wraps. H.F. Witherby's set.
          (Wheldon & Wesley) **£275 [≈$527]**

Rieder, Hermann
- Atlas of Urinary Sediments ... Edited and Annotated by A. Sheridan Delepine. London: 1899. 1st English translation. 111 pp. 36 cold plates. Orig bndg.   *(Fye)* **$200 [≈£104]**

Riley, Henry A.
- An Atlas of the Basal Ganglia, Brain Stem, and Spinal Cord. Baltimore: 1943. 1st edn. Oblong 4to. 708 pp. Cloth, scuffed, 1 inch tear at ft of spine.   *(Goodrich)* **$175 [≈£91]**

Rindfleisch, Eduard
- A Manual of Pathological Histology to serve as an Introduction to the Study of Morbid Anatomy. Translated by E. Buchanan Baster. London: New Sydenham Society, 1872. 2 vols. 8vo. Cloth, worn.
          (Goodrich) **$95 [≈£49]**

Ring, John
- An Answer to Dr Moseley, containing a Defence of Vaccination. London: Murray, 1805. 1st edn. 8vo. vii,291 pp, inc half-title. 2 lib stamps. V pale spotting. Old half calf.
          (Bickersteth) **£145 [≈$278]**

Rinne, F.
- Crystals and the Fine-Structure of Matter. New York: Dutton, 1922. 8vo. ix,195 pp. 12 plates, 202 text figs. V.g. ex-lib. Cloth.
          (Gemmary) **$50 [≈£26]**

Ripley, William Z.
- The Races of Europe. A Sociological Study. London: Kegan Paul ..., 1900. 1st edn. 8vo. Num ills. Orig cloth. *(Young's)* **£40 [≈$76]**

Ritchie, A.T.
- The Dynamical Theory of the Formation of the Earth. London: 1850. 2 vols. 8vo. vii, 562; viii, 632 pp. Sm lib stamps. Cloth, vol 2 backstrip relaid.   *(Henly)* **£28 [≈$53]**

Robberds, J.W.
- Geological and Historical Observations on the Eastern Vallies of Norfolk. Norwich: 1826. 8vo. xiii,76 pp, errata leaf. Fldg map. Orig roan backed bds, piece missing from ft of

spine.   *(Henly)* **£65 [≈ $124]**

Roberts, Austin
- The Mammals of South Africa. London: 1954. 2nd edn. Lge 4to. Num cold & other plates. Marg tear in title & next 2 pp. Sl foxed. Dw (sl frayed).
                    (Grayling) **£60 [≈ $115]**

Roberts, Job
- The Pennsylvania Farmer; being a Selection from the most Approved Treatises on Husbandry, interspersed with Observations and Experiments. Phila: 1804. 1st edn. v,[2]-224 pp. Foxed. Old stamp on endsheet. Contemp calf, some wear to extremities.
                    (Reese) **$450 [≈ £234]**

Roberts, John
- Surgical Delusions and Follies. Phila: 1884. 1st edn. 55 pp. Orig bndg. *(Fye)* **$125 [≈ £65]**
- The Surgical Treatment of Disfigurements and Deformities of the Face. Phila: 1901. 2nd edn. 72 pp. Num photo plates. Orig bndg.
                    (Fye) **$250 [≈ £130]**

Roberts, W.H.
- The British Wine-Maker and Domestic Brewer. A Complete, Practical and Easy Treatise on the Art of Making and Managing British Wines and Liqueurs ... Edinburgh: 1847. 4th edn. 8vo. xv,384,16 pp. Orig cloth.
                    (Young's) **£70 [≈ $134]**

Robertson, J.H.
- The Story of the Telephone. A History of the Telecommunications Industry of Britain. London: 1947. viii,299 pp. Spine & rear cvr sl faded.   *(Whitehart)* **£15 [≈ $28]**

Robertson, James
- General View of the Agriculture in the County of Inverness ... London: for Richard Phillips ..., 1808. 8vo. lxvi,447,[4 ctlg] pp. 2 fldg maps. Mod soft calf gilt.
                    (Hollett) **£120 [≈ $230]**

Robertson, John
- Tables of Difference of Latitude and departure. Phila: Joseph Cruikshank, 1790. 1st edn. 8vo. [i],90 pp. Later wraps.
                    (Bookpress) **$225 [≈ £117]**

Robertson, Robert
- An Essay on Fevers ... London: !790. 1st edn. 286 pp. Ex-lib. Leather, lacks backstrip, spine scorched.   *(Fye)* **$150 [≈ £78]**

Robinson, D.H.
- The Dangerous Sky. A History of Aviation Medicine. Henley: 1973. 8vo. xxiv,292 pp. Orig bndg.   *(Goodrich)* **$50 [≈ £26]**

Robinson, H.N.
- A Treatise on Surveying and Navigation. New York: Ivison, Phinney, 1862. 8vo. 246,101 pp. Text figs. Leather, hinges cracked.   *(Gemmary)* **$75 [≈ £39]**

Robinson, Judith
- Tom Cullen of Baltimore. London: 1949. 8vo. xii,435 pp. Ills. Cloth.
                    (Bickersteth) **£18 [≈ $34]**

Robinson, M.
- The New Family Herbal: comprising a Description, and the Medical Virtues of British and Foreign Plants. London: [ca 1870]. 12mo. 480 pp. 24 cold plates. Orig cloth gilt. *(Wheldon & Wesley)* **£45 [≈ $86]**

Robinson, Nicholas
- A Compleat Treatise of the Gravel and Stone, with all their Causes, Symptoms, and Cures ... Second Edition, with large Additions. London: B. Cowse, 1723. 8vo. [24], 284, [10], [8 advt] pp. Some damp staining mainly at the end. Contemp calf. *(Spelman)* **£140 [≈ $268]**

Robinson, S.
- A Catalogue of American Minerals. Boston: Cummings, Hilliard, 1825. Roy 8vo. 316 pp. Half leather.   *(Gemmary)* **$275 [≈ £143]**

Robinson, Thomas
- An Essay towards a Natural History of Westmorland and Cumberland ... London: J.L. for W. Freeman, 1709. 1st edn. [xiv],118,[2 advt] pp. Old calf, rebacked, new endpapers. Earl of derby's b'plates (dated 1702).   *(Hollett)* **£225 [≈ $431]**

Robison, S.S.
- Manual of Wireless Telegraphy 1911. 1911. 2nd edn. 2127 pp. 112 ills. Orig bndg.
                    (New Wireless) **$65 [≈ £33]**
- Robison's Manual of Radio Telegraphy and Telephony 1918. 1918. 4th edn. 256 pp. 30 photos, 121 ills. Orig bndg.
                    (New Wireless) **$45 [≈ £23]**
- Robison's Manual of Radio Telegraphy and Telephony 1919. 1919. 5th edn. 307 pp. 33 photos, 121 ills. Orig bndg.
                    (New Wireless) **$55 [≈ £28]**

Robson, J., et al.
- Canaries, Hybrids and British Birds in Cage and Aviary. Edited by S̓.H. Lewer. London: 1911. 4to. x,421 pp. 18 cold plates, num other ills. Orig dec cloth, trifle used.
  (Wheldon & Wesley) £60 [≈ $115]

Rockwell, A.D.
- The Medical and Surgical Uses of Electricity. 1896. 2nd edn. 612 pp. 200 ills. Leather, front hinge weak.
  (New Wireless) $125 [≈ £65]

Rodd, E.H.
- The Birds of Cornwall, and the Scilly Islands. Edited by J.E. Harting. London: 1880. 8vo. lvi,320 pp. Port, map. Sl foxed. Cloth, trifle used. *(Wheldon & Wesley)* £60 [≈ $115]

Rodway, L.
- The Tasmanian Flora. Hobart: 1903. Roy 8vo. xx,320 pp. 50 plates. Orig bds.
  (Wheldon & Wesley) £75 [≈ $143]

Rodwell, James
- The Rat. Its History and Destructive Character, with Numerous Anecdotes. London: [ca 1860]. New edn. Frontis. 19th c half calf. *(Grayling)* £60 [≈ $115]

Roesler, Hugo
- Atlas of Cardio-Roentgenology. Springfield: 1940. 1st edn. Folio. 124 pp. 166 ills. Orig bndg. *(Fye)* $100 [≈ £52]

Rokitansky, Carl
- A Manual of Pathological Anatomy. London: Sydenham Society, 1854. 1st English translation. 4 vols. 8vo. Foxed. Orig cloth, faded & sunned. *(Goodrich)* $250 [≈ £130]
- A Manual of Pathological Anatomy. Phila: 1855. 1st Amer edn. 2 vols. 267; 320 pp. Orig bndg. *(Fye)* $400 [≈ £208]

Rolfe, G.W.
- The Polariscope in the Chemical Laboratory. New York: Macmillan, 1905. Cr 8vo. vii,320 pp. 38 text figs. Cloth.
  (Gemmary) $45 [≈ £23]

Romanes, George John
- Darwin and after Darwin, an Exposition of the Darwinian Theory. London: 1892-97. 3 vols. Cr 8vo. 3 ports, 1 diag, 129 text figs. Cloth. *(Wheldon & Wesley)* £60 [≈ $115]
- Jelly-Fish, Star-Fish and Sea-Urchins being a Research on Primitive Nervous Systems. London: 1885. 1st edn. 323 pp. Orig bndg.

(Fye) $150 [≈ £78]
- The Life and Letters of George John Romanes. Edited by his Wife. London: 1896. 1st edn. 8vo. x,360 pp. 3 plates. A few pencil notes. Cloth.
  (Wheldon & Wesley) £45 [≈ $86]
- The Life and Letters of George John Romanes. Edited by his Wife. London: 1896. 2nd edn. 8vo. x,360 pp. 3 plates. Orig cloth, trifle used. *(Wheldon & Wesley)* £40 [≈ $76]

Ronayne, Philip
- A Treatise of Algebra in Two Books ... Second Edition with Additions. London: Innys, 1727. 8vo. [viii], v, [iii], 160, 177-461, [3 advt] pp. Text diags. Contemp sprinkled calf, worn, upper jnt cracked.
  (Gaskell) £375 [≈ $719]

Roosevelt, Theodore, et al.
- The Deer Family. USA: 1902. 8vo. Ills. Dw.
  (Grayling) £35 [≈ $67]

Roscoe, Sir Henry E.
- Spectrum Analysis: Six Lectures delivered in 1868 before the Society of Apothecaries of London. Fourth Edition Revised and Considerably Enlarged ... London: 1885. 8vo. xvi,452 pp. Frontis, 3 cold & 2 plain plates, text ills. Orig dec cloth gilt, t.e.g.
  (Bow Windows) £40 [≈ $76]

Rose, T.K.
- Precious Metals comprising Gold Silver and Platinum. London: Constable, 1909. 8vo. xvi,295 pp. 46 text figs. Cloth, sl loose.
  (Gemmary) $150 [≈ £79]

Rose, T.K. & Newman, W.A.C.
- The Metallurgy of Gold. London: Charles Griffin, 1894. 1st edn. 8vo. xvi,461 pp. 235 ills. Cloth, loose. *(Gemmary)* $125 [≈ £65]
- The Metallurgy of Gold. London: Charles Griffin, 1896. 2nd edn. 8vo. xviii,495 pp. 235 ills. Cloth, loose. *(Gemmary)* $125 [≈ £65]
- The Metallurgy of Gold. London: Charles Griffin, 1902. 4th edn. 8vo. xvi,554 pp. 94 ills. Cloth, new endpapers.
  (Gemmary) $150 [≈ £78]
- The Metallurgy of Gold. London: Charles Griffin, 1937. 7th edn. 8vo. xiii,561 pp. 235 ills. Cloth, loose. *(Gemmary)* $125 [≈ £65]

Rose, William
- The Surgical Treatment of the Fifth Nerve (Tic Douloureux). London: Bailliere, 1892. 8vo. viii,85 pp. Orig cloth, new spine.
  (Goodrich) $295 [≈ £153]

Rosen, Dr.
- The Reformed Practice of Medicine; A Practical Treatise on the Prevention and Cure of Disease without the Use of Mineral or Vegetable Poisons. Glasgow: [ca 1860]. 1st edn (?). 12mo. 114 pp. Port, 15 cold plates. Sm flaw in 1 leaf. Orig pict cloth.
(Gough) £35 [≈$67]

Ross, J. (ed.)
- The Book of the Red Deer. London: 1925. 4to. Ills. Some foxing. Orig bndg, spine somewhat snagged. *(Grayling)* £35 [≈$67]

Ross, T.
- A Compendious System of Geography, as connected with Astronomy and Illustrated by the Use of the Globes, with an Appendix ... Edinburgh: 1804. 780 pp. 8 maps (7 fldg). Contemp bds, uncut, rebacked, bds sl rubbed & worn. *(Whitehart)* £35 [≈$67]

Ross, W.A.
- The Blow-Pipe in Chemistry, Mineralogy & Geology. London: Crosby Lockwood, 1889. 2nd edn. Cr 8vo. xv,214,advt pp. 120 text figs, tables. Dec cloth.
(Gemmary) $100 [≈£52]

Ross-Craig, Stella
- Drawings of British Plants. London: 1948-73. Orig issue. 31 parts. 8vo. 1317 plates. Stiff wraps. *(Wheldon & Wesley)* £90 [≈$172]
- Drawings of British Plants ... L: 1979. 2nd edn. 8 vols. 8vo. 1299 plates. Cloth. Dws.
(Henly) £125 [≈$239]

Rossiter, William
- A First Book of Botany, for the Use of Schools and Private Families. Second Edition, revised and corrected. London: 1867. 12mo. viii, [2] pp. 20 plates (14 hand cold), over 220 text figs. Orig cloth, dull & marked, spine ends sl worn.
(Bow Windows) £35 [≈$67]

Rotch, Thomas
- Pediatrics: the Hygienic and Medical Treatment of Children. Phila: 1896. 1st edn. 1124 pp. Orig leather, fine.
(Fye) $200 [≈£104]

Roth, Irving
- Cardiac Arrhythmias, Clinical Features & Mechanism of the Irregular Heart. New York: 1928. 1st edn. 4to. 210 pp. Ills. Orig bndg. *(Fye)* $200 [≈£104]

Roth, M.
- The Prevention and Cure of many Chronic Diseases by Movements. London: 1851. 1st edn. 303 pp. Inner marg of title stained. Rec qtr leather, new endpapers. *(Fye)* $150 [≈£78]

Rotheram, J.
- Edinburgh New Dispensatory. Containing the Elements of Pharmaceutical Chemistry, The Materia Medica ... Edinburgh: 1801. 6th edn. xxxi, 622 pp. 3 plates. Contemp leather, rebacked, crnrs sl worn.
(Whitehart) £95 [≈$182]

Rothschild, M. & Clay, T.
- Fleas, Flukes and Cuckoos; a Study of Bird Parasites. London: Collins New Naturalist, 1952. 1st edn (reprint). 8vo. xiv,304,2 pp. 40 plates. Orig cloth. Dw. *(Henly)* £35 [≈$67]

Rousseau, Jean Jacques
- Letters on the Elements of Botany. Addressed to a Lady. Translated into English with Notes and Twenty-Four Additional Letters ... by Thomas Martyn. London: White, 1785. 1st edn in English. 8vo. xxiv,503,[28] pp. Fldg table. Contemp calf, v faint mark back bd.
(Gough) £125 [≈$239]
- Letters on the Elements of Botany. Addressed to a Lad. With Notes, and Twenty-Four Additional Letters, fully explaining the System of Linnaeus. London: 1787. Translated by T. Martyn. xxv,500,[28] pp. Fldg table. Contemp calf, rebacked.
(Whitehart) £85 [≈$163]

Rowe, N.L. & Killey, H.C.
- Fractures of the Facial Skeleton. Edinburgh: 1955. xxxvi,923 pp. Num text ills. Cloth, sl marked. *(Whitehart)* £35 [≈$67]

Rowlette, Robert J.
- The Medical Press and Circular, 1839-1939; A Hundred Years in the Life of a Medical Journal. London: MPC, 1939. 4to. Ills. Cloth bds. *(Emerald Isle)* £55 [≈$105]

Royal College of Physicians of London
- Catalogue of the Library. London: 1912. [vi], 1354 pp. Lib bndg, hinges sl weak.
(Whitehart) £40 [≈$76]

Royal College of Surgeons of England
- Catalogue of the Hunterian Collection in the Museum. London: 1830-31. 6 vols. 4to. Sl foxing. Contemp cloth. Only fasc I of Part 4 was published.
(Wheldon & Wesley) £100 [≈$191]

Royal Horticultural Society

- Dictionary of Gardening. Edited by J.F. Chittenden. London: 1951-69. 1st edn. 4 vols. 2316 pp. Ills. [With] Supplement. 2nd edn. Together 5 vols. 4to. Orig cloth.
(Henly) **£90 [≈ $172]**
- Dictionary of Gardening. Edited by Fred J. Chittenden. Oxford: Clarendon Press, 1956. 2nd edn. 5 vols. Num ills. Dws (sl chipped).
(Gough) **£135 [≈ $259]**

Royal Society

- Biographical Memoirs of the Royal Society. London: 1955-86. Vols 1-32. Complete run. Orig cloth. Mostly with dws.
(Whitehart) **£280 [≈ $537]**
- Obituary Notices of Fellows of the Royal Society, 1941-53 [with] Biographical Memoirs of Fellows of the Royal Society, 1955-80. Together 39 annual vols, lacking the vol for 1954, with the index vol 1951-60. Orig wraps & orig blue buckram.
(Claude Cox) **£120 [≈ $230]**

Ruhmer, Ernst

- Wireless Telephony. Translated by James Erskine Murray. 1908. 1st English edn. 225,64 ctlg pp. 145 ills. Orig bndg, spine sl worn. *(New Wireless)* **$195 [≈ £101]**

Rumpel, O.

- Cystoscopy as adjuvant in Surgery with an Atlas of Cytoscopic Views and Concomitant Text for Physicians and Students. New York: 1910. 1st English translation. 4to. 131 pp. 85 mtd cold ills. Orig bndg. *(Fye)* **$150 [≈ £78]**

Rundell, Maria Eliza

- Modern Domestic Cookery ... Carefully Revised. London: Milner & Co, [ca 1890?]. Ills. Sl browned. Orig red cloth, sl dulled.
(Jarndyce) **£15 [≈ $28]**
- A New System of Domestic Cookery: formed upon Principles of Economy ... New Edition, corrected. London: Murray, 1808. Lge 12mo. [22], xxx, 28*/29*, 351, [1 advt] pp. Frontis, 9 plates. Minor browning, occas foxing. Contemp tree calf, gilt label, lower jnt cracked. *(Spelman)* **£120 [≈ $230]**
- A New System of Domestic Cookery, formed upon Principles of Economy: and adapted to ... the United States. By a Lady. Second Edition. New York: 1815. xxiii, [25]-316, [1] pp. Frontis, plates. Occas foxing. Lib b'plate. Mod lib buckram. Anon.
(Reese) **$300 [≈ £156]**
- A New System of Domestic Cookery; formed upon Principles of Economy ... By a Lady.

New Edition, Corrected. London: Murray, 1819. 12mo. Frontis, plates. Some spotting. Red half calf, dark green label. Anon.
(Jarndyce) **£85 [≈ $163]**
- A New System of Domestic Cookery; formed upon Principles of Economy ... New Edition, Corrected. London: Murray, 1827. 12mo. liv, 449 pp. Frontis, 9 plates (damp marked). Some spotting. Contemp calf, backstrip relaid. Anon. *(Gough)* **£60 [≈ $115]**
- A New System of Domestic Cookery: formed upon Principles of Economy ... Sixty-Third Edition, corrected and augmented ... London: Murray ..., 1839. 8vo. liv,448 pp. Frontis, 9 plates. Orig cloth, ptd label. Anon.
(Burmester) **£65 [≈ $124]**

Rural Oeconomy ...

- See Young, Arthur.

Rush, Benjamin

- Medical Inquiries and Observations. Phila: 1818. 5th edn. 2 vols. 273; 249 pp. Lacks free endpapers. Orig leather, lacks labels, 1-inch missing from hd of vol 1 spine.
(Fye) **$250 [≈ £130]**

Ruskin, Arthur

- Classics in Arterial Hypertension. Springfield: 1956. 1st edn. 358 pp. Orig bndg. *(Fye)* **$100 [≈ £52]**

Russel, A.

- The Salmon. Edinburgh: 1864. 8vo. viii,248 pp. Cloth. *(Wheldon & Wesley)* **£25 [≈ $47]**

Russell, Sir E.J.

- The World of the Soil. London: Collins New Naturalist, 1957. 1st edn. 8vo. xiv,237,4 pp. 2 cold & 24 plain plates. Orig cloth.
(Henly) **£24 [≈ $46]**
- The World of the Soil. London: Collins New Naturalist, 1959. 2nd edn. 8vo. xiv,237,4 pp. 2 cold & 24 plain plates. Orig cloth.
(Henly) **£20 [≈ $38]**

Russell, E.S.

- The Interpretation of Development and Heredity. Oxford: 1930. [vii],312 pp. Few sl pencil notes. Cloth, sl marked.
(Whitehart) **£25 [≈ $47]**

Russell, Joseph

- A Treatise on Practical and Chemical Agriculture ... Warwick: E. Foden, for the author, 1831. 1st edn. 8vo. xvi,396 pp. Some spotting. Orig bds, uncut, rebacked.
(Burmester) **£120 [≈ $230]**

Russell, K.F.
- British Anatomy, 1525-1800. A Bibliography. Parkville, Victoria: 1963. One of 750 sgnd. xvii,254 pp. Frontis, sev plates. Orig bndg. *(Whitehart)* **£45 [≈ $86]**

Russell, R.
- On Hail. London: 1893. xv,224 pp. 2 woodburytypes of hailstones. Cloth sl dull, sm lib label on front cvr & endpaper.
(Whitehart) **£25 [≈ $47]**

Russell, Richard
- Dissertation concerning the Use of Sea Water in Diseases of the Glands ... Oxford: At the Theatre, 1753. 1st edn containing both parts. xvi,398,[2] pp. Licence leaf, errata at end. 7 plates. Contemp calf, spine extremities sl rubbed. *(Karmiole)* **$400 [≈ £208]**
- A Dissertation of the Use of Sea-Water in the Diseases of the Glands ... Third Edition, revised and corrected ... London: for W. Owen, 1755. 8vo. Frontis, plate. 1 marg tear. Sl spotting. Contemp calf, gilt, sl rubbed, wear at spine ends, splits in hinge.
(Jarndyce) **£140 [≈ $268]**
- The Oeconomy of Nature in Acute and Chronical Diseases of the Glands ... London: 1755. 1st edn. 8vo. [iv], 253, [1 blank,1 advt, 1 blank] pp. 1 plate. Old jotting on title verso. Old calf, rebacked, crnrs worn.
(Bow Windows) **£175 [≈ $335]**

Russell, T.
- Meteorology Weather, and Methods of Forecasting Description of Meteorological Instruments and River Flood Predictions in the United States. New York: 1895. xxiii,277 pp. 50 maps, 29 text figs. Few pp sl nicked at hd. Orig bndg. *(Whitehart)* **£25 [≈ $47]**

Rutherford, Sir Ernest
- Radioactive Substances and their Radiations. Cambridge: 1913. viii,699 pp. 5 plates, num text figs. Orig cloth, sl worn, prize label, endpapers sl discold. *(Whitehart)* **£40 [≈ $76]**

Rutherford, Sir Ernest, et al.
- Radiations from Radioactive Substances. Cambridge: UP, 1930. 1st edn. 8vo. xi,588 pp. 140 text figs. Orig cloth.
(Gough) **£45 [≈ $86]**
- Radiations from Radioactive Substances. Cambridge: (1931) 1951. xi,588 pp. 12 plates, 140 text figs. Orig cloth. Dw (torn & marked). *(Whitehart)* **£40 [≈ $76]**

Rutherforth, Thomas
- A System of Natural Philosophy ... Cambridge: J. Bentham, 1748. 1st edn. 2 vols. 4to. [24], 496; [4], 497-1105, [7] pp. Subscribers. Fldg map, 31 plates. Minimal browning. Contemp tree calf, elab gilt spine (sl worn). *(Rootenberg)* **$500 [≈ £260]**

Rye, E.C.
- British Beetles ... London: Lovell Reeve, 1866. 1st edn. xv,280,16 ctlg pp. 16 cold plates. Orig pict maroon cloth gilt, spine faded & sl marked. *(Gough)* **£30 [≈ $57]**
- British Beetles: an Introduction to the Study of our Indigenous Coleoptera. London: Lovell Reeve, 1866. 1st edn. 8vo. xvi,280,16 ctlg pp. 16 hand cold plates. Orig cloth, minor fading. *(Claude Cox)* **£35 [≈ $67]**

S., J.
- The Shepherd's Kalendar, or the Citizen's and Countryman's Daily Companion ... The Twelfth Edition, with Additions. London: J. Hollis, [ca 1807?]. 12mo. 94,2 advt pp. W'cut frontis, 4 w'cut text figs. Sl age-browning. Contemp bds, uncut, recased. Preface sgnd J.S. *(Beech)* **£130 [≈ $249]**

S., M.E. & S., K.R.
- Sir Joseph Wilson Swan F.R.S. 1929. 1st edn. 183 pp. 6 photos. Orig bndg, spine worn at ft.
(New Wireless) **$45 [≈ £23]**

Sabine, Wallace Clement
- Collected Papers on Acoustics. 1922. 1st edn. 279 pp. Orig bndg.
(New Wireless) **$85 [≈ £45]**

Safian, Joseph
- Corrective Rhinoplastic Surgery. New York: 1935. 1st edn. 218 pp. Ills. Orig bndg.
(Fye) **$200 [≈ £104]**

Sahli, H.
- A Treatise on Diagnostic Methods of Examination. London: 1906. 1008 pp. 12 plates, 383 text figs. Sl marg tears in last few pp. Orig cloth. *(Whitehart)* **£25 [≈ $47]**

St. John, C.
- Our Canaries, a thoroughly Practical and Comprehensive Guide to the Successful Keeping, Breeding, nd Exhibiting of every known Variety. London: [1911]. 4to. 382 pp. 32 cold & 32 plain plates. Cloth, trifle worn.
(Wheldon & Wesley) **£60 [≈ $115]**

St. John, Thomas M.
- Wireless telegraphy for Amateurs and Students. 1906. 1st edn. 171 pp. 155 ills. Orig bndg, cvrs stained, edges worn.
(New Wireless) **$65 [≈ £34]**

Sale catalogues
- The Honeyman Collection of Scientific Books and Manuscripts. London: Sotheby Parke Bernet, 1978-81. 7 parts. 4to. Ills. Wrappers.   *(Gemmary)* **$275 [≈ £143]**
- The Sir John Findlay Collection ... Scientific Instruments (Part 1). London: Sotheby, 1961. 8vo. 69,26,8 pp. Plates. Cloth.
(Gemmary) **$200 [≈ £104]**

Salisbury, Sir E.J.
- Downs and Dunes. Their Plant Life and Environment. London: 1952. 8vo. xiii,328 pp. Num ills. Cloth.
(Wheldon & Wesley) **£25 [≈ $47]**
- Weeds and Aliens. London: Collins New Naturalist, 1961. 1st edn. 8vo. 1 cold & 16 plain plates. Orig cloth. *(Henly)* **£45 [≈ $86]**
- Weeds & Aliens. London: New Naturalist, 1961. 384 pp. Cold frontis, ills. Title sl foxed. Orig cloth.   *(Baldwin)* **£40 [≈ $76]**

Salisbury, William
- Hints Addressed to Proprietors of Orchards, and to growers of Fruit ... London: Longman, & the author, 1816. 1st edn. 8vo. xviii, [iv], 188 pp. 2 fldg plates (sl spotted). Orig bds, spine ends worn. *(Burmester)* **£75 [≈ $143]**

Sallander, Hans
- Bibliotheca Walleriana. The Books Illustrating the History of Medicine and Science. Collected by Dr. Erik Waller ... Compiled by Hans Sallander. Stockholm: 1955. 2 vols. 8vo. Dws.
(Goodrich) **$450 [≈ £234]**

Salmon, C.E.
- Flora of Surrey. London: 1931. 8vo. 688 pp. 2 cold maps, port, 8 plates. Cloth.
(Wheldon & Wesley) **£36 [≈ $69]**

Samouelle, George
- The Entomological Cabinet; being a Natural History of British Insects. London: 1841. 2nd edn. Post 8vo. 156 hand cold plates. Sl dust soiling. Mod half calf.
(Wheldon & Wesley) **£150 [≈ $287]**
- The Entomologist's Useful Compendium; or an Introduction to the Knowledge of British Insects. London: 1824. New edn. 8vo. 496 pp. 12 plain plates. Trifle foxed. Half leather,

worn but sound.
(Wheldon & Wesley) **£35 [≈ $67]**
- The Entomologist's Useful Compendium; or An Introduction to the Knowledge of British Insects ... London: Longman, Hurst ..., 1824. 8vo. 496 pp. 20 plates (12 hand cold). Mor gilt, elab gilt spine, a.e.g.
(Hollett) **£120 [≈ $230]**

Samuelson, J. & Hicks, J.B.
- Humble Creatures: Part I. The Earthworm and the Common Housefly ... With Microscopic Illustrations ... Second Edition. London: 1860. Sm 8vo. viii,79 pp. 8 plates. Tiny marg worm hole in a few ff. Sl marks. Orig cloth.   *(Bow Windows)* **£25 [≈ $47]**

Sanborn, Kate
- Educated Dogs of To-day. An Illustrated Record of Canine Intelligence Marking an Advance with the Modern Movement of Man. Boston: privately ptd, 1916. Lge 4to. 80 pp. Num ills. Orig bds, pict onlay, sl water stained.   *(Karmiole)* **$75 [≈ £39]**

Sanctorius, Sanctorius
- Medicina Statica: being the Aphorisms ... Translated into English with large Explanations ... By John Quincy. London: for William Newton, 1712. 1st edn. 8vo. lvi,[312] pp. Final page mispaginated 112. Frontis, fldg plate. Faintly browned. Contemp calf, sl worn.   *(Finch)* **£150 [≈ $287]**
- Medicina Statica: being the Aphorisms ... Translated into English with large Explanations ... added, Dr. Keil's Medicina Statica ... Essays ... by John Quincy ... London: 1723. 3rd edn. 8vo. viii, 344, xxiv, 116 pp. Frontis, fldg plate. Orig calf, rebacked.   *(Bickersteth)* **£85 [≈ $163]**
- Medicina Statica: being the Aphorisms ... Translated into English with large Explanations ... By John Quincy ... added, Dr. Keil's Medicina Statica ... London: 1737. 5th edn. 463 pp. Fldg plate. Leather, rebacked, new endpapers.
(Fye) **$400 [≈ £208]**

Sappington, John
- The Theory and Treatment of Fevers. Arrow Rock, MO: 1844. 1st edn. 216 pp. Leather.
(Fye) **$250 [≈ £130]**

Sarjeant, W.A.S.
- Geologists and the History of Geology. An International Bibliography from the Origins to 1978. London: 1980. 5 vols. Orig cloth.
(Baldwin) **£230 [≈ $441]**

Sarton, George
- A History of Science. Cambridge: 1959-60. Vol 1 3rd printing, vol 2 1st printing. 2 vols, all published. Dws. *(Goodrich)* **$75 [≈ £39]**

Saunders, H.
- Manual of British Birds. Revised by W.E. Clarke. London: 1927. 3rd (last) edn. viii, 834 pp. 405 figs. New cloth, t.e.g.
(Whitehart) **£25 [≈ $47]**

Saunders, J.B. & O'Malley, C.D.
- Vesalius. The Illustrations from his Works ... with Annotations, Translations, a Discussion of the Plates and their Background, Authorship and Influence, and a Biographical Sketch. New York: 1950. 4to. Ills. Dw.
(Goodrich) **$75 [≈ £39]**

Saunders, John Cunningham
- A Treatise on some Practical Points relating to the Diseases of the Eye ... A Short Account of the Author's Life, and his Method of Curing the Congenital Cataract. London: Longman, 1811. 1st edn. 8vo. xliii, [1], 216 pp. Frontis port, 8 plates. Sl used. Contemp half calf. *(Rootenberg)* **$550 [≈ £286]**

Saunders, William
- A Treatise on the Structure, Economy, and Diseases of the Liver ... London: 1793. 1st edn. 232 pp. Wormhole affecting marg of 25 ff. Rec qtr leather. *(Fye)* **$250 [≈ £130]**
- A Treatise on the Structure, Economy, and Diseases of the Liver; together with an Inquiry into the Properties and Component Parts of the Bile and Biliary Concretions. London: 1795. 2nd edn. xxvi,261 pp. Few sm ink stains. Half leather, rebacked, sl worn.
(Whitehart) **£90 [≈ $172]**

Savage, C.
- The Mandarin Duck. London: 1952. 4to. ix, 78 pp. Cold frontis by Peter Scott, 16 plates, 41 text figs. Cloth.
(Wheldon & Wesley) **£35 [≈ $67]**

Savage, Henry
- The Surgery, Surgical Pathology and Surgical Anatomy of the Female Pelvic Organs in a Series of Plates taken from Nature. New York: 1880. 3rd edn. 115 pp. 32 engvd plates. Orig bndg. *(Fye)* **$100 [≈ £52]**

Saville-Kent, W.
- A Manual of the Infusoria. London: 1881-82. 3 vols in 2. Roy 8vo. Cold frontis, 52 plates (1-51, 48a). Sl foxing. Half mor, spines faded.

(Wheldon & Wesley) **£160 [≈ $307]**

Savoury, T.H.
- The Spiders and Allied Orders of the British Isles. L: 1935. 1st edn. Post 8vo. xvi,176 pp. 15 cold & 80 plain plates. Cloth gilt.
(Henly) **£24 [≈ $46]**
- The Spider's Web. L: 1952. 1st edn. Post 8vo. 154 pp. 8 cold & 19 plain plates. Cloth gilt. *(Henly)* **£24 [≈ $46]**

Sawyer, Arthur Robert
- Accidents in Mines, in the North Staffordshire Coalfield ... Hanley: Allbut & Daniel, 1886. Tall 8vo. 101 pp. Over 300 figs, some in 2 colours, many in fldg plates. Orig cloth gilt, spine faded, rather used. Author's pres inscrptn. *(Hollett)* **£55 [≈ $105]**

Say, T.
- Descriptions of New Species of Heteropterous Hemiptera of North America. New-Harmony, Indiana: 1831. 8vo. 39 pp. Blind stamp on title. Bds, rebacked.
(Wheldon & Wesley) **£100 [≈ $191]**

Sayre, Lewis
- Lectures on Orthopedic Surgery and Diseases of the Joints. New York: 1885. 2nd edn. 569 pp. Rvsd edn. 324 ills. Orig bndg.
(Fye) **$150 [≈ £78]**

Scalpel, Aesculapius
- Dying Scientifically ... see Berdoe, Edward.

Scammon, C.M.
- The Marine Mammals of the North-Western Coast of North America, described and illustrated, together with an Account of the American Whale-Fishery. San Francisco: 1874. 4to. 319,v pp. 27 litho plates, text figs. Some blind stamps. New half mor.
(Wheldon & Wesley) **£900 [≈ $1,727]**

Schaefer, E.A. (ed.)
- Text-Book of Physiology. Edinburgh: Young J. Pentland, 1898-1900. 2 vols. Lib stamp on titles. Orig cloth, recased, rubbed.
(Goodrich) **$350 [≈ £182]**

Schall, W.E.
- X Rays: Their Origin, Dosage and Practical Application. 1928. 3rd edn. 307 pp. 139 ills. Orig bndg, front cvr stained.
(New Wireless) **$45 [≈ £24]**

Schellen, H.
- Spectrum Analysis in its Application to

Terrestrial Substances, and the Physical Constitution of the Heavenly Bodies. New York: Appleton, 1872. 1st edn. 8vo. xvii,455 pp. Plates, ills. Cloth, loose.
(Gemmary) **$100 [≈ £52]**

- Spectrum Analysis ... London: Longmans, Green, 1885. 2nd edn. 8vo. xxiv,626 pp. Cold plates, ills. Ex-lib. Cloth, loose.
(Gemmary) **$100 [≈ £52]**

Scheuchzer, John Gaspar
- An Account of the Success of Inoculating the Small-Pox in Great britain, for the Years 1727 and 1728 ... London: J. Peele, 1729. 63 pp. Some ff trimmed sl close. Rec wraps.
(C.R. Johnson) **£160 [≈ $307]**
- An Account of the Success of Inoculating the Small-Pox in Great Britain, for the Years 1727 and 1728 ... London: for J. Peele ..., 1729. 1st edn. 8vo. 63 pp. Page numerals & 1 catchword partly cropped. Wraps.
(Young's) **£290 [≈ $556]**

Schilling, C.W. & Werts, M.F.
- An Annotated Bibliography on Diving and Submarine Medicine. London: 1971. vii,622 pp.
(Whitehart) **£35 [≈ $67]**

Schoeller, W.R. & Powell, A.R.
- The Analysis of Minerals and Ores of the Rare Elements. London: Charles Griffin, 1919. 1st edn. 8vo. x,239 pp. Cloth.
(Gemmary) **$55 [≈ £28]**
- The Analysis of Minerals and Ores of the Rare Elements. London: Charles Griffin, 1940. 2nd edn. 8vo. xv,308 pp. Cloth.
(Gemmary) **$65 [≈ £33]**

Schouten, J.
- The Rod and Serpent of Asklepios. Amsterdam: 1967. 1st English translation. 260 pp. Num ills. Orig bndg.
(Fye) **$90 [≈ £46]**

Schouw, J.F.
- The Earth, Plants, and Man. Popular Pictures of Nature ... Translated and edited by A. Henfrey. London: 1852. Sm 8vo. [iv],402 pp. Cold frontis map. Dark green polished calf gilt, inside gilt borders, a.e.g.
(Bow Windows) **£45 [≈ $86]**

Schrodinger, E.
- Space-Time Structure. Cambridge: UP, 1950. 8vo. viii,119 pp. Cloth. Dw.
(Gemmary) **$35 [≈ £18]**
- What is Life? The Physical Aspects of the Living Cell. Cambridge: 1944. Cr 8vo. viii,91

pp. 4 plates, text figs. Cloth. Dw.
(Wheldon & Wesley) **£35 [≈ $67]**

Schullian, D.M. & Sommer, F.E.
- A Catalogue of Incunabula and Manuscripts in the Army Medical Library. New York: 1948. 8vo. 361 pp. Ills. Orig bndg.
(Goodrich) **$65 [≈ £33]**
- A Catalogue of Incunabula and Manuscripts in the Army Medical Library. New York: Henry Schuman, [1949]. Med 8vo. 12 plates.
(Georges) **£50 [≈ $95]**

Schupbach, William
- The Paradox of Rembrandt's 'Anatomy of Dr. Tulp'. London: Wellcome Institute, 1982. 1st edn. Sm 4to. xiv,110 pp. 45 plates, 13 text figs. Orig cloth.
(Gough) **£20 [≈ $38]**

Schuster, A.
- An Introduction to the Theory of Optics. London: Edward Arnold, 1904. 8vo. xv,340 pp. 180 text figs. Ex-lib. Cloth.
(Gemmary) **$50 [≈ £26]**

Schwann, Theodor
- Microscopical Researches into the Accordance in the Structure and Growth of Animals and Plants. London: 1847. 1st English translation. 268 pp. Ex-lib. Rebound in buckram.
(Fye) **$150 [≈ £78]**

Schwartzenberg, F.A.
- Alexander Von Humboldt; or, What may be Accomplished in a Lifetime. London: Robert Hardwicke, 1866. Half-title, 207, advt pp. Orig green cloth. *(C.R. Johnson)* **£35 [≈ $67]**

Scofield, Samuel
- A Practical Treatise on Vaccina or Cowpock. New York: Southwick & Pelsue, 1810. Only edn. 12mo. 139,[1] pp. Hand cold plate. Occas foxing. Contemp calf, front hinge weak.
(Rootenberg) **$450 [≈ £234]**

Scoresby-Jackson, R.E.
- Note-Book of Materia Medica, Pharmacology and Therapeutics. Edinburgh: 1866. xii,632 pp. Page edges soiled. Cloth, dusty & sl worn, inner hinge cracked. *(Whitehart)* **£38 [≈ $72]**
- On the Influence of Weather upon Disease and Mortality. Edinburgh: Neill & Co, 1863. 1st edn. 4to. 54 pp. Frontis map, 3 fldg tables, 4 fldg charts. Orig cloth.
(Chapel Hill) **$150 [≈ £78]**

Scott, D.H.
- Studies in Fossil Botany. London: 1920-23.

3rd edn. 2 vols. 8vo. 326 text figs. Cloth, spines faded, sl worn at hd.
(Wheldon & Wesley) **£30 [≈ $57]**

Scott, Harold
- A History of Tropical Medicine. Baltimore: 1939. 1st edn. 2 vols. 1165 pp. Ex-lib. Orig bndg. *(Fye)* **$200 [≈ £104]**

Scott, Robert
- A Treatise on the Ventilation of Coal Mines; together with a Narrative of Scenes and Incidents ... London: Spon, 1863. 1st edn. 8vo. Disbound. *(Young's)* **£26 [≈ $49]**

Scott-Brown, W.G.
- Diseases of the Ear, Nose and Throat. London: 1952. 2 vols. 27 cold plates, 598 text figs. Orig bndg. *(Whitehart)* **£25 [≈ $47]**

Scott-Elliot, G.F.
- The Flora of Dumfriesshire, including part of the Stewartry of Kirkcudbright. Dumfries: 1896. 8vo. xl,219 pp. Fldg map. Good ex-lib. Cloth. *(Wheldon & Wesley)* **£30 [≈ $57]**

Scott-Taggart, John
- Elementary Text-Book on Wireless Vacuum Tubes. 1922. 4th edn. 232 pp. 136 ills. Orig bndg, some wear to spine.
(New Wireless) **$40 [≈ £20]**
- Thermionic Vacuum Tubes in Radio Telegraphy and Telephony. 1921. 1st edn. 424 pp. 344 ills. Orig bndg.
(New Wireless) **$45 [≈ £23]**

Scrivenor, J.B.
- The Geology of Malaya. London: 1931. xx, 217 pp. Lge fldg map in pocket, 33 text figs. Orig cloth, sl marked.
(Whitehart) **£18 [≈ $34]**

Scrope, George J. Paulett
- The Geology and Extinct Volcanoes of Central France. London: 1858. 2nd edn. 8vo. xvii, 258 pp. 2 fldg maps in pocket, 17 plates, 10 text figs. Orig cloth, new endpapers.
(Henly) **£120 [≈ $230]**
- Volcanos. The Character of their Phenomena ... With a Descriptive Catalogue of all known Volcanos ... Second Edition, Revised and Enlarged. London: 1862. 8vo. xi,[1],490,[2 blank] pp. Frontis, fldg map, num text ills. Orig cloth gilt. *(Fenning)* **£95 [≈ $182]**

Searle, Henry
- A Treatise on the Tonic System of Treating Affections of the Stomach and Brain. London:

Richard & John E. Taylor, 1843. 1st edn. 8vo. [iv], 308 pp. Orig cloth, faded.
(Burmester) **£75 [≈ $143]**

Searle, John
- A New and Improved Method of Constructing Bee-Houses and Bee-Hives, and the Management of the same. Concord (NH): Asa McFarland, 1839. 1st edn. 8vo. 4 w'cut diags. Sl foxing. Disbound.
(Ximenes) **$325 [≈ £169]**

Seaward, A.C.
- Plant Life through the Ages. A Geological and Botanical Retrospect. Cambridge: 1931. 8vo. xxi,601 pp. 140 figs. Orig cloth.
(Henly) **£42 [≈ $80]**
- Plant Life through the Ages. A Geological and Botanical Retrospect. London: 1941. 3rd edn. New endpapers. *(Henly)* **£18 [≈ $34]**

Seebohm, Henry
- The Birds of Siberia. A Records of a Naturalist's Visits to the Valleys of the Petchora and Yenesei. London: Murray, 1901. 1st edn. 8vo. xix,512 pp. Fldg map, num ills. Orig dec cloth.
(Frew Mackenzie) **£70 [≈ $134]**
- Coloured Figures of the Eggs of British Birds. Sheffield: Pawson & Brailsford, 1896. 1st edn. 8vo. xiv,304 pp. Port, 59 cold plates. V occas marg spotting to some plates. Orig cloth gilt, somewhat marked & rubbed.
(Gough) **£35 [≈ $67]**

Seguin, Edward
- Idiocy: and its Treatment by the Physiological Method. New York: 1866. 1st edn. 457 pp. Orig bndg. *(Fye)* **$350 [≈ £182]**

Seitz, A.
- Macrolepidoptera of the World. Vol 9. Indo-Australian Butterflies. Stuttgart: [1908-] 1927. 2 vols. 4to. 1184 pp. 177 (1-175, 146B, 150B) cold plates. Titles creased. Orig half mor. *(Wheldon & Wesley)* **£750 [≈ $1,439]**
- Macrolepidoptera of the World. Vol 9. Indo-Australian Bombyces and Sphinges. Stuttgart: 1933-34. 4to. 909 pp. 104 cold plates. Half mor.
(Wheldon & Wesley) **£600 [≈ $1,151]**

Selby, Prideaux John
- A History of Forest Trees; Indigenous and Introduced. London: Van Voorst, 1842. xx,540 pp. Num text w'engvs. Contemp green half mor, t.e.g., gilt spine (faded).
(Gough) **£95 [≈ $182]**

- The Naturalist's Library: Parrots. London: Bohn, [ca 1850]. Sm 8vo. [vi], 17-207, 189-219 pp, correct for this edn. Port, cold vignette, 30 hand cold plates. Orig red cloth, spine sl worn.
(*Wheldon & Wesley*) **£100 [≈ $191]**
- The Naturalist's Library: Pigeons. Edinburgh: [ca 1850]. Sm 8vo. [vi], 17-252 pp, correct. Port, cold vignette, 30 cold plates. Orig red cloth.
(*Wheldon & Wesley*) **£90 [≈ $172]**

Select Essays on Husbandry ...
- Select Essays on Husbandry. Extracted from the Museum Rusticum, and Foreign Essays on Agriculture ... Experiments ... in Scotland. Edinburgh: Balfour, 1767. 1st edn. 8vo. viii, 408 pp. Advt leaf after title. 2 plates, fldg table. Some (mostly marg) stain. Contemp calf, rubbed.   (*Finch*) **£135 [≈ $259]**

Senn, Nicholas
- Intestinal Surgery. Chicago: 1889. 1st edn. 269 pp. Orig bndg.   (*Fye*) **$225 [≈ £117]**
- A Nurse's Guide for the Operating Room. Chicago: 1932. 1st edn. 131 pp. Ills. Orig bndg.   (*Fye*) **$100 [≈ £52]**

Servetus, Michael
- Michael Servetus. A Translation of his Geographical, Medical and Astrological Writings with Introductions and Notes by C.D. O'Malley. Phila: 1953. 208 pp. Port, 4 plates.   (*Whitehart*) **£25 [≈ $47]**

Seth-Smith, D.
- Parrakeets. A Handbook to the Imported Species. London: 1903. Roy 8vo. xix,281 pp. 20 cold (19 hand cold) plates, 24 text figs. Cloth.   (*Wheldon & Wesley*) **£325 [≈ $623]**

Seton, E.T.
- Lives of Game Animals ... New York: 1925-28. One of 177 deluxe. 4 vols. 4to. 55 maps, 450 plates, 128 ills. Sm blind stamp on titles, 1 sm tear reprd. Orig buckram, sl used, 1 jnt worn.
(*Wheldon & Wesley*) **£375 [≈ $719]**

Seward, A.C.
- Fossil Plants, a Text Book for Students of Botany and Geology. Cambridge: 1898-1919. 4 vols. 8vo. Cloth, vol 2 spine faded.
(*Wheldon & Wesley*) **£75 [≈ $143]**

Sharp, Samuel
- A Critical Enquiry into the Present State of Surgery. Second Edition. London: Tonson,

1750. 8vo. [8],294 pp. Contemp unlettered calf, lacks f.e.p.   (*Spelman*) **£160 [≈ $307]**
- A Treatise on the Operations of Surgery, with a Description and Representation of the Instruments used ... Eighth Edition. London: Tonson, 1761. 8vo. [viii],liv,234 pp. 14 plates. Contemp calf, spine sl rubbed & chipped at hd.
(*Frew Mackenzie*) **£285 [≈ $547]**
- A Treatise on the Operations of Surgery, with a Description and Representation of the Instruments used in performing them ... London: 1761. 8th edn. 234 pp. Plates. Rec qtr leather.   (*Fye*) **$400 [≈ £208]**

Sharpe, R. Bowdler
- A Hand-List of the Genera and Species of Birds. London: BM, 1899-1912. 6 vols. 8vo. Ex-lib, trifle used but unstamped. Orig cloth.
(*Wheldon & Wesley*) **£85 [≈ $163]**
- Sketch-Book of British Birds. London: SPCK, 1898. 1st edn. Sm 4to. xx,255 pp. 1 plain & 303 colour-printed plates & text ills by A.F. & C. Lydon. Orig pict green cloth, gilt spine, fine.   (*Gough*) **£65 [≈ $124]**
- Wonders of the Bird World. London: Wells, Gardner, Darton, 1898. 1st edn. xvi,399 pp. 104 b/w ills. Occas sl spotting. Orig pict green cloth gilt, t.e.g., fine. (*Gough*) **£30 [≈ $57]**

Shaw, G.
- General Zoology. Vols 1 and 2, Mammalia. London: 1800-01. 2 vols in 4. 8vo. 235 engvd plates. Occas foxing. Diced calf, 1 vol rebacked. (*Wheldon & Wesley*) **£180 [≈ $345]**

Shaw, J.C.M.
- The Teeth, the Bony Palate and the Mandible in Bantu Races of South Africa ... London: 1931. 1st edn. Lge 8vo. xvi,134 pp. Frontis, 54 ills. Orig cloth.
(*Bow Windows*) **£30 [≈ $57]**

Shaw, Peter
- The Dispensatory of the Royal College of Physicians in Edinburgh. London: 1727. xii, 281 pp. Sl foxing. New leather.
(*Whitehart*) **£150 [≈ $287]**
- A New Practice of Physic ... London: Longman, 1753. 7th edn. 2 vols. 8vo. [xvi], 415; [ii], 413-712, [22] pp. Contemp calf, spines sl darkened, some hinges starting.
(*Bookpress*) **$325 [≈ £169]**

Shaw, Thomas George
- Wine, The Vine, and the Cellar. London: Longman, Green ..., 1863. xvi,505,[2 advt] pp. 28 text w'cuts. Advt slip tipped in on

front endpaper. Orig pict cloth gilt.
(Hollett) £120 [≈ $230]

Sheild, A. Marmaduke
- A Clinical Treatise on Diseases of the Breast.
London: 1898. 1st edn. 510 pp. Ills. Qtr
leather, front inner hinge broken.
(Fye) $150 [≈ £78]

Sheldon, H. Horton & Griswood, E.N.
- Television: Present Methods of Picture
Transmission. 1930. 1st edn. 2nd printing.
194 pp. 129 ills. Orig bndg.
(New Wireless) $120 [≈ £62]

Sheldon, J.P.
- Dairy Farming ... London: Cassell, Petter &
Galpin, [1880]. 1st edn. 4to. xxii,570 pp. 25
chromolitho plates, 250 other plates & ills.
Contemp calf gilt, fine.
(Gough) £275 [≈ $527]

Sheppard, Edgar
- Lectures on Madness in its Medical, Legal,
and Social Aspects. London: 1873. 1st edn.
186 pp. Orig bndg, front inner hinge cracked.
(Fye) $150 [≈ £78]

Sheppard, Thomas
- Geological Rambles in East Yorkshire.
London: A. Brown & Sons, n.d. 1st edn. xi,
235, [6 advt] pp. Fldg cold geological map, 53
ills. F.e.p. sl damaged. Orig cloth gilt, sm
mark on spine. *(Hollett)* £35 [≈ $67]
- Geological Rambles in East Yorkshire.
London: [1903]. xi,235, advt] pp. Cold
geological map, 52 figs. Orig cloth.
(Baldwin) £30 [≈ $57]

Shepperley, W.
- A History of Photography. London: [1929].
vii,100 pp. Frontis, 24 plates. Orig linen
backed bds, sl dust stained.
(Whitehart) £35 [≈ $67]

Sherborn, C.D.
- Index Animalium 1758-1800. London: 1902.
lix,1191 pp. Ex-lib. Browning of page edges.
Orig cloth. *(Baldwin)* £60 [≈ $115]
- Where is the --- Collection? An Account of
Various Natural History Collections.
London: 1940. 8vo. Limp bds.
(Wheldon & Wesley) £50 [≈ $95]

Sherrington, Sir Charles
- The Brain and Its Mechanism. The Rede
Lecture ... Cambridge: 1933. Sm 8vo. 35 pp.
Orig ptd wraps. *(Bickersteth)* £22 [≈ $42]

- The Endeavour of Jean Fernel with a List of
the Editions of his Writings. Folkestone:
(1946) 1974. x,223 pp. 27 ills inc frontis. Orig
bndg. *(Whitehart)* £25 [≈ $47]
- The Endeavours of Jean Fernel. With a List
of the Editions of his Writings. Cambridge:
1948. 8vo. 223 pp. Dw (worn).
(Goodrich) $75 [≈ £39]
- The Integrative Action of the Nervous
System. London: Constable, 1911. 1st edn.
2nd issue, with cancelled title-page. 8vo. 411
pp. Occas underlining. Later cloth.
(Goodrich) $395 [≈ £205]
- The Integrative Action of the Nervous
System. New Haven: 1918. 5th printing. Orig
cloth, a bit worn. *(Goodrich)* $150 [≈ £78]
- The Integrative Action of the Nervous
System. Cambridge: 1947. 2nd edn. 433 pp.
Orig bndg, fine. *(Fye)* $150 [≈ £78]
- Man on his Nature. New York: 1941. 1st edn.
413 pp. Orig bndg. *(Fye)* $100 [≈ £52]
- Selected Writings ... Edited by D. Denny-
Brown. London: 1939. 1st edn. xiv,532 pp.
85 figs. Orig bndg. *(Whitehart)* £45 [≈ $86]
- Selected Writings. London: 1939. 1st edn.
532 pp. Dw. *(Fye)* $300 [≈ £156]
- Selected Writings. New York: 1940. 1st Amer
edn. 532 pp. Ex-lib. Orig bndg.
(Fye) $200 [≈ £104]

Sherrington, Sir Charles, et al.
- Reflex Activity of the Spinal Cord. London:
1938. 2nd printing. 8vo. Dw.
(Goodrich) $100 [≈ £52]

Shiras, G.
- Hunting Wild Life with Camera and
Flashlight. A Record of Sixty-Five Years'
Visits to the Woods and Waters of North
America. Washington: Nat Geog Soc, (1936).
2nd edn. 2 vols. Lge 8vo. 950 photo ills. Orig
cloth. *(Bow Windows)* £30 [≈ $57]

Shockley, William
- Electrons and Holes in Semiconductors.
1951. 1st edn, 2nd printing. 558 pp. Orig
bndg. *(New Wireless)* $115 [≈ £60]
- Electrons and Holes in Semiconductors.
1956. 1st edn. 6th printing. 558 pp. Orig
bndg. *(New Wireless)* $110 [≈ £57]

A Short History of Insects ...
- See Lever, Lady.

Short, Thomas
- The Natural, Experimental, and Medicinal
History of the Mineral Waters of Derbyshire,

Lincolnshire, and Yorkshire, particularly those of Scarborough ... London: 1734. [xx], xxii, 362 pp. 4 plates. Last few ff sl wormed. Reversed calf, v sl worn.
(Whitehart) **£250 [≈ $479]**
- The Natural, Experimental, and Medicinal History of the Mineral Waters. London: for the author, 1734. 1st edn. Cr 4to. [xx], xxii, 362 pp. 5 plates. 1 leaf sl flawed. Lacks addtnl disclaimer leaf Uu2 found in BL copy. Mod half calf.   *(Ash)* **£125 [≈ $239]**

Shorten, Monica
- Squirrels. London: Collins New Naturalist, 1954. 1st edn. 8vo. Ills. Dw.
(Wheldon & Wesley) **£30 [≈ $57]**
- Squirrels. London: Collins New naturalist Series, 1954. 1st edn. 8vo. xii,212 pp. 15 plates. Ends sl foxed. Orig cloth. Dw (reprd).
(Henly) **£36 [≈ $69]**
- Squirrels. London: Collins New Naturalist, 1954. 1st edn. 8vo. 212 pp. Maps, ills. Orig cloth gilt. Dw (v sm chip hd of spine).
(Hollett) **£75 [≈ $143]**

Shortridge, G.C.
- The Mammals of South-West Africa. A Biological Account. London: 1934. 2 vols. Roy 8vo. Num ills & maps. Cloth, spines faded.   *(Wheldon & Wesley)* **£75 [≈ $143]**

Shuckard, W.E.
- British Bees ... London: L. Reeve, [1866]. 1st edn. xvi,371,16 ctlg pp. 16 hand cold plates. Orig pict maroon cloth gilt, spine trifle faded.
(Gough) **£45 [≈ $86]**
- British Bees. London: 1866. 8vo. xvi,371 pp. 16 hand cold plates. Orig cloth, rebacked.
(Wheldon & Wesley) **£40 [≈ $76]**

Sibly, Ebenezer
- The Medical Mirror. Or Treatise on the Impregnation of the Human Female. Shewing the Origin of Diseases ... Second Edition. London: for the author ..., [plates dated 1794]. 8vo. 184,8 pp. Port frontis, 4 plates. Orig bds, uncut, sl soiled, spine defective at ft.   *(Finch)* **£140 [≈ $268]**
- A New and Complete Illustration of the Celestial Science of Astrology ... In Four Books ... London: for the proprietor & sold by W. Nicoll, 1784-88. 1st edn of the 4 parts. 4to. 1126,[4] pp. Frontis, 29 plates. Some wear & tear. Contemp style half calf.
(Gough) **£295 [≈ $566]**

Sidgwick, N.V.
- The Electronic Theory of Valency. Oxford:

[1927] 1929. Reprint. xii,310 pp. Occas sl foxing.   *(Whitehart)* **£15 [≈ $28]**
- Some Physical Properties of the Covalent Link in Chemistry. Ithaca, New York: 1933. 1st edn. [7],249 pp. Frontis port, sev text diags. Cloth sl dust stained.
(Whitehart) **£30 [≈ $57]**
- Some Physical Properties of the Covalent Link in Chemistry. Ithaca, New York: 1933. 1st edn. [7],249 pp. Frontis port, sev text diags. Cloth sl worn at crnrs. Sgnd by the author.   *(Whitehart)* **£35 [≈ $67]**

Sidney, S.
- The Book of the Horse ... London: Cassell & Co Ltd, [ca 1880]. 4to. 25 chromolitho plates. Occas spotting. Orig half roan.
(Frew Mackenzie) **£320 [≈ $614]**
- The Book of the Horse ... Second Edition. London: Cassell, Petter, Galpin & Co, [ca 1880]. 4to. 608 pp. 25 chromolithos, num w'engvs. Contemp half calf gilt, sl worn & scraped.   *(Hollett)* **£250 [≈ $479]**
- The Book of the Horse ... London: Cassell, [1884-86]. 3rd edn, enlgd. 4to. x,680 pp. 28 chromolitho plates, num w'engvs in text. Orig red half mor, dec gilt spine, a.e.g.
(Sotheran's) **£298 [≈ $572]**

Siegle, Emil
- The Treatment of Diseases of the Throat and Lungs by Inhalations. Cincinnati: 1868. 8vo. 136, illust advt pp. Ex-lib. Cloth, worn.
(Goodrich) **$65 [≈ £33]**

Siemens, C. William
- On the Conservation of Solar Energy. A Collection of Papers and Discussions. London: Macmillan, 1883. 1st edn. 8vo. xx,111 pp. Ills. Orig cloth.
(Young's) **£75 [≈ $143]**

Sigerist, Henry
- The Great Doctors. New York: 1933. 1st English translation. 436 pp. Orig bndg.
(Fye) **$100 [≈ £52]**
- A History of Medicine. Vols 1 & 2. New York: 1951-61. 2 vols. 8vo. Occas underlining. Foredge creased in vol 1. Orig bndgs.   *(Goodrich)* **$75 [≈ £39]**
- A History of Medicine. Volume 1. Primitive and Archaic Medicine. Oxford: (1951) 1955. xxi, 564 pp. 48 plates. Endpapers sl discold. Orig cloth.   *(Whitehart)* **£28 [≈ $53]**
- Man and Medicine: an Introduction to Medical Knowledge. New York: 1932. 1st English translation. 340 pp. Orig bndg.
(Fye) **$75 [≈ £39]**

Silvertop, C.

- A Geological Sketch of the Tertiary Formation in the Provinces of Granada and Murcia, Spain, with Notices respecting Primary, Secondary, and Volcanic Rocks in the same District and Sections. London: 1836. 8vo. 236 pp. Frontis, 7 plates. Half calf gilt. *(Wheldon & Wesley)* **£75 [≈ $143]**

Simmons, Samuel Foart

- An Account of the Tenia, and Method of Treating It. London: J. Wilkie, 1778. 2nd edn. 8vo. (iii)-xxi,77 pp. 2 fldg plates. Lacks half-title. Later bds. Anon.
(Bookpress) **$275 [≈ £143]**
- Elements of Anatomy and the Animal Economy. From the French of M. Person. Corrected ... Augmented with Notes. London: Wilie, 1775. 1st edn. 8vo. xii,396 pp, errata leaf. 3 plates. Light pencilling. Old qtr calf, worn. *(Goodrich)* **$75 [≈ £39]**

Simms, E.

- British Thrushes. London: Collins New Naturalist, 1978. 1st edn. 8vo. 304 pp. 24 plates. Orig cloth. Dw. *(Henly)* **£15 [≈ $28]**
- Woodland Birds. London: Collins New Naturalist, 1971. 1st edn. 8vo. xxii,391 pp. 4 cold & 24 plain plates. Orig cloth. Dw.
(Henly) **£30 [≈ $57]**

Simms, F.W.

- Practical Tunnelling ... as exemplified by the particulars of the Bletchingley and Saltwood Tunnels. London: 1844. 4to. xii,174 pp. Frontis, 12 fldg plates, w'engvs in text. Orig blind stamped cloth, rough linen label.
(Whitehart) **£200 [≈ $383]**
- A Treatise on the Principal Mathematical Instruments employed in Surveying, Levelling, and Astronomy ... London: 1850. 8th edn. xi, 130, [x], [16 Troughton & Simms ctlg] pp. Ills. 3 lib blind stamps. Orig cloth, rather faded, sl worn.
(Whitehart) **£38 [≈ $72]**

Simon, Andre

- Wine and the Wine Trade. London: Pitman, 1934. 2nd edn, rvsd. 8vo. 129 pp. Ills. Name. Dw (chipped). *(Respess)* **$45 [≈ £23]**

Simon, John

- General Pathology; as conducive to the Establishment of Rational Principles for the Diagnosis and Treatment of Disease ... London: Henry Renshaw, 1850. 1st edn. 8vo. xi, 288 pp. Orig cloth, backstrip relaid.
(Gough) **£48 [≈ $92]**

Simon, Sir John

- English Sanitary Institutions, Reviewed in their Course of Development, and in Some of their Political and Social Relations. London: Cassell, 1890. 1st edn. 12 ctlg pp. Orig cloth, spine sl marked. *(Jarndyce)* **£120 [≈ $230]**

Simonin, L.

- Underground Life; or, Mines and Miners. Translated, Adapted ... and Edited by H.W. Bristowe. London: 1869. Roy 8vo. xix,522 pp. 14 cold geological maps, frontis, 16 cold plates, num w'engvs. Blind stamp on title & plates. New bds.
(Wheldon & Wesley) **£125 [≈ $239]**

Simpson, James Y.

- The Obstetric Memoirs and Contributions of James Y. Simpson, M.D., F.R.C.E. Edited by W.O. Priestly ... and Horatio R. Storer. Phila: Lippincott, 1855. 2 vols. 8vo. 756; 733 pp. Num text ills. Foxed. Orig cloth, backstrips relaid. *(Goodrich)* **$175 [≈ £91]**

Simpson, N.D.

- A Bibliographical Index of the British Flora. Bournemouth: 1960. One of 750. Imperial 8vo. xix,429 pp. Cloth, spine faded.
(Wheldon & Wesley) **£48 [≈ $92]**

Simpson, R.R.

- Shakespeare and Medicine. Edinburgh: 1959. vii,267 pp. 2 plates. Name stamp on title. Dw. *(Whitehart)* **£25 [≈ $47]**

Simpson, Thomas, 1710-61

- The Doctrine and Application of Fluxions ... Second Edition, revised and carefully corrected. London: for John Nourse, 1776. 2 vols. 8vo. xii,274,[2 advt]; [ii],275-576 pp. Name torn from hd of vol 2 title. Contemp sheep, rebacked, sides scuffed.
(Burmester) **£175 [≈ $335]**
- Elements of Geometry; with their Application to the Mensuration of Superficies and Solids ... London: 1800. 5th edn. xii,276 pp. Figs. Occas marks. Orig leather, rubbed, worn & dust stained. *(Whitehart)* **£30 [≈ $57]**
- Essays on Several Curious and Useful Subjects, in Speculative and Mix't Mathematicks ... London: H. Woodfall, for J. Nourse, 1740. 1st edn. 4to. viii,142,[1 errata], [1 advt] pp. W'cut text diags. Contemp panelled calf, label chipped, spine & crnrs sl worn. *(Gaskell)* **£400 [≈ $767]**
- Essays on Several Curious and Useful Subjects, in Speculative and • Mix'd Mathematicks. London: H. Woodfall, for J.

Nourse, 1740. 1st edn. 4to. viii,142,[2] pp.
Errata. Ctlg. W'cut diags. Rec half calf gilt.
(Rootenberg) **$750 [≈ £390]**
- Select Exercises for Young Proficients in the
Mathematics ... A New Edition ... Account of
the Life and Writings of the Author, by
Charles Hutton. London: for F. Wingrave,
1792. 8vo. [4],iv, xxiii, [i],252 pp. Ink
splashes on 4 pp. Contemp calf.
(Fenning) **£45 [≈ $86]**
- Trigonometry, Plane and Spherical; with the
Construction and Application of Logarithms.
Phila: 1810. 125 pp. 7 fldg plates (offset).
Occas foxing throughout. Contemp leather,
rebacked.   *(Whitehart)* **£35 [≈ $67]**

Simson, Robert
- Elements of the Conic Sections ... The First
Three Books, translated from the Latin
Original ... Edinburgh: for Charles Elliot ...,
1775. 1st edn in English. 8vo. [vi],255 pp. 14
fldg plates. Contemp calf backed bds, vellum
crnrs, jnts rubbed.   *(Gaskell)* **£125 [≈ $239]**

Simson, Thomas, 1696-1764
- An Inquiry how far the Vital and Animal
Actions of the more Perfect Animals can be
accounted for Independent of the Brain.
Edinburgh: 1752. 1st edn. 4to. [4],16,270,[2]
pp. Errata after title. 2 fldg plates. V sl
browning. Contemp calf, rebacked.
(Rootenberg) **$650 [≈ £338]**

Sinclair, W.J.
- Semmelweis. His Life and His Doctrine. A
Chapter in the History of Medicine.
Manchester: 1909. 8vo. 369 pp. Cloth, worn.
3 quite interesting other items inserted.
(Goodrich) **$175 [≈ £91]**

Singer, Charles
- The Discovery of the Circulation of the
Blood. London: 1922. 1st edn. 80 pp. Orig
wraps.   *(Fye)* **$50 [≈ £26]**
- The Discovery of the Circulation of the
Blood. London: 1922. 8vo. 80 pp. Ills. Orig
bndg.   *(Goodrich)* **$45 [≈ £23]**
- The Evolution of Anatomy. A Short History
of Anatomical and Physiological Discovery to
Harvey ... New York: 1925. 1st Amer edn.
xii, 211 pp. 22 plates, 117 text figs. Cloth, sl
worn & marked, inner hinge sl cracked.
(Whitehart) **£38 [≈ $72]**
- The Evolution of Anatomy: A Short History
of Anatomical and Physiological Discovery to
Harvey. New York: 1925. 1st edn. 209 pp.
Orig bndg.   *(Fye)* **$100 [≈ £52]**
- From Magic to Science. Essays on the

Scientific Twilight. London: 1928. xix,253
pp. 14 plates, 109 figs. Cloth sl discold, inner
hinge cracked but bndg firm.
(Whitehart) **£60 [≈ $115]**
- From Magic to Science: Essays on the
Scientific Twilight. London: 1928. 1st edn.
253 pp. Ills. Orig bndg.   *(Fye)* **$100 [≈ £52]**
- Greek Biology & Medicine. Oxford: 1922. 1st
edn. 128 pp. Orig bndg.   *(Fye)* **$50 [≈ £26]**
- A Short History of Biology. Oxford: 1931.
8vo. 194 ills. Orig bndg.
(Wheldon & Wesley) **£25 [≈ $47]**
- A Short History of Medicine. New York:
1928. 1st edn. 368 pp. Orig bndg.
(Fye) **$50 [≈ £26]**
- A Short History of Medicine. Oxford: 1928.
1st edn. 368 pp. Half leather, raised bands.
(Fye) **$100 [≈ £52]**
- Studies in the History and Method of
Science. Oxford: (1917) 1955. 8vo. xiv,304
pp. Frontis, 40 plates. Orig cloth.
(Goodrich) **$75 [≈ £39]**

Singer, Charles, et al.
- A History of Technology. Edited by Charles
Singer et al. Oxford: 1957-59. Later printing.
5 vols. 8vo. Orig blue cloth.
(Goodrich) **$250 [≈ £130]**
- A History of Technology. OUP: 1978-80.
Complete set. 7 vols. Sm 4to. Plates, text figs.
Dws.   *(Georges)* **£300 [≈ $575]**
- A History of Technology. Volume I. From
Early Times to the Fall of Ancient Empires.
New York & London: 1954. Cold frontis, 18
dble-sided plates, 8 maps, 570 text figs. Cloth
spotted. Dw.   *(Whitehart)* **£45 [≈ $86]**
- A History of Technology. Volume II. The
Mediterranean Civilizations and the Middle
Ages. New York & London: 1956. Cold
frontis, 22 dble-sided plates, 695 text figs.
Cloth sl spotted. Dw.
(Whitehart) **£45 [≈ $86]**
- A History of Technology. Volume III. From
the Renaissance to the Industrial Revolution
... New York & London: 1957. Cold frontis,
16 dble-sided plates, 426 text figs. Cloth sl
spotted.   *(Whitehart)* **£45 [≈ $86]**
- A History of Technology. Volume IV. The
Industrial Revolution ... New York &
London: 1958. Cold frontis, 24 dble-sided
plates, 349 text figs. Cloth sl spotted. Dw.
(Whitehart) **£45 [≈ $86]**
- A History of Technology. Volume V. The
Late Nineteenth Century ... New York &
London: 1958. Cold frontis, 22 dble-sided
plates, 415 text figs. Cloth sl spotted. Dw.
(Whitehart) **£45 [≈ $86]**

- A History of Technology. Volume V. The Late Nineteenth Century c.1850 to c.1900. Oxford: 1958. xxxviii,888 pp. 22 plates, 415 text diags, other ills. Lib stamp on title & endpaper. V sm nick in spine.
(Whitehart) **£25 [≈ $47]**
- Studies in the History and Method of Science. Oxford: 1917-21. 2 vols. Imperial 8vo. 96 plates (12 cold). Buckram.
(Wheldon & Wesley) **£80 [≈ $153]**

Singer, Charles & Rabin, C.
- A Prelude to Modern Science. Being a Discussion of the History, Sources & Circumstances of the Tabulae Anatomicae Sex of Vesalius. London: 1946. 8vo. 6 plates, 59 text figs. Orig bndg.
(Goodrich) **$195 [≈ £101]**

Sisley, R.
- Epidemic Influenza: Note on its Origin and Method of Spread. London: 1891. xi,150 pp. 17 diags. Cloth, worn. Author's inscrptn.
(Whitehart) **£25 [≈ $47]**

Sitwell, Sacheverell, Buchanan, H., & Fisher, J.
- Fine Bird Books, 1700-1900. A Bibliographical Record of Coloured Plate Books. London: 1953. Folio. 104 pp. 16 cold (1 dble) & 24 collotype plates. Half buckram, trifle used.
(Wheldon & Wesley) **£450 [≈ $863]**

Skey, Frederic Carpenter
- Hysteria ... Six Lectures ... London: Longman, 1867. 1st edn. 8vo. viii,107 pp. Orig cloth, spine sl rubbed & dull.
(Burmester) **£60 [≈ $115]**

Skoda, Joseph
- Auscultation and Percussion. Translated by W.O. Markham. Phila: 1854. 1st Amer edn. 380 pp. Front bd & prelims detached.
(Fye) **$250 [≈ £130]**

Slagg, Charles
- Sanitary Work in the Smaller Towns and in Villages. London: Crosby Lockwood, 1876. 1st edn. 4 advt, 32 ctlg pp. Orig brown cloth, spine rubbed.
(Jarndyce) **£40 [≈ $76]**

Slater, J.W.
- Handbook of Chemical Analysis for Practical Men ... London: 1861. xvi,384 pp. 17 text diags. Endpapers foxed. Deleted sgntr on title. Three qtr roan, mrbld bds, rubbed.
(Whitehart) **£35 [≈ $67]**

Sloane, T. O'Conor
- Electric Toy Making. 1901. 12th edn. 140 pp. 52 ills. Orig bndg.
(New Wireless) **$40 [≈ £21]**

Small Arms ...
- Textbook of Small Arms. London: HMSO, 1929. Enlgd edn. Roy 8vo. viii,427,22 advt pp. Corrigenda slip. 72 plates, num text ills. Orig cloth.
(Fenning) **£65 [≈ $124]**

Smart, C.E.
- The Makers of Surveying Instruments in America since 1700. Troy, New York: Regal Art Press, 1962. 8vo. xxiv,282 pp. Num ills. Cloth.
(Gemmary) **$150 [≈ £78]**

Smeaton, John
- Experimental Enquiry concerning the Natural Powers of Wind and Water to Turn Mills and Other Machines ... Second Edition. London: I. & J. Taylor, 1795. Tall 8vo. 5 fldg plates, 2 fldg tables. Advt leaf at end. 3 ff soiled. Rec calf, v sl bowed.
(Georges) **£350 [≈ $671]**

Smedley, J.
- Practical Hydropathy ... London: 1866. 444, 8 advt pp. 160 figs. Lacks front free endpaper. Occas foxing. Cloth, faded, edges sl worn, inner hinges cracked.
(Whitehart) **£25 [≈ $47]**

Smee, A.
- General Debility and Defective Nutrition: Their Causes, Consequences, and Treatment. London: 1862. 2nd edn. xi,117 pp. Few sm pencil lines. Orig cloth, sl dusty & worn.
(Whitehart) **£35 [≈ $67]**

Smellie, John
- Shipbuilding and Repairing in Dublin. A Record of Work carried out by Dublin Dockyard Co., 1901-1923. Glasgow: McCorquodale, 1923. 8vo. Ills. Cloth bds.
(Emerald Isle) **£35 [≈ $67]**

Smethurst, G.
- Tables of Time: whereby the Day of the Month ... Manchester: 1749. Sm 8vo. viii, 132, 48 pp. Sev lib blind stamps. Later lib cloth, spine dull.
(Whitehart) **£40 [≈ $76]**

Smialowski, Arthur & Currie, Donald
- Photography in Medicine. Springfield: 1960. 1st edn. 330 pp. 282 ills. Dw.
(Fye) **$100 [≈ £52]**

Smiles, Samuel
- The Life of George Stephenson, Railway Engineer. Fifth Edition, Revised, with Additions. London: 1858. 8vo. xvi,557 pp. Port. Sm lib stamp on title. Few marks. Rec half mor.   *(Bow Windows)* **£45 [≈$86]**
- Lives of Boulton and Watt. Principally from the Original Soho Mss. comprising also a History of the Invention and Introduction of the Steam-Engine. London: Murray, 1865. Lge 8vo. xvi, 521, [8 advt] pp. 2 ports, text ills. Sl wear & tear. Mod half mor gilt.
        (Hollett) **£75 [≈$143]**

Smillie, I.S.
- Injuries of the Knee Joint. Edinburgh: 1946. xi,320 pp. 350 figs. Sm lib stamp on endpaper.   *(Whitehart)* **£25 [≈$47]**

Smith, C.H.
- Horses. London: Bohn, Jardine's Naturalist's Library, 1866. Sm 8vo. 352 pp. Port, vignette, 30 cold & 3 plain plates. Contemp half calf.   *(Wheldon & Wesley)* **£50 [≈$95]**

Smith, Cecil
- The Birds of Somersetshire. London: Van Voorst, 1869. 1st edn. 8vo. xii,643 pp. Orig green cloth, sl rubbed & marked.
        (Claude Cox) **£38 [≈$72]**
- The Birds of Somersetshire. London: Van Voorst, 1869. 1st edn. xi,643 pp. Orig cloth gilt.   *(Gough)* **£60 [≈$115]**

Smith, D.E. & De Morgan, Augustus
- Rara Arithmetica. A Catalogue of the Arithmetics written before the year MDCI with a Description of those in the Library of George Arthur Plimpton of New York. New York: 1970. 4th edn. xviii,725 pp. Ills.
        (Whitehart) **£30 [≈$57]**

Smith, E.
- The Life of Sir Joseph Banks ... London: 1911. 8vo. xvi,348 pp. 16 plates. Sl foxing. Cloth, spine faded.
        (Wheldon & Wesley) **£50 [≈$95]**

Smith, E.A.
- The Sampling and Assay of the Precious Metals. London: Charles Griffin, 1947. 2nd edn. 8vo. xvi,505 pp. Num text figs. Cloth.
        (Gemmary) **£100 [≈$52]**

Smith, E.C.
- A Short History of Naval and Marine Engineering. Cambridge: 1937. xix,376 pp. 16 plates, 46 text figs. Orig cloth, sl stained.

        (Whitehart) **£25 [≈$47]**

Smith, Eliza
- The Compleat Housewife: or Accomplish'd Gentlewoman's Companion: being a Collection of Upwards of Six Hundred of the most Approved Receipts in Cookery ... Eighth Edition ... London: 1737. 8vo. [xviii], 354, xv, [3 advt] pp. Frontis, 6 fldg plates. Rec qtr calf.   *(Burmester)* **£275 [≈$527]**
- The Compleat Housewife: or, Accomplish'd Gentlewoman's Companion ... London: for J. & J. Pemberton, 1737. 8th edn. [xvi], 354, xv, [4 advt] pp. Frontis, 6 fldg plates. Sm worm track edge of frontis. Contemp calf, rather worn, jnts cracked.   *(Hollett)* **£240 [≈$460]**

Smith, Francis
- The Canary; its Varieties, Management and Breeding ... London: Groombridge, 1868. 1st edn. 8vo. viii,146 pp. 12 cold plates by Benjamin Fawcett. Occas spotting & thumbing. Orig gilt dec blue cloth, a.e.g., presumably recased.
        (de Beaumont) **£78 [≈$149]**

Smith, Sir Frederick
- The Early History of Veterinary Literature and its British Development. Vol. II [only, of 4]. The Eighteenth Century. London: Bailliere, Tindall & Cox, 1924. Med 8vo. Orig bndg.   *(Georges)* **£50 [≈$95]**

Smith, G. Munro
- A History of the Bristol Royal Infirmary. London: 1917. xiii,507 pp. 86 ills. Orig bndg.
        (Whitehart) **£35 [≈$67]**

Smith, George, of Kendal
- A Compleat Body of Distilling, explaining the Mysteries of that Science ... Second Edition. London: for Henry Linton sic, 1731. 8vo. Intl advt leaf. Frontis. Contemp sheep, hinges sl cracked.   *(Jarndyce)* **£360 [≈$691]**

Smith, Henry
- Anatomical Atlas Illustrative of the Structure of the Human Body. Phila: 1859. 200 pp. 634 ills. Strip cut from hd of title. Orig bndg, front hinge cracked.   *(Fye)* **$100 [≈£52]**

Smith, J.
- Tables for Calculating Interest at 5 per Cent on any Sum from £.1 to £.20,000 ... Edinburgh: 1810. [14],392 pp. B'plate. Half leather, spine sl worn.
        (Whitehart) **£35 [≈$67]**

Smith, J.B.
- A Treatise upon Wire. Its Manufacture and Uses ... London: 1891. 4to. xxii,347 pp. 95 figs, 33 tables. Orig cloth, sl stained, sm nick on spine. *(Whitehart)* **£25 [≈ $47]**

Smith, J.L.
- Mineralogy and Chemistry. Louisville: John P. Morton, 1873. 8vo. 401 pp. Text figs. Rebound in buckram.
(Gemmary) **$125 [≈ £65]**

Smith, James
- The Panorama of Science and Art ... Liverpool: for Nuttall, Fisher, 1815. 1st edn. 2 vols. 8vo. x,626; xii,862,[2] pp. Frontis, 49 plates. Occas sl browning. Rec bds.
(Fenning) **£95 [≈ $182]**

Smith, Sir James Edward
- A Grammar of Botany ... Second Edition. London: Longman ..., 1826. 8vo. xxii,240 pp. 21 plates. Contemp black half calf, gilt dec spine. *(Gough)* **£30 [≈ $57]**
- An Introduction to Physiological and Systematical Botany. Third Edition. London: Longman ..., 1814. 8vo. xxiii,408 pp. 15 plates. Contemp gilt panelled calf.
(Gough) **£48 [≈ $92]**
- An Introduction to Physiological and Systematical Botany ... London: Longmans ..., 1819. 4th edn. 8vo. xix,407 pp. 15 hand cold plates. Calf, rebacked.
(Young's) **£60 [≈ $115]**
- Memoir and Correspondence of the late Sir James Edward Smith, edited by Lady Smith. London: 1832. 2 vols. 8vo. Port, 9 plates. Occas foxing. 1 plate sl water stained. Qtr roan, trifle faded, minor spine wear.
(Wheldon & Wesley) **£120 [≈ $230]**

Smith, John
- A Treatise on the Artificial Growth of Cucumbers and Melons ... Asparagus, Rhubarb ... Ipswich: Edward Shalders, 1833. 1st edn. 12mo. [2],60,[2] pp. Litho plate. Sl browning. Orig cloth backed bds, uncut, rubbed, sl soiled. *(Claude Cox)* **£45 [≈ $86]**

Smith, Kenneth M. & Markham, Roy
- Mumps Measles and Mosaics. London: Collins New Naturalist Series, 1954. 1st edn. 8vo. 160 pp. Ills. Orig cloth gilt, few spots to edges. Dw (1 v sm nick lower edge).
(Hollett) **£95 [≈ $182]**
- Mumps, Measles and Mosaics. London: Collins New Naturalist, 1954. 1st edn. 8vo. xii,160,4 advt pp. 1 cold & 16 other plates.

Orig cloth. *(Henly)* **£28 [≈ $53]**
- Mumps, Measles and Mosaics. London: Collins New Naturalist, 1954. 1st edn. 8vo. xii,160 pp. Cold frontis, 16 plain plates. Orig cloth. Dw (trifle worn).
(Wheldon & Wesley) **£40 [≈ $76]**

Smith, M.
- The British Amphibians and Reptiles. London: Collins New Naturalist, 1951. 1st edn. 8vo. xiv,318,4 pp. 16 cold & 16 plain plates. Orig cloth. *(Henly)* **£18 [≈ $34]**

Smith, Nathan
- Medical and Surgical Memoirs. Edited with an Addenda by Nathan R. Smith, M.D. Baltimore: 1831. 8vo. vii,374.errata pp. Port. Foxing. Orig bds, uncut, rebacked.
(Goodrich) **$195 [≈ £101]**
- Medical and Surgical Memoirs. Baltimore: 1831. 1st edn. 374 pp. Leather, most of backstrip missing, bds detached.
(Fye) **$250 [≈ £130]**

Smith, Nathan Ryno
- Treatment of Fractures of the Lower extremity by the Use of the Anterior Suspensory Apparatus. Baltimore: 1867. 1st edn. 70 pp. Orig bndg. *(Fye)* **$300 [≈ £156]**

Smith, Noble
- The Surgery of Deformities. London: 1882. 1st edn. 280 pp. 118 ills. Orig bndg, ex-lib but fine. *(Fye)* **$150 [≈ £78]**

Smith, O.C.
- Identification and Qualitative Chemical Analysis of Minerals. New York: Van Nostrand, 1953. 2nd edn. 8vo. ix,385 pp. 28 cold plates. Cloth. *(Gemmary)* **$60 [≈ £31]**

Smith, Robert Angus
- Memoir of John Dalton, and History of the Atomic Theory up to his Time. London: H. Bailliere, Manchester Lit & Phil Soc 2nd Series Vol 13, 1856. 8vo. xii,316 pp. Port frontis. Lib stamp on title verso. Mod half mor gilt. *(Hollett)* **£65 [≈ $124]**

Smith,   Robert,   Rat-Catcher   to   the Princess Amelia
- The Universal Directory for Taking Alive and Destroying Rats, and all other Kinds of Four-Footed and Winged Vermin ... London: for the author, 1768. 1st edn. 8vo. vii,218 pp. Author's note pasted to title verso. Sl wear & marks. 6 plates. Orig calf, rebacked.
(Bickersteth) **£130 [≈ $249]**

Smith, S.
- The Yellow Wagtail. London: Collins New Naturalist, 1950. 1st edn. 8vo. xiv,178 pp. 8 cold & 4 plain plates. Endpapers spotted. Orig cloth, spine faded. *(Henly)* **£20 [≈ $38]**

Smith, W.
- The Rise and Extension of Submarine Telegraphy. London: 1891. 4to. xiii,390 pp. Frontis, fldg chart, text diags. Orig pict cloth gilt, partly unopened, rear jnt cracked but firm. *(Whitehart)* **£95 [≈ $182]**

Smyth, A.L.
- John Dalton 1766-1844. A Bibliography of Works by and about him. Manchester: 1966. Roy 8vo. 11 plates. Orig bndg.
(Georges) **£25 [≈ $47]**

Smyth, Charles Piazzi
- Madeira Meteorologic. Being a Paper on the above Subject read before the Royal Society, Edinburgh, on the 1st May 1882. Edinburgh: 1882. viii,83 pp. Frontis, 3 ills. Orig cloth, partly unopened, v sl stained.
(Whitehart) **£25 [≈ $47]**

Smyth, Henry DeWolf
- Atomic Energy for Military Purposes. The Official Report on the Development of the Atom Bomb under the Auspices of the United States Government, 1940-1945. Princeton: UP, 1945. 1st edn. 8vo. 8 ills. Orig wraps, backstrip sl bleach spotted.
(Young's) **£90 [≈ $172]**
- Atomic Energy for Military Purposes ... London: HMSO, 1945. 1st English edn. 8vo. Orig bndg. *(Young's)* **£17 [≈ $32]**
- Atomic Energy. A General Account of the Development of Methods of using Atomic Energy for Military Purposes under the Auspices of the United States Government. London: HMSO, 1945. 1st UK edn (code 10/45). 144 pp. Diags. Orig ptd wraps (sl marked by rusty staples).
(Whitehart) **£25 [≈ $47]**

Smyth, James Carmichael
- The Effects of the Nitrous Vapour in Preventing and Destroying Contagion ... made chiefly by the Surgeons of His Majesty's Navy ... with an Introduction ... on Jail or Hospital Fever ... Phila: Dobson, 1799. 8vo. 174 pp. Fldg table. Foxed. Early sheep, rebacked. *(Goodrich)* **$165 [≈ £85]**

Smyth, W.H.
- A Cycle of Celestial Objects Observed,

Reduced and Discussed ... Revised, Condensed and greatly Enlarged by G.F. Chambers. Oxford: 1881. 2nd edn. xxii,696 pp. Cold frontis, a few text figs. 1st few pp sl stained. Cloth, dull, faded, new endpapers.
(Whitehart) **£45 [≈ $86]**

Smythies, B.E.
- The Birds of Borneo. London: 1960. 1st edn. Roy 8vo. xvi,562 pp. Map, 99 plates (52 cold). Cloth.
(Wheldon & Wesley) **£100 [≈ $191]**
- Birds of Burma. Rangoon: 1940. 1st edn. Roy 8vo. xxx,589 pp. Fldg map, 31 cold plates. Orig cloth.
(Wheldon & Wesley) **£325 [≈ $623]**
- The Birds of Burma. London: 1953. 2nd rvsd edn. Roy 8vo. xliii,668 pp. Fldg map, 31 cold plates. Cloth.
(Wheldon & Wesley) **£100 [≈ $191]**

Snow, D.W.
- A Study of Blackbirds. L: 1958. 8vo. 192 pp. Text ills. Dw. *(Henly)* **£28 [≈ $53]**

Snow, W.B.
- Currents of High Potential of High and Other Frequencies. New York: 1911. 2nd edn. xiv,275 pp. Frontis, 63 text figs. New cloth.
(Whitehart) **£25 [≈ $47]**

A Snowdrop (pseudonym)
- The Berries and Heaths of Rannoch ... see Cross, J.E.

Snyder, L.L.
- Arctic Birds of Canada. Toronto: UP, 1957. 1st edn. Ills. Dw. *(Walcot)* **£32 [≈ $61]**

Soderberg, P.M.
- Foreign Birds for Cage and Aviary. London: 1956. 4 vols. 8vo. Cold & other ills. Cloth.
(Wheldon & Wesley) **£30 [≈ $57]**

Soederberg, R.
- Studies of the Birds in North West Australia. Stockholm: 1918. 4to. 116 pp. 5 plates (1 cold). New bds.
(Wheldon & Wesley) **£35 [≈ $67]**

Solly, S.E.
- A Handbook of Medical Climatology ... London: 1897. 470 pp. 11 plates. Few blue pencil underlinings. Cloth, sl worn, inner hinges cracked. *(Whitehart)* **£45 [≈ $86]**

Somervell, John
- Water-Power Mills of South Westmorland ...

Kendal: Titus Wilson, 1930. 1st edn. 8vo. 4 plates. Orig cloth gilt. *(Hollett)* **£80 [≈ $153]**

Somerville, Mary
- On Connexion of the Physical Sciences. Fourth Edition. London: Murray, 1837. Sm 8vo. xv, 499 pp. Frontis, 4 plates. Orig cloth, spine faded, jnts sl worn.
(Bickersteth) **£28 [≈ $53]**
- Personal Recollections from Early Life to Old Age. London: 1873. vi,377 pp. Frontis port. New cloth. *(Whitehart)* **£38 [≈ $72]**

Sommerfeld, A.
- Atomic Structure and Spectral Lines. New York: Dutton, 1923. 8vo. xiii,626 pp. Cloth.
(Gemmary) **$90 [≈ £46]**

Sotbene, Oswold
- The Shrine of Aesculapius. Cleveland: 1905. 277 pp. 4 ills. Orig bndg. *(Fye)* **$100 [≈ £52]**

Soulsby, B.
- A Catalogue of the Works of Linnaeus ... in the Libraries of the British Museum. London: 1933. 2nd edn. 4to. xi,246,68 pp. 7 plates. [With] Index to Authors other than Linneaus, by C.D. Sherborn. London: 1936. 59 pp. Together 2 vols. 4to. Cloth & wraps.
(Wheldon & Wesley) **£70 [≈ $134]**

South, J.F.
- A Description of the Bones ... Third Edition enlarged and corrected. London: 1837. Sm 8vo. [vi],145, [1],[16 advt dated Jan 1837] pp. Frontis, text figs. Few sl marks. Orig cloth.
(Bow Windows) **£55 [≈ $105]**
- Household Surgery; or, Hints on Emergencies. London: 1847. xvi,340 pp. Frontis, sev ills. Orig cloth gilt, backstrip relaid, sl worn. *(Whitehart)* **£35 [≈ $67]**

South, Richard
- The Butterflies of the British Isles. London: Warne, Wayside and Woodland Series, 1906. 1st edn. 12mo. x,204 pp. 450 cold figs & num b/w plates & text ills. Tiny ink mark ft of some pp. Orig pict blue cloth gilt.
(Gough) **£40 [≈ $76]**
- The Moths of the British Isles. London: Warne, Wayside and Woodland Series, 1907. 1st edn. 2 vols. 12mo. 1543 cold figs, num b/w plates & text ills. Orig pict blue cloth gilt, fine. *(Gough)* **£60 [≈ $115]**

Southern, H.N.
- The Handbook of British Mammals. L: 1964. 1st edn. 8vo. xxi,465 pp. 32 plates, 51 text

ills. Cloth.   *(Henly)* **£24 [≈ $46]**

Southgate, Frank
- Wildfowl & Waders. Nature & Sport in the Coastlands, depicted by the late Frank Southgate ... and Described by Hugh B.C. Pollard. London: (1928). 1st ltd edn, one of 950. 4to. viii,83 pp. 16 cold plates, 48 ills. Occas sl foxing. Orig qtr vellum, t.e.g.
(Bow Windows) **£175 [≈ $335]**

Sowerby, George Brettingham, the elder
- A Conchological Manual. London: 1852. 4th edn. 8vo. vii,337 pp. 2 fldg tables, 29 hand cold plates, 98 text figs. Sound ex-lib. Title sl foxed. Orig cloth, sl worn, rebacked.
(Wheldon & Wesley) **£110 [≈ $211]**
- A Conchological Manual. London: 1852. 4th edn. 8vo. vii,337 pp. 2 fldg tables, 29 plain plates, 98 text figs. Sl foxing. Orig cloth, trifle worn, spine faded.
(Wheldon & Wesley) **£40 [≈ $76]**

Sowerby, Henry
- Popular Mineralogy, comprising a Familiar Account of Minerals and their Uses. London: 1850. Sq 8vo. viii,344 pp. 20 hand cold plates. Lib b'plates, blind stamps on plates. Orig cloth, rebacked.
(Wheldon & Wesley) **£65 [≈ $124]**

Sowerby, James
- British Mineralogy: or Coloured Figures intended to elucidate the Mineralogy of Great Britain. London: the author, 1806-11. 5 vols. 8vo. xii,223; 199; 209; 184; 281,xxiii pp. 550 hand cold plates. New half leather.
(Gemmary) **$6,500 [≈ £3,385]**
- The British Miscellany: or Coloured Figures of New, Rare or Little Known Animal Subjects ... London: [1804-06-] 1875. 8vo. vi, 137, 31 pp. 76 hand cold plates. Ex-lib. Orig cloth, orig wraps to the 12 parts bound in. With the title & index, as issued by Quaritch in 1875. *(Henly)* **£480 [≈ $921]**
- Coloured Figures of English Fungi or Mushrooms. London: 1797-1803. 3 vols in one. Folio. 400 hand cold plates. Contemp calf gilt, rather worn. Without the unfinished supplement published in 1809-15 with 40 plates.
(Wheldon & Wesley) **£2,750 [≈ $5,279]**
- English Botany ... Third Edition Revised, Edited by J.T. Boswell-Syme. London: 1899. 12 vols, with supplement to vols 1-4, together 13 vols. Roy 8vo. 2 plain & 1950 hand cold plates (16 dble page). Qtr mor, sl rubbed.
(Henly) **£850 [≈ $1,631]**

- English Botany ... Third Edition ... by T. Boswell Syme. 12 vols. 1937 hand cold plates. [With] Supplement (to vols 1-4) by N.E. Brown. 13 cold & 2 plain plates. London: 1901. Together 13 vols, all published. Roy 8vo. Contemp half mor. Plate 1834* not present as often.
(Wheldon & Wesley) £750 [≈ $1,439]

Sowerby, John Edward & Johnson, C.
- British Poisonous Plants. London: 1861. 2nd edn. 8vo. iv,76 pp. 32 hand cold plates. Cloth gilt, unopened.   *(Henly) £112 [≈ $215]*
- British Poisonous Plants ... see also under Johnson, C.
- The Ferns of Great Britain. London: 1855. 1st edn. 8vo. 87 pp. 49 partly hand cold plates. Cloth, spine sl faded.
(Henly) £45 [≈ $86]
- The Ferns of Great Britain. London: 1855. 8vo. 87 pp. 49 partly hand cold plates. Orig cloth, sound ex-lib.
(Wheldon & Wesley) £35 [≈ $67]
- The Ferns of Great britain. London: 1855. 8vo. 88 pp. 49 (fully) cold plates. Occas foxing & offsets. Binder's cloth, sl worn.
(Wheldon & Wesley) £40 [≈ $76]

Soyer, Alexis
- The Modern Housewife of Menagere. Comprising One Thousand Receipts for the Economic and Judicious Preparation of Every Meal of the Day ... London: Simpkin, 1849. 1st edn. 8vo. Frontis, 1 plate. Rebound with orig cvrs laid down. *(Young's) £85 [≈ $163]*

Spallanzani, Lazzaro
- Dissertations relative to the Natural History of Animals and Vegetables. Translated from the Italian. A New Edition, Corrected and Enlarged. London: Murray, 1789. 2nd English edn. 2 vols. 8vo. 3 fldg plates. 1st vol sl spotted. Rec calf antique.
(Bickersteth) £225 [≈ $431]
- Tracts on the Natural History of Animals and Vegetables. Translated by J.G. Dalyell. Edinburgh: 1803. 2nd edn. 2 vols. 8vo. 11 plates (foxed). Crimson mor.
(Wheldon & Wesley) £150 [≈ $287]

Sparrow, John
- A Mechanical Dissertation upon the Lues Venerea. Proving not only the possibility, but certainty of curing that Disease ... By J.S. Surgeon. London: Richard King ..., 1731. 1st edn. 43,[1] pp. Wraps (sl worn).
(Wreden) $249.50 [≈ £130]

Spectacle de la Nature ...
- See Pluche, Noel Antoine.

Speechly, William
- A Treatise on the Culture of the Pine Apple and the Management of the Hot-House ... York: 1779. 1st edn. Roy 8vo. xvii,[v],186 pp. Subscribers 5 pp. 2 plates. Sl soiling, lib b'plate. Cloth.
(Wheldon & Wesley) £180 [≈ $345]
- A Treatise on the Culture of the Vine ... New Hints on the Formation of Vineyards in England ... Dublin: 1791. 1st Dublin edn. 8vo. xxi,[i blank], 307,[iv misbound after p 306] pp. 5 plates (1 fldg with sm marg tear). Contemp calf, gilt spine, mor label.
(Finch) £180 [≈ $345]

Speedy, Tom
- The Natural History of Sport in Scotland with Rod and Gun. Edinburgh: Blackwood, 1920. 1st edn. xxviii,440 pp. Port frontis, num ills by J.G. Millais. Title sl spotted. Orig cloth gilt, rather worn. *(Hollett) £35 [≈ $67]*

Speert, Harold
- Iconographia Gyniatrica: A Pictorial History of Gynecology and Obstetrics. Phila: 1973. 1st edn. 4to. 540 pp. Num ills. Orig bndg.
(Fye) $200 [≈ £104]
- Obstetric and Gynecologic Milestones: Essays and Eponyms. New York: 1958. 1st edn. 700 pp. Orig bndg. *(Fye) $150 [≈ £78]*

Spence, J.
- Lectures on Surgery. London: 1875-76. 2 vols. 58 cold plates, 157 figs. Orig cloth, sl worn, vol 2 backstrip relaid.
(Whitehart) £58 [≈ $111]

Spencer, Herbert R.
- The History of British Midwifery from 1650 to 1800. London: John Bale, Sons & Danielson, 1927. 8vo. 9 plates. Orig bndg.
(Georges) £25 [≈ $47]

Spiers, W.
- Nature through the Microscope or Rambles and Studies of a Microscopist. London: Robert Culley, [ca 1909]. 8vo. 355 pp. 99 plates (10 cold), 300 text figs. Some foxing. Ex-lib. Dec cloth.   *(Gemmary) $65 [≈ £33]*

Spitta, E.J.
- Microscopy. The Construction, Theory and Use of the Microscope. London: 1920. 3rd edn. xxviii,537 pp. 83 plates, 255 text ills. Orig cloth, sl faded, spine ends worn, front

inner hinge sl cracked but firm.
(Whitehart) **£25 [≈ $47]**

Spottiswoode, W.
- Polarisation of Light. London: Macmillan, 1874. Cr 8vo. ix,129 pp. 2 cold plates, 29 text figs. Cloth, sl loose. *(Gemmary)* **$60 [≈ £31]**

Sprat, Thomas
- The History of the Royal Society of London ... Third Edition Corrected. London: Knapton ..., 1722. Sm 4to. [xvi],438 pp. Frontis with imprimatur on recto, 2 fldg plates. Title & prelims sl fingered. Period panelled calf, sl worn.
(Rankin) **£125 [≈ $239]**

Spurr, J.E.
- The Ore Magmas. A Series of Essays on Ore Deposition. New York: McGraw-Hill, 1923. 1st edn. 2 vols. 8vo. 175 text figs. Cloth, vol 2 cvr spotted. *(Gemmary)* **$125 [≈ £65]**

Spurzheim, J.G.
- Observations on the Deranged Manifestations of the Mind, or Insanity. First American Edition, with Notes, Improvements, and Plates. With an Appendix by A. Brigham. Boston: 1833. 8vo. viii,260 pp. Errata slip. 4 plates. Some foxing. Orig cloth, sl worn.
(Bow Windows) **£115 [≈ $220]**
- Observations on the Deranged Manifestations of the Human Mind, or Insanity ... With an Appendix by A. Brigham. Boston: 1836. 272 pp. 4 plates. Orig bndg, fine.
(Fye) **$250 [≈ £130]**

Stables, Gordon
- Our Friend the Dog ... London: Dean & Son, [ca 1900-10]. 7th edn. 8vo. xii,369 pp, inc 17 pp advts. 32 plates, ills. Orig dec cloth.
(Beech) **£14 [≈ $26]**

Stainton, H.T.
- British Butterflies and Moths. London: L. reeve, [1867]. 1st edn. xii,292,16 advt pp. 16 colour-printed plates finished by hand, sev text ills. Orig red pict cloth gilt, spine faded.
(Gough) **£30 [≈ $57]**
- A Manual of British Butterflies and Moths. London: Van Voorst, 1857. 1st edn. 2 vols. Num w'cut ills. Orig purple cloth, spines faded. *(Gough)* **£40 [≈ $76]**

Stamp, L. Dudley
- Britain's Structure and Scenery. London: Collins New Naturalist, 1946. 1st edn. 8vo. xvi,255 pp. 32 cold & 32 plain plates, 74 text

figs. End sl foxed. Orig cloth.
(Henly) **£8 [≈ $15]**
- Man and the Land. London: Collins New Naturalist, 1955. 1st edn. 8vo. xvi,272 pp. 24 cold & 32 plain plates. Orig cloth.
(Henly) **£18 [≈ $34]**
- Man and the Land. London: Collins New Naturalist, 1955. 1st edn. Ills. Inscrptn on endpaper. Dw (sl worn).
(Wheldon & Wesley) **£25 [≈ $47]**
- Nature Conservation in Britain. London: Collins New Naturalist, 1969. 1st edn. 8vo. xiv,273 pp. 23 plates. Orig cloth. Dw.
(Henly) **£22 [≈ $42]**

Stanley, Rupert
- Textbook on Wireless Telegraphy. 1914. 1st edn. 344 pp. 201 ills. Orig wraps.
(New Wireless) **$35 [≈ £18]**
- Text-Book on Wireless Telegraphy. London: 1919-23. New edn. 2 vols. xiii,471; xi,394 pp. 2 ports, fldg plate, num other ills. Cloth dust stained. *(Whitehart)* **£35 [≈ $67]**

Stark, A.C. & Sclater, W.L.
- The Fauna of South Africa: The Birds of South Africa. London: 1900-06. 4 vols. 8vo. Port, fldg map, 468 text figs. Orig green cloth, recased, new endpapers.
(Wheldon & Wesley) **£450 [≈ $863]**

Stark, Robert M.
- A Popular History of British Mosses. London: 1860. 2nd edn. xx,348 pp. 20 hand cold plates. Orig cloth, trifle used.
(Wheldon & Wesley) **£20 [≈ $38]**
- A Popular History of British Mosses ... London: Routledge, [ca 1870]. 2nd edn. 12mo. xx, 348 pp. 20 cold plates. Some spotting. Orig blue cloth, sl faded, elab gilt spine. *(Gough)* **£30 [≈ $57]**

Starobinski, J.
- A History of Medicine. New York: 1964. Roy 8vo. 108 pp. Ills. Dw. *(Goodrich)* **$45 [≈ £23]**

Starr, Louis (ed.)
- An American Textbook of the Diseases of Children ... by American Teachers ... London & Phila: 1894. 2 vols. 8vo. 1195 pp. Sheep, v worn, jnts split, front fly lacking.
(Goodrich) **$75 [≈ £39]**

Staveley, E.F.
- British Insects. London: 1871. 8vo. xvi, 392 pp. 16 hand cold plates. Labels on title & inside front cvr. Orig cloth, spine faded.
(Wheldon & Wesley) **£30 [≈ $57]**

- British Spiders: an Introduction to the Study of the Araneidae. London: [1866]. Cr 8vo. xvi,280 pp. 14 hand cold & 2 plain plates. Title trifle foxed. Orig cloth.
(Wheldon & Wesley) **£30** [≈ $57]

Stavely, S.W.
- The New Whole Art of Confectionary ... New Edition. To which are added several New and Useful Receipts ... Derby: [ca 1827]. 8vo. vi, [i], 8-60 pp. Advts on inside cvrs. Some creasing to crnrs & sl dusty. Orig ptd wraps.
(Spelman) **£95** [≈ $182]

Stebbing, T.R.R.
- A History of Crustacea, recent Malacostraca. London: Intl Scientific Series, 1893. 1st edn. Sm 8vo. xviii,466 pp. 19 plates, 32 text figs. Orig dec cloth, partly unopened.
(Bow Windows) **£35** [≈ $67]

Steenstrup, J.J.S.
- On the Alternation of Generations. London: Ray Society, 1845. 8vo. viii,132 pp. 3 plates. Sl foxing. Cloth.
(Wheldon & Wesley) **£40** [≈ $76]

Steers, J.A.
- The Sea Coast. London: Collins New Naturalist, 1953. 1st edn. 8vo. xii,276 pp. 8 cold & 24 plain plates. Orig cloth, fore edges of cvrs affected by damp. *(Henly)* **£12** [≈ $23]

Steinmetz, Charles Proteus
- Four Lectures on Relativity and Space. 1923. 1st edn. 126 pp. 33 ills. 7 stereo views in back pocket. Orig bndg.
(New Wireless) **$65** [≈ £33]
- Theory and Calculation of Alternating Current Phenomena. London: 1908. 4th edn. xxii, 746 pp. 262 text figs. Orig cloth, dull.
(Whitehart) **£18** [≈ $34]

Step, Edward
- Bees, Wasps, Ants and Allied Insects of the British Isles. L: 1932. 1st edn. Post 8vo. xxv,238 pp. 67 plates (44 cold). Cloth gilt.
(Henly) **£22** [≈ $42]
- Shell Life. An Introduction to the British Mollusca. London: Warne, 1901. 1st edn. 414 pp. 32 photo plates, num text ills. Occas sl foxing. Orig pict cloth gilt.
(Gough) **£35** [≈ $67]
- Shell Life. An Introduction to British Mollusca. L: 1945. Post 8vo. 443 pp. 25 cold & 7 plain plates. Cloth. *(Henly)* **£18** [≈ $34]
- Wayside and Woodland Blossoms ... London: Warne, 1895-96. 1st edn. 2 vols. 12mo. 286 cold figs, num b/w ills. Orig pict red cloth, sl rubbed & faded.
(Gough) **£40** [≈ $76]
- Wayside and Woodland Trees ... London: Warne, 1904. 1st edn. 12mo. 182 pp. 127 b/w photo plates, num text ills. Orig green pict cloth gilt, jnts v sl rubbed.
(Gough) **£25** [≈ $47]
- Wild Flowers Month by Month in their Natural Haunts. L: 1905-06. 2 vols. Sm 4to. vi,199; vi,200 pp. Cold frontises, num photo ills. Ends sl foxed. Pict cloth gilt.
(Henly) **£18** [≈ $34]

Stephens, Henry
- The Book of the Farm. Edinburgh: Blackwood, 1849-52. 2nd edn. 2 vols. Roy 8vo. Num text ills. Endpapers foxed. Orig pict gilt cloth (not uniform colour, reprd).
(Stewart) **£75** [≈ $143]
- Book of the Farm ... Revised and largely re-written by James MacDonald. Edinburgh: Blackwood, 1908-09. 3 vols. Lge 8vo. 60 animal ports, 777 ills. Orig roan backed cloth gilt, some jnts cracking.
(Hollett) **£75** [≈ $143]

Stephens, J.F.
- Illustrations of British Entomology. London: 1828-46. 12 vols, complete inc Supplement vol. 8vo. 95 hand cold plates. Sl foxing. New bds. *(Wheldon & Wesley)* **£700** [≈ $1,343]

Stephens, J.W.W.
- Blackwater Fever; A Historical Survey and Observations made over a Century. Liverpool: UP, 1937. 1st edn. 8vo. xvi,727 pp. 2 plates. Dw (chipped).
(Gough) **£30** [≈ $57]

Stephens, James Francis
- Illustrations of British Entomology ... London: Baldwin & Cradock, Bohn ..., 1828-46. 1st edn. 12 vols (inc Supplement). Bohn's 94-page ctlg at end of Supplement. 95 hand cold plates. Contemp half mor, gilt spines (strengthened at ends).
(Gough) **£495** [≈ $950]

Stephenson, John
- Medical Zoology, and Mineralogy ... London: John Churchill, 1838. 1st edn. vi,350 pp. 44 hand cold lithos & 2 plain plates. Occas mostly sl spotting. Contemp half calf, gilt dec spine, a.e.g.
(Gough) **£395** [≈ $758]

Sterland, W.J.
- The Birds of Sherwood Forest ... London: L:

Reeve, 1869. 1st edn. xi,244,24 ctlg pp. 1 plain & chromolithograph plates. Orig cloth, backstrip relaid. *(Gough)* £35 [≈ $67]

Sterland, W.J. & Whitaker, J.
- Descriptive List of the Birds of Nottinghamshire. Mansfield: William Gouk, 1879. 1st edn. 71 pp. Orig dec cloth, sl faded.
(Gough) £25 [≈ $47]

Stern, F.C.
- A Study of the Genus Paeonia. London: 1946. Imperial 4to. viii,155 pp. 8 maps, 15 cold plates by Lilian Snelling. Ends v sl foxed. Cloth gilt. *(Henly)* £245 [≈ $470]

Steuart, Henry
- The Planter's Guide ... being an Attempt to Place the Art ... on Phytological and Fixed Principles ...Edinburgh: 1828. 2nd edn, enlgd. 8vo. [6],xxxvii, [i],527 pp. 6 litho plates. Half-title. Advt slip. Orig linen backed bds. *(Spelman)* £160 [≈ $307]
- The Planter's Guide ... being an Attempt to Place the Art ... on Phytological and Fixed Principles ...Edinburgh: 1828. 2nd edn, enlgd. 8vo. [6],xxxvii, [i],527 pp. 6 litho plates. Some marg dustiness. Orig linen backed bds, uncut, bds evenly soiled.
(Spelman) £120 [≈ $230]
- The Planter's Guide ... New York: 1832. 1st Amer edn. xxxix, [41]-422 pp. Frontis, plates. Light to heavy foxing. Orig cloth, leather label, spotted & worn. *(Reese)* $150 [≈ £78]
- The Planter's Guide ... New York: 1832. 1st Amer edn. 8vo. 422 pp. Frontis, 3 plates. Title & ends sl foxed. Cloth.
(Henly) £65 [≈ $124]

Stevens, R.W.
- On the Stowage of Ships and their Cargoes ... London: 1869. 5th edn. 712 pp. Lge fldg frontis, 16 plates. Marg ink notes. New cloth.
(Whitehart) £25 [≈ $47]

Stevenson, Henry
- The Birds of Norfolk. London: Van Voorst, 1866-70. 1st edn. 2 vols. 8vo. lxxii,445; x,449,[2 advt] pp. 5 litho plates (2 hand cold). Plates somewhat foxed. Orig cloth. A supplement was published later.
(Gough) £60 [≈ $115]

Stevenson, James
- Advice Medical, and Economical, relative to the Purchase and Consumption of Tea, Coffee, & Chocolate; Wines and Malt Liquors ... London: Westley, 1830. 1st edn. xvi,204

pp. Orig dec bds, crnrs bumped, front jnt starting. *(Wreden)* $95 [≈ £49]

Stevenson, John, 1778-1846?
- On the Nature and Symptoms of Cataract, and on the Cure of that Disease ... London: Whittaker, 1824. 1st edn. 8vo. ix,[3],234,2 advt pp. Orig bds, uncut, paper label, somewhat worn. *(Rootenberg)* $400 [≈ £208]

Stevenson-Hamilton, J.
- Animal Life in Africa. London: 1912. 1st edn. 538 pp. Num ills. Orig bndg.
(Trophy Room) $200 [≈ £104]

Stigand, C.H.
- Central African Game and Its Spoor. London: 1906. 4to. Num ills. Orig bndg, sl stained, title on spine faded.
(Central Africana) £295 [≈ $566]
- Central African Game and Its Spoor. London: Horace Cox, 1909. 2nd edn. 4to. xii, 315 pp. Num photo ills & ills by D.D. Lyell. Orig cloth, soiled, wrinkled.
(Frew Mackenzie) £200 [≈ $383]
- The Game of British East Africa. London: Horace Cox, 1909. 1st edn. Lge 4to. x, 310, advt pp. Num photo plates. Orig pict green cloth gilt, front edge of cvr sl frayed.
(Terramedia) $350 [≈ £182]
- The Game of British East Africa. London: Horace Cox, 1909. 1st edn. 4to. x,310,[8 advt] pp. Num photo ills. Orig cloth, sm tear hd of spine. *(Frew Mackenzie)* £250 [≈ $479]
- The Game of British East Africa. London: 1913. 2nd edn. 4to. 310 pp. 76 ills. Half leather. *(Trophy Room)* $275 [≈ £143]

Stille, Alfred
- Epidemic Meningitis, or Cerebro-Spinal Meningitis. Phila: 1867. 1st edn. 178 pp. Orig bndg. *(Fye)* $175 [≈ £91]

Stillingfleet, Benjamin
- Miscellaneous Tracts relating to Natural History, Husbandry, and Physick. Translated from the Latin ... with Notes. London: 1759. 1st edn. 8vo. xxx,[1],230 pp. Sl water stain at ends. Half calf, trifle used.
(Wheldon & Wesley) £200 [≈ $383]
- Miscellaneous Tracts relating to Natural History, Husbandry, and Physick ... The Second Edition ... London: 1762. 8vo. xxxi, 391 pp. Lib stamp on title. 11 plates. Contemp calf, rebacked. Author's pres copy.
(Goodrich) $145 [≈ £75]
- See also Linnaeus, C.

Stillwell, M.B.
- The Awakening Interest in Science during the First Century of Printing 1450-1550. New York: Bibl. Soc of America, 1970. One of 1500. Roy 8vo. xxix,399 pp. Cloth.
(Gemmary) **$100 [≃ £52]**

Stirling, William
- Some Apostles of Physiology being an Account of their Lives and Labours ... London: Waterlow & Sons, 1902. iv,129 pp. 32 plates. Owner's name stamp, owner's name on title. Orig cloth gilt, v soiled, spine torn.
(Hollett) **£75 [≃ $143]**
- Some Apostles of Physiology, being an Account of their Lives and Labours ... London: privately Printed, 1902. Folio. 129 pp. 31 plates, 30 text ills. Orig white cloth, v sl bump hd of spine. *(Hemlock)* **$150 [≃ £78]**

Stoddart, Richard
- Tables for computing the Solid Contents of Timber, from 2 to 48 3/4 inches square ... Leith: for the author, 1818. Thin 8vo. Sl soiled, notes on endpaper. Contemp calf, crnrs worn. *(Stewart)* **£45 [≃ $86]**

Stoerck, Anthony
- An Essay on the Use and Effects of the Root of the Colchicum Autumnale, or Meadow Saffron ... with an Appendix concerning the Cicuta, or Hemlock ... London: Becket & De Hondt, 1764. 1st edn in English. 8vo. 47 pp. Fldg frontis. Later mor backed bds.
(Burmester) **£170 [≃ $326]**

Stokes, R., et al.
- A Text-Book of Rand Metallurgical Practice. London: Charles Griffin, 1926. 3rd edn. 2 vols. 8vo. xxi,564; xxii,438,[76 advt] pp. 128 + 455 text figs. Sl foxing. Orig cloth, worn.
(Gemmary) **£150 [≃ £78]**

Stokes, William
- The Diseases of the Heart and Aorta. Phila: 1855. 1st Amer edn, 2nd printing. 710 pp. Leather, fine. *(Fye)* **$500 [≃ £260]**
- The Diseases of the Heart and Aorta. Phila: 1855. 1st Amer edn, 2nd printing. 710 pp. Date erased from title. Leather, front hinge cracked, ft of spine soiled.
(Fye) **$400 [≃ £208]**
- Selected Papers on Operative and Clinical Surgery. With a Memoir of the Author by Alexander Ogston. Edited by W. Taylor. London: 1902. xxv,484 pp. Frontis port, 21 plates, 52 text figs. Sl foxing.
(Whitehart) **£35 [≃ $67]**

- A Treatise on the Diagnosis and Treatment of Diseases of the Chest - Part I. Diseases of the Lung and Windpipe. London: New Sydenham Soc, 1882. lv,596 pp. Port. Orig cloth, 2-inch tear hd of spine.
(Whitehart) **£40 [≃ $76]**
- A Treatise on the Diagnosis and Treatment of Diseases of the Chest. Part 1. Diseases of the Lung and Windpipe. London: 1882. 596 pp. Orig bndg, backstrip defective, rear hinge cracked. *(Fye)* **$75 [≃ £39]**

Stone, Ellery W.
- Elements of Radio Communication. 1923. 2nd edn. 318 pp. 39 photos, 145 ills. Orig bndg. *(New Wireless)* **$35 [≃ £18]**
- Elements of Radiotelegraphy. 1922. 1st edn. 267 pp. 33 photos, 125 ills. Orig bndg.
(New Wireless) **$45 [≃ £23]**

Stone, Thomas, surveyor
- An Essay on Agriculture, with a View to Inform Gentlemen of Landed Property, whether their Estates are managed to the Greatest Advantage. Lynn: W. Whittingham, 1785. 261 pp. Contemp qtr calf, mrbld bds. Matthew Boulton's copy.
(C.R. Johnson) **£160 [≃ $307]**

Stone, Thomas, M.D.
- Observations on the Phrenological Development of Burke, Hare and other atrocious Murderers ... Edinburgh: 1829. [iv], 75 pp. Half-title. V sl spotting. Mod wraps. *(Buccleuch)* **£60 [≃ $115]**

Stonehenge (J.H. Walsh)
- The Dog in Health and Disease ... London: Longman ..., 1859. 1st edn. xvi,468 pp. Advt on endpapers. Num text engvs. Qtr red mor, gilt dec spine, rubbed, sl frayed & faded.
(Bookline) **£50 [≃ $95]**

Stones, M. & Curtis, W.
- The Endemic Flora of Tasmania. London: 1967-68. 6 vols. Folio. 155 cold plates. Orig cloth. Dws.
(Wheldon & Wesley) **£500 [≃ $959]**

Stoney, B.B.
- The Theory of Strains in Girders and Similar Structures, with Observations on the Application of Theory to Practice and Tables ... London: 1873. New edn, rvsd & enlgd. xxxi, 632 pp. 5 fldg tables, 123 text figs. Orig cloth, spine relaid. *(Whitehart)* **£35 [≃ $67]**

Stonham, Charles
- The Birds of the British Islands. London: Grant Richards, 1906. 1st edn. 5 vols. Lge 4to. 318 hand cold plates. Contemp half mor, uncut.   *(Gough)* **£1,850 [≈ $3,551]**

Stookey, Byron
- A History of Colonial Medical Education in the Province of New York ... (1767-1830). Springfield: 1962. 8vo. 286 pp. Ills. Orig bndg.   *(Goodrich)* **$45 [≈ £23]**

Stopes, H.
- Malt and Malting. An Historical, Scientific, and Practical Treatise ... London: Lyon, 1885. 1st edn. 8vo. 150 ills. Orig bndg.
                    (Young's) **£100 [≈ $191]**

Storer, H.R.
- Medicina in Nummis. A Descriptive List of the Coins - Medals - Jetons relating to Medicine, Surgery and the Allied Sciences. Boston, MA: privately ptd, 1931. 1146 pp. 16 plates.   *(Whitehart)* **£200 [≈ $383]**

Story, A.T.
- The Story of Wireless Telegraphy. 1912. 2nd edn. 225 pp. 11 photos, 57 ills. Orig bndg, cvrs soiled.   *(New Wireless)* **$80 [≈ £42]**

Strahan, A.
- Isle of Purbeck & Weymouth. London: 1898. xi,278 pp. Map, 11 plates, 183 figs. Orig cloth gilt.   *(Baldwin)* **£48 [≈ $92]**

Strahan, John
- The Diagnosis and Treatment of Extra Uterine Pregnancy. Phila: 1889. 1st edn. 8vo. Name cut from top of title. Cloth bds.
                    (Emerald Isle) **£45 [≈ $86]**

Straker, E.
- Wealden Iron. A Monograph on the former Ironworks in the Counties of Sussex, Surrey and Kent ... London: 1931. 1st edn. 8vo. xiv, 487 pp. Cold maps, ills. Orig cloth.
                    (Bow Windows) **£55 [≈ $105]**

Strauss, E.
- Sir William Petty. Portrait of a Genius. London: Bodley Head, 1954. 8vo. Port frontis. Orig bndg.   *(Georges)* **£35 [≈ $67]**

Stricker, Solomon
- Manual of Human and Comparative Histology. Translated by Henry Power. London: New Sydenham Society, 1870. 3 vols. 8vo. Orig bndgs, worn, 1 recased.

(Goodrich) **$115 [≈ £59]**

Strickland, F.
- A Manual of Petrol Motors and Motor Cars. Comprising the Designing, Construction and Working of Petrol Motors. London: 1907. viii, 376 pp. 329 ills, 15 tables. Occas sl soiling. Orig cloth, sl stained, new endpapers.
                    (Whitehart) **£40 [≈ $76]**

Strother, Edward
- Criticon Febrium: or, a Critical Essay on Fevers ... London: Rivington, 1716. 1st edn. 8vo. [xii],211,[1] pp. Contemp calf, hinges cracked.   *(Bookpress)* **$375 [≈ £195]**
- An Essay on Sickness and Health. London: 1725. 1st edn. 8vo. lxviii,463,[1] pp. Contemp calf, split in lower hinge. The Plesch copy.   *(Hemlock)* **$375 [≈ £195]**
- Pharmacopoeia Radcliffeana ... see Radcliffe, John.

Strumpfell, Adolf
- A Textbook of Medicine ... Translated ... Notes by F.C. Shattuck. New York: 1891. 8vo. 981 pp. Ills. Sheep, worn, jnts weak.
                    (Goodrich) **$95 [≈ £49]**

Strutt, J.G.
- Sylva Britannica, or Portraits of Forest Trees. London: [1830]. 4to. xvi,151 pp. Engvd title, 49 plates on india paper. Some foxing. Half calf, rebacked, rubbed.
                    (Henly) **£110 [≈ $211]**
- Sylva Britannica, or Portraits of Forest Trees. London: [1830-36]. Imperial 8vo. viii, 151 pp. Addtnl engvd title, 49 plates. Plate margs spotted. Qtr calf.   *(Henly)* **£60 [≈ $115]**

Struve, Christian August
- A Practical Essay on the Art of Recovering Suspended Animation: together with a Review of the ... Means to be adopted in Cases of Imminent Danger. Albany: 1803. 1st edn in English. 12mo. Contemp calf, jnts cracked.   *(Goodrich)* **$150 [≈ £78]**

Stubbe, Henry
- The Miraculous Conformist: or An Account of several Marvailous Cures performed by the Stroaking of the Hands of Mr. Valentine Greatarick ... In a Letter to ... Robert Boyle ... Oxford: Hall, 1666. Sm 4to. 44 pp. Some blank crnrs chewed. New qtr calf. Wing S.6062.   *(Goodrich)* **$1,495 [≈ £778]**
- The Miraculous Conformist: or an Account of several Marvellous Cures performed by the stroking of the Hands of Mr Valentine

Greatarick ... Oxford: H. Hall, 1666. 1st edn.
Sm 4to. [vi],44,[2 blank] pp. Sl browned. 19th
c mor gilt, a.e.g. Wing S.6062.
(Finch) **£750 [≈ $1,439]**

Stubbs, S.G. Blaxland & Bligh, E.W.
- Sixty Centuries of Health and Physic; The
Progress of Ideas from Primitive Magic to
Modern Medicine. London: Sampson Low
..., [1931]. 1st edn. 8vo. xvi,253 pp. Cold
frontis, 63 plates. Orig cloth, edges sl rubbed.
(Gough) **£30 [≈ $57]**

Suckling, C.W.
- On the Treatment of Diseases of the Nervous
System. London: 1890. [v],285,[iv] pp. Cloth,
sl dusty.   *(Whitehart)* **£35 [≈ $67]**

Sudoff, Karl
- Essays in the History of Medicine. Translated
by Various Hands and Edited ... by Fielding
H. Garrison. New York: 1926. 8vo. 397 pp.
Frontis port. Orig bndg, spine sunned.
(Goodrich) **$85 [≈ £44]**

Suffolk, W.T.
- On Microscopical Manipulations. London:
Henry Gillman, 1875. 2nd edn. Cr 8vo.
xv,227 pp. 7 plates, 48 text figs. Cloth, sl
water stained.   *(Gemmary)* **$60 [≈ £31]**

Summerhayes, V.S.
- Wild Orchids of Britain, with a Key to the
Species. London: Collins New Naturalist,
1951. 1st edn. 8vo. 48 cold & 24 plain plates.
Orig cloth.   *(Henly)* **£18 [≈ $34]**

Summers-Smith, J.D.
- The House Sparrow. London: Collins New
Naturalist, 1963. 1st edn. 8vo. xvi,269 pp. 1
cold & 24 plain plates. Orig cloth. Dw.
(Henly) **£50 [≈ $95]**
- The House-Sparrow. London: Collins New
Naturalist, 1963. 1st edn. 8vo. xvi,269 pp.
Ills. Dw (sl torn).
(Wheldon & Wesley) **£40 [≈ $76]**

The Surgeon's Vade-Mecum ...
- The Surgeon's Vade-Mecum: containing the
Symptoms, Causes, Diagnosis, Prognosis,
and Treatment of Surgical Diseases ...
London: 1824. 3rd edn. xvi,395 pp. 12 plates.
Marg water stain at front. Binder's cloth.
(Whitehart) **£60 [≈ $115]**

Sutcliffe, G. Lister (ed.)
- The Principles and Practice of Modern
House Construction ... London: 1898. 6 vols.

1031 pp. 750 ills & diags, many cold. 1
endpaper sl scarred. Orig cloth, sl dust
stained.   *(Whitehart)* **£40 [≈ $76]**

Sutherland, G.A.
- The Heart in Early Life. London: 1914. 1st
edn. 211 pp. Orig bndg. *(Fye)* **$100 [≈ £52]**

Sutton, Thomas
- A Practical Account of a Remittent Fever,
frequently occurring among the Troops in
this Climate. Canterbury: ptd by James
Simmons, sold by G. Robinson, London,
1806. 1st edn. 8vo. 42 pp. Title sl spotted &
with old stamp. Disbound.
(Burmester) **£45 [≈ $86]**

Swainson, W.
- The Birds of Western Africa. London: Bohn,
Jardine's Naturalist's Library, [ca 1850]. 2
vols. Sm 8vo. 2 ports, 2 cold title vignettes, 64
hand cold plates. Orig red cloth.
(Wheldon & Wesley) **£100 [≈ $191]**
- The Natural History of the Birds of Western
Africa ... Edinburgh: Jardine's Naturalist's
Library, 1837-43. 1st edn. 2 vols. Sm 8vo. 2
ports, 2 cold title vignettes, 64 hand cold
plates. 2 ff reprd. Title sl stained. Orig cloth,
recased, hd of spines reprd.
(Wheldon & Wesley) **£130 [≈ $249]**
- A Preliminary Discourse on the Study of
Natural History. London: 1834. Post 8vo.
viii, 462 pp. Cloth.
(Wheldon & Wesley) **£30 [≈ $57]**

Swan, Joseph
- A Demonstration of the Nerves of the Human
Body. London: 1834. 1st 4to edn. 83 pp. 25
plates. Half leather, rebacked, new
endpapers.   *(Fye)* **$500 [≈ £260]**

Swediaur, Francois
- Practical   Observations   on   Venereal
Complaints. New York: Samuel Campbell,
1788. 1st Amer edn. 8vo. [iv],128 pp.
Browned. Contemp sheep, sl worn.
(Bookpress) **$650 [≈ £338]**
- A Complete Treatise of the Symptoms,
Effects, Nature and Treatment of Syphilis.
Translated from the Fourth Edition by
Thomas T. Hewson. Phila: 1815. 8vo. vii,539
pp. Some browning & foxing. Sheep, rubbed.
(Goodrich) **$75 [≈ £39]**

Swete, E.H.
- Flora Bristoliensis. London: 1854. 8vo.
xxvi,138 pp. Map in pocket, 2 plates. Cloth,
trifle worn *(Wheldon & Wesley)* **£35 [≈ $67]**

Swinnerton, H.H.
- Fossils. London: Collins New Naturalist, 1960. 1st edn. 8vo. xiv,274 pp. 1 cold & 34 plain plates. Orig cloth. Dw.
(Henly) £28 [≈ $53]

Swinton, A.H.
- Insect Variety: its Propagation and Distribution. Treating of the Odours, Dances, Colour and Music ... bearing of the Science of Entomology on Geology. London: [1880]. x, 323, [4] pp. Frontis, 7 plates, text figs. Orig cloth, sl stained & worn, inner front hinge cracked but firm.
(Whitehart) £20 [≈ $38]

Swinton, W.E.
- The Dinosaurs. London: 1934. 1st edn. xii,233 pp. 25 plates, 20 figs. Orig blue cloth.
(Baldwin) £30 [≈ $57]

Switzer, Stephen
- The Practical Fruit-Gardener. London: Thomas Woodward, 1724. 1st edn. 8vo. [xxvii], 333, [17] pp. 3 fldg plates. Occas v sl foxing. Contemp calf, minor chipping & cracking to spine. *(Bookpress)* $450 [≈ £234]

Sydenham, Thomas
- The Whole Works ... Translated from the Original Latin, by John Pechy ... London: Richard Wellington, 1696. 1st edn in English. 8vo. [xxiv],248, 353-592 pp. Title dusty & creased, marg tears to 1st 2 ff. Sl marks. Rec half calf. Wing S.6305.
(Clark) £380 [≈ $729]
- The Whole Works. London: for Wellington & Castle, 1696. 1st edn in English. Transl. by John Pechy. Post 8vo. [xxiv],1-248, 353-592 pp, complete. 1st 2 ff sl chipped. Some browning. Mod half calf.
(Ash) £250 [≈ $479]
- The Entire Works ... Newly made English ... Notes ... By John Swan. London: Edward Cave, 1742. 1st edn of this translation. 8vo. [ii],xi, [i],xxiii, [vii],623, [xv] pp. Few pp sl dusty. Old calf, extremities sl worn, lacks label. *(Clark)* £200 [≈ $383]
- The Works ... Translated from the Latin Edition of Dr. Greenhill with a Life of the Author by R.G. Latham, MD. London: Sydenham Society, 1848-50. 2 vols. 8vo. New cloth. *(Goodrich)* £95 [≈ £49]
- The Works ... Translated from the Latin Edition of Dr. Greenhill with a Life of the Author by R.G. Latham, MD. London: Sydenham Society, 1848. 2 vols. 8vo. Orig cloth, hd of vol 2 spine cracked, lib b'plate.

(Goodrich) $95 [≈ £49]

Syme, James
- Observations in Clinical Surgery. Edinburgh: 1862. 2nd edn. 217 pp. Orig bndg, fine.
(Fye) $200 [≈ £104]

Symons, G.J. (ed.)
- The Eruption of Krakatoa and Subsequent Phenomena. London: 1888. 4to. xvi,494 pp. 47 plates (2 cold). Sm blind stamps on plates. Orig cloth, reprd.
(Wheldon & Wesley) £320 [≈ $614]

Symons, William
- The Practical Gager ... All the Necessary Rules for Gaging and fixing the Utensils of Victuallers, Common Brewers, Distillers, and Maltsters ... New Edition ... London: for Wingrave & Collingwood, 1815. 8vo. xii,384 pp. Orig sheep, upper cvr held on the cords.
(Claude Cox) £25 [≈ $47]

Tahourdin, C.B.
- Native Orchids of Britain ... Croydon: H.R. Grubb, [1925]. 1st edn. xiv,114 pp. Num b/w plates & ills. Orig cloth gilt.
(Gough) £25 [≈ $47]
- Native Orchids of Britain. Descriptive Notes on all Species ... Croydon: 1925. Num photo ills. Orig bndg. *(Grayling)* £25 [≈ $47]

Tait, P.G.
- An Elementary Treatise on Quaternions. Oxford: 1847. 1st edn. xviii,320 pp. A few figs. Spine chipped at hd & cracked down half one side. *(Whitehart)* £35 [≈ $67]
- An Elementary Treatise on Quaternions. Oxford: 1873. 2nd edn. xx,296 pp. A few figs. Cloth sl worn, spine faded.
(Whitehart) £40 [≈ $76]
- Sketch of Thermodynamics. Edinburgh: Edmonston & Douglas, 1868. 8vo. vii,128 pp. Ex-lib. Orig cloth. *(Gemmary)* $90 [≈ £46]

Tait, W.C.
- The Birds of Portugal. London: 1924. 8vo. xii,260 pp. Fldg map, 10 plates. Inscrptn on endpaper, sl foxing, few pencil notes. Cloth.
(Wheldon & Wesley) £50 [≈ $95]

Talbot, B.
- The New Art of Land Measuring; or, a Turnpike Road to Practical Surveying ... Wolverhampton: for the author ..., 1779. 1st edn. 8vo. xxiv,412 pp. 13 plates, fldg table. Contemp qtr calf, sl rubbed.
(Burmester) £360 [≈ $691]

Talbot, C.H. & Hammond, E.A.
- The Medical Practitioners in Medieval England; A Biographical Register. London: Wellcome, 1965. 1st edn. 8vo. x,503 pp. Dw.
(Gough) £20 [≈ $38]
- The Medical Practitioners in Medieval England. A Biographical Register. London: 1965. x,503 pp. Orig bndg.
(Whitehart) £40 [≈ $76]

Talbot, J.H.
- A Biographical History of Medicine. Excerpts and Essays of the Men and Their Work. New York: 1970. 8vo. 1211 pp. Num ills. Orig bndg.   *(Goodrich)* $125 [≈ £65]

Tansley, A.G.
- The British Islands and their Vegetation. Cambridge: 1939. 1st edn. Roy 8vo. xxxviii, 930 pp. 418 photos, 179 text figs. Cloth, trifle faded.   *(Wheldon & Wesley)* £40 [≈ $76]
- The British Islands and their Vegetation. London: 1949. 2 vols. 8vo. 162 plates of 418 photos, 179 text figs. Cloth.
(Henly) £60 [≈ $115]
- The British Islands and their Vegetation. Cambridge: (1949) 1965. 2 vols. Roy 8vo. 970 pp. 162 plates of 418 photos, 179 text figs. Cloth.   *(Wheldon & Wesley)* £55 [≈ $105]

Taplin, William
- The Gentleman's Stable Directory; or, Modern System of Farriery ... London: for G. Kearsley, 1788-91. 6th edn vol 1, 1st edn vol 2. 2 vols. 8vo. xxiii,448; viii,424 pp. Half-titles. Early 19th c calf, sometime rebacked.
(Young's) £110 [≈ $211]

Tarleton, F.A.
- An Introduction to the Mathematical Theory of Attraction. New York: Longmans, Green, 1899. 8vo. xii,290 pp. Ex-lib. Cloth, unopened.   *(Gemmary)* $35 [≈ £18]

Tate, G.H.H.
- Mammals of Eastern Asia. New York: 1947. Cr 8vo. xiv,366 pp. 79 ills. Cloth.
(Wheldon & Wesley) £30 [≈ $57]

Tate, R.
- Rudimentary Treatise on Geology. London: 1879-85. 3rd & 2nd edns. 2 vols in one. 12mo. viii,215; viii,244, [16,32 advt] pp. 2 plates, text ills. New cloth.   *(Henly)* £24 [≈ $46]

Taussig, Helen
- Congenital Malformations of the Heart. New York: 1947. 1st edn, 2nd printing. 618 pp.

Orig bndg.   *(Fye)* $150 [≈ £78]
- Congenital Malformations of the Heart. New York: 1947. 1st edn, 4th printing. 618 pp. Orig bndg, rubbed.   *(Fye)* $60 [≈ £31]

Tayler, C.
- Elements of Algebra, compiled from Garnier's French Translations of Leonard Euler. To which are added, Solutions of several Miscellaneous Problems ... London: 1824. iv,338 pp. Occas foxing on endpapers & title. Contemp three qtr leather, sl worn.
(Whitehart) £35 [≈ $67]

Taylor, Adam
- A Treatise on the Ananas or Pine-Apple, containing Plain and Easy Directions for raising this most excellent Fruit without Fire ... Devizes: 1769. 8vo. [2],vi,62 pp. 2 fldg hand cold plates. Rec half calf, gilt spine.
(Spelman) £240 [≈ $460]

Taylor, Alfred
- Birds of a County Palatine. Being a Camera Record of Birds found ... in the County of Lancaster. London: "Wild Life" Publishing Co, 1913. 4to. 148 pp. 30 mtd photo ills, num ills. Orig pict cloth gilt, rubbed.
(Hollett) £50 [≈ $95]
- Birds of a County Palatine; Being a Camera Record of Birds ... in the County of Lancaster. London: Wild Life Publ Co, 1913. 1st edn. 4to. 148 pp. 29 mtd photo plates, num other plates & ills. Orig pict buckram gilt.   *(Gough)* £30 [≈ $57]

Taylor, Charles F.
- Spinal Irritation or, the Causes of Backache among American Women. New York: Wood, 1864. Reprint. 8vo. 32 pp. 15 ills. Ptd wraps in later bds.   *(Goodrich)* $75 [≈ £39]

Taylor, E.G.R.
- The Haven-Finding Art. London: Hollis & Carter, 1956. 8vo. xii,295 pp. 25 plates, 28 text figs. Cloth.   *(Gemmary)* $75 [≈ £39]

Taylor, E.H.
- Operative Surgery. The Head and Neck, the Thorax and the Abdomen. London: 1914. Lge 4to. xi,524 pp. 300 figs. Endpapers foxed.   *(Whitehart)* £35 [≈ $67]

Taylor, G.
- Australian Meteorology. A Text-Book including Sections on Aviation and Climatology. Oxford: 1920. xi,312 pp. Moveable model at front, 229 ills. Orig cloth,

dull. *(Whitehart)* £18 [≈ $34]

Taylor, H.V.
- The Apples of England. London: Crosby Lockwood, 1945. 2nd edn. 4to. 206,30 advt pp. Cold frontis, 17 plates. Orig cloth. Dw (defective). *(Claude Cox)* £20 [≈ $38]

Taylor, J.
- The Forest, or Rambles in the Woodland. L: 1835. 3rd edn. Cr 8vo. iv,288,viii advt pp. 36 plates. Qtr calf. *(Henly)* £35 [≈ $67]

Taylor, John
- Geological Essays, and Sketch of the Geology of Manchester. London: Simpkin, Marshall, 1864. 1st edn. 8vo. ix,282 pp. Text figs. Endpapers stuck together at crnrs & rather roughly separated. Orig cloth gilt.
(Hollett) £35 [≈ $67]

Taylor, William
- The Ready Reckoner, or, Trader's Correct Guide ... Birmingham: ptd by J. Belcher ..., 1792. 1st edn. 12mo. x,[ii], 202,[2] pp. Occas sl marks. Contemp sheep, worn, lower jnt tender. *(Burmester)* £25 [≈ $47]

Teacher, J.H.
- Catalogue of the Anatomical and Pathological Preparations of Dr. William Hunter in the Hunterian Museum, University of Glasgow. By J.H. Teacher. Glasgow: 1900. 2 vols. Frontis port (sl marg water stain). 1 sm lib stamp. Cloth, sl dusty.
(Whitehart) £150 [≈ $287]

Teale, T.P.
- Dangers to Health: A Pictorial Guide to Domestic Sanitary Defects. London: 1881. 3rd edn. xix,170 pp. 70 plates. Some underlining. Orig pict cloth.
(Whitehart) £28 [≈ $53]

Teall, J.J. Harris
- British Petrography: with Special reference to the Igneous Rocks. London: 1888. 1st edn. Lge 8vo. vii,[1],469 pp. 47 cold plates, all but 2 with plain key plate as called for. Few marks. Orig cloth, worn, recased, new endpapers. *(Bow Windows)* £75 [≈ $143]
- British Petrography, with Special reference to Igneous Rocks. London: 1888. Imperial 8vo. viii,469 pp. 47 plates (46 cold), 45 key plates. Cloth, trifle used.
(Wheldon & Wesley) £70 [≈ $134]

Tebb, W.
- The Recrudescence of Leprosy and its Causation. A Popular Treatise. London: 1893. 408 pp. Orig cloth, sl dust stained.
(Whitehart) £25 [≈ $47]

Tegetmeier, W.B.
- Pheasants, their Natural History and Practical Management. London: 1904. 4th edn. 8vo. xii,255 pp. 6 cold & 16 plain plates. Cloth, trifle used.
(Wheldon & Wesley) £35 [≈ $67]
- Pheasants, their Natural History and Practical Management. New Edition by E. Parker. London: [1931]. 8vo. xv,268 pp. 20 plates (1 cold). Cloth.
(Wheldon & Wesley) £30 [≈ $57]

Telliamed; or, the World Explain'd ...
- See Maillet, Benoit de.

The Temperate Man ...
- See Cornaro, Luigi, et al.

Temple, R.
- Practice of Physic ... London: 1798. xiv, 344 pp. Interleaved with blanks. Occas sl foxing, ink notes on some blanks. New qtr leather.
(Whitehart) £240 [≈ $460]

Templeton, W.
- The Operative Mechanic's Workshop Companion. London: Weale, 1845. 1st edn. 12mo. viii,172 pp. Orig qtr mor, a.e.g.
(Bookpress) $110 [≈ £57]

Tennent, John
- Physical Enquiries. London: Andrew Millar, 1742. 1st edn. Sm 8vo. [x],69,[1] pp. Later half calf. *(Bookpress)* $750 [≈ £390]

Terpstra, P. & Codd, L.W.
- Crystallometry. London: Longmans, Green, 1961. Roy 8vo. xv,420 pp. 274 text figs. Cloth. *(Gemmary)* $65 [≈ £34]

Tesla, Nikola
- Experiments with Alternate Currents of High Potential and High Frequency. 1904. 2nd edn. 162 pp. 6 photos, 35 ills. Orig bndg.
(New Wireless) $125 [≈ £65]

Thacher, James
- American Medical Biography: or Memoirs of Eminent Physicians who have flourished in America ... Boston: 1828. 2 vols in one. 8vo. 15 plates. Some browning & marg damp staining. Orig half calf, rebacked.

(Goodrich) **$275 [≈£143]**
- American Medical Practice: or, a Simple Method of Prevention and Cure of Diseases ... Boston: 1817. 1st edn. 8vo. 744 pp. Some foxing. Unabused ex-lib. Sheep.
(Goodrich) **$125 [≈£65]**
- American New Dispensatory. Fourth Edition. Boston: Thomas B. Wait, 1821. 8vo. 736 pp. Foxed. Lacks front free endpaper. Calf, rubbed.   *(Schoyer)* **$125 [≈£65]**
- Observations on Hydrophobia, produced by the Bite of a Mad Dog, or Other Rabid Animal ... Plymouth (MA): Joseph Avery, 1812. 1st edn. 8vo. 1 hand cold plate. Sl foxing. Contemp tree sheep, gilt spine, a little rubbed.   *(Ximenes)* **$350 [≈£182]**

Thayer, Gerald H.
- Concealing-Coloration in the Animal Kingdom, an Exposition of the Laws of Disguise through Color and Pattern ... New York: Macmillan, 1909. xix,260 pp. Num ills. Orig cloth, spotted & worn.
(McGilvery) **$125 [≈£65]**

Thomas, K.B.
- The Development of Anaesthetic Apparatus. A History based on the Charles King Collection of the Association of Anaesthetists of Great Britain and Ireland. Oxford: 1975. x,268 pp. Plates, text ills. Orig bndg.
(Whitehart) **£48 [≈$92]**

Thomas, Robert
- Medical Advice to the Inhabitants of Warm Climates, on the Domestic Treatment of all the Diseases incidental thereon ... Nassau, New-Providence: John Wells, 1794. 12mo. [4], 192 pp. Sm ownership stamps. Contemp calf. Bound with sev other unimportant pieces.   *(Reese)* **$12,500 [≈£6,510]**
- The Modern Practice of Physic ... With an Appendix by Edward Miller. New York: 1811. 1st Amer edn. 697 pp. Leather.
(Fye) **$200 [≈£104]**
- The Modern Practice of Physic ... With an Appendix by Edward Miller. Second American from the Third London Edition. New York: Collins & Co, 1813. [xii], 697, 3 advt pp. Foxed. Calf, spine rubbed.
(Schoyer) **$125 [≈£65]**

Thomas, T. Gaillard
- Abortion and its Treatment, from the Stand-Point of Practical Experience. New York: 1890. 1st edn. 112 pp. Orig bndg.
(Fye) **$100 [≈£52]**

Thomas-Stanford, Charles
- Early Editions of Euclid's Elements. London: Bibliographical Society, 1926. 4to. vii, 67 pp. 12 plates. Orig linen backed bds.
(Whitehart) **£55 [≈$105]**
- Early Editions of Euclid's Elements. London: Bibliographical Society, 1926. 4to. 13 plates. Orig linen backed bds, t.e.g., a trifle soiled.
(Georges) **£75 [≈$143]**

Thompson, C.J.S.
- The Quacks of Old London. London: 1928. 356 pp. 19 plates, 16 ills. Cloth, sl wrinkled.
(Whitehart) **£38 [≈$72]**
- The Quacks of Old London. London: 1928. 356 pp. Frontis, 6 plates, sev text ills. Dw.
(Whitehart) **£50 [≈$95]**
- The Quacks of Old London. London: [1928]. xvi, 356 pp. Frontis, 18 plates, text figs. Orig linen backed ptd bds.
(Whitehart) **£35 [≈$67]**

Thompson, Edward P.
- Roentgen Rays and Phenomena of the Anode and Cathode. New York: Van Nostrand, [1896]. 1st edn. 8vo. [2],xviii,190,[6] pp. Frontis port, photo ills, illust advts. Orig cloth, sl soiled.   *(Rootenberg)* **$300 [≈£156]**

Thompson, H.C.
- The Story of the Middlesex Hospital Medical School ... London: 1935. 1st edn. xiii, 182 pp. Frontis, 21 plates. Sm sgntr on title, few pencil notes.   *(Whitehart)* **£25 [≈$47]**

Thompson, H.S.
- Sub-Alpine Plants or Flowers of the Swiss Woods and Meadows. London: 1912. 8vo. xv,325 pp. 33 cold plates. Orig cloth gilt.
(Henly) **£18 [≈$34]**

Thompson, Harry V. & Worden, Alastair N.
- The Rabbit. London: Collins New Naturalist, 1956. 1st edn. 8vo. Maps, ills. Orig cloth gilt (few damp spots). Price-clipped dw.   *(Hollett)* **£65 [≈$124]**

Thompson, Henry
- The Diseases of the Prostate, from the Stand-Point of Practical Experience. London: 1861. 364 pp. Litho ills. Orig bndg.
(Fye) **$150 [≈£78]**

Thompson, J.S. & H.G.
- Silvanus Phillips Thompson. His Life and Letters. London: [1920]. ix,372 pp. 13 plates. Front blank removed. Orig cloth, sl faded & marked.   *(Whitehart)* **£18 [≈$34]**

Thompson, J.V.
- A Catalogue of Plants growing in the Vicinity of Berwick upon Tweed. London: 1807. 8vo. xxiv,[1],132 pp. Cold title vignette, hand cold plate. Stamp on title. New cloth.
(Wheldon & Wesley) £80 [≈ $153]

Thompson, R.C.
- A Dictionary of Assyrian Chemistry and Geology. Oxford: 1936. xlviii,266 pp. Sev sm marg lib stamps. *(Whitehart)* £35 [≈ $67]

Thompson, Robert
- The Gardeners Assistant; Practical and Scientific ... London: [1859]. 8vo. xv,774 pp. 12 hand cold plates. Sl foxing throughout. Lower marg of last 12 pp damp stained. Half calf, sl worn. *(Henly)* £150 [≈ $287]
- The Gardener's Assistant; Practical and Scientific ... New Edition. London: Blackie & Son, [1859]. 8vo. xv,774 pp. 12 hand cold plates. Orig cloth gilt, jnts sl rubbed.
(Gough) £95 [≈ $182]
- The Gardener's Assistant; Practical and Scientific. New Edition by T. Moore. London: 1881. Roy 8vo. 956 pp. 32 plates (12 cold). Cold plates foxed. Orig cloth, recased, reprd. *(Wheldon & Wesley)* £50 [≈ $95]

Thompson, Robert Luther
- Wiring a Continent. 1947. 1st edn. 544 pp. 73 ills. Dw. *(New Wireless)* £50 [≈ $26]

Thompson, Sylvanus P.
- Dynamo-Electric Machinery. 1902. 5th edn. 2 vols. 835 pp. 20 fldg plates, 520 ills. Orig bndgs, spines sl worn.
(New Wireless) £95 [≈ $50]
- The Electromagnet and Electromagnetism. London: 1892. 2nd edn. xxiv,452 pp. 213 figs. Occas foxing. Front endpaper sl loose.
(Whitehart) £25 [≈ $47]
- Elementary Lessons in Electricity & Magnetism. New York: Macmillan, 1909. 2nd edn. 8vo. xv,638 pp. Cloth.
(Gemmary) $30 [≈ £15]
- Light Visible and Invisible. A Series of Lectures delivered at the Royal Institution of Great Britain at Christmas 1896. London: 1897. 1st edn. xii,294 pp. 158 figs, some on plates. Orig cloth, sl marked & worn. Inscrbd by the author. *(Whitehart)* £35 [≈ $67]
- Light Visible and Invisible. London: Macmillan, 1897. 8vo. xii,294 pp. 158 text figs. Sl foxed. Ex-lib. Cloth.
(Gemmary) $65 [≈ £33]
- Michael Faraday His Life and Work. New York: Cassell, 1898. Cr 8vo. 308 pp. 22 text

figs. Sl foxing. Cloth.
(Gemmary) $35 [≈ £18]

Thompson, Theophilus
- Annals of Epidemic Catarrhal Fever in Great Britain from 1510 to 1837. London: Sydenham Soc, 1852. xvi,406 pp. Traces of label removal, lib stamps on title. Orig cloth, spine reprd, front hinge cracked.
(Whitehart) £40 [≈ $76]
- Annals of Influenza or Epidemic Catarrhal Fever in Great Britain from 1510 to 1817. London: 1852. 1st edn. 406 pp. Orig bndg.
(Fye) $100 [≈ £52]

Thomson, Adam
- Time and Timekeepers. London: T. & W. Boone, 1842. 1st edn. Sm 8vo. xii,195 pp. 54 text ills. Occas sl browning. Orig cloth gilt.
(Fenning) £55 [≈ $105]

Thomson, Alexis
- On Neuroma and Neuro-Fibromatosis. Edinburgh: 1900. 1st edn. 4to. 168 pp. Num photo ills. Orig bndg. Author's ptd pres slip.
(Fye) $100 [≈ £52]

Thomson, Anthony Todd
- Atlas of Delineations of Cutaneous Eruptions; illustrative of the Descriptions in the Practical Synopsis of Cutaneous Diseases of Thomas Bateman. London: Longman ..., 1829. 8vo. vii,[1],112 pp. 27 cold plates. Sm repr to title. Contemp cloth, faded, rubbed.
(Rootenberg) $350 [≈ £182]
- The Domestic Management of the Sick-Room ... London: Longman ..., 1841. 8vo. cloth, spine faded & hd worn.
(Stewart) £100 [≈ $191]

Thomson, D'A.W.
- On Growth and Form. Cambridge: (1942) 1968. 2nd edn, rvsd & enlgd. 2 vols. 8vo. 1116 pp. 2 plates, 554 text figs. Cloth.
(Wheldon & Wesley) £105 [≈ $201]

Thomson, David
- Handy Book of the Flower-Garden. Edinburgh: Blackwood, 1868. 1st edn. Cr 8vo. xii,364,20 pp. Fldg plans. Orig dec cloth gilt, extremities v sl rubbed.
(Ash) £40 [≈ $76]

Thomson, G.M.
- The Ferns and Fern Allies of New Zealand. Melbourne & Dunedin: 1882. 8vo. viii,132 pp. 5 plates. Cloth.
(Wheldon & Wesley) £25 [≈ $47]

Thomson, George Malcolm
- The Naturalisation of Animals & Plants in New Zealand. London: Cambridge, 1922. 8vo. x, 607 pp. Minor cvr spotting.
  (McBlain) **$85 [≈ £44]**

Thomson, J.G.
- Researches on Blackwater Fever in Southern Rhodesia. London: London School of Tropical Medicine Research Memoir 6, 1924. viii,148 pp. 10 plates, 12 charts. Sm lib stamp title verso. Orig ptd wraps, dusty & worn.
  (Whitehart) **£25 [≈ $47]**

Thomson, Sir J.J.
- Beyond the Electron; A Lecture given at Girton College ... Cambridge: UP, 1928. 1st edn thus. 8vo. 43 pp. Orig wraps, edges sl frayed.
  (Gough) **£25 [≈ $47]**
- Conduction of Electricity through Gases. Cambridge: UP, 1903. 1st edn. vi,[2],566 pp. 183 text figs. Orig cloth gilt, extremities somewhat rubbed & sl soiled.
  (Karmiole) **$60 [≈ £31]**
- Conduction of Electricity through Gases. Cambridge: UP, 1906. 2nd edn. 8vo. viii,678 pp. 205 text figs. Ex-lib. Cloth.
  (Gemmary) **$125 [≈ £65]**
- The Electron in Chemistry. Phila: The Franklin Institute, 1923. Roy 8vo. 144 pp. Ex-lib. Cloth.   *(Gemmary)* **$50 [≈ £26]**
- Elements of the Mathematical Theory of Electricity and Magnetism. Cambridge: UP, 1904. 3rd edn. 8vo. viii,544 pp. Ex-lib. Cloth.
  (Gemmary) **$60 [≈ £31]**
- Elements of the Mathematical Theory of Electricity and Magnetism. Cambridge: UP, 1909. 4th edn. 8vo. viii,550 pp. Cloth.
  (Gemmary) **$60 [≈ £31]**
- Notes on Recent Researches in Electricity and Magnetism. London: Dawsons, 1968. Reprint of 1898 edn. 8vo. xvi,578 pp. 144 text figs. Cloth.   *(Gemmary)* **$50 [≈ £26]**
- Rays of Positive Electricity and their Application to Chemical Analyses. London: 1921. 2nd edn. x,237 pp. 9 plates, text diags. Orig bndg.   *(Whitehart)* **£35 [≈ $67]**
- Recent Researches in Electricity and Magnetism. Intended as a Sequel to Professor Clerk-Maxwell's Treatise on Electricity and Magnetism. Oxford: Clarendon Press Series, 1893. xvi,578 pp. 144 figs. Orig bndg.
  (Whitehart) **£65 [≈ $124]**
- Recollections and Reflections. London: G. Bell & Sons, 1936. Roy 8vo. viii,451 pp. 2 plates, 8 text ills. Cloth.
  (Gemmary) **$25 [≈ £13]**

Thomson, James
- Tables of Interest, at 3, 4, 4 1/2 and 5 per Cent. From One Pound to Ten Thousand ... London: 1833. vii,532 pp. Mod half leather.
  (Whitehart) **£30 [≈ $57]**
- The Universal Calculator; or, The Merchant's, Tradesman's, and family's Assistant ... New Edition. Edinburgh: Murray & Cochrane ..., 1793. Sgnd on title verso by compiler. Contemp sheep, hd of spine chipped, splits in hinges.
  (Jarndyce) **£30 [≈ $57]**

Thomson, T.
- An Outline of the Sciences of Heat and Electricity. London: Baldwin & Cradock, 1830. 8vo. xii,583 pp. Text figs. Ex-lib. Rebound in cloth. *(Gemmary)* **$150 [≈ £78]**

Thomson, Sir William & Tait, P.G.
- Treatise on Natural Philosophy. Cambridge: 1890. New rvsd edn. 2 vols. xvii,508; xxv,527 pp. Text figs. Orig cloth.
  (Whitehart) **£38 [≈ $72]**
- See also Kelvin, William Thomson, 1st Baron

Thonner, F.
- The Flowering Plants of Africa, an Analytical Key to the Genera of African Phanerogams. London: (1916) 1962. xvi,647 pp. Map, 150 plates.   *(Wheldon & Wesley)* **£65 [≈ $124]**

Thorburn, Archibald
- British Birds. London: 1915-16. 1st edn. 4 vols. 4to. 80 cold plates. Virtually unfoxed. Stamp on title versos. Orig red cloth, trifle faded. H.F. Witherby b'plate.
  (Wheldon & Wesley) **£600 [≈ $1,151]**
- British Birds. London: 1916. Vols 1 & 2 2nd edn, vols 3 & 4 1st edn. 4 vols. Roy 8vo. 80 cold plates. text somewhat foxed as usual. Without the 2 Supplementary Plates issued separately in wraps. Orig cloth.
  (Wheldon & Wesley) **£600 [≈ $1,151]**
- British Birds. Third Edition. London: Longmans Green, 1917. 4 vols. 4to. 82 cold plates. Orig red cloth, t.e.g., 2 spines dulled.
  (Sotheran's) **£698 [≈ $1,340]**
- British Birds. London: 1925-26. New edn. 4 vols. 8vo. 192 cold plates. Margs of 2 plates trimmed, occas sl soiling. Orig red cloth.
  (Wheldon & Wesley) **£60 [≈ $115]**
- British Mammals. London: 1920-21. 2 vols. 4to. 50 cold plates. Lib stamp on endpapers. Orig red cloth, lib mark on spines.
  (Wheldon & Wesley) **£350 [≈ $671]**
- A Naturalist's Sketch Book. London: 1919. Roy 4to. viii,72 pp. 24 cold & 36 collotype

plates. Sl foxing. Orig red cloth, trifle faded.
(Wheldon & Wesley) **£375 [≈ $719]**
- A Naturalist's Sketchbook. London: Longmans Green, 1919. 1st edn. 4to. 60 plates (24 cold). Lib b'plate. Lib stamps on title & verso of plates. Unbrowned. Contemp red buckram.   *(Claude Cox)* **£150 [≈ $287]**
- A Naturalist's Sketchbook. London: Longmans, Green, 1919. 1st edn. 4to. 60 plates (24 cold). Sl foxing. Orig red cloth, t.e.g.   *(Sotheran's)* **£598 [≈ $1,148]**
- A Naturalist's Sketchbook. London: Longmans Green, 1919. 1st edn. 4to. 60 plates (24 cold). Unspotted. Orig cloth, t.e.g., spine sl darkened.
(Claude Cox) **£450 [≈ $863]**

Thornton, Robert John
- Elements of Botany. London: 1812. 2 vols in one. Roy 8vo. viii,90,73 pp. 172 plates. Tears in 2 plates (no loss), plates numbered in ink. Mod half calf.   *(Henly)* **£70 [≈ $134]**
- A New Family Herbal ... London: 1810. 8vo. xvi, 901 pp. 283 w'cuts by Thomas Bewick after Henderson. Contents leaf & index foxed as usual. 1 leaf sl frayed & soiled. Half mor, trifle rubbed.
(Wheldon & Wesley) **£150 [≈ $287]**
- A New Family Herbal ... The Plants drawn from Nature by Henderson: and engraved on Wood, by Thomas Bewick. London: for Richard Phillips, 1810. Lge 8vo. xvi,888 pp. Half-title. W'cuts. Sl wear & tear. old calf, rebacked lib style calf, worn & rubbed.
(Hollett) **£120 [≈ $230]**
- Thornton's Temple of Flora, with Plates faithfully reproduced from the Original Engravings and the Work described by G. Grigson ... H. Buchanan ... W.T. Stearn. London: 1951. One of 250. Folio. 12 cold & 25 other plates. Edges trifle foxed. Orig half mor. Slipcase.
(Wheldon & Wesley) **£150 [≈ $287]**

Thorpe, Sir Edward
- Essays in Historical Chemistry. New Edition. London: Macmillan, 1931. 8vo. xii, 601 pp. Orig cloth.   *(Gough)* **£20 [≈ $38]**

A Thousand Memorable Things ...
- See Lupton, Thomas.

Thrush, P.W.
- A Dictionary of Mining, Mineral, and Related Terms. Washington, D.C.: 1968. 4to. vii,1269 pp. Cloth. *(Gemmary)* **$70 [≈ £37]**

Thurston, Albert P.
- Elementary Aeronautics, or the Science and Practice of Aerial Machines. London: Whittaker, 1911. 1st edn. 8vo. vii,126 pp. 126 ills. Orig cloth. *(Fenning)* **£28.50 [≈ $55]**

Thwaites, G.H.K. & Hooker, J.D.
- Enumeratio Plantarum Zeylaniae: an Enumeration of Ceylon Plants. London: [1858-] 1864. 8vo. viii,483 pp. Good ex-lib. Buckram. *(Wheldon & Wesley)* **£95 [≈ $182]**

Ticehurst, C.B.
- A History of the Birds of Suffolk. London: 1932. 1st edn. 8vo. xii,502 pp. Fldg map, 18 plates, 3 pp Swan Marks. Orig cloth.
(Bow Windows) **£48 [≈ $92]**

Ticehurst, Norman F.
- A History of the Birds of Kent. London: Witherby, 1909. 1st edn. 8vo. lvi,568 pp. Fldg map, 24 photo plates. Orig cloth, foredges of bds sl damp stained.
(Gough) **£55 [≈ $105]**

Tillyard, R.J.
- The Insects of Australia and New Zealand. Sydney: 1926. Roy 8vo. xiii,560 pp. 44 plates (8 cold), num text figs. Orig cloth.
(Wheldon & Wesley) **£90 [≈ $172]**

Tilney, Frederick & Riley, Henry A.
- The Forms and Functions of the Central Nervous System. New York: 1921. 8vo. 1020 pp. Cloth, rubbed, shaken, inner front jnt taped.   *(Goodrich)* **$95 [≈ £49]**

Tiltman, Ronald F.
- Television for the Home. 1927. 1st edn. 106 pp. 8 photos. Orig bndg.
(New Wireless) **$110 [≈ £57]**

Tinbergen, Niko
- The Herring Gull's World. London: Collins New Naturalist, 1953. 1st edn. 8vo. xvi,255 pp. 31 plates. Orig cloth. *(Henly)* **£36 [≈ $69]**
- The Herring Gull's World. London: Collins New Naturalist, 1953. 1st edn. 8vo. xvi,255 pp. 52 plates. Dw (torn with loss).
(Gough) **£25 [≈ $47]**

Tissot, Samuel A.D.
- Advice to the People in General, with Regard to their Health ... Translated from the French ... by J. Kirkpatrick. London: Becket & De Hondt, 1765. 1st edn. 8vo. xxxii, 608, [4] pp. Rec contemp style calf.
(Young's) **£140 [≈ $268]**

- Advice to the People in General, with regard to their Health ... Translated by J. Kirkpatrick ... London: 1766. 2nd edn. xxxvi, 620 pp. Contemp leather, rubbed, sl marked.
(Whitehart) **£180 [≈ $345]**
- Advice to the People in General with Regard to their Health ... Translated from the French ... by J. Kirkpatrick. Third Edition. London: 1768. 8vo. 620 pp. Calf, jnts weak.
(Goodrich) **$60 [≈ £31]**
- Advice to People in General, with Respect sic to their Health. Edinburgh: A Donaldson, 1768. 2 vols. 12mo. xxi,261, vi,364 pp. Contemp calf.   *(Bookpress)* **$285 [≈ £148]**

Titchmarsh, E.C.
- Introduction to the Theory of Fourier Integrals. Oxford: Clarendon Press, 1937. 1st edn. Roy 8vo. x,390 pp. Cloth. Dw.
(Gemmary) **$100 [≈ £52]**

Todd, Robert Bentley
- Clinical Lectures of Paralysis, Diseases of the Brain, and other Affections of the Nervous System. Phila: 1855. 1st Amer edn. 311 pp. Orig bndg.   *(Fye)* **$275 [≈ £143]**
- Clinical Lectures on Certain Diseases of the Urinary Organs: and on Dropsies. Phila: 1857. 1st Amer edn. 283 pp. Orig bndg, fine.
(Fye) **$100 [≈ £52]**
- Clinical Lectures on Certain Acute Diseases. London: 1860. 8vo. xl,487 pp. Cloth, soiled.
(Goodrich) **$145 [≈ £75]**

Todd, Robert Bentley (ed.)
- The Cyclopaedia of Anatomy and Physiology. London: Longman ..., 1835-59. 1st edn. 5 vols in 6. 8vo. [18], 813,[1]; [6], 1015,[1]; [4], 1028 (errata slip present); [6], 800; [4], 801-1543; [6], 890 pp. Half-titles. Num text ills. Half calf, edges sl worn.
(Rootenberg) **$650 [≈ £338]**

Todd, W.E.C.
- Birds of the Labrador Peninsula and Adjacent Areas. Toronto: 1963. Demy 4to. 834 pp. 9 cold & num other plates. Cloth.
(Wheldon & Wesley) **£60 [≈ $115]**

Todhunter, Isaac
- Researches in the Calculus of Variations. Principally on the Theory of Discontinuous Solutions. London: 1871. 1st edn. viii,278 pp. Text figs. Orig cloth, sl stained.
(Whitehart) **£35 [≈ $67]**
- Researches in the Calculus of Variations ... London: Macmillan, 1871. 1st edn. 8vo. viii, 278 pp. Orig cloth.   *(Gough)* **£48 [≈ $92]**

- William Whewell, D.D. An Account of his Writings with Selections from his Literary and Scientific Correspondence. London: 1876, reprint Farnborough: 1970. 2 vols. xxxi,416; 439 pp. Orig bndg.
(Whitehart) **£40 [≈ $76]**

Tomes, J.
- A System of Dental Surgery. London: 1897. 4th edn. x,717 pp. 289 ills. Half-title soiled, few sm marks elsewhere. New cloth.
(Whitehart) **£25 [≈ $47]**

Tomlinson, Charles
- Cyclopaedia of Useful Arts, Mechanical and Chemical, Manufacturing, Mining, and Engineering. London: George Virtue, 1854. 1st edn. 2 vols in 9 parts. 4to. xvi, clx,832; iv, 1052, [8 advt] pp. Addtnl engvd titles, 42 plates, 2399 ills. Orig red cloth gilt.
(Fenning) **£125 [≈ $239]**
- Cyclopaedia of Useful Arts ... Vol.III. Appendix. - Abaca to Wool. London: Virtue & Co, 1866. 4to. [2],740 pp. Addtnl engvd title, 29 plates, 644 ills. Orig blue cloth gilt.
(Fenning) **£75 [≈ $143]**

Tousey, Sinclair
- Medical Electricity and Rontgen Rays. 1910. 1st edn. 1116 pp. 16 cold plates, 750 ills. Three qtr leather.
(New Wireless) **$140 [≈ £73]**

Townshend, Chauncy Hare
- Facts in Mesmerism. With Reasons for a Dispassionate Inquiry into It. London: Longman, 1840. 1st edn. 8vo. Orig cloth, recased.   *(Young's)* **£70 [≈ $134]**

Toynbee, Joseph
- The Diseases of the Ear. Phila: 1860. 1st Amer edn. 440 pp. Orig bndg, fine.
(Fye) **$300 [≈ £156]**

Trade catalogues
- Allen & Hanbury's Ltd: Abridged Catalogue of Surgical Instruments and Appliances, Aseptic Hospital Furniture and Electro-Medical Apparatus. London: [1925]. xii,739 pp. Num ills. Endpapers sl foxed, front endpaper split. Cloth rather dust stained & sl worn.   *(Whitehart)* **£55 [≈ $105]**
- Allen & Hanbury's Ltd: Reference List of Surgical Instruments and Medical Appliances ... London: 1930. [xvi], 1974, lxxxix pp. Frontis, 8 dble-sided plates, num text ills. Orig bndg.   *(Whitehart)* **£35 [≈ $67]**
- Allen & Hanburys Ltd: A Reference List of

Surgical Instruments and Medical Appliances ... London: 1930. [xvi], 1974, lxxxix pp. Num ills. Stamp on sev ff. 2 ff carelessly opened. Sellotape marks on endpapers. Orig bndg,
(Bow Windows) **£30 [≈ $57]**

- American Optical Co.: Illustrated Catalogue of Spectacles and Eyeglasses, in 8-K, 10-K and 14-K Gold, Platinum, Silver, Aluminium ... Southbridge: 1894. 8vo. 96 pp. Num ills. Orig cloth. *(Bickersteth)* **£195 [≈ $374]**

- American Optical Co.: Spencer Scientific Instruments. Buffalo: [1945?]. Roy 8vo. 207 pp. Num text figs. Cloth.
(Gemmary) **$50 [≈ £26]**

- Armstrong & Co, William H.: Catalogue of Surgical Instruments, Deformity Apparatus, Aseptic Furniture and Hospital Supplies. Indianapolis: 1901. 4th edn. 800 pp. Num ills. Orig bndg. *(Fye)* **$300 [≈ £156]**

- Ashe, Sons & Co, Claudius: Vulcanizers, Flasks, Presses, Lathe Brushes, Carborundum ... London: 1908. 8vo. 108 pp. 1 cold plate, ills. Orig ptd wraps, lacks backstrip. *(Bickersteth)* **£55 [≈ $105]**

- Baird & Tatlock (London) Ltd: Standard Catalogue Vol. 1. Chemistry including Apparatus for the Teaching of and Research Work in Organic and Inorganic Chemistry. London: 1928. Abridged edn. [viii], 75-544, xix pp. Num ills. Cloth sl worn.
(Whitehart) **£25 [≈ $47]**

- Banks, James: Illustrated and Descriptive Catalogue of Iron Manufactures, Machinery, etc ... Liverpool: 1864. Sm 4to. [2],62 pp. 2 fldg ff. Folded leaf loosely inserted. Ills. Ptd wraps, vertical crease throughout has been flattened. *(Beech)* **£40 [≈ $76]**

- Bausch & Lomb Optical Co.: Microscopes & Accessories. New York: 1919. 8vo. xiii,318 pp. Text ills. Ex-lib. Cloth gilt.
(Gemmary) **$50 [≈ £26]**

- Bausch & Lomb Optical Co.: Microscopes & Accessories. New York: 1929. 8vo. xiii,318 pp. Text ills. Cloth gilt.
(Gemmary) **$60 [≈ £31]**

- Bausch & Lomb Optical Co.: Scientific Instruments. Catalog D-111. New York: 1940. 4to. 286 pp. Num ills. Cloth.
(Gemmary) **$45 [≈ £23]**

- Benjamin & Rackerby: Catalogue of Surgical Instruments of Superior Quality. Sacramento: 1935. 24th edn. 511 pp. Num ills. Orig bndg, inner hinges cracked. *(Fye)* **$100 [≈ £52]**

- Braun-Knecht-Heimann Co.: Assay and Mining Laboratory Supplies and Chemicals. Catalog A-2. San Francisco: 1933. 4to. 168 pp. Text figs. Wraps.
(Gemmary) **$75 [≈ £40]**

- Browne, Albert, Ltd: Illustrated Catalogue of Surgical Instruments and Appliances; Electro-Medical Apparatus, Enamelled Steel Goods, Sterilizers, etc. Sixth Edition. London: [1928]. Sm 4to. xxxvi,991 pp. Ca 5000 ills. Price list in pocket. Orig cloth, sl worn. *(Gough)* **£50 [≈ $95]**

- Casella, Louis: An Illustrated and Descriptive Catalogue of Surveying, Philosophical, Mathematical, Optical, Photographic, and Standard Meteorological Instruments. London: [D. Lane, 1871]. 8vo. vii, 260 pp. Ills. Orig cloth. *(Rootenberg)* **$400 [≈ £208]**

- Chicago Apparatus Co.: Laboratory Equipment. Catalog No.45. Chicago: 1936. 4to. 500 pp. Num text figs. Cloth.
(Gemmary) **$40 [≈ £20]**

- Cooke, Troughton & Simms Ltd: Cooke Microscopes. London: [1946]. 207 pp. Num ills. Price list. Orig cloth, sl dust stained.
(Whitehart) **£18 [≈ $34]**

- Crofts (Engineers) Ltd: Catalogue & Price List. Power Transmitting Machinery & Appliances. Bradford: [ca 1900]. Cr 8vo. 814, [1] pp. Num ills. Orig cloth gilt.
(Fenning) **£45 [≈ $86]**

- Crolius, Tucker & Allen: Illustrated Catalogue of Surgical Instruments, Galvanic and Faradic Batteries, Microscopes, Artificial Limbs ... Minneapolis: [1892]. 1st edn. 344 pp. Num ills. Orig bndg. *(Fye)* **$300 [≈ £156]**

- Cuxson, Gerrard & Co.: Price List of Antiseptic Surgical Dressings, Instruments & Appliances ... Birmingham: 1903. Super roy 8vo. Title, 8 ff of photos, Preface leaf, 342, [1], xvii pp. Num ills. Orig cloth.
(Bickersteth) **£145 [≈ $278]**

- Dollond, P. & G.: A Catalogue of Optical, Mathematical, and Philosophical Instruments ... London: [ca 1800]. Sm folio. Single sheet, ptd on 1 side only. *(Burmester)* **£150 [≈ $287]**

- Down Bros & Mayer & Phelps Ltd: Oto-Rhino-Laryngology. Surgical Instruments, Appliances and Hospital Equipment ... London: 1952. [viii], 402-945, xxiii pp. Price list. Num ills. Orig bndg.
(Whitehart) **£40 [≈ $76]**

- Down Bros Ltd: A Catalogue of Surgical Instruments & Appliances, also Aseptic Hospital Furniture. London: 1901. xliv,1345 pp. 8 plates, num ills. Priced. Title sl discold. Lacks both endpapers. Orig cloth, some edge & crnr wear. *(Whitehart)* **£95 [≈ $182]**

- Down Bros Ltd: A Catalogue of Surgical Instruments and Appliances. Also of Aseptic Furniture ... London: 1906. iv,2247 pp. Num ills. Cloth a little worn, new endpapers.
(Whitehart) **£65 [≈ $124]**

- Down Bros Ltd: A Catalogue of Surgical Instruments and Appliances with Appendix ... London: July 1929. 3028,lxxvii pp. Num ills. Cloth sl worn, spine dust stained.
(Whitehart) **£55 [≈ $105]**
- Eimer & Amend: Biological, Chemical and Metallurgical Apparatus. New York: Eimer & Amend, 1927. 4to. xxiii,871 pp. Num text figs. Cloth.   *(Gemmary)* **£60 [≈ £31]**
- Evans & Wormull: Illustrated Catalogue of Surgical Instruments, Apparatus and Appliances.. London: 1893. xxxvi,720 pp. Frontis, 2503 text figs. Sl marg water stain. Cloth, sl marked & worn, water stain along bottom edge.   *(Whitehart)* **£150 [≈ $287]**
- Fannin & Co: Catalogue of Medical and Surgical Appliances. Dublin: 1887. 8vo. 170,advt pp. Ills. Cloth bds.
(Emerald Isle) **£48 [≈ $92]**
- Fannin & Co: Illustrated Catalogue and Price List of Surgical Instruments and Medical Appliances. Dublin: Fannin, 1908. Roy 8vo. 448 pp. Ills. Cloth bds.
(Emerald Isle) **£75 [≈ $143]**
- Fannin & Co Ltd: Surgical Instruments and Medical Appliances. London: 1926. xxvi,415 pp. Num ills. Lacks price list from pocket. Orig cloth.   *(Whitehart)* **£40 [≈ $76]**
- Fisher Scientific Co.: Laboratory Apparatus and Reagents. Pittsburgh: 1926. 4to. viii,630 pp. Num text figs. Cloth, sl worn.
(Gemmary) **$60 [≈ £31]**
- Furst & Bradley Manufacturing Co: Catalogue of Valuable Information, Tables, Recipes, etc. Chicago: 1876. 12mo. 64 pp. Ills of ploughs, harrows, &c. Orig ptd wraps.
(Spelman) **£35 [≈ $67]**
- Griffin & Tatlock: Scientific Apparatus Catalogue No. 70E. London: [ca 1940]. 4to. 264 pp. Num text figs. Bds.
(Gemmary) **$45 [≈ £23]**
- Keuffel & Esser Co.: Catalogue. New York: 1921. 36th edn. 8vo. viii,482 pp. Num text figs. Cloth.   *(Gemmary)* **$35 [≈ £18]**
- Keuffel & Esser Co.: Catalogue. New York: 1927. 37th edn. 8vo. viii,482 pp. Num text figs. Cloth.   *(Gemmary)* **$35 [≈ £18]**
- Kuhlman & Co., A.: Catalogue of Surgical Instruments, Hospital Equipment and Supplies. Detroit: 1931. 458 pp. Num ills. Price list. Orig bndg.   *(Fye)* **$100 [≈ £52]**
- McArthur Wirth & Co: Butchers, Packers and Sausage Makers. Fixtures, Tools, Machinery and Supplies ... Refrigerators ... Ice Boxes. Syracuse, New York: 1900. 4to. 81,[3] pp. Ills. Orig ptd paper wraps, some marking of cvrs. *(de Beaumont)* **£48 [≈ $92]**

- Negretti & Zambra: Catalogue of Meteorological Instruments. London: 1950. Roy 8vo. 100 pp. Num text figs. Cloth.
(Gemmary) **$40 [≈ £20]**
- Pettingell-Andrews Co: Catalogue of Electrical Merchandise. Boston: 1905. Lge 8vo. 666,xiv pp. Num ills. Orig cloth.
(Karmiole) **$75 [≈ £39]**
- Sharp & Smith: Catalog of General Surgical Supplies. Chicago: 1926. 865 pp. Ills. Orig bndg.   *(Fye)* **$100 [≈ £52]**
- Surgical Manufacturing Co Ltd: Illustrated Catalogue of Surgical Instruments and Appliances ... London: 1925. 6th edn. 1072 pp. Num ills. Cloth v sl worn & marked.
(Whitehart) **£55 [≈ $105]**
- Thackray, C.F.: A Catalogue of Surgical Instruments, Surgical Appliances, Hospital Equipment ... Leeds & London: [ca 1936]. Sm cr 4to. xxxvii, 472 pp. Num ills. Cloth bndg.   *(Bow Windows)* **£35 [≈ $67]**
- Ward, Charles H.: Catalogue of Human Skeletons, Anatomical Models, Anthropology, Ethnology. Rochester, New York: Charles H. Ward, 1913. 143,[1] pp. Cold plates, num photo ills. Orig dec wraps, a few crnrs creased.   *(Wreden)* **$75 [≈ £39]**
- Watson, W., & Sons: Microscopes and Accessories. London: [ca 1935]. 35th edn. 8vo. 174 pp. Num text figs. Wraps.
(Gemmary) **$45 [≈ £23]**
- Welch, W.M.: Physics-Chemistry Catalog "G". Chicago: W.M. Welch Scientific Co, 1919. 8vo. 313 pp. Num text figs. Wraps.
(Gemmary) **$60 [≈ £31]**

Traherne, John P.
- The Habits of the Salmon. London: Chapman & Hall, 1889. 1st edn. 8vo. 163,[1] pp. Orig pict gilt cloth, 1 crnr bumped.
(Chapel Hill) **$85 [≈ £44]**

Trail, William
- Account of the Life and Writings of Robert Simson, M.D. late Professor of Mathematics in the University of Glasgow. Bath: ptd by R. Cruttwell, for Nicol, London, 1812. 1st edn. 4to. [iv], vii,[i], 191,[1] pp, errata leaf. 1 plate. Orig bds, uncut, rebacked.
(Gaskell) **£285 [≈ $547]**

Traill, C.P.
- Studies of Plant Life in Canada. Toronto: 1906. New & rvsd edn. 8vo. xvii,227 pp. Port, 8 cold & 12 plain plates. Orig cloth.
(Wheldon & Wesley) **£35 [≈ $67]**

Trall, R.T.
- The Hydropathic Encyclopedia: A System of Hydropathy and Hygiene ... New York: Fowler & Wells, 1857. 8vo. xi,460,504,4 advt pp. Num, ills. Sl stains, occas spotting. Orig cloth, pict gilt spine. *(Hemlock)* **$175 [≈£91]**

Trease, G.E.
- Pharmacy in History. London: 1964. vii,265 pp. 51 figs. Date stamps on rear endpaper. Boards, sl marked, rear hinge cracked.
(Whitehart) **£35 [≈$67]**

A Treatise on Practical Surveying ...
- A Treatise on Practical Surveying, and Topographical Plan Drawing. London: Murray, 1829. 1st edn. 8vo. 191 pp. Errata slip. 6 plates. Orig purple muslin, paper label, unopened.   *(Chapel Hill)* **$165 [≈£85]**

Trevert, Edward
- The A-B-C of Wireless Telegraphy. 1902. 1st edn. 82 pp. 22 ills. Orig bndg.
(New Wireless) **$90 [≈£46]**

Treves, Sir F.
- The Elephant Man and Other Reminiscences. London: 1923. reprint. 222 pp. Orig cloth, 1 side of spine sl worn.
(Whitehart) **£25 [≈$47]**

Trimen, Roland
- South-African Butterflies: A Monograph of the Extra-Tropical Species ... London: Trubner, 1887-89. 1st edn. 3 vols. Lge 8vo. xiv,356; [6],242; [6],438 pp. 13 plates (12 hand cold), fldg map. Orig cloth, gilt spines.
(Karmiole) **$350 [≈£182]**

Trimmer, J.
- Practical Geology and Mineralogy. London: John W. Parker, 1841. 8vo. xxvi,519 pp. 212 text figs. 1st & last pp water stained. Half leather, worn.   *(Gemmary)* **$40 [≈£20]**
- Practical Geology and Mineralogy. Phila: Lea & Blanchard, 1842. 8vo. 527 pp. 212 text figs. Cloth, cvrs detached, lacks backstrip.
(Gemmary) **$40 [≈£20]**

Trimmer, Kirby
- Flora of Norfolk ... London: Hamilton, Adams, 1866. 1st edn. 12mo. xxxvi,[iv], 195 pp. Orig cloth.   *(Lamb)* **£40 [≈$76]**

Tripp, F.E.
- British Mosses ... London: 1874. 2nd edn. 2 vols. 4to. Cold titles, 39 cold plates. Lib b'plates, lib blind stamps in text. Buckram.

(Henly) **£65 [≈$124]**
- British Mosses ... New Edition. London: George Bell & Sons, 1888. 2 vols. 37 cold plates. 1 gathering sl sprung. Orig pict green cloth gilt.   *(Gough)* **£95 [≈$182]**

Troeltsch, Anton Friedrich & Helmholtz, Hermann
- The Surgical Diseases of the Ear; The Mechanism of the Ossicles ... Translated from the German by James Hinton. London: New Sydenham Society, 1874. 1st edn in English of both titles. 8vo. vii,[3],160 pp. 1 plate, text ills. Orig cloth, spine ends chipped.
(Rootenberg) **$185 [≈£96]**

Troup, R.S.
- Silvicultural Systems. London: 1928. Roy 8vo. xii,199 pp. Plates, text figs. Cloth.
(Henly) **£35 [≈$67]**

Trousseau, A.
- Lectures on Clinical Medicine delivered at the Hotel-Dieu, Paris. London: Sydenham Society, 1867-72. 5 vols. 8vo. Orig cloth, worn, jnts cracking. *(Goodrich)* **$125 [≈£65]**

Trow, A.H.
- The Flora of Glamorgan. Vol. 1 [all published]. Cardiff: [1907-] 1911. 8vo. 209 pp. Endpapers foxed. Cloth, recased.
(Wheldon & Wesley) **£30 [≈$57]**

True, Frederick W.
- The Whalebone Whales of the Western North Atlantic. Washington: Smithsonian Contribs to Knowledge vol 33, 1904. 4to. 332 pp. 50 plates. Cloth.
(Wheldon & Wesley) **£75 [≈$143]**
- The Whalebone Whales of the Western North Atlantic compared with those occurring in European Waters ... Washington: Smithsonian Contribs to Knowledge Vol 33, 1904. Folio. xi,vii,332 pp. 50 plates, text ills. 2 lib stamps. Orig cloth.   *(High Latitude)* **$140 [≈£72]**

Truscott, S.J.
- A Text-Book of Ore Dressing. London: Macmillan, 1923. 8vo. xi,680 pp. 446 text figs. Cloth.   *(Gemmary)* **$50 [≈£26]**

Trusler, J.
- The Honours of the Table ... With the Whole Art of Carving ... Second Edition. London: Literary Press, 1791. 12mo. 120 pp. 28 w'cut ills. Contemp calf, spine roughly reprd. Anon.   *(Karmiole)* **$125 [≈£65]**

Tryon, Thomas
- The Way to Health, Long Life and Happiness ... added, a Treatise of most Sorts of English Herbs ... London: Andrew Sowle, 1683. 1st edn. 8vo. [xvi],669,[3 advt] pp. Sm rust hole in 1 leaf. Contemp calf, sm chips spine ends, crnrs worn. Wing T.3200.
(Gaskell) **£1,200 [≈ $2,303]**
- The Way to Health, Long Life and Happiness ... [Bound & continuously signed with] A Dialogue between an East-Indian Brackmanny ... and a French Gentleman ... London: D. Newman, 1691. 2nd edns. 8vo. [xiv], 500; [2], 19 pp. Some worming. New sheep. Wing T.3201.
(Bookpress) **$425 [≈ £221]**

Tubbs, E.M.
- The New Hampshire Kitchen, Fruit, and Floral Gardener. Peterboro (NH): K.C. Scott, 1852. 1st edn. 8vo. W'cut text ills. Some foxing & sl browning. Orig light brown ptd wraps, minor chipping of crnrs.
(Ximenes) **$500 [≈ £260]**

Tugwell, George
- A Manual of the Sea-Anemones commonly found on the English Coast. London: Van Voorst, 1856. 1st edn. [viii],123 pp. 1 plain & 6 chromolitho plates. Occas v sl spotting. Orig blue cloth, gilt spine.
(Gough) **£40 [≈ $76]**

Tuke, Daniel Hack
- Illustrations of the Influence of the Mind upon the Body in Health and Disease. Designed to Elucidate the Action of the Imagination. London: Churchill, 1872. 1st edn. 8vo. xvi, 444 pp. Pres blind stamp on title. Orig cloth, faded, sl spotted, hd of spine sl worn.
(Bickersteth) **£45 [≈ $86]**

Tull, Jethro
- Horse-Hoeing Husbandry. London: A. Millar, 1751. 3rd edn. 8vo. xvi,432 pp. 7 plates. Contemp calf.
(Bookpress) **$900 [≈ £468]**
- The Horse-Hoeing Husbandry ... London: published [and edited] by William Cobbett, 1829. 1st edn thus. 8vo. Orig cloth, paper label (blank edge chipped), unopened.
(Ximenes) **$450 [≈ £234]**

Tully, J.D.
- The History of Plague as it has lately appeared in the Islands of Malta, Gozo, Corfu, Cephalonia &c. ... Means adopted for its Eradication. London: Longman ..., 1821. 1st edn. 8vo. xi,292 pp. Orig bds, rebacked.
(Frew Mackenzie) **£375 [≈ $719]**

Turner, Daniel
- A Discourse concerning Fevers. In Two Letters to a Young Physician. London: John Clarke, 1739. 3rd edn. 8vo. xii,364 pp. Frontis. Contemp calf, hinges cracked, wear to spine & tips. *(Bookpress)* **$285 [≈ £148]**
- Syphilis. A Practical Dissertation on the Venereal Disease ... Second Edition, revised ... London: 1724. 8vo. 16 ff, 376 pp, 4 ff. Contemp calf. *(Hemlock)* **$275 [≈ £143]**
- Syphilis. A Practical Dissertation on the Venereal Disease, in Two Parts. The Fourth Edition, still farther improved ... London: 1732. 8vo. [xxvi],476 pp. Port. Contemp panelled calf, rubbed, head of spine worn.
(Bickersteth) **£120 [≈ $230]**
- Siphylis. A Practical Dissertation on the Venereal Disease. London: J. Walthoe ..., 1732. 4th edn. 8vo. [xxvi],476 pp. Frontis. Contemp calf, sl worn.
(Bookpress) **$350 [≈ £182]**

Turner, G.L'E.
- Nineteenth-Century Scientific Instruments. Berkeley, CA: Univ of Calif Press, 1983. 4to. 320 pp. Cloth. Dw. *(Gemmary)* **$70 [≈ £36]**

Turner, L.M.
- Contributions to the Natural History of Alaska ... Washington: GPO, 1886. 4to. 226 pp. 26 plates (inc 11 cold lithos of birds).
(Walcot) **£60 [≈ $115]**

Turner, Richard
- The Heavens Survey'd, and the True System of the Universe delineated, so as to form a curious Astronomical Instrument. London: for S. Crowder, 1783. 1st edn. Folio. [ii],ii,53 pp. 3 plates, 2 text engvs. Sl used. Contemp wraps, worn, spine defective.
(Gaskell) **£225 [≈ $431]**

Turner, William
- Sound Anatomiz'd, in a Philosophical Essay on Musick ... London: William Pearson, for the author ..., 1724. 1st edn. Sm 4to. Errata leaf. Fldg engvd plate of music. Sl foxing. 19th c cloth backed mrbld bds, a bit worn.
(Ximenes) **$1,500 [≈ £781]**

Turrill, W.B.
- British Plant Life. London: Collins New Naturalist, 1948. 1st edn. 8vo. xvii,315 pp. 48 cold & 24 plain plates. Ends spotted. Orig cloth. *(Henly)* **£12 [≈ $23]**

Tuson, Edward William
- A Supplement to Myology; containing the Arteries, Veins, Nerves, and Lymphatics of the Human Body ... London: Callow & Wilson, 1828. 1st edn. Folio. [2],9 ff. 9 hand cold plates, each with flaps & explanation ff. Calf backed bds, orig label front cvr.
(Rootenberg) **$2,000 [≈ £1,041]**

Tusser, Thomas
- Five Hundred Points of Good Husbandry ... Corrected, better ordered, and newly augmented to a fourth part more ... London: T.R. & M.D. for the Company of Stationers, 1672. Sm 4to. 146,[ii] pp. Num early MS notes. 18th c calf, jnt cracked. Wing T.3369.
(Bickersteth) **£145 [≈ $278]**
- Thomas Tusser, 1557 Floruit; His Good Points of Husbandry. Compiled and Edited by Dorothy Hartley. London: Country Life, 1931. 1st edn thus. Sm 4to. 195 pp. Cold frontis, num ills. Dw. *(Gough)* **£35 [≈ $67]**

Tutt, J.W.
- A Natural History of the British Lepidoptera. London: 1899-1914. 9 vols, complete (vols 1-5 Moths, vols 8-11 Butterflies, vols 6 & 7 not published). 8vo. Orig cloth, 2 backstrips relaid.
(Wheldon & Wesley) **£160 [≈ $307]**

Tutton, A.E.H.
- Crystalline Form and Chemical Composition. London: Macmillan, 1910. 8vo. vii,252 pp. 54 text figs. V.g. ex-lib. Cloth.
(Gemmary) **$50 [≈ £26]**
- The Natural History of Crystals. London: Kegan Paul ..., 1924. 1st edn. 8vo. xii,287 pp. 32 plates, 134 text figs. Cloth.
(Gemmary) **$75 [≈ £39]**
- The Natural History of Ice and Snow Illustrated from the Alps. London: Kegan Paul ..., 1927. 8vo. xvi,319 pp. 191 ills. Cloth.
(Gemmary) **$45 [≈ £23]**

Tweedie, A. (ed.)
- A System of Practical Medicine comprised in a Series of Original Dissertations. London: 1840. 5 vols. Contemp half roan, v rubbed & worn, spines sl defective.
(Whitehart) **£35 [≈ $67]**

Twenhoffel, W.H.
- Treatise on Sedimentation. Baltimore: 1926. 1st edn. 8vo. xxv,661 pp. 34 plates, text figs. Cloth.
(Henly) **£32 [≈ $61]**

Tyas, Robert
- Favourite Field Flowers; or, Wild Flowers of

England Popularly Described ... London: Houlston & Stoneman, 1848. 1st edn. 12mo. xi, 196 pp. 12 hand cold plates. Orig pict green cloth gilt, a.e.g., spine ends sl rubbed.
(Gough) **£110 [≈ $211]**
- Popular Flowers: their Cultivation, Propagation, and General Treatment ... Second Series. London: 1844. 12mo. 11 hand cold plates. Orig cloth, faded. Anon.
(Wheldon & Wesley) **£35 [≈ $67]**

Tyers, Paul D.
- Television Reception Technique. 1937. 1st edn. 144 pp. 85 ills. Orig bndg.
(New Wireless) **$35 [≈ £18]**

Tyler, Kingdon S.
- Telecasting and Color. 1946. 1st edn. 213 pp. 31 photos, 20 ills. Dw.
(New Wireless) **$45 [≈ £23]**

Tyndall, John
- Contributions to Molecular Physics in the Domain of Radiant Heat. London: Longmans ..., 1872. 1st edn. 8vo. x,446, [ii],24 advt pp. Orig cloth, spine faded. *(Gough)* **£50 [≈ $95]**
- Contributions to Molecular Physics in the Domain of Radiant Heat. New York: Appleton, 1885. 8vo. xiv,446 pp. 3 plates, 31 text figs. Cloth, spine worn.
(Gemmary) **$90 [≈ £46]**
- Essays on the Floating Matter of the Air in relation to Putrefaction and Infection. New York: Appleton, 1895. Cr 8vo. xix,338 pp. 23 text figs. Cloth, 1 edge worn).
(Gemmary) **$60 [≈ £31]**
- Faraday as a Discoverer. London: Longmans, Green, 1868. 8vo. viii,171 pp. Cloth, sl shaken. *(Gemmary)* **$50 [≈ £26]**
- Faraday as a Discoverer. 1868. 1st edn. 171 pp. Orig bndg. *(New Wireless)* **$115 [≈ £59]**
- Heat A Mode of Motion. London: Longmans, Green ..., 1870. 4th edn. 8vo. xxiii,575 pp. 1 plate, 109 text figs. Cloth gilt, spine torn. *(Gemmary)* **$60 [≈ £31]**
- Heat A Mode of Motion. New York: Appleton, 1905. 6th edn. Cr 8vo. xix,591 pp. 125 text figs. Cloth. *(Gemmary)* **$75 [≈ £39]**
- Lectures on Light. New York: 1873. 1st edn. 194 pp. Orig bndg. *(Fye)* **$75 [≈ £39]**
- New Fragments. London: Longmans, Green, 1892. 8vo. 500 pp. Cloth.
(Gemmary) **$25 [≈ £13]**
- Notes on Light. London: Longmans, Green, 1870. Cr 8vo. viii,74 pp. 3 text figs. Water stained & foxed. Cloth.
(Gemmary) **$45 [≈ £23]**

- Notes on Light. London: Longmans, Green, 1872. 4th edn. Cr 8vo. viii,74 pp. 3 text figs. Cloth.   *(Gemmary)* **$60** [≈ £31]
- On Radiation. The 'Rede' Lecture delivered in the Senate House before the University of Cambridge ... London: Longman ..., 1865. 1st edn thus. 8vo. 62,32 ctlg pp. Frontis. Orig cloth gilt.   *(Gough)* **£45** [≈ $86]
- Six Lectures on Light. Delivered in America in 1872-1873. Second Edition. London: Longman, Green, 1875. 8vo. [xix],272 pp. Port, 1 plate, text figs. Orig cloth, sl worn.   *(Bickersteth)* **£28** [≈ $53]
- Six Lectures on Light delivered in the United States in 1872-1873. London: Longmans, Green, 1882. 3rd edn. 8vo. ix,264 pp. Port frontis, 1 plate, 57 text figs. Cloth.   *(Gemmary)* **$75** [≈ £39]
- Six Lectures on Light. Delivered in the United States in 1872-1873. Third Edition. London: 1882. Sm 8vo. xii,264 pp. 2 plates, 57 figs. Half calf, gilt spine, mor label, by Mudie.   *(Bow Windows)* **£36** [≈ $69]
- Six Lectures on Light delivered in the United States in 1872-1873. London: Longmans, Green, 1885. 4th edn. 8vo. ix,244 pp. Port frontis, 57 text figs. Ex-lib. Cloth.   *(Gemmary)* **$75** [≈ £39]
- Six Lectures on Light delivered in the United States in 1872-1873. New York: Appleton, 1886. 2nd (US) edn. 8vo. xvii,272 pp. 2 plates. Cloth, sl worn.   *(Gemmary)* **$65** [≈ £33]
- Sound. 1873. 1st edn. 335 pp. 169 ills. Orig bndg, some wear to spine, chipped at hd.   *(New Wireless)* **$55** [≈ £29]
- Sound. London: Longmans, Green, 1875. 8vo. xxxii, 420 pp. 2 plates (foxed), 190 text figs. Ex-lib. Cloth.   *(Gemmary)* **$45** [≈ £23]

Tyrrell, Frederick
- A Practical Work on the Diseases of the Eye, and their Treatment ... London: Churchill, 1840. Sole edn. 2 vols. 8vo. lviii, 533; xii, 566 pp. 8 cold & 1 other plates. Orig half calf, sl rubbed.   *(Bickersteth)* **£380** [≈ $729]

Tyson, Edward
- Orang-Outang, sive Homo Sylvestris: or, The Anatomy of a Pygmie compared with that of a Monkey, an Ape, and a Man ... London 1699. reprinted with an Introduction by Ashley Montagu. London: 1966. 4to. Port, 8 fldg plates. Orig cloth.   *(Bow Windows)* **£48** [≈ $92]

The Universal Instructor ...
- The Universal Instructor in the Art of

Brewing Beer. London: Harvey & Darton, [ca 1820]. 1st edn. 12mo. 126,[3] pp. Orig ptd bds, minor wear & soiling.   *(Bookpress)* **$285** [≈ £148]

The Universal Family Physician ...
- The Universal Family Physician, and Surgeon ... Liverpool: 1810. vi,760 pp. Frontis. Occas foxing. Sm hole in endpaper. Limp half pink leather, orig label, mrbld bds.   *(Whitehart)* **£40** [≈ $76]

Ure, Andrew
- A Dictionary of Arts, Manufactures, and Mines ... London: 1839. 1st edn. vii,1334 pp. 1241 w'engvs. Occas sl foxing. Contemp three qtr leather, rather worn, hd of spine defective & sl damp stained.   *(Whitehart)* **£90** [≈ $172]
- A Dictionary of the Arts, Manufactures, and Mines ... London: Longman, Orme ..., 1839. 1st edn. Thick 8vo. viii,1334 pp. 1241 text figs. Contemp half calf, rubbed, hinges splitting.   *(Claude Cox)* **£65** [≈ $124]
- A Dictionary of Arts, Manufacture, and Mines ... London: 1843. 3rd edn. vii,1334 pp. 1240 w'engvs. Half mor, v rubbed & worn.   *(Whitehart)* **£60** [≈ $115]

Urquhart, John W.
- Electric Light Fitting. 1890. 1st edn. 226, 62 ctlg pp. 89 ills. Orig bndg.   *(New Wireless)* **$65** [≈ £33]
- Electric Light. 1893. 5th edn. 412 pp. 153 ills. Orig bndg.   *(New Wireless)* **$60** [≈ £31]

Ussher, R.J. & Warren, R.
- The Birds of Ireland ... London: Gurney & Jackson, 1900. 8vo. 419 pp. Cold frontis, maps, ills. Cloth bds, sl stain on cvr.   *(Emerald Isle)* **£55** [≈ $105]

Vallancey, Charles
- The Art of Tanning and Currying Leather: With an Account of all the Different Processes Made Use of in Europe and Asia, for Dying Leather Red and Yellow ... London: reptd for J. Nourse, 1780. 12mo. [ii], xx, 259, [i] pp. Antique style qtr calf. Anon.   *(Finch)* **£400** [≈ $767]

Vallemont, Pierre le Lorrain de
- Curiosities of Nature and Art in Husbandry and Gardening. London: D. Brown ..., 1707. 1st edn in English. 8vo. [xvi],352 pp. 12 plates. Contemp calf, rebacked, some wear.   *(Bookpress)* **$550** [≈ £286]

Vancouver, Charles
- General View of the Agriculture of the County of Devon ... London: for Richard Phillips ..., 1808. 8vo. xii, 479, 2 advt, 2 ctlg of seeds, [i errata] pp. Fldg hand cold map, 28 plates. Old polished calf gilt, edges & spine rubbed, upper bd rather loose.
(Hollett) **£140 [≈ $268]**

Van Kampen, Nicholas, & Son
- The Dutch Florist: or, True Method of Managing All Sorts of Flowers with Bulbous Roots. The Second Edition, to which is added the particular Method of treating the Guernsey Lily. London: Baldwin, 1764. 8vo. [8], 104 pp. Half calf, extremities v sl rubbed.
(Beech) **£60 [≈ $115]**

Van Someren, R.A.L. & V.G.L.
- Studies of Birdlife in Uganda. London: 1911. 4to. 22 pp. 25 photo plates. Orig portfolio.
(Wheldon & Wesley) **£40 [≈ $76]**

Vasey, G.
- Illustrations of North American Grasses. Washington: 1891-93. 2 vols. Imperial 8vo. 200 plates. Lib stamp on title & reverse of plates. New cloth.
(Wheldon & Wesley) **£80 [≈ $153]**

Veitch, J., & Son
- A Manual of the Coniferae. London: 1881. 1st edn. 8vo. 342 pp. 21 plates, 63 text figs. 1 plate reprd at fold. Orig pict cloth gilt.
(Henly) **£46 [≈ $88]**

Velikovsky, Immanuel
- Worlds in Collision. New York: Macmillan, 1950. 1st edn. Orig blue cloth, extremities sl rubbed. Dw (sl soiled & chipped).
(Bromer) **$125 [≈ £65]**

Velpeau, A.
- An Elementary Treatise on Midwifery. Phila: 1831. 1st English translation. Leather.
(Fye) **$250 [≈ £130]**
- New Elements of Operative Surgery ... augmented ... and with Notes and Observations by valentine Mott. New York: 1847. 1st English translation. 3 vols. 851; 992; 1162 pp. W'cut ills. Leather. Lacks atlas vol.
(Fye) **$400 [≈ £208]**
- A Treatise on Diseases of the Breast. Phila: 1841. 1st English translation. 83 pp. Leather.
(Fye) **$150 [≈ £78]**

Venn, J.
- The Logic of Chance. London: Macmillan,

1888. 3rd edn. Cr 8vo. xxix,508 pp. Ex-lib. Cloth, partly unopened.
(Gemmary) **$75 [≈ £39]**

Verdon, W.
- Angina Pectoris. Brighton: 1920. xv,414 pp. Inscrptn on title. Cloth, sl worn & dusty, new endpapers.
(Whitehart) **£35 [≈ $67]**

The Vermin Killer ...
- The Vermin Killer. Being a Compleat and Necessary Family-Book. London: W. Owen, [17--?]. 12mo. 84 pp. Disbound.
(Bookpress) **$425 [≈ £221]**

Verrill, A. Hyatt
- Harper's Wireless Book. 1913. 1st edn. 184 pp. 129 ills. Orig bndg.
(New Wireless) **$35 [≈ £18]**

Vesalius, Andreas
- Vesalius on the Human Brain. Edited and Translated by Charles Singer. Oxford: 1952. 8vo. 151 pp. Orig bndg.
(Goodrich) **$95 [≈ £49]**

Vesey-Fitzgerald, B.
- British Game. London: Collins New Naturalist, 1946. 2nd edn. 8vo. xv,240 pp. 24 cold & 48 plain plates. Orig cloth.
(Henly) **£12 [≈ $23]**

Vestiges of the Natural History of Creation ...
- See Chambers, Robert.

Vicaire, G.
- Bibliographie Gastronomique. London: 1954. 2nd edn. 8vo. Orig cloth.
(Young's) **£50 [≈ $95]**

A View of Sir Isaac Newton's Philosophy ...
- See Pemberton, Henry.

Vigo, John
- The Whole Worke of that Famous Chirurgion Maister John Vigo; newly Corrected by men skilfull in that Arte ... Compiled and Published by Thomas Gale ... London: Thomas East, 1586. Sm thick 4to. [10],455 ff. Engvd title border. Black Letter. Early calf, rebacked.
(Goodrich) **$6,500 [≈ £3,385]**

Villamil, R. de
- Newton the Man. London: [1931]. vi,111 pp. Port. Ink scribble on 1 page. Orig cloth, spine faded.
(Whitehart) **£18 [≈ $34]**

Vince, Samuel
- The Elements of Astronomy. Phila: Kimber & Conrad, 1811. 1st Amer edn. 8vo. 242 pp. text figs. Sl foxed. New leather.
	(Gemmary) **$75** [≈ £39]
- A Treatise on Plane and Spherical Trigonometry ... Cambridge: UP ..., 1805. 2nd edn. 8vo. [ii],148 pp. 2 fldg plates. Disbound.		*(Burmester)* **£25** [≈ $47]

Vincent, Benjamin
- A New Classified Catalogue of the Library of the Royal Institution of Great Britain ... London: sold at the Royal Institution ..., 1857. 1st edn. 8vo. xx,928 pp. Contemp roan backed cloth, headcap chipped.
	(Gaskell) **£80** [≈ $153]

Virchow, Rudolf
- Cellular Pathology as Based upon the Physiological and Pathological Histology. Translated ... by Frank Chance. New York: [1867]. 2nd Amer edn. 554 pp. Orig bndg, hinges torn, tear in backstrip.
	(Fye) **$150** [≈ £78]

Von Ardenne, Manfred
- Cathode Ray Tubes. 1939. 1st English edn. 530 pp. 465 ills. Orig bndg.
	(New Wireless) **$45** [≈ £23]

Von Kobell, F.
- Mineralogy Simplified. Phila: Henry Carey Baird, 1867. Cr 8vo. vii,206 pp. 10 text w'cuts. Cloth, spine torn.
	(Gemmary) **$50** [≈ £26]

Von Laue, M. & Von Mises, R.
- Stereoscopic Drawings of Crystal Structures. London: Blackie & Son, 1926. Cr 8vo. 43,24 pp. 24 slides in pockets. Wrappers. Slipcase.
	(Gemmary) **$150** [≈ £78]

Von Marilaun, A.K. & Oliver, F.W.
- The Natural History of Plants ... London: Blackie & Son, 1894. 1st edn in English. 2 vols. Sm 4to. 16 cold plates, ca 2000 ills. Prelims sl spotted. Contemp half mor, elab gilt dec spines, t.e.g., fine.
	(Gough) **£145** [≈ $278]
- See also Kerner von Marilaun, A.K.

Von Neumann, J.
- Mathematical Foundations of Quantum Mechanics. Princeton: UP, 1955. 8vo. xii,455 pp. Wraps.		*(Gemmary)* **$40** [≈ £20]

Von Zittel, K.A.
- History of Geology and Palaeontology to the End of the Nineteenth Century. London: Walter Scott, 1901. Cr 8vo. xiii,562 pp. 13 ports. "Fine ex-lib". New qtr leather.
	(Gemmary) **$150** [≈ £78]

Voous, K.H.
- Atlas of European Birds. London: 1960. Folio. Maps, photo ills. Dw (frayed).
	(Grayling) **£35** [≈ $67]

Voronoff, Serge
- Rejuvenation by Grafting. Translation edited by Fred. F. Imianitoff. London: 1925. 1st edn in English. 8vo. 224 pp. 38 plates. Orig cloth.
	(Bickersteth) **£48** [≈ $92]
- Rejuvenation by Grafting. Translation edited by Fred. Imianitoff. New York: 1925. 1st edn in English. 8vo. 38 plates. Orig bndg.
	(Young's) **£30** [≈ $57]

Vyvyan, R.N.
- Wireless Over 30 Years. 1933. 1st edn. 256 pp. 16 photos, 12 ills. Dw.
	(New Wireless) **$75** [≈ £39]

W., The Hon. Mrs.
- See Ward, Hon. Mrs. Mary.

Waddell, J.A.L.
- Bridge Engineering. New York: 1916. 2 vols. lxxv,2177 pp. Num figs & diags, some fldg. Orig cloth.		*(Whitehart)* **£35** [≈ $67]

Wagner, Rudolph
- Elements of the Comparative Anatomy of the Vertebrate Animals ... Edited from the German by Alfred Tulk. London: Longman ..., 1845. 1st edn in English. 8vo. iv,[ii],264 pp. Few sm lib stamps. Orig cloth, uncut, spine ends worn, jnt ends cracked.
	(Bickersteth) **£45** [≈ $86]

Wailes, Rex
- The English Windmill. London: Routledge, 1954. 1st edn. xxiii,246 pp. Frontis, 72 photo plates, 64 text ills. Dw (sl chipped).
	(Gough) **£35** [≈ $67]

Wait, W.E.
- Manual of the Birds of Ceylon. Colombo: 1931. 2nd edn. 8vo. xxxiii,494 pp. Map. Orig cloth, trifle worn.
	(Wheldon & Wesley) **£30** [≈ $57]

Wakefield, E.M. & Dennis, R.W.G.
- Common British Fungi. London: [1950]. Roy

8vo. ix,290 pp. 111 cold plates. Orig cloth, trifle soiled.   *(Henly)* **£22 [≈ $42]**
- Common British Fungi. London: [1950]. Roy 8vo. ix,290 pp. 111 cold plates. Cloth.
(Wheldon & Wesley) **£28 [≈ $53]**

Wakefield, Priscilla
- An Introduction to Botany. London: 1818. 8th edn. 8vo. xii,187 pp. 9 plates. Half calf, trifle rubbed.
(Wheldon & Wesley) **£20 [≈ $38]**
- An Introduction to the Natural History and Classification of Insects ... London: Darton, Harvey & Darton, 1816. 8vo. x,192 pp. 12 plates. Occas foxing. Period calf gilt, sl worn.
(Rankin) **£75 [≈ $143]**
- An Introduction to the Natural History and Classification of Insects, in a Series of Familiar Letters. London: 1816. 1st edn. Sm 8vo. x,192 pp. 12 hand cold plates. Mod bds.
(Wheldon & Wesley) **£30 [≈ $57]**

Wakely, Andrew
- The Mariner's Compass Rectified ... Enlarged ... by J. Atkinson ... Revised ... by John Adams ... London: for Mount & Page, 1784. Lge 12mo. 272 pp. W'cut volvelle, w'cut ill. Title dusty. Contemp calf.
(Vanbrugh) **£175 [≈ $335]**

Wakeman, Geoffrey
- Aspects of Victorian Lithography, Anastatic Printing and Photozincography. Wymondham: Brewhouse Press, 1970. 1st edn. One of 250. 4to. 64 pp. 3 mtd specimens. Orig half leather & mrbld bds.
(Oak Knoll) **$325 [≈ £169]**

Walcott, Mary Vaux
- North American Wild Flowers. Washington: Smithsonian, 1925. One of 500. Lge 4to. Loose sgntrs & plates with accompanying caption ff, as issued. Blank prelims sl insect nibbled. Half mor fldg slipcases (ft of spines sl rubbed).   *(Reese)* **$950 [≈ £494]**
- North American Wild Flowers. Washington: 1925. One of 500. Imperial 4to. 400 cold plates, each with a page of text. Orig half mor portfolios.
(Wheldon & Wesley) **£500 [≈ $959]**

Walker, E.
- Terrestrial and Cosmical Magnetism. The Adams Prize Essay for 1865. London: 1866. iv, 336, vi pp. 10 fldg plates. Title sl foxed. Orig cloth, dull & dust stained.
(Whitehart) **£25 [≈ $47]**

Walker, J.
- Folk Medicine in Modern Egypt ... London: 1934. 128 pp. 4 plates. Sl foxing. Cloth, sl dusty.   *(Whitehart)* **£25 [≈ $47]**

Walker, J. & C.
- A Geological Map of England and Wales and a Part of Scotland ... London: 1837. Fldg hand cold map, in 36 linen backed sections. 1432 x 995 mm, fldg to 250 x 160 mm. Contemp pull-off box. *(Henly)* **£340 [≈ $652]**

Walker, Obadiah
- Propositions concerning Optic-Glasses ... Oxford: at the theater, 1679. 1st edn. 4to. [iv], 46 pp. Text diags. Faint water stains in inner crnrs. Mod qtr mor. Wing W.409. Anon.
(Gaskell) **£550 [≈ $1,055]**

Walker, R.
- The Flora of Oxfordshire and its Contiguous Counties ... Oxford: 1833. 8vo. cxxxv, 338 pp. Fldg table (torn), 12 plates (foxed). Few pencil notes. Orig cloth, trifle used.
(Wheldon & Wesley) **£65 [≈ $124]**

Walker, R.C. & Lance, T.M.C.
- Photoelectric Cell Applications. 1935. 2nd edn. 245 pp. 90 photos, 155 ills. Dw.
(New Wireless) **$40 [≈ £20]**

Walker, W.
- Memoirs of the Distinguished Men of Science of Great Britain living in the Years 1807-08. With an Introduction by Robert Hunt ... London: 1862. xii,228 pp. Frontis (creased). Cloth sl worn, spine ends sl defective.   *(Whitehart)* **£35 [≈ $67]**

Wallace, Alfred Russell
- Contributions to the Theory of Natural Selection. London: Macmillan, 1870. 1st edn. 8vo. xvi,384,[43 advt dated Jan 1870] pp. Orig cloth.   *(Rootenberg)* **$500 [≈ £260]**
- Darwinism an Exposition of the Theory of Natural Selection with some of its Applications. London: 1889. 1st edn. 8vo. xvi,494,[2] pp. Port, fldg map, figs. Minor spotting. Orig cloth, upper cvr marked.
(Bow Windows) **£105 [≈ $201]**
- Darwinism: an Exposition of the Theory of Natural Selection with some of its Applications. London: Macmillan, 1889. 8vo. Orig cloth, sl shaken.
(Waterfield's) **£75 [≈ $143]**
- The Geographical Distribution of Animals ... London: Macmillan, 1876. 1st edn. 2 vols. 8vo. xxi,[3], 503,[1]; viii,[4], 607,[1] pp.

Errata. 7 cold maps, 20 plates. Orig green cloth, new endpapers.
                    (Rootenberg) **$600 [≈ £312]**
- The Geographical Distribution of Animals ... London: 1876. 1st edn. 2 vols. 8vo. 7 cold maps, 20 plates. Sound ex-lib. Some spotting. Orig cloth.
           (Wheldon & Wesley) **£200 [≈ $383]**
- The Geographical Distribution of Animals ... London: Macmillan, 1876. 1st edn. 2 vols. 7 cold maps, 20 plates. Sl spotting. Orig dec green cloth gilt, t.e.g., fine.
              (Gough) **£275 [≈ $527]**
- Island Life or the Phenomena and Causes of Insular Faunas and Floras ... Second and Revised Edition. London: Macmillan, 1892. 8vo. xx,563 pp. 26 ills & maps. Near contemp red prize calf gilt.
       (Frew Mackenzie) **£65 [≈ $124]**
- A Narrative of Travels on the Amazon and Rio Negro ... London: Reeve & Co, 1853. 1st edn. viii,541,26 advt pp. Chromolitho frontis, map, fldg table, 8 plain plates, 2 text ills. V occas sl spotting. Orig cloth, spine v sl faded, recased.   *(Gough)* **£425 [≈ $815]**
- Natural Selection and Tropical Nature: Essays on Descriptive and Theoretical Biology. London: 1891. 1st edn thus. 8vo. xii, 492 pp. Orig cloth, sl marked, spine ends trifle rubbed. *(Bow Windows)* **£65 [≈ $124]**
- Palm Trees of the Amazon and their Uses. London: 1853. 8vo. viii,129 pp. Map, 47 litho plates. Lib stamps on title & reverse of plates. Orig green cloth, rebacked.
          (Wheldon & Wesley) **£250 [≈ $479]**
- Tropical Nature, and Other Essays. London: Macmillan, 1878. 1st edn. 8vo. xiii,[3],356 pp,advt leaf. Orig cloth.
              (Rootenberg) **$300 [≈ £156]**

Wallace, R.L.
- British Cage Birds. Full Directions for Breeding, Rearing, and Managing the Various British Birds that can be kept in Confinement. London: [ca 1880]. 15 cold litho plates, 16 (of 17) plain plates. Spine sl rubbed & snagged. *(Grayling)* **£55 [≈ $105]**
- British Cage Birds. London: 1887. 8vo. viii, 504 pp. 15 cold & 17 plain plates. Reverse of frontis foxed. Orig dec cloth, a.e.g.
              (Wheldon & Wesley) **£30 [≈ $57]**
- The Canary Book. London: [1893]. 3rd edn. 8vo. viii,429 pp. 6 cold & 16 plain plates. Some sl offsetting. New cloth.
              (Wheldon & Wesley) **£30 [≈ $57]**

Wallace, William
- Researches respecting the Medical Powers of

Chlorine ... London: Longman, Hurst ..., 1822. 1st edn. xiv,148 pp. Sm marg stain on a few ff. Rec bds.   *(Fenning)* **£65 [≈ $124]**

Waller, Augustus D.
- Eight Lectures on the Signs of Life. London: 1903. 1st edn. 175 pp. Orig bndg.
                    (Fye) **$200 [≈ £104]**
- Lectures on Physiology. First Series: On Animal Electricity. London: 1897. 1st edn. 144 pp. Orig bndg.   *(Fye)* **$300 [≈ £156]**

Waller, Erik
- Bibliotheca Walleriana ... see Sallander, Hans.

Wallis, George
- The Art of Preventing Diseases, and Restoring Health ... London: Robinson, 1793. 8vo. xx,850,[12] pp. Tree calf, front jnt cracked.   *(Goodrich)* **$145 [≈ £75]**

Wallis, P. & R.
- Newton and Newtoniana 1672-1975. Kent: Dawson, 1977. 4to. xxiv,362 pp. Cloth.
                    (Gemmary) **$70 [≈ £36]**
- Newton and Newtoniana, 1672-1975. London: 1977. xxiv,362 pp. Orig bndg.
                    (Whitehart) **£35 [≈ $67]**

Wallis-Tayler, A.J.
- Aerial or Wire Rope-Ways. London: Crosby Lockwood, 1911. 1st edn. 155 ills. Orig bndg.   *(Young's)* **£60 [≈ $115]**
- Aerial or Wire-Rope Tramways. Their Construction and Management. London: Crosby Lockwood, 1898. 1st edn. 8vo. 81 ills. Title sl spotted. Orig bndg.
                    (Young's) **£58 [≈ $111]**

Walmsley, R.M.
- Electricity in the Service of Man. A Popular and Practical Treatise on the Application of Electricity to Modern Life. London: [1921]. 4 vols. 2214,lii pp. 21 fldg plates, over 3300 ills. Orig cloth, v sl worn.
                    (Whitehart) **£45 [≈ $86]**

Walpole-Bond, John
- A History of Sussex Birds. London: Witherby, 1938. 1st edn. 3 vols. 53 cold plates by Philip Rickman. Foredges v sl spotted. Dws.   *(Gough)* **£350 [≈ $671]**

Walsh, James
- Psychotherapy including the History of the Use of Mental Influence, Directly and Indirectly, in Healing ... New York: 1912. 1st

edn. 806 pp. Orig bndg. *(Fye)* **$75 [≃ £39]**

Walsh, James J.
- The Popes and Science. The History of the Papal Relations to Science during the Middle Ages and down to our own Times. New York: 1908. 8vo. 431 pp. Occas discoloration due to inserted clippings. Orig bndg.
(Goodrich) **$55 [≃ £28]**

Walshe, Sir Francis
- Further Critical Studies in Neurology and Other Essays and Addresses. London: 1965. 1st edn. 8vo. viii,248 pp. Orig cloth. Dw.
(Bickersteth) **£15 [≃ $28]**

Walton, W.
- A Collection of Problems in Illustration of the Principles of Elementary Mechanics. Cambridge: 1858. xii,247 pp. 5 fldg plates. Orig cloth, backstrip relaid.
(Whitehart) **£35 [≃ $67]**

Ward, H.
- The Microscope (Microscope Teachings). London: Groombridge, [ca 1870]. 8vo. vi,154 pp. 7 cold plates, 25 text figs. Cloth gilt, a.e.g.
(Gemmary) **$60 [≃ £31]**

Ward, John
- The Young Mathematician's Guide. Being a Plain and Easy Introduction to the Mathematicks ... The Fourth Edition, Carefully Corrected ... London: 1724. [8],456 pp. Frontis port, text diags. Orig panelled calf, spine with a lacquer-like coat.
(Karmiole) **$225 [≃ £117]**
- The Young Mathematician's Guide: being a Plain and Easy Introduction to the Mathematicks. London: 1734. 6th edn. viii,456 pp. Frontis port. A few pp stained at edges, some browned. Panelled calf, rebacked.
(Whitehart) **£50 [≃ $95]**

Ward, The Hon Mrs Mary
- A World of Wonders Revealed by the Microscope. By the Hon. Mrs. W. London: Groombridge, 1858. 1st published edn. 8vo. [iv], 56, [8 advt dated 1858] pp. 14 cold plates. Occas sl offsetting. Orig elab gilt cloth, a.e.g., recased, rebacked. *(de Beaumont)* **£50 [≃ $95]**

Ward, N.B.
- On the Growth of Plants in Closely Glazed Cases. London: 1842. 8vo. vii,95,[3] pp. Marg stain on 2 ff. Orig cloth, reprd.
(Wheldon & Wesley) **£70 [≃ $134]**

Ward, R.
- The Design and Equipment of Hospitals. London: 1949. xvi,360 pp. Num diags. Traces of label removal endpaper. Spine reprd.
(Whitehart) **£25 [≃ $47]**

Ward, Rowland
- A Naturalist's Life Study in the Art of Taxidermy ... London: Rowland Ward, for private circulation, 1913. 4to. Port frontis, num text ills. Orig buckram, pict cloth label, t.e.g., trivial soiling, minor repr to label. *(Frew Mackenzie)* **£300 [≃ $575]**

Wardrop, James
- Essays on the Morbid Anatomy of the Human Eye. Volume 2 [only, of 2]. London: 1818. 1st edn. 274 pp. 8 hand cold plates. Qtr leather.
(Fye) **$350 [≃ £182]**

Ware, James
- Observations on the Cataract, and Gutta Serena ... London: 1812. 3rd edn. 460 pp. Paper backed bds, backstrip missing, front bd detached. *(Fye)* **$150 [≃ £78]**

Waring, Edward
- Pharmacopoeia of India. London: 1868. 1st edn. 503 pp. Qtr leather, orig backstrip relaid.
(Fye) **$175 [≃ £91]**

Warren, Sir Charles
- The Ancient Cubit and Our Weights and Measures. London: Palestine Exploration Fund, 1903. 1st edn. 8vo. xx,131 pp. Orig cloth gilt, lettering sl dulled.
(Hollett) **£45 [≃ $86]**

Warren, J. Mason
- Surgical Observations, with Cases and Operations. New York: 1867. 1st edn. 630 pp. Litho ills, some cold. Orig bndg, fine.
(Fye) **$600 [≃ £312]**

Warren, John C.
- Etherization; with Surgical Remarks. Boston: Ticknor, 1848. 8vo. [2],v, [2], 100, advt pp. Marg damp staining. Orig cloth, faded & spotted. *(Goodrich)* **$795 [≃ £414]**

Waterfield, M.
- Flower Grouping in English, Scotch and Irish Gardens. London: 1907. 4to. xiii,237 pp. 56 cold plates. Orig dec cloth gilt, sl worn.
(Henly) **£48 [≃ $92]**

Watkins, E.T.
- Watkins' Telegraphic Code 1881, and

Appendix, 1884. 1884. 1st edn. 936 pp. Orig dec leather, some wear to spine.
(New Wireless) **$95 [≈ £49]**

Watson, H.C.
- The New Botanist's Guide to the Localities of the Rarer Plants of Britain. London: 1835-37. 2 vols. Cr 8vo. Orig cloth.
(Wheldon & Wesley) **£60 [≈ $115]**
- Topographical Botany, being Local and Personal Records towards shewing the Distribution of British Plants. London: 1883. 2nd edn. 8vo. xlvii,612 pp. Fldg cold map. Orig cloth, unopened.   *(Henly)* **£18 [≈ $34]**

Watson, J. Madison
- Watson's Manual of Calisthenics. A Systematic Drill Book without Apparatus ... With Music to accompany the Exercises ... New York: 1864. 1st edn. 8vo. 144,[4] pp. Orig cloth, some wear, 1 hinge cracked.
(Hemlock) **$125 [≈ £65]**

Watson, James D.
- The Double Helix. A Personal Account of the Discovery of the Structure of DNA. London: Weidenfeld & Nicolson, [1968]. 1st edn. 8vo. xvi,226,[9] pp, inc figs & photo ills. Orig cloth. Dw.   *(Bickersteth)* **£120 [≈ $230]**
- The Double Helix. A Personal Account of the Discovery of the Structure of DNA. London: 1968. 1st edn. xvi,226 pp. 21 photos & 11 diags in text. Orig bndg. Dw.
(Whitehart) **£15 [≈ $28]**

Watson, John Selby
- The Reasoning Power in Animals. London: Reeve & Co, 1867. 1st edn. Cr 8vo. [2],viii, 471,24 advt pp. Orig cloth gilt, remains of lib label on upper bd.   *(Fenning)* **£35 [≈ $67]**

Watson, Richard
- Chemical Essays ... Third Edition. London: for T. Evans, 1784-87. Vols 1-3 3rd edn, 4 & 5 1st edn. 5 vols. 8vo. Contemp calf, red & green mor labels.
(Waterfield's) **£300 [≈ $575]**

Watson, T.
- Lectures on the Principles and Practice of Physic: delivered at King's College, London. London: 1857. 4th edn. 2 vols. 2 plates. Edge of 1st few pp vol 1 sl water stained, 1 page edge reprd. New cloth.
(Whitehart) **£35 [≈ $67]**

Watson, W.C.R.
- Handbook of the Rubi of Great Britain and

Ireland. Cambridge: 1958. 8vo. xi,274 pp. 50 ills. Cloth.   *(Wheldon & Wesley)* **£17 [≈ $32]**

Watson, William
- Orchids: Their Culture and Management, with a Description of all the Kinds in General Cultivation. London: Upcott Gill, 1890. Num cold plates & engvs. Orig pict green cloth, a.e.g., sl worn.   *(Boswell)* **$80 [≈ £41]**

Watson-Jones, R.
- Fractures and other Bone Joint Injuries. Edinburgh: 1940. xiii,723 pp. 1040 text ills. Cloth, sl worn & stained.
(Whitehart) **£25 [≈ $47]**
- Fractures and Joint Injuries. Edinburgh: 1943. 3rd edn. 2 vols. 1353 figs (many cold). Dws.   *(Whitehart)* **£40 [≈ $76]**

Watson-Watt, Sir Robert
- The Pulse of Radar. 1959. 1st edn. 438 pp. Orig bndg. Dw. *(New Wireless)* **$45 [≈ £24]**

Watt, A. & Philip, A.
- The Electro-Plating and Electro-Refining of Minerals. London: Crosby Lockwood, 1911. 2nd edn. 8vo. xxiv,680 pp. 160 text figs. Cloth.   *(Gemmary)* **$75 [≈ £40]**

Watt, G.
- Dictionary of the Economic Products of India. London & Calcutta: 1889-93. 6 vols in 9. 8vo. Sound ex-lib. Half calf, vol 3 not uniform, 2 vols reprd. Without the general index publ in 1896.
(Wheldon & Wesley) **£240 [≈ $460]**

Watt, James
- Correspondence of the late James Watt on his Discovery of the Theory and Composition of Water ... Edited by J.P. Muirhead. London: 1846. cxxvii,264 pp. Port, 2 text figs. Num marg lib stamps, some erasures. Lib bndg.
(Whitehart) **£60 [≈ $115]**

Watts, Henry
- A Dictionary of Chemistry and the Allied Branches of Other Sciences. London: Longmans, Green, 1866-81. 1st edn, with all supplements. 8 vols in 9 (5 vols & 4 supplements). Ca 10,000 pp. Half-titles. 4 fldg tables, num text ills. 1 title soiled, 1 half-title reprd. Cloth. *(Rootenberg)* **$500 [≈ £260]**

Watts, Isaac
- The Knowledge of the Heavens and the Earth made easy; or, the First Principles of Astronomy and Geography explain'd by the

Use of Globes and Maps ... London: 1728. 2nd edn. xi, 222 pp. 6 fldg plates. Contemp calf, rebacked, edges sl worn.
(Whitehart) **£85 [≈ $163]**
- The Knowledge of the Heavens and the Earth made easy ... The fourth edition, corrected. London: for T. Longman ..., 1744. 8vo. xiii, [i], 222, [12] pp. 30 figs on 6 fldg engvd plates. Contemp calf, gilt ruled sides & spine, mor label.
(Gaskell) **£125 [≈ $239]**

Weaver, William D.
- See Wheeler Gift Catalog.

Webb, T.W.
- Celestial Objects for Common Telescopes. London: Longmans, Green, 1911. 5th edn. 2 vols. Cr 8vo. xx,235; iv,280 pp. Plates, text figs. Cloth.
(Gemmary) **$75 [≈ £39]**

Weber, M. & de Beaufort, L.F.
- The Fishes of the Indo-Australian Archipelago. Leiden: 1911-62. 11 vols. 8vo. Cloth, 1 spine worn.
(Wheldon & Wesley) **£380 [≈ $729]**

Webster, A.D.
- British Orchids ... Second Edition, Enlarged and Illustrated. London: J.S. Virtue, 1898. xii,132 pp. 40 b/w ills. Title page & frontis spotted. Orig pict green cloth gilt.
(Gough) **£20 [≈ $38]**
- British Orchids. London: 1898. 2nd edn. 8vo. xii, 132, 3 pp. Frontis, 39 text ills. Cloth.
(Henly) **£36 [≈ $69]**

Webster, Charles
- Facts tending to show the Connection of the Stomach with Life, Disease, and Recovery. London: Murray, 1793. 59 pp. Rec wraps.
(C.R. Johnson) **£85 [≈ $163]**

Webster, J.C.
- Researches in Female Pelvic Anatomy. Edinburgh: 1892. [xi],129 pp. 26 plates. Cloth, sl marked & worn, inner hinge sl weak.
(Whitehart) **£40 [≈ $76]**

Wegmann, Edward
- The Design and Construction of Dams ... Sixth Edition, revised and enlarged. New York: Wiley, 1911. 4to. xvi,529,[4 advt] pp. 158 fldg & other plates, 198 ills. Orig cloth gilt.
(Fenning) **£32.50 [≈ $63]**

Weismann, A.
- Essays upon Heredity and Kindred Biological Problems. Edited by A.E. Shipley and others.

Oxford: 1891-92. 2 vols. Occas foxing. Sm lib stamp. Cloth, vol 1 marked. Sgnd by Shipley.
(Whitehart) **£40 [≈ $76]**
- The Germ-Plasm: a Theory of Heredity. London: 1893. xxiii,477 pp. 24 text figs. Prelims loose. Orig cloth, sl marked & worn, inner hinge cracked. *(Whitehart)* **£40 [≈ $76]**

Welch, C.
- History of the Cutlers' Company of London and of the Minor Cutlery Crafts with Biographical Notices of Early London Cutlers. London: privately ptd, 1916-23. 2 vols. 2 frontis, 44 plates. A few sl marks. Orig green cloth, sl worn, vol 2 rebacked.
(Whitehart) **£45 [≈ $86]**

Welch, William
- Papers and Addresses. Baltimore: 1920. 3 vols. Tall 4to. Sl lib marks. Orig bndg, uncut.
(Goodrich) **$195 [≈ £101]**

Wellcome Library
- A Catalogue of Printed Books in the Wellcome Library ... London: 1962-66-76. 3 vols. Lge 4to. Orig bndgs.
(Goodrich) **$450 [≈ £234]**

Wells, Edward
- The Young Gentleman's Astronomy, Chronology, and Dialling ... Third Edition, Revised, and Corrected, with Additions. London: Knapton, 1725. 8vo. [viii],148, [viii],85, [viii],43 pp. 27 plates. Marg piece torn from 1 title. Orig calf, rubbed, label defective. *(Bickersteth)* **£110 [≈ $211]**
- The Young Gentleman's Astronomy, Chronology, and Dialling ... Fourth Edition, Revised, and Corrected, with Additions. London: Knapton, 1736. 8vo. [viii],148, [viii],86, [viii],54 pp. 25 plates. Sl foxing on plates. Contemp calf gilt, cracks to jnts.
(Rankin) **£75 [≈ $143]**

Wells, H.G. & Huxley, Julian
- The Science of Life. New York: Doubleday, Doran, 1931. 1st edn. 2 vols. Orig blue cloth gilt. Dws. *(MacDonnell)* **$75 [≈ £39]**

Wells, T. Spencer
- On Ovarian and Uterine Tumours, their Diagnosis and Treatment. London: 1882. 1st edn. 530 pp. Ills. Orig bndg, fine.
(Fye) **$300 [≈ £156]**

Wells, W.C.
- An Essay on Dew, and several appearances connected with it. Phila: 1838. 71 pp. Foxed.

New cloth, garish endpapers.
(Whitehart) **£40 [≈ $76]**

Wentzel, G.
- Quantum Theory of Fields. New York: Interscience Publ, 1949. 8vo. ix,224 pp. Cloth. Dw.   *(Gemmary)* **$50 [≈ £26]**

West, A.G.D.
- Television Today. 1935. 1st edn. 2 vols. 776 pp. Num ills. Orig bndg, sm stain cvr vol 2.
(New Wireless) **$195 [≈ £102]**

West, Charles
- Lectures on the Diseases of Infancy and Childhood. London: Longman ..., 1848. 1st edn. 8vo. xxiii,488 pp. Intl advt leaf, 16 pp ctlg at end. Orig cloth, sl worn, new endpapers.   *(Bickersteth)* **£450 [≈ $863]**

West, G.
- The Practical Principles of Plain Photo-Micrography. Dundee: Campbell & Sons, for the author, 1916. 1st edn. 4to. 146,4 advt pp. 8 plates, 5 figs. Wraps. *(Savona)* **£30 [≈ $57]**

Westermarck, Edward
- Ethical Relativity. London: 1932. 1st edn in English. 8vo. xviii,301 pp. Orig cloth, marked.   *(Bow Windows)* **£60 [≈ $115]**
- The History of Human Marriage. Fifth Edition, revised. New York: Allerton Book Co, 1922. 3 vols. Orig cloth gilt, lettering faded & inked in.   *(Hollett)* **£120 [≈ $230]**
- The History of Human Marriage. London: 1894. 2nd edn. 644 pp. Orig bndg.
(Fye) **$100 [≈ £52]**

Westofen, W.
- The Forth Bridge. Reprinted from "Engineering", February 28, 1890. Third Edition, Revised, with an Appendix. London: [ca 1890]. Folio. [4],72 pp. 19 plates, 157 ills. Orig limp cloth gilt.   *(Fenning)* **£35 [≈ $67]**

Weston, Richard
- The English Flora [with] The Supplement to the English Flora. London: 1775-80. 2 vols in one. 8vo. [xvi],259; [xii],120 pp. Contemp calf.   *(Wheldon & Wesley)* **£80 [≈ $153]**
- The Gardner's and Planter's Calendar ... Second Edition, corrected and enlarged. London: for T. Carnan, 1778. Lge 12mo. [12], 336 pp. Contemp calf bds, rebacked.
(Beech) **£65 [≈ $124]**

Westwood, J.O.
- The Entomologist's Text Book ... London:

Wm. S. Orr, 1838. 8vo. x,432 pp. 5 hand cold plates. Orig cloth gilt, spine faded.
(Hollett) **£60 [≈ $115]**
- An Introduction to the Modern Classification of Insects ... London: Longman ..., 1839-40. 1st edn. 2 vols. xii,462; xi, 587, 158 pp. Hand cold frontis, ca 2000 text figs. Orig green cloth, spines faded.   *(Gough)* **£100 [≈ $191]**

Weymouth, A.
- Through the Leper Squint. A Study of Leprosy from pre-Christian Times to the Present Day. London: [1938]. 286 pp. 2 maps, 25 ills. Occas sl foxing.
(Whitehart) **£20 [≈ $38]**

Wheeler Gift
- Wheeler Gift Catalog. Edited by William D. Weaver. Volume I [only, of 2]. 1909. 1st edn. 504 pp. 60 ills. Orig bndg.
(New Wireless) **$115 [≈ £59]**

Wheldon, H.J.
- A Key to the British Agaricineae. Darwen, Lancs.: 1914. 4 plates (1 hand cold). Orig cloth backed bds, sl worn.
(Grayling) **£25 [≈ $47]**

Wheldon, J.A. & Wilson, A.
- The Flora of West Lancashire. Eastbourne: 1907. 8vo. vi,511 pp. Map, 15 plates. Good ex-lib. Cloth.
(Wheldon & Wesley) **£35 [≈ $67]**

Whetham, W.C.D.
- The Recent Development of Physical Science. London: Murray, 1904. 8vo. xvi,347 pp. 39 text figs. Ex-lib. Cloth.
(Gemmary) **$40 [≈ £20]**

Whewell, William
- Astronomy and General Physics considered with reference to Natural Theology. London: William Pickering, 1834. 8vo. [10 advt], xv, 381, [3] pp. Some browning & other marks. Contemp publisher's cloth, maroon spine label.   *(Bow Windows)* **£55 [≈ $105]**
- Astronomy and General Physics considered with reference to Natural Theology. London: William Pickering, 1839. 8vo. xv,381 pp. Leather gilt, v sl worn.
(Gemmary) **$125 [≈ £65]**
- An Elementary Treatise on Mechanics ... Cambridge: John Smith for J. & J.J. Deighton, 1833. 4th edn, with addtns. 8vo. 280 pp. 9 plates. Orig cloth, paper label, unopened.   *(Chapel Hill)* **$125 [≈ £65]**
- History of the Inductive Sciences, from the

Earliest to the Present Times. London: John W. Parker; Cambridge: Deighton, 1837. 1st edn. 3 vols. 8vo. xxxvi,437, errata leaf; xii,534, errata leaf; xii,624 pp. Contemp polished calf gilt, mor labels. The Currer set.
(Gaskell) £285 [≈ $547]

- An Introduction to Dynamics, containing the Laws of Motion and the First Three Sections of the Principia. Cambridge & London: 1832. 8vo. New wraps. Author's pres inscrptn.
(Sanders) £60 [≈ $115]

- The Mechanical Euclid ... Cambridge: Parker for Deighton, 1837. 1st edn. 12mo. viii, 182 pp, errata leaf, errata slip. Text diags. Sl browned. Lib stamp p iii. Contemp half mor, gilt arms on front bd, jnts & spine rubbed. *(Gaskell)* £100 [≈ $191]

- On the Free Motion of Points and on the Universal Gravitation. Cambridge: Pitt Press, 1836. 8vo. xxviii,238 pp. 3 plates. Rebound in cloth. *(Gemmary)* $100 [≈ £52]

- On the Free Motion of Points, and on Universal Gravitation ... The First Part of a Treatise on Dynamics. Cambridge: 1836. 3rd edn. xxviii, 238 pp. 3 fldg plates. Sl foxing. Binder's cloth. *(Whitehart)* £40 [≈ $76]

- On the Philosophy of Discovery, Chapters Historical and Critical ... London: John W. Parker ..., 1860. 1st edn. 8vo. xvi,532,12 advt pp. Prize inscrptn. Orig cloth.
(Gaskell) £50 [≈ $95]

Whitaker, J.I.S.
- The Birds of Tunisia ... London: 1905. One of 250. 2 vols. Roy 8vo. 2 cold maps, 4 plates of views, 15 hand cold plates. Orig half mor, t.e.g. *(Wheldon & Wesley)* £750 [≈ $1,439]

Whitaker, W.
- Geology of London and of Part of the Thames Valley. London: Geol Survey, 1889. 2 vols. 8vo. Fldg table, num text figs. Cloth.
(Wheldon & Wesley) £75 [≈ $143]

Whitcombe, Charles Edward
- The Canadian Farmer's Manual of Agriculture ... Toronto: 1879. 1st edn. 8vo. 571. Appears to have been bound without a table of contents. Sev ills. Orig cloth, rubbed.
(Young's) £120 [≈ $230]

White, Alain & Sloane, Boyd L.
- The Stapeliaceae. Pasadena, CA: 1937. 2nd edn, enlgd. 3 vols. 4to. 39 cold plates, 1233 photos, 2 fldg maps, ills. Orig cloth, sl rubbed. *(Karmiole)* $200 [≈ £104]

White, Charles
- Cases in Surgery, with Remarks. Part the First [all published] ... added, An Essay on the Ligature of Arteries, by J. Aiken. London: 1770. 1st edn. 8vo. xv,198,[4] pp. 7 fldg plates. Contemp calf, extremities v sl bumped, sm splits in jnt.
(Hemlock) $875 [≈ £455]

- A Treatise on the Management of Pregnancy and Lying-in Women ... with some Directions concerning the Delivery of the Child ... Third Edition, revised and enlarged. London: Dilly, 1785. 3rd edn. 8vo. xix,475 pp. 2 plates. Sl browning. Rec bds. *(Hemlock)* $400 [≈ £208]

White, Daniel T.
- White's New Cook-Book, embracing Temperate and Economical Receipts for Domestic Liquors and Cookery ... Cincinnati: 1840. 24mo. 96 pp. Some marg damp stains, occas foxing. Contemp wraps, worn, spine defective. *(Reese)* $750 [≈ £390]

White, E. & Humphrey, J.
- Pharmacopoeia. A Commentary on the British Pharmacopoeia 1898. London: 1904. New issue with addtns & crrctns. 4to. xxii,692 pp. 46 plates. Some reprs & notes. Orig cloth, dull & faded, spine worn.
(Whitehart) £30 [≈ $57]

White, F.B.W.
- The Flora of Perthshire. Edited by J.W.H. Trail. Edinburgh: 1898. One of 500. 8vo. lix, 407 pp. Port, cold map. Orig cloth.
(Wheldon & Wesley) £45 [≈ $86]

White, Gilbert
- The Natural History of Selborne ... The Naturalist's Calendar, Miscellaneous Observations, and Poems. London: 1822. 2 vols. 8vo. 1 cold & 3 plain plates. Occas foxing, endpapers dust marked. Old tree calf, rebacked, crnrs worn.
(Bow Windows) £135 [≈ $259]

White, J.C. & Bruce, A.N.
- Pain. Its Mechanisms and Neurosurgical Control. Springfield: 1955. xxiv,736 pp. 134 figs. Sm sgntr on title. Sl marg water stain towards end. Orig bndg.
(Whitehart) £30 [≈ $57]

White, J.W., et al.
- Cases Illustrative of the Practical Application of the Rontgen Rays in Surgery. Reprinted AJMS 1896. 8vo. 23 pp. 12 skiagraphic plates. Orig bndg. *(Goodrich)* $495 [≈ £257]

White, Stephen
- Collateral Bee-Boxes; or, a New, Easy and Advantageous Method of Managing Bees ... Third Edition improved. London: Davis & Reyners, 1764. 8vo. ix,47 pp. Plate. Marg reprs to plate & last leaf not affecting text. Mod qtr mor.   *(Lamb)* £75 [≈ $143]

Whitehead, Alfred & Russell, Bertrand
- Principia Mathematica. Cambridge: UP, 1910-13. 1st edns. 3 vols. Lge 8vo. xiii,[3], 666; xxxiv,772; x,491, [1] pp. Errata leaf in each vol. Orig blue cloth, possibly new endpapers, fine. Half mor box.
          (Rootenberg) $20,000 [≈ £10,416]

Whitehead, G.K.
- The Deer of Great Britain and Ireland. An Account of their History, Status and Distribution. London: 1964. 8vo. Ills.
          (Grayling) £65 [≈ $124]
- The Deer of Great Britain and Ireland. An Account of their History, Status and Distribution. London: 1964. 8vo. Ills. Dw (faded).   *(Grayling)* £70 [≈ $134]
- Deer of the World. London: 1972. Roy 8vo. xii,194 pp. Cold frontis, 27 maps, 32 plates. Cloth.   *(Wheldon & Wesley)* £40 [≈ $76]

Whitehead, T.H. & Eastwood, T.
- Southern Part of the South Staffordshire Coalfield. London: 1927. xx,218 pp. 13 plates, 5 figs. Orig cloth gilt, spine sl dull.
          (Baldwin) £45 [≈ $86]

Whitehurst, John
- An Inquiry into the Original State and Formation of the Earth ... London: for the author by J. Cooper, 1778. 1st edn. 4to. [xii],ii, [ii],199 pp. 9 plates on 4 ff (2 fldg). B'plate removed. Contemp polished calf gilt, edges sl worn & scraped, upper hinge cracked.
          (Hollett) £375 [≈ $719]

Whitley, N.
- The Application of Geology to Agriculture and to the Improvement and Valuation of Land; with the Nature and Properties of Soils, and the Principles of Cultivation. London: 1843. 1st edn. 162,[1],32 pp. Fldg chart. New cloth. *(Whitehart)* £55 [≈ $105]

Whitlock, H.P.
- Calcites of New York. Albany: New York State Education Dept, 1910. 4to. 190 pp. 27 plates (1 in back pocket). Orig green cloth.
          (Gemmary) $150 [≈ £78]

Whitney, Elijah & A.B.
- Asiatic Cholera ... New York: M.W. Dodd, 1866. 12mo. 214 pp. Orig cloth, spine faded & worn at ends.   *(Schoyer)* $75 [≈ £39]

Whittaker, E.
- A History of the Theories of Aether and Electricity. The Classical Theories. London: 1951. Rvsd edn. xiv,434 pp. Orig bndg.
          (Whitehart) £35 [≈ $67]
- History of the Theories of Aether and Electricity. New York: Thomas Nelson & Sons, 1951. New edn. 8vo. xiv,434 pp. Cloth.
          (Gemmary) $90 [≈ £46]

Whymper, Charles
- Egyptian Birds for the most part seen in the Nile Valley. London: A. & C. Black, 1909. 1st edn. Lge 8vo. 51 cold plates. Few spots to foredge & prelims. Orig dec cloth gilt, upper jnt cracking.   *(Hollett)* £120 [≈ $230]

Widdess, J.D.H.
- A History of the Royal College of Physicians of Ireland 1654-1963. Edinburgh: 1963. xii,255 pp. 10 plates. Dw.
          (Whitehart) £25 [≈ $47]

Wiener, Norbert
- Cybernetics or Control and Communication in the Animal and the Machine. Paris: Herman & Cie, 1948. Tall 8vo. 194,[2] pp. Later buckram.   *(Karmiole)* $100 [≈ £52]

Wiggers, Carl
- Modern Aspects of the Circulation in Health and Disease. Phila: 1915. 1st edn. 376 pp. Ex-lib. Inner margs of title taped. Orig bndg.
          (Fye) $100 [≈ £52]

Wild Flowers and their Teachings ...
- See Howard, M.M.

Wilder, Alexander
- History of Medicine. A Brief Outline of Medical History from the Earliest Historic Period ... Augusta: 1904. 8vo. 946 pp. Frontis. Orig bndg. *(Goodrich)* $65 [≈ £33]

Wildman, Thomas
- A Treatise on the Management of Bees ... London: for the author, & sold by T. Cadell, 1768. 1st edn. 4to. xx,169 pp. 3 fldg plates. Title trifle foxed. Near contemp qtr calf, unsophisticated copy. *(Gough)* £395 [≈ $758]
- A Treatise on the Management of Bees ... London: 1778. 3rd edn. xx,325,16 pp. 3 fldg plates. Occas foxing. Mod leather backed bds.

(Whitehart) **£140 [≃ $268]**

Wilkins, John
- Mathematicall Magick ... London: M.F. for Sa: Gellibrand, 1648. 1st edn, 1st issue. 8vo. [xiv],295 pp. Lacks A1 blank. 33 text w'cut figs, 8 engvd plates in text. Title sl browned, sm marg tear. Calf antique. Wing W.2198.
(Bickersteth) **£550 [≃ $1,055]**

Wilkinson, Charles Henry
- Analytical Researches into the Properties of the Bath Waters ... Bath: ptd by Wood & Cunningham, B. Crosby, London, 1811. 1st edn. Sm 8vo. viii,148,[2] pp. Old wraps.
(Burmester) **£120 [≃ $230]**

Wilkinson, S.J.
- The British Tortrices. London: Van Voorst, 1859. 1st edn. viii,328 pp. 4 plates. Orig green cloth gilt.   *(Gough)* **£45 [≃ $86]**

Wilks, S. & Bettany, G.T.
- A Biographical History of Guy's Hospital. London: 1892. viii,500 pp. Plates. Occas foxing page edges.   *(Whitehart)* **£40 [≃ $76]**

Wilks, S. & Moxon, W.
- Lectures on Pathological Anatomy. London: 1875. 2nd edn. xxiii,672 pp. 7 plates. Sev marg pencil notes. Cloth, sl worn, inner hinge sl cracked.   *(Whitehart)* **£25 [≃ $47]**
- Lectures on Pathological Anatomy. London: 1889. 3rd edn. xx,672 pp. Cloth sl worn & dusty, sm label on spine, inner hinge cracked.
(Whitehart) **£28 [≃ $53]**
- Lectures on Pathological Anatomy. London: 1889. 3rd edn. xx,672 pp. Cloth backed bds, sl worn.   *(Whitehart)* **£25 [≃ $47]**

Willan, Robert
- On Vaccine Inoculation. London: 1806. 1st edn. 108,liv pp. 2 cold plates. Orig cloth backed mrbld bds, front outer hinge weak.
(Fye) **$500 [≃ £260]**

Willard, Emma
- A Treatise on the Motive Powers which produce the Circulation of the Blood. New York & London: 1846. 1st edn. 8vo. xiv,170,[6 ctlg] pp. S sm lib stamps. Orig cloth, hd of spine v sl bumped.
(Hemlock) **$275 [≃ £143]**

Willey, A.
- Zoological Results based on Material from New Britain, New Guinea, Loyalty Islands and elsewhere, collected 1895-97. London:

1898-1902. 6 parts. 4to. 830 pp. Map, 83 plates, text figs. Orig bds.
(Wheldon & Wesley) **£150 [≃ $287]**

William, Prince of Sweden
- Wild African Animals I Have Known. London: 1923. 4to. xiv,315 pp. 211 photo plates. Orig cloth, sl soiled & worn.
(Henly) **£22 [≃ $42]**

Williams, Archibald
- Telegraphy and Telephony. 1928. 1st edn. 340 pp. 30 photos, 88 ills. Orig bndg.
(New Wireless) **$55 [≃ £29]**

Williams, B.
- The Orchid-Grower's Manual ... London: 1877. 5th edn, rvsd & enlgd. Fldg cold frontis, num fldg plates. Mod half mor.
(Grayling) **£80 [≃ $153]**

Williams, C.B.
- Insect Migration. London: Collins New Naturalist, 1958. 1st edn. 8vo. xiii,235,6 pp. 8 cold & 16 plain plates. Orig cloth.
(Henly) **£18 [≃ $34]**

Williams, C.J.B.
- Principles of Medicine. An Elementary View of the Causes, Nature, Treatment, Diagnosis, and Prognosis of Diseases ... A New American from the Third London Edition. Phila: 1857. 8vo. 496 pp. Sheep, rubbed.
(Goodrich) **$95 [≃ £49]**

Williams, G.F.
- The Diamond Mines of South Africa. New York: 1906. 2 vols. Roy 8vo. xvii,359; xv,353 pp. 15 maps, 28 plates (3 cold), num text ills. Rec half mor, largely unopened.
(Henly) **£210 [≃ $403]**

Williams, J.
- The Natural History of the Mineral Kingdom. Edinburgh: Longman ..., 1810. 2nd edn. 2 vols. 8vo. xi,562; vi,597 pp. Engvd text figs. V.g. ex-lib. Contemp qtr leather.   *(Gemmary)* **$650 [≃ £338]**

Williams, J. Whitridge
- Obstetrics. New York: 1906. 1st edn, reprinted. 845 pp. 630 ills. Orig bndg.
(Fye) **$250 [≃ £130]**

Williams, Stephen
- American Medical Biography ... Greenfield: 1845. 1st edn. 664 pp. Ports. Orig cloth.
(Fye) **$175 [≃ £91]**

Williams, W.M.
- The Fuel of the Sun. London: 1870. xx,222 pp. Orig cloth.   *(Whitehart)* **£20 [≈ $38]**

Williamson, Hugh
- Observations on the Climate in Different Parts of America ... Being an Introductory Discourse to the History of North-Carolina. New York: Swords, 1811. 1st edn. 8vo. 199 pp. Some foxing. 19th c cloth, mor label.
        (Chapel Hill) **$400 [≈ £208]**

Williamson, R.T.
- Diseases of the Spinal Cord. Oxford: 1908. xi,432 pp. 7 plates, 183 text figs. Lib stamp on endpaper, half-title & title. Orig cloth, spine sl marked.   *(Whitehart)* **£25 [≈ $47]**
- Diseases of the Spinal Cord. London: 1911. 1st edn, 2nd imp. 432 pp. Orig bndg.
        (Fye) **$100 [≈ £52]**

Willich, A.F.M.
- Lectures on Diet and Regimen ... chiefly for the Use of Families ... Second Edition, improved and enlarged ... London: Longman & Rees, 1799. 8vo. [iv],708 pp,2 advt ff. Orig bds, uncut, new paper spine.
        (Bickersteth) **£160 [≈ $307]**
- Lectures on Diet and Regimen. London: 1809. 4th edn. xxiii,448 pp. Orig bds, new paper label.   *(Whitehart)* **£50 [≈ $95]**

Willis, Bailey
- East African Plateaus and Rift Valleys. Studies in Comparative Seismology ... Washington: Carnegie Inst, 1936. 1st edn. 4to. x,358 pp. Cold frontis, 73 plates, 16 text figs. Some marks & spots. Orig cloth, stained & marked, sl worn. Pres slip.
        (Bow Windows) **£75 [≈ $143]**

Willis, Thomas
- The London Practice of Physic ... London: for Thomas Basset & William Crooke, 1685. 1st edn. 8vo. [x],672,[16] pp. Errata leaf. Port frontis. Sl browning, some edges a bit ragged. New qtr calf.   *(Goodrich)* **$1,750 [≈ £911]**

Willius, Fredrick & Dry, Thomas
- A History of the Heart and Circulation. 1948. 1st edn. 456 pp. Orig bndg.
        (Fye) **$150 [≈ £78]**

Wilmer, William
- Atlas Fundus Oculi. New York: 1934. 1st edn. 100 chromolitho plates. Orig bndg.
        (Fye) **$250 [≈ £130]**

Wilson, A.
- The Flora of Westmorland ... London: 1938. 8vo. 413 pp. Fldg cold map in pocket, 37 plates. Orig cloth gilt.   *(Henly)* **£65 [≈ $124]**

Wilson, Dr. A.
- Wild Animals & Birds. Their Haunts and Habits. London: 1883. 2nd edn. 4to. Num engvd plates by J. Wolf & F. Specht, text engvs. Orig pict cloth gilt.
        (Grayling) **£45 [≈ $86]**

Wilson, E.H.
- The Lilies of Eastern Asia, a Monograph. London: (1925) 1929. 4to. xiv,110 pp. Frontis, 16 plates. Cloth.
        (Wheldon & Wesley) **£75 [≈ $143]**

Wilson, Edward
- Edward Wilson's Birds of the Atlantic. London: Blandford Press, 1967. 1st edn. 4to. 191 pp. 102 ills (60 cold). Dw (worn).
        (Parmer) **$95 [≈ £49]**

Wilson, Erasmus
- On Diseases of the Skin. London: 1847. 2nd edn. 482 pp. 7 hand cold ills. Orig bndg, backstrip loose.   *(Fye)* **$150 [≈ £78]**

Wilson, George
- Healthy Life and Healthy Dwellings: a Guide to Personal and Domestic Hygiene. London: Churchill, 1880. 1st edn. Half-title. Orig brown cloth.   *(Jarndyce)* **£48 [≈ $92]**
- The Life of the Hon. Henry Cavendish, including Abstracts of his more important Scientific Papers ... London: Cavendish Society, 1851. 1st edn. 8vo. xiv,478 pp. Frontis, port, 2 w'engvs. Contemp prize tree calf, hd of spine reprd.
        (Claude Cox) **£25 [≈ $47]**

Wilson, J.A.
- Memoir of George Wilson, MD, FRSE. Edinburgh: 1860. xii,536 pp. Frontis port (offset). Occas sl foxing. Orig cloth, sl stained, spine faded.   *(Whitehart)* **£25 [≈ $47]**
- Memoir of George Wilson. Edinburgh: 1860. xii,536 pp. Port, few text ills. Occas v sl foxing. Leather, gilt spine.
        (Whitehart) **£35 [≈ $67]**

Wilson, James
- The Natural History of Quadrupeds and Whales ... Edinburgh: Adam & Charles Black, 1837. 1st edn. 4to. (120) pp. 17 plates. Orig cloth, sl spotted.
        (Chapel Hill) **$110 [≈ £57]**

Wilson, O.S.
- The Larvae of the British Lepidoptera and their Food Plants. London: 1880. Roy 8vo. xxix,367 pp. 40 cold plates. Cloth, trifle used.
(Wheldon & Wesley) **£100 [≈ $191]**

Wilson, P. & Webb, G.W.
- Modern Gramaphones and Electrical Reproducers. 1929. 1st edn. 272 pp. 116 ills. Orig bndg.
(New Wireless) **$65 [≈ £33]**

Wilson, S.A. Kinnier
- Neurology. Baltimore: 1955. 2nd edn. 3 vols. 2160 pp. Num photo ills. Orig bndg.
(Fye) **$200 [≈ £104]**

Wilson, S.A.K. & Bruce, A.N.
- Neurology. London: 1954-55. 3 vols. 279 figs. Sev lib stamps, traces of label removal. Cloth, sl worn, vol 1 inner hinges sl weak.
(Whitehart) **£140 [≈ $268]**

Wilson, William
- Bryologia Britannica, containing the Mosses of Great Britain and Ireland ... London: 1855. 8vo. xx,445 pp. 61 cold plates. Orig cloth.
(Wheldon & Wesley) **£100 [≈ $191]**
- Bryologia Britannica; containing the Mosses of Great Britain and Ireland ... being a New (Third) Edition ... of the Muscologia Britannica of Messrs. Hooker and Taylor. London: Longman ..., 1855. xx,445 pp. 61 hand cold plates. Half mor gilt, a.e.g.
(Hollett) **£180 [≈ $345]**

Winckel, F.
- Diseases of Women. A Handbook for Physicians and Students. Translated by J.H. Williamson. Phila: 1887. 1st US edn. Text ills. Orig bndg, sl rubbed.
(Young's) **£45 [≈ $86]**

Wingate, Edmund
- Mr. Wingate's Arithmetick ... Revised by J. Kersey. London: 1699. [xii],544 pp. Occas foxing. Contemp mottled Cambridge calf, sl worn, sm old lib label on spine.
(Whitehart) **£95 [≈ $182]**
- Mr. Wingate's Arithmetick ... With New Supplement ... by George Shelley. London: for J. Phillips & J. & J. Knapton, 1726. 15th edn. 8vo. A few marg stains. New cloth.
(Stewart) **£120 [≈ $230]**

Winslow, Forbes
- On Obscure Diseases of the Brain, and Disorders of the Mind ... Phila: 1860. 1st Amer edn. 576 pp. Orig bndg, fine.

(Fye) **$250 [≈ £130]**

Winter, George
- Animal Magnetism. History of its Origin, Progress and Present State ... Bath: George Routh ..., [1801]. 1st edn. 8vo. [viii],223 pp. Orig bds, spine ends & bd edges worn.
(Burmester) **£150 [≈ $287]**

Winton, John G. & Millar, W.J.
- Modern Steam Practice and Engineering. A Guide to Approved Methods of Construction and the Principles relating thereto ... London: 1883. 2 vols. Sm 4to. xiii,1120 pp. 13 plates, ca 800 text figs. Half leather, rubbed, sl worn, sm cracks in hinges.
(Whitehart) **£55 [≈ $105]**
- Modern Steam Practice and Engineering: A Guide to Approved Methods of Construction and the Principles relating thereto ... London: Blackie, 1883. 1st edn. One vol in 2. Roy 8vo. xiii,[2],529; [1],530-1120 pp. 14 plates, ca 800 ills. Sl foxing. Orig half calf, rubbed & worn but strong.
(Fenning) **£75 [≈ $143]**

Wise, T.A.
- Commentary on the Hindu System of Medicine. Calcutta: Thacker, 1845. 8vo. xx, 431 pp. 2 plates. Contemp qtr calf & mrbld bds.
(Goodrich) **$395 [≈ £205]**

Wiseman, Richard
- Severall Chirurgicall Treatises. London: 1686. 2nd edn. Folio. [xvi],577,[13] pp. Inner marg of title & dedic leaf remargd. Rec half mor, new endpapers.
(Fye) **$1,000 [≈ £520]**

Wistar, Caspar
- A System of Anatomy ... Phila: Dobson, 1817. 2nd Amer edn. 2 vols. 8vo. 13 plates. text foxed. Orig calf, rubbed, jnts cracked.
(Goodrich) **$125 [≈ £65]**

Witherby, H.F., et al.
- The Handbook of British Birds. London: 1938-41. 1st edn. 5 vols. 8vo. 147 plates, text figs & maps. Orig cloth. Dws.
(Henly) **£100 [≈ $191]**
- The Handbook of British Birds. London: 1938-43. 1st edn. 5 vols. 8vo. 157 plates, text figs & maps. Cloth.
(Wheldon & Wesley) **£120 [≈ $230]**
- The Handbook of British Birds. London: 1946. 5 vols. 8vo. 157 cold & other plates. Cloth.
(Wheldon & Wesley) **£90 [≈ $172]**
- The Handbook of British Birds. London: 1948. 5 vols. 8vo. 157 cold & other plates. Cloth.
(Wheldon & Wesley) **£90 [≈ $172]**

- A Practical Handbook of British Birds. London: 1920. 2 vols. Cold & other plates. Orig bndg.   *(Grayling)* **£35 [≈ $67]**

Withering, William
- An Account of the Foxglove, and some of its Medical Uses ... London: 1949. Facs of the 1785 edn. One of 250. xxii,208 pp. Hand cold frontis, fldg plate. *(Whitehart)* **£60 [≈ $115]**
- An Arrangement of British Plants ... Sixth Edition. London: Cadell & Davies, 1818. 4 vols. 8vo. 34 plates. Contemp black half calf, mrbld bds.   *(Gough)* **£80 [≈ $153]**
- A Systematic Arrangement of British Plants. London: 1801. 4th edn. 4 vols. 8vo. 32 plates (1 cold). Half calf.
        (Wheldon & Wesley) **£40 [≈ $76]**

Withers, Thomas
- Observations on Chronic Weakness. York: Ward, 1777. 8vo. ix,[1],169 pp. Rec contemp style bds.   *(Goodrich)* **$165 [≈ £85]**

Wolf, Abraham
- A History of Science, Technology, and Philosophy in the 16th and 17th Centuries. London: 1935. xxvii,692 pp. Frontis, 316 ills. Orig cloth, sl dust stained, spine faded.
        (Whitehart) **£35 [≈ $67]**
- A History of Science, Technology, and Philosophy in the 16th and 17th Centuries. New York: Macmillan, 1935. xxvii,692 pp. 316 ills. Cloth.   *(Gemmary)* **$80 [≈ £41]**
- A History of Science, Technology, and Philosophy in the Eighteenth Century. New York: Macmillan, 1939. 8vo. 814 pp. 345 text figs. Cloth.   *(Gemmary)* **$75 [≈ £39]**
- A History of Science, Technology, and Philosophy in the Eighteenth Century. London: Allen, (1962). 2nd edn. 2 vols. 8vo. Plates. Cloth. Dws (sl soiled).
        (Bookpress) **$85 [≈ £44]**

Wolley, J.
- Ootheca Wolleyana: an Illustrated Catalogue of the Collection of Birds' Eggs ... London: 1864-1907. 2 vols. Roy 8vo. Map, port, 23 cold & 14 plain plates. New cloth.
        (Wheldon & Wesley) **£500 [≈ $959]**

Wolley-Dod, A.H.
- Flora of Sussex. Hastings: 1937. 1st edn. 8vo. lxxiii,571 pp. 2 maps (1 in pocket), 6 plates. Top crnr nibbled by a mouse, not affecting text. Orig cloth.   *(Henly)* **£18 [≈ $34]**
- Flora of Sussex. Hastings: 1937. 1st edn. 8vo. lxxiii,571 pp. 2 maps (1 in pocket), 6 plates. Cloth.   *(Henly)* **£36 [≈ $69]**

Wood, Alexander
- Thomas Young. Natural Philosopher 1773-1829 ... completed by Frank Oldham ... Cambridge: UP, 1954. 1st edn. 8vo. xx,355 pp. Text ills. Orig cloth. Dw.
        (Frew Mackenzie) **£25 [≈ $47]**

Wood, Casey A.
- The Fundus Oculi of Birds especially as viewed by the Ophthalmoscope. Chicago: 1917. 180 pp. 61 cold ills on plates, 145 text figs. Traces of label removal. Sm marg water stain. Cloth, sl marked.
        (Whitehart) **£85 [≈ $163]**
- An Introduction to the Literature of Vertebrate Zoology. Hildesheim, 1974. Reprint of the Oxford 1931 edn. Roy 8vo. xix,643 pp. Cloth.
        (Wheldon & Wesley) **£55 [≈ $105]**

Wood, E.J.
- Giants and Dwarfs. London: 1868. xii,472 pp. Orig cloth, sl faded, spine darkened, new endpapers.   *(Whitehart)* **£40 [≈ $76]**

Wood, H.C.
- A Study of the Nature and Mechanism of Fever. Washington: 1875. lii,45 pp. Later cloth. Sgnd by the author.
        (Whitehart) **£25 [≈ $47]**

Wood, J.M.
- Natal Plants. Descriptions and Figures of Natal Indigenous Plants, with Notes on their Distribution, Economic Value, Native Names ... Durban: 1899-1912. 6 vols in the orig 22 parts. 4to. 600 plates (1 in facs). Wraps, some sl used. *(Wheldon & Wesley)* **£500 [≈ $959]**

Wood, John George
- Common British Beetles. London: Routledge, [ca 1870]. 12mo. 174 pp. 12 cold plates. Orig pict brown cloth gilt, fine.
        (Gough) **£40 [≈ $76]**
- The Common Moths of England. London: Routledge, [ca 1880]. 187 pp. 12 cold plates, num text ills. V occas sl spotting. Orig elab pict blue cloth gilt.   *(Gough)* **£30 [≈ $57]**
- The Common Objects of the Country. London: Routledge, 1858. 1st edn. Fcap 8vo. iv,182, [vi] pp. Cold plates (Edmund Evans), text ills. Orig gilt dec cloth, v sl rubbed, sl shaken.   *(Ash)* **£50 [≈ $95]**
- Common Objects of the Microscope. London: Routledge, [ca 1870]. 12mo. 188 pp. 12 cold plates, sev text ills. Sl spotting. Orig pict red cloth gilt, trifle faded.
        (Ash) **£35 [≈ $67]**

- Common Objects of the Microscope. London: [ca 1875]. Cr 8vo. iv,132 pp. Advt endpapers. 12 plates, text ills. Pict bds.
(Henly) **£28 [≈ $53]**
- The Common Shells of the Sea-Shore. London: Warne, 1865. 1st edn. 12mo. iv,132 pp. 12 hand cold plates. Orig pict green cloth gilt, a.e.g., fine.   *(Ash)* **£45 [≈ $86]**
- The Fresh and Salt-Water Aquarium. London: Routledge, [ca 1870]. viii,182 pp. 3 plain & 8 cold plates. Occas sl spotting. Orig pict green cloth gilt.   *(Ash)* **£40 [≈ $76]**
- The Natural History of Man ... London: 1870. Lge thick 8vo. Num w'engvd ills. Minor spots, 1 sm tear. Half calf.
(Bow Windows) **£75 [≈ $143]**

Wood, Neville
- British Song Birds ... London: John W. Parker, 1836. 1st edn. 12mo. xii,411 pp. Contemp blue cloth.   *(Gough)* **£50 [≈ $95]**

Wood, P.
- Diseases of the Heart and Circulation. London: (1956) 1963. 2nd edn. xxxviii,1005 pp. Num text ills & diags. Orig bndg.
(Whitehart) **£40 [≈ $76]**
- Diseases of the Heart and Circulation. London: (1968) 1969. 3rd edn. xlvii,1164 pp. Num ills. Orig bndg. *(Whitehart)* **£25 [≈ $47]**

Wood, T. & Pycraft, W.P.
- The British Bird Book. London: 1921. Cr 4to. xvi,269 pp. 44 plates (20 cold), num text figs. Orig cloth.
(Wheldon & Wesley) **£35 [≈ $67]**

Wood, T.W.
- Curiosities of Entomology. London: Groombridge, [ca 1870]. 1st edn. 64 pp. 10 chromolitho plates. Some foxing to text. Orig elab dec blue cloth gilt, a.e.g., fine. Anon.
(Gough) **£70 [≈ $134]**

Wood, W.
- General Conchology: or, a Description of Shells arranged according to the Linnean System. Vol. 1 [all published]. London: 1815. 8vo. [iv],7, lxi,246 pp. 60 (1-59, 4*) hand cold plates. Half mor, trifle rubbed.
(Wheldon & Wesley) **£300 [≈ $575]**
- General Conchology; or a Description of Shells, arranged according to the Linnean System. Volume 1 [all published]. London: 1815. iv,lxi, 7,246 pp. 60 hand cold plates. Orig bds, rebacked. *(Baldwin)* **£190 [≈ $364]**
- Illustrations of the Linnaean Genera of Insects. London: 1821. 2 vols. 12mo. 86 hand cold plates. Orig bds, rebacked.
(Wheldon & Wesley) **£185 [≈ $355]**
- Index Entomologicus; or, a Complete Illustrated Catalogue ... of the Lepidopterous Insects of Great Britain. New and Revised Edition by J.O. Westwood. London: 1854. Roy 8vo. vii,ii,298,21 pp. 59 hand cold plates. New cloth.
(Wheldon & Wesley) **£150 [≈ $287]**
- Zoography; or, the Beauties of Nature displayed in Select Descriptions from the Animal, and Vegetable, with Additions from the Mineral, Kingdom ... London: 1807. 3 vols. 8vo. 60 plates. Contemp calf, reprd.
(Wheldon & Wesley) **£170 [≈ $326]**

Woodall, Percy H.
- Intra-Pelvic Technic or Manipulative Surgery of the Pelvic Organs. Kansas City: [1926]. 1st edn. 8vo. 198,[iii] pp. Text figs. Orig cloth.   *(Bickersteth)* **£22 [≈ $42]**

Woodforde, J.
- A Catalogue of the Indigenous Phenogamic Plants growing in the Neighbourhood of Edinburgh ... Edinburgh: 1824. 12mo. xi,86 pp. A few lib stamps, sl foxing. Orig bds, uncut, trifle worn, lacks backstrip.
(Wheldon & Wesley) **£50 [≈ $95]**

Woodhouse, R.
- The Principles of Analytical Calculation. Cambridge: 1803. 1st edn. [3],xxxiv,219 pp. Title sl browned at edges. Contemp tree calf, rebacked.   *(Whitehart)* **£180 [≈ $345]**
- A Treatise on Plane and Spherical Trigonometry. Cambridge: 1822. 4th edn. v,v, [1],264 pp. Mod old-style cloth, uncut.
(Whitehart) **£25 [≈ $47]**

Woods, George
- An Account of the Past and Present State of the Isle of Man ... London: for Robert Baldwin & William Blackwood, 1811. Large Paper. 365, advt pp. Hand cold map (recto soiled, a faint blind stamp). 1st few ff sl damp stained. Lib qtr cloth, uncut.
(Hollett) **£140 [≈ $268]**

Woods, James
- Elements and Influence of the Weather ... including a Brief Memoir of the late Lieut. George Mackenzie of the Perth Royal Militia with a Synopsis of his Discoveries ... London: Hodson, 1861. 8vo. xvi,114 pp. Fldg plate. Sm lib stamps. Orig cloth.
(Lamb) **£20 [≈ $38]**

Woodward, Horace B.
- Geology of East Somerset and the Bristol Coal-Fields ... Memoirs of the Geological Survey. London: Longmans, Green, 1876. x,271 pp. Hand cold map frontis, 8 plates (some cold). Few blind stamps. Orig cloth gilt, faded, piece missing from hd of spine.
(Hollett) **£55 [≈ $105]**
- The Geology of England and Wales: a Concise Account of the Lithological Characters ... London: 1876. xx,476 pp. Fldg geol map, 26 text w'cuts. Orig cloth, spine sl marked. *(Whitehart)* **£18 [≈ $34]**
- The History of the Geological Society of London. London: 1907. xix,336 pp. Ills. Foxed. Orig cloth, sl soiled.
(Baldwin) **£33 [≈ $63]**
- The History of the Geological Society of London. London: 1908. xix,336 pp. Ills. Orig cloth. *(Baldwin)* **£40 [≈ $76]**
- Stanford's Geological Atlas of Great Britain. London: 1904. Cr 8vo. x,139 pp. Cold geological map, cold index, 34 dble page maps, 16 plates, 17 text figs. Cloth, recased.
(Henly) **£48 [≈ $92]**

Woodward, John
- An Essay Toward a Natural History of the Earth and Terrestrial Bodies. London: Wilkin, 1695. 1st edn. 8vo. [xvi],277,[2] pp. Contemp calf, lacks free endpapers.
(Bookpress) **$475 [≈ £247]**

Woodward, S.P.
- A Manual of the Mollusca. London: 1851-56. 8vo. xvi,486 pp. Frontis, map, 24 plates, 272 text figs. Sl foxing. Cloth.
(Wheldon & Wesley) **£20 [≈ $38]**

Wooldridge, S.W. & Goldring, F.
- The Weald. London: Collins New Naturalist, 1953. 1st edn. 8vo. x,276,2 pp. 16 cold & 24 plain plates. Orig cloth. *(Henly)* **£22 [≈ $42]**

Wooster, David
- Alpine Plants ... London: 1872. 1st edn. 8vo. viii,152 pp. 54 cold plates. Sl damp stain hd of some plates. Orig bndg, a.e.g., spine ends & jnts torn & reprd, inner hinges strained.
(Bow Windows) **£80 [≈ $153]**
- Alpine Plants ... London: Bell & Daldy, 1872-74. 1st edn. 2 vols. 108 chromolithos. Some foxing, mostly light, affecting some plates. Orig pict green cloth gilt, a.e.g.
(Gough) **£275 [≈ $527]**
- Alpine Plants ... London (& Driffield: Benjamin Fawcett) 1874. Vol 1 2nd edn. 2 vols. Roy 8vo. 108 cold plates. Sm water stain

in inner crnrs of 23 plates. Orig cloth, rebacked. *(Wheldon & Wesley)* **£200 [≈ $383]**

Wootton, A.C.
- Chronicles of Pharmacy. London: 1910. 2 vols. xii,428; [viii],332 pp. Sev ills. Lacks half-titles. Orig cloth.
(Whitehart) **£50 [≈ $95]**

Worlidge, John
- Vinetum Britannicum: or a Treatise of Cider, and other Wines and Drinks extracted from Fruits growing in this Kingdom ... Third impression, much enlarged. London: for Thomas Dring, 1691. 8vo. 2 frontis, 3 plates. Contemp sheep, spine sl rubbed. Wing W.3610. *(Ximenes)* **$1,250 [≈ £651]**

Worms, Henry de
- The Earth and Its Mechanism: being an Account of the Various Proofs of the Rotation of the Earth. With a Description of the Instruments used in the Experimental Demonstrations ... London: 1862. 1st edn. 8vo. xiv,296 pp. Num text figs. Orig cloth, sm slit in 1 jnt. *(Bickersteth)* **£65 [≈ $124]**

Wright, Horace J. & Walter, P.
- Beautiful Flowers and How to Grow Them ... London: Jack, 1909. 2 vols. 4to. 100 cold plates, text ills. Orig green cloth gilt.
(Beech) **£45 [≈ $86]**

Wright, J.
- The Fruit-Growers Guide. London: 1924. New & rvsd edn. 2 vols. Imperial 8vo. 24 cold plates, num text figs. V sl staining at start of vol 2. Orig cloth, trifle used, cvrs trifle stained. *(Wheldon & Wesley)* **£65 [≈ $124]**

Wright, Lewis
- The Illustrated Book of Poultry. London: Cassell, Petter & Galpin, [1873]. 1st edn. 4to. viii,591 pp. 50 cold plates. Sl foxing, mainly at ends. Contemp half mor gilt, trifle rubbed.
(Wheldon & Wesley) **£650 [≈ $1,247]**
- The Illustrated Book of Polutry ... New Edition, Revised ... . London: Cassell & Co, 1890. 4to. viii,591 pp. 50 chromolitho plates, num plain plates & text ills. V occas sl marg spotting. Contemp brown half mor gilt, fine.
(Gough) **£900 [≈ $1,727]**

Wright, R.P. (ed.)
- The Standard Cyclopedia of Modern Agriculture and Rural Economy. By the Most Distinguished Authorities and Specialists ... London: 1908-11. 12 vols. 8vo. 33 cold & 188 other plates, num text ills, 3 cold models with

overlays. Orig pict cloth, sl used.
(Bow Windows) **£50 [≈ $95]**

Wrigley, John
- Notes on the Bird Life of Formby. Liverpool: Rockliff Bros, for private circulation, [1893]. Sm 4to. 61 pp. 4 plates. Orig cloth, rather rubbed & marked. *(Gough)* **£100 [≈ $191]**

Wurtz, Ad.
- The Atomic Theory. Translated by E. Cleminshaw. London: International Scientific Series, 1880. 1st English edn. viii,339 pp. Fldg plate at end. Orig cloth.
(Whitehart) **£25 [≈ $47]**

Wyeth, John
- A Text-Book on Surgery, General, Operative, and Mechanical. New York: Appleton, 1887. 8vo. Num ills. Orig sheep, rebacked.
(Goodrich) **$395 [≈ £205]**

Wyman, Morrill
- Autumnal Catarrh (Hayfever) with Three Maps. New York: 1872. 1st edn. 173 pp. 3 maps. Orig bndg, water stain affecting hd & ft of front cvr & extreme edge of some ff.
(Fye) **$150 [≈ £78]**

Wynter, Andrew
- Subtle Brains and Lissom Fingers. being Some of the Chisel-Marks of our Industrial and Scientific Progress. And Other Papers. London: Robert Hardwicke, 1863. 1st coll edn. 8vo. vii,[1],446,[1] pp. Orig cloth, bndg discold. *(Fenning)* **£35 [≈ $67]**

Wynter, H. & Turner, A.
- Scientific Instruments. New York: Scribner's, 1975. 4to. 239 pp. 285 ills. Cloth. Dw.
(Gemmary) **$300 [≈ £156]**

Wythes, J.H.
- The Microscopist; or A Complete Manual on the Use of the Microscope. Phila: 1853. 2nd edn. 12mo. viii,212,4 pp. 2 plates, 63 text ills. Cloth gilt, spine faded. *(Henly)* **£32 [≈ $61]**

Yarrell, William
- A History of British Fishes. London: Van Voorst, 1836. 1st edn. 2 vols. Roy 8vo. Ca 400 ills. Some foxing of prelims. Endpapers replaced. Contemp calf gilt, rebacked.
(Ash) **£250 [≈ $479]**
- A History of British Fishes ... Second Edition. London: Van Voorst, 1841. 2 vols. 8vo. 500 w'engvs. Orig cloth, uncut.
(Claude Cox) **£75 [≈ $143]**

- A History of British Fishes. Third Edition, edited by Sir John Richardson. London: 1859. 2 vols. 8vo. Port, 522 w'engvs. Sm blind stamp on title & port. Green mor elab gilt, a.e.g., by Hayday, trifle rubbed.
(Wheldon & Wesley) **£95 [≈ $182]**

Yates, Raymond Francis
- ABC of Television or Seeing by Radio. 1929. 1st edn. 210 pp. 21 photos, 78 ills. Orig bndg.
(New Wireless) **$145 [≈ £75]**

Yates, William & Maclean, Charles
- A View of the Science of Life; on the Principles established in the Elements of Medicine, of the late celebrated John Brown ... Phila: 1797. 8vo. 232 pp. Foxing. Old bds, rebacked. *(Goodrich)* **$75 [≈ £39]**

Yerkes, R.M. & A.W.
- The Great Apes. New Haven, Conn.: 1929. Roy 8vo. xix,652 pp. 172 ills. Cloth.
(Wheldon & Wesley) **£50 [≈ $95]**

Yonge, C.M.
- Oysters. London: Collins New Naturalist, 1960. 1st edn. 8vo. xiv,209 pp. 15 plates, 72 text figs. Orig cloth. Dw. *(Henly)* **£22 [≈ $42]**
- The Sea Shore. London: Collins New Naturalist, 1949. 1st edn. 8vo. xvi,311 pp. 40 cold & 32 plain plates. Orig cloth.
(Henly) **£15 [≈ $28]**

Youatt, William
- Cattle; their Breeds, Management and Diseases; with an Index. London: Baldwin & Cradock, 1838. 8vo. viii,600 pp. Title vignette, w'engvs. Sl spotting. Contemp half calf, rubbed, lacks 1 label.
(Claude Cox) **£35 [≈ $67]**
- The Horse; with a Treatise on Draught; and a Copious Index. London: Baldwin & Craddock, 1831. 1st edn. 8vo. 472 pp. Text ills. Orig cloth, some wear & soil, crnrs bumped. *(Chapel Hill)* **£175 [≈ $91]**
- The Horse ... Revised and Enlarged by E.N. Gabriel. London: Longman ..., 1860. x,601,2 advt pp. W'cut ills. Pp 13-18 torn at top, not affecting text. Orig cloth, spine sl split at hd.
(Bookline) **£45 [≈ $86]**
- Sheep, their Breeds, Management, and Diseases ... [with] the Mountain Shepherd's Manual. New Edition. London: Edward Low, 1859. 8vo. viii,568, 36,12 advt pp. W'cuts. Signs of use. Rec bds.
(Fenning) **£28.50 [≈ $55]**

Youden, Y.Y.
Computer Literature Bibliography 1946-1963.
1965. National Bureau of Standards, 1965.
1st edn. 463 pp. Orig bndg.
                    (New Wireless) **$85 [≈ £45]**

Youle, Joseph
- An Inaugural Dissertation on Respiration ...
New York: T. & J. Swords, 1793. 8vo. 39,[1]
pp. Mod qtr calf.   *(Hemlock)* **$175 [≈ £91]**

Young, Arthur
- The Farmer's Guide in Hiring and Stocking
Farms ... By the Author of the Farmer's
Letters. London: for W. Strahan ..., 1770. 1st
edn. 2 vols. 8vo. Advt leaf at end of vol 1. 10
plates in vol 2. Orig bds, uncut, new paper
spines & labels. Anon.
                  (Bickersteth) **£220 [≈ $422]**
- General View of the Agriculture of the
County of Sussex; with Observations on the
Means of its Improvement. London: 1793.
4to. 97 pp. Fldg hand cold map, 2 hand cold
plates (cropped with some loss of text). Mor
backed bds.   *(Henly)* **£110 [≈ $211]**
- Rural Oeconomy. London: for T. Becket,
1770. 1st edn. Demy 8vo. [ii],520 pp. Sl
browning. Contemp calf, armorial device,
rebacked. Anon.   *(Ash)* **£200 [≈ $383]**

Young, Arthur
- Axial Polarity of Man's World-Embodied
Ideas and its Teachings. London: Kegan Paul
..., 1887. 1st edn. 4to. 242,[1] pp. Sl foxing.
Orig cloth, spine darkened.
                   (Chapel Hill) **$75 [≈ £39]**

Young, Francis C.
- Every Man His Own Mechanic. A Complete
and Comprehensive Guide to Every
Description of Constructive and Decorative
Work ... Appendix ... Tenth Edition.
London: 1893. Thick 8vo. x,924, [14 advt]
pp. 3 lge sheets, 850 ills. Few sm tears &
marks. Orig dec cloth gilt.
                   (Bow Windows) **£40 [≈ $76]**

Young, John Radford
- Modern Scepticism, viewed in relation to
Modern Science ... Colenso, Huxley, Lyell,
and Darwin ... Origin of Species. London:
Saunders, otley, 1865. 1st edn. 8vo. xvi,229
pp, advt leaf. Orig cloth, hd of spine sl worn.
                   (Bickersteth) **£185 [≈ $355]**
- Theory and Solution of Algebraical
Equations. London: 1843. 2nd edn. xxiii,476

pp. A few pp underlined in red ink. New
cloth.   *(Whitehart)* **£40 [≈ $76]**

Zaanen, A.C.
- Linear Analysis. Measure and Integral,
Banach and Hilbert Space, Linear Integral
Equations. New York: 1953. vii,601 pp. Sm
lib stamps. Inner hinge cracked but firm.
                   (Whitehart) **£25 [≈ $47]**

Zeller, H.
- Wild Flowers of the Holy Land. London:
1883. 3rd edn. Roy 8vo. xiv pp. 54 cold
plates. Front free endpaper removed, occas v
sl foxing. Orig cloth.
                (Wheldon & Wesley) **£85 [≈ $163]**

Zenneck, J.
- Wireless Telegraphy. 1915. 1st English edn.
443 pp. 470 ills. Orig bndg.
                   (New Wireless) **$55 [≈ £28]**

Zilboorg, Gregory & Henry, George W.
- A History of Medical Psychology. New York:
W.W. Norton, 1941. 8vo. Plates. Orig bndg.
                   (Georges) **£35 [≈ $67]**

Zittel, K.A. von
- History of Geology & Palaeontology to the
End of the Nineteenth Century. London:
1901. xiii, 562 pp. 13 plates. Orig cloth.
                   (Baldwin) **£65 [≈ $124]**
- History of Geology and Palaeontology.
Translated by M.O. Gordon. London: (1901)
1962. xvi,562 pp. Orig bndg.
                (Wheldon & Wesley) **£19 [≈ $36]**
- History of Geology & Palaeontology to the
End of the Nineteenth Century. London:
(1901) 1962. Reprint. xiii,562 pp. 13 plates.
Orig cloth.   *(Baldwin)* **£25 [≈ $47]**

The Zoist ...
- The Zoist: A Journal of Cerebral Physiology
& Mesmerism, and their Applications to
Human Welfare. London: Bailliere; Paris ...
Leipzig ... London, 1844-56. 13 vols, all
published. 8vo. Over 6200 pp. Frontis port,
16 plates, fldg diag. Some browning. Half
calf.   *(Rootenberg)* **$5,000 [≈ £2,604]**

Zornlin, Rosina M.
- Recreations in Geology. London: John W.
Parker, 1839. 1st edn. Sm 8vo. lxi,224 pp.
Frontis, text figs. Orig cloth.
                   (Bickersteth) **£38 [≈ $72]**

Catalogue Booksellers Contributing to IRBP

The booksellers who have provided catalogues during 1990 specifically for the purpose of compiling the various titles in the *IRBP* series, and from whose catalogues books have been selected, are listed below in alphabetical order of the abbreviation employed for each. This listing is therefore a complete key to the booksellers contributing to the series as a whole; only a proportion of the listed names is represented in this particular subject volume.

The majority of these booksellers issue periodic catalogues free, on request, to potential customers. Sufficient indication of the type of book handled by each bookseller can be gleaned from the individual book entries set out in the main body of this work and in the companion titles in the series.

Agvent	=	Charles Agvent, R.D.2, Box 377A, Mertztown, PA 19539, U.S.A. (215 682 4750)
Alphabet	=	Alphabet Bookshop, 145 Main Street West, Port Colborne, Ontario L3K 3V3, Canada (416 834 5323)
Antic Hay	=	Antic Hay Rare Books, P.O. Box 2185, Asbury Park, NJ 07712, U.S.A. (201 774 4590)
Any Amount	=	Any Amount of Books, 62 Charing Cross Road, London WC2H 0BB, England (071 240 8140)
Ars Artis	=	Ars Artis, 31 Abberbury Road, Oxford OX4 4ET, England (0865 770714)
Ars Libri	=	Ars Libri, Ltd., 560 Harrison Avenue, Boston, Massachusetts 02118, U.S.A. (617 357 5212)
Ash	=	Ash Rare Books, 25 Royal Exchange, London EC3V 3LP, England (071 626 2665)
Baldwin	=	Stuart A. Baldwin, Fossil Hall, Boars Tye Road, Silver End, Witham, Essex CM8 3QA, England (0376 83502)
Bates & Hindmarch	=	Bates and Hindmarch, Antiquarian Bookseller, Fishergate, Boroughbridge, North Yorkshire Y05 9AL, England (0423 324258)
Beech	=	John Beech Rare Books, 63 Station Road, Histon, Cambridge CB4 4LQ, England (0223 232210)
Bell	=	Peter Bell, Bookseller & Publisher, 4 Brandon Street, Edinburgh EH3 5DX, Scotland (031 556 2198)
Bernett	=	F.A. Bernett Inc., 2001 Palmer Avenue, Larchmont, N.Y. 10538, U.S.A. (914 834 3026)
Between the Covers	=	Between the Covers, 575 Collings Avenue, Collingswood, NJ 08107, U.S.A. (609 869 0512)
Bickersteth	=	David Bickersteth, 4 South End, Bassingbourn, Royston, Hertfordshire SG8 5NG, England (0763 45619)
Black Sun	=	Black Sun Books, P.O. Box 7916 - F.D.R. Sta., New York, New York 10150-1915, U.S.A. (212 688 6622)
Blakeney	=	Adam Blakeney, Apartment 8, 59 Devonshire Street, London W1N 1LT, England (071 323 0937)
Book Block	=	The Book Block, 8 Loughlin Avenue, Cos Cob, Connecticut 06807, U.S.A. (203 629 2990)
Bookline	=	Bookline, 35 Farranfad Road, Downpatrick BT30 8NH, Northern Ireland (039687 712)
Bookmark	=	Bookmark, Children's Books, Fortnight, Wick Down, Broad Hinton, Swindon, Wiltshire SN4 9NR, England (0793 731693)
Bookpress	=	The Bookpress Ltd., Post Office Box KP, Williamsburg, Virginia 23187, U.S.A. (804 229 1260)

Boswell	=	Boswell Books and Prints, 44 Great Russell Street, London WC1B 3PA, England (071 580 7200) or Boswell Books and Prints, 2261 Market Street, Suite 288, San Francisco, CA 94114, U.S.A. (415 431 3021)
Bow Windows	=	Bow Windows Book Shop, 128 High Street, Lewes, East Sussex BN7 1XL, England (0273 480780)
Bromer	=	Bromer Booksellers, 607 Boylston Street, at Copley Square, Boston, MA 02116, U.S.A. (617 247 2818)
Paul Brown	=	Paul Brown, 3 Melbourne Terrace, Melbourne Grove, London SE22 8RE, England (081 299 4195)
Buccleuch	=	Buccleuch Books, 40 Buccleuch Street, Edinburgh EH8 9LP, Scotland (031 6681353)
Buckley	=	Brian & Margaret Buckley, 11 Convent Close, Kenilworth, Warwickshire CV8 2FQ, England (0926 55223)
Burmester	=	James Burmester, Manor House Farmhouse, North Stoke, Bath BA1 9AT, England (0272 327265)
Central Africana	=	Central Africana, The Coach House, Serpentine Road, Sevenoaks TN13 3XP, England (071 242 3131)
Chapel Hill	=	Chapel Hill Rare Books, P.O. Box 456, Carrboro, NC 27510, U.S.A. (919 929 8351)
Clark	=	Robert Clark, 6a King Street, Jericho, Oxford OX2 6DF, England (0865 52154)
Clearwater	=	Clearwater Books, 19 Matlock Road, Ferndown, Wimborne, Dorset BH22 8QT, England (0202 893263)
Claude Cox	=	Claude Cox, The White House, Kelsale, Saxmundham, Suffolk IP17 2PQ, England (0728 602786)
Dalian	=	Dalian Books, David P. Williams, 81 Albion Drive, London Fields, London E8 4LT, England (071 249 1587)
de Beaumont	=	Robin de Beaumont, 25 Park Walk, Chelsea, London SW10 0AJ, England (071 352 3440)
Dermont	=	Joseph A. Dermont, 13 Arthur Street, P.O. Box 654, Onset, MA 02558, U.S.A. (508 295 4760)
Dramatis Personae	=	Dramatis Personae, 71 Lexington Avenue, New York, New York 10010, U.S.A. (212 679 3705)
Dyke	=	Martin Dyke, 4 Gordon Road, Clifton, Bristol BS8 1AP, England (0272 742090)
Edrich	=	I.D. Edrich, 17 Selsdon Road, London E11 2QF, England (081 989 9541)
Egret	=	Egret Books, 6 Priory Place, Wells, Somerset BA5 1SP, England (0749 679312)
Ellis	=	Peter Ellis, 31 Museum Street, London WC1A 1LH, England (071 637 5862)
Emerald Isle	=	Emerald Isle Books, 539 Antrim Road, Belfast BT15 3BU, Northern Ireland (0232 370798)
Fenning	=	James Fenning, 12 Glenview, Rochestown Avenue, Dun Laoghaire, County Dublin, Eire (01 857855)
Finch	=	Simon Finch Rare Books, Clifford Chambers, 10 New Bond Street, London W1Y 9PF, England (071 499 0974)
First Issues	=	First Issues Ltd, 17 Alfoxton Avenue, London N15 3DD, England (081 881 6931)
Frew Mackenzie	=	Frew Mackenzie plc, 106 Great Russell Street, London WC1B 3NA, England (071 580 2311)
Fye	=	W. Bruce Fye, Antiquarian Medical Books, 1607 North Wood Avenue, Marshfield, Wisconsin 54449, U.S.A. (715 384 8128)
Gage	=	Gage Postal Books, P.O. Box 105, Westcliff-on-Sea, Essex SS0 8EQ, England (0702 715133)

Gaskell	=	Roger Gaskell, 17 Ramsey Road, Warboys, Cambridgeshire PE17 2RW, England (0487 823059)
Gemmary	=	The Gemmary, Inc, PO Box 816, Redondo Beach, CA 90277, U.S.A. (213 372 5969)
Georges	=	Georges, 52 Park Street, Bristol BS1 5JN, England (0272 276602)
Glyn's	=	Glyn's Books, 4 Bryn Draw Terrace, Wrexham, Clwyd LL13 7DF, Wales (0978 364473)
Goodrich	=	James Tait Goodrich, Antiquarian Books & Manuscripts, 214 Everett Place, Englewood, New Jersey 07631, U.S.A. (201 567 0199)
Gough	=	Simon Gough Books, 5 Fish Hill, Holt, Norfolk, England (026371 2650)
Grayling	=	David A.H. Grayling, Lyvennet, Crosby Ravensworth, Penrith, Cumbria CA10 3JP, England (09315 282)
Green Meadow	=	Green Meadow Books, Kinoulton, Nottingham NG12 3EN, England (0949 81723)
Gretton	=	John R. Gretton, 5 Quebec Road, Dereham, Norfolk NR19 2DP, England (0362 692707)
Hadley	=	Peter J. Hadley, 20th Century Books, 132 Corve Street, Ludlow, Shropshire SY8 2PG, England (0584 874441)
Halsey	=	Alan Halsey, The Poetry Bookshop, 22 Broad Street, Hay-on-Wye, Via Hereford HR3 5DB, England (0497 820 305)
Hannas	=	Torgrim Hannas, 29a Canon Street, Winchester, Hampshire SO23 9JJ, England (0962 862730)
Hatchwell	=	Richard Hatchwell, The Old Rectory, Little Somerford, Chippenham, Wiltshire SN15 5JW, England (0666 823261)
Hazeldene	=	Hazeldene Bookshop, A.H. & L.G. Elliot, 61 Renshaw Street, Liverpool L1 2SJ, England (051 708 8780)
Hemlock	=	Hemlock Books, 170 Beach 145th Street, Neponsit, New York 11694, U.S.A. (718 318 0737)
Henly	=	John Henly, Bookseller, Brooklands, Walderton, Chichester, West Sussex PO18 9EE, England (0705 631426)
Heritage	=	Heritage Book Shop, Inc., 8540 Melrose Avenue, Los Angeles, California 90069, U.S.A. (213 659 3674)
High Latitude	=	High Latitude, P.O. Box 11254, Bainbridge Island, WA 98110, U.S.A. (206 598 3454)
Hollett	=	R.F.G. Hollett and Son, 6 Finkle Street, Sedbergh, Cumbria LA10 5BZ, England (05396 20298)
Holmes	=	David J. Holmes, 230 South Broad Street, Third Floor, Philadelphia, Pennsylvania 19102, U.S.A. (215 735 1083)
Horowitz	=	Glenn Horowitz, 141 East 44th Street, Suite 808, New York, New York 10017, U.S.A. (212 557 1381)
Houle	=	George Houle, 7260 Beverly Boulevard, Los Angeles, California 90036, U.S.A. (213 937 5858)
Humber	=	Humber Books, 688 Beverley Road, Hull, North Humberside HU6 7JH, England (0482 802239)
James	=	Marjorie James, The Old School, Oving, Chichester, West Sussex PO20 6DG, England (0243 781354)
Janus	=	Janus Books, Post Office Box 40787, Tucson, Arizona 85717, U.S.A. (602 881 8192)
Jarndyce	=	Jarndyce, Antiquarian Booksellers, 46 Great Russell Street, Bloomsbury, London WC1B 3PA, England (071 631 4220)
C.R. Johnson	=	C.R. Johnson, 21 Charlton Place, London N1 8AQ, England (071 354 1077)
Michael Johnson	=	Michael Johnson Books, Oak Lodge, Kingsway, Portishead, Bristol BS20 8HW, England (0272 843798)

Karmiole	=	Kenneth Karmiole, Bookseller, 1225 Santa Monica Mall, Santa Monica, California 90401, U.S.A. (213 451 4342)
King	=	John K. King, P.O. Box 33363, Detroit, Michigan 48232-5363, U.S.A. (313 961 0622)
Lamb	=	R.W. & C.R. Lamb, Talbot House, 158 Denmark Rd., Lowestoft, Suffolk NR32 2EL, England (0502 564306)
Larkhill	=	Larkhill Books, Larkhill House, Tetbury, Gloucestershire GL8 8SY, England (0666 502343)
Lewis	=	John Lewis, 35 Stoneham Street, Coggeshall, Essex CO6 1UH, England (0376 561518)
Lewton	=	L.J. Lewton, Old Station House, Freshford, Bath BA3 6EQ, England (0225 723351)
Limestone Hills	=	Limestone Hills Book Shop, P.O. Box 1125, Glen Rose, Texas 76043, U.S.A. (817 897 4991)
Lloyd-Roberts	=	Tom Lloyd-Roberts, Old Court House, Caerwys, Mold, Clwyd CH7 5BB, Wales (0352 720276)
Lopez	=	Ken Lopez, Bookseller, 51 Huntington Road, Hadley, MA 01035, U.S.A. (413 584 4827)
McBlain	=	McBlain Books, P.O. Box 5062 Hamden, CT 06518, U.S.A. (203 281 0400)
McCann	=	Joey McCann, 76 Oliver Road, Cowley, Oxford OX4 2JF, England (0865 715001)
MacDonnell	=	MacDonnell Rare Books, 9307 Glenlake Drive, Austin, Texas 78730, U.S.A. (512 345 4139)
McGilvery	=	Laurence McGilvery, Post Office Box 852, La Jolla, California 92038, U.S.A. (619 454 4443)
Marlborough B'Shop	=	Marlborough Bookshop, 6 Kingsbury Street, Marlborough, Wiltshire, England (0672 514074)
Mendelsohn	=	H.L. Mendelsohn, Fine European Books, P.O. Box 317, Belmont, Massachusetts 02178, U.S.A. (617 484 7362)
Meyer Boswell	=	Meyer Boswell Books, Inc., 982 Hayes Street, San Francisco, CA 94117, U.S.A. (415 346 1839)
Moon	=	Michael Moon, Antiquarian, Booksellers & Publishers, 41, 42 & 43 Roper Street, Whitehaven, Cumbria CA28 7BS, England (0946 62936)
Moorhouse	=	Hartley Moorhouse Books, 142 Petersham Road, Richmond, Surrey TW10 6UX, England (081 948 7742)
Mordida	=	Mordida Books, P.O. Box 79322, Houston, Texas 77279, U.S.A. (713 467 4280)
Newnham	=	Anthony Newnham, 72 Dundas Street, Edinburgh EH3 6QZ, Scotland (031 556 3705)
New Wireless	=	New Wireless Pioneers, Box 398, Elma N.Y. 14059, U.S.A. (716 681 3186)
Nouveau	=	Nouveau Rare Books, Steve Silberman, P.O. Box 12471, 5005 Meadow Oaks Park Drive, Jackson, Mississippi 39211, U.S.A. (601 956 9950)
Oak Knoll	=	Oak Knoll Books, 414 Delaware Street, New Castle, Delaware 19720, U.S.A. (302 328 7232)
Offenbacher	=	Emile Offenbacher, 84-50 Austin Street, P.O. Box 96, Kew Gardens, New York 11415, U.S.A. (718 849 5834)
Parmer	=	J. Parmer, Booksellers, 7644 Forrestal Road, San Diego, CA 92120, U.S.A. (619 287 0693)
Patterson	=	Ian Patterson, 21 Bateman Street, Cambridge CB2 1NB, England (0223 321658)
Petrilla	=	R. & A. Petrilla, Roosevelt, NJ 08555-0306, U.S.A. (609 426 4999)
Pettler & Liebermann	=	Pettler & Liebermann, 8033 Sunset Blvd. #977, Los Angeles, CA 90046, U.S.A. (213 474 2479)

Phillips	=	Phillips of Hitchin, (Antiques) Ltd., The Manor House, Hitchin, Hertfordshire, England (0462 432067)
Pickering	=	Pickering & Chatto, 17 Pall Mall, London SW1Y 5NB, England (071 930 8627)
Polyanthos	=	Polyanthos Park Avenue Books, P.O. Box 343, Huntington, NY 11743, U.S.A. (516 271 5558)
Rankin	=	Alan Rankin, 72 Dundas Street, Edinburgh EH3 6QZ, Scotland, Scotland (031 556 3705)
Reese	=	William Reese Company, 409 Temple Street, New Haven, Connecticut 06511, U.S.A. (203 789 8081)
David Rees	=	David Rees, 18A Prentis Road, London SW16 1QD, England (081 769 2453)
Reference Works	=	Reference Works, 12 Commercial Road, Dorset BH19 1DF, England (0929 424423)
Respess	=	L. & T. Respess Books, PO Box 236, Bristol, RI 02809, U.S.A. (401 253 1639)
Roberts	=	John Roberts Bookshop, 43 Triangle West, Clifton, Bristol BS8 1ES, Scotland (2 268568)
Robertshaw	=	John Robertshaw, 5 Fellowes Drive, Ramsey, Huntingdon, Cambridgeshire PE17 1BE, England (0487 813330)
Rootenberg	=	B. & L. Rootenberg, P.O. Box 5049, Sherman Oaks, California 91403-5049, U.S.A. (818 788 7765)
Rostenberg & Stern	=	Leona Rostenberg and Madeleine, Stern, Rare Books, 40 East 88 Street, New York, N.Y. 10128., U.S.A. (212 831 6628)
Sanders	=	Sanders of Oxford Ltd., 104 High Street, Oxford OX1 4BW, England (0865 242590)
Savona	=	Savona Books, 9 Wilton Road, Hornsea, North Humberside HU18 1QU, England (0964 535195)
Schoyer	=	Schoyer's Books, 1404 South Negley Avenue, Pittsburgh, PA 15217, U.S.A. (412 521 8464)
Sclanders	=	Andrew Sclanders, 73 Duckett Road, London N4 1BL, England (081 340 6843)
Sklaroff	=	L.J. Sklaroff, The Totland Bookshop, The Broadway, Totland, Isle of Wight PO39 0BW, England (0983 754960)
Sotheran's	=	Henry Sotheran Ltd., 2 Sackville Street, Piccadilly, London W1X 2DP, England (071 439 6151)
Spelman	=	Ken Spelman, 70 Micklegate, York YO1 1LF, England (0904 624414)
Stewart	=	Andrew Stewart, 11 High Street, Helpringham, Sleaford, Lincolnshire NG34 9RA, England (052 921 617)
Sumner & Stillman	=	Sumner & Stillman, P.O. Box 225, Yarmouth, ME 04096, U.S.A. (207 846 6070)
Michael Taylor	=	Michael Taylor Rare Books, The Gables, 8 Mendham Lane, Harleston, Norfolk IP20 9DE, England (0379 853889)
Peter Taylor	=	Peter Taylor, 4A Ye Corner, Aldenham Road, Watford, Hertfordshire WD1 4BS, England (0923 50342)
Temple	=	Robert Temple, 65 Mildmay Road, London N1 4PU, England (071 254 3674)
Terramedia	=	Terramedia Books, 19 Homestead Road, Wellesley, MA 02181, U.S.A. (617 237 6485)
Tiger Books	=	Tiger Books, Yew Tree Cottage, Westbere, Canterbury, Kent CT2 0HH, England (0227 710030)
Trophy Room Books	=	Trophy Room Books, Box 3041, Agoura, CA 91301, U.S.A. (818 889 2469)
Vanbrugh	=	Vanbrugh Rare Books, Pied Bull Yard, Bury Place, Bloomsbury, London EC1A 2JR, England (071 404 0733)

Virgo	=	Virgo Books, Little Court, South Wraxall, Bradford-on-Avon, Wiltshire BA15 2SE, England (02216 2040)
Walcot	=	Patrick Walcot, 60 Sunnybank Road, Sutton Coldfield, West Midlands B73 5RJ, England (021 382 6381)
Washton	=	Andrew D. Washton, 411 East 83rd Street, New York, New York 10028, U.S.A. (212 751 7027)
Waterfield's	=	Waterfield's, 36 Park End Street, Oxford OX1 1HJ, England (0865 721809)
West Side	=	West Side Books, 113 W. Liberty, Ann Arbor, MI 48103, U.S.A. (313 995 1891)
Wheldon & Wesley	=	Wheldon & Wesley Ltd., Lytton Lodge, Codicote, Hitchin, Hertfordshire SG4 8TE, England (0438 820370)
Whitehart	=	F.E. Whitehart, Rare Books, 40 Priestfield Road, Forest Hill, London SE23 2RS, England (081 699 3225)
Whiteson	=	Edna Whiteson, 66 Belmont Avenue, Cockfosters, Hertfordshire EN4 9LA, England (081 449 8860)
Willow	=	Willow House Books, 58-60 Chapel Street, Chorley, Lancashire PR7 1BS, England (02572 69280)
Woolmer	=	J. Howard Woolmer, Revere, Pennsylvania 18953, U.S.A. (215 847 5074)
Words Etcetera	=	Words Etcetera, Julian Nangle, Hod House, Child Okeford, Dorset DT11 8EH, England (0258 73338)
Worldwide	=	Worldwide Antiquarian, Post Office Box 391, Cambridge, MA 02141, U.S.A. (617 876 6220)
Wreden	=	William P. Wreden, 206 Hamilton Avenue, P.O. Box 56, Palo Alto, CA 94302-0056, U.S.A. (415 325 6851)
Ximenes	=	Ximenes: Rare Books, Inc., 19 East 69th Street, New York, NY 10021, U.S.A. (212 744 0226)
Young's	=	Young's Antiquarian Books, Tillingham, Essex CM0 7ST, England (062187 8187)
Zwisohn	=	Jane Zwisohn Books, 524 Solano Drive N.E., Albuquerque, New Mexico 87108, U.S.A. (505 255 4080)